Prentice Hall Brief Review

MW00993195

United States History and Government

Bonnie-Anne Briggs / Catherine Fish Petersen

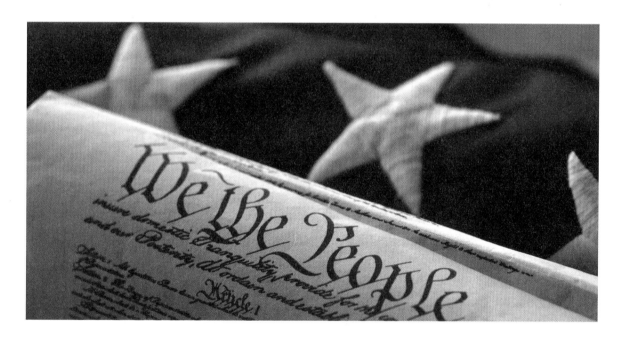

Ordering Information

Send orders to:
Pearson
PO Box 6820
Chandler, AZ 85246

or call toll free:
1-800-848-9500
(8:00 A.M.-6:00 P.M. EST)

School orders:
k12.oasis.pearson.com

Individual orders:
pearsonschool.com/nybriefreviews

 Pearson

Acknowledgments appear on pages I-17–I-18, which constitute an extension of this copyright page.

Regents Examinations and questions appear courtesy of the New York State Education Department/ New York Regents Exam.

Document-Based Essay Question Writers: Fran Legum and Jane Librett, Department of Instructional Programs and Alternative Schools, Nassau BOCES

13-digit ISBN 978-0-328-98339-1
10-digit ISBN   0-328-98339-X

3 18

Table of Contents

New York Standards

Standard   Key Idea

KEY **4.2**

Table of Contents

New York Standards

> Standard 1 and 2 1.1, 1.2, 2.2

> Standard 1 1.3, 1.4

> Standard 1 1.1, 1.4

> Standard 1 and 5 5.3, 5.4, 1.4

> Standard 1 and 2 1.3, 2.3, 2.4

> Standard 1

About This Book

This book has been written to help you, the student, review your course in order to take the New York State Regents Examination in United States History and Government. The purpose of this book is to:

- help you focus on the key facts, themes, and concepts tested on the Regents Examination.
- familiarize you with the format of the Regents Examination.
- provide you with the test-taking skills you need to succeed.

Content Review

Just like the New York State Core Curriculum, this book is organized into seven units. The concepts and content that are consistently tested are emphasized in this text, with special emphasis given to the second unit on United States government and constitutional history to 1865. The charts, maps, cartoons, timelines, and graphic organizers in this text will help reinforce your understanding of the content. *The Big Idea* notes at the beginning of each section organize the content at a glance. *Key Themes and Concepts* notes summarize important content and link it to the key themes and concepts of United States history and government.

Test-Taking Skills

You can practice your test-taking skills on a variety of Regents Examination questions throughout the book.

- A Pre-Test assessment helps you to measure your basic social studies skills and understandings.
- Every multiple-choice question has been on a New York State Regents Examination.
- Document-Based Questions, Thematic Essay Questions, and multiple-choice questions are provided in each history and government unit of the book.
- **Six** Regents Examinations are provided for additional practice.
- An extensive Test-Taking Strategies section teaches you the skills and strategies you need for the exam.
- *Preparing for the Exam* notes in the margins help reinforce test-taking strategies.
- The Reference Section provides charts that summarize the actions of each United States President, list important people in United States history, explain decisions in each of the Landmark Supreme Court Cases, and includes a Glossary.

Transition to the New New York 9-12 Social Studies Framework

Pearson is committed to supporting the New York State K12 Social Studies Framework. With that in mind, this Brief Review contains new and updated *Preparing for the Exam* and Strategy boxes to reinforce Social Studies Practices from the new Framework and help you prepare for exam day.

About the Authors

Bonnie-Anne Briggs

Bonnie-Anne Briggs is a graduate of Nazareth College of Rochester and the State University of New York at Brockport. She is retired from her position as teacher and Teacher-in-Charge of Social Studies (department head) at Gates Chili High School in suburban Rochester. She was an adjunct professor in social studies education at the State University of New York at Brockport for seventeen years. Miss Briggs is a past President of the Rochester Area Council for the Social Studies. She is also a past officer of both the New York State Social Studies Supervisory Association and the New York State Council for the Social Studies. Miss Briggs is a recipient of the Rochester Area Council Distinguished Educator Award, the New York State Social Studies Supervisory Association Supervisor of the Year Award, the New York State Council for the Social Studies Distinguished Educator Award, and the Outstanding Alumni Award from Nazareth College of Rochester. She has been inducted into the Gates Chili High School Alumni Hall of Fame, and in 1993, she was a semifinalist for the New York State Teacher of the Year Award. Miss Briggs is currently a very active docent at the Susan B. Anthony House in Rochester, New York.

Catherine Fish Petersen

Catherine Fish Petersen is a graduate of Wellesley College, Harvard University, and the State University of New York at Stony Brook. Ms. Petersen was the consultant to the New York State Education Department on the *Social Studies Resource Guide* and was their social studies consultant for the New York State Academy for Teaching and Learning. She also was an editor of the State publication, *Social Studies Instructional Strategies & Resources Pre K–Grade Six*. Before retirement, she chaired the Department of Humanities (Social Studies and English) in the East Islip School District on Long Island. Ms. Petersen is a past president of the New York State Social Studies Supervisory Association. She is also a past president, treasurer, and executive secretary of the Long Island Council for the Social Studies. She served on the Board of Directors of the New York State Council for the Social Studies. Ms. Petersen is a recipient of the Long Island Council for the Social Studies Presidential Leadership Award and its Gus Swift Outstanding Service to Social Studies Education Award, the New York State Social Studies Supervisory Association Supervisor of the Year Award and that organization's Special Service Award, as well as the Distinguished Social Studies Service Award from the New York State Council for the Social Studies.

How to Succeed on the Regents Exam in United States History and Government

This section of the book is intended to help you prepare to take the Regents Examination itself. Other parts of the book review the contents of the course you have studied. This section includes hints about preparing for and actually taking the examination based on test-taking skills you have probably been developing for years in social studies classes. Read and think carefully about all parts of this section as you prepare for the examination.

Preparing to take the Regents Examination

1. **Attend review sessions.** If review sessions are offered by your teacher or school, attend them. You will probably be reminded of something you studied earlier in the year and have not thought of since then. Review sessions also help you bring together the main ideas of the whole course.
2. **Find a study partner.** Two heads can be better than one. Try to review with a friend or a family member who can give you the chance to explain various parts of this course. You will have a better chance of remembering details if you have already explained them correctly to someone else. It has been said that the best way to learn something is to teach it to someone else.
3. **Do not "over-study."** As important as it is to review carefully and over a period of time for your exams, do not make the mistake of "over-studying" or cramming at the last minute. This could leave you exhausted and unable to think clearly during the exam itself. This exam is important enough for you to ask your employer for time off right before the test.
4. **Eat a good meal.** Eat something before the exam so your energy level stays high.
5. **Know the exam site.** Be sure you know the correct time and place of the examination. Arriving half an hour late can make the difference between passing and failing. Be sure someone else at your house has a schedule of your exams.
6. **Be prepared.** Bring several dark ink pens and pencils.
7. **Wear a watch, if possible.** You will need to pay close attention to the time during the exam, and you might be seated where you cannot see a clock.
8. **Stay for the full allotted time.** Come to the exam prepared to stay for the full three-hour examination period. Do not tell someone to pick you up in two hours—you will need all the time allowed. Don't sacrifice a year's worth of work to get outside faster on a nice day.

Taking the Regents Examination

1. **Arrive on time.** Use a reliable method of getting to school so you can arrive early in the exam room. This will allow you to get your mind on the task at hand.
2. **Select a seat.** If you are allowed to select your own seat, be sure to choose one with the least distraction. Choose one away from doors or windows.
3. **Dress comfortably.** You will be sitting in one place for a long period of time, so be sure you are comfortably dressed.
4. **Listen to instructions.** Pay full attention to all instructions given by the proctor(s).

5. **Read directions carefully.** Read all directions written on the test booklet as you take the exam. If you have reviewed well, you will be familiar with the terms *discuss, explain, show,* and *describe.* Nonetheless, take the time to read carefully the instructions given to you on the test.

6. **Be an active test-taker.** Become a participant in the exam, not a spectator. You may write on the exam. Underline key ideas. You may write in the margins as you think about the questions. The idea is for you to interact with the exam. Other hints are given as you review the multiple-choice questions from the practice examination.

7. **DON'T leave blanks.** No credit can be given for a blank on either multiple-choice or essay questions. Write something. Write anything, but never leave an answer blank.

The Multiple-Choice Section

Part I of the Regents Examination is made up of 50 multiple-choice questions. These questions tend to fall into certain categories that you can identify as you take an examination. The following is about identifying these categories and improving your ability to answer certain types of questions. These questions come from the June 2000 exam.

Data-Based Questions

Data-based questions provide specific information to be used in answering a question or questions. You will probably not be able to answer the question(s) without this information, and you will also need to know some social studies background to help interpret the information. There are several types of data-based questions.

Reading Passages Some questions on the practice exam are based on a selected reading passage. These questions often require an ability to recognize opinions expressed in a passage.

If there are words you are unsure of in the selection, try to find a root word you know. Be sure to look for dates or other historical references to help you. You may write notes in the margin near the selection.

Example:

"To take a single step beyond these specific [Constitutional] limits to the powers of Congress is to grasp unlimited power.

"The power to create a [national] bank has not, in my opinion, been delegated to Congress by the Constitution. Supporters of the Bank Bill argue that a [national] bank would be a great convenience in collecting taxes. Even if this argument were true, the Constitution allows only for laws which are 'necessary,' not those which are merely 'convenient' for carrying out delegated powers."

The speaker is basing his argument mainly on a strict interpretation of which provision of the federal Constitution?
(1) Preamble
(2) elastic clause
(3) judicial review
(4) apportionment of representatives

Test-Taking Strategies

Answer: The correct answer is 2. The phrase "laws which are 'necessary'" near the end of the reading passage should help you make an association with the elastic clause or "necessary and proper" clause. As you read this book, you will find key vocabulary and social studies phrases highlighted throughout.

Speaker Questions Speaker questions present different reading passages by different people on the same topic. When answering speaker questions, follow these steps:

- Determine the theme or topic that all of the speakers are addressing.
- Read the questions before you study the speakers' statements too closely; often you do not have to read each speaker's viewpoint to answer a question.
- Be sure you are reading the correct speaker when answering each question.
- Take your time when answering speaker questions. You will probably need to go back and forth among the readings as you analyze the difference between speakers.

Example:

> *Speaker A:* "We cannot make the same mistakes that led to the sinking of the *Lusitania*. Freedom of the seas is important, but we must keep our ships away from possible danger."

> *Speaker B:* "We should encourage Great Britain and France to follow a policy of appeasement."

> *Speaker C:* "Continued isolation is the only alternative. Whichever way we turn in this conflict, we find an alien ideology."

> *Speaker D:* "The future of the free world depends now on the United States and Great Britain. We must not only help win this war, but also ensure that no others occur in the future."

> The speakers are most likely discussing the situation facing the United States just before
> (1) the American Revolution
> (2) the Spanish-American War
> (3) World War II
> (4) the Korean War

Answer: The correct answer is 3, World War II. Underline all hints such as the phrases *mistake of the* Lusitania, *freedom of the seas, Great Britain and France, appeasement, continued isolation,* and *future of the free world*. The correct answer cannot be the American Revolution or the Spanish-American War, because the sinking of the *Lusitania* occurred after both of those wars. The correct answer cannot be the Korean War, because the United States had abandoned its isolationist policy before the Korean War. All of the hints together indicate that these speakers are discussing the situation facing the United States just before World War II.

Graphs Graphs may appear in several forms—bar graphs, line graphs, or pie graphs. Some graphs may provide all of the information that you need to answer the question. Others may require you to draw upon your knowledge of social studies to interpret the graph.

Example:

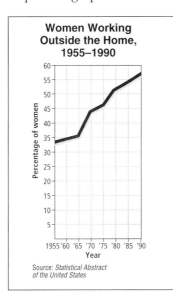

Women Working Outside the Home, 1955–1990

Source: *Statistical Abstract of the United States*

The trend shown in the graph was mainly the result of
(1) increases in immigration
(2) demands for more schoolteachers
(3) a buildup in the defense industry
(4) new social attitudes

Answer: The correct answer is 4. The graph indicates a steady increase in the number of women working outside the home between 1955 and 1990. You must draw upon your knowledge of U.S. history to provide the reason for this trend.

Tables Some questions require you to draw conclusions from information provided in tables. Be *very* careful to base your conclusions only on the information in the table unless the question specifically asks you to do otherwise. Be sure to note the source and date of the information given in the table.

Which statement is best supported by the chart?
(1) In the early 1900s, there was an increase in the number of immigrants who became farmers.
(2) In the early 1900s, people who lived in cities were more likely to vote than those who lived in rural areas.
(3) In 1920, more people lived in cities than on farms.
(4) In 1920, there were fewer women working in factories than on farms.

Example:

Rural and Urban Populations in the United States		
Year	Rural (thousands)	Urban (thousands)
1860	25,227	6,217
1870	28,656	9,902
1880	36,026	14,130
1890	40,841	22,106
1900	45,835	30,160
1910	49,973	41,999
1920	51,553	54,158

Source: *Bureau of the Census*

Answer: The correct answer is 3. This question tests your ability to read the table, as well as your understanding of the words *urban* and *rural*. To answer a question such as this, eliminate all possible answers that do not have information given in the chart. For example, answer 1 mentions immigrants, but the table provides no information about immigrants.

Political Cartoons Some questions ask you to analyze and interpret a political cartoon. When analyzing a political cartoon, follow these steps:

- Study the caption.
- Look for a date.
- Read all words in the cartoon. Look closely for any small print written on figures or objects in the cartoon.
- Identify the symbolism used by the cartoonist.

Example:

Declined with Thanks

The Antis—"Here take a dose of this anti-fat and get thin again!"
Uncle Sam—"No, Sonny! I never did take any of that stuff, and I'm too old to begin."

Source: J. S. Pugh, *Puck*, September 5, 1900 (adapted)

Which foreign policy is the main issue of this cartoon?
(1) containment   (3) internationalism
(2) imperialism   (4) neutrality

The correct answer is 2, imperialism. When analyzing this cartoon, be sure to look very carefully at all parts of the cartoon: the caption under the figures in the cartoon, the writing on the large figure representing Uncle Sam, the writing on the tailor (McKinley) and the material behind him, and the writing on the containers that the men at the door are carrying. The date of the cartoon (1900) is also an important hint about the answer.

Outlines Some questions ask you to complete a hypothetical outline.

Example:

> In an outline, one of these entries is a main topic and three are subtopics. Which is the main topic?
> (1) Alexander Hamilton's Economic Program
> (2) The Rise of National Political Parties
> (3) The Constitution's First Tests
> (4) John Adams's Stormy Presidency

Answer: In this question, you are simply asked to determine the main topic. Look for the most general answer. Recognize that the other choices would be subheads on the outline under the main topic. The right choice is 3 because 1, 2, and 4 are examples of the Constitution's first tests.

Quotation Interpretation This type of question asks you to explain the idea of a given quotation. Sometimes the date and speaker of the quotation are identified and sometimes not.

Example:

> "(Sec. 4.) Every person presenting himself for registration shall be able to read and write any section of the Constitution in the English language, and before he shall be entitled to vote, he shall have paid on or before the first day of March of the year in which he proposes to vote his poll tax as prescribed by law for the previous year."
> —*Public Laws of North Carolina, 1899, chapter 218*
>
> The principle purpose of this law was to
> (1) assure equality of voting rights for all peoples
> (2) encourage literacy for former enslaved people
> (3) prevent African Americans from using their suffrage rights
> (4) promote the racial integration of Southern society

Answer: The correct answer is 3. The date and place of origin of this quotation are important clues, which should remind you that Jim Crow laws were legal in much of the South at the end of the 1800s.

Maps When maps are given, be sure to look for the following:

- A key explaining any symbols used
- Dates
- Specific place locations
- Compass point for directions

Timelines A timeline is a graphic way of showing relationships among events over time. Questions dealing with timelines often ask you to draw a conclusion about a series of events. When answering timeline questions, be careful to focus on the time period shown; do not jump to a different era to answer the question.

Other Multiple-Choice Questions

Many other types of multiple-choice questions appear on the Regents Examination.

Headline Questions In this type of question, you are given a few sample headlines that usually have to do with a common event. Your goal is to determine the connection between the headlines.

Example:

> "Raise Tariffs!"
> "Buy American!"
> "Impose Import Quotas!"
>
> Which policy do these slogans reflect?
> (1) militarism   (3) isolationism
> (2) protectionism   (4) détente

Answer: The correct answer is 2. The subject of all three headlines is economics and trade. The words and phrases *tariffs, buy American,* and *import quotas* suggest foreign trade. The only possible answer that deals with foreign trade is protectionism.

Recall Questions These questions require you to know specific information about people, events, topics, concepts, and vocabulary studied in the course. Throughout this review book, you will find many suggestions about test-taking strategies, as well as references to the many important people and events covered in this course. There is also a glossary at the end of this book to help you with vocabulary.

Example:

> At the Constitutional Convention of 1787, a bicameral legislature was proposed as the solution to the disagreement over
> (1) taxation within each state
> (2) control of interstate commerce
> (3) limits on the treaty-making power of a President
> (4) state representation in the national government

Answer: The correct answer is 4. The key to answering this question correctly is understanding the meaning of the term *bicameral legislature* and the reason for its proposal.

Cause-and-Effect Questions These questions test your understanding of the concepts of cause and effect. A cause is an event or action that brings about another event or action—an effect. Your study of history will have revealed that almost everything is either the cause or result of some event.

Example:

> Which factor contributed most directly to the settlement and development of the Great Plains after the Civil War?
> (1) freeing of the enslaved people in Southern states
> (2) construction of railroads west of the Mississippi River
> (3) influx of immigrants from eastern and southern Europe
> (4) hospitality of the American Indian tribes inhabiting the region

Answer: The correct answer is 2. The use of the newly developed railroad as transportation was key to the western development (choice 2). Choice 1 is wrong because the freed enslaved people did not move west, and 3 is wrong because those immigrants generally stayed in urban areas to work in factories. Note the word *hospitality* in choice 4. Few of the American Indian tribes welcomed the arrival of the settlers on the plains.

Time Reference or Chronology Questions These are questions that make reference to a particular time period. You rarely need to identify specific dates on Regents exams. However, you often do need to know the time sequence or order of events.

Example:

In the period between World War I and World War II, which group made the greatest gains in political rights?
(1) African Americans
(2) women
(3) new immigrants
(4) Native Americans

Answer: The correct answer is 2. With a question like this, it is a good idea to write the dates of the period above the question so that you can focus on that specific time. Remember, a condition that was true in one time period may cease to exist in another time period. When answering this question, you should remember that the Nineteenth Amendment granting women the right to vote was passed in 1920 (between the wars). Not until well after World War II did the other groups make great gains in their political rights.

Generalizations These questions require you to make a general statement about a particular event, time period, or body of information. You are really being asked to draw a conclusion.

Example:

A primary aim of the writers of the United States Constitution was to
(1) strengthen the power of the central government
(2) change from a government based on division of powers to one based on a single power
(3) develop a governmental system based on the principle of supremacy of the states
(4) weaken the power of the executive

Answer: The correct answer is 1. This question asks you to explain why the Constitution was written. To do so, you need to recall the problems of the Articles of Confederation. Choice 1 is correct because the Constitution does establish a strong central government.

Fact and Opinion These questions require you to find a statement that is clearly either fact or opinion. If you keep in mind that certain words such as *most important, most significant,* and *greatest contribution* signal opinions, you should have no trouble with this type of question. It is difficult to make true statements that include the words *always, never, all,* or *none.*

Test-Taking Strategies

Sources and References Some questions test your ability to identify a valid source of information. A primary source is one written or told by someone who was present at an event. These sources can be biased, but they can also give a special insight into an event. Secondary sources, such as textbooks, are those that are written after an event.

Questions About Social Scientists Some questions ask about the jobs of certain types of social scientists. These might include the following:

Historian: a person who studies the past and makes judgments about why events happened and how they affected other events

Economist: a person who studies the monetary systems of countries or cultures. The work of economists is important to our understanding of events such as the Great Depression.

Political scientist: a person who studies the workings of government and politics. For example, political scientists analyze the results of elections to determine trends in voting patterns.

The Thematic Essay

There will be one thematic essay on your examination. The score on the thematic essay ranges from 0 to 5 points, using a generic scoring rubric. You should become familiar with this rubric as you prepare for the exam, because it will help you learn how to write the most effective essay possible.

You will not have a choice of theme or topic, but you will have many choices within the provided list of suggested examples you may draw upon in writing your essay. You may choose examples that are not on the list of suggestions, but that approach may not be a good idea. The most frequently studied examples are the ones that are usually given in the suggestions. As an example, we will use the Thematic Essay Question from the June 2004 exam:

Answers to the essay questions are to be written in the separate essay booklet.

Directions: Write a well-organized essay that includes an introduction, several paragraphs addressing the task below, and a conclusion.

Theme: **Geography and United States Government Actions**

> Geographic factors often influence United States government actions, both foreign and domestic. Some of these factors include location, physical environment, movement of people, climate, and resources.

Task:

> Identify *two* actions taken by the United States government that were influenced by geographic factors, and for *each* action
> - Discuss the historical circumstances that resulted in the government action
> - Discuss the influence of a geographic factor on the action
> - Describe the impact of the government action on the United States

From your study of United States history, you may use any federal government action that was influenced by geography. Some suggestions you might wish to consider include the Louisiana Purchase (1803), issuance of the Monroe Doctrine (1823), passage of the Homestead Act (1862), decision to build the transcontinental railroad (1860s), acquisition of the Philippines (1898), decision to build the Panama Canal (early 1900s), and passage of the Interstate Highway Act (1956).

You are *not* limited to these suggestions.

Guidelines:

In your essay, be sure to
- Develop all aspects of the task
- Support the theme with relevant facts, examples, and details
- Use a logical and clear plan of organization, including an introduction and a conclusion that are beyond a restatement of the theme

In developing your answer, be sure to keep these general definitions in mind:

(a) <u>discuss</u> means "to make observations about something using facts, reasoning, and argument; to present in some detail"
(b) <u>describe</u> means "to illustrate something in words or tell about it"

Blocking Essay Answers

Blocking an essay will help you organize your ideas before you write your answer. Organizing your thoughts before writing will help you earn more points on the essay and avoid leaving out parts of the essay. Experts in helping students prepare for tests know that the more involved you become with a test, the better you will do on it.

Steps in Blocking an Essay

1. Underline the words that tell you what you need to do: *discuss, describe, explain,* and so on.
2. Study the directions next to each bulleted point (•).
3. Use those directions to form headings for your block.
4. Under each section of your block, write facts to help you answer that part of the question.
5. Review to see if you have completed all parts of the *Task*.
6. Check to see that your introduction and conclusion show thought and are not just a repetition of the ones you are given in the question.
7. When you have arranged all your facts in the section of the block, check to be sure you have not left any blocks empty.

Test-Taking Strategies

Sample Block

This chart blocks only one of the two required actions for the Thematic Essay Question that was on the June 2004 Regents examination.

As an example, we will use the June 2004 exam:	Action	Discuss historical circumstances that resulted in government actions.	Discuss influence of a geographic factor (location, physical environment, actions, movement of people, climate resources)	Impact of action on United States.
	Louisiana Purchase	France wanted and needed to sell area much cheaper than the United States expected to buy; President Jefferson decided the government could purchase the land.	United States could expand to the west and end French presence on U. S. western border.	Gave United States chance to double size of territory to allow for future growth and exploration for new resources. United States set precedent that it could add additional territory.

Generic Thematic Essay Scoring Rubric

Score of 5:	Score of 4:	Score of 3:
• Thoroughly develops all aspects of the task evenly and in depth • Is more analytical than descriptive (analyzes, evaluates, and/or creates* information) • Richly supports the theme with many relevant facts, examples, and details • Demonstrates a logical and clear plan of organization; includes an introduction and a conclusion that are beyond a restatement of the theme	• Develops all aspects of the task but may do so somewhat unevenly • Is both descriptive and analytical (applies, analyzes, evaluates, and/or creates information) • Supports the theme with relevant facts, examples, and details • Demonstrates a logical and clear plan of organization; includes an introduction and a conclusion that are beyond a restatement of the theme	• Develops all aspects of the task with little depth or develops most aspects of the task in some depth • Is more descriptive than analytical (applies, may analyze, and/or evaluate information) • Includes some relevant facts, examples, and details; may include some minor inaccuracies • Demonstrates a satisfactory plan of organization; includes an introduction and a conclusion that may be a restatement of the theme

Score of 2:	Score of 1:	Score of 0:
• Minimally develops all aspects of the task or develops some aspects of the task in some depth • Is primarily descriptive; may include faulty, weak, or isolated application or analysis • Includes few relevant facts, examples, and details; may include some inaccuracies • Demonstrates a general plan of organization; may lack focus; may contain digressions; may not clearly identify which aspect of the task is being addressed; may lack an introduction and/or a conclusion	• Minimally develops some aspects of the task • Is descriptive; may lack understanding, application, or analysis • Includes few relevant facts, examples, or details; may include inaccuracies • May demonstrate a weakness in organization; may lack focus; may contain digressions; may not clearly identify which aspect of the task is being addressed; may lack an introduction and/or a conclusion	Fails to develop the task or may only refer to the theme in a general way; *OR* includes no relevant facts, examples, or details; *OR* includes only the theme, task, or suggestions as copied from the test booklet; *OR* is illegible; *OR* is blank

Document-Based Question

There will be one document-based question (DBQ) on the examination. The score on the document-based essay question ranges from 0 to 5 points, using a generic scoring rubric. You should become familiar with this rubric as you prepare for the exam, because it will help you learn how to write the most effective essay possible. The DBQ from the June 2004 exam is included here for you.

The DBQ has two important parts. Part A includes the scaffolding questions in which you examine documents individually and complete short-answer questions. Part B is the essay question in which you draw upon your analysis of the documents and your knowledge of United States history and government to write the essay. You must complete all sections of both parts. There are several steps you should take to ensure success in answering the DBQ:

- **Read the *Historical Context* section carefully.** This sets the time frame in which all parts of the question are set. It also limits the time period that you can write about in your answer. Remember to highlight or underline important data.

- **Read and understand the *Task*.** Read this part carefully to be sure that you complete all parts. Underline any parts of the test that you do not want to forget or overlook.

- **Do not leave any blanks on the scaffolding question section.** Any blanks you leave will cause you to lose points automatically.

- **Keep track of main ideas/block your essay.** As you work through the scaffolding questions, write down the main idea or ideas of each document on your scrap paper. Briefly listing the main ideas of each document will help you organize your thoughts so that you can successfully support your viewpoint in the essay. You may choose to organize the main ideas by creating a simple chart.

Document-Based Question

In developing your answer, be sure to keep this general definition in mind:

<u>discuss</u> means "to make observations about something using
facts, reasoning, and argument; to present in some detail"

This question is based on the accompanying documents (1–8). The question is designed to test your ability to work with historical documents. Some of the documents have been edited for the purposes of the question. As you analyze the documents, take into account both the source of each document and any point of view that may be presented in the document.

Historical Context:

The Civil War and the period of Reconstruction brought great social, political, and economic changes to American society. The effects of these changes continued into the twentieth century.

Task: Using information from the documents and your knowledge of United States history, answer the questions that follow each document in Part A. Your answers to the questions will help you write the Part B essay in which you will be asked to

> • Identify and discuss *one* social, *one* political, **AND** *one* economic change in American society that occurred as a result of the Civil War or the period of Reconstruction

Part A: Short-Answer Questions

Directions: Analyze the documents and answer the short-answer questions that follow each document in the space provided.

Document #1

" . . . *All persons born or naturalized in the United States, and subject to the jurisdiction thereof, are citizens of the United States and of the State wherein they reside. No State shall make or enforce any law which shall abridge the privileges or immunities of citizens of the United States; nor shall any State deprive any person of life, liberty, or property, without due process of law; nor deny to any person within its jurisdiction the equal protection of the laws. . . .*"

—**Fourteenth Amendment, Section 1, 1868**

1*a.* How does the Fourteenth Amendment define citizenship? [1]

_____

_____

Score ☐

b. During Reconstruction, how was the Fourteenth Amendment intended to help formerly enslaved persons? [1]

_____

_____

Score ☐

Document #2

" . . . History does not furnish an example of emancipation under conditions less friendly to the emancipated class than this American example. Liberty came to the freedmen of the United States not in mercy, but in wrath [anger], not by moral choice but by military necessity, not by the generous action of the people among whom they were to live, and whose good-will was essential to the success of the measure, but by strangers, foreigners, invaders, trespassers, aliens, and enemies. The very manner of their emancipation invited to the heads of the freedmen the bitterest hostility of race and class. They were hated because they had been slaves, hated because they were now free, and hated because of those who had freed them. Nothing was to have been expected other than what has happened, and he is a poor student of the human heart who does not see that the old master class would naturally employ every power and means in their reach to make the great measure of emancipation unsuccessful and utterly odious [hateful]. It was born in the tempest and whirlwind [turmoil] of war, and has lived in a storm of violence and blood. When the Hebrews were emancipated, they were told to take spoil [goods or property] from the Egyptians. When the serfs of Russia were emancipated [in 1861], they were given three acres of ground upon which they could live and make a living. But not so when our slaves were emancipated. They were sent away empty-handed, without money, without friends, and without a foot of land to stand upon. Old and young, sick and well, were turned loose to the open sky, naked to their enemies. The old slave quarter that had before sheltered them and the fields that had yielded them corn were now denied them. The old master class, in its wrath, said, "Clear out! The Yankees have freed you, now let them feed and shelter you! . . .""

Source: Frederick Douglass, *Life and Times of Frederick Douglass*, Park Publishing Co., 1881

2. According to this document, what did Frederick Douglass identify as a problem with the way the United States government emancipated the enslaved persons? [1]

_____

_____

_____

Score [ ]

Document #3

> " . . . We believe you are not familiar with the description of the Ku Klux Klans riding nightly over the country, going from county to county, and in the county towns, spreading terror wherever they go by robbing, whipping, ravishing, and killing our people without provocation [reason], compelling [forcing] colored people to break the ice and bathe in the chilly waters of the Kentucky river."
>
> "The [state] legislature has adjourned. They refused to enact any laws to suppress [stop] Ku-Klux disorder. We regard them [the Ku-Kluxers] as now being licensed to continue their dark and bloody deeds under cover of the dark night. They refuse to allow us to testify in the state courts where a white man is concerned. We find their deeds are perpetrated [carried out] only upon colored men and white Republicans. We also find that for our services to the government and our race we have become the special object of hatred and persecution at the hands of the Democratic Party. Our people are driven from their homes in great numbers, having no redress [relief from distress] only [except] the United States court, which is in many cases unable to reach them."
>
> "We would state that we have been law-abiding citizens, pay our taxes, and in many parts of the state our people have been driven from the polls, refused the right to vote. Many have been slaughtered while attempting to vote. We ask, how long is this state of things to last? . . ."
>
> **—Petition to the United States Congress, March 25, 1871,**
> **Miscellaneous Documents of the United States Senate, 42nd Congress, 1st Session, 1871**

3a. Based on this document, identify *one* way the Ku Klux Klan terrorized African Americans. [1]

_____

Score [ ]

b. According to this document, how did the actions of the Ku Klux Klan affect African Americans' participation in the political process? [1]

_____

Score [ ]

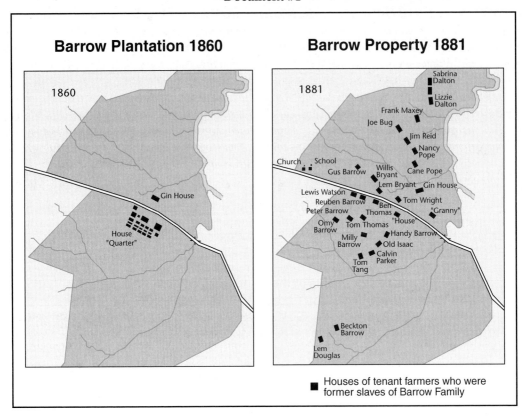

Barrow Plantation 1860

Barrow Property 1881

- Houses of tenant farmers who were former slaves of Barrow Family

4. According to these illustrations, how did the economic role of African Americans change between 1860 and 1881? [1]

_____

_____

Score

Document #5

" . . . When we come to the New Industrial South the change is marvellous, and so vast and various that I scarcely know where to begin in a short paper that cannot go much into details. Instead of a South devoted to agriculture and politics, we find a South wide-awake to business, excited and even astonished at the development of its own immense resources in metals, marbles, coal, timber, fertilizers, eagerly laying lines of communication, rapidly opening mines, building furnaces, foundries [workplace where melted metal is poured into molds], and all sorts of shops for utilizing the native riches. It is like the discovery of a new world. When the Northerner finds great foundries in Virginia using only (with slight exceptions) the products of Virginia iron and coal mines; when he finds Alabama and Tennessee making iron so good and so cheap that it finds ready market in Pennsylvania; and foundries multiplying near the great furnaces for supplying Northern markets; when he finds cotton-mills running to full capacity on grades of cheap cottons universally in demand throughout the South and Southwest; when he finds small industries, such as paper-box factories and wooden bucket and tub factories, sending all they can make into the North and widely over the West; when he sees the loads of most beautiful marbles shipped North; when he learns that some of the largest and most important engines and mill machinery were made in Southern shops; when he finds in Richmond a "pole locomotive," made to run on logs laid end to end, and drag out from Michigan forests and Southern swamps lumber hitherto inaccessible; when he sees worn out highlands in Georgia and Carolina bear more cotton than ever before by help of a fertilizer the base of which is the cotton seed itself (worth more as a fertilizer than it was before the oil was extracted from it); when he sees a multitude of small shops giving employment to men, women, and children who never had any work of that sort to do before; and when he sees Roanoke iron cast in Richmond into car irons, and returned to a car factory in Roanoke which last year sold three hundred cars to the New York and New England Railroad—he begins to open his eyes. The South is manufacturing a great variety of things needed in the house, on the farm, and in the shops, for home consumption, and already sends to the North and West several manufactured products. With iron, coal, timber contiguous [adjoining] and easily obtained, the amount sent out is certain to increase as the labor becomes more skillful. The most striking industrial development today is in iron, coal, lumber, and marbles; the more encouraging for the self-sustaining life of the Southern people is the multiplication of small industries in nearly every city I visited. . . ."

Source: Charles Dudley Warner, "The South Revisited,"
Harper's New Monthly Magazine **(March 1887)**

5. According to this passage, what was *one* economic change that had occurred in the South by 1887? [1]

_____

_____

Score

Document #6

A Public Fountain in North Carolina, 1950

—Photograph by Elliott Erwitt
Source: Steve Kashwer, The Civil Rights Movement:
A Photographic History, 1954–68, *Abbeville Press*

6. What does this photograph show about the treatment of African Americans in the South after Reconstruction? [1]

_____

_____

Score ☐

Document #7

" . . . Since 1868 there has been a steady and persistent determination to eliminate us from the politics of the Southern States. We are not to be eliminated. Suffrage is a federal guaranty and not a privilege to be conferred [given] or withheld by the States. We contend for the principle of manhood suffrage as the most effective safeguard of citizenship. A disfranchised citizen [one who is deprived of the right to vote] is a pariah [outcast] in the body politic. We are not opposed to legitimate restriction of the suffrage, but we insist that restrictions shall apply alike to all citizens of all States. We are willing to accept an educational or property qualification, or both; and we contend that retroactive legislation depriving citizens of the suffrage rights is a hardship which should be speedily passed upon by the courts. We insist that neither of these was intended or is conserved [protected] by the new constitutions of Mississippi, South Carolina or Louisiana. Their framers intended and did disfranchise a majority of their citizenship [deprived them of the right to vote] because of "race and color" and "previous condition," and we therefore call upon the Congress to reduce the representation of those States in the Congress as provided and made mandatory by Section 2 of Article XIV of the Constitution. We call upon Afro-Americans everywhere to resist by all lawful means the determination to deprive them of their suffrage rights. If it is necessary to accomplish this vital purpose to divide their vote in a given State we advise that they divide it. The shibboleth [custom] of party must give way to the shibboleth of self-preservation. . . ."

— **Afro-American Council public statement, 1898**
Source: Francis L. Broderick and August Meier, *Negro Protest Thought in the Twentieth Century,*
Bobbs-Merrill Company

7. What political problem is being described in this passage? [1]

_____

_____

Score ☐

Document #8

Source: Robert Divine et al., America Past and Present, Addison Wesley (adapted)

Parade in New York City sponsored by the NAACP in 1917

8. What was the general goal of the marchers shown in this photograph? [1]

_____

_____

Score ☐

Part B
Essay

Directions: Write a well-organized essay that includes an introduction, several paragraphs, and a conclusion. Use evidence from *at least **five*** documents in your essay. Support your response with relevant facts, examples, and details. Include additional outside information.

Historical Context:

The Civil War and the period of Reconstruction brought great social, political, and economic changes to American society. The effects of these changes continued into the twentieth century.

Task: Using information from the documents and your knowledge of United States history, write an essay in which you

- Identify and discuss *one* social, *one* political, **AND** *one* economic change in American society that occurred as a result of the Civil War or the period of Reconstruction

Guidelines:

In your essay, be sure to
- Develop all aspects of the task
- Incorporate information from *at least **five*** documents
- Incorporate relevant outside information
- Support the theme with relevant facts, examples, and details
- Use a logical and clear plan of organization, including an introduction and a conclusion that are beyond a restatement of the theme

Sample Block or Prewriting Outline

The chart below blocks the Document-Based Question from the June 2004 Regents examination used here.

Writing the Document-Based Question

Use the list you created while answering the scaffolding questions to help guide the writing of your essay. Using the question from the June 2004 Regents, you should have a list of social, political, and economic changes from the given documents. Be sure to note that not all of the changes have to be positive and that some changes definitely had a negative impact on the United States.

In your essay, you should take care to draw as much information out of the documents as you can. However, you should also include other information from your knowledge of United States history if that information helps support your viewpoint. In the document-based question from the sample Regents examination, for example, you could also include information about other changes that occured such as the work of Martin Luther King, Jr., Rosa Parks, Civil Rights legislation of the 1960s, and so on.

Be sure to study carefully the *Guidelines* that are provided in the instructions on writing the document-based question. These *Guidelines* will remind you of what you must include in order to score the full five points for the essay.

Document (number and source)	Type of Change (social, political, economic)	Specific Application
1 14th Amendment	political	gave persons natural born or naturalized citizenship
2 F. Douglass	economic	formerly enslaved persons that were not given land, money or other assistance to help them get started as free citizens
3 Senate document	social and political	KKK depriving former enslaved persons of basic human rights, i.e. life, liberty as well as new political right to vote
4 Plantation map	economic	enslaved persons had a right to be tenant farmers, big plantations had been subdivided, therefore change for the old "elite" or Master too
5 Harper's Magazine	economic and social	multiple examples of new types of businesses in the south in 1887, iron foundries, cotton mills, train car production
6 separate drinking fountain	social	illustrates separate AND unequal public facilities as recent as the 1950s and 60s
7 Afro-American Council	political	changes did not always happen when they should have, some Southern states made their own laws to deprive African Americans of voting rights
8 NAACP Parade	social, political, and economic	shows that in 1917 African Americans were using parades and demonstrations to protest their lack of right to be truly equal (note formal, business dress on marchers)

Generic Document Based Question Essay Scoring Rubric

Score of 5:	Score of 4:	Score of 3:
• Thoroughly develops all aspects of the task evenly and in depth • Is more analytical than descriptive (analyzes, evaluates, and/or creates information) • Incorporates relevant information from *at least* xxx* documents • Incorporates substantial relevant outside information • Richly supports the theme with many relevant facts, examples, and details • Demonstrates a logical and clear plan of organization; includes an introduction and a conclusion that are beyond a restatement of the theme	• Develops all aspects of the task but may do so somewhat unevenly • Is both descriptive and analytical (applies, analyzes, evaluates, and/or creates information) • Incorporates relevant information from at least xxx* documents • Incorporates relevant outside information • Supports the theme with relevant facts, examples, and details • Demonstrates a logical and clear plan of organization; includes an introduction and a conclusion that are beyond a restatement of the theme	• Develops all aspects of the task with little depth *or* develops most aspects of the task in some depth • Is more descriptive than analytical (applies, may analyze, and/or evaluate information) • Incorporates some relevant information from some of the documents • Incorporates limited relevant outside information • Includes some relevant facts, examples, and details; may include some minor inaccuracies • Demonstrates a satisfactory plan of organization; includes an introduction and a conclusion that may be a restatement of the theme
Score of 2:	Score of 1:	Score of 0:
• Minimally develops all aspects of the task *or* develops some aspects of the task in some depth • Is primarily descriptive; may include faulty, weak, or isolated application or analysis • Incorporates limited relevant information from the documents or consists primarily of relevant information copied from the documents • Presents little or no relevant outside information • Includes few relevant facts, examples, and details; may include some inaccuracies • Demonstrates a general plan of organization; may lack focus; may contain digressions; may not clearly identify which aspect of the task is being addressed; may lack an introduction and/or a conclusion	• Minimally develops some aspects of the task • Is descriptive; may lack understanding, application, or analysis • Makes vague, unclear references to the documents or consists primarily of relevant and irrelevant information copied from the documents • Presents no relevant outside information • Includes few relevant facts, examples, or details; may include inaccuracies • May demonstrate a weakness in organization; may lack focus; may contain digressions; may not clearly identify which aspect of the task is being addressed; may lack an introduction and/or a conclusion	Fails to develop the task or may only refer to the theme in a general way; *OR* includes no relevant facts, examples, or details; includes only the historical context and/or task as copies from the test booklet; *OR* includes only entire documents copied from the test booklet; *OR* is illegible; *OR* is blank

* *xxx* means that the required number of documents varies by question but almost always means one more than half of the total number of documents given.

Unit Pre-Tests

This section consists of seven Pre-Tests, one for each of the units in the New York State Core Curriculum in United States History and Government. In constructing these Pre-Tests, the authors' objective was to give you the opportunity to determine what you know about each unit before you begin to review the unit. The questions cover a range of topics within each unit. They focus on major understandings and often tested information. In addition, the Pre-Tests offer practice in social studies reading skills with the inclusion of many outline, headline, and speaker questions. The Pre-Tests can be supplemented with the maps, charts, graphs, cartoons, and accompanying questions throughout each unit that provide further opportunities to strengthen social studies skills.

These Pre-Tests are composed only of multiple choice questions that have appeared on previous Regents examinations. They do not duplicate any *Questions for Regents Practice* at the end of each unit, nor any multiple choice question on the six Regents Examinations in the book. Therefore, the Pre-Tests may also be used as additional practice questions following your review of the unit.

Unit 1 Pre-Test

Name _____   **Date** _____

Directions Review the Test-Taking Strategies section of this book. Then answer the following questions, drawn from actual Regents examinations. For each statement or question, choose the number of the word or expression that, of those given, best completes the statement or answers the question.

1. Which type of map shows the most detailed information about Earth's natural features, such as rivers, lakes, and mountain ranges?
   (1) political   (3) weather
   (2) demographic   (4) physical

2. • Jamestown, founded in 1607
   • Plymouth colony, founded in 1620
   • New Amsterdam, founded in 1625

   These early colonial settlements were similar in that each was located
   (1) at the base of a mountain range
   (2) near the coastline
   (3) in an arid climate
   (4) on offshore islands

3. Because of the fertile land and long growing season, plantations in the Thirteen Colonies developed in
   (1) New England
   (2) the Middle Atlantic region
   (3) the South
   (4) the upper Mississippi River valley

4. Which geographic feature contributed the most to the development of commerce throughout colonial America?
   (1) mountains   (3) natural harbors
   (2) grasslands   (4) interior lakes

5. Which heading best completes the partial outline below?

   > I. _____
   >
   >   A. Villages with town meetings
   >   B. Small farms and commercial fishing
   >   C. First American college

   (1) New England colonies
   (2) Middle colonies
   (3) Southern colonies
   (4) Spanish colonies

6. Which group benefited most from the United States acquisition of the port of New Orleans?
   (1) farmers in the Ohio River Valley
   (2) American Indians in the Southwest
   (3) fur trappers in the Columbia River valley
   (4) gold miners in Northern California

7. Acquiring New Orleans as part of the Louisiana Purchase was considered important to the development of the Mississippi and Ohio River Valleys because the city
   (1) provided protection from attacks by the Spanish
   (2) provided migrant workers for river valley farms
   (3) served as a port for American agricultural goods
   (4) served as the cultural center for the nation

8. In the early 1800s, the need for a water route to help farmers ship their products to market was one reason for the
   (1) Gadsden Purchase
   (2) Louisiana Purchase
   (3) Mexican Cession
   (4) Missouri Compromise

9. The relatively flat grassy region of the United States between the Mississippi River and the Rocky Mountains is known as the
   (1) Great Plains   (3) Coastal Plain
   (2) Great Basin   (4) Piedmont

10. In the 1800s, the Great Plains region of the United States was characterized primarily by
    (1) exceptionally high amounts of annual rainfall
    (2) heavily wooded forests covering most of the area
    (3) an extensive system of navigable rivers
    (4) vast expanses of native grasses

Unit 2 Pre-Test

Name _____ **Date** _____

Directions Review the Test-Taking Strategies section of this book. Then answer the following questions, drawn from actual Regents examinations. For each statement or question, choose the number of the word or expression that, of those given, best completes the statement or answers the question.

1. Which heading best completes the partial outline below?

   > I. _____
   >   A. Committees of Correspondence
   >   B. Nonimportation Agreements
   >   C. Boston Tea Party
   >   D. First Continental Congress

   (1) Protests Against Slavery in the American Colonies
   (2) British Parliamentary Actions to Punish Colonial Americans
   (3) Colonial Responses to British Mercantile Policies
   (4) Colonial Attempts to End the British Policy of Salutary Neglect

2. In writing the *Declaration of Independence*, Thomas Jefferson was influenced most by John Locke's idea of
   (1) due process of law
   (2) natural rights
   (3) the rights of the accused
   (4) the right to privacy

3. The Northwest Ordinance of 1787 set a precedent for other western territories by
   (1) allowing slavery
   (2) including voting rights for women
   (3) providing a method for the creation of new states
   (4) setting aside land for churches

   Base your answers to questions 4 and 5 on the statements below and on your knowledge of social studies.

   Speaker A: A leader is not ultimately responsible to the people but to God, from whom the leader derives the right to govern.

   Speaker B: Each citizen is entitled to a voice in government. Therefore, government should be run by those representatives elected directly by the citizens so that the will of the citizens is expressed.

   Speaker C: History has taught us that the concentration of political power leads to the abuse of that power. Therefore, power should be divided among national, state, and local governments.

   Speaker D: Life is a struggle. Those who seize and maintain political power represent the strongest and most competent of that society and earn the right to govern.

4. The principle of federalism contained in the Constitution of the United States is most consistent with the ideas of Speaker
   (1) *A*   (3) *C*
   (2) *B*   (4) *D*

5. Over the course of its history, the United States has advanced the goal of Speaker B by
   (1) upholding the separation of church and state
   (2) adding constitutional amendments to expand voting rights
   (3) expanding the role of the Supreme Court in government
   (4) providing for the direct election of the President

6. **"New Congress to Have Two Houses"**
   "Slaves to Count as Three-Fifths of a Person"
   "President to be Chosen by Electoral Vote"

   Which conclusion about the Constitutional Convention is best supported by these headlines?
   (1) The Framers of the Constitution were able to compromise on important issues.
   (2) States that were small in area would lose power in the new Constitution.
   (3) States with large populations controlled the outcome of the convention.
   (4) The President and Congress would have equal power under the new constitution.

Name _____   Date _____

7. Which newspaper headline shows the operation of the system of checks and balances?

   (1) "Senate Rejects President's Choice of Supreme Court Justice"
   (2) "Florida To Gain Two Seats in the United States House of Representatives"
   (3) "Albany County Receives $4 Million from Congress for Transportation Development"
   (4) "New York State Rejects Federal Regulations on Drug Testing"

8. Which statement from the United States Constitution is referred to as the elastic clause?

   (1) "All legislative powers herein granted shall be vested in a Congress of the United States. . . . "
   (2) "Congress shall make no law respecting an establishment of religion. . . . "
   (3) "All bills for raising revenue shall originate in the House of Representatives. . . . "
   (4) "Congress shall have power . . . to make all laws which shall be necessary and proper for carrying into execution the foregoing powers. . . . "

9. The decision in *Marbury* v. *Madison* (1803) expanded the power of the Supreme Court by

   (1) restricting the use of the elastic clause
   (2) establishing the power of judicial review
   (3) upholding the constitutionality of the National Bank
   (4) interpreting the interstate commerce clause

10. The major reason Antifederalists opposed ratification of the Constitution was because they believed

   (1) amending the Constitution was too easy
   (2) too much power was given to the states
   (3) a federal court system would be too weak
   (4) individual rights were not adequately protected

11. Which heading best completes the partial outline below?

   I. _____
   A. Political parties
   B. Committee system in Congress
   C. Judicial review
   D. President's cabinet

   (1) Unwritten Constitution
   (2) Constitutional Amendments
   (3) Electoral Process
   (4) Checks and Balances

12. Washington's Proclamation of Neutrality (1793), Jefferson's Embargo Act (1807), and the Monroe Doctrine (1823) were all efforts to

   (1) avoid political conflicts with European nations
   (2) directly support European revolutions
   (3) aid Great Britain in its war against France
   (4) promote military alliances

13. The slogan "Fifty-four forty or fight!," the annexation of Texas, and the Mexican War all relate to the

   (1) theory of nullification
   (2) practice of secession
   (3) belief in Manifest Destiny
   (4) idea of due process

14. As the United States acquired more land between 1803 and 1850, controversy over these territories focused on the

   (1) need for schools and colleges
   (2) failure to conserve natural resources
   (3) expansion of slavery
   (4) construction of transcontinental railroads

15. As the Civil War began, President Abraham Lincoln stated that his primary goal was to

   (1) end slavery
   (2) set new national boundaries
   (3) increase congressional powers
   (4) preserve the Union

Name _____ **Date** _____

Directions Review the Test-Taking Strategies section of this book. Then answer the following questions, drawn from actual Regents examinations. For each statement or question, choose the number of the word or expression that, of those given, best completes the statement or answers the question.

1. Constitutional amendments adopted during Reconstruction were intended to
   (1) provide legal and political rights for African Americans
   (2) end property and religious qualifications for voting
   (3) correct problems with the electoral college system
   (4) limit the number of terms of the President

2. In the South, the passage of Jim Crow laws in the 1870s and 1880s led directly to the
   (1) racial integration of public schools
   (2) decline of the Democratic party
   (3) organization of the Ku Klux Klan
   (4) segregation of public facilities

3. In an outline, which main topic would include the other three?
   (1) Erie Canal
   (2) Nineteenth-Century Internal Improvements
   (3) Transcontinental Railroad
   (4) National Road

4. The growth of big business in the late 1800s resulted in
   (1) a reduction in child labor
   (2) the elimination of the middle class
   (3) the widening of the economic gap between rich and poor
   (4) a shift in transportation investment from railroads to canals

5. Mark Twain labeled the late 1800s in the United States the "Gilded Age" to describe the
   (1) end of the practice of slavery
   (2) absence of international conflicts
   (3) extremes of wealth and poverty
   (4) achievements of the labor movement

6. During the late nineteenth century, which practices were used by employers against workers?
   (1) boycotts and lockouts
   (2) picketing and walkouts
   (3) blacklists and yellow-dog contracts
   (4) mass rallies and sit-down strikes

Base your answers to questions 7 and 8 on the speakers' statements below and on your knowledge of social studies.

Speaker A: "When demand ran high, and markets were scarce, he showed little mercy, broke his contracts for delivery and raised prices."

Speaker B: "The man of wealth must hold his fortune 'in trust' for the community and use it for philanthropic and charitable purposes."

Speaker C: "It is cruel to slander the rich because they have been successful. They have gone into great enterprises that have enriched the nation and the nation has enriched them."

Speaker D: "The fruits of the toil of millions are boldly stolen to build up colossal fortunes for the few, unprecedented in the history of mankind."

7. Which two speakers would most likely label late nineteenth-century industrialists as *robber barons*?
   (1) A and B   (3) B and C
   (2) A and D   (4) C and D

8. The most valid conclusion that can be drawn from the different viewpoints of these speakers is that industrialists of the late nineteenth century
   (1) benefited and harmed society
   (2) treated their workers fairly
   (3) used illegal means to gain wealth
   (4) generally opposed the free-enterprise economic system

Name _____ **Date** _____

9. In the last half of the 1800s, which development led to the other three?

(1) expansion of the middle class
(2) growth of industrialization
(3) formation of trusts
(4) creation of labor unions

10. Which action by the federal government during the late 1800s is an example of nativism?

(1) passage of the Chinese Exclusion Act
(2) creation of tribal reservations in the East
(3) grants of financial aid to western farmers
(4) support for the construction of transcontinental railroads

Base your answers to questions 11 and 12 on the speakers' statements below and on your knowledge of social studies.

Speaker A: "Our nation has grown and prospered from the ideas and labor of immigrants. The nation has been enriched by immigrants from different nations who brought new ideas and lifestyles, which have become part of American culture."

Speaker B: "United States industries are competing with established European manufacturers. To prosper, American industries need the vast supply of unskilled labor that is provided by immigrants."

Speaker C: "Immigrants are taking jobs at low wages without regard for long hours and workers' safety. American workers must unite to end this unfair competition."

Speaker D: "Immigrants arrive in American cities poor and frightened. They are helped to find jobs or housing. These newcomers should show their gratitude at voting time."

11. Which speaker is most clearly expressing the melting pot theory?

(1) A   (3) C
(2) B   (4) D

12. Speaker D is expressing an opinion most like that of a

(1) labor union member
(2) religious leader
(3) factory owner
(4) political party boss

13. The Gentlemen's Agreement, literacy tests, and the quota system were all attempts by Congress to restrict

(1) immigration
(2) property ownership
(3) voting rights
(4) access to public education

14. In the ten years following the Civil War, a large numbers of former slaves earned a living by becoming

(1) conductors on the Underground Railroad
(2) workers in Northern factories
(3) sharecroppers on Southern farms
(4) gold miners in California

15. The tragedy of the Triangle Shirtwaist Company fire of 1911 drew national attention to the need to

(1) restrict immigration from southern Europe
(2) establish full-time fire departments
(3) protect the safety of workers
(4) improve conditions for tenement dwellers

16. During the late 1800s, many farmers supported the idea that free and unlimited coinage of silver would

(1) end farm subsidies
(2) help farmers to repay their loans
(3) lead to lower prices for consumer goods
(4) decrease prices for farmland

Unit 4 Pre-Test

Name _____   **Date** _____

Directions Review the Test-Taking Strategies section of this book. Then answer the following questions, drawn from actual Regents examinations. For each statement or question, choose the number of the word or expression that, of those given, best completes the statement or answers the question.

1. Which development led to the other three?

(1) growth of tenements and slums

(2) shift from a rural to an urban lifestyle

(3) rapid industrial growth

(4) widespread use of child labor

2. During the Progressive Era, muckrakers published articles and novels primarily to

(1) advance their own political careers

(2) make Americans aware of problems in society

(3) help the federal government become more efficient

(4) provide entertainment for readers

3. Which heading best completes the partial outline below?

```
I. _____
   A. Secret ballot
   B. Direct election of senators
   C. Recall
   D. Referendum
```

(1) Checks and Balances

(2) Unwritten Constitution

(3) Progressive Reforms

(4) Universal Suffrage

4. Which long-awaited goal of the women's rights movement was achieved during the Progressive Era?

(1) right to vote

(2) right to own property

(3) equal pay for equal work

(4) equal access to employment and education

Base your answer to question 5 on the speakers' statements below and on your knowledge of social studies.

Speaker A: It is more important now to focus on vocational training and economic opportunities than on removing obstacles to social equality for African Americans.

Speaker B: The Constitution is color-blind and recognizes no superior class in this country. All citizens are equal before the law.

Speaker C: The American Negro [African American] must focus on the achievement of three goals: higher education, full political participation, and continued support for civil rights.

Speaker D: African Americans should return home to Africa to establish their own independent nation free from white control.

5. During the early 1900s, reform leaders tried to advance the goals of Speaker C by

(1) supporting passage of Jim Crow laws

(2) forming the Tuskegee Institute in Alabama

(3) avoiding attempts to overturn racial segregation in the courts

(4) creating the National Association for the Advancement of Colored People (NAACP)

6. A similarity between the Bank of the United States, created in 1791, and the present-day Federal Reserve System is that both were established to

(1) set tariff rates

(2) regulate the money supply

(3) achieve balanced budgets

(4) restrict the gold supply

7. The Spanish-American War (1898) marked a turning point in United States foreign policy because the United States

(1) developed a plan for peaceful coexistence

(2) emerged as a major world power

(3) pledged neutrality in future European conflicts

(4) refused to become a colonial power

Name _____   **Date** _____

8. Which heading best completes the partial outline below?

> I. _____
> A. Sea power is the key to national greatness.
> B. United States missionaries spread Christian principles.
> C. The Anglo-Saxon civilization is the best in the world.
> D. Sugar plantations in Hawaii were developed by Americans.

(1) Reasons to Declare War on Spain
(2) Justification for American Imperialism
(3) Theodore Roosevelt's Political Platform
(4) Yellow Journalism in Newspapers

9. What was a major reason for United States entry into World War I?

(1) to overthrow the czarist government of Russia
(2) to keep Latin America from being attacked by Germany
(3) to maintain freedom of the seas
(4) to break up the colonial empires of the Allies

Base your answers to questions 10 and 11 on the statements below that discuss immigration laws in the early twentieth century, and on your knowledge of social studies.

Speaker A: A literacy test as a requirement for immigration to the United States is reasonable. Great numbers of uneducated workers take jobs and good wages from our workers.

Speaker B: Requiring literacy of immigrants is unfair. It will keep people out because they lacked the opportunity to gain an education.

Speaker C: A literacy test will allow more people from northern and western Europe to enter. They are similar to the majority of the United States population.

Speaker D: Literacy is not an issue. The real purpose of this law is to discriminate against immigrants from certain parts of the world.

10. Supporters of literacy tests to restrict immigration would most likely favor the views of Speakers

(1) A and C   (3) B and D
(2) B and C   (4) A and B

11. The immigrants referred to by Speaker D were mainly from

(1) Canada and Mexico
(2) South America
(3) western Europe
(4) southern and eastern Europe

12. In the case *Schenck v. United States* (1919), the United States Supreme Court settled the issue of limits on individual freedoms during wartime by establishing the

(1) clear and present danger test
(2) states' rights principle
(3) separate but equal doctrine
(4) popular sovereignty principle

13. One goal for a lasting peace that president Woodrow Wilson included in his Fourteen Points was

(1) establishing a League of Nations
(2) maintaining a permanent military force in Europe
(3) returning the United States to a policy of isolationism
(4) blaming Germany for causing World War I

14. Many senators who opposed United States membership in the League of Nations argued that joining the League would

(1) involve the nation in future military conflicts
(2) reduce freedom of the seas
(3) end the country's free-trade policy
(4) endanger the nation's military preparedness

Unit 5 Pre-Test

Name _____ **Date** _____

Directions Review the Test-Taking Strategies section of this book. Then answer the following questions, drawn from actual Regents examinations. For each statement or question, choose the number of the word or expression that, of those given, best completes the statement or answers the question.

1. Improved mass-production techniques affected the American economy of the 1920s by
   (1) reducing prices of consumer goods
   (2) lowering the quality of most products
   (3) causing higher unemployment
   (4) decreasing the quantity of manufactured products

2. During most of the 1920s, which group experienced the most severe economic problems?
   (1) owners of small family farms
   (2) workers in the automobile industry
   (3) bankers in urban centers
   (4) entertainers in the field of radio

3. The Harlem Renaissance of the 1920s can best be described as
   (1) an organization created to help promote African American businesses
   (2) a movement that sought to draw people back to the inner cities
   (3) a relief program to provide jobs for minority workers
   (4) a period of great achievement by African-American writers, artists, and performers

4. The influence of nativism during the 1920s is best illustrated by the
   (1) increase in the popularity of the automobile
   (2) emergence of the flappers
   (3) expansion of trusts and monopolies
   (4) growth of the Ku Klux Klan

5. "Public Ignores Prohibition Restrictions"
   "Evolution and Creation Debated in Scopes Trial"
   "Women Bring Change to the Industrial Workforce"

   What do headlines such as these from the 1920s illustrate?
   (1) conflict between traditional and modern values
   (2) trend toward mass consumption of consumer goods
   (3) hostility of certain groups toward ethnic minorities
   (4) debate over the role of government in the economy

6. The Red Scare, the National Origins Acts of the 1920s, and the verdict in the Sacco and Vanzetti trial are examples of negative American attitudes toward
   (1) immigrants
   (2) business leaders
   (3) African Americans
   (4) labor union leaders

7. Statistics such as the gross domestic product, consumer price index, and unemployment rate are used to measure the
   (1) condition of the economy
   (2) amount of the federal budget deficit
   (3) balance of international trade
   (4) productivity of industry

8. Which heading would be most appropriate for the partial outline below?

I. _____
A. Wages lagging behind the cost of living
B. Overproduction of consumer goods
C. Excessive buying on credit

   (1) Mercantilist Economic Theory
   (2) Features of a Bull Stock Market
   (3) Monopolistic Business Practices
   (4) Causes of the Great Depression

Name _____   **Date** _____

9. New Deal programs such as the Civilian Conservation Corps (CCC) and the Works Progress Administration (WPA) were primarily intended to help

(1) farmers
(2) homeowners
(3) businesses
(4) unemployed workers

10. Critics of the New Deal claimed that the Tennessee Valley Authority (TVA) and the Social Security System threatened the United States economy by

(1) applying socialist principles
(2) imposing unfair working hours
(3) decreasing government spending
(4) eroding antitrust laws

11. The Federal Deposit Insurance Corporation (FDIC) and the Securities and Exchange Commission (SEC), established during the New Deal, were important because they

(1) increased the supply of money in the economy
(2) guaranteed loans to failing businesses and banks
(3) attempted to restore public confidence in financial institutions
(4) provided grants to unemployed workers

12. President Franklin D. Roosevelt tried to pack the United States Supreme Court, but Congress did not support him. This situation is an example of

(1) Congress undermining the separation of powers
(2) the President using the unwritten constitution
(3) the use of the system of checks and balances
(4) how federalism was preserved by one branch of government

13. The National Labor Relations Act (Wagner Act) of 1935 strengthened labor unions because it legalized

(1) collective bargaining
(2) blacklisting
(3) the open shop
(4) the sit-down strike

14. The New Deal tried to solve many problems of the Great Depression by

(1) providing federal aid to many sectors of the economy
(2) reducing taxes on big business to stimulate job creation
(3) lowering federal spending to maintain a balanced budget
(4) decreasing foreign competition by raising tariffs

15. One similarity in the presidential administrations of Abraham Lincoln, Franklin D. Roosevelt, and Lyndon Johnson is that each

(1) maintained a foreign policy of neutrality
(2) expanded the power of the presidency
(3) removed Supreme Court Justices from office
(4) decreased the size of the military

16. A lasting effect of the New Deal has been a belief that government should

(1) own the principal means of producing goods and services
(2) allow natural market forces to determine economic conditions
(3) maintain a balanced federal budget during hard economic times
(4) assume responsibility for the well-being of its citizens

Name _____   **Date** _____

Directions Review the Test-Taking Strategies section of this book. Then answer the following questions, drawn from actual Regents examinations. For each statement or question, choose the number of the word or expression that, of those given, best completes the statement or answers the question.

1. **"Arms Sales to Warring Nations Banned"**
"Americans Forbidden to Travel on Ships of Warring Nations"
"Loans to Nations at War Forbidden"
"War Materials Sold Only on Cash-and-Carry Basis"

These headlines from the 1930s reflect the efforts of the United States to

(1) maintain freedom of the seas
(2) send military supplies to the League of Nations
(3) limit the spread of international communism
(4) avoid participation in European wars

2. The Neutrality Acts passed by Congress in the mid-1930s were efforts to

(1) avoid mistakes that led the country into World War I
(2) create jobs for the unemployed in the military defense industry
(3) support the League of Nations efforts to stop wars in Africa and Asia
(4) help the democratic nations of Europe against Hitler and Mussolini

3. Why was the United States called the "arsenal of democracy" in 1940?

(1) The leaders in the democratic nations of Europe were educated in the United States.
(2) Most of the battles to defend worldwide democracy took place on American soil.
(3) The United States supervised elections in European nations before the war.
(4) The United States provided much of the weaponry needed to fight the Axis powers.

4. Shortly after entering World War II, the United States began the Manhattan Project to

(1) work on the development of an atomic bomb
(2) increase economic production to meet wartime demands
(3) defend New York City against a nuclear attack
(4) recruit men for the military services

5. A controversial issue that resulted from World War II was the

(1) future role of the League of Nations
(2) morality of nuclear warfare
(3) commitment of troops without congressional approval
(4) civilian control of the military

6. A main purpose of government-ordered rationing during World War II was to

(1) increase foreign trade
(2) limit the growth of industry
(3) conserve raw materials for the war effort
(4) encourage women to enter the workforce

7. The experiences of African Americans serving in the military forces during World War II influenced their postwar decision to

(1) renew support for the principle of separate but equal
(2) join the armed forces in record numbers
(3) increase efforts to end racial discrimination
(4) move back to the rural south

8. Which factor contributed to the internment of Japanese Americans during World War II?

(1) labor shortage during the war
(2) influence of racial prejudice
(3) increase of terrorist activities on the West Coast
(4) fear of loss of jobs to Japanese workers

9. The decision of the Supreme Court in *Korematsu* v. *United States* (1944) upheld the power of the president during wartime to

(1) ban terrorists from entering the country
(2) limit a group's civil liberties
(3) stop mistreatment of resident legal aliens
(4) deport persons who work for enemy nations

Name _____   **Date** _____

10. The GI Bill affected American society after World War II by
    (1) eliminating child labor
    (2) expanding voting rights
    (3) increasing spending on space exploration
    (4) extending educational and housing opportunities

11. Following World War II, Eleanor Roosevelt was most noted for her
    (1) support of racial segregation in the United States military
    (2) role in creating the United Nations Universal Declaration of Human Rights
    (3) opposition to the Truman Administration
    (4) efforts to end the use of land mines

12. The main foreign policy objective of the Marshall Plan (1948–1952) was to
    (1) stop communist aggression in Korea
    (2) fight poverty in Latin America
    (3) rebuild the economies of European nations
    (4) provide jobs for unemployed Americans

13. Which foreign policy decision by President Harry Truman is an example of the policy of containment?
    (1) relieving General MacArthur of his Korean command
    (2) recognizing the new nation of Israel
    (3) supporting the trials of war criminals in Germany and Japan
    (4) providing military aid to Greece and Turkey

14. During the Korean War, President Harry Truman removed General Douglas MacArthur from command because MacArthur
    (1) called for an immediate end to the war
    (2) refused to serve under the United Nations
    (3) lacked the experience to provide wartime leadership
    (4) threatened the constitutional principle of civilian control of the military

15. Which foreign policy term would be the most appropriate title for the partial outline below?

I. _____
A. Truman Doctrine
B. Marshall Plan
C. Berlin Blockade
D. Korean War

    (1) Imperialism   (3) Noninvolvement
    (2) Appeasement   (4) Containment

16. What was a major outcome of the Korean War (1950–1953)?
    (1) Korea continued to be a divided nation.
    (2) North Korea became an ally of the United States.
    (3) South Korea became a communist nation.
    (4) Control of Korea was turned over to the United Nations.

17. McCarthyism in the early 1950s resulted from
    (1) new commitments to civil rights for African Americans
    (2) opposition to the Marshall Plan
    (3) charges that Communists had infiltrated the United States government
    (4) increased public support for labor unions

18. During the early 1950s, the tactics of Senator Joseph McCarthy were criticized because he
    (1) violated important constitutional liberties
    (2) displayed racial prejudice in his questions
    (3) opposed the use of loyalty oaths
    (4) ignored evidence of Soviet spying

Name _____   **Date** _____

Directions Review the Test-Taking Strategies section of this book. Then answer the following questions, drawn from actual Regents examinations. For each statement or question, choose the number of the word or expression that, of those given, best completes the statement or answers the question.

1. In 1957, President Dwight D. Eisenhower sent federal troops to Little Rock, Arkansas, to
   (1) protect civil rights marchers
   (2) help African Americans register to vote
   (3) enforce a Supreme Court decision to desegregate public schools
   (4) end race riots resulting from a bus boycott

2. Which strategy did African American students use when they refused to leave a "whites only" lunch counter in Greensboro, North Carolina, in 1960?
   (1) economic boycott
   (2) hunger strike
   (3) petition drive
   (4) civil disobedience

3. The Equal Pay Act, the Title IX education amendment, and the proposed Equal Rights amendment (ERA) were primarily efforts to improve the status of
   (1) African Americans
   (2) American Indians
   (3) migrant workers
   (4) women

4. One reason for the creation of the Peace Corps by President John F. Kennedy was to
   (1) stop the spread of AIDS in Africa and Asia
   (2) gain control of territory in Latin America
   (3) provide workers for industrial nations
   (4) give support to developing nations

5. A major goal of President Lyndon Johnson's Great Society program was to
   (1) control economic inflation
   (2) end poverty in the United States
   (3) repeal several New Deal social programs
   (4) return responsibility for welfare programs to the states

6. "Batista Driven from Power"
   "Bay of Pigs Invasion Fails"
   "U-2 Planes Reveal Soviet Missiles"
   These headlines refer to the relationship between the United States and
   (1) Canada   (3) Mexico
   (2) Cuba   (4) Panama

7. United States involvement in the Vietnam War was based in part on a desire to
   (1) prevent renewed Japanese expansionism in the Pacific
   (2) assure access to an adequate supply of oil from the Middle East
   (3) contain communism in Southeast Asia
   (4) protect American business interests in China

8. The main goal of President Richard Nixon's foreign policy of détente was to
   (1) assure American victory in Vietnam
   (2) resolve conflicts in the Middle East
   (3) abolish the North Atlantic Treaty Organization (NATO)
   (4) improve relations with the Soviet Union

9. Which statement best describes an impact of the Watergate scandal on American society?
   (1) The modern environmental movement began.
   (2) Public trust in government declined.
   (3) Voter turnout in elections increased.
   (4) An economic recession ended.

10. A major policy of President Ronald Reagan's administration was to
    (1) reduce defense spending
    (2) lower federal income tax rates
    (3) end desegregation of public facilities
    (4) promote regulation of small businesses

Name _____   **Date** _____

11. **"Gorbachev Proposes Nuclear Arms Reductions"**
"Berliners Travel Freely Between East and West"
"Russia Seeks To Join NATO"

These headlines are most closely associated with the

(1) military arms race
(2) decline of Cold War hostilities
(3) failures of the containment policy
(4) successes of communism in the Soviet Union

12. The North American Free Trade Agreement (NAFTA) and the General Agreement on Trade and Tariffs (GATT) have encouraged countries to

(1) participate in the global economy
(2) create a uniform international currency
(3) accept similar wage and price controls
(4) regulate multinational corporations

13. *The Jungle* by Upton Sinclair and *Unsafe at Any Speed* by Ralph Nader were both intended to

(1) publicize the growing violence in American society
(2) suggest that a poor person could get rich with hard work
(3) encourage immigration reform
(4) make the public aware of the poor quality of certain products

14. The dispute over counting Florida voter ballots in the presidential election of 2000 was settled by

(1) an order of the governor of Florida
(2) an agreement between the candidates
(3) a vote of the United States Senate
(4) a United States Supreme Court decision

15. The United States intervened in Haiti and Bosnia during the 1990s to

(1) gain access to new markets
(2) acquire colonies for an economic empire
(3) stop conflicts within those nations
(4) disrupt international drug trafficking

16. As the average age of the nation's population increases, there will be a need to

(1) create more child care facilities
(2) address the financing of Medicare
(3) increase the number of public schools
(4) reform immigration laws

Geography and the Development of the United States

Unit Overview

This unit provides a general review of the physical and cultural geography of the United States. It also reviews some of the ways in which geography has influenced the history of the country. Geographers use five themes to study an area. The five themes are location, place, movement, regions, and human-environment interaction.

These are some of the key questions relating to the nation's geography. Each question relates to one of the five geographic themes:

- Where is the United States located, both absolutely and relatively? How has the country's relative location changed over time?
- What are the physical and human characteristics of the United States?
- How have people, goods, and ideas moved between places?
- How are places within the United States similar to and different from other places?
- How have people in the United States interacted with the natural environment?

Geography and the Development of the United States

Key Themes and Concepts

As you review this unit, take special note of the following key themes and concepts:

Physical Systems: How have the nation's systems of mountains and waterways influenced the development of the United States?

Immigration and Migration: What have been the major patterns of immigration and movement of people over the course of the country's history?

Places and Regions: What different types of regions exist within the United States?

Key Terms

geographers	Mississippi River	Manifest Destiny
geography	Appalachian	Sun Belt
demographic	Mountains	Pacific Northwest
Great Plains	Rocky Mountains	Great Lakes
Central Plains	population density	Middle Atlantic
Midwest	New England	Region

Location

Geographers describe the location of an area in both absolute and relative terms. An atlas is the best source for identifying both physical and political place locations as well as other demographic information.

Absolute Location

In terms of its absolute location, the United States is located in the Northern and Western hemispheres. With the exception of Hawaii, the country is located on the continent of North America. The country is bordered by the Atlantic Ocean on the east and the Pacific Ocean on the west.

Relative Location

Geographers also consider an area's relative location, or where it is located in relation to other places. For example, the United States is located south of Canada and north of Mexico. California is west of New York.

The relative location of a place can also change over time. For much of the country's history, Americans felt relatively isolated from Europe and Asia. Likewise, people in the West felt relatively isolated from the East.

Changes in transportation and communication technologies changed these perceptions. For example, the number of post offices in the nation leaped from 75 in 1790 to 8,450 in 1830. Regular mail delivery made it easier for people in distant places to communicate with one another. Improved communication and transportation helped tie together different parts of the country as it grew in both size and population.

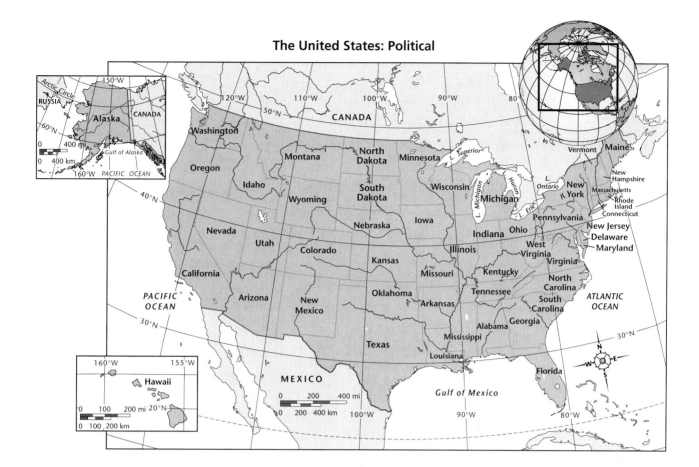

The United States: Political

Place

Geographers study both the physical and human characteristics of places. Both physical and human characteristics of the **geography** of the United States have had a huge impact on the development of the country. Geographers use a number of types of maps. Physical maps show land features such as rivers and mountains. Political maps illustrate state or country boundaries and various political divisions such as counties and cities. **Demographic** maps show the placement of groups of people by different categories such as age or income level or education. The ability to develop maps forecasting weather conditions has improved dramatically with the use of modern technology.

Physical Characteristics

Physical characteristics include landforms, water bodies, vegetation, and climate. Because of its size, the United States has a wide variety of landforms. As the map on this page shows, the **Great Plains** and the **Central Plains** occupy the central regions of the country, also known as the **Midwest.** The rich soils and climate of the Midwest encouraged Americans to move to these regions, where they could acquire inexpensive farmland. The **Mississippi River** cuts through the Central Plains as it flows south to the Gulf of Mexico. Boats traveling along the Mississippi allowed farmers and traders to transport their goods to markets throughout the country.

Two mountain ranges run from north to south on either side of the Central Plains region. In the east are the lower, older **Appalachian Mountains.** In the west are the **Rocky Mountains.** The Rockies are a cordillera, or a related set of mountain ranges, that stretches from northern Alaska to Mexico, forming the longest mountain chain in North America.

Analyzing Documents

This map shows the fifty states of the United States.

- Where is New York located in relation to Florida?

- What types of regions are shown on this map?

- What two foreign countries share their borders with the United States?

The United States and Canada: Physical

KEY

Elevation

Feet	Meters
Over 13,000	Over 3,960
6,500–13,000	1,980–3,960
1,600–6,500	480–1,980
650–1,600	200–480
0–650	0–200
Below sea level	Below sea level

Lambert Azimuthal Equal-Area Projection

Analyzing Documents

Study the map on this page; then answer the following questions.

- What major landform occupies the central region of the United States?

- Which mountain range is higher, the Appalachian Mountains or the Rocky Mountains?

Human Characteristics

Several waves of immigration have created a unique cultural mix of people in the United States. People from every region of the world have settled in the United States. As a result, the nation's human characteristics, such as language, religion, and customs, are varied. About half of all African Americans live in the South. About nine percent of southern residents are of Latino origin.

In general, **population density** is greater in the eastern half of the country. The most densely settled region of the country is the Northeast Corridor, which stretches along the east coast from Washington, D.C., to Boston, Massachusetts.

Compared with those in many nations of the world, people in the United States have long life expectancies, high per capita incomes, and high literacy rates.

Movement

Geographers study the movement of people, goods, and ideas within an area. The movement of people into and within the United States over the course of history can be broken into the following large patterns.

Bering Strait Land Bridge

Geographers believe that during the Ice Ages—between about 20,000 and 12,000 years ago—much of the earth's water was frozen into glaciers and ice sheets. As a result, ocean levels dropped, exposing a flat bridge of land between Alaska and eastern Asia where the Bering Strait is today. Over thousands of years, hunters from East Asia crossed the land bridge and gradually spread out over North and South America. These Paleo-Indians were the first humans in the Americas, ancestors of all the Native American peoples.

European Exploration and Slavery

By the 1500s, better ships and navigation methods allowed European explorers to find their way to North America. The first European newcomers, mainly from Spain, settled in what are now Florida, the Southwest, and Mexico. About a century later, people from France and Great Britain set up colonies on the eastern coast of North America. In addition, millions of Africans were enslaved and brought unwillingly to North America. In the 1600s the earliest English settlements in the New World, from Plymouth in Massachusetts to New Amsterdam in New York to Jamestown, Virginia, were all located near the coastline or on rivers. **New England** earned its name as it is the location of some of the earliest colonies, Massachusetts, Rhode Island, and Connecticut and later New Hampshire, Vermont, and Maine. The geography of this area encouraged small farms and commercial fishing, whereas much further south, fertile land and a long growing season encouraged the development of plantations producing tobacco, cotton, rice, and indigo. Geographically, the Appalachian Mountains limited the movement of colonists westward until the middle of the eighteenth century. Later in the century by the end of the Revolutionary War, the western border of the United States was the Mississippi River.

Movement and Migration

Time Period	Location	Reason/s	Results:
20,000 B.C. to 12,000 B.C.	Bering Strait, between Alaska and eastern Asia	Hunters in search of food and warmer climate	Settlement by Native Americans from Alaska south and west along the coastline
1500s (A.D.)	Florida, Mexico	Spanish in search of gold, glory for their nation, and to spread Christianity	Spanish language and heritage in the settled areas, eventually including California and the American Southwest
1600s–early 1700s	Coastal New England, New York, the Middle Atlantic and Southern colonies to Georgia	Religious freedom, farmland, coastal fishing resources, furs, minerals,	The Thirteen original British colonies developed
1700s	Expansion westward over the Appalachian Mountains to the Mississippi River Valley	Population growth encouraged expansion westward	The concept of the frontier as the western boundary of the new country was extended further west
1800s	Across the Great Plains and the Rocky Mountains to California	Continued growth of population, immigration	Manifest Destiny accepted as American right, acquisition of additional territory

United States Territorial Expansion, 1783–1853

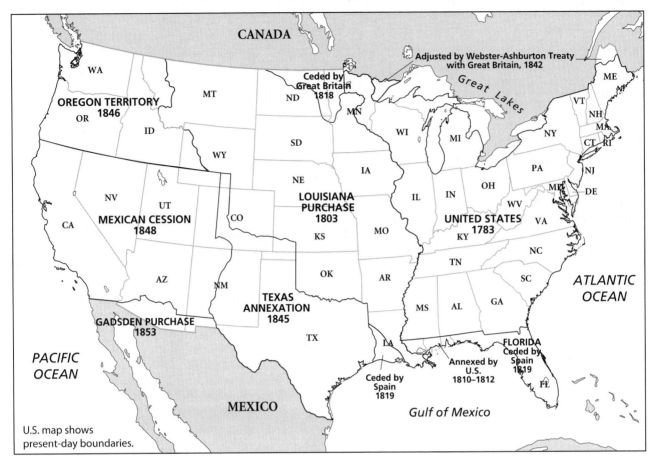

U.S. map shows present-day boundaries.

Analyzing Documents

The movement of people from east to west put pressure on the government to expand the territory of the United States. Study the map above; then answer the following questions.

- What was the date of the Louisiana Purchase?

- When were the lands of the present-day states of Washington and Oregon added to the country's territory?

- Using the information on this map, describe the acquisition of present-day California.

Migration from East to West

During the 1800s, the promise of land and gold led many Americans of European descent to move westward. Farmers along the Ohio and Mississippi River Valleys benefitted from the Louisiana Purchase and the acquisition of New Orleans as a port for American agricultural goods. Native Americans were forced from their lands to locations even further west. Rivers, turnpikes, canals, and railroads all played a part in the movement of people to the frontiers of the west. The flat grassy region between the Mississippi River and the Rocky Mountains is known as the Great Plains. This fertile farmland was a great attraction, and the Homestead Act of 1862 provided for the development of additional farms in the area. **Manifest Destiny** was the concept that expressed the American belief that the United States was destined to expand across North America. Throughout the seventeenth, eighteenth, and nineteenth centuries, the American frontier shifted further and further westward. The Atlantic Ocean to the east and the Pacific Ocean to the west enhanced the ability of the United States to maintain a policy of political neutrality for many years.

African American Migration

African Americans moved from the South to the Northeast and Midwest in search of economic opportunities from about 1890 to 1920 and again during the 1940s.

The Rise of the Sun Belt

Beginning around 1950, many Americans moved from the industrial cities of the North and Midwest to the so-called **Sun Belt**—the southern states stretching from Florida to California. Newcomers were attracted by job opportunities and warmer climates.

This population shift, along with its corresponding reapportionment of congressional seats, has given the South greater influence in American politics. Once a stronghold for Democrats, the South has become more strongly Republican and conservative.

Regions

The continental United States from east to west covers a distance of over three thousand miles. The states of Hawaii in the Pacific Ocean and Alaska in the North Pacific expand the country's geographic dimensions. Given this huge size, it is not surprising that geographers can identify hundreds of regions within the country.

Different Types of Regions

Geographers describe regions as places having at least one common characteristic. Regions can be defined by physical characteristics, such as landforms or climate. They can also be defined by cultural characteristics, such as the economy of the area or the political organization of the area. The map below shows regions that share similar economies or land use patterns. Political regions include towns, counties, cities, states, and the United States as a whole.

In the United States, geographers use terms to describe groups of states. They use "Midwest" to describe states such as Ohio, Indiana, and Illinois. They use **"Pacific Northwest"** to describe Oregon and Washington. They also refer to the states where the Rocky Mountains are as the "Rocky Mountain area." Climatic conditions can cause a region to be identified for its frequency of tornadoes, hurricanes, or snowstorms. The cultural characteristics of people might also designate a region, such as the region around Lancaster, Pennsylvania, where many Amish people live. As you study the history and development of the United States, think about how various immigrant groups gave certain regions distinctive names, for example, New York City's Chinatown.

Analyzing Documents

Study the land-use map on this page; then answer the following questions.

- What is the major land use activity in the Midwest?

- How do the economic activities of the Pacific Northwest compare with those of the Northeast?

- Where are the most concentrated areas of manufacturing and trade located?

Land Use in the United States

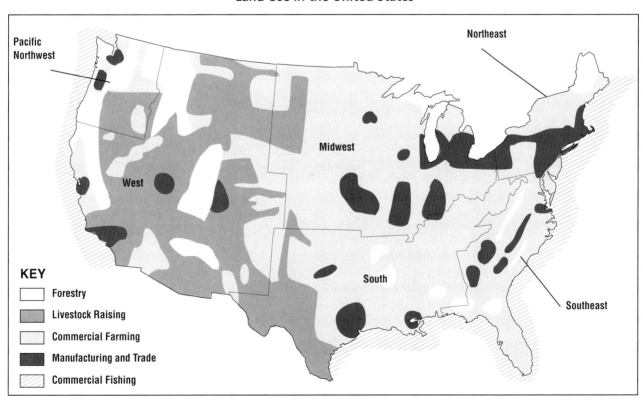

KEY
- ☐ Forestry
- ▨ Livestock Raising
- ☐ Commercial Farming
- ■ Manufacturing and Trade
- ▨ Commercial Fishing

Regions Within New York State

In New York State, some examples of regions include the **Great Lakes** region, the Adirondack Mountains, Long Island, the Finger Lakes, Manhattan, and the Capital District around Albany.

Human-Environment Interaction

When studying an area, geographers also examine how people use the environment and how they have changed it. What are the consequences of those changes?

Early Land Use Patterns

From the earliest days of settlement, Americans have been interacting with their environment to survive. When the Europeans began to settle along the Atlantic coast, they faced a range of climatic and geographic conditions. At various points in this nation's history, these conditions both encouraged and discouraged settlement. In some places, Native Americans assisted the Europeans in adapting to their unfamiliar surroundings.

Key Themes and Concepts

Places
- Why did some cities develop as ports?
- Why might Chicago and St. Louis be considered port cities also?

The great Atlantic coastal plain fostered agricultural development in the **Middle Atlantic Region,** while further to the south, the long, hot summers gave rise to the tobacco and cotton industries. Settlers of coastal South Carolina drained swamps to create thriving rice plantations. The rocky soil of New England discouraged extensive farming, but the rich coastal waters encouraged the development of fishing and shipbuilding. The waterfalls in the area and elsewhere in the Middle Atlantic states encouraged the development of factories that could benefit from water power. These factories produced goods that were then traded all over the world. Port cities, such as Boston, New York, Charleston, Savannah, and New Orleans, developed as centers of this trade. Even today population density is impacted by geographic features. Coastal areas and river valleys tend to attract development much faster than deserts or mountainous areas.

Tourism and Conservation

In addition to the land-use patterns on the previous page, tourism is another form of land use. The national parks are an example of human-environment interaction in which the landscape and natural resources are preserved for the enjoyment of future generations. Niagara Falls, New York, leads a double life as a tourist attraction for its natural beauty and as a major source of hydroelectric power.

It was only in the late twentieth century that many people began to realize the need to protect and preserve the environment for future generations. Today, geographic issues include waste disposal, air and water pollution, energy sources, and energy use, and topics related to demographics, such as the changing composition of the population, the "graying" of America, and the effects of the baby boom generation.

21st Century Geographic Concerns and Interests

The availability of clean water will be an increasing concern into the 21st century. Some parts of the United States, such as the Southwest, are usually very dry, and other areas have experienced extreme seasonal droughts. The Great Lakes area is a tremendous source of fresh water but has been plagued by industrial pollution for many years. Currently there are serious efforts to correct this situation on local, state, and national levels. Some of the drier areas of the United States have expressed interest in the possibility of accessing this water source. As you might imagine, this is a controversial topic.

Looking Ahead

As you continue through this review book, you will have many opportunities to utilize the concepts of location, place, movement, regions, and human-environment interaction. Use the maps located in this unit and elsewhere in this text to help you draw conclusions about the impact geography has had and continues to have on the development of the United States.

In recent years the Regents examination has included multiple-choice questions, one Thematic Essay Question, and one Document-Based Question. This unit includes one Thematic Essay Question. To succeed on the Regents examination, you may need to review these pages after you have completed your United States History and Government course. If you are using this text as a review aid, try to answer as many of these questions as you can before you refer to the other sections of the text.

Analyzing Documents

Study the climate map on this page; then answer the following questions.`

• Much of the southwestern United States has a hot, dry, arid climate and receives less than 10 inches of rainfall each year. Many people have been moving to this region in recent decades. How do you think climate affects the human-environment interaction in this region?

• Describe the climate of the southeastern half of the United States.

The United States and Canada: Climate Regions

KEY

- Tropical wet
- Tropical wet and dry
- Semiarid
- Arid
- Mediterranean
- Humid subtropical
- Marine west coast
- Humid continental
- Subarctic
- Tundra
- Highlands

Lambert Azimuthal Equal-Area Projection

Thematic Essay Question

Directions: Write a well-organized essay that includes an introduction, several paragraphs addressing the task below, and a conclusion.

Theme: **Influence of Geographic Factors on Governmental Actions**

> Actions taken by the United States government have often been influenced by geographic factors. Some of these factors include location, climate, natural resources, and physical features.

Task:

> Identify *two* actions taken by the United States government that have been influenced by geographic factors and for *each*
>
> - State *one* reason the United States took the action
> - Describe how a geographic factor influenced the action
> - Discuss the impact of the action on the United States

You may use any action taken by the United States government that was influenced by a geographic factor. Some suggestions you might wish to consider include the Lewis and Clark expedition (1804–1806), issuance of the Monroe Doctrine (1823), Mexican War (1846–1848), Commodore Perry's opening of Japan (1853), passage of the Homestead Act (1862), purchase of Alaska (1867), construction of the Panama Canal (1904–1914), entry into World War II (1941), passage of the Interstate Highway Act (1956), and involvement in the Persian Gulf War (1991).

You are *not* limited to these suggestions.

Guidelines:

In your essay, be sure to:

- Develop all aspects of the task
- Support the theme with relevant facts, examples, and details
- Use a logical and clear plan of organization, including an introduction and a conclusion that are beyond a restatement of the theme

In developing your answer, be sure to keep these general definitions in mind:

(a) **describe means "to illustrate something in words or tell about it"**
(b) **discuss means "to make observations about something using facts, reasoning, and argument; to present in some detail"**

Constitutional Foundations for the United States Democratic Republic

Section 1: The Constitution: The Foundation of American Society

Section 2: The Constitution Tested: Nationalism and Sectionalism

Unit Overview

Unit 2 covers the period from the first English settlement in 1607 through the end of the Civil War in 1865. The focus of the unit is the Constitution of the United States—its historical and constitutional foundations, including the ways in which the nation's government, based on the Constitution, developed and was then tested.

Some of the key questions about the United States government and constitutional history through 1865 include:

- What was the influence of the colonial settlement pattern, colonists' experience living in the American colonies, colonial slavery, and Enlightenment thought on the development of the United States Constitution?

- What opinions about government were discussed and debated by the Framers? What compromises did they reach in order to create the Constitution and ensure approval by the states?

- What is the structure of the United States Constitution, and how does the government it describes function?

- What are the basic constitutional principles of American democracy? Why were they important when the Constitution was written? Why have they remained critical principles throughout United States history?

- How did the new nation go about putting its constitution into effect? What helped to build nationalism? What conflicting opinions about government were discussed and debated in those early years?

- How did sectionalism and slavery bring on a constitutional crisis that led the nation to civil war?

The Constitution: The Foundation of American Society

Section Overview

For centuries, North America was inhabited solely by Native Americans. Beginning in the sixteenth century, Europeans, mainly from Spain, France and England, came to the continent. The United States of America developed from thirteen colonies along the North American Atlantic coast, settled in the 1600s and 1700s by English and other Europeans, as well as by Africans brought as slaves.

In 1763, following the end of the French and Indian War, tensions between the colonies and England increased sharply. In 1776, after a year of fighting the British, the colonies issued the Declaration of Independence. The American Revolution resulted in victory for the former colonies.

They established a weak government under the Articles of Confederation, but in 1787 the leaders of the new nation wrote the United States Constitution. After ratification, the first government under the Constitution was formed. In its early years the new nation struggled to define itself, as political parties entered the debate over the meaning of the Constitution and how best to implement it.

Key Themes and Concepts

Take special note of the following key themes and concepts:

Diversity: In what ways did the Native Americans, the Europeans, and the Africans who met in North America differ?

Change Why did the Thirteen British Colonies become an independent nation?

Government What is the basic structure and function of the government created by the United States Constitution?

Constitutional Principles: What are the basic principles that are the foundation of our democratic form of government?

Citizenship Under the Constitution, what are the basic rights and responsibilities of a citizen of the United States?

Foreign Policy What were the major influences on United States foreign policy in the first years of the new nation?

Key People

Be sure you understand the significance of these key people:

John Locke	Patrick Henry	George Washington
Baron de Montesquieu	Samuel Adams	James Madison
Jean-Jacques Rousseau	Thomas Jefferson	Alexander Hamilton
Voltaire	Benjamin Franklin	John Marshall
John Peter Zenger	John Adams	James Monroe

Key Terms

Iroquois Confederacy
indentured servants
triangular trade
Middle Passage
democracy
republic
Magna Carta
writ of *habeas corpus*

Parliament
representative
   government
rule of law
natural rights
Enlightenment
social contract

charter
Mayflower Compact
salutary neglect
mercantilism
Articles of
   Confederation

Key Supreme Court Cases

Marbury v. *Madison*, 1803
McCulloch v. *Maryland*, 1819
Gibbons v. *Ogden*, 1824

Part 1 The Historical Foundations of American Society and Government

Before examining the Constitution of the United States and the features that make it unique, it is important to understand the roots of the ideas in the document. To do that, we must start with the historical origins of the United States of America.

The People and Peopling of the Thirteen American Colonies

The historical origins of the United States of America date from the settlement, in the seventeenth and eighteenth centuries, of thirteen English colonies along the North American Atlantic coast. There, the cultures of three different peoples came together—Native Americans (the original inhabitants), Europeans, and Africans (brought as enslaved people).

Native Americans

Native Americans were the first people to occupy the Western Hemisphere. In the late 1400s, they numbered as many as 15 million in North America alone. The way of life of Native Americans was heavily influenced by the **environment.** The Native American lifestyle in present-day northeastern and southeastern United States was based on agriculture, hunting, and fishing. Trade was an important part of this economic system. Strong social organizations rested on ties between extended families, with women in positions of some power in those tribes that were agricultural.

The Iroquois Confederacy

The most powerful government of the Eastern Woodlands Native Americans was the **Iroquois Confederacy,** formed in 1570, and made up of first five and then six Iroquois nations located in central and western New York. The Confederacy made it possible for the Iroquois to hold onto its lands against European pressure for almost two centuries, playing the English and French against each other.

Trade and Alliances

Relations between colonists and Native Americans centered around trade and exchange, alliances, or warfare. The survival of **Jamestown,** founded in 1607 as

Geography in History

• How did the environment influence the culture of Native Americans?

Preparing for the Exam

On the examination, you will need to have a thorough understanding of important United States historical and governmental terms.

• What is a confederacy?

• What are two examples of confederacies in United States history?

the first permanent English settlement in North America is credited in part to the food supplied, in return for weapons, by the Algonquin tribes that made up the Powhatan Confederacy. Native Americans also offered food to the **Plymouth Colony,** settled in 1620, in order to gain the colony as an ally against other tribes. In the 1600s, the Iroquois fought the Hurons, the Eries, and then the French for control of the fur trade between the Great Lakes region and New York. The wars with France ended in 1701 when the Iroquois adopted a policy of neutrality toward both France and England.

Interactions between Native Americans and the settlers led to outbreaks of diseases, such as measles and smallpox, which decimated the Native American population. As the Native Americans became increasingly dependent on European products, their traditional culture weakened.

Different Views and Values

Possession of the land was at the center of conflict between Native Americans and colonists. Native Americans held land in common and believed it should be used for the good of all. It could not be bought or sold, although the rights to the use of land could be transferred. The English valued individual ownership and had a tradition of buying and selling land.

There were other cultural differences. The European colonists believed in the superiority of their way of life and acted accordingly. They attempted to convert the Native Americans to Christianity and assumed that they would adopt an English lifestyle.

Preparing for the Exam

Stimulus Based Question: Political Cartoon
Examine the cartoon, then answer the following questions.

- Which groups do the speakers in this cartoon represent?

- What is the point of view of the cartoonist as shown in this document?

- What is the cartoonist's purpose for creating this document?

Warfare

In the 1600s, European settlers and Native Americans engaged in wars caused by the expansion of English settlements and fears of Native Americans for the survival of their culture. In tidewater Virginia, profitable tobacco farming led settlers to move westward into Native American lands. By 1646, after two wars, the Powhatan Confederacy was destroyed, unable to hold back the settlers' movement. In 1675 in New England, an alliance of Native American tribes launched King Philip's War. The colonists eliminated most Native Americans in southern New England. However, for the next 50 years, colonial expansion in New England was slowed.

In the 1700s, France and England competed for world power, fighting four wars for control in Europe, Asia, and North America. Because the French entered regions to trade furs, building forts rather than settlements, Native Americans tended to support them rather than the British who settled and farmed the land. **The French and Indian War** (1756–63) erupted when the English challenged the French for control of the land that is now Ohio and western Pennsylvania. The war pitted the British army and colonists against the French and their Native American allies. Toward the end of the war, the Iroquois, influenced by their earlier conflict with the French over trade, ended their neutrality and supported the British.

Analyzing Documents

"I am now grown old, and must soon die; . . . Why should you take by force that from us which you can have by love? Why should you destroy us, who have provided you with food? . . . What is the cause of your jealousy? You see us unarmed, and willing to supply your wants, if you come in a friendly manner, not with swords and guns, as to invade an enemy."
—King Powhatan, 1609

• Answer Powhatan's question, "What is the cause of your jealousy?"

• Cite specific textual evidence of the impact of European colonization on Native Americans.

The Colonists

The oldest settlement in what is now the United States is Saint Augustine, in Florida (1565). Founded by the Spanish, it did not become part of the United States until 1819. What was to become the United States began with the settlement of Virginia in 1607. By 1732, with the charter of Georgia, there were a total of 13 British colonies.

The Colonial Experience, 1607–1732

Analyzing Documents

• How many years were there between the settling of the first and the last of the 13 English colonies?

• What was the impact on the colonial experience of the political events shown on the chart?

Who Came to the Colonies

The settlers were a diverse group. They included Africans brought against their will, Scots-Irish from northern Ireland, Germans, Portuguese, Swedes, Dutch, French, Welsh, Irish, Scots, Belgians, and Swiss. In the colonial period, a large number of European immigrants came as **indentured servants** who contracted to work as many as seven years to repay the cost of their passage.

Most of each colony's population, however, was English. This fact would greatly affect the nature of the government that developed in the United States.

Why They Came

Just as the colonists represented many ethnic backgrounds, their motivations for coming to the colonies also varied.

Examine the map below then answer the following questions.

- By 1776, two thirds of the population of the English colonies lived no more than 50 miles from the ocean. Why?
- Which ethnic groups had the largest settlements in 1770? Which had the smallest settlements?
- Which natural harbors in the Thirteen Colonies contributed to the development of **commerce,** or trade between cities, states, and nations?

Religious Reasons Some colonies were founded for religious reasons, but the colonists represented different religions and had different motivations. Massachusetts, for example, was founded by Pilgrims, or Separatists, who had left the Church of England, and Puritans who wanted to reform it. Colonies controlled by the Puritans allowed no religious freedom. Rhode Island, on the other hand, permitted all religions including Judaism. Pennsylvania was founded as a refuge for Quakers and Maryland as a refuge for Roman Catholics.

Economic Reasons Economic motives were a major factor in the founding of Virginia, Delaware, and New Netherlands (later New York), as well as North and South Carolina. Georgia, the last of the colonies to be founded, was settled by debtors. Settlers in all colonies were drawn by the availability of land and the opportunity to own it.

Political Reasons Political events in seventeenth-century England influenced patterns of migration. Separatists and Puritans came to North America after having fallen into political disfavor because of their objections to the established Church of England and the king who headed it. After the monarchy was restored in 1660, colonies that included New Jersey and the Carolinas were founded on land granted by the king to his loyal supporters. Quakers, Catholics, French Huguenots, and Jews came to escape religious intolerance as well as governmental persecution.

Colonial Settlement by Ethnic Group in 1770

Map legend:
- English
- African
- Scots-Irish
- German and Swiss
- Scottish
- W Welsh
- Dutch
- French
- S Swedish

0   150   300 Miles
0   150   300 Kilometers

What Influenced Their Experiences

Geography was a primary influence on the colonial way of life. So were the practices colonists brought from their homelands. Ethnic groups tended to settle together. Large distances and difficult transportation encouraged continuing family patterns, gender roles, and farming methods brought from Europe, although these were sometimes modified by the new environment. Native American and African cultures also influenced changes in colonial lifestyles.

New England

Every aspect of New England life was influenced by religion in the early colonial period. Church membership was a requirement for participation in government. Strict moral codes were enforced.

The cold climate and poor soil of New England challenged Puritan farmers, who grew crops mostly for their own families' consumption. Only when they reached the Connecticut River Valley with its richer soil were they successful at commercial farming.

New England developed a diversified economy. Although farming was the most common occupation, New England also became the center of colonial shipping, with major ports at Boston and Salem. Fishing and ship building were among the related industries. Merchants and professionals made up the wealthiest social class.

The Middle Colonies

The middle colonies had a diverse population, including Dutch, Germans, and Scots-Irish. These colonies, especially New York and Pennsylvania, benefited from more fertile soil. They exported wheat and corn, and this trade helped build New York and Philadelphia. Large numbers of tenant farmers—who rented rather than owned the land—lived in the Hudson River Valley of New York and in New Jersey.

The Southern Colonies

In the southern colonies a warmer climate, rich soil, and long growing season led to the development of the plantation system. This agricultural economy was based on tobacco, rice and indigo crops grown for export, cultivated first by indentured servants and then by enslaved Africans.

The wealthiest social class included Chesapeake tobacco planters and the owners of the Carolina rice plantations. The central role of plantation agriculture led to a growing dependence on slavery to support the economic, social, and political systems of the southern colonies.

Comparing the Thirteen Colonies 1607–1760

	New England Colonies MA, RI, CT, NH	Middle Colonies NY, NJ, PA, DE	Southern Colonies VA, MD, NC, SC, GA
Geography	cold winters, rocky soil, short growing season, mountains, forests, rivers, natural harbors	less severe winters, fertile soil, rivers, natural harbors	mild, long growing season, fertile soil, tidal rivers, wide coastal plain
Early Colonists	English Pilgrims, mostly English Puritans	Dutch, English, Welsh, Germans, Scots-Irish, Irish, Swedes, French	English, enslaved Africans
Economy 17th to Mid-18th Centuries	diverse economy included small-scale farming, fishing, fur trade, shipbuilding, lumbering, trade and commerce, crafts, and industry. Major City: Boston	economy included medium-scale farming for cash crops of wheat, corn, and flax, as well as fur trade, trade, crafts, and industry. Major Cities: Philadelphia, New York	highly agricultural: economy included large plantations, which used indentured servants or slave labor, to produce cash crops of tobacco, rice, and indigo. Major City: Charleston, SC
Lifestyle	high literacy level, Protestant work ethic, town meetings; Colonial colleges: Harvard (the oldest), Yale, College of RI (Brown), Dartmouth	most regional diversity in religion and nationalities; Colonial colleges: Princeton, Pennsylvania, Columbia (King's), Rutgers (Queen's)	self-sufficient plantation life, few cities, least populated and developed region, small farmers largest social group; Colonial college: William and Mary
Influences on Gov't	1620: Mayflower Compact (MA) 1639: Fundamental Orders of CT	1683: NY Chapter of Liberties	1619: House of Burgesses (VA) 1649: Act of Toleration (MD)

The Africans

By 1700, the institution of slavery—primarily involving Africans—already served to highlight the regional differences in the colonies.

Origins of the Atlantic Slave Trade

The first enslaved people in the Americas were Native Americans. In the 1500s, the Spanish and Portuguese forced them to work in mines and on sugar plantations. After the Native American population declined as a result of European diseases, the Spanish, Portuguese, and French began enslaving West Africans. With the growth of tobacco, indigo, and rice plantations, the British colonies also began to participate in the slave trade. By the early 1700s, England controlled the Atlantic slave trade.

There was a two-way trade between England and the colonies for goods such as grains, fish, fur, wood products, tobacco, indigo, and rice, which the colonies exchanged for English manufactured goods. The slave trade, however, was a

triangular trade. New England merchants traded rum for enslaved people in West Africa. The enslaved people were sold in the West Indies for molasses or sugar, which was shipped to New England to make more rum.

Geography in History

- Find a trade pattern that is an example of mercantilism.
- Find an example of the triangular trade.

Reading Strategy

Analyzing Patterns of Cause and Effect

- Use multiple sources such as text, maps, charts, to examine the impact of geography on the patterns of colonial settlement and the development of colonial economic systems.

- Identify and analyze specific examples of the relationship between environment and human activities.

Development of Slavery in the Colonies

The first African enslaved people were brought to Virginia in 1619. At this time, most were considered indentured servants and were considered free when their contracts ended.

By 1700, a race-based definition of a slave that included restrictions and punishments, was written into law. Soon a **system of permanent slavery** was in place. It was a legal system that both discriminated against and exploited the Africans and African Americans. The slave system became central to the economic system of the South. It influenced not only the economy but also the social and political systems, affecting southerners of both races.

Slavery

- This legalization of slavery coincided with an increased market for tobacco in **Virginia and the Chesapeake region,** and difficulty in obtaining European indentured servants. Working conditions on the Southern plantations alienated free workers.

- Slavery in **South Carolina and Georgia** was based on that of the Caribbean plantation system. Many of the settlers, along with their slaves, came from the West Indies. The Africans were enslaved from the time of their arrival. They were brought there to work on huge rice plantations. The slave code was the strictest in the colonies.

- Beginning in the 1800s, the **lower Mississippi Valley** contained the largest number of plantations, with 100 or more enslaved people. Cotton profits related directly to the amount of land cultivated, encouraging the slave system to grow.

- In contrast, the diverse economy, climate, and smaller farms in the **middle and northern colonies** meant slavery there was less common. At the end of the colonial period on the eve of the American Revolution, there were 50,000 enslaved people in the North compared with 400,000 in the South. While most enslaved people in the North, like those in the South, worked in agriculture, enslaved people in northern cities were often skilled tradesmen, domestic workers, and laborers. The slave codes were also milder than those of the southern colonies.

Slave Resistance

Throughout the period in which slavery was legal, Africans and African Americans resisted their enslavement. On the slave ships during the voyage from Africa to America (called the **Middle Passage**), some staged revolts. Others chose starvation or drowning as an alternative to enslavement.

Even in the face of severe punishment, some enslaved Africans attempted escape. Small communities of escaped enslaved people formed in Spanish Florida, South Carolina, Georgia, and Virginia. Other enslaved people offered more subtle resistance, such as slowing down at work, pretending illness, or damaging tools and crops.

In colonial America, open rebellion was not very common. Two notable colonial revolts took place in New York City in 1712 and at the Stono River near Charleston, South Carolina, in 1739. Both rebellions were put down by local militia. Most of the enslaved people who survived were later executed.

The Influence of Africa and African American Culture on Colonial Cultures

With succeeding generations, slaves lost some of their ethnic identity but many elements of their West African traditions became the basis of African American culture. Particularly important was maintenance of an extended family network that provided some stability in their lives. Some African words found their way into the English language, as did certain farming methods, foods, folk literature, and folk art. African building traditions of multiple small dwellings, front porches, and decorative iron work influenced southern colonial architecture. Some African musical styles and instruments, such as the banjo, continued to be incorporated into religious music and work songs. African musical traditions later influenced many forms of American music.

Major Historical Influences on American Government

The government of each of the 13 colonies reflected ideas that came from the heritage of Western civilization. Those ideas were then modified by centuries of English thought and practice and by the American colonial experience.

Ideas From Ancient Greece

The concept of **democracy,** or government by the people, began in the city-state of Athens (in what is now Greece) between 750 B.C. and 550 B.C. Athens had a direct democracy, one in which all eligible citizens participated in government.

Ideas From Ancient Rome

The concept of republican government was established by the ancient Romans. In a **republic,** voters elect representatives who speak and act for other citizens in the business of government. These representatives are supposed to work for the common good. This form of government is sometimes called representative democracy.

Preparing for the Exam

Organizing Information
- Many enslaved Africans found both peaceful and violent ways to resist their enslavement.

- What are two peaceful ways that slaves resisted?

1.

2.

- What are two violent ways that they resisted?

1.

2.

- What are two 19th century examples of these patterns of resistance?

Key Themes and Concepts

Civic Values
American political rights and governmental institutions had three major sources:

1. British constitutional, political, and historical traditions

2. Seventeenth- and eighteenth-century Enlightenment ideas

3. American colonial experience

- What is an example of how each source influenced the political rights and governmental institutions in the United States?

Reinforcing Main Ideas
• Why is the writ of *habeas corpus* called the "Great Writ of Liberty"?

• Which two rights guaranteed in the U.S. Constitution can be traced directly to the English Bill of Rights?

Influence of English Events and Documents

Other basic concepts of government and **common law** were established in England before or during the colonial period in America. The common-law system developed in England from customs and traditions enforced by court decisions. It became the basis of the legal system in nations that England colonized.

Magna Carta In 1215, English noblemen forced King John of England to agree to the Magna Carta, or Great Charter, a document that placed limits on his power to rule. For example, this document established the right to a trial by jury—but only for nobles.

Petition of Right In 1628, King Charles I signed the Petition of Right. It put in writing certain basic rights and legal traditions, such as a **writ of** *habeas corpus*— a court order requiring that a person be brought before a court and the court shown evidence why the person should be held for trial. It prevents arrest and imprisonment without a trial.

The English Bill of Rights In 1689, the Glorious Revolution ended a decades-long power struggle between the English **Parliament** and the monarchy. Parliament overthrew James II and replaced him with William and Mary, who were required to agree to the English Bill of Rights. This established that **representative government** and the **rule of law** outweighed the power of any monarch.

Foundations of American Rights

Rights	Sources of Rights			
	Magna Carta (1215)	English Bill of Rights (1689)	Virginia Declaration of Rights (1776)	Bill of Rights (1791)
Trial by jury	✔	✔		✔
Due process	✔	✔		✔
Private property	✔			✔
No unreasonable searches or seizures			✔	✔
No cruel punishment		✔	✔	✔
No excessive bail or fines		✔		✔
Right to bear arms		✔		✔
Right to petition		✔		✔
Freedom of speech			✔	✔
Freedom of the press			✔	✔
Freedom of religion			✔	✔

17th- and 18th-Century Enlightenment Thought

The Framers of the Constitution were also strongly influenced by the ideas of the philosophers of the **Enlightenment.** This intellectual movement held that reliance on reason and experience would lead to social progress.

John Locke John Locke's ideas influenced the Declaration of Independence, state constitutions, and the United States Constitution.

• **Locke** believed that people were born free with certain **natural rights,** including the rights to life, liberty, and property.

• Such rights predate any government and exist in the "state of nature."

- Locke stated that a **social contract** was formed between the people and their government in which people agree to form a state and grant to its government the powers necessary to protect their natural rights.
- Therefore, governments exist only with the **consent of the governed.**
- When a government fails to protect these rights, the contract has been broken and the people are free to change or even to replace or overthrow that government.

The Baron de Montesquieu The French philosopher Baron de Montesquieu believed that the British political system was successful because the power to govern was divided among the monarch and the two houses of Parliament. This division helped balance political power among the branches, so that no one branch had too much power.

Jean-Jacques Rousseau Another French philosopher, Jean-Jacques Rousseau, developed further the idea of a social contract. His arguments in support of government by the consent of the governed influenced the U.S. Declaration of Independence.

Voltaire A third important French philosopher, Voltaire, wrote *Philosophical Letters*, praising British institutions and rights. He wrote against religious intolerance and persecution.

The Colonial Experience: Political Rights and Mercantile Relationships

During the colonial period, two important forces helped shape a uniquely American way of life:

- political ideas based on the English experience and on Enlightenment thinking,
- the colonists' experience thousands of miles from their home country.

Colonial Charters and Self-Government

Twelve of the thirteen original colonies were founded based on charters issued by the British government. A **charter** provided legal authority to companies or individuals to start a colony. Most of the colonies were originally self-governing private enterprises, but by 1730, most became royal colonies. Even after England later centralized control, the colonies remained largely self-governing and independent.

Colonial Principles and Practices of Government

The beliefs that colonists held about the proper role of government had a strong influence over the way they structured their governments.

Limits on Government The colonists believed that the power of government should be limited, in accordance with English laws and traditions. The colonists wrote laws based on the principle that government existed to protect people's natural rights. The rights to life, liberty, and protection of property were most often mentioned. As early as 1641 in Massachusetts, the right to own property and protect it from being illegally seized by the government was written into law. The right to vote helped to protect property rights.

Enforceable Contracts Colonists believed in the right to enter into contracts. Enforceable contracts between parties can be traced to the idea of a political compact, or contract. After the United States won independence, decisions of the Marshall Court protected individuals' right to enter into contracts.

Analyzing Documents

Men being, . . . by Nature, all free, equal and independent, no one can be …subjected to the Political Power of another, without his own Consent. …For when any number of Men have, by the consent of every individual, made a Community, they have made that community one Body, with a Power to Act as one Body, which is only by the will and determination of the majority . . .
Two Treatises on Government
John Locke, 1690

- Compare this statement to the Mayflower Compact (1620) and to the Declaration of Independence (1776).

- What principle, basic to a democracy, do you find in all three documents?

Key Themes and Concepts

Constitutional Principles
The following two cases deal with property rights and economic policy:

Fletcher v. *Peck* (1810) established that a state cannot interfere with constitutionally protected contract rights.

Dartmouth College v. *Woodward* (1819) extended constitutional protection of contracts to corporate charters.

- Why are *Fletcher* v. *Peck* and *Dartmouth College* v. *Woodward* important to economic freedom?

Analyzing Documents

Reading a Primary Source
"We whose names are underwritten . . . covenant and combine ourselves together into a civil body politic, for our better ordering and preservation and furtherance of the ends aforesaid; and by virtue hereof to enact, constitute, and frame such just and equal laws, ordinances, acts, constitutions, offices from time to time as shall be thought most meet and convenient for the general good of the colony; unto which we promise all due submission and obedience."
—Mayflower Compact

- What words indicate that this is a contract or compact?

- What textual evidence is there that the intent is to establish a limited government?

Freedom of the Press Colonists believed there should be legal limits on government attempts to control what is written. In 1735, **John Peter Zenger,** a German immigrant to New York, was tried for **seditious libel** for accusing the governor of the colony of wrongdoing. Zenger's lawyer argued that no crime was committed when what Zenger had printed was true, and the jury found Zenger not guilty. Later, this case helped establish the principle of freedom of the press in the United States.

Contract Theory of Government: Mayflower Compact In 1620, before landing at Plymouth in present-day Massachusetts, an area outside of existing English authority, the Pilgrims signed the **Mayflower Compact.** This compact was a contract in which the colonists consented to be governed by a government that they created. It was the first plan for self-government and majority rule in the colonies. **The Fundamental Orders of Connecticut,** adopted in 1639, is another example of a colonial compact.

Self-Government: Colonial Assemblies and Local Governments

The importance of self-government—of participation in government by representatives of the people—is seen in the colonial assemblies established in each colony. As early as 1619, Virginia colonists took the first step toward republican government when they instituted the colonies' first representative lawmaking body, the **House of Burgesses.** Most colonies established a bicameral, or two-house, legislature modeled after the two-house English Parliament.

Colonists also recognized the need for local governments. The county was the center of local government in most of the colonies. In New England, local government was at the town level, where the **town meeting** allowed citizens to govern themselves through **direct democracy.**

Separation of Powers A system of **separation of powers** developed in the colonies. Colonial charters divided government into three branches—the legislative, the executive, and the judicial. However, since colonial governors were usually appointed by the king and the judges by the governors, it was primarily through the colonial legislatures, elected by the people, that the colonists received their training in self government.

Events Leading to the American Revolution

1754 French and Indian War begins; Albany Plan of Union		**1763** France and Great Britain sign Treaty of Paris	**1765** Parliament passes Stamp Act	**1773** Tea Act; Boston Tea Party
1750	1755	1760	1765	1770	1775
	1759 British capture Quebec	**1764** Sugar Act	**1766** Parliament repeals Stamp Act	**1774** Intolerable Acts; First Continental Congress

The Causes of the American Revolution

For almost a century before the outbreak of the American Revolution in 1775, England and France were involved in a rivalry for power, not only in Europe, but wherever the two nations had colonies. Preoccupied with France, England governed the colonies under a policy known as **salutary neglect,** or a healthy ignoring of the colonies. This policy resulted in the colonists gaining more independence in their trade practices and Great Britain benefiting from the colonies' economic prosperity. The colonies also exercised a large degree of self-government.

Before the Revolution, colonists saw themselves as British subjects and as New Yorkers, or Rhode Islanders, or Virginians. In 1754, Benjamin Franklin tried to get the colonies to join together as protection against the French. His **Albany Plan of Union,** modeled on the Iroquois Confederacy, was rejected by the colonies because each feared loss of power and independence.

The Treaty of Paris of 1763, marked Great Britain's victory over France in the Seven Years (or French and Indian) War. It also shifted the way power was distributed in North America. With French land in North America now in British hands, Native Americans could no longer benefit from balancing French and English interests against one another. The colonists felt their war efforts earned them the right to move into the newly acquired lands and saw less need for the protection of the British government. However, with the French wars ended, England changed its imperial policy toward the colonies. The **Proclamation of 1763** prohibited expansion west of the ridge of the Appalachian Mountains. The British aim was to avoid conflicts between the colonists and Native Americans. The colonists deeply resented the Proclamation and often ignored it. In 1775, colonial resistance to post-1763 British policies resulted in the American Revolution.

JOIN, or DIE.

Analyzing Documents

Ben Franklin published this political cartoon in 1754.
- Why?

- What point of view does he express?

- How was his message received?

- What was the response to this cartoon in 1765 when the Stamp Act was issued?

Cause and Effect
Turning Point

- Why is the Treaty of Paris of 1763 considered a turning point in history?

Land Claims After the French and Indian War, 1763

British territory

French territory

Spanish territory

Hudson Bay

Proclamation Line of 1763
prohibited colonial settlement west of the Appalachians.

ROCKY MOUNTAINS

Missouri R.

St. Lawrence R.

Mississippi R.

Ohio R.

APPALACHIAN MTS.

ATLANTIC OCEAN

Gulf of Mexico

PACIFIC OCEAN

0   500 Miles

0   500 Kilometers

Key Themes and Concepts

Change:
- What caused the changes in British imperial policy after 1763?

- Why did the colonists resist those changes?

- What was the result of that resistance?

Organizing Information
The American Revolution had economic, political, and social and ideological causes. List these causes by category: category; then identify those you consider the most significant.

1. Economic

2. Political

3. Social and Ideological

In May 1765, Patrick Henry voiced his opposition to the Stamp Act with a speech to the Virginia House of Burgesses. In that speech, he said:

"Caesar had his Brutus; Charles the First, his Cromwell; and George the Third . . . may profit by their example. If this be treason, make the most of it."

Brutus assassinated Caesar, and Cromwell defeated Charles I and had him beheaded.

- What is Patrick Henry's message or point of view?

- What might Patrick Henry have been implying but would not say?

- What textual evidence makes Patrick Henry's message quite clear?

Economic Causes of the Revolution

By 1763, while Great Britain had secured control of a large portion of the continent, it had a huge war debt to repay and needed money to maintain forces in the colonies in case of another French threat. Believing that the colonies should pay for their own defense, the British Parliament began to enforce its policy of mercantilism, an economic system practiced by European trading nations in the 16th, 17th, and 18th centuries.

Mercantilism held that a nation's power was based on how much gold and silver it accumulated. To that end a nation sought a favorable balance of trade by protecting manufacturing and promoting exports while limiting imports. Colonial economies were controlled to benefit the mother country. Colonies were to supply raw materials and serve as markets while restrictions limited their manufacturing and commerce. For example, the Navigation Acts (1650-1673) required that most colonial trade occurred only within the British Empire and that certain goods could be shipped only to Great Britain.

In 1764, Parliament passed the **Sugar Act** and in 1765 the **Stamp Act,** requiring a tax stamp on printed material, from newspapers to wills. While often evading the **Navigation Acts**, the colonists had accepted the right of England to regulate trade. But the primary objective of the two new acts was to raise money, and the colonists forced their repeal. The 1767 **Townshend Acts** taxed imports but again, producing revenue was the objective. In reaction, imports dropped. **Writs of Assistance**— open-ended, transferable search warrants—were issued to look for smuggled goods in merchants' ships, warehouses, and homes.

Political Causes of the Revolution

The money raised by the Townshend Acts acts would be used to pay some of the English officials in the colonies. Colonial legislatures believed this undermined their power to exert control over officials by withholding their salaries. The colonists reacted to the new taxes with petitions, boycotts, and other more violent protests. The Bill of Rights' protection against unreasonable search and seizure reflects the anger against the Writs of Assistance. **Samuel Adams,** a Boston political organizer and journalist, helped create the Sons of Liberty and the Massachusetts Committee of Correspondence.

Colonists viewed these new taxes as a threat to their liberties, including the right to property. They charged that Great Britain had violated their **natural rights** as British citizens. Because they had no representation in Parliament, colonists reasoned that taxation could come only from the colonial legislatures. Great Britain insisted that Parliament represented all of its subjects.

Social and Ideological Causes of the Revolution

Leaders in Great Britain failed to understand the colonists' fears of the power of the British government. They also did not recognize that the colonists had developed independent political lives and thoughts.

- Separation by 3,000 miles of ocean had led to a sense of self sufficiency and independence in the colonists.

- This feeling was reinforced by the colonists' belief in their natural rights as English citizens.

- The Great Awakening, a religious movement, had encouraged people to question authority and increased a sense of equality among people. Because of the abundance of land, as much as 90 percent of the white male population held enough land to qualify them for the right to vote.

The American Revolution and the Declaration of Independence

Resistance Leads to Crisis and War

In 1773, the issue of **taxation without representation** rose again when Parliament passed the Tea Act, which made British tea less expensive than tea imported by colonial tea merchants. Colonists protested by destroying three shiploads of British tea in the **Boston Tea Party.** The British government punished Massachusetts with the Coercive Acts of 1774. Labeled the **"Intolerable Acts"** by the colonists, the acts closed the port of Boston, forbid town meetings, reduced the powers of the legislature, and sent more British troops to the colony to enforce the acts. The colonies responded with support for Boston and unity in opposition.

The American Revolution and the Declaration of Independence, 1775–1783

1775
Second Continental Congress; Battles of Lexington and Concord

1777
Battle of Saratoga

1783
Treaty of Paris

1775 | 1777 | 1779 | 1781 | 1783

1776
Common Sense published; Declaration of Independence signed

1781
Cornwallis surrenders at Yorktown

Colonial Efforts at Union

In the late summer of 1774, 12 of the colonies sent representatives to Philadelphia to plan a response to these British actions. This meeting became known as the **First Continental Congress.** After the start of the American Revolution in 1775 at Lexington and Concord, a **Second Continental Congress** met and took charge of the war effort.

While the colonies moved toward war and demands for independence, colonists were divided. Those known as **Tories** or **Loyalists** supported the king and obedience to English laws. Opposing independence, thousands left the United States at the end of the Revolution, including large numbers from New York.

Decision for Independence

The decision to declare independence was made over a year after the American Revolution began. **Thomas Paine,** in his pamphlet, *Common Sense,* was influential in persuading the colonists to end their relationship with Great Britain.

In June 1776, Richard Henry Lee of Virginia presented a resolution to the Second Continental Congress calling for independence from Great Britain. The Congress appointed a committee (including Thomas Jefferson, Benjamin Franklin, and John Adams) to draft a formal declaration. The resulting **Declaration of Independence** was almost entirely the work of Thomas Jefferson. In writing the Declaration, Jefferson relied heavily on the Enlightenment ideas of John Locke's social contract theory and belief in natural rights. The delegates adopted the Declaration of Independence on July 4, which marks the birth of the United States of America.

The Declaration of Independence

The PURPOSE of the Declaration:	The Declaration's KEY IDEAS OF GOVERNMENT:
• To announce to the world that the colonies were now a new, independent nation • To explain and justify the reasons that the united colonies had decided to become the United States of America	• People have natural rights, including the rights to "Life, Liberty, and the pursuit of Happiness." • When governments receive their power to govern "from the consent of the governed" by social contract or compact, that power is for the fundamental purpose of protecting the people's natural rights.
The THREE PARTS of the Declaration:	
• A theory of government • A list of grievances against the King • A formal resolution declaring independence	• When a government fails to protect and respect those rights, it is the "Right of the People to alter or to abolish" that government.

The Ideals of the Declaration of Independence

The ideals of the Declaration of Independence are still a goal for our nation. In 1791 the Bill of Rights again emphasized the importance of individual liberties and limits on government power first stated in the Declaration of Independence. Those ideals have also served to inspire people in other nations at other times during the French Revolution of the late 1700s, the South American independence movement in the early 1800s, and even twentieth century independence movements in Africa and Asia.

There was a fundamental contradiction between slavery and the Declaration's ideals of freedom and liberty. Locke's compact theory stated that no person may rule another without the consent of the other person. The colonists protested their treatment by England and chose freedom. Few made comparisons with the institution of slavery.

Fighting the War for Independence

During the American Revolution, the Second Continental Congress served as the national government. The Congress had no constitutional basis but was created in a crisis and supported by popular opinion. It remained in place until 1781 when the Articles of Confederation went into effect.

The American Revolution pitted Great Britain, then the world's most powerful nation, against thirteen former colonies without financial resources and a regular army. The British army was larger in number, better trained, and aided by the Creek, Cherokee, and Shawnee in the South and most Iroquois in the North. It was disadvantaged by its use of European military techniques in America and by the behavior of its troops, which alienated many colonists in the territories it occupied.

Cause and Effect
Turning Point

• Why is the Battle of Saratoga considered a turning point in the war?

Assembling and training the continental army (the colonists' army) was the achievement of **George Washington,** the colonial commander in chief. The continental army was reinforced as it moved from region to region by an untrained militia or home guard defending their homes.

The colonists were aided by an alliance with France, negotiated by Benjamin Franklin. Motivated by its ongoing rivalry with Great Britain, France supplied the colonists with military arms, troops, and naval support and engaged Great Britain in war elsewhere in the world.

The American victory at Saratoga helped bring the French into the war. They saw that the colonists might possibly win the war. The victory also prevented the

British from isolating New England from the rest of the colonies by taking control of the Hudson River Valley and the area north of it to Canada.

The American Revolution lasted from 1775 to the surrender of the British at Yorktown in Virginia in 1781. A peace treaty, the **Treaty of Paris,** was negotiated by John Adams, John Jay, and Benjamin Franklin and was signed in 1783. In it Great Britain recognized the independence of the United States. The new nation's boundaries were set at Canada to the north, Spanish Florida to the south, and the Mississippi River to the west.

Slavery, African Americans, and the Outcome of the American Revolution

Although African Americans fought on both sides during the American Revolution, more fought on the British side because of British promises of freedom from slavery. After first hesitating, Washington and the Continental Congress eventually recruited African Americans, as did state militias.

Some Effects of the American Revolution

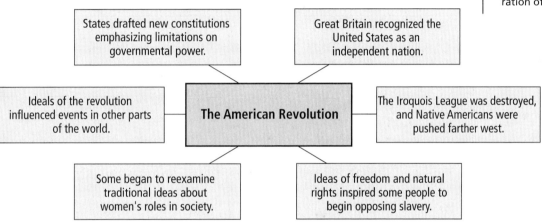

The Revolution had important consequences for many groups of people.

During the Revolution, some enslaved Africans in the South successfully escaped. Others were freed in return for military service. Some left the country with the British army, while others settled in northern cities and became part of a growing free African American population.

An antislavery movement led by Quakers started in the North before the Revolution. After the war, northern states passed laws that immediately or gradually abolished slavery. Although free, African Americans in the North still faced discrimination. Many were not allowed to vote, except in New England. There was segregation in public places, housing, and transportation.

The Articles of Confederation, 1781–1789

The first constitution, or basic framework of a national government of the United States, was the Articles of Confederation. This constitution, proposed by the Second Continental Congress in 1777, went into effect in 1781 after all 13 states had ratified, or approved, it. The Articles of Confederation reflected the colonists' fear of a strong central government and the desire of the individual states to protect their powers. As a result, the Articles created a weak national government.

An Alliance of Independent States

The Articles set up a confederation among the 13 states. A confederation is an alliance of independent states in which the states give as much power as they choose to the central government, while keeping the greater part of the power and remaining sovereign. The Articles were more like a treaty among the states than a plan of centralized government.

The Articles of Confederation, 1781–1789

Achievements of the Confederation Government

The government under the Articles of Confederation had the power to make treaties, declare war, and receive ambassadors. The Confederation Congress is credited with several notable achievements:

Cause and Effect
Turning Point

- Why is the Northwest Ordinance a turning point in history?

- How did that law affect the development of the rest of our nation?

1. Successful conclusion of the American Revolution.
2. Negotiation of the Treaty of Paris of 1783, ending the war and setting U.S. borders at Canada, the Mississippi River, and Florida.
3. Passage of the **Land Ordinance of 1785** and the **Northwest Ordinance of 1787** pass, that
   - set a pattern of development of the Northwest Territory.
   - provided the guidelines by which new states could join the nation on a basis of equality with the thirteen original states.
   - prohibited slavery in the Northwest Territory.

Weaknesses of the Confederation Government

The Confederation government proved too weak to deal with the problems during the **Critical Period** of the 1780s. There was no single national currency, because the states could also coin money. The Congress could not tax the people directly but had to ask the states for funds. The government lacked a president to direct operations. There was no national judiciary. Congress could raise an army only by requesting troops from the states.

Preparing for the Exam

- Why was the period 1781–1789 under the Articles of Confederation called the "critical period"?

The new nation soon suffered severe economic problems, while its government was unable to command respect at home or abroad. However, all 13 states had to agree before the Articles could be changed, so it was nearly impossible to change them.

State Governments Based on Republican Principles

Between 1776 and 1787, 11 of the 13 states adopted new constitutions. State constitutions were based on republican principles creating a government grounded in representation of the people, and formed with the consent of the governed. Special state conventions were called so that the constitutions could be written by the people. When complete, they were ratified or approved by the voters.

Fears of a strong executive power led the Framers of the first state constitutions to emphasize limitations on power. The New York Constitution of 1777, which even included the text of the Declaration of Independence, gave most of the power to the legislature, rather than to a single person such as a governor. In New York as in most states, the legislature remained bicameral, rather than unicameral.

Some states granted more people the right to vote by lowering property qualifications. Some states gave the right to vote to property-owning African Americans and Native Americans. State constitutions, including the New York State Constitution, protected some individual rights, such as the right to religious freedom. In addition, the State government could not give money to any religion. This was part of a national movement to disestablish churches, which meant the end of government endorsement and financial support of any single religious group.

Analyzing Documents

Reading for Evidence
- How were the state constitutions that were adopted after the American Revolution affected by the conflict and war with Great Britain?

- What ideas and features from state constitutions were included in the U.S. Constitution?

- What provision in the U.S. Constitution expressly supports disestablishment?

Part 2 Writing and Ratifying the Constitution, 1787–1789

Key Terms

Constitutional Convention
representation
Great Compromise or Connecticut Plan

bicameral legislature
Three-Fifths Compromise
Commerce Compromise
Presidency Compromise

Federalists
ratification
Anti-Federalists
The Federalist Papers
Bill of Rights

Calling for a Constitutional Convention

By the mid-1780s, the Articles of Confederation government had increasing difficulty in regulating trade and dealing with the nation's debt. Concern also grew that state legislatures were too powerful, and that freedom versus order and stability were imbalanced. In 1786–1787, **Shays' Rebellion** of debt-stricken farmers in Massachusetts exposed the basic weaknesses of the Articles while fueling fears of national collapse and mob rule. More Americans saw the need for a stronger national government and supported the call for a **Constitutional Convention** in Philadelphia in May, 1787 for "the sole and express purpose of amending the Articles of Confederation."

The Constitutional Convention

The Framers of the Constitution

Fifty-five delegates, representing all the states except Rhode Island, met in the Pennsylvania State House (now known as Independence Hall) in Philadelphia in May 1787 at the Constitutional Convention. The delegates were prominent lawyers, planters, and merchants at a time when most of the population were small farmers.

The most famous delegate was **George Washington,** who was elected president of the Constitutional Convention. Another well-known figure was **James Madison,** whom some consider to have had the most influence on the Constitution. Also attending were Benjamin Franklin and Alexander Hamilton, a strong nationalist from New York.

Some famous Americans from the Revolution were noticeably absent. Thomas Jefferson and John Adams were serving the country as diplomats in Europe. A few patriots, such as Patrick Henry, refused to attend because they suspected that

Key Themes and Concepts

Diversity
Certain groups of people were not represented at the Constitutional Convention.

- How does their absence explain some sections of the Constitution?

- Why were these groups absent?

Reading
Strategy

Make Inferences and Draw
Conclusions from Evidence
• What evidence is there
  that the writers of the
  Articles of Confederation
  had different objectives
  than the writers of the
  Constitution?

• What evidence indicates
  that historical context
  influenced the writers of
  each document?

• What evidence is there of
  continuity between the
  two documents?

the convention would try to create a strong national government, which they opposed. Still others were not selected by their states.

In addition, no women, Native Americans, African Americans, or poorer white men attended the Constitutional Convention. At that time, these groups had limited political and legal rights.

Governments of the United States: 1781 and 1789

How the Weaknesses of the Articles of Confederation Were Corrected by the Constitution	
Articles of Confederation	**Constitution of the United States**
• Confederacy: States, not national government, have most of the power. • Congress lacked power to enforce laws. • No executive officer to carry out the laws of Congress. • No national courts. Only state courts exist. • Congress is responsible to the states. • Laws must be approved by 9 of 13 states. • Congress has no power to tax. • Congress can not regulate trade among the states. • Each state coins its own money. There is no national currency. • All 13 states must agree to an amendment.	• Federal system: Power to govern is divided between national and state government. • The Constitution and acts of Congress take supremacy. • A President heads the executive branch of the government. • Both federal and state courts exist. • Congress is responsible to the people. • Laws require a majority vote in both houses of Congress. • Congress has the power to levy and collect taxes. • Congress is given sole control over interstate and foreign trade. • Only the national government has the power to coin money. • Amendment process involves both federal and state governments.

Key Compromises at the Convention

The delegates agreed that discussions would be kept secret in order to debate freely without outside pressure. They also decided not to revise the Articles of Confederation, but to write a new constitution instead.

Most of what we know about the Convention comes to us from Madison's notes. The delegates' task was to create a government with enough authority to govern effectively while protecting individual liberties. The debates involved much conflict and much compromise. In fact, the United States Constitution has been called a "bundle of compromises." Four key compromises made the Constitution possible.

Key Themes
and Concepts

Individuals, Groups, Institutions
At the Constitutional Convention, four major compromises were achieved.

• For each issue, how did the compromise satisfy each side?

• Why were the compromises necessary?

• Why was slavery an issue in two compromises?

The Great Compromise, or Connecticut Plan

The first issue to be resolved was that of **representation.** The delegates from Virginia proposed the Virginia Plan, which called for a bicameral legislature. A state's representation in each house would be based on its population. Larger states supported this plan. The smaller states favored the New Jersey Plan. This plan called for a unicameral legislature in which each state had equal representation.

The Virginia Plan served as the basis for much of the new Constitution. However, the matter of representation had to be settled by what is known as the **Great Compromise** or the **Connecticut Plan,** which gave something to both large and small states. The compromise created the Congress, a **bicameral legislature.** The states had equal representation in the upper house, or the Senate. In the lower house, or the House of Representatives, representation was based on population. In addition, all bills dealing with money would have to start in the House, but would need the approval of the Senate.

The Three-Fifths Compromise

Meanwhile, a bitter debate continued over slavery and power. Southerners wanted enslaved people to be counted for purposes of deciding representation in the House, but not for purposes of determining taxes. The **Three-Fifths Compromise** stated that three fifths of the enslaved African Americans in a state would be counted for both representation and taxation purposes.

The Commerce Compromise

Northerners wanted a government that could regulate trade. Southerners, however, feared that the importing of African slaves would be prohibited and that their agricultural exports would be taxed. Under the **Commerce Compromise** the delegates agreed that no export duties could be passed by Congress and that Congress could not prohibit the slave trade for 20 years.

The Presidency Compromise

The delegates favoring a strong national government wanted a President elected directly by the people with a long term of office. Those favoring states' rights wanted a short term of office with state legislatures selecting the President. In the **Presidency Compromise,** the two sides agreed on a four-year term and the indirect election of the President through the **Electoral College** system.

Reading Strategy

Examining Points of View
- Which groups stood in opposition to each other on the major issues at the Constitutional Convention?
- Why did they take their particular positions?
- How has each of the Constitutional compromises experienced change and/or continuity across time?

Major Compromises of the Constitutional Convention

Compromise	Issue	Solution
Connecticut Plan or Great Compromise	Equal or proportionate representation in Congress	Through a bicameral legislature, States would have equal representation in Senate, and representation in the House would depend on State's population.
Three-Fifths Compromise	Counting enslaved people within population to determine representation	Enslaved people were counted as three-fifths of one person, both for representation and taxation.
Commerce Compromise	Granting Congress the power to regulate foreign and interstate trade	Congress was forbidden to tax a State's exports, or take action against the slave trade for 20 years.
Presidency Compromise	Length of President's term of office and method of election	President would serve a four-year term and be elected by Electoral College rather than popular election, or selection by Congress or State governors.

Ratification of the Constitution

After months of debate in Philadelphia, delegates approved the Constitution of the United States. On September 17, 1787, thirty-nine of the delegates remaining in Philadelphia signed the Constitution. The fact that three, including George Mason, author of the Virginia Declaration of Rights, refused to sign gave an indication of the coming debate. The Framers had written that 9 of the 13 states must approve the Constitution for it to go into effect. Approval would be done through special conventions called in each state rather than through the state legislatures.

Key Themes and Concepts

Government
- Why was it essential that Virginia and New York be among those states that ratified the Constitution?
- In which states was there strong division of opinion about ratification?

The Great Debate

The Federalist Arguments	The Anti-Federalist Arguments
• Wanted a strong national government to provide order and protect the rights of people.	• Wanted a weak national government so that it would not threaten the rights of the people or the powers of the states.
• Claimed that a bill of rights was unnecessary because the new government's powers were limited by the Constitution.	• Wanted to add a bill of rights to protect the people against abuses of power by the federal government.

Reading Strategy

Craft and Structure

"Ambition must be made to counteract ambition . . . If men were angels, no government would be necessary. If angels were to govern men, neither external nor internal controls on government would be necessary. In framing a government which is to be administered by men over men, the great difficulty lies in this: you must first enable the government to control the governed; and in the next place oblige it to control itself."
—James Madison,
The Federalist Papers No. 51

• Based on this quote, what was James Madison's view of the relationship between human nature and good government?

• Anti-Federalists opposed ratification because the Constitution shifted the balance of power between the national and state governments. How would Madison respond to this concern?

The Great Debate and Ratification

Two groups formed in each state: the **Federalists,** who favored **ratification,** and the **Anti-Federalists,** who opposed it.

The first five states ratified the Constitution within a few months. By June 1788, nine states had given their approval—enough for ratification. But these did not include the states of Virginia and New York. The success of the new government depended upon acceptance of the Constitution by these two key states.

In Virginia, James Madison led the fight for ratification against the opposition of George Mason and Patrick Henry. Virginia approved the Constitution by ten votes but only with suggested amendments. New York was the next battleground. Here, **The Federalist Papers**—a series of pro-ratification essays by Alexander Hamilton, John Jay, and James Madison—helped turn the tide against the Anti-Federalists, led by Governor George Clinton. Ratification was by a margin of three votes. *The Federalist Papers* remains one of the finest statements on government and the Constitution ever written.

When the new government took office in 1789, Congress acted in response to concerns of the Anti-Federalists about the need for a **Bill of Rights** in the Constitution. James Madison prepared the first draft of these first ten amendments. By 1791 the states had ratified them.

Part 3 What You Need to Know About the U.S. Constitution and Government

Key Terms

Preamble	unwritten constitution	census
popular sovereignty	delegated powers	Electoral College system
limited government	implied powers	bureaucracy
separation of powers	concurrent powers	jurisdiction
federal sysytem	reserved powers	judicial review
checks and balances	legislative	amendment
elastic clause	executive	due process of law
"necessary and proper"	judicial	equal protection clause

Preamble to the Constitution

The United States Constitution is a fundamental plan, or framework, clearly defining and limiting the powers of government. In the **Preamble,** or introduction, to the Constitution, the Framers defined their reasons for writing the document:

• To create a better, stronger national government
• To ensure a system of justice

- To provide for peace at home
- To provide for the defense of the nation
- To promote the well being of the people
- To secure liberty to the people and to future generations

Basic Principles of the Constitution

The Constitution of the United States includes a number of important basic principles, which are listed below.

Popular Sovereignty

The Preamble states the principle of **popular sovereignty,** meaning that the source of all power or authority to govern is the people. *Popular* means "of or by the people." *Sovereignty* means "supreme power." In this way the Constitution creates a **democracy,** or government by the consent of the governed.

Limited Government

Governmental powers are defined by the Constitution. In this way our government is limited by law. The U.S. Constitution, as well as state constitutions, places limits on state and national governments and governmental officials as well. No person is considered above the law.

Federalism

The Constitution divides the power to govern between the states and the national government. This division of power between levels of government creates a **federal system** of government.

Analyzing Documents

"We the People of the United States . . . do ordain and establish this Constitution for the United States."
—Preamble to the U.S. Constitution

- According to the Preamble, who is creating this Constitution?

- In what other documents have we seen a concept that is restated here?

System of Federalism

National Government

State Governments

Delegated Powers
- Maintain army and navy
- Declare war
- Coin money
- Regulate trade between states and with foreign nations
- Make all laws necessary for carrying out delegated powers

Concurrent Powers
- Enforce laws
- Establish courts
- Borrow money
- Protect the safety of the people
- Build roads
- Collect taxes

Reserved Powers
- Conduct elections
- Establish schools
- Regulate businesses within a state
- Establish local governments
- Regulate marriages
- Assume other powers not given to the national government or denied to the states

Separation of Powers

The Constitution establishes the **separation of powers,** meaning that power to govern is divided among the legislative, executive, and judiciary branches to ensure that no single branch can dominate the government. Each branch takes its power directly from the Constitution, not from another branch.

Three Branches of U.S. Government

Legislative	Executive	Judicial
Senate **House of Representatives**	**President** **Vice President**	**Supreme Court** **Federal Courts**
Makes laws	**Enforces laws and treaties**	**Explains and interprets laws**
• Overrides presidential vetoes • Approves presidential appointments • Approves treaties • Taxes to provide services • Provides for defense, declares war • Regulates money and trade • Impeaches officials	• Can veto laws • Appoints high officials • Conducts foreign policy • Enforces laws and treaties • Commander in chief of the military • Recommends bills to Congress • Reports the state of the Union to Congress	• Settles legal disputes between states • Settles State and federal disputes • Settles disputes between States and foreign countries • Hears cases with ambassadors of foreign governments • Settles disputes between individuals and Federal Government

Source: U.S. Department of Justice

Checks and Balances

In addition to separation of powers among the three branches of government, the constitution includes a system of **checks and balances.** Each branch of the national government has ways to check, or control, the other branches. This prevents one branch from gaining too much power.

The Checks and Balances System

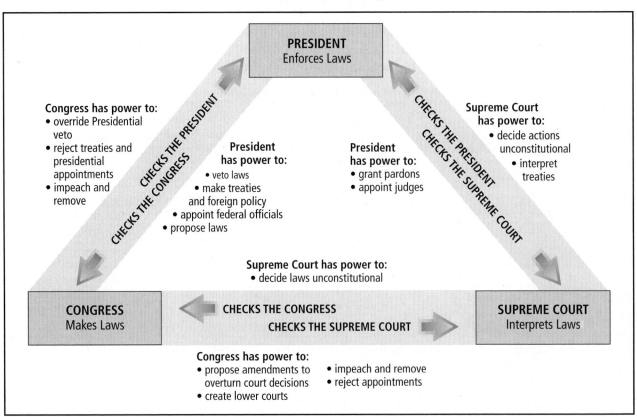

PRESIDENT
Enforces Laws

Congress has power to:
• override Presidential veto
• reject treaties and presidential appointments
• impeach and remove

CHECKS THE PRESIDENT
CHECKS THE CONGRESS

President has power to:
• veto laws
• make treaties and foreign policy
• appoint federal officials
• propose laws

President has power to:
• grant pardons
• appoint judges

Supreme Court has power to:
• decide actions unconstitutional
• interpret treaties

CHECKS THE PRESIDENT
CHECKS THE SUPREME COURT

Supreme Court has power to:
• decide laws unconstitutional

CONGRESS
Makes Laws

CHECKS THE CONGRESS
CHECKS THE SUPREME COURT

SUPREME COURT
Interprets Laws

Congress has power to:
• propose amendments to overturn court decisions
• create lower courts
• impeach and remove
• reject appointments

Flexibility

The Constitution's flexibility allows it to meet changing conditions.

The Elastic Clause Article I, Section 8, Clause 18, known as the **elastic clause,** states that Congress can make all laws **"necessary and proper"** for carrying out the tasks listed in the Constitution.

The Amendment Process The Constitution may be formally changed with approval of both Congress and the states.

Judicial Interpretation The Supreme Court and lower federal courts review cases that involve possible conflicts with the Constitution and federal laws. This involves interpreting local, state, and federal laws, as well as executive actions.

Unwritten Constitution Congressional and executive interpretations and actions, court decisions, customs, and traditions form a so-called **unwritten constitution** to allow for Constitutional change and flexibility.

Federalism in the Constitution

The Constitution divides the power to govern between the national and the state governments. Disputes between the national and state governments are settled by the courts, but the **Supremacy Clause** of Article VI of the Constitution makes the Constitution, federal laws, and treaties superior to state laws.

The Supremacy Clause

Delegated Powers Certain powers of the national government are spelled out in the Constitution. Most of these delegated powers are listed in Article I, Section 8. One example is the power of the national government to declare war.

Implied Powers Certain powers of the national government are not stated in writing. Their existence is implied by the **Elastic Clause.** One example of an implied power is the regulation of child labor; this power is implied by the delegated power to regulate interstate commerce.

Denied Powers Certain powers are denied to the national government, for example, the power to pass an export tax. Other powers are denied to the states, for example, the power to print money. Still other powers are denied to both national and state governments, for example, the power to deny the right to vote because of sex or race.

Concurrent Powers Certain powers belong to both national and state governments. One example of such a concurrent power is the power to tax.

Reserved Powers The reserved powers are neither delegated to the national government nor denied to the states. One example is the power to make divorce laws.

Federalism in Article IV is seen in the guarantee to each state of a republican form of government and protection against invasion and domestic violence. The amendment process in Article V, requires approval of both Congress and three quarters of the states. Article VII states that the new Constitution must first be approved or ratified by conventions of nine of the states.

The Basic Organization and Functions of Government Under the Constitution

The first three articles of the Constitution describe and define the powers of the **legislative, executive,** and **judicial** branches of the national government. These articles detail the separation of powers, while showing how each branch can check and balance the others.

Federal Officeholders

Office	Number	Term	Selection	Requirements
Representative	at least 1 per state; based on state population	2 years	elected by voters of congressional district	• age 25 or over • citizen for 7 years • resident of state in which elected
Senator	2 per state	6 years	original Constitution-elected by state legislature Amendment 17-elected by voters	• age 30 or over • citizen for 9 years • resident of state in which elected
President and Vice President	1	4 years	elected by Electoral College	• age 35 or over • natural-born citizen • resident of U.S. for 14 years
Supreme Court Justice	9	Life	appointed by President with approval of the Senate	• no requirements in Constitution

Article I: The Legislative Branch

Article I establishes the United States Congress with its two houses—the Senate and the House of Representatives. Congress is the legislative, or lawmaking, branch of government. Article I gives the qualifications for election to Congress, the rights and privileges of members of Congress, and some basic operating procedures of both houses. The article also lists the powers delegated to Congress. These include the **"necessary and proper" or elastic clause,** which enables the government to adapt to changing times. Each house of Congress also has special duties that it alone can perform.

Special Powers of the House and Senate

House	Senate
• To select the President if no candidate receives a majority of the electoral vote	• To select the Vice President if no candidate has a majority of the electoral vote
• To bring impeachment charges	• To act as jury in cases of impeachment
• To originate all revenue (money) bills	• To ratify treaties (by a two-thirds vote)
	• To approve presidential appointments, including federal judges (by a majority vote)

Article I briefly outlines how a bill becomes a federal law. This process requires the approval of each house and of the President. A presidential **veto,** or rejection, of a bill can be overridden by a two-thirds vote of each house. As the diagram on the next page shows, the process today is quite complex, and a bill must pass through numerous committees before becoming a law.

Congress does much of its work through committees—an important part of the **unwritten constitution.** Committees control what bills include and which come to the floor for a vote.

Due to its size, debate in the House is limited. The Senate usually permits unlimited debate on a bill. At times, a minority of senators **filibuster,** or keep talking, in an attempt to force a Senate majority to change or even drop a bill. On major bills in the Senate, **cloture,** the votes of sixty senators, is required to end a filibuster or a filibuster threat. But Senate rules changed in 2013 and in 2017 to allow approval of executive nominations, including all federal judgeships by a simple majority vote.

The Powers of Congress as Stated (by Clause) in Article I, Section 8 of the United States Constitution

Expressed Powers
Peace Powers

1. To lay taxes
   a. Direct (not used since the War Between the States, except income tax)
   b. Indirect (customs [tariffs], excise for internal revenue)
2. To borrow money
3. To regulate foreign and interstate commerce
4. To establish naturalization and bankruptcy laws
5. To coin money and regulate its value; to regulate weights and measures
6. To punish counterfeiters of federal money and securities
7. To establish post offices and post roads
8. To grant patents and copyrights
9. To create courts inferior to the Supreme Court
10. To define and punish piracies and felonies on the high seas; to define and punish offenses against the law of nations
11. To exercise exclusive jurisdiction over the District of Columbia; to exercise exclusive jurisdiction over forts, dockyards, national parks, federal buildings, and the like

War Powers
12. To declare war; to grant letters of marque and reprisal; to make rules concerning captures on land and water 13. To raise and support armies 14. To provide and maintain a navy 15. To make laws governing land and naval forces 16. To provide for calling forth the militia to execute federal laws, suppress insurrections, and repel invasions 17. To provide for organizing, arming, and disciplining the militia, and for its governing when in the service of the Union
Implied Powers

18. To make all laws necessary and proper for carrying into execution the foregoing powers, such as:
   a. To define and provide punishment for federal crimes
   b. To establish the Federal Reserve System
   c. To improve rivers, canals, harbors, and other waterways
   d. To fix minimum wages, maximum hours of work

How Bills Become Laws

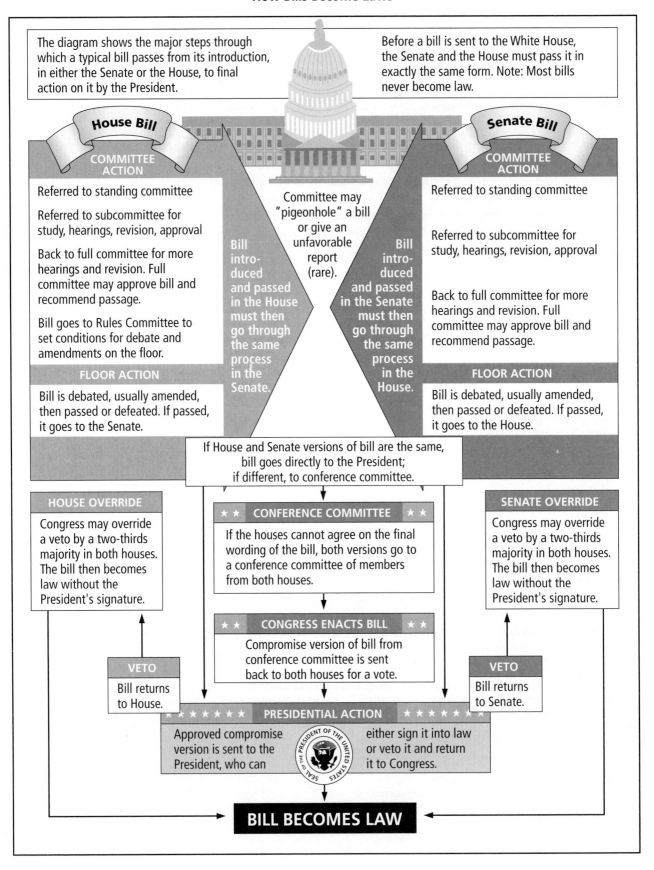

The diagram shows the major steps through which a typical bill passes from its introduction, in either the Senate or the House, to final action on it by the President.

Before a bill is sent to the White House, the Senate and the House must pass it in exactly the same form. Note: Most bills never become law.

House Bill

COMMITTEE ACTION

Referred to standing committee

Referred to subcommittee for study, hearings, revision, approval

Back to full committee for more hearings and revision. Full committee may approve bill and recommend passage.

Bill goes to Rules Committee to set conditions for debate and amendments on the floor.

FLOOR ACTION

Bill is debated, usually amended, then passed or defeated. If passed, it goes to the Senate.

Bill introduced and passed in the House must then go through the same process in the Senate.

Committee may "pigeonhole" a bill or give an unfavorable report (rare).

Bill introduced and passed in the Senate must then go through the same process in the House.

Senate Bill

COMMITTEE ACTION

Referred to standing committee

Referred to subcommittee for study, hearings, revision, approval

Back to full committee for more hearings and revision. Full committee may approve bill and recommend passage.

FLOOR ACTION

Bill is debated, usually amended, then passed or defeated. If passed, it goes to the House.

If House and Senate versions of bill are the same, bill goes directly to the President; if different, to conference committee.

HOUSE OVERRIDE

Congress may override a veto by a two-thirds majority in both houses. The bill then becomes law without the President's signature.

★ ★ CONFERENCE COMMITTEE ★ ★

If the houses cannot agree on the final wording of the bill, both versions go to a conference committee of members from both houses.

SENATE OVERRIDE

Congress may override a veto by a two-thirds majority in both houses. The bill then becomes law without the President's signature.

★ ★ CONGRESS ENACTS BILL ★ ★

Compromise version of bill from conference committee is sent back to both houses for a vote.

VETO

Bill returns to House.

VETO

Bill returns to Senate.

★ ★ ★ ★ ★ ★ PRESIDENTIAL ACTION ★ ★ ★ ★ ★ ★

Approved compromise version is sent to the President, who can

either sign it into law or veto it and return it to Congress.

BILL BECOMES LAW

Article II: The Executive Branch

Article II outlines the workings of the executive branch, including the method of electing the President as well as the powers and duties of the office.

Electing the President

Article II describes the process by which the president is elected. The Twelfth, Twentieth, Twenty-second, Twenty-third, and Twenty-fifth Amendments have changed this process.

- A key compromise of the Constitutional Convention involved the method of electing the president. Under the resulting **Electoral College system,** voters cast their ballots for electors. Those electors cast the actual votes for President and Vice President. Each state was granted as many presidential electors as it had senators plus representatives. A candidate needs a majority of the electoral votes to become President. Today, that means 270 votes, a number that is one more than half of 538:
- the total number of senators (2 per state to equal 100)
- plus representatives (set at 435 in 1929 with number of seats per state reallocated after each census)
- plus the three electoral votes given to Washington, D.C. by the 23rd amendment.

The Constitution requires that a **census,** or counting of the population, be taken every ten years. Changes to reflect shifts in population are then made in the number of representatives per state, which in turn affects the electoral vote. Census data is also used to make decisions about other national needs.

Customs and precedents influenced how the President is elected. After Washington's two terms, the formation of **political parties** forced changes in the election process. No longer did electors exercise their own judgments. Rather, they pledged in advance to vote for the presidential candidate of their party. Today, while the names of the presidential candidates appear on the ballot, voters are actually casting their ballots for electors chosen by each candidate's party.

By 1832, national conventions had become the method of selecting party candidates. Today **presidential primaries** and **caucuses** are held in each state to select most of the delegates to the national convention. Both parties also name their officials and office holders as delegates. At the start of each 2016 presidential convention about 85% of the delegates were pledged to a candidate.

Debating the Electoral College System

From the days of the Constitutional Convention, people have argued over the method of selecting the president.

Reasons to Change the System There are three major arguments against the Electoral College system.

1. Except for two states it is a "winner-take-all" system. A winning candidate gets all the electoral votes in a state, no matter how close the popular vote. Five times—in 1824, 1876, 1888, 2000, and 2016—the winner of the **popular vote** lost the presidency because he or she failed to win a majority of the **electoral vote**.
2. The less populated states are over-represented in the electoral college because every state has two electors for its two senators. It is estimated that the ten smallest states have a population of 189,000 to 333,000 per electoral vote while the ten largest states have a population of 619,000 to 679,000 per electoral vote.
3. In 21 states the electors for the candidate who wins that state's popular vote have no legal requirements on how they vote.

Reading Strategy

Analyzing Cause and Effect: Census
The U.S. Constitution requires that a census of the population be taken every 10 years. The census is used to determine how many representatives each state will send to the House.

- What impact does the census have on the Electoral College?

- How have the 2010 census results affected each of the following states in the House of Representatives and in the Electoral College? Florida, New York, Ohio, Texas, Nevada, Washington

- What is the pattern of these population shifts?

- What are the major causes of this changing population pattern?

Reading Strategy

Integration of Knowledge and Ideas
Use the text and the chart, "The Path to the Presidency," to determine what steps to the presidency are part of the Constitution and which have developed from custom.

The Path to the Presidency

First Step in a Presidential Campaign: Announcing Intention to Run

- Announces candidacy in person, or by video, phone call, or tweet often a year plus before election.
- Organizes national and state campaign staffs; seeks financial support and endorsements.

The Campaign for Delegates Begins

- Candidate works to win state party delegates to national nominating convention. Most states now hold primary elections to select some or all delegates but some states and U.S. territories still use caucuses.
- In 2008 and 2012 both parties passed rules to control front-loading - the push by states to vote early in order to have more influence. In 2016 only 4 states were allowed to hold primaries in February; the rest had to wait until March-June with the majority selecting March and April primary dates.
- Population and party loyalty in previous elections determine the number of delegates allotted to each state.

Raising Money for the Primaries and General Election

- Candidate raises money with meetings, rallies, dinners, letters, phone calls, and Internet appeals.
- In 2016 as in 2012 neither presidential candidate accepted the public funding provided by the Federal Election Campaign Act (1976) and last used by John McCain in 2008.
- In 2010 *Citizens United* v. *FEC* ruled that the 1st amendment allowed corporations, unions, and individuals (See *Buckley* v. *Valeo*; also *SpeechNOW.org* v. *FEC*) to spend unlimited amounts of money on candidates if these "independent expenditures" do not go directly to and are not coordinated with the candidate or political party. Decision led to formation of Super PACS required to disclose donors and finances to FEC, and to non-profit "social welfare" organizations not "primarily engaged" in election activity and exempt from naming their donors.
- In 2014 *McCutcheon v. FEC*, while keeping the base contribution limit, removed the aggregate limit - the total amount of money an individual could give directly to multiple federal candidates, parties and committees within a two year election cycle.
- An estimated 2 billion dollars was spent on the 2016 presidential election.

The National Convention: Selecting the Party Nominees

- Party nominees are chosen at conventions held in summer before November election.
- Having already won a majority of delegate votes, nominee is usually known before convention.

The Presidential Campaign

- Candidate plans strategy to win the majority (270 of 538) of the electoral votes required to become president. Each state's electoral vote equals the number of its senators (2) plus its representatives to total 535 plus 3 votes for Washington D.C. (See 23rd Amendment)
- The 2010 census mirrored the 2000 census pattern moving another 12 House seats from Eastern and Midwestern states to Western and Southern states in a population trend that also shifts electoral votes.
- Candidate focuses time, money, and media attention on "contested" rather than "safe" states.
- In 2016 candidates increased use of targeted digital communication to reach voters.

Election Day: Voters Choose the Electors Who Elect the President

- Voters cast ballots for president on the Tuesday following first Monday in November in years divisible by four, selecting which party's electors in each state will vote for its presidential slate on the Monday following the second Wednesday in December.
- The new President is sworn in (inaugurated) on January 20.

Reasons to Keep the System Despite such criticisms, the Electoral College system remains in use for three key reasons:

1. It is very difficult to amend the Constitution.
2. Small states would lose the advantage they now have of being over-represented in the electoral college; they would, therefore, oppose any change. It is also argued that at this time, the 11 most populous states control a majority of the Electoral College votes.
3. Changes in the Electoral College system might threaten the two-party political system. The fact that a presidential candidate needs a majority of the Electoral College vote, critics believe, prevents the creation of a multi-party system with no candidate winning a clear majority vote.

Presidential Roles and Powers

Article II describes the powers and duties of the President of the United States. Since power in the executive branch centers in one individual, a president can act swiftly in times of war and national crisis. In carrying out the duties of office, the president fills several different roles.

Chief Executive In this role, the President has the power to

- enforce or put the laws into effect.
- act as administrator of the huge federal bureaucracy.
- issue executive orders that have the effect of laws.
- appoint judges, diplomats, and other high government officials—some with Senate approval and others without.
- remove appointed government officials within the executive branch.

Chief Diplomat In this role, the President has the power to

- make treaties with the advice and consent of the Senate.
- make executive agreements with nations without Senate approval.
- extend or withdraw diplomatic recognition to a nation.

Commander in Chief In this role, the President has broad military powers that are shared with Congress. In times of war, these powers are even stronger.

Chief Legislator In this role of lawmaker, the President has the power to

- recommend legislation to Congress.
- veto potential laws.

Chief of State In addition to being head of the government, the President is also chief of state, the ceremonial head of government, and the symbol of all the people of the nation. He fills this role in such ceremonies as the laying of a wreath on the Tomb of the Unknowns.

Judicial Powers The President can grant reprieves, pardons, and amnesties, or pardons extended to groups rather than individuals.

Head of the Party The President is also the leader of the political party in power. The duties of this role are not mentioned in the Constitution because the party system developed through custom, making it part of the unwritten constitution.

The Federal Bureaucracy

The federal **bureaucracy** consists of the administrative agencies and staff that put the decisions or policies of the government into effect. Such a bureaucracy has developed through legislation, executive action, and custom.

Key Themes and Concepts

Government
In the presidential election of 2016, Donald J. Trump became the fifth president to win the presidency without winning the popular vote. The other presidents were John Quincy Adams, elected in 1824; Rutherford B. Hayes, elected in 1876; Benjamin Harrison, elected in 1888; and George W. Bush, elected in 2000.

Key Themes and Concepts

Government
The executive branch is the largest branch of the government, as shown in the chart **The Government of the United States Under the Constitution** on the next page.

- Why is the executive branch so large?

- How were the departments and agencies shown created?

Most of the bureaucracy is part of the executive branch and includes the White House staff, 15 executive departments, and more than 200 independent agencies. This bureaucracy is explained in more detail in the following chart.

The Government of the United States Under the Constitution

Legislative	Executive	Judicial
THE CONGRESS	**THE PRESIDENT** **THE VICE PRESIDENT**	**THE SUPREME COURT** **OF THE UNITED STATES**
Senate House	**Executive Office of the President**	
• Architect of the Capitol • General Accountability Office • Government Printing Office • Library of Congress • United States Botanic Garden • Office of Technology Assessment • Congressional Budget Office	• White House Office • Office of the Vice President • Office of Management and Budget • Council of Economic Advisers • National Security Council • Office of National Drug Control Policy • Office of the United States Trade Representative • Council on Environmental Quality • Office of Science and Technology Policy • Office of Administration • Office of Policy Development	• Courts of Appeals • District Courts • Federal Claims Court • Court of Appeals for the Federal Circuit • Court of International Trade • Territorial Courts • Court of Appeals—Armed Forces • Court of Veterans Appeals • Administrative Office of the United States Courts • Federal Judicial Center • United States Tax Court • U.S. Sentencing Commission

Executive Departments

• State • Treasury • Defense • Justice • Interior	• Agriculture • Commerce • Labor • Health and Human Services • Housing and Urban Development	• Transportation • Energy • Education • Veterans Affairs • Homeland Security

Selected Independent Establishments and Government Corporations

• Central Intelligence Agency • Commission on Civil Rights • Consumer Product Safety Commission • Corporation for National and Community Service • Defense Nuclear Facilities Safety Board • Environmental Protection Agency • Equal Employment Opportunity Commission • Export-Import Bank of the U.S. • Farm Credit Administration • Federal Communications Commission	• Federal Deposit Insurance Corporation • Federal Election Commission • Federal Housing Finance Board • Federal Maritime Commission • Federal Mediation and Conciliation Service • Federal Reserve System • Federal Trade Commission • General Services Administration • National Science Foundation • U.S. International Trade Commission • Merit Systems Protection Board • National Aeronautics and Space Administration	• National Labor Relations Board • National Transportation Safety Board • Nuclear Regulatory Commission • Office of Government Ethics • Securities and Exchange Commission • Selective Service System • Small Business Administration • Social Security Administration • Tennessee Valley Authority • U.S. Postal Service

Article III: The Judicial Branch

Article III of the Constitution creates the Supreme Court and gives Congress the power to create lower federal courts. The role of this judicial branch is to interpret the law. In addition to this national court system, each of the 50 states has its own court system.

Jurisdiction

With two court systems—federal and state—the Constitution had to define the **jurisdiction,** or authority, of the federal courts in order to make clear which cases go to federal courts and which to state courts. The court that has the authority to hear a case is determined by two factors:

Subject Matter Federal courts hear cases involving federal laws, treaties, maritime law, and interpretation of the Constitution.

Parties Federal courts are directed to have jurisdiction if cases involve certain parties, or participants in a case. For example, cases involving representatives of foreign governments or states suing other states are tried in federal courts.

The Constitution states that in some types of cases, the Supreme Court will have original jurisdiction. This means the Supreme Court will hear the case first and make a decision. In most cases, the Supreme Court has appellate jurisdiction. This means that, in a lower court, if the losing side believes a judge made a mistake in applying the law in a case, that case may be appealed to a higher court. The Supreme Court hears only about 90 cases of the more than 8,000 appealed to it each year.

Judicial Review

The most important power of the federal courts is the right of **judicial review.** This power enables the courts to hear cases involving the application and interpretation of law and to declare state laws and acts of Congress and of the executive branch unconstitutional and void if judged not in keeping with the Constitution's intent. The Supreme Court is the final voice in interpreting the Constitution. The right of judicial review strengthened the judiciary against the other two branches of government. Chief Justice John Marshall first applied the doctrine of judicial review in *Marbury* v. *Madison* **(1803)**, voiding parts of the **1789 Judiciary Act**.

Amending the Constitution

Article V describes methods of amending, or formally changing, the Constitution. The purpose of an **amendment** process is to ensure that the government meets the

Reading Strategy

Problem Solving
- The process of amending the Constitution is an excellent example of federalism in practice. Why?

The Formal Amendment Process (Four Methods)

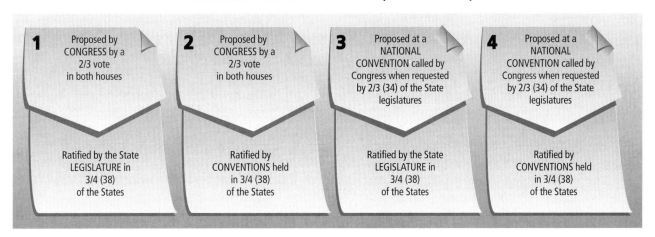

1 Proposed by CONGRESS by a 2/3 vote in both houses → Ratified by the State LEGISLATURE in 3/4 (38) of the States

2 Proposed by CONGRESS by a 2/3 vote in both houses → Ratified by CONVENTIONS held in 3/4 (38) of the States

3 Proposed at a NATIONAL CONVENTION called by Congress when requested by 2/3 (34) of the State legislatures → Ratified by the State LEGISLATURE in 3/4 (38) of the States

4 Proposed at a NATIONAL CONVENTION called by Congress when requested by 2/3 (34) of the State legislatures → Ratified by CONVENTIONS held in 3/4 (38) of the States

**Analyzing
Documents**

*"I may detest what you say, but
will defend to the death your
right to say it."*
—Voltaire

• What basic civil liberty is
  Voltaire defending?

nation's changing needs. In accordance with the principle of federalism, both national and state governments are involved in the amendment process. In the most common method of amendment, Congress approves a proposed amendment by a two-thirds vote in each house. The amendment then goes to the state legislatures. If three quarters of them ratify it, the amendment becomes part of the Constitution. Twenty-six of the constitutional amendments have been adopted by this method. To date, only the Twenty-first Amendment has been ratified by special conventions called in the states.

The Bill of Rights

The Bill of Rights is the name given to the first ten amendments to the Constitution adopted in 1791. They were added at the insistence of the Anti-Federalists. These amendments guarantee certain basic or fundamental rights of the people against the power of the federal government.

The Bill of Rights

Amendment	Subject
1st	Guarantees freedom of religion, of speech, and of the press; the right to assemble peacefully; and the right to petition the government.
2nd	Protects the right to possess firearms.
3rd	Declares that the government may not require people to house soldiers during peacetime.
4th	Protects people from unreasonable searches and seizures.
5th	Includes protection against self incrimination and double jeopardy; guarantees due process of law.
6th	Guarantees the right to a speedy, public trial, to confront witnesses, and to legal counsel.
7th	Guarantees the right to trial by jury in most civil cases.
8th	Prohibits excessive bail, fines, and "cruel and unusual" punishments.
9th	Declares that rights not mentioned in the Constitution belong to the people.
10th	Declares that powers not given to the national government belong to the states or to the people.

Extending Constitutional Protections

In the 200 years since the Bill of Rights was added to the Constitution, the rights of the people have been expanded by court decisions, by other amendments, and even by presidential actions. The Fourteenth Amendment contains the equal protection clause. Court interpretations have held that the Fourteenth Amendment extends the protections of most of the Bill of Rights against the states as well as the national government.

The courts have held that civil rights (as defined in the Bill of Rights and other amendments) are relative, not absolute. The courts have thus tried to balance an individual's rights against the rights of society and other individuals. In recent years, Bill of Rights issues such as privacy versus national security have been debated. Sometimes basic civil rights conflict with each other. For example, the Sixth Amendment right of the accused to confront witnesses might clash with a reporter's First Amendment, the right of freedom of the press to protect news sources. In such conflicts, the courts must decide the issue.

Additional Constitutional Amendments

Between 1795 and 1992, an additional 17 amendments have been added to the Constitution. Note that the Thirteenth, Fourteenth, and Fifteenth Amendments were passed after the Civil War so that formerly enslaved people could become citizens, and to give them the right to vote. Four amendments—the Fifteenth, Nineteenth, Twenty-third, and Twenty-sixth—have expanded the right to vote.

Amendments 11–27

Amendment	Year Ratified	Subject
11th	1795	Grants states immunity from certain lawsuits
12th	1804	Separates voting for President and Vice President
13th	1865	Abolishes slavery
14th	1868	Defines citizenship; prohibits states from denying people due process and equal protection of the law
15th	1870	Grants voting rights for African American men
16th	1913	Gives Congress power to tax incomes
17th	1913	Requires election of U.S. Senators by people of a state, not the state legislature
18th	1919	Prohibits manufacture, sale, and transportation of alcoholic beverages
19th	1920	Grants voting rights for women
20th	1933	Shortens amount of time between election of a president and of Congress and start of their term of office
21st	1933	Repeals Eighteenth Amendment
22nd	1951	Limits president to two terms
23rd	1961	Grants electoral votes and right to vote in presidential elections for the District of Columbia
24th	1964	Abolishes poll taxes as qualification for voting in federal elections
25th	1967	Sets procedure for determining presidential disability and succession, and for filling a vice-presidential vacancy
26th	1971	Lowers voting age to 18
27th	1992	Bans mid-term congressional pay raises

Extending the Right to Vote

Year	People Allowed to Vote
1789	White men over age 21 who meet property requirements (state laws)
Early 1800s–1850s	All white men over age 21 (state laws)
1870	African American men (15th Amendment)
1920	Women (19th Amendment)
1961	Citizens in the District of Columbia in presidential elections (23rd Amendment)
1971	Citizens age 18 or over (26th Amendment)

Analyzing Documents

- Based on the chart what has been the most common way of extending the right to vote to more people?

New York State Government Compared to the Federal Government

The government of New York has many similarities to the federal government. New York has a constitution and a Bill of Rights. The New York government has three branches. The executive branch is headed by the governor. The bicameral legislature has a Senate and an Assembly. The highest court in the judicial branch is the Court of Appeals.

Part 4 The Thirteen Basic Constitutional Principles

Thirteen basic constitutional principles have endured since the ratification of the Constitution. These principles continue to be important to the development of American government and society.

Constitutional Principle 1
National Power—Limits and Potential

The powers of the federal government are limited. The Constitution states the powers held by each branch of government. The powers that are not delegated to the national government are reserved to the states or to the people (Tenth Amendment). The Bill of Rights also limits the government's interference with basic rights.

However, the powers of all three branches of the federal government have grown.
- Has the national government become too powerful?
- Do the limits placed on the national government make it incapable of dealing with the problems of the modern age?

Examples of This Principle as a Recurring Theme in U.S. History

Need for a strong central government: debate over ratification

Loose vs. strict interpretation of the Constitution: Hamilton's financial plan, Louisiana Purchase

Conflict over slavery: 1820–1860

Civil War: establishing federal supremacy over the states

Imperialism: Spanish-American War, acquiring an overseas empire

Progressive movement: Theodore Roosevelt and Woodrow Wilson

Elastic clause: Pure Food and Drug Act, Social Security

Commerce clause: expanding powers of government

New Deal: expanding role of government

Great Society: demand for reform

New Federalism: less government involvement

Constitutional Principle 2
Federalism—Balance Between Nation and State

The Constitution created a new federal government that divided power between the states and the national government. The Constitution reserved certain powers to the states and to the people, but the Constitution and the laws and treaties of the United States are supreme to state laws.

- Is the power still balanced, or has it tilted to the federal government?
- Has the shift of power to the federal government become greater since the New Deal, or did Reagan's New Federalism reverse this trend?

Examples of This Principle as a Recurring Theme in U.S. History

Marshall Supreme Court cases: *McCulloch* v. *Maryland, Gibbons* v. *Ogden*

John C. Calhoun: nullification, states' rights

Conflict over slavery: 1820–1860

Civil War: establishing federal supremacy over the states

Reconstruction: greater federal supremacy; 13th, 14th, and 15th Amendments

Populists and Progressive reform
New Deal legislation

Rights of minorities: *Brown* v. *Board of Education*

Fourteenth Amendment: extends Bill of Rights protections to states

Great Society, mid-1960s

New Federalism, 1980s

Constitutional Principle 3
The Judiciary—Interpreter of the Constitution or Shaper of Public Policy

The Judiciary interprets the law (Article III) and has the power to declare laws unconstitutional. This power of judicial review dates from Marshall's decision in *Marbury* v. *Madison,* which was based on Article III, and the supremacy clause in Article VI, which states that the Constitution is the "supreme law of the land."

- By acting when Congress has not acted, or by reversing congressional actions to favor the states, have the courts become lawmakers instead of law interpreters?
- If the courts did not have the power to shape public policy, would the Bill of Rights and democracy itself be endangered?

Examples of This Principle as a Recurring Theme in U.S. History

Marbury v. *Madison:* judicial review strengthened judiciary, government, and national unity

Federal vs. state powers: *McCulloch* v. *Maryland, Gibbons* v. *Ogden*

Limiting protections and rights: *Dred Scott* v. *Sanford, Civil Rights Cases*

Reversals of decisions: *Plessy* v. *Ferguson, Brown* v. *Board of Education*

State vs. federal powers: *United States* v. *E.C. Knight Co., Lochner* v. *New York, Schechter Poultry* v. *United States*

Rights of accused: *Miranda* v. *Arizona, Gideon* v. *Wainwright*

First Amendment cases (freedom of speech, press, religion, assembly): *Engel* v. *Vitale, Schenck* v. *United States, New York Times Co.* v. *United States, Tinker* v. *Des Moines Independent Community School District, Citizens United* v. *F.E.C.*

Ninth Amendment privacy cases: *Roe* v. *Wade; Cruzan* v. *Director, MO Dept. of Health; Griswold* v. *CT*

Checks and balances: *Watkins* v. *United States, United States* v. *Nixon*

Constitutional Principle 4
Civil Liberties—Protecting Individual Liberties From Government Abuses; the Balance Between Government and the Individual

A problem unique to a democratic government is how to balance the rights of the individual and the needs of society. The Constitution's Bill of Rights and Fourteenth Amendment guarantee certain basic rights, rights which predate any government. But these rights are not unlimited.

- What are the rights of the individual?
- Should government protect and/or extend the rights of the individual?
- Should government decide where the balance should be between individual and societal rights?

Examples of This Principle as a Recurring Theme in U.S. History

Right to dissent: Alien & Sediton Acts; Virginia & Kentucky Resolutions

Equal protection clause: Fourteenth Amendment—*Civil Rights Cases, Heart of Atlanta Motel* v. *United States*

Freedom of speech v. "clear and present danger": *Schenck* v. *United States*

Relocation of Japanese Americans: *Korematsu* v. *United States*

Red Scare, McCarthyism: fear of subversion, the erosion of liberties *Watkins* v. *United States*

Testing for drug use: *Vernonia School District* v. *Acton*

Rights of individuals: effects of technology

Individual's rights v. security against terrorism: *Patriot Act, Foreign Intelligence Surveillance Act*

Constitutional Principle 5
Criminal Procedures—The Balance Between the Rights of the Accused and the Protection of the Community and Victims

This is a question of balancing the rights of individuals accused of crimes and those of citizens to be safe and secure.
- Why does an individual accused of a crime have rights?

- Are those rights easily defined?
- What are the rights of a victim of a crime?
- When do the rights of the accused interfere with society's ability to maintain law and order?

Examples of This Principle as a Recurring Theme in U.S. History

Free press vs. the rights of the accused

Death penalty: individual rights v. rights of society

Writ of *habeas corpus:* purpose

Due process of law, search and seizure: *Mapp* v. *Ohio*

Students' rights and search and seizure: *New Jersey* v. *T.L.O.; Vernonia School District* v. *Acton*

Rights of the accused: *Miranda* v. *Arizona, Gideon* v. *Wainwright*

Constitutional Principle 6
Equality—Its Historic and Present Meaning as a Constitutional Value

This issue involves questions of who is equal and in what ways. When Jefferson wrote that "all men are created equal," he referred to the equality before the law of white, property-owning males. The equal protection clause of the Fourteenth Amendment and the due process clause of the Fifth Amendment were later interpreted to make equal justice more of a reality for all Americans.

- According to the Constitution, who is equal: men and women? All races? Rich and poor? Young and old?
- How has the Constitution expanded equality?
- Has equality been achieved?
- How are people equal: equal in opportunity? Before the law? In entitlements?

Examples of This Principle as a Recurring Theme in U.S. History

Conflict over slavery: Constitutional Convention; 1820–1860
Passage of 13th, 14th, and 15th Amendments
Equal protection clause: 14th Amendment
Jim Crow laws: legal basis for segregation
Plessy v. *Ferguson*
Brown v. *Board of Education*
Martin Luther King, Jr.: Civil Rights Movement

19th-century women's rights movement
19th Amendment
1960s women's rights movement
Treatment of Native Americans: *Worcester* v. *Georgia*
Native American movement
New Deal: relief of human suffering
Great Society: help for less fortunate
Affirmative action: court decisions

Constitutional Principle 7
The Rights of Women Under the Constitution

Women are not mentioned in the Constitution except in the Nineteenth Amendment, which protects their right to vote.
- What is the historic and present meaning of equality for women as a constitutional value?

- How were these changes achieved?
- Are federal laws and court rulings sufficiently protective of the rights of women?
- Was there a need for the defeated Equal Rights Amendment?

Examples of This Principle as a Recurring Theme in U.S. History

Elizabeth Cady Stanton and Susan B. Anthony: Women's suffrage movement
Seneca Falls: Women's rights movement
Effects of industrialization on the role of women

1960s women's rights movement
Roe v. *Wade:* Ninth amendment, right to privacy, abortion
Affirmative action and women

Constitutional Principle 8
The Rights of Ethnic and Racial Minority Groups Under the Constitution

The Constitution has not always protected ethnic, racial, and other minority groups. When first ratified, in fact, the Constitution contained clauses that protected slavery and the rights of slaveholders.
- Has the Constitution protected the rights of ethnic and racial minority groups?

- Has the Constitution protected the rights of economically powerful groups better than those of minority groups?
- Are the gains that minorities have made secure, or do such groups need more protection of their rights?
- How do we balance minority rights and rule by a majority?

Examples of This Principle as a Recurring Theme in U.S. History

Conflict over slavery: Constitutional Convention; 1820–1860
Frederick Douglass: abolition movement
Dred Scott v. *Sanford*
Civil War: Emancipation Proclamation
Reconstruction: 13th, 14th, and 15th Amendments
Jim Crow laws, *Plessy* v. *Ferguson*: legal basis for segregation
Equal protection clause: 14th Amendment

Brown v. *Board of Education*
Martin Luther King, Jr.: Civil Rights Movement of 1960s
Restrictions on immigration: quota system, exclusion of Chinese and Japanese
Relocation of Japanese Americans: *Korematsu* v. *United States*
Native Americans: treaty rights, *Worcester* v. *Georgia*, Dawes Act, citizenship in 1924
Native American movement

Constitutional Principle 9
Presidential Power in Wartime and in Foreign Affairs

The Constitution gives the President the power to make treaties, as well as other major foreign-policy responsibilities. The President is also the commander in chief of the armed forces. The powers of the President have grown since the early days of the United States government, and they are even greater in wartime.

- Does the President have too much power, particularly since the Civil War?
- Are broad presidential powers necessary to conduct war and foreign affairs?

Examples of This Principle as a Recurring Theme in U.S. History

George Washington: expanded governmental powers, Proclamation of Neutrality

Increase of presidential power during wartime by Lincoln, Wilson, and FDR.: *Schenck v. United States, Korematsu v. United States*

T. Roosevelt: increase of presidential power because of U.S. involvement in world affairs

T. Roosevelt: Roosevelt Corollary to Monroe Doctrine

Truman: decision to drop atomic bomb

Korean and Vietnam Wars: expanded presidential wartime powers

Kennedy: Cuban missile crisis

War Powers Act: a check on presidential power

Carter: Camp David Accords

G.H.W. Bush: Persian Gulf Crisis

Clinton: Somalia, Bosnia, Haiti, Yugoslavia

G.W. Bush: Bush Doctrine; presidential powers in wartime: writ of *Habeas Corpus*, wiretapping

Constitutional Principle 10
The Separation of Powers and the Effectiveness of Government

The Constitution established three branches of government with separate powers, as well as a system of checks and balances among them.

- Has the system of separation of powers and of checks and balances been effective in preventing dominance by one branch?

- Is this system necessary, or has it resulted in a badly-run government that is slow to respond to the needs of the people and the nation?

Examples of This Principle as a Recurring Theme in U.S. History

Checks and balances: presidential veto

Judicial review: *Marbury v. Madison*

Reconstruction: period of legislative power

Checks and balances: Treaty of Versailles

Checks and balances: FDR and Supreme Court reorganization

Checks and balances: Vietnam War

Checks and balances: *Watkins v. United States, United States v. Nixon*

War Powers Act: check on presidential power

Watergate: government based on laws and not on an individual

Clinton: impeachment and acquittal

Constitutional Principle 11
Avenues of Representation

Since the Constitution was ratified, there has been a continuing expansion of the right to vote. However, while the system has become more democratic and more reflective of majority rule, the power of political parties and special interest groups has grown, as has the influence of technology.

- Has the federal government become more or less representative of "we the people"?

Examples of This Principle as a Recurring Theme in U.S. History

Great Compromise: representation in Congress

Electoral college system

Direct election of senators

Passage of 15th, 19th, 24th, and 26th Amendments

19th-century and Progressive reform movements

Populist and Grange movements

Women's suffrage movement

Third parties' effect on the political process

"One man, one vote": effect on representative government

Campaign financing: public v. private, individual rights, rights of lobbyists and other special interests

Effects of technology: electronic voting; the Internet

Constitutional Principle 12
Property Rights and Economic Policy

The Constitution gives the government responsibility for promoting the general welfare and Congress the power to regulate commerce and taxes.	• Has government balanced its two roles as the promoter of capitalism and free enterprise and as the protector of the public from the abuses of business?

Examples of This Principle as a Recurring Theme in U.S. History

Hamilton: government encouragement of business, national bank	Antitrust activities: Sherman Antitrust Act, T. Roosevelt and W. Wilson, *Northern Securities Co.* v. *United States*, Clayton Antitrust Act
Andrew Jackson: second national bank	Federal Reserve: regulating monetary system
Expanded interstate commerce clause: *Gibbons* v. *Ogden*; *Wabash, St. Louis & Pacific R.R.* v. *Illinois*	Government action for environmental and consumer protection
Weakened interstate commerce clause: *United States* v. *E.C. Knight Co.*, *Lochner* v. *New York*, *Schechter Poultry* v. *United States*	New Deal: government farm price supports
	New Deal: collective bargaining, Wagner Act
Interstate commerce clause used against labor: *In Re Debs*	Reagan: supply side economics, budget deficits

Constitutional Principle 13
Constitutional Change and Flexibility

The Constitution has adapted to changing circumstances over the years because of certain provisions built into it, such as the necessary and proper clause and the interstate commerce clause. • Has the Constitution proven adaptable to changing times?	• Should the Constitution be easier to change? • Has the amendment process, combined with judicial interpretation and the implied powers of the executive and legislative branches, kept the Constitution able to meet the challenges of the modern world?

Examples of This Principle as a Recurring Theme in United States History

Washington: the unwritten constitution	Amendments and court decisions used to expand rights
Hamilton's bank plan: implied powers	Cabinet and congressional committees: custom and precedent
Commerce clause: expansion of government authority, regulation of business, Federal Reserve System	Role of political parties

Part 5 Putting the Constitution Into Effect

Key Terms

unwritten constitution	protective tariff	loose constructionists
cabinet	neutrality	judicial review
"advise and consent"	Alien and Sedition Acts	Federalists
assumption	committee system	Democratic-Republicans
national bank	lobbying	foreign policy
excise tax	strict constructionists	Monroe Doctrine

The Constitution was implemented, or put into effect, beginning in 1789 with George Washington's administration. Our leaders first needed to:

- create a sound financial foundation for the new nation.
- establish a solid political system.
- insure national security through foreign policy decisions.

Not all the actions that shaped our government in its early years grew directly out of the plan set down in the Constitution. From the time of our first presidents an **unwritten constitution** developed in response to changing times and circumstances. This unwritten constitution resulted from a combination of:

- executive interpretations and actions.
- congressional interpretations and actions.
- court decisions, especially judicial review.
- customs and traditions.
- the actions of political parties.

First Years of the New Government, 1789–1820

1792	1795	1798	1801	1803
Kentucky becomes state	Jay's Treaty; Treaty of Greenville	XYZ Affair; Alien and Sedition Acts	John Marshall named Chief Justice	*Marbury* v. *Madison*; Louisiana Purchase

1785 1790 1795 1800 1805 1810 1815 1820

1789	1794	1796	1800	1819
George Washington becomes president	Whiskey Rebellion	John Adams elected president	Jefferson elected president	*McCulloch* v. *Maryland*

Executive Interpretation, Action, and Custom

Executive Decision-Making

Presidents follow a precedent started by George Washington that, when developing policy, they seek advice from the heads of the executive departments, who are called the President's **cabinet**. Today, the White House staff also plays a major role in this advisory process. The President appoints cabinet members with Senate approval but can dismiss a cabinet member without Senate approval.

The early presidents also consulted with congressional leaders when developing policies. Such **"advise and consent"** consultation is an informal procedure. Today, the Senate's official role often seems more "to consent" than "to advise" on presidential decisions. This method of advising the President has become custom.

Developing a Financial Plan

With Washington's support, Alexander Hamilton, the first secretary of the treasury, set out to put the government on a sound economic footing. He proposed a plan that included four key elements:

Assumption Hamilton wanted the national government to pay off American Revolution war debts run up by the Continental Congress as well as the wartime debts of the states. Hamilton believed that this **assumption** of debt would establish the credit of the nation. Congress approved this plan.

A National Bank Hamilton wanted Congress to create a national bank, which he believed would win the government the support of the business community. Such a bank would also aid the government in all of its financial dealings, as well as help ensure the economic stability of the nation. Congress chartered a national bank in 1791.

An Excise Tax Hamilton proposed that the government raise operating revenues through an excise tax on whiskey.

Key Themes and Concepts

Government: Unwritten Constitution
In the early years of the new nation, the United States government grew from the basic framework of the Constitution to a functioning governmental system. Provide an example of how interpretation, action, and custom each contributed to this process.

Interpretation:

Action:

Custom:

Analyzing Documents

Hamilton used the **"necessary and proper"** clause to justify creating a national bank. Read the clause below, then answer the question.

"[The Congress shall have the power] to make all laws which shall be necessary and proper for carrying into execution the foregoing powers, and all other powers vested by this Constitution in the government of the United States, or in any department or officer thereof."
—U.S. Constitution, Article I, Section 8, Clause 18

- Was Hamilton justified in using the "necessary and proper" clause to create a national bank?

- Did the Supreme Court support his argument?

A Protective Tariff Hamilton called for a protective tariff to shield products of the nation's infant industries from foreign competition. Congress rejected the protective tariff but passed other tariffs to generate income for the government.

The Hamilton plan raised controversy, but it put the new nation on a sound financial footing. It also encouraged the wealthy to support the government and built a solid foundation for the nation's future as an industrial power.

The Whiskey Rebellion

In 1794, western Pennsylvania farmers refused to pay excise tax on the whiskey they made from grain. Washington called out state militias and put down this "Whiskey Rebellion." There is debate today over how serious a threat this rebellion really was, but Washington's actions demonstrated that the new government intended to enforce federal law - the supreme law of the land.

Foreign Policy in the Federalist Era

Preparing for the Exam

Geographic Reasoning
"It is our true policy to steer clear of permanent alliances with any portion of the foreign world. . . ."
—Washington's Farewell Address, September 17, 1796

• Why did Washington make this foreign policy?

• How did geography make it possible for the United States to follow Washington's policy for over a hundred years?

From 1789 to 1815, the French Revolution and the European wars that grew out of it put many pressures on the young nation. To protect the new nation Washington set the precedent of neutrality as U.S. foreign policy, when in 1793 he issued a **Proclamation of Neutrality**. In 1795 Washington supported the unpopular **Jay's Treaty,** an agreement designed to resolve conflicts with Great Britain and keep the United States from going to war. His **Farewell Address** in 1796 warned of the danger of permanent alliances with other nations.

John Adams, the first vice president and second president, also understood the importance of keeping the nation out of war. He chose to settle rather than expand an undeclared naval war with France (1798–1800). His actions divided his own Federalist Party, contributing to his failure to win a second term. But Adams, in resisting internal and external pressures for war and ending the 1778 alliance with France, maintained the nation's neutrality and security.

Reacting to Dissent: The Alien and Sedition Acts

Taking advantage of the emotions stirred up by the French Revolution, the Federalists passed the **Alien and Sedition Acts** (1798), four acts designed to strengthen the Federalist Party and weaken the Republican opposition. The Alien Acts made it more difficult to become a citizen and easier to arrest and deport any noncitizens thought to endanger national security. The Sedition Act made it easier to arrest a person for criticizing the government. Writing anonymously, Madison and Jefferson in the **Virginia and Kentucky Resolutions** opposed the acts as a threat to First Amendment rights of freedom of speech and of the press. They also declared the acts a danger to representative government, charged that the federal government had exceeded its authority and claimed that each state had the right to interpret the constitutionality of a federal law.

The Two-Term Presidency

Key Themes and Concepts

Presidential Decisions and Actions
• What impact did Franklin D. Roosevelt's decision to run for a third and fourth term eventually have on the U.S. Constitution?

Washington rejected a third term as president. In doing so, he established a tradition that was not broken until 1940 and 1944, when Franklin D. Roosevelt won a third and then a fourth term. Unhappiness over Roosevelt's break with tradition led to the passage of the **Twenty-second Amendment** that limits a President to two terms or no more than ten years in office.

Congressional Interpretation, Action, and Custom
Creating Structures of Government

The Constitution supplied few details of how the machinery of government would operate, so early congressional actions helped set up that machinery. For example, the Constitution established only a Supreme Court. Congress, therefore, passed the **Judiciary Act of 1789,** creating the rest of the federal court system. Congress also created the first five executive departments—State, Treasury, War (Defense), Attorney General (Justice), and Postmaster General. Today, there are 15 departments and more than 200 independent agencies.

In 1789, Congress began the custom of assigning bills to committees. This developed into today's **committee system,** in which standing committees review all bills before sending them on to the full House or Senate. Congressional committees can also operate as investigative committees, gathering information in order to determine the need for new laws or to examine how current laws are working.

Lobbying

Custom has led to **lobbying** by people representing special-interest groups who act to influence legislation and elect people who support the lobby group's views. Lobbying is protected by the First Amendment's right to petition but also regulated by federal law. The National Rifle Association and the National Association of Realtors are two examples of over 4,600 Political Action Committees (PACs) funded by lobby groups to seek access and influence.

Strict vs. Loose Construction

Hamilton's Financial Plan Hamilton's proposal for a national bank started the first national debate between "strict" and "loose" constructionists. **Strict constructionists** favor a narrow interpretation of the Constitution, holding that government can do only those things the document specifically spells out. **Loose constructionists** favor a freer reading of the Constitution that gives government more room to act. Despite objections of such strict constructionists as Jefferson and Madison, Congress established the bank using the implied powers of the elastic clause.

The Louisiana Purchase In 1803, Jefferson had the chance to double the size of the nation through the **Louisiana Purchase.** However, supporting the purchase meant adopting a loose interpretation of the Constitution. Jefferson overcame his reluctance and backed the purchase. In addition to adding new lands, the

Preparing for the Exam

- What types of PACs are involved in election campaigns and what methods do they use to elect their candidates?

- How does federal law attempt to limit PACs?

- How has the Supreme Court decision in *Citizens United* v. *FEC* affected presidential election campaigns?

The Louisiana Purchase, 1803

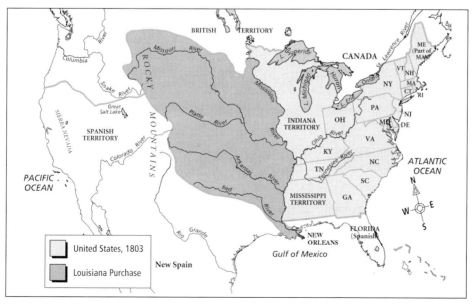

United States, 1803

Louisiana Purchase

Geography in History

". . . is on the globe one spot, the possessor of which is our natural and habitual enemy. It is New Orleans, through which the produce of three-eighths of our territory must pass to market. . ."
— *Thomas Jefferson to Robert Livingston*

Does evidence on the map support or contradict Jefferson's statement?

- Use geographic evidence to determine if the possessor of New Orleans is "our natural and habitual enemy."

Louisiana Purchase gave the United States control of the vital port of New Orleans and the Mississippi River. This opened up a water route for Ohio River Valley farmers and others to ship their products to market.

Judicial Interpretation of the Constitution

Under Chief Justice **John Marshall,** (1801–1835) a series of Supreme Court decisions strengthened the power of the national government and the authority of the judicial branch of government.

The Marshall Court

- First, and most critically, Marshall led the Court in the 1803 decision in ***Marbury v. Madison.*** This decision established the court's most significant right—that of **judicial review**, the power to rule on the constitutionality of a law.
- The decision in ***McCulloch v. Maryland,*** 1819, upheld the creation of a national bank. The decision strengthened federal supremacy over state law, the use of the elastic clause, and national economic interests.
- Similarly, in 1824, the Marshall Court verdict in ***Gibbons v. Ogden*** expanded the powers of the national government in the area of commerce through a broad interpretation of the Congressional power to regulate interstate commerce. (Article I, Section 8)

Activism v. Restraint

Those favoring **judicial activism** believe the Court should use this power to help make public policy. Those favoring **judicial restraint** believe that this power should be used only when there is an obvious violation of a particular part of the Constitution, opposing a policy-making role for the Court. In our history, the Court has been activist and restrained, irrespective of whether the Court was considered conservative or liberal. The Court has also been influenced by changes in the nation's social and political climate.

Actions of Political Parties

Political parties developed through custom and tradition. The debate between **Federalists** and **Anti-Federalists** over ratification revealed the existence of differences of opinion on government. These differences led to the formation of the first two political parties—the **Federalists** and the **Democratic-Republicans,** also known as the Republicans.

The formation of political parties led to constitutional changes in the method of electing the president. Party politics also gave rise to nominating conventions and the pledging of electoral votes to a candidate. Today, due to the growth of primaries and party caucuses, the presidential candidate has usually been selected before the delegates attend the nominating convention.

In the first half of the 1800s, many more men had the right to vote, and the campaign techniques and organization of political parties changed to appeal to this broader electorate.

While major political parties have changed infrequently, the nation has seen many influential "third parties." Such parties have offered criticisms and suggested reforms later adopted by the major parties when in power.

Key Themes and Concepts

Government
Supreme Court decisions have affected the separation of powers in the federal system.

- How did *Marbury* v. *Madison* (1803) affect the separation of powers?

- Based on the Marshall Court's rulings, do you think Marshall was a Federalist or a Democratic-Republican?

Analyzing Documents

In *McCulloch* v. *Maryland,* (1819) the Court rejected the right of Maryland to tax the national bank. Chief Justice Marshall wrote, "The power to tax is the power to destroy." What did he mean?

The First Political Parties

Federalists	Democratic-Republicans
1. Led by Alexander Hamilton, John Adams	1. Led by Thomas Jefferson, James Madison
2. Wealthy and well-educated should lead nation	2. Believed people should hold the political power
3. Believed in strong federal government	3. Believed in smaller government and strong state's rights
4. Favored order and unity	4. Favored individual rights
5. Favored economy based on manufacturing, shipping, and trade	5. Favored economy based on agriculture
6. Favored loose interpretation of Constitution	6. Favored strict interpretation of Constitution
7. Were pro-British, but pro-neutrality	7. Pro-French, but pro-neutrality
8. Favored national bank	8. Opposed national bank
9. Favored protective tariff	9. Opposed protective tariff

Foreign Policy: 1800–1823

Events in Europe from 1789 to 1815 influenced domestic and foreign policies of the United States. With the Atlantic Ocean providing a 3000 mile buffer, Presidents maintained a **foreign policy** of American neutrality. The United States tried to balance neutrality with its right and need as a sovereign nation to trade with European nations because America's economic well-being depended on such trade.

United States Exports, 1800–1820

Embargo of 1807

War of 1812

Source: *Historical Statistics of the United States, Colonial Times to 1970*

Analyzing Documents

Jefferson left instructions that his gravestone be inscribed:

"Author of the Declaration of Independence, the Statute of Virginia for Religious Freedom, and father of the University of Virginia."

• What does this tell you about a man who was both president and vice president of the United States, governor of Virginia, the first secretary of state, and the second minister to France?

Preparing for the Exam

National self-interest is the prime motivation behind a nation's foreign policy.

• Did the motives behind American foreign policy change after the War of 1812? Why or why not?

Analyzing Documents

Compare and Contrast
U.S. exports dropped sharply in 1807–08 and again in 1812–1814.

• What are the similarities and differences in the causes and effects of these losses?

Reading Strategy

Reading for Evidence
Is the War of 1812 best described as

- a second war for independence?

- a war of expansion?

- a war for rights on the seas?

Explain your answer.

- How did geography affect whether a region of the United States supported or opposed the War of 1812?

War of 1812

Meanwhile, Great Britain and France remained at war, and Great Britain outraged Americans by seizing American merchant ships trying to reach France. In an attempt to avoid war and to force Great Britain and France to lift their blockades, Congress passed the **Embargo Act of 1807**. It prohibited the export of goods from the United States. New England, with its trade-based economy, was hit the hardest. In 1809 protests due to the economic impact of the law led to its repeal.

Great Britain continued to violate American freedom of the seas, seizing American ships and impressing or forcing American sailors to serve in the British navy. Meanwhile, western and southern "War Hawks"—interested in expanding into British Canada and Spanish Florida—urged war. In 1812, Congress declared war on Great Britain. The war, however, was not supported by all Americans and provoked disputes among different sections of the nation.

Although the war ended in a draw in 1814, it produced some significant long-term results.

- The war reinforced the American belief that a policy of neutrality regarding European affairs was justified.
- Native American tribes in the West lost their ally, Great Britain, and were much less able to stand up to American expansion.
- American manufacturing began to grow, particularly in New England, when the United States was cut off from European imports.
- Opposing the war, in the face of a growing sense of nationalism weakened the Federalist Party, which soon ceased to be a major factor in national politics.
- In Andrew Jackson and William Henry Harrison, the nation gained new war heroes. "The Star Spangled Banner" was inspired by the bombarding of Fort McHenry.

Foreign Policy After the War of 1812

The new national self-confidence is also seen in the field of diplomacy. John Quincy Adams, secretary of state for President James Monroe, settled the border between the United States and Canada. He acquired Florida from Spain and reached an agreement with that nation on the southern boundary of the Louisiana Purchase. Adams was also Monroe's chief advisor for the Monroe Doctrine.

Monroe Doctrine

The 1823 **Monroe Doctrine,** became the foundation of the United States' foreign policy in the Western Hemisphere. It was issued to prevent former colonial powers from attempting to regain South American colonies that had recently declared their independence. The Monroe Doctrine called for

- an end to European colonization in the Western Hemisphere.
- no intervention by Europe in existing nations in this hemisphere.
- a declaration that European interference was "dangerous to our peace and safety."
- a promise of noninterference by the United States in European affairs and European colonies.

In 1823, the United States lacked the military might to enforce this doctrine. However, Great Britain, acting in its own national interest, agreed to support the United States if European nations challenged the new doctrine. By the end of the 1800s, the United States was actively enforcing the policy on its own.

Preparing for the Exam

On the examination, you will need to understand the changing influences on United States foreign policy.

- How was the Monroe Doctrine influenced by each of the following?

- geography

- isolationism and neutrality

- United States national interests

- concerns of the new Latin American republics

Questions for Regents Practice

Multiple Choice

Directions: Review the Test-Taking Strategies section of this book. Then answer the following questions, drawn from actual Regents examinations. For each statement or question, choose the *number* of the word or expression that, of those given, best completes the statement or answers the question.

1 "We hold these truths to be self-evident, that all men are created equal, that they are endowed by their Creator with certain unalienable rights, that among these are life, liberty, and the pursuit of happiness."

This quotation reflects beliefs mainly derived from

(1) the Magna Carta
(2) the divine right monarchs of Europe
(3) John Locke's theory of natural rights
(4) Marxist philosophy

Base your answers to questions 2 and 3 on the quotation below and on your knowledge of social studies.

"That to secure these rights, governments are instituted among men, deriving their just powers from the consent of the governed; that whenever any form of government becomes destructive of those ends, it is the right of the people to alter or abolish it, and to institute new government. . . ."

2 This quotation presents a justification for

(1) anarchy
(2) revolution
(3) despotism
(4) laissez faire

3 According to the quotation, governments get their authority from

(1) the people
(2) powerful leaders
(3) the justice system
(4) political parties

4 "The individual can be free *only* when the power of one governmental branch is balanced by the other two."

—*Baron de Montesquieu, 1735 (adapted)*

The idea expressed in this quotation is best illustrated by which aspect of the United States government?

(1) existence of a Cabinet
(2) separation of powers
(3) elastic clause
(4) executive privilege

5 In the colonial era, developments such as the New England town meetings and the establishment of the Virginia House of Burgesses represented

(1) colonial attempts to build a strong national government
(2) efforts by the British to strengthen their control over the colonies
(3) steps in the growth of representative democracy
(4) early social reform movements

6 "The only representatives of the people of these colonies are persons chosen therein by themselves; and that no taxes ever have been, or can be constitutionally imposed on them but by their respective legislatures."

—*Statement by the Stamp Act Congress, 1765*

What is a valid conclusion that can be drawn from this quotation?

(1) The colonial legislatures should be appointed by the English King with the consent of Parliament.

(2) Only the colonists' elected representatives should have the power to levy taxes.

(3) The English King should have the right to tax the colonists.

(4) The colonists should be opposed to all taxation.

7 One way in which the United States Constitution differed from the Articles of Confederation was that the Constitution

(1) created a national government having three branches

(2) provided for the direct election of the President by the voters

(3) made the amendment process more difficult

(4) increased the powers of the states

Base your answers to questions 8 and 9 on the discussion below and on your knowledge of social studies.

Speaker A: States must be represented in the national government solely on the basis of population. It is indeed the only fair situation.

Speaker B: The national legislature must be based on equal representation of the states to protect the interests of the small states.

Speaker C: States must accept the supremacy of the national government on all issues; otherwise, the system will fail.

Speaker D: The national Congress should consist of two houses: one in which representation is based on population, and one in which states are equally represented.

8 Which document was being written when this discussion most likely occurred?

(1) Declaration of Independence

(2) United States Constitution

(3) Covenant of the League of Nations

(4) Charter of the United Nations

9 Which speaker's idea about representation was actually included in the document that was written?

(1) A

(2) B

(3) C

(4) D

10 "We should consider we are providing a constitution for future generations of Americans, and not merely for the particular circumstances of the moment."

—*Delegate at the Constitutional Convention of 1787*

The writers of the Constitution best reflected this idea when they provided that

(1) Senators should be elected directly by the people

(2) three fifths of the slaves should be counted as part of the total population

(3) Congress shall make all laws necessary and proper to carry out its constitutional powers

(4) political parties should be established to represent various viewpoints

11 During the debates over the ratification of the United States Constitution, Federalists and Anti-Federalists disagreed most strongly over the

(1) division of powers between the national and state governments

(2) provision for admitting new states to the Union

(3) distribution of powers between the Senate and the House of Representatives

(4) method of amending the Constitution

12   The main purpose of the Bill of Rights is to

(1) prevent governmental abuse of power

(2) increase the power of the Federal judiciary

(3) provide for separation of powers

(4) create a bicameral legislature

13   The fact that the United States Constitution provided for federalism and a system of checks and balances suggests that

(1) the original thirteen states sought to dominate the national government

(2) its writers desired the national government to rule over the states

(3) its writers feared a concentration of political power

(4) the American people of that time supported a military government

14   The United States Supreme Court is sometimes said to fulfill a legislative function because

(1) its members are appointed by the President

(2) its judgments may determine the effect of the law

(3) its members serve only so long as Congress approves

(4) it meets regularly with Congress to advise on the appropriateness of proposed laws

15   Which quotation taken from the United States Constitution provides for limiting the power of government?

(1) "All persons born or naturalized in the United States . . . are citizens of the United States . . ."

(2) "This Constitution . . . shall be the supreme law of the land . . ."

(3) "The President shall be commander in chief of the army and navy . . ."

(4) "Congress shall make no law respecting an establishment of religion . . . or abridging the freedom of speech, or of the press . . ."

16   Which action is an example of lobbying by a special interest group?

(1) labor union members threatening to strike if their company opens a factory in a foreign nation

(2) members of Congress introducing a bill that will provide for low-interest college loans

(3) a congressional committee investigating the activities of organized crime

(4) several lumber companies asking Senators to allow logging on Federal lands

17   If the President has vetoed a bill, the United States Constitution provides that the bill will become a law when the bill is

(1) declared constitutional by the Supreme Court

(2) passed again by two-thirds of both houses of Congress

(3) approved by three-fourths of the State legislatures

(4) approved by a joint committee of Congress

18   In the United States, the electoral college system affects the campaigns of major-party presidential candidates by influencing candidates to

(1) concentrate upon the states with large populations

(2) place more emphasis on controversial issues than on personality

(3) focus upon the states where winning by a large plurality is likely

(4) appeal to the electoral college members rather than to the general public

19   The decision of President George Washington to use the state militia to put down the Whiskey Rebellion in 1794 demonstrated that the

(1) states were still the dominant power in the new nation

(2) President was becoming a military dictator

(3) Federal Government had no authority to impose an excise tax

(4) new National Government intended to enforce Federal laws

Questions for Regents Practice

20 In United States history, which statement best represents the political ideology of Alexander Hamilton and the Federalists?

(1) Only the wealthy will survive in the economic system.

(2) A strong central government is essential for the economic growth of the nation.

(3) No one should have to pay taxes to the National Government.

(4) Elected officials should give public jobs to those who helped them into office.

21 The major role of political parties in the United States is to

(1) protect the American public from corrupt public officials

(2) insure that free and honest elections are held

(3) nominate candidates for public office and conduct campaigns

(4) meet constitutional requirements for choosing the President

22 The term "judicial review" refers to the power of

(1) the Supreme Court to determine the constitutionality of laws

(2) Congress to pass laws over the veto of the President

(3) the states to approve amendments to the Constitution

(4) the President to veto bills passed by Congress

23 In deciding to purchase the Louisiana Territory, President Thomas Jefferson had to overcome the problem of

(1) obtaining the support of Western settlers

(2) passing the constitutional amendment necessary to authorize the purchase

(3) avoiding a possible war with England over the purchase

(4) contradicting his belief in a strict interpretation of the Constitution

24 "The great rule of conduct for us in regard to foreign nations is, in extending our commercial relations to have with them as little political connection as possible."

—George Washington, Farewell Address, 1796

This statement helped establish the United States foreign policy called

(1) containment

(2) internationalism

(3) imperialism

(4) neutrality

25 The Monroe Doctrine declared that the United States would

(1) prevent the establishment of new European colonies anywhere in the world

(2) help colonies in North and South America adopt a democratic form of government

(3) view European interference in the Americas as a threat to the national interest of the United States

(4) prevent other nations from trading with South American nations

26 "Many, if not most, of our Indian wars have had their origin in broken promises and acts of injustice on our part."

The author of this statement would most likely agree that the history of United States treatment of Native Americans was primarily the result of

(1) prejudice toward Native American religions

(2) the desire for territorial expansion

(3) a refusal of Native Americans to negotiate treaties

(4) opposing economic and political systems

27 Which was the most important reason for the social mobility that existed in the English colonies of North America during the 18th century?

(1) absence of racial prejudice among the colonists

(2) existence of a strong cultural heritage

(3) early emphasis on rapid industrialization

(4) availability of land

28 Under mercantilism, the thirteen American colonies were expected to provide Great Britain with

(1) finished American-manufactured goods

(2) raw materials and markets for British products

(3) officials to represent colonial interests in Parliament

(4) laborers to work in British factories

29 Which feature of the United States government is based upon principles found in the Magna Carta and the Petition of Right?

(1) the levying of a personal income tax

(2) the power of Congress to declare war

(3) the power of the House of Representatives to originate all revenue bills

(4) Presidential veto power

30 In the eighteenth century, the British colonies in North America were most similar to Great Britain in their

(1) common law legal system

(2) countrywide established church

(3) opportunities for social mobility

(4) dependence upon manufacturing as the economic base

31 Which was most influential in making the idea of separation of church and state a part of the United States political tradition?

(1) the democratic heritage of ancient Athens

(2) the Roman Republic's principles of religious freedom

(3) practices of European colonial governments

(4) the diversity of the new nation's population

32 Which idea had a major influence on the authors of the Articles of Confederation?

(1) A strong central government threatens the rights of the people and the states.

(2) All people must be granted the right to vote.

(3) Three branches of government are needed to protect liberty.

(4) The central government must have the power to levy taxes and to control trade.

33 At the Constitutional Convention of 1787, the Three-fifths Compromise and the Great Compromise dealt with the issue of

(1) amendments to the Constitution

(2) women's rights

(3) representation in Congress

(4) the rights of the accused

34 In the 1780s, the publication of *The Federalist Papers* was intended to

(1) justify the American Revolution to the colonists

(2) provide a plan of operation for the delegates to the Constitutional Convention

(3) encourage ratification of the United States Constitution

(4) express support for the election of George Washington to the presidency

35 Under the United States Constitution, those powers not delegated to the federal government are

(1) exercised only by state governors

(2) concerned only with issues of taxation

(3) reserved to the states or to the people

(4) divided equally between the states and the national government

36 "The accumulation of all powers, legislative, executive, and judicial, in the same hands . . . may justly be pronounced the very definition of tyranny."

The writers of the United States Constitution intended to prevent the situation described in this quotation by

(1) developing a system of checks and balances

(2) relying on an electoral college

(3) establishing political parties

(4) including the implied powers clause

37 Only a small number of amendments have been added to the United States Constitution mainly because the

(1) executive branch has feared a loss of power

(2) Constitution has been broadly interpreted and applied

(3) public has not objected to the government's use of its power

(4) Constitution is clear in its original intent and seldom needs amending

38 "The privilege of the writ of *habeas corpus* shall not be suspended, unless when in cases of rebellion or invasion the public safety may require it."

This provision is evidence that the writers of the United States Constitution

(1) wanted the President to have unlimited power during wartime

(2) wanted to balance individual liberty with the needs of the nation

(3) did not trust the common people to obey the laws

(4) expected the American people to oppose most government policies

Four statements dealing with the formation of a new government are given below. Base your answers to questions 39 and 40 on these statements and on your knowledge of social studies.

Statement A: Each person must be able to voice his or her concerns on all issues that involve this new nation and bear the responsibility for the decisions made.

Statement B: The power of this new nation must rest in a strong, stable group that makes important decisions with the approval, but not the participation, of all.

Statement C: There must be several governments within one nation to ensure adequate voice and responsibility to all.

Statement D: Individuals must not allow their freedoms to be swallowed by an all-powerful government.

39 Which statement best shows the desire for safeguards such as those in the Bill of Rights?

(1) A   (3) C

(2) B   (4) D

40 Which statement best represents the ideas of federalism?

(1) A   (3) C

(2) B   (4) D

Directions: Write a well-organized essay that includes an introduction, several paragraphs addressing the task below, and a conclusion.

Theme: **The Constitution and Change**

> The United States Constitution not only provides a basic framework government, but also allows for the flexibility to adapt to changes over time.

Task:

> - Identify *two* basic constitutional principles and discuss how each principle allows the government to adapt to changes in the United States
> - For *each* constitutional principle you discuss, describe a specific historical circumstance when the principle was used to meet the needs of American political, social, *or* economic life

You may use any constitutional principle from your study of United States history. Some suggestions you might wish to consider include: the amendment process; judicial review; equality; civil liberties; presidential power in foreign affairs; presidential power during wartime.

You are *not* limited to these suggestions.

Guidelines:

In your essay, be sure to
- Develop all aspects of the task
- Support the theme with relevant facts, examples, and details
- Use a logical and clear plan of organization, including an introduction and a conclusion that are beyond a restatement of the theme

In developing your answer, be sure to keep these general definitions in mind:

(a) <u>describe</u> means "to illustrate something in words or tell about it"
(b) <u>discuss</u> means "to make observations about something using facts, reasoning, and argument; to present in some detail"

Thematic Essay Question 2

Directions: Write a well-organized essay that includes an introduction, several paragraphs addressing the task below, and a conclusion.

Theme: **Constitutional Principles and the Supreme Court**

> Throughout United States history, Supreme Court decisions concerning conflicts over constitutional issues have had a long-term effect on the nation.

Task:

> From your study of United States history, identify two Supreme Court decisions concerning conflicts over constitutional issues which have had a long-term effect on the nation. For each Supreme Court decision identified:
> - Describe the historical circumstances surrounding the Supreme Court decision
> - Discuss the extent to which the Supreme Court decision resolved the conflict over the constitutional issue
> - Discuss the long term impact of the Supreme Court decision

You may use any Supreme Court decision concerning conflicts over constitutional issues that has had a long-term effect on the nation. Some suggestions you might wish to consider include: *McCulloch v. Maryland* (1819) (federalism); *Marbury v. Madison* (1803) (role of the judiciary); *Gibbons v. Ogden* (commerce); *Dred Scott v. Sanford* (separation of powers); *Schenck v. United States* (freedom of expression); *Gideon v. Wainwright* (right to legal counsel); *Heart of Atlanta Motel v. United States* (equal protection under the law).

You are *not* limited to these suggestions.

Guidelines:

In your essay, be sure to
- Develop all aspects of the task
- Support the theme with relevant facts, examples, and details
- Use a logical and clear plan of organization, including an introduction and a conclusion that are beyond a restatement of the theme

In developing your answer, be sure to keep these general definitions in mind:

(a) <u>describe</u> means "to illustrate something in words or tell about it"
(b) <u>discuss</u> means "to make observations about something using facts, reasoning, and argument; to present in some detail"

The Constitution Tested: Nationalism and Sectionalism

Section Overview

In the first half of the 1800s, the United States grew in size and population. The North, blessed with natural resources and a growing population, began industrializing. In the agricultural South, cotton became the dominant crop, and slavery became more firmly rooted in place.

As a new age of mass politics and reform dominated the 1830s and 1840s, tensions grew among the regions, pulling the North and the South apart. The southern states began to see their power and influence decreasing, and soon after the election of 1860, 11 states seceded from the Union. The Civil War that followed settled the constitutional question of federal supremacy versus states rights on the battlefields of Antietam and Gettsyburg.

Key Themes and Concepts

Factors of Production: How did the transportation and industrial revolutions affect life in the United States?

Civic Values: What factors strengthened nationalism and democracy?

Reform Movement: What reform movements developed and what was their impact?

Immigration and Migration: How did immigration and migration west affect the development of our nation?

Constitutional Principles: What three constitutional principles were debated in the first half of the nineteenth century?

Diversity: What caused the sectionalism that led to the Civil War?

Government: How was the conflict over federalism resolved?

Change: What changes took place during the Civil War?

The Big Idea

In the early to mid-nineteenth century:

- the North and South developed different patterns of life and philosophies of government.

- immigration and territorial expansion produced growth and change.

- reform movements attempted to correct many of the injustices of American society.

- sectional differences led to a Civil War testing the Constitution.

Key People

John C. Calhoun	Elizabeth Cady	James Polk
Andrew Jackson	Stanton	John Brown
Martin Van Buren	Lucretia Mott	Abraham Lincoln
William Lloyd Garrison	Susan B. Anthony	Robert E. Lee
Frederick Douglass	Dorothea Dix	Ulysses S. Grant
Harriet Tubman	Meriwether Lewis	
Sojourner Truth	and William Clark	

Key Terms

Whig Party	slavery	Women's Rights
Democratic Party	spoils system	Convention
American System	tariffs	Manifest Destiny
Industrial Revolution	National Bank	popular sovereignty
Transportation	Removal Policy	secede
Revolution	Trail of Tears	Confederate States
immigration	abolitionist	of America
nativism	Underground	Emancipation
potato famine	Railroad	Proclamation

Key Supreme Court Cases

Worcester v. *Georgia* (1832)
Dred Scott v. *Sanford* (1857)

Part 1 Testing the Constitution: Stress and Crisis

In the decades before the Civil War, some forces contributed to national unity, while others began splitting the nation apart.

Nationalism and Sectionalism, 1820–1865

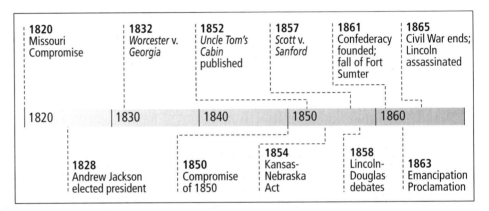

Factors Unifying the United States

Reading Strategy

Organizing Information
List three factors that unified the United States between 1789 and 1861.

1.

2.

3.

The factors that unified the United States include the first and second two-party systems, the market economy and interstate commerce, and decisions of the Marshall Court.

Both the **first and second two-party systems** helped to unify the United States in part because they were national, not sectional, parties. The first two-party system consisted of the **Federalists** and the **Democratic-Republicans**, parties that offered different political philosophies and proposals for action, disagreeing over interpretation of the Constitution. The second two-party system developed in 1834, when the new **Whig Party** opposed Andrew Jackson's party, now called the **Democratic Party.** Both parties ran campaigns that attracted interest and increased the numbers of those voting and involved in national issues.

The development of a **market economy** and **increased interstate** commerce helped to stimulate economic growth nationwide. In the 1800s, revolutions in transportation and technology led to industrialization and urbanization. Specialization was possible because people could now purchase what they did not make or grow. Banks expanded to provide the capital for investment and the funds needed for exchange of goods and services. Southern and western crops were exchanged for northern manufactured goods.

Decisions of the Marshall Court also promoted national unity. These decisions helped to encourage a national economy by expanding interstate commerce and protecting the validity of contracts.

Comparing Household and Market Economies

	Household Economy	Market Economy
Producers	Household	Industries
Labor	Members of the household produce a variety of goods at home.	Workers specialize in producing a certain product outside the home. They exchange their labor for cash.
Goods	Goods are made primarily to be used by the household.	Goods are sold on the open market for a profit.

Preparing for the Exam

Stimulus Based Question
Based on the table at left and your knowledge of American history, answer the following questions.

- How were workers affected by the change to a market economy?

- How did the shift to a market economy promote nationalism?

The American System Supports a National Economy

Senator Henry Clay, supported by John Quincy Adams, designed a legislative program called the **"American System."** The program benefited the North, the South, and the West, and unified the nation by:

- establishing a better national transportation system to aid trade and national defense.
- setting the first protective tariff to encourage American manufacturing and provide funds for improved national transportation networks.
- creating a second national bank to promote the necessary financial support.

Urban and Industrial Patterns in the North

The use of new technologies in manufacturing—particularly steam engines and machines to spin thread and weave cloth—gave rise to the **Industrial Revolution** in Great Britain during the 1700s. By the early 1800s, these new technologies reached the United States. Factory builders flocked to the North, particularly New England, because of its abundant supplies of iron, coal, and swiftly flowing rivers used for water power to operate machinery.

By 1860, northern factories had entered a worldwide competition for markets. While agriculture, especially in its westernmost states, continued to be a major part of its economy, the North began to take on a new identity as an urban manufacturing and commercial area. About 70 percent of national manufacturing was located in the North.

The Transportation Revolution

A **Transportation Revolution** brought new technologies, innovations, and inventions that stimulated the development of transportation systems. Canals, steam transport, and then railroads connected northern markets to western farmlands and westward migration accelerated. In 1825 in New York the **Erie Canal** linked the Atlantic Ocean at New York City through the Great Lakes to the vast interior of the United States. As a result, shipping costs dropped sharply. Population in upstate New York as well as in New York City increased rapidly while industry grew and commerce boomed. Railroads later connected New York to other major cities and to the West. By 1840 New York city was the nation's major port as well as its financial, commercial and industrial center.

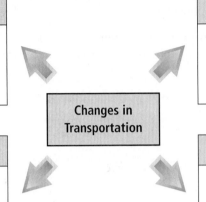

The Transportation Revolution

Steam Power
- In 1807, Robert Fulton's *Clermont* steamed up the Hudson River.
- Steamships helped farmers ship their goods to markets around the world.

Canals
- Erie Canal connected Lake Erie to New York City in 1825.
- By 1840, 3,000 miles of canals are in use.

Changes in Transportation

Roads
- By 1833, the Cumberland Road ran from Maryland to Ohio.
- New roads of stone and gravel helped Americans move west.

Railroads
- In 1828, the B & O railroad line became nation's first railroad.
- By 1840, United States had more miles of railroad track than any other country in the world.

The Factory System

By 1850, most American manufacturing was no longer done in homes and small shops, but instead in factories by workers using machines. This was called the factory system. The first mills were in New England, with the "model" Lowell mill the most well known. It employed white, teenage farm girls as its labor force, offering them an opportunity for financial independence. The girls lived at the mill in a highly regulated environment. Most planned to stay only a few years. Here the first work protests and strikes were organized against wage cuts.

By the 1840s and 1850s, the mills acquired a more permanent work force—Irish immigrant women who needed to work to help support their families. Working conditions were dictated by a strict routine. Twelve-hour days and six-day weeks were the routine. Gains made by the first union movements often were lost when demand for goods dropped in the fluctuating business cycle.

Urban Problems

By 1860, nine of the ten largest cities in the nation were in the North. After 1840, immigrants made up the majority of the population in some cities. The gap between rich and poor widened, as a distinctive rich upper class and a poor working class developed in the cities. Private companies provided sanitation and water only to those who could afford to pay for these services. Cities were unsafe, and police forces did not begin to appear until the mid-1830s.

Middle-Class and Working-Class Life in the North

Industrialization changed family life and gender roles. Previously, families worked together at home and on the farm, taking on different tasks according to gender. After industrialization, both working-class men and women worked, and their jobs also differed depending on their gender. More women worked as servants, more men in factories. The lives of middle-class men were often centered in the new business world, while middle-class women found their lives defined by the home. One of the few jobs considered proper for a single middle-class woman was teaching.

Working-class children usually had to make economic contributions to the family, but middle-class children did not. Childhood, as a specific stage in one's life, received new attention. Middle-class parents supported the growing movement for public schools.

Urban and Rural Populations, 1800–1850

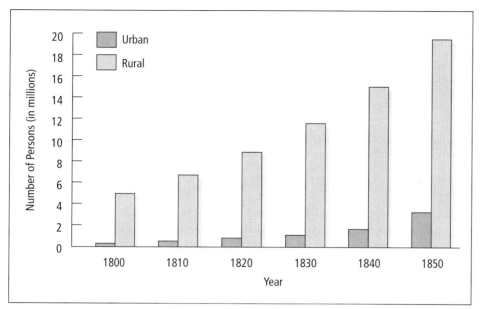

Source: *Historical Statistics of the United States, Colonial Times to 1970*

Both urban and rural populations grew rapidly in the early 1800s. By 1850, 12 percent of the total population lived in urban areas.

Free African Americans in the North continued to face racism and legal restrictions. Public places remained segregated. African Americans also faced discrimination in hiring. Women were more likely than men to find permanent work, most often as household helpers.

Immigration

Until about 1850, most immigrants came from northern and western Europe, particularly Ireland and Germany. The Germans included many who were Jewish. Scandinavians, Dutch, Swiss, and English also immigrated. They generally settled in the North and the West because of greater economic opportunities there. The industrial economy was creating jobs so that there were few restrictions on **immigration.**

Reasons for Immigration Between 1845 and 1850, millions of Irish people came to the United States because of the **potato famine,** a period of mass starvation caused by failure of the potato crop. Many Germans came seeking peace and stability after the failed 1848 Revolution in Germany. Most immigrants arrived in search of better economic opportunities.

Areas of Settlement The Irish tended to settle in northeastern cities. Some Germans also stayed in cities, but many moved west to start farms, as did many Scandinavian immigrants.

Difficulties They Faced Irish and German Catholic immigrants often faced hostility from native-born Americans, some of whom feared economic competition from the newcomers. Others resented the Catholic or Jewish immigrants at a time when the nation was mostly Protestant. **Nativism,** or anti-immigrant feelings, was so strong that a political party called the **"Know Nothings,"** was formed to support the nativist political program. It campaigned to restrict immigration, electing as many as 100 congressmen. The party did very well in local elections in northern states.

Continuity and Change

Migrations
Throughout United States history there have been movements of people (migrations), voluntary and involuntary, into and within the nation. Some examples are:

- colonial settlement (1600s–1700s)
- forced migration of Native Americans (1800–1880)
- westward expansion (1840–1890)
- rural to urban migration (1870s–1920s)
- European immigration (1840–1860 and 1880–1910)
- migration of African Americans from the South to North (1900–1929)
- migration west from the Dust Bowl (1930s)
- suburbanization (1945–1960s)
- migration to the Sun Belt (1950-present)
- illegal immigration (1990- present)
- For each migration identify the: primary cause, participants, influence of geographic and economic factors, historical context, and the short-term and long-term effects on the migrants and on the United States.
- Evaluate patterns of historical continuity and change over time.

Key Themes and Concepts

Immigration and Migration
- Where did the immigrants of the first half of the nineteenth century come from?

- What reaction did these new immigrants face from native-born Americans?

Contributions Immigrants made significant contributions to the growth of this nation. Irish workers helped build railroads and labored in factories. Germans and Scandinavians brought advanced farming techniques and new ideas on education, such as kindergarten.

Patterns of Southern Development

In contrast to the North, the South remained agricultural. Its wealth continued to be invested in land and slaves, and its economy was dependent chiefly on its cotton crop grown with slave labor. The southern population grew slowly because it failed to attract immigrants.

Growth of a Cotton Economy

The climate and topography of the South favored the plantation system of agriculture. Rice, tobacco, and sugar were grown. It was **Eli Whitney's** 1793 invention of the **cotton gin,** which removed the seeds from cotton, that transformed cotton into a successful commercial crop. The opportunity for wealth afforded by cotton had several direct effects:

- It stimulated the growth of **slavery,** linking it even more firmly to the Southern economy.
- It spurred westward migration of planters with their slaves, looking for new land on which to grow cotton. Movement was into the Old Southwest, Alabama and Mississippi, and later even further west into Louisiana, Arkansas, and Texas.
- Cotton became important to the national economy, making up half of all exports.
- However, its agricultural base kept the South economically dependent on the North, both as a market for its crops and as a source of needed manufactured goods.

Preparing for the Exam

Stimulus Based Question
- Examine the graphic organizer at the right.

- Why did the South become increasingly dependent on slavery in the first half of the nineteenth century?

The Growth of "King Cotton"

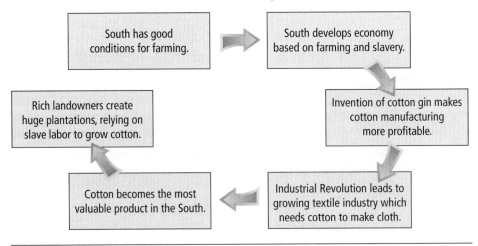

In the early 1800s, cotton became the South's most important crop.

Men and Women on Plantations

Slaveholding men dominated political, economic, and social life in the South. Planters' wives and daughters were responsible for the domestic sphere. They managed the care, feeding, and clothing of their families and the slave families as well.

Life Under Slavery

Daily life for most slaves was very difficult. They had no control over their own lives or their children's lives, and they were at the mercy of the slaveholders or overseers. Slaves who worked as field hands often worked from dawn to sunset, while those who were house servants often worked long past sunset.

Slaves generally ate inexpensive food and wore rough clothing. Cabins housed one or two families. However, slaves were also a financial investment, and this affected their treatment. After the importing of slaves ended, the economic value of slaves increased, and their health care improved.

Slaves could not legally marry, but families remained central to the African American community. Parents instilled the importance of family in their children, while preparing them to cope with a life of slavery. Children were not educated and began work as young as eight years old. As planters moved westward in search of new lands for growing cotton, slave families were often tragically broken up.

The religious practices of slaves were a mixture of Protestant Christian and African elements. Music was an important part of worship services. Religion provided slaves with comfort and hope for salvation.

Resistance

Resistance against slavery took many forms. Most protests took the forms of escape, self-mutilation, sabotage, or work slowdowns. Although open rebellions were rare, they instilled fear within the white slaveholding society. There were several notable slave revolts.

- In 1800, Gabriel Prosser's Conspiracy in Virginia, led by urban skilled workers, was discovered.
- In 1822, Denmark Vesey's plans to lead a South Carolina revolt were uncovered.
- In 1831, Nat Turner led a revolt in Virginia.

Rebellions led southern lawmakers to pass increasingly strict laws to maintain slavery. Freeing slaves became more difficult, and teaching a slave to read and write became illegal.

The Age of Jackson

Andrew Jackson was twice elected President of the United States, serving from 1829 to 1837. He was the first president elected from a state other than one of the 13 original states. Jackson ran unsuccessfully for president in 1824. Out of four presidential candidates, none received a majority of the electoral votes. Although Jackson had the most popular votes and the most electoral votes, the House of Representatives selected **John Quincy Adams** as president. Jackson's party, the Democrats, got its support from middle-class and small farmers of the South and the West, and urban workers. Adams' party was strongest in the North.

The Rise of Mass Politics

By the mid-1820s, most states had dropped their property qualifications for voting. In 1828, the number of voters was three times larger than it had been in 1824. Andrew Jackson, a popular hero of the War of 1812, appealed to these new voters and won both the electoral and the popular vote.

Selecting a presidential candidate became more democratic in 1832. Candidates were chosen for the first time by a national nominating convention, rather than a few party leaders.

Reading Strategy

Key Ideas and Details
- What were some of the effects of the expansion of slavery?

Analyzing Documents

"This Fourth of July is yours, not mine. You may rejoice, I must mourn. . . . What, to the American slave, is your 4th of July? I answer; a day that reveals to him, more than any other days in the year, the gross injustice and cruelty to which he is the constant victim."
—Frederick Douglass, Rochester, New York, 1852

- Why does Douglass find it impossible to celebrate the Fourth of July?

- How did slavery contradict the civic values expressed in the Declaration of Independence?

Preparing for the Exam

- What is the difference between the popular and the electoral vote?

- How was each of the presidential elections of 1800, 1824, 1876, 2000 and 2016 resolved?

Rallies, slogans, and often vicious written attacks marked the advent of mass politics. "Secret" ballots became popular, but parties printed them in colors so it was easy to tell for whom a person voted. Only after the Civil War did the truly secret ballot come into general use.

The Spoils System and Civil Service Reform

The **spoils system,** which dates from the presidency of Andrew Jackson, gave government jobs to people who had worked to help their political party win the election. This method was called the spoils system because of the saying "To the victor belong the spoils (rewards)." In 1881, a party worker who had failed to get a government job killed President James Garfield. At that point, people began to demand reform, and the new president, Chester Arthur, supported it. The **Pendleton Act** of 1883 marked the beginning of **civil service reform.** The Act:

- provided that competitive exams be used to hire some government workers.
- set up a commission to administer the tests.
- banned the common practice of forcing government employees to give money to political parties.

Growing Sectionalism

Sectionalism also developed in the United States during the first half of the nineteenth century as economic, social, and political differences pulled the nation in opposite directions.

States' Rights v. Federal Supremacy

Debate raged over how the balance of power between the states and the federal government should be achieved. From 1820 to 1865 this debate focused on nullification, protective tariffs and the spread of slavery.

The Tariff Issue Southern states opposed protective **tariffs,** which resulted in higher prices paid for imported manufactured goods. The agricultural South saw northern industries as the chief beneficiaries of such tariffs.

With passage of the high **Tariff of 1828**, called the Tariff of Abominations in the South, tensions increased. Vice President John C. Calhoun of South Carolina argued that a state had the right to **nullify,** or declare void, any federal law that the state considered unconstitutional. In 1798 in the Virginia and Kentucky Resolutions Madison and Jefferson had made a similar argument regarding a state's right to interpret federal laws. However, in 1803 the Supreme Court established its right of judicial review.

Then, in response to a slightly lower 1832 tariff South Carolina enacted an Ordinance of Nullification, voiding both the 1828 and the 1832 tariffs in the State. President Andrew Jackson:

- defended federal supremacy and denounced nullification as treasonous.
- requested a Force Bill to allow him to use federal troops in South Carolina to enforce the law.
- proposed the Compromise Tariff of 1833 that gradually lowered tariffs.

Jackson's solution resolved the immediate crisis. South Carolina withdrew its tariff nullification, then nullified the Force Bill. The fundamental issue remained.

The National Bank Issue—The Bank War

The Second Bank of the United States also provoked sectional differences. Most opposition to the **National Bank** came from southerners and westerners, who wanted a greater supply of money in circulation. They also resented the national bank's control over state banking.

Key Themes and Concepts

Economic Systems
- Why did the South believe that the North benefited from a protective tariff?

- How did this debate increase sectional conflict?

Preparing for the Exam

What is an example of a conflict in the pre-Civil War period involving each concept below?

Supremacy Clause, State's Rights, sectionalism, nationalism, nullification, secession

In 1832, President Jackson vetoed a bill to recharter the bank. He then withdrew federal money from the bank, effectively killing it. To Jackson and many of his followers, **the Second Bank of the United States** had symbolized privilege and the power of special northern interests.

The Presidency of Andrew Jackson

President Andrew Jackson

Fired more than 2,000 government workers and replaced them with his own supporters
Vetoed more acts of Congress than all six previous presidents combined
Closed Bank of the United States
Threatened to send huge army to South Carolina to force the state to obey tariff laws
Used Indian Removal Act to force 100,000 Native Americans from their homelands

Jackson's forceful actions earned him both strong support and angry opposition throughout the country.

Relations With Native Americans

As American settlers moved ever westward in the 1800s, conflict continued with the Native Americans who lived in these territories.

Native American Cultural Survival Strategies

Native Americans tried a variety of strategies to cope and retain their land and culture.

- In the early 1800s, two Shawnee brothers, Prophet and Tecumseh, tried to build a **Pan-Indian Movement** in the Old Northwest, but this movement died with Tecumseh in the War of 1812.

- Meanwhile, a Seneca named Handsome Lake urged the Iroquois to adopt a lifestyle based on temperance, education, farming, and peace. This lifestyle became known as cultural revitalization.

- In 1813, Creeks attacked settlers in Georgia and Alabama in a series of raids, but in 1814, they were defeated at Horseshoe Bend, Alabama. The Southwest was then opened to settlement.

- The Cherokees attempted to survive and retain their culture through **cultural adaptation,** combining elements of Native American and European culture, including a written constitution. This strategy, however, did not save them.

The Removal Policy

The federal government used a combination of treaties and force to move **Native Americans** to lands west of the Mississippi River. The treaties were worthless, because Native Americans were forced repeatedly to give up their land even though ownership was guaranteed by treaty.

In the 1830s, President Andrew Jackson began his **Removal Policy** that forced all Native Americans to move west of the Mississippi. In 1832, the Cherokee went to court to prevent Georgia from taking their land. In ***Worcester* v. *Georgia,*** Chief Justice John Marshall ruled that Georgia had no authority over Cherokee territory, but Georgia simply ignored the ruling. In 1838, the U.S. Army rounded up the Cherokee and moved them west in a forced march known as the **Trail of Tears.**

Analyzing Documents

"The consequences of a speedy removal will be important. . . . It will separate the Indians from immediate contact with settlements of whites; . . . and perhaps cause them . . . to cast off their savage habits and become an interesting, civilized, and Christian community."
—*President Andrew Jackson, 1830*

- What does this quote reveal about Jackson's attitude toward Native Americans?

Analyzing Documents

"We wish to remain on the land of our fathers. We have a perfect and original right to remain without interruption."
—*Cherokee public appeal, July 17, 1830*

- What does this quote reveal about how the Cherokee viewed their possession of the land?

The Seminole of Florida were also faced with removal. A group fought the effort in the Second Seminole War. Many remained in Florida. By the 1840s, however, only scattered groups of Native Americans still lived in the East.

Native American Land Transfer Before 1850

Analyzing Documents

Compare the map at right with the Territorial Expansion map on page 76.

• How does the map at right relate to the territorial expansion of the United States?

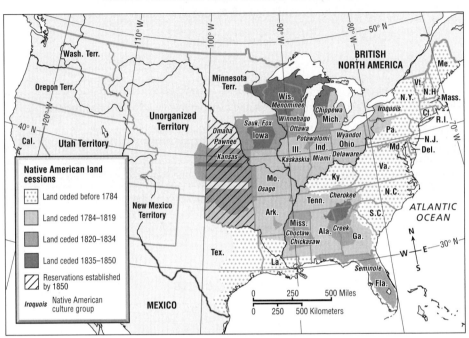

The American Reform Tradition

In the early 1800s, great changes affected the way people lived and interacted with each other. The Industrial Revolution, urbanization, growth in immigration, westward expansion, and the cotton-based southern economy created opportunities as well as serious problems.

The Second Great Awakening, a religious revival movement, motivated reform with its emphasis on self-reliance, on one's ability to affect one's future and to improve the world. The movement called for self-improvement and for joining to fight forces of evil. The religious feelings that drove reform were reinforced by the Republican political belief in civic virtue—that a good citizen acts for the common good.

Reform Movements

Many areas of American life inspired reform movements, including education and care of the mentally ill.

Public Schools Reformers recognized that if the people were to govern, they needed to be educated. Under the leadership of Horace Mann, Massachusetts led the nineteenth century drive for public education. Mann believed that every human being had the right to an education, and he developed an educational system with grade levels and teacher training. His ideas spread rapidly. By 1860, most people had at least an elementary education in all regions but the South. Educational opportunities for girls and young women also expanded.

Care of the Mentally Ill In the early 1800s, most mentally ill people were kept locked up in prisons. In the 1840s, a Massachusetts reformer named Dorothea Dix studied the poor treatment of the mentally ill and reported her findings to the state legislature, which authorized funds for state mental hospitals. Dix later worked with several other states that followed the example of Massachusetts.

Other Reforms Reformers also pushed for the creation of prisons, hospitals, orphanages, and institutions to care for physically disabled people. In addition, a strong temperance movement was organized to eliminate alcohol consumption.

Abolition

In the 1820s, the antislavery movement grew as cotton production became more profitable and slavery spread. In 1833 the American Anti-Slavery Society was formed to support immediate rather than gradual abolition of slavery. The movement attracted a wide variety of activists – men, women, religious leaders, freed slaves, wealthy and poor – including Frederick Douglass, Sojourner Truth, Angelina and Sarah Grimké, and William Lloyd Garrison.

Abolitionists organized the **Underground Railroad,** a series of safe houses where escaping slaves could rest safely as they made their way north and into Canada. **Harriet Tubman,** who made 19 trips to escort runaways, was a leader of the Underground Railroad.

By 1840 the abolitionist movement had 2000 chapters in the North but not all northerners supported it. Some northern merchants feared that the abolition movement would further sour relations between the North and the South and harm trade. White workers feared the competition from escaped or freed slaves willing to work for lower wages.

Women's Rights

By the 1830s, reform-minded women recognized that they faced discrimination, even within their own organizations. The Grimke sisters faced objections to women speaking publicly. **Elizabeth Cady Stanton** and Lucretia Mott, women delegates attending the 1840 World Anti-Slavery Convention, were not allowed to participate in the convention.

The women's rights movement began officially in 1848, when Stanton and Mott organized the **Women's Rights Convention** in **Seneca Falls,** New York. There, the **Declaration of Sentiments** was issued. The first goal of this chiefly middle class movement was to end legal inequalities faced by married women. At this time, a husband had the legal right to control his wife's property, earnings, and children.

In 1853, **Susan B. Anthony** joined Stanton in the drive for women's rights. By the 1850s, the women's rights movement began focusing on winning the vote for women. Women's right to vote in national elections was not won until 1920.

Territorial Expansion

From 1803 to 1853, the United States expanded to its present continental boundaries.

Manifest Destiny

Many Americans believed in **Manifest Destiny,** the conviction that the United States had a divine mission:

- to expand to the Pacific Ocean and even to possess the entire North American continent.
- to spread the ideals of freedom and democracy.

What Americans saw as Manifest Destiny was viewed quite differently by the Native American and Mexican peoples, who were in possession of these western lands. Expansion increased national pride, but by raising serious questions about slavery, it also contributed to growing sectional tensions.

Analyzing Documents

Key Ideas and Details
On this subject, I do not wish to think, or speak, or write, with moderation. No!, no! Tell a man whose house is on fire, to give a moderate alarm; . . . tell the mother to gradually extricate [pull out] her babe from the fire into which it has fallen;—but urge me not to use moderation in a cause like the present. I am in earnest . . .—I will not retreat a single inch—AND I WILL BE HEARD.
—William Lloyd Garrison, The Liberator, 1831

- How does Garrison use words and phrases to convey his anti-slavery views?

Analyzing Documents

Craft and Structure
We hold these truths to be self-evident: that all men and women are created equal. . . . The history of mankind is a history of repeated injuries and usurpations [seizure of power] on the part of man toward woman, . . . [to establish] absolute tyranny over her. . . .
—Declaration of Sentiments, 1848

- Cite textual evidence to analyze how this document is structured and why.

People and Westward Expansion

Often using river systems, the first Americans to move westward were **explorers,** such as Meriwether Lewis, William Clark, and Zebulon Pike, and naturalists, trappers, traders, and missionaries. They were followed by trailblazers and settlers who traveled along routes such as the Santa Fe and Oregon Trails. **Mormons,** led by **Brigham Young,** settled at the Great Salt Lake in 1846. In order to escape religious persecution, they selected a spot which placed them far from others. Discovery of gold and silver in California and other western territories accelerated settlement in those regions. Most settlers chose more prosperous lands in the far West, leaving the flat but dry and treeless Great Plains to be settled only after the 1860s.

Territorial Expansion of the United States and Other Acquisitions

Geography in History

Using the map at right and the map on page 74, answer the following questions.

- What was the effect of the Appalachian Mountains and Rocky Mountains on settlement?

- Why was the Great Plains the last region to be settled?

- How did the arid conditions affect the settlement of parts of the Mexican Cession?

Analyzing Documents

In the 1840s, songs, writings, and slogans expressed responses to **Manifest Destiny.** Connect each example below to Manifest Destiny.

- James Polk: Fifty-four forty or fight!

- California: The Bear Flag Republic

- Henry D. Thoreau: *Civil Disobedience*

- U.S. Marines: "From the halls of Montezuma. . ."

Lands Acquired Between 1783–1853

By 1853, the continental United States had expanded to its present boundaries.

Louisiana Purchase (1803) Stretching from the Rocky Mountains to the Mississippi River, and including the Great Plains, this territory was bought from France for $15 million. In 1803 President Jefferson sent Meriwether Lewis and William Clark to seek a water route to the Pacific Ocean, to explore the economic resources, and to strengthen U.S. control of the territory. Their data and maps contributed to the nation's expansion by increasing understanding of the vast area.

Florida (1819) This territory was acquired by treaty from Spain, satisfying southern expansionists. In the Adams-Onís Treaty, Spain also gave up its claims to the Pacific Northwest in return for the United States giving up its claims to Texas.

Texas (1845) The United States acquired Texas and what is now parts of New Mexico, Oklahoma, Colorado, Wyoming, and Kansas from Mexico by annexation. The Spanish had long established missions and settlements in Texas. After Mexico declared its independence from Spain in 1821, southern slaveholders and other American settlers moved into Texas. In 1836, the settlers declared independence from Mexico and created the Republic of Texas. Soon, Texas requested admission to the Union. However, President Jackson and then President **Martin Van Buren**

were concerned about the political effects of admitting another slave state as well as the diplomatic effects of admitting land claimed by Mexico. In 1845, after nine years of controversy, Texas joined the Union as a slave state during the administrations of President John Tyler and of President James K. Polk.

Oregon Country (1846) What is now Oregon, Washington, Idaho, and parts of Montana and Wyoming, was gained from Great Britain in a compromise that continued the northern border set at the 49th parallel all the way to the coast.

Mexican Cession (1848) What is now California, Nevada, Utah, Arizona, and parts of New Mexico, Colorado, and Wyoming became part of the United States by the Treaty of Guadalupe Hidalgo, which ended the **Mexican War (1846–1848).** Mexico strongly objected to the Texas annexation. Tensions increased when President James Polk sent an envoy to Mexico with an offer to buy California and moved federal troops into the Rio Grande area that was at the center of a border dispute between the United States and Mexico. When fighting occurred there, war was declared. National opinion was divided. Expansionists welcomed an opportunity to acquire more land. Northerners feared the future addition of more slave states. Some, such as Abraham Lincoln, saw it as a "war of conquest," others saw it as fulfilling *"Manifest Destiny."*

Gadsden Purchase (1853) This piece of land in southern Arizona and New Mexico was purchased from Mexico as a possible railroad route.

Preparing for the Exam

While a treaty requires a two-thirds vote of the Senate, a joint resolution of Congress requires a majority of each house.

• Why were Texas and Hawaii each annexed by joint resolution instead of by treaty?

Part 2 The Constitution in Jeopardy: The American Civil War

Differences between the North and the South finally threatened the existence of the nation. The debate that followed on how slavery should be treated in new lands centered on constitutional issues.

Great Constitutional Debates: The Slavery Issue

Until the Civil War, the Constitution had recognized and protected slavery in three ways: the Three-Fifths Compromise, the provision that Congress could not end the importing of slaves before 1808, and the fugitive slave clause. These compromises had been made in order to encourage southern states to ratify the Constitution. With the expansion of American territory in the West, controversy brewed over whether these new territories should allow slavery or not.

Northern Views

Northerners who sought to stop the spread of slavery used several arguments:

1. The Constitution gave Congress jurisdiction, or power, over the territories.
2. Precedent, or previous acts, justified congressional action. Precedents included
   • the **Northwest Ordinance,** by which the Confederation Congress had banned slavery in the territory north of the Ohio River.
   • the **Missouri Compromise** of 1820, which had banned slavery in that part of the Louisiana Purchase north of 36° 30′ latitude.

Southern Views

Because of the earlier constitutional compromises, Southerners insisted that slavery be permitted in the new territories. Constitutional equality, they said, applied only to whites. Slavery in the territories, they claimed, was legal for the following reasons:

Reading Strategy

Organizing Information Below are eight events that led to the Civil War.

• Place them in chronological order

• Identify how the events are related to each other chronologically.

• Compromise of 1850

• Confederacy formed

• *Dred Scott* v. *Sanford* decision

• John Brown's raid

• Kansas-Nebraska Act

• Lincoln elected president

• Missouri Compromise

• South Carolina secedes

Constitutional Principles
In 1836, southern members
of Congress succeeded in
passing the so-called gag
rule, which prohibited the
reading of any antislavery
petitions in the House. The
gag rule stayed in place for
eight years.

• Why might abolitionists
point to the gag rule as an
example of how slavery
threatened the rights of
all Americans?

Government
Compromise is essential
to democratic government.

• How did the Missouri
Compromise postpone
the clash between the
North and the South?

• Why did the Compromise
of 1850 satisfy neither
side?

1. Congress had no authority to prevent the extension of slavery into the territories.
2. Congress had a constitutional duty to protect slavery.

Differences Between the North and the South

	Northern States	Southern States
Population	21.5 million	9 million
Number of Factories	110,100	20,600
Miles of Railroad	21,700	9,000
Bank Deposits	$207 million	$47 million
Cotton Production	4 thousand bales	5 million bales

During the 1850s, differences between the North and the South continued to grow.

The Compromise of 1850

Until 1850, with an equal number of slave and free states in the Union, the South maintained a balance of power in the Senate. That year, this balance was threatened when California, its rapid growth aided by the Gold Rush, applied to become a free state. The issue of slavery in the new territories was settled for a brief time by the **Compromise of 1850,** which included four key laws:

1. California entered the Union as a free state.
2. A stricter **Fugitive Slave Law** required that escaped slaves be returned.
3. Slave trade was prohibited in Washington D.C.
4. **Popular sovereignty,** or a vote of the people living in the territory, would determine whether a territory in the Mexican Cession was to be slave or free.

The Compromise of 1850 pleased no one. Some Northerners engaged in civil disobedience against the Fugitive Slave Law by protesting the return of runaway slaves and aiding slaves trying to reach the safety of Canada. The passage of this act is said to have motivated **Harriet Beecher Stowe** to write *Uncle Tom's Cabin.* The bestselling book of the nineteenth century, it influenced many to oppose slavery. The popular sovereignty provision was unclear. Would the vote to make a territory slave or free be held at the time the territory was settled or when it applied to become a state? This uncertainty led to further conflict.

The Kansas-Nebraska Act

In 1820, the **Missouri Compromise** had prohibited slavery in the lands that made up Kansas and Nebraska. The Kansas-Nebraska Act of 1854 overturned the Missouri Compromise by allowing those territories to decide the question of slavery by popular sovereignty.

Violence erupted when pro- and antislavery people rushed into Kansas to vote on the issue. The territory was called **Bleeding Kansas** after a pro-slavery mob destroyed homes, stores, and offices in Lawrence, and John Brown's group killed pro-slavery settlers at Pottawatomie Creek. Violence extended to the U.S. Senate when, angered at a speech Sumner made, southern congressman Preston Brooks beat abolitionist Senator Charles Sumner in the Senate chamber.

Rise of the Republican Party

Reactions to the Kansas-Nebraska Act led to changes in the political party system. One major party, the Whigs, split into northern and southern wings and soon died out. The Democrats were seriously weakened in the North. A new party, the Republicans, was founded to oppose the spread of slavery. It was a sectional rather than a national party and proclaimed a platform of "Free Soil, Free Labor, Free Men."

The Dred Scott Case

In 1857 in *Dred Scott* v. *Sanford* ruled that Dred Scott remained a slave although he had lived in a free state and free territory because:

- African Americans were not citizens and therefore had no right to sue in federal court or seek constitutional protection.
- Congress could not deprive citizens of their right to property (slaves) by banning slavery in any territory. The Missouri Compromise was unconstitutional.

The Lincoln-Douglas Debates

In Illinois in 1858, Abraham Lincoln, a Republican, challenged the well-known Senator Stephen A. Douglas, author of the **Kansas-Nebraska Act,** in the campaign for U.S. Senate. A series of debates were held, then the Illinois legislature reelected Douglas to the Senate. The **Lincoln-Douglas Debates** weakened Douglas in the South while making Lincoln a national political figure unacceptable to the South because of his position against the extension of slavery. Lincoln had accepted the Republican Senate nomination with a speech that included the famous lines:

"A house divided against itself cannot stand. I believe this government cannot endure, permanently half *slave* and half *free*. I do not expect the Union to be *dissolved*—I do not expect the house to *fall*—but I *do* expect it will cease to be divided. It will become *all* one thing or *all* the other."

John Brown's Raid at Harper's Ferry

In 1859, John Brown led a small group in a raid against a federal arsenal in what is now West Virginia. His plan was to seize weapons and lead a slave uprising. Although he was unsuccessful and was later executed for treason, he became a Northern hero. The incident increased Southern distrust of the North.

The Election of 1860

The election of 1860 showed clearly how divided the United States had become. The only remaining national party, the Democratic Party, split between the North and the South with each wing running a candidate. Abraham Lincoln, the first Republican to be elected President, received only 39 percent of the popular vote.

The election of a Northerner who opposed the extension of slavery drove some Southerners to threaten secession. To prevent secession, Senator John Crittenden of Kentucky proposed the **Crittenden Compromise,** which would have divided the nation, slave versus free territory, all the way to California, along the Missouri Compromise line. The compromise was defeated because congressional Republicans would not support it. Some did not believe that the South would go through with their threats to leave the Union.

The Secession Crisis

In December 1860, South Carolina decided to **secede** from, or leave, the Union. By February 1861, six more Southern states seceded and, with South Carolina, formed the **Confederate States of America.**

President James Buchanan took no action to stop them. He stated that neither he nor Congress had the power to preserve the Union because it "rests upon public

Preparing for the Exam

Stimulus Based Question
It is the opinion of the Court that the Act of Congress which prohibited a citizen from holding and owning property of this kind in the territory of the United States north of the line . . ., is not warranted by the Constitution, and is therefore void. . . .
—Dred Scott v. Sanford, 1857

- What is meant by "property of this kind"?
- What were the Supreme Court's reasons for declaring the Missouri Compromise unconstitutional?
- What role did the Northwest Ordinance (1787) play in the Dred Scott decision?

Preparing for the Exam

- Why did the "House Divided" speech hurt Lincoln in his Senate race but help him to be elected president?

The Election of 1860 can be considered a turning point in United States history. Examine the chart below and answer the question that follows.

Election of 1860 Popular Vote

Candidate	Popular Vote	% of Popular Vote
Lincoln	1,865,593	39.5
Douglas	1,382,713	29.5
Breckinridge	848,356	18
Bell	592,906	13

Election of Vote

Candidate	Electoral Vote	% of Electoral Vote
Lincoln	180	59
Douglas	12	4
Breckinridge	72	24
Bell	39	13

- Citing specific data, analyze why the southern states responded to the 1860 election by seceding from the Union.

opinion and can never be cemented by the blood of its citizens shed in war." Lincoln disagreed and denied that states could secede. In his First Inaugural Address in March 1861, Lincoln stated that "in view of the Constitution and the law, the Union is unbroken."

The Union and the Confederacy, 1861

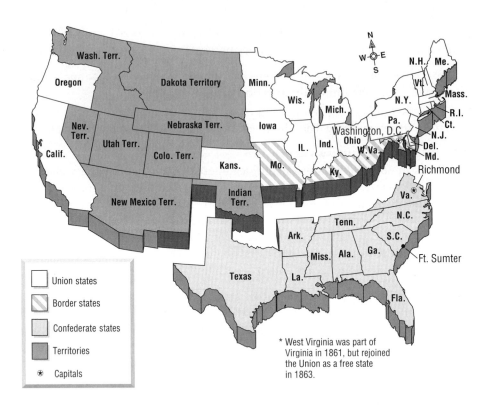

Union states
Border states
Confederate states
Territories
⊛ Capitals

* West Virginia was part of Virginia in 1861, but rejoined the Union as a free state in 1863.

Stimulus Based Question
Review the chart on page 78 and the map on this page.

- What advantages did the South have at the beginning of the Civil War? What advantages did the North have?

- How can the differences in the two areas best be explained?

- What advantages did each side have that are not seen on either the chart or the map?

- Why does the map show the border states differently? With which side did these states align?

The Civil War

Lincoln's policy was to oppose secession but to take no military action until the South started fighting. In April 1861, the South seized Fort Sumter in Charleston Harbor, South Carolina. Lincoln called for troops to put down the rebellion. Four more southern states, including Virginia, seceded. The Civil War had begun.

Great Constitutional Debates: Preservation of the Union

Once a state had entered the United States, did it have the right to leave? From the Southern view, the South had the right to secede because the United States had not protected Southern rights. (In this case, only the rights of the white population were being considered.) Lincoln took the position that states could not leave the Union. No minority could act to destroy the nation and its government.

Lincoln's Aims and Actions

From the beginning of the secession crisis, Lincoln's goal was to preserve the Union. He took bold executive action to achieve this aim.

- He called out state militias, increased the size of the navy, ordered a naval blockade of the South, and approved funds for military expenses while Congress was not in session. Congress later gave its approval of these actions.

- He ordered the arrest of Southern sympathizers in Maryland and Delaware to prevent secession of those states. Failure to act might have meant the encircling of the capital by Confederate states.

- He suspended the writ of *habeas corpus* in areas not in rebellion. He later won congressional approval for this step.
- He declared martial law, which led to the arrests of thousands for suspected disloyalty.
- He censored newspapers and arrested publishers and editors.

Constitutional Questions

Lincoln's actions broadened the power of the executive. They also raised troubling questions: Were such actions constitutional? Did they fall within the scope of the President's war powers, or were they dictatorial? Did the fact that some Northerners sympathized with the rebelling South justify the limiting of their civil rights? Did Lincoln set precedents for expanded executive action that later presidents might use in more questionable circumstances?

Other Government Policies During the War

In order to help to finance the Civil War, a new federal banking system was created, establishing a national currency. The currency was backed by government bonds and issued by the new federal banks.

In 1862, the Congress passed three major acts to facilitate economic growth after the war ended, primarily by encouraging development of the Midwest and far west. Congress:

- passed the Pacific Railway Act authorizing the building of the **transcontinental railroad,** financed with public land grants and cash loans.
- passed the **Homestead Act,** providing for the settlement of western lands.
- approved the **Morrill Land Grant Act,** which gave public lands to states and territories to found agriculture, mechanical arts, and military science colleges.

Military Strategy

The Confederate war strategy was to attack the Union army repeatedly, inflicting casualties and wearing it down until it lost the will to fight. The Confederacy hoped to gain aid and diplomatic recognition from Great Britain and France, two nations that relied on Southern cotton. Neither strategy was successful.

The Union relied on its superior resources and technology. Union ships blockaded Southern ports, preventing the Confederacy from importing food and military supplies. In 1863, General Ulysses S. Grant led the victorious Union forces at Vicksburg, Mississippi, giving the North control of the Mississippi and dividing the South. In 1864, Lincoln appointed Grant to head the Union forces. As the new commander, Grant's strategy was to destroy not only the Confederate army but also all Southern resources that supported the war effort.

The Human Cost

The Civil War was the bloodiest war the United States has ever known. Some 600,000 Americans lost their lives as new military technologies and old diseases struck down soldiers and civilians. Families along the border between the Union and the Confederacy were particularly devastated, as family members fought on opposite sides. The dead included Lincoln himself, assassinated within days of the war's end.

The worst single day of the war occurred in 1862 at the **Battle of Antietam** in Maryland, where the Southern commander General Robert E. Lee attempted to invade Maryland. Some 5,000 soldiers died and more than 17,000 were wounded. In 1863, the three-day **Battle of Gettysburg** in Pennsylvania was the most costly battle of the war, leaving more than 50,000 dead and wounded on both sides.

Key Themes and Concepts

Constitutional Principles
Historically, presidential powers increase in times of war.

- How did Lincoln's presidential power increase during the Civil War?

- Name three other examples of increased presidential powers during wartime.

- Historically, how has the increase of presidential power during wartime been a threat to civil liberties?

The Emancipation Proclamation

On January 1, 1863 Lincoln's Emancipation Proclamation, a military order based on his war powers, went into effect. It decreed that all slaves in those areas still in rebellion against the Union "shall be then, thenceforward, and forever free." Because the proclamation exempted 750,00 slaves in the four border states and in sections of the South that were under Union control some saw it as largely symbolic. In fact, the proclamation helped to satisfy Northern abolitionists and averted British recognition of the Confederacy. It undermined the economic foundation of the Confederacy by accelerating the number of ex-slaves leaving the plantations and their work behind the military lines. With 185,00 to 200,000 African American enlistments, Northern manpower increased. Lincoln called the proclamation "an act of justice." In addition to a war to restore the Union, the Civil War had become a fight to end slavery.

Permanent emancipation depended on a final military victory and on a Constitutional amendment. On January 31, 1865 the House followed the Senate and approved the Thirteenth Amendment. On April 8th the war ended. A week later Lincoln was killed. In December final state ratification of the amendment abolished slavery.

The Gettysburg Address

In November 1863, Lincoln dedicated the Union military cemetery at Gettysburg. His short speech summarized the meaning of the Civil War.

The End of the War

The Battle of Gettysburg was the turning point in the war. It was the last time that the South attempted to invade the North. From then on, Lee fought a defensive war. The war ended in 1865 with Lee's surrender at Appomattox Court House.

The Civil War on the Home Front

In the North, production in factories and on farms increased during the Civil War. Women and African Americans took more factory jobs to replace the white men who had gone to war. Women also ran the farms and raised money to help the wounded soldiers.

On both sides, women served as nurses, even in field hospitals. However, medicine was seen as a male profession, and even Clara Barton, founder of the American Red Cross, met with resistance.

The South lacked industrial support and a good transportation network. Furthermore, the Confederate government, led by Jefferson Davis, met opposition when calling for a military draft or attempting to collect food for the army.

In the South, the Northern blockade led to food shortages. Inflation soared. As in the North, women took over the work on the farms. On the plantations, they supervised the slaves. They worked as government clerks and as teachers.

Major Results of the Civil War

- The issue of secession was settled and the Union preserved, but a legacy of resentment, bitterness, and divisiveness remained.
- With the passage of the 13th Amendment, the enslaved people were freed, but the reality of their civil and political rights was unresolved.
- The supremacy of the federal government was upheld and its power strengthened.
- The war stimulated economic growth and increased manufacturing in the North.
- The South was economically and financially devastated.

Questions for Regents Practice

Multiple Choice

Directions: Review the Test-Taking Strategies section of this book. Then answer the following questions, drawn from actual Regents examinations. For each statement or question, choose the *number* of the word or expression that, of those given, best completes the statement or answers the question.

1   Base your answer to question 1 on the cartoon below and on your knowledge of social studies.

"King Andrew the First"

The cartoonist is most clearly accusing President Jackson of which behavior?

(1) involving the United States in European wars

(2) exceeding the constitutional limits of his authority

(3) using government funds to support an extravagant lifestyle

(4) violating the Federal Constitution by granting titles of nobility

2   Which was most characteristic of the early factory systems in the United States?

(1) Factories provided workers with a voice in management and employment conditions.

(2) Women and children were not allowed to work in factories.

(3) Unsafe working conditions were common.

(4) Many workers had the opportunity to move up in social class.

Base your answers to questions 3 and 4 on the quotation below and on your knowledge of social studies.

"How can an industrialized Northeast, a plantation South, and a small farms West peacefully share the same nation?"

3   This quotation best describes the United States during which time period?

(1) Federal Era (1789–1800)

(2) Pre-Civil War (1820–1860)

(3) Era of Overseas Expansion (1898–1914)

(4) Great Depression of the 1930s

4   Which term can be most accurately applied to the situation in the quotation?

(1) sectionalism

(2) protectionism

(3) liberalism

(4) militarism

5   Which was most responsible for the rapid economic growth of New York City during the nineteeth century?

(1) presence of the New York Stock Exchange

(2) rise of domestic and foreign commerce

(3) rise of urban mass transportation

(4) migration of blacks from the rural South

6   In the United States, the belief in Manifest Destiny was most similar to later demands for

(1) restrictions on immigration

(2) a laissez-faire economic policy

(3) regulation of interstate commerce

(4) imperialistic expansion

7   In United States history, which characteristic was common to the War of 1812, the Mexican War, and the Spanish-American War?

(1) They were fought to promote democratic principles.

(2) Their aim was expansion of United States self-interest.

(3) They reflected conditions in Western Europe.

(4) They were necessary to protect national security.

Base your answers to questions 8 and 9 on your knowledge of social studies and on the quotation below, from a speech made by a United States Senator in 1847.

"What is the territory, Mr. President, which you propose to wrest from Mexico? It is consecrated to the heart of the Mexican by many a well-fought battle with his old Castilian master. His Bunker Hills, and Saratogas, and Yorktowns are there and shall he surrender that consecrated home of his affection to the Anglo-Saxon invaders? What do we want with it? The Senator from Michigan says he must have this. Why, my Christian brother, on what principle of justice?"

8   The parallel between the United States and Mexico which the Senator indicated in his speech was that both

(1) claimed Oregon

(2) disliked England

(3) had a revolutionary heritage

(4) were overcrowded

9   With which position would the speaker most likely have agreed?

(1) The United States should pressure Great Britain out of Oregon.

(2) The pursuit of a policy of manifest destiny is unfair.

(3) The annexation of Texas is justified because most of its population are settlers from the United States.

(4) The extension of United States democracy to parts of Mexico is divinely intended.

10   Laws requiring individuals to pass civil service examinations to obtain government jobs were enacted to

(1) eliminate patronage and corruption in government hiring

(2) allow the government to compete with private industry for employees

(3) support the development of public employee labor unions

(4) encourage the growth of local political parties

11   During the nineteenth century, the expansion of the population of the United States affected the lives of the Native Americans in that most

(1) moved to urban areas in large numbers

(2) sought to form alliances with other minority groups

(3) were forced to move westward

(4) chose to adopt the culture of the settlers

12 The reason for ending the importation of enslaved persons in the United States after 1807 was the

(1) success of the American colonial revolution against Great Britain

(2) rapid industrialization of the South

(3) replacement of slave labor by immigrant workers from eastern Europe

(4) passage of legislation that forbid the practice

13 The activities of Nat Turner and Denmark Vesey in the United States indicated that

(1) slave revolts occurred in the South

(2) cotton was a profitable crop

(3) political rivalries existed in the North

(4) slavery could be extended into the territories

14 A similarity between the pre-Civil War abolitionist movement and the Progressive movement is that both

(1) were mainly concerned with improving the status of African Americans

(2) worked to reduce income taxes

(3) contributed directly to the start of a major war

(4) sought to improve the conditions of poor or oppressed peoples

15 The main goal of the Seneca Falls Convention (1848) was to

(1) obtain equal rights for women

(2) make the public aware of environmental problems

(3 correct the abuses of big business

(4) organize the first labor union in the United States

16 "To the Honorable Senate and House of Representatives in Congress Assembled: We the undersigned, citizens of the United States, but deprived of some of the privileges and immunities of citizens, among which is the right to vote, beg leave to submit the following Resolution: . . ."

—*Susan B. Anthony, Elizabeth Cady Stanton (1873)*

This statement is an example of a citizen's constitutional right to

(1) petition for a redress of grievances

(2) seek election to public office

(3) receive a speedy, public trial

(4) assemble peacefully

Base your answers to questions 17 and 18 on this excerpt from a resolution adopted at the Seneca Falls Convention in 1848 and on your knowledge of social studies.

"We hold these truths to be self-evident: that all men and women are created equal; that they are endowed by their Creator with certain inalienable rights; that among these are life, liberty, and the pursuit of happiness. . . ."

17 Which document served as the most direct model for this resolution?

(1) Articles of Confederation

(2) Emancipation Proclamation

(3) United States Constitution

(4) Declaration of Independence

18 The philosophy stated in this resolution was based on the

(1) idea of rugged individualism

(2) natural rights theory

(3) theory of separation of powers

(4) "necessary and proper" clause of the United States Constitution

19 "Compromise Enables Maine and Missouri to Enter Union" (1820)

"California Admitted to Union as Free State" (1850)

"Kansas-Nebraska Act Sets Up Popular Sovereignty" (1854)

Which issue is reflected in these headlines?

(1) enactment of protective tariffs

(2) extension of slavery

(3) voting rights for minorities

(4) universal public education

20 "By the 1850s, the Constitution, originally framed as an instrument of national unity, had become a source of national discord."

This quotation suggests that

(1) vast differences of opinion existed over the issue of States rights

(2) the federal government had become more interested in foreign affairs than in domestic problems

(3) the Constitution had no provisions for governing new territories

(4) the Southern states continued to import slaves

21 Which event was the immediate cause of the secession of several Southern states from the Union in 1860?

(1) the Dred Scott decision, which declared that all prior compromises on the extension of slavery into territories were unconstitutional

(2) the Missouri Compromise, which kept an even balance between the number of free and slave states

(3) the raid on the federal arsenal at Harper's Ferry, which was led by the militant abolitionist John Brown

(4) the election of President Abraham Lincoln, who opposed the spread of slavery into the territories

22 "You have no oath registered in heaven to destroy the government, while I shall have the most solemn one to 'preserve, protect, and defend' it."

—Abraham Lincoln, Inaugural Address, 1861

When President Abraham Lincoln made this statement, he indicated his commitment to

(1) allow the Southern states to leave the Union

(2) defend the institution of slavery throughout the United States

(3) take strong action to maintain the Union

(4) make fundamental changes in the United States government

23 "Restriction of free thought and free speech is the most dangerous of all subversions. It is the one un-American act that could easily defeat us."

In the United States, the danger identified in this statement was the greatest during the

(1) Age of Jackson

(2) Civil War

(3) Spanish-American War

(4) New Deal Era in the 1930s

24 A major result of the Civil War was that the

(1) economic system of the South came to dominate the United States economy

(2) federal government's power over the states was strengthened

(3) members of Congress from Southern states gained control of the legislative branch

(4) nation's industrial development came to a standstill

25 In the United States during the 1800s, the growth of industrialization resulted in

(1 the end of rural life and values

(2) a decline in the influence of big business

(3) a decrease in child labor

(4) the rising influence of the middle class

26 Which statement best explains why candidates for President of the United States are nominated during national nominating conventions?

(1) It is mandated by the U.S. Constitution.

(2) It is mandated by state constitutions.

(3) It is part of the United States political tradition.

(4) It was instituted by an act of Congress.

27 During the period from 1800 to 1865, the issues of states rights, tariffs, and slavery led most directly to the growth of

(1) imperialism

(2) sectionalism

(3) national unity

(4) industrialization

28 The United States Supreme Court decision in *Dred Scott* v. *Sanford* (1857) was important because it

(1) strengthened the determination of abolitionists to achieve their goals

(2) caused the immediate outbreak of the Civil War

(3) ended the importation of slaves into the United States

(4) increased the power of Congress to exclude slavery from the territories

29 Which argument did President Abraham Lincoln use against the secession of the Southern states?

(1) Slavery was not profitable.

(2) The government was a union of people and not of states.

(3) The Southern states did not permit their people to vote on secessions.

(4) As the Commander in Chief, he had the duty to defend the United States against foreign invasion.

30 Which situation was an immediate result of the United States Civil War?

(1) Women gained the right to vote as an acknowledgment of their role in the conflict.

(2) Secession was no longer regarded as an option to be exercised by states.

(3) Sectionalism disappeared as a force in American economic and political life.

(4) The South retained its pre-Civil War economic and social structure.

Base your answer to questions 31 and 32 on the speakers' statements below and on your knowledge of social studies.

Speaker A: "Secession from the Union caused this war, and all those who supported it must now be punished."

Speaker B: "The nation's wounds will heal most quickly if we forgive the Southerners and welcome them back into the Union."

Speaker C: "The freedmen must be given economic assistance and guaranteed the constitutional right to protect themselves."

Speaker D: "The war may have ended, but the fight must continue to preserve the system of white supremacy in the South."

31 Which speakers best represent the attitudes of the Radical Republicans who controlled Congress during Reconstruction?

(1) A and D

(2) A and C

(3) B and C

(4) B and D

32 The position taken by *Speaker B* is closest to the beliefs expressed by

(1) Abraham Lincoln

(2) Thaddeus Stevens

(3) the carpetbaggers

(4) the Ku Klux Klan

Thematic Essay Question

Directions: Write a well-organized essay that includes an introduction, several paragraphs addressing the task below, and a conclusion.

Theme: **Government: Federalism**

> The United States Constitution created a new type of government—federalism—that divided power between the states and the national government. The proper balance of power under federalism has been debated throughout the history of the United States.

Task:

> From your study of United States history, identify *two* time periods in which there was an important debate about federalism. For *each* era or time period identified:
> - Identify a specific disagreement that occurred concerning the principle of federalism.
> - Discuss the historical circumstances surrounding the disagreement over federalism.
> - Describe the actions taken by each side during the disagreement over federalism.
> - Discuss the extent to which these actions were successful in resolving the disagreement.

You may use any time period in United States history in which there was an important debate about federalism. Some suggestions you might wish to consider include: the Supreme Court under John Marshall (1801–1835); the extension of slavery (1820–1860); Civil War (1861–1865); Reconstruction (1865–1876); Populist and Progressive reform movements (1890–1920); Franklin D. Roosevelt's New Deal (1933–1945); Civil Rights Movement (1950–1970); Ronald Reagan's New Federalism (1981–1989).

You are *not* limited to these suggestions.

Guidelines:

In your essay, be sure to
- Develop all aspects of the task
- Support the theme with relevant facts, examples, and details
- Use a logical and clear plan of organization, including an introduction and a conclusion that are beyond a restatement of the theme

In developing your answer, be sure to keep these general definitions in mind:

(a) <u>describe</u> means "to illustrate something in words or tell about it"
(b) <u>discuss</u> means "to make observations about something using facts, reasoning, and argument; to present in some detail"

Document-Based Question

In developing your answers, be sure to keep this general definition in mind:

(a) <u>discuss</u> means "to make observations about something using facts, reasoning, and argument; to present in some detail"

This question is based on the accompanying documents. The question is designed to test your ability to work with historical documents. Some of these documents have been edited for the purposes of this question. As you analyze the documents, take into account the source of each document and any point of view that may be presented in the document.

Historical Context:

In May 1787, fifty-five delegates came together in Philadelphia to amend the Articles of Confederation. What they did was create a new Constitution, a plan of government designed to solve the governmental problems experienced under the Articles of Confederation. The Constitution they created has remained a flexible, living document that continues to guide this nation today.

Task: Using the information from the documents and your knowledge of United States history and government, answer the questions that follow each document in Part A. Your answers to the questions will help you write the Part B essay, in which you will be asked to

> Discuss how the Constitution was both:
> - a product of its time
> - a document that has had enough flexibility to meet the challenges of the future

Document-Based Question

Part A: Short Answer Questions

Document #1

> *"The United States in Congress assembled shall never engage in a war, . . . nor enter into any treaties or alliances, nor coin money, nor regulate the value thereof, . . . nor borrow money on the credit of the United States, nor appropriate money, . . . nor appoint a commander in chief of the army or navy, unless nine States assent [agree]."*
>
> **—The Articles of Confederation**

1. Why might it be difficult for the government under the Articles of Confederation to be effective?

_____

_____

_____

Document #2

Year Ratified	Amendment Number	Excerpt from the Amendment
1870	15	"The right of the citizens of the United States to vote shall not be denied or abridged...on account of race, color, or previous condition of servitude."
1920	19	"The right of citizens of the United States to vote shall not be denied or abridged...on account of sex."
1971	26	"The right of citizens of the United States, who are eighteen years of age or older, to vote, shall not be denied or abridged..."

2. How do these amendments demonstrate the ability of the Constitution to adapt to a change in attitude about who should have the right to vote?

_____

_____

_____

Document #3

> "Representatives . . . shall be determined by adding to the . . . number of free persons . . . three fifths of all other persons [slaves]."
>
> —**U.S. Constitution, Article I, Section 2**

3. How was the debate over the counting of slaves for representation resolved in the Constitution?

_____

_____

_____

Document #4

> "The accumulation of all powers, legislative, executive, and judiciary, in the same hands, whether one, a few, or many . . . may justly be pronounced the very definition of tyranny [cruel or unjust use of power]."
>
> —**James Madison, *The Federalist Papers* No. 47**

4. How might the system of checks and balances address the fears expressed in the quote by James Madison?

_____

_____

_____

Document #5

> "So if a law be in opposition to the Constitution, if both the law and the Constitution apply to a particular case . . . the court must decide that case conformably [in agreement] to the law, disregarding the Constitution or conformably to the Constitution, disregarding the law, the court must determine which of these conflicting rules governs the case. This is the very essence of judicial duty. If, then, the courts are to regard the Constitution, and the Constitution is superior to any ordinary act, the Constitution and not such ordinary act, must govern the case to which both apply."
>
> —*Marbury v. Madison* (1803)

5. How did the ruling in *Marbury* v. *Madison* expand the power of the Supreme Court?

_____

_____

_____

Document #6

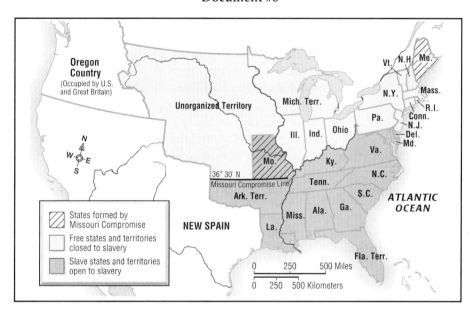

6. How does the map above demonstrate the ability of Congress to make laws to deal with the extension of slavery?

_____

_____

_____

Part B

Essay

Directions: Write a well-organized essay that includes an introduction, several paragraphs, and a conclusion. Use evidence from *at least **four*** documents in your essay. Support your response with relevant facts, examples, and details. Include additional outside information.

Historical Context:

In May 1787, 55 delegates came together in Philadelphia to amend the Articles of Confederation. Instead they created a new Constitution, a plan of government designed to solve the governmental problems caused by the Articles of Confederation. The Constitution they created has remained a flexible, living document that continues to guide this nation today.

Task: Using information from the documents and your knowledge of United States history and government, write an essay in which you

> Discuss how the Constitution was both:
> - a product of its time
> - a document that has had enough flexibility to meet the challenges of the future

Guidelines:

In your essay, be sure to
- Develop all aspects of the task
- Incorporate information from *at least **four*** documents
- Incorporate relevant outside information
- Support the theme with relevant facts, examples, and details
- Use a logical and clear plan of organization, including an introduction and a conclusion that are beyond a restatement of the theme

Industrialization of the United States

Unit Overview

The Civil War had torn the United States apart. With Union victory came the task of putting the nation back together. Yet the rebuilt nation would be a very different one. This unit reviews those changes that the Civil War brought to the United States. It also highlights how the shift from an agrarian to an industrial economy changed the United States and its people.

Some key questions to help you focus on the industrialization of the United States include:

- What social, political, and economic changes occurred as the nation sought to rebuild after the Civil War?
- What factors in the United States led to the shift from an agrarian to an industrial society, and what were the results of this shift?
- How did patterns of immigration to the United States change in the nineteenth and early twentieth centuries, and what did those changes mean for American society?

The Reconstructed Nation

The
Big Idea

Reconstruction followed the Civil War in the South. During this period:

- President Abraham Lincoln was assassinated.

- President Andrew Johnson was impeached.

- African Americans won voting and political rights.

- Southern whites regained political control.

Section Overview

After the Civil War, the nation faced the immense task of restoring the Union. Conflicting plans for Reconstruction produced bitter political battles that led to the impeachment of a president. Enormous resources were poured into rebuilding the shattered Southern economy. Meanwhile, new political gains for African Americans were gradually rolled back in the South as whites regained power.

Key Themes and Concepts

As you review this section, take special note of the following key themes and concepts:

Change How did the nation rebuild and reunify after the Civil War?

Citizenship How did African Americans win political rights in the South?

Places and Regions How did white Southerners react to the terms of Reconstruction?

Key People

As you review this section, be sure you understand the significance of these key people:

Andrew Johnson	Samuel Tilden	Thomas Nast
Ulysses S. Grant	Rutherford B. Hayes	W.E.B. Du Bois
William "Boss" Tweed	Booker T. Washington	

Key Terms

Reconstruction	Compromise of 1877
Radical Republicans	black codes
Radical Reconstruction	Ku Klux Klan
scalawags	poll taxes
carpetbaggers	literacy tests
Thirteenth Amendment	Freedmen's Bureau
Fourteenth Amendment	grandfather clauses
Fifteenth Amendment	segregation
solid South	Jim Crow laws

Key Supreme Court Cases

As you review this section, be sure you understand the significance of these key Supreme Court cases:

The Civil Rights Cases (1883)
Plessy v. *Ferguson* (1896)
Brown v. *Board of Education of Topeka, Kansas* (1954)

The effort to rebuild the Southern states and restore the Union was known as **Reconstruction,** a period that lasted from 1865 to 1877. Reconstruction required the rebuilding of the nation's economy as well as its government. With so much at stake, rival political factions—with competing plans for the future—waged bitter battles in Washington.

Plans of Reconstruction

Several different plans for Reconstruction emerged during and after the war. Much debate about differing plans centered on who would control Reconstruction—the president or Congress.

Lincoln's Plan

President Lincoln had begun planning for the restoration of the South long before the end of the war. His plan of Reconstruction was based on the idea that the Southern states had never legally left the Union. It featured the following elements:

- pardons to Southerners who swore oaths of loyalty to the United States
- recognition of new Southern state governments when 10 percent of those who had voted in the 1860 election took these oaths and when the states adopted new constitutions abolishing slavery
- concern that healing the nation's wounds quickly was essential

Lincoln was open to suggestions from Congress for changes in his plan, but his assassination in April 1865 meant he would never carry out his program.

Johnson's Plan

Vice President Andrew Johnson became president after Lincoln's death. He intended to follow the broad outlines of Lincoln's plan. Johnson recognized four Southern state governments and prepared to readmit the others. These states would participate fully in Congress.

Radical Republicans, however, controlled Congress, and they wanted harsher terms for Reconstruction. Johnson's failure to consider congressional views on Reconstruction and his efforts to block radical plans finally led Republicans in Congress to attempt to impeach him. In 1868, the House charged the president with "high crimes and misdemeanors"—specifically, for violating the Tenure of Office Act. The Senate fell one vote short of the two-thirds vote required by the Constitution to remove a president from office. Although Johnson was acquitted, his political power was gone.

Radical Reconstruction

Now the Republican-controlled Congress dictated the terms of Reconstruction. The chief features of this so-called Radical Reconstruction included:

- the division of the South into five military districts controlled by the U.S. Army, while new state constitutions and governments were being set up.
- the requirement of the new state governments to grant African American males the right to vote.
- the requirement of Southern states to ratify the Fourteenth Amendment. In addition to addressing several fundamental civil rights issues, the amendment prohibited many former Confederate government officials from holding office.

Turning Point

- Why is President Lincoln's assassination considered a turning point in history?

Reading Strategy

Reinforcing Main Ideas
- Why did Congress impeach President Johnson?

Reading Strategy

Organizing Information
During Radical Reconstruction, some groups of people exerted great power over the terms of Reconstruction, while others had very little power.

- Which groups had the largest roles in the Radical Reconstruction?
- Which had the smallest roles?

Key Themes and Concepts

Government
• Which plan limited the voting rights of former Confederate officers?

State Governments During Reconstruction

Immediately after the Civil War ended, white Southerners who had served in leadership positions before and during the Civil War tried to reassert their control of state and local governments. They were especially concerned with limiting the freedom and movement of former slaves.

When the radical plan of Reconstruction took effect, most of the former Confederate leaders—largely Democrats—were barred from holding office and voting. Republicans headed the new state governments that emerged and they were overwhelmingly supported by African Americans, who had recently won the right to vote. In many cases, African Americans themselves won election to office.

Many white Southerners deeply resented the federal government's imposition of Radical Reconstruction. They also resented the new Reconstruction governments and the role of African Americans in them. They branded the few white Southerners active in those governments as **scalawags** and the Republican Northerners who came to the South to take part in Reconstruction as **carpetbaggers.** White southerners sometimes used terror and violence in efforts to keep African Americans from taking part in government.

New Constitutional Amendments

During the Reconstruction period, the states ratified three amendments to the Constitution:

Key Themes and Concepts

Government
During Reconstruction, three new amendments to the Constitution were ratified. In the space below, name these three amendments and provide the major provisions of each.

1.

2.

3.

• **Thirteenth Amendment** (1865)—abolished slavery in the United States
• **Fourteenth Amendment** (1868)—(1) declared that all native-born or naturalized people, including African Americans, were citizens; (2) forbade states to make laws that "abridge the privileges . . . of citizens" or that "deprive any person of life, liberty, or property, without due process of law" or that "deny to any person . . . the equal protection of the laws"; (3) limited the rights of former Confederate officers and government officials; and (4) promised to pay Civil War debts owed by the federal government, but declared Confederate debts to be void
• **Fifteenth Amendment** (1870)—declared that states could not keep citizens from voting because of "race, color, or previous condition of servitude" (slavery)

President Grant

The first presidential election after the end of the Civil War took place in 1868. Union war hero General Ulysses S. Grant ran as a Republican and won. Grant's strengths, however, were those of a military leader, not those of a politician or government leader. Scandals and corruption damaged Grant's administration, as business owners in the booming postwar economy offered bribes to politicians who would do favors for them. Among the most notorious scandals were:

Reading Strategy

Analyzing Cause and Effect
• Why were scandals common during President Grant's administration?

• *Crédit Mobilier Scandal:* Railroad officials impoverished the railroad, then bribed members of Congress to block any investigation.
• *"Salary Grab":* Congress voted itself a 50 percent pay raise and added two years of "back pay." Public outcry forced repeal of this act.
• *"Whiskey Ring":* Whiskey distillers paid graft to federal tax collectors rather than pay tax on their liquor.

Political corruption was also common at state and local levels. Perhaps the most notorious figure was William "Boss" Tweed, who ran the Tammany Hall political machine in New York City in the 1860s and 1870s. The artist Thomas Nast attacked Tweed's behavior in a series of stinging cartoons that helped turn public opinion against Tweed.

The End of Reconstruction

Corruption in the Grant administration weakened the political strength of the Republican party. In addition, by the early 1870s, all but a handful of former Confederates could vote again. Most of these white Southern males now voted Democratic in reaction to Radical Republican Reconstruction. For most of the next century, the Democratic party would dominate voting in the South, giving rise to the term **solid South.**

While nearly dying out in the South, the Republican party remained strong in the North and the Midwest. It focused on issues of interest to businessmen and farmers, such as keeping the money supply tight and tariffs on imports high.

The Election of 1876

The emergence of the solid South gave the Democrats greater power in politics at the national level. In 1876, Democrats nominated Samuel Tilden, the governor of New York, to run for president against Republican Rutherford B. Hayes, the governor of Ohio.

Tilden clearly won the popular vote, but the electoral vote was contested. Four states sent in disputed election returns. Which votes were counted would determine the outcome of the election.

A special electoral commission was named to count the votes. The Republican majority on the commission gave all the electoral votes in question to Hayes, thus guaranteeing his victory.

In the **Compromise of 1877,** Democrats agreed to go along with the commission's decision in return for promises by Hayes to:

- withdraw remaining federal troops from the Southern states, thus ending the Reconstruction period.
- name a Southerner to his cabinet.
- support federal spending on internal improvements in the South.

The Compromise of 1877 effectively weakened the North's political victory in the Civil War, restoring to power many of the Southern families who, 16 years before, had formed the Confederacy and led it into war.

Geography in History

- How did voting patterns in the South affect the presidential election of 1876?

Preparing for the Exam

On the examination, you will need to understand the influences that brought Reconstruction to an end.

- Why do you think the Democrats agreed to support the Compromise of 1877?

Analyzing Documents

Analyze Data
Examine the timeline, then answer these questions.

- How many years passed between the end of the Civil War and the states' ratification of the Fifteenth Amendment?

- Which event occurred first: the impeachment of President Johnson or the election of President Hayes?

The Reconstructed Nation, 1865–1876

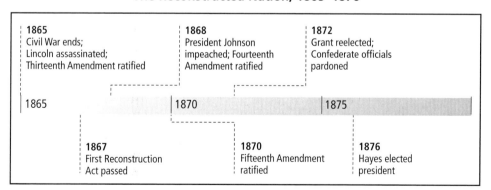

1865
Civil War ends;
Lincoln assassinated;
Thirteenth Amendment ratified

1868
President Johnson impeached; Fourteenth Amendment ratified

1872
Grant reelected;
Confederate officials pardoned

1865   1870   1875

1867
First Reconstruction Act passed

1870
Fifteenth Amendment ratified

1876
Hayes elected president

White Control in the South

The withdrawal of federal troops enabled white Southerners to eliminate any political advances African Americans had made during Reconstruction. Various methods were used to curb the rights of African Americans, and by 1900, their civil rights had been sharply limited.

Black Codes These measures, passed in most Southern states immediately after the Civil War, were based on old slave codes and aimed at keeping African Americans in conditions close to slavery. The black codes produced an angry reaction in the North that helped passage of the Radical Reconstruction program. Reconstruction governments in the South overturned these codes.

Key Themes and Concepts

Individuals, Groups, Institutions
• Why did some white Southerners form secret societies such as the Ku Klux Klan?

Secret Societies White Southerners originally formed groups like the **Ku Klux Klan** to try to frighten African Americans and their supporters out of taking part in Reconstruction governments. The lawlessness and brutality demonstrated by these groups led the federal government to use the army against the societies. With the end of Reconstruction and the growth of white political power, the Klan and other similar groups played a less active role in the South. Such organizations, however, remain in existence to this day.

Poll Taxes Southern states imposed a tax on every voter. Those who were too poor to pay poll taxes—including many African Americans—could not vote.

Literacy Tests Some states required citizens to demonstrate that they could read and write before they voted. Often literacy tests involved interpreting a difficult part of the Constitution. Few African Americans could pass these tests because they had received little schooling. While the **Freedmen's Bureau,** created by Congress in 1865 to aid former slaves, established many schools for young African Americans, the bureau lasted only a few years. Thereafter, state laws forced African American children to attend separate schools that were poorly equipped and funded.

Reading Strategy

Reading for Evidence
• Reread the section entitled "White Control in the South." What were five major ways in which white Southerners reasserted their control in the South after Reconstruction?

Grandfather Clauses Poll taxes and literacy tests might have also kept poor and uneducated whites from voting. To prevent this, Southern states added grandfather clauses to their constitutions. These clauses allowed the son or grandson of a man eligible to vote in 1866 or 1867 to vote himself even if he could neither pay the tax nor pass the test. Since few African Americans could vote in 1867, the clause benefited whites almost exclusively.

Jim Crow Laws Southern states also passed laws establishing social as well as legal **segregation,** or the separation of people on the basis of race. Such Jim Crow laws forbade African Americans from sharing facilities with whites, such as railroad cars or water fountains. The passage of Jim Crow laws in the South after Reconstruction was aided in part by a narrow interpretation of the Fourteenth Amendment by the United States Supreme Court.

Jim Crow laws were a part of everyday life in the South after Reconstruction.

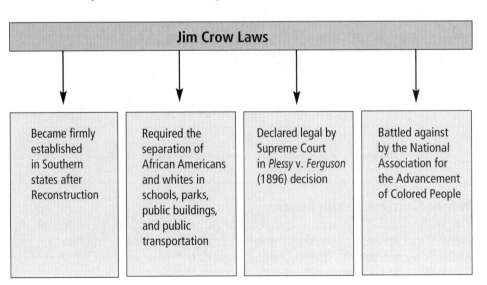

Jim Crow Laws

Became firmly established in Southern states after Reconstruction	Required the separation of African Americans and whites in schools, parks, public buildings, and public transportation	Declared legal by Supreme Court in *Plessy* v. *Ferguson* (1896) decision	Battled against by the National Association for the Advancement of Colored People

The Supreme Court's Response

The Supreme Court did not interfere with efforts to restore white control in the South. In the 1883 *Civil Rights Cases*, the Court ruled that the Thirteenth Amendment abolished slavery but did not prohibit discrimination and that the Fourteenth Amendment prohibited discrimination by government but not by individuals. Later, in the landmark case of *Plessy v. Ferguson* (1896), the Court ruled that segregation was legal as long as African Americans had access to "equal but separate" facilities.

The Court's ruling in the *Plessy* case set a precedent that justified segregation in all public facilities—schools, hospitals, passenger terminals, and more—until the 1950s. It was not until the pivotal case of *Brown v. Board of Education of Topeka, Kansas* (1954) that the Supreme Court reversed the finding in *Plessy v. Ferguson* (1896). The *Brown* decision stated that educational facilities separated solely on the basis of race were by their nature unequal.

African Americans Debate Their Future

Two prominent leaders offered contrasting strategies to improve the lives of African Americans. Booker T. Washington argued that African Americans should temporarily put aside their desire for political equality and instead focus on building economic security by gaining useful vocational skills. W.E.B. Du Bois called for the brightest African Americans to gain an advanced liberal arts education (rather than a vocational education) and then demand social and political equality. However, widespread discrimination against African Americans made either strategy difficult to follow.

W.E.B. Du Bois

Booker T. Washington

The Rise of American Business, Industry, and Labor—1865–1920

The Big Idea

The United States developed a prosperous new economy based on the mass production of goods. During this period:

- economic development expanded in the North, but weakened in the South.

- entrepreneurs became wealthy and powerful.

- government began to regulate business.

- labor unions formed to improve working conditions.

Section Overview

From Reconstruction through World War I, the United States developed a prosperous industrial economy that revolutionized American society. New machines made possible the mass production of goods. Industrial growth led to a new type of business, the corporation, headed by a rising class of enterprising industrialists such as Henry Ford. With little government interference, these corporate giants created new business structures, some legal and some not, that brought them fabulous wealth. They used their riches both to benefit society and to increase their power. Industries attracted a new type of laborer, the factory worker, who often worked long hours in hazardous conditions. These conditions spurred the growth of labor unions, which gradually gained the right to bargain with employers.

Key Themes and Concepts

As you review this section, take special note of the following key themes and concepts:

Science and Technology How did technological developments lead to the growth of industrialization?

Government How did the government respond to the growth of powerful industries and to complaints about business practices?

Factors of Production What factors led to the growth of the labor movement, and what strategies did unions pursue?

Key People

As you review this section, be sure you understand the significance of these key people:

Andrew Carnegie	Henry Ford	Charles Darwin
John D. Rockefeller	Horatio Alger	Terence Powderly
J. Pierpont Morgan	Adam Smith	Samuel Gompers

Key Terms

transcontinental railroad	entrepreneurs
New South	assembly line
sharecroppers	laissez faire
tenant farmers	free enterprise system
capital	robber barons
corporations	Sherman Antitrust Act
monopoly	collective bargaining
merger	Haymarket Riot
trust	boycotts

Key Supreme Court Cases

As you review this section, be sure you understand the significance of these key Supreme Court cases:

Munn v. *Illinois* (1877)
Wabash, St. Louis & Pacific Railway v. *Illinois* (1886)
United States v. *E. C. Knight Company* (1895)
In re Debs (1895)

The Civil War changed the economies of the northern and southern regions of the United States. The Civil War stimulated economic growth in the North. Meanwhile, the South struggled to recover from the devastation of the war.

Economic Developments in the North

The industrialization that had started before the war accelerated as northern factories rushed to keep up with the Union's demand for guns, ammunition, uniforms, and other necessary products. Improvements in railroad systems helped speed troop movements. Since so many northern farm workers entered the army, farms became more heavily mechanized, using fewer workers to produce more crops. Little of the fighting took place in the North, and the region was spared much physical destruction from the war.

Growing northern factories looked to overseas markets for their goods. Completion of the **transcontinental railroad**, authorized by the Pacific Railway Act of 1862, opened new markets in the West and brought products of western farms and mines east. The federal government encouraged the building of the transcontinental railroads by giving land to the railroad companies who in turn sometimes sold the land at a profit.

Economic growth attracted new waves of immigrants to the United States. Some sought farms in the West, but many found employment in the booming industries of the North.

Economic Developments in the South

The Civil War ruined the South's economy. It ended slavery, thus killing the plantation system on which southern wealth was based. During the fighting, plantations had been burned, railroads ripped up, and the region's few factories destroyed.

After the war, many farmers and planters had to sell off parts of their land to pay off debts or to start over. These land-owners often found themselves in debt to banks or merchants. Yet despite such hardships, southern farmers again began to produce cotton and tobacco.

Some Key Economic Issues in the Post-Civil War Era

	NORTH	SOUTH
industries	continued rapid development financed by wartime growth; new interest in overseas markets	began slowly after the war, especially in textile and steel production; urban areas needed major reconstruction
railroads	crucial to economy; new transcontinental routes allowed the development of western markets	destroyed during the war; needed to be rebuilt, along with roads and bridges
land use and agriculture	farms began to mechanize and to increase production, providing food for the growing urban areas	plantation economy based on slavery ended; land destroyed by fighting; former slaves competed with destitute whites in search of land; tenant farming and sharecropping began

Geography in History

Geographic Reasoning
• What factors contributed to the development of factories in the North?

Preparing for the Exam

On the examination, you will need to understand important economic developments.

• What is the transcontinental railroad?

• How did it contribute to economic growth?

Key Themes and Concepts

Places and Regions
New manufacturing technologies were less commonly used in the South than in the North. Why?

Some southern leaders, however, believed that the South's economy should not rest simply on agriculture. They began to create a **New South,** with rebuilt railroads, new textile and steel mills, and, later, new industries, such as oil and coal production.

Despite these changes, the South lagged behind the North in economic growth. Agriculture still offered the most jobs, and many southerners, including large numbers of former slaves, had to farm land owned by others. These landless farmers included **sharecroppers,** who gave part of each year's crop to the landowner and received the rest as payment. Sharecropping emerged in the South primarily as a way to provide a labor supply to plantation owners. **Tenant farmers** paid cash to rent land. A negative effect of the sharecropping system was that it kept formerly enslaved persons economically dependent. Beginning in the 1880s, African Americans began a migration to the North in search of better jobs. This migration accelerated during and after World War I.

Business Developments

Before the Civil War, sole proprietors, or single owners, and partnerships had controlled most American businesses. The mills and factories that came with industrialization, however, usually required greater **capital,** or money for investment, than one person or a few partners could raise.

The Growth of Corporations

To raise capital for expansion, many businesses became corporations. A corporation is a business in which many investors own shares, usually called stocks. In exchange for their investment, each stockholder receives a dividend, or part of the corporation's profits.

Besides paying dividends, the corporations also limited investor losses. If a corporation failed, an investor lost only his or her investment and was not responsible for the corporation's debts.

The money raised by corporations speeded the growth of American industry. Among the fastest growing industries were transportation (railroads, urban transportation, and, later, automobiles), building materials (steel), energy (coal, oil, and electricity), and communications (telegraph and telephone).

Other Forms of Business Organization

As the nation's economy boomed and industries grew larger in the late 1800s, other ways of organizing business appeared. Often the aim of such business organizations was to eliminate competition and dominate a particular area of the economy.

Monopoly A company or small group of companies that has complete control over a particular field of business is a monopoly. One example of a monopoly in the late 1800s was the E. C. Knight Sugar Company. Having a monopoly in a field often allowed a company to raise prices to almost any level it desired. Such abuses led to federal legislation aimed at curbing monopolies.

Some monopolies are permitted today. Public utility companies that provide gas, water, and electricity are examples of private companies that often have monopolies in their fields. Government agencies closely monitor the operations of such utilities.

Conglomerate A corporation that owns a group of unrelated companies is a conglomerate. Such conglomerates are usually formed by **merger,** the process by which one company acquires legal control over another. Mergers and

Key Themes and Concepts

Individuals, Groups, Institutions
As the southern economy grew after the Civil War, some groups lagged behind others.

- Who were the sharecroppers?

- How did sharecroppers differ from tenant farmers?

Key Themes and Concepts

Economic Systems
- What do you call a business in which many investors own shares?

Name two kinds of businesses that speeded the growth of American industry:

1.

2.

- What do you call a company that has complete control over a particular kind of business?

Name two examples:
1.

2.

- What do you call the merger of a group of unrelated companies?

Name an example:
1.

conglomerates are both legal and common today. General Electric, for example, is a conglomerate that has acquired many different divisions through mergers.

Pool Sometimes competing companies in one field entered into agreements to fix prices and divide business. Such an agreement was a pool. Railroad companies in the late 1800s formed such pools, which were later outlawed.

Trust A group of corporations in the same or related fields sometimes agreed to combine under a single board of trustees that controlled the actions of all the member corporations. This was a trust. Shareholders in the corporations received dividends from the trust but lost any say in its operation. The Standard Oil Trust was one example of such a combination. Trusts were later made illegal. Both trusts and pools were used by big business in an effort to limit competition.

Holding Company To get around the outlawing of trusts, corporations formed holding companies. The holding company bought controlling amounts of stock in different corporations rather than take operations over directly as a trust did.

Innovations and Business Developments, 1868–1913

Key Themes and Concepts

Economics
Vertical trusts controlled all aspects of the production, from beginning to sale.

Horizontal trusts grouped related industries for maximum profits.

- Give an example of each type of trust.

Analyzing Documents

Analyze data
Examine the timeline, then answer these questions.

- How many years passed between the formation of Standard Oil Trust and the formation of Carnegie Steel?

- Which event occurred first: the invention of the telephone or the introduction of the assembly line?

Innovation

While these new forms of business organization helped young industries to get started and to maximize profits, other innovations enabled businesses to market their products more effectively. In urban areas, new department stores offered customers a wide variety of goods under one roof. For rural areas, retailers developed mail-order catalogs that saved customers a trip to faraway stores. The items offered in these stores and catalogs expanded as well, thanks to new inventions such as the vacuum cleaner, the telephone, the electric light bulb, the electric iron, and the safety razor.

Entrepreneurs

These new forms of business organization and innovative ideas from inventors helped American industry grow in the late 1800s and early 1900s. Yet without the business knowledge and daring of certain individuals, that growth would have been much slower.

These individuals were **entrepreneurs,** people who take responsibility for the organization and operation of a new business venture. Entrepreneurs often risk large sums of venture capital in hopes of making enormous profits. The business decisions made by turn-of-the-century entrepreneurs had a great impact on the lives of most Americans. Some of the key entrepreneurs of the late 1800s and early 1900s are listed below.

Andrew Carnegie An immigrant from Scotland, Andrew Carnegie started work in a textile factory at age 12. He worked his way up through a variety of jobs and

Reading Strategy

Organizing Information
In the space below, name four key entrepreneurs of the late 1800s and early 1900s and the industries each operated.

1.

2.

3.

4.

Key Themes and Concepts

Technology
New production techniques increased efficiency in many industries such as steel and automotive.

• Explain how one of these techniques worked to increase efficiency.

J. Pierpont Morgan
Courtesy of the Library of Congress

Preparing for the Exam

• What system was based on the principle that private individuals should make economic decisions?

Key Themes and Concepts

Human Systems
Charles Darwin's theory of natural selection was simplified by philosophers and turned into a philosophy called Social Darwinism.

• How was Social Darwinism applied to business competition?

invested his money shrewdly. At age 38, Carnegie entered the steel industry, which was booming because of the growth of railroads. Carnegie sought to control all aspects of steelmaking and built his company into the world's largest steelmaker.

Carnegie sold his company in 1901 for a quarter billion dollars. He believed the wealthy had a duty to society and gave hundreds of millions to charities. He also underwrote the founding of free public libraries all across the country.

John D. Rockefeller Industrialist John D. Rockefeller entered the oil-refining business during the Civil War. He believed competition was wasteful and used ruthless methods to eliminate competitors. By 1882, his Standard Oil Company controlled over 90 percent of American oil refining. In 1882, he formed the Standard Oil Trust to control more aspects of oil production. Rockefeller also gave away hundreds of millions to charity.

J. Pierpont Morgan Trained as a banker, J. Pierpont Morgan profited by making loans to growing businesses. He took control of many bankrupt railroads in the late 1800s, reorganized them, and made a profit. He also controlled electrical, insurance, and shipping companies. Morgan bought Carnegie Steel in 1901, merged it with other companies, and created the United States Steel Corporation, the world's largest.

Henry Ford Entrepreneur Henry Ford revolutionized auto-making in 1913 by using a moving **assembly line** that permitted the mass production of cars, significantly lowering the cost of production. Ford also paid workers higher wages and set a standard that enabled laborers to afford such purchases.

Attitudes Toward Business

Industrialization and the changes associated with it caused American attitudes toward business to alter in the late 1800s. Traditional attitudes, of course, still existed. They could be found in books by the popular writer Horatio Alger. Alger's novels describe poor boys who become rich through hard work and luck.

Alger's novels illustrate what is known as the Puritan work ethic. This is the belief, brought with the Puritans to colonial New England and embodied in the preaching of Puritan minister Cotton Mather, that hard work builds character and is its own reward.

The tremendous wealth some entrepreneurs gained during the late 1800s, as well as the cut-throat business methods they used, led some Americans to rethink their ideas on the meaning of business success. New philosophies tried to explain and justify both the accumulation of wealth and the practices used to achieve it.

Laissez Faire Many supporters of late 1800s business growth restated the older principle of laissez faire, or noninterference. Economist Adam Smith, in his 1776 book, *The Wealth of Nations,* and many other writers had supported this principle, which holds that government should not interfere in the economic workings of a nation. They believed that a **free enterprise system,** in which private individuals make the economic decisions, is most efficient.

During the late 1800s, economists restated the importance of laissez faire policies to economic growth. Government interference with business was minimal for much of this period, and entrepreneurs expanded their businesses and earned great wealth. Businesses in the eastern part of the United States profited from large farms in the west.

Social Darwinism Laissez faire capitalists found justification for their beliefs in new scientific theories being developed at that time. Naturalist Charles Darwin had developed a theory of evolution that described how animal species live or die by a process of natural selection. Other writers simplified Darwin's theories and created a philosophy called Social Darwinism.

Social Darwinists held that life was a struggle for the "survival of the fittest." Unregulated business competition would see weak businesses fail and healthy businesses thrive. Government action regulating business practices would interfere with the process of natural selection. Likewise, any government programs to aid the poor or workers would also violate natural "laws."

Robber Barons or Philanthropists? The philosophies described above and the growing gulf between rich and poor led some Americans to criticize laissez faire policies and those who profited from them. Critics condemned the wealthy entrepreneurs as robber barons, those who gained their wealth by ruthless methods in their dealings with competitors at the expense of the poor and the working class. The lavish lifestyles of the wealthy at this time fed such criticism. During this so-called Gilded Age, the rich spent freely to show off their wealth, a practice known as conspicuous consumption.

Public criticism and a sense of social responsibility led entrepreneurs to use a part of their wealth to aid society. People like Carnegie and Rockefeller became philanthropists, donating vast sums of money to charities and institutions such as schools, museums, libraries, and orchestras.

Government Policies Toward Business

The federal government generally held a laissez faire attitude toward business for much of this period. Expanding industries and growing foreign trade seemed to justify such an attitude. In addition, many business leaders made financial contributions, legal and illegal, to the politicians who set federal policies.

A number of government policies were designed to aid the growth of business. These included loans and land grants to large railroad companies, high tariffs that discouraged competition from foreign manufacturers, tight limits on the amount of money in circulation, and few limits on immigration.

Steps Toward Government Regulation

Several factors led the government to take the first steps in the late 1800s toward regulating business:

- periodic downturns in the national economy
- growing criticism of practices that saw big business profit at the expense of the poor and working class
- increasing grassroots political pressure for change

Although government intervention at this time had limited impact, it did set the course for more federal actions in years to come.

Supreme Court Decisions During the late 1800s, railroads developed a number of policies that discriminated against farmers and small shippers. These groups pressured some states to pass laws regulating railroad practices. The railroads sued to have such laws overturned.

In the 1877 case *Munn* v. *Illinois,* the Supreme Court upheld an Illinois law controlling grain elevator rates. The Court ruled that the Constitution recognized a state's right to a "police power" that permitted regulation of private property "affected with a public interest."

Reading Strategy

Reinforcing Main Ideas
- What factors led the government toward regulating business in the late 1800s?

Key Themes and Concepts

Constitutional Principles
Two landmark Supreme Court cases dealt with railroad regulation: *Munn* v. *Illinois* (1877) and *Wabash, St. Louis and Pacific Railway* v. *Illinois* (1886).

- How did these two cases influence railroad regulation?

In the 1886 case *Wabash, St. Louis & Pacific Railway Co.* v. *Illinois*, however, the Court ruled that states could not regulate railroad rates on portions of interstate routes that lay within their borders. Under the Constitution, only the federal government can regulate interstate trade. This decision meant that states could do little to regulate the railroads.

Interstate Commerce Commission In 1887, public pressure for reform of railroad policies led Congress to pass the Interstate Commerce Act. The act set up the Interstate Commerce Commission, an agency charged with ending such railroad abuses as pools and rebates, discounts only available to special customers. Although court decisions kept the commission ineffective for several years, its establishment set a precedent for federal regulation of interstate commerce.

Sherman Antitrust Act By the late 1800s, some large corporations and trusts had eliminated most competition and won almost total monopolies in their fields. Politicians heeded the public protests over the ensuing abuses. One result was the Sherman Antitrust Act of 1890. The act prohibited monopolies by declaring illegal any business combination or trust "in restraint of trade or commerce."

Yet when the federal government tried to enforce the act, the Supreme Court, in *United States* v. *E.C. Knight Company*, 1895, ruled that many businesses were exempt from the new law. In addition, some other corporations circumvented the act by forming holding companies rather than trusts. Once again, the precedent set by the act proved more important than the act itself.

Labor Organizations

Business growth in the late 1800s brought generally higher wages to American workers. Yet periodic unemployment and poor working conditions remained a fact of life for workers. In addition, employers held enormous power over the lives of their workers and could lower wages and fire employees at will.

The Growth of Unions

To improve conditions, increasing numbers of American workers formed labor unions beginning in the 1820s. As working conditions changed with industrialization, many more workers became interested in unions. "Eight hours for work, eight hours for sleep, eight hours for what we will" was a popular slogan that promoted a major goal of labor unions.

Americans had long understood the values of cooperation and association, and labor unions provided a means to put these values into action. In **collective bargaining,** union members representing workers negotiated labor issues with management. Instead of each worker trying to achieve individual aims, a united group would put pressure on management. Several early unions helped advance the cause of labor.

Knights of Labor Under the direction of Terence Powderly, the Knights of Labor, formed in 1869, welcomed skilled and unskilled workers as well as women and African Americans. The Knights fought for broad social reforms such as an eight-hour day for workers, an end to child labor, and equal opportunities and wages for women. As a rule, the union opposed strikes, but a successful strike against railroads in 1885 brought many new members. However, an antilabor feeling swept the nation after the **Haymarket Riot** in late 1886. The Knights declined in influence due to a series of unsuccessful strikes and competition from the American Federation of Labor.

Key Themes and Concepts

Power
• The Sherman Antitrust Act was an attempt to reduce the power of business owners in an effort to protect individual workers and consumers.

Key Themes and Concepts

Interdependence
• What do you call the process through which union members represent workers in labor negotiations with management?

American Federation of Labor In 1886, Samuel Gompers formed the American Federation of Labor (AFL). The AFL was a collection of many different craft unions, unions of skilled workers in similar trades. In contrast to the Knights of Labor, the AFL fought for immediate goals such as better wages, hours, and working conditions. This policy is known as *bread-and-butter unionism.* AFL membership reached about a million by 1900, making the AFL the most powerful union in the nation. Nevertheless, groups such as women, immigrants, and African Americans generally were not welcome. The AFL specifically focused on the needs of skilled workers.

International Ladies' Garment Workers Union Women made up the majority of workers in the garment industries. In 1900, the International Ladies' Garment Workers Union (ILGWU) was formed to represent the laborers who toiled in sweatshops. After a successful strike in 1910, the ILGWU soon became an important part of the AFL. In March 1911 a horrific fire at the Triangle Shirtwaist Company in New York City caused the deaths of almost 150 people, mostly young immigrant women. Dozens leapt to their deaths from upper stories to escape the burning building due to locked exits and inadequate fire escapes. This event gave further impetus to the work of the ILGWU.

Labor Conflict

If collective bargaining failed, labor unions sometimes used **boycotts** against the employer or resorted to strikes, or work stoppages, to achieve their aims. Boycotts are still used today. They are an organized refusal to buy or use a product or service or to deal with a company or a group of companies. This type of protest is used as a means of forcing action by a company. Strikes sometimes ended in union victories; often, however, they led to violence as business owners sought state and even federal support to end walkouts. The strikes and labor-associated violence described below sometimes advanced the cause of labor and sometimes set it back. During the late 1800s when most efforts at **collective bargaining** failed, big business often used court injunctions against labor unions to force workers back to work. Other tactics used by big business were **blacklists** and **yellow dog contracts**. If a worker's name was put on a blacklist, it meant that the name was circulated to other companies or employers so that the person would not be hired because of his or her actions or beliefs. Big business also used yellow dog contracts, which forced workers to sign agreements stating that they would never join a labor union.

Great Railway Strike In 1877, a series of pay cuts for railroad workers led to a strike that spread across several states. At the request of state governors, President Rutherford B. Hayes sent federal troops to help end the strike. The workers gained little benefit from the strike, and owners took a harder position against unions.

Haymarket Riot A labor rally called by Chicago anarchists in 1886 ended with a bomb blast and riot that left many people dead, including seven police officers. Although the Knights of Labor had no responsibility for the violence, some public opinion blamed them.

Homestead Strike In 1892, union members at the Carnegie steel plant in Homestead, Pennsylvania, went on strike to protest a wage cut. Management brought in security guards to protect the plant. In the violence that followed, 16 people were killed. The National Guard finally ended the fighting and the strike. Fewer than 25 percent of the striking workers got their jobs back. The strike halted the union movement in the steel industry for 20 years.

Reading Strategy

Organizing Information
American workers began to form a number of labor unions in the 1800s. In the space below, name three different labor unions and describe the workers who joined each of them.

1.

2.

3.

Preparing for the Exam

For the examination, you will need to understand the history of labor conflict in the United States.

Identify the outcome of each of the following strikes:

- Great Railway Strike (1877)

- Haymarket Riot (1886)

- Homestead Strike (1892)

- Pullman Strike (1894)

- Lawrence Textile Strike (1912)

Pullman Strike

Pullman Strike In 1894, a strike by railway-car makers in Illinois spread and tied up other rail lines. President Grover Cleveland sent in federal troops to end the strike. Union leader Eugene V. Debs was jailed for his involvement. (The Supreme Court, in the 1895 case *In re Debs*, ruled that the president had the right to deploy the troops, even over the objection of the governor of Illinois.) Cleveland's action confirmed the belief of many that government favored the interests of business over those of labor. Both the Homestead Steel Strike and the Pullman Strike ended sooner than expected as a result of direct government intervention.

Lawrence Textile Strike The Industrial Workers of the World (IWW), a radical union of skilled and unskilled laborers, led a huge strike against the textile mills in Lawrence, Massachusetts, in 1912. The strike proved one of the greatest successes of that era, and workers won most of their demands.

An Era of Strikes, Late 1800s

Preparing for the Exam

A flowchart shows the steps in a process. Based on the text and the flowchart, answer the question.

• What were three reasons for tensions between workers and business owners?

1.

2.

3.

Increasing tensions between workers and employers led to large, often violent strikes.

American Society Adjusts to Industrialization

Section Overview

Industrialization and new building technologies triggered an explosion of urban growth that brought social changes, both good and bad. A prosperous middle class emerged, while urban crowding and disease took a heavy toll on the working poor, many of whom were immigrants. New arrivals came in waves, first from western Europe and Africa, then from eastern Europe and Asia. Despite widespread discrimination, many immigrants prospered. A growing United States population and a demand for new lands and resources lured Americans westward, reducing the Native American population and forcing them into ever-shrinking parcels of land. Western land was gobbled up by miners, ranchers, and a growing political force: farmers.

Key Themes and Concepts

As you review this section, take special note of the following key themes and concepts:

Change What effects did industrialization and urbanization have on American culture, work life, and family life?

Immigration and Migration How did patterns of immigration change from colonial times through the early 1900s?

Places and Regions What types of land, resources, and economic opportunities caused Americans to move farther and farther westward?

Key People

As you review this section, be sure you understand the significance of these key people:

John Dewey   William Jennings Bryan

Jane Addams   William McKinley

Frederick Jackson Turner

Key Terms

tenements   reservations

political machines   Dawes Act

settlement house movement   Agricultural Revolution

company towns   Grange

suffrage   Populist Party

ghettos   free silver

nativism

The Big Idea

Immigration and urbanization changed the United States dramatically. During the late 1800s:

- a prosperous middle class developed.

- cities became crowded and workers lived in unhealthful conditions.

- immigrants arrived from eastern Europe and Asia.

- women and other workers became a larger part of the workforce.

- settlers continued to move westward.

Cities offered the best and the worst of life for newcomers from the countryside and from abroad. The dazzling skyscrapers and bustling streets were symbols of the new opportunities for prosperity in America. Yet behind the dazzle grew a darker side of city life.

Industrialization and Urbanization

Industrialization and urbanization, the growth of cities, went hand in hand. Cities offered large numbers of workers for new factories. Cities provided transportation for raw materials and finished goods. As more plants were built, more workers moved to cities seeking jobs. In 1880, about a quarter of Americans lived in cities. By 1900, roughly 40 percent did. By 1920, more than half of all Americans lived in cities. This shift from rural to urban life had both positive and negative effects.

Negative Effects of City Growth

Some of the negative effects of urbanization included crowded, unsanitary living conditions for workers, as well as corrupt city politics.

Housing Construction of decent housing often lagged behind the growth of city populations. Much city housing consisted of multifamily buildings called **tenements**. Immigrant and working-class families, who could pay little for rent, crowded into such buildings. These poorly maintained tenements deteriorated, and whole neighborhoods became slums. Crime flourished in such poor, congested neighborhoods.

Health Urban crowding helped spread disease. Water and sanitation facilities were often inadequate. Poor families could not afford proper diets and lacked knowledge of basic health procedures.

Politics **Political machines** took control of many city governments, partly by providing help to the growing number of poor immigrant voters and thereby gaining their support. Corruption increased, and money that could have been spent on public works often ended up in private pockets.

Positive Effects of City Growth

Urbanization was aided and improved by new technologies in transportation, architecture, utilities, and sanitation. In addition, cities offered new cultural opportunities.

New Technologies Builders turned to new technologies to meet the challenge posed by huge numbers of people living together. Subways, elevated trains, and streetcars provided mass transportation. Steel girders and elevators made possible high-rise skyscrapers. Gas and electric lights brightened city streets and made them safer. Growing health problems forced officials to design and build new water and sewage systems.

Cultural Advances Public and private money funded new museums, concert halls, theaters, and parks. New printing presses turned out mass-circulation newspapers, magazines, and popular novels by authors such as Mark Twain and Horatio Alger. Public schools educated more students than ever before. Reformers, including the philosopher and educator John Dewey, improved the quality of teaching.

Reading Strategy

Analyzing Cause And Effect
- How was industrialization related to urbanization?
- Did one process lead to the other, or were these processes interdependent?

Reading Strategy

Predicting Content
The growth of cities had both positive and negative effects. Some of the negative effects included crowded and unsanitary living conditions for workers.
- How might these conditions change over time?
- How might they stay the same?

An Urban Classroom

Community Improvement Other reformers founded groups intended to correct the problems of society. In Chicago, Jane Addams started Hull House, a model project that led a **settlement house movement** to provide education and services to the poor. Political reformers sought to unseat corrupt political machines and see that public money was spent on improved services such as police and fire departments and new hospitals, rather than on graft.

Urban and Rural Population, 1850–1900

Source: *Historical Statistics of the United States*

Preparing for the Exam

Some examination questions require you to read and interpret charts. Study the chart and answer these questions.

- Approximately how much did the urban (city) population in the United States grow between 1860 and 1900?

- Did the rural population increase or decrease between 1870 and 1890?

- Between 1850 and 1900 was the population primarily rural or urban?

The Urban Mixture

The people of these growing cities generally could be divided into three broad groups.

Workers and the Poor The largest group contained the workers and the poor. Most immigrants belonged to this group, whose members lived in slums and poorer neighborhoods. (Living conditions generally were better in the **company towns,** which were built and owned by a single employer, but workers in these towns were dependent on their employer for everything from housing to food to police protection.) Often workers lacked the time and money to go to theaters or museums or use other resources that cities provided.

The Middle Class As a result of industrialization, doctors, lawyers, office workers, and skilled laborers made up a growing middle class. Middle-class neighborhoods offered more spacious, better maintained housing. The middle-class people had both money and leisure time. Their homes contained the new consumer goods becoming available, such as sewing machines and phonographs. They could afford to go to concerts, attend increasingly popular football, basketball, or baseball games, and save money for their children's higher education.

The Wealthy Entrepreneurs and wealthy business people usually made the city their chief residence, although they often had summer estates outside it. The rich made up the smallest segment of urban society. They lived in large mansions or elegant apartment buildings. They often contributed to charities and cultural institutions such as opera companies and libraries. They could enjoy the broadest range of benefits of city life.

Changes for Women, Families, and Workers

Industrialization and urbanization brought changes to the lives of women in all the classes. Many Americans had long held the view that the ideal woman devoted herself to home and family, instilling in her husband and children high moral

Reading Strategy

Organizing Information
- Into which three groups can the urban population of the late 1800s be divided?
- Which group was the largest?
- Which group was the smallest?

Key Themes and Concepts

Change
In the late 1800s, more women began to seek paid employment outside the home.

- What reasons led to this change?

- What kinds of new jobs did women seek outside the home?

values. In fact, usually only wealthy women could dedicate themselves full-time to such tasks.

In the late 1800s, more women began taking jobs outside the home, some out of economic necessity and others out of a desire for a larger role in society. These jobs provided added income and personal fulfillment but sometimes produced added stress for family members. For example, women who worked outside the home also were expected to continue performing most of the jobs in the home, and children often had to be cared for by relatives or neighbors during the day.

New Employment Opportunities for Women Working-class women often had to hold jobs outside the home. In addition to jobs women had traditionally filled, such as household services, sewing, or laundering, women took some new jobs created by recent inventions such as the typewriter and telephone.

Middle- and upper-class women also sought jobs. Many of these women had long been active in reform movements, including abolition and temperance, and had attended college in increasing numbers through the 1800s. They sought to apply their educations and social concerns in the job market. Women took jobs as teachers, social workers, doctors, and lawyers, often struggling against public disapproval.

Women thus became an ever-larger part of the workforce. Between 1880 and 1910, the number of working women grew from 2.6 million to more than 7 million. Conditions women met in the workplace—hostility, laws that barred them from certain jobs, unequal pay—led more women to seek legal remedies. To gain the political power to force change, however, women first needed to win the right to vote, called **suffrage.** The women's suffrage movement grew more active.

Other Groups of Workers Groups besides women faced problems in the workplace. Employers regularly discriminated against African American workers and workers who were older or disabled, refusing to hire them or keeping them in low-paying jobs.

Nor did laws protect children from dangerous and unhealthful work, such as in mines and factories. Nevertheless, many families were forced to send their children to work rather than school in order to help make ends meet.

Immigration

The United States has always been a nation of immigrants. After the Civil War, however, industrialization drew an even greater flood of immigrants. From 1865 to 1900, some 13.5 million people arrived from abroad. During much of the nineteenth century, there were few restrictions on immigration as the growing numbers of factories provided job opportunities for cheap labor. Not until the 1920s would the numbers begin to dwindle. Immigration to the United States can be divided into three stages.

Colonial Immigration

This period lasted from the arrival of the first people from England through the Declaration of Independence. The following features characterize this period of immigration.

Colonial Immigrants People from England made up the largest part of these immigrants. However, Scotch-Irish, German, Swedish, and Dutch also came in significant numbers. Large numbers of Africans were also part of the colonial immigration.

Reading Strategy

Problem Solving
- How much did the number of working women grow between 1880 and 1910?
- What challenges did women face in the workplace?
- How did some women address those challenges?

Key Themes and Concepts

Individuals, Groups, Institutions
- What other groups of workers also began working in the late 1800s? What kinds of conditions did they face?

Key Themes and Concepts

Immigration and Migration
During the colonial period, a huge number of immigrants arrived in the United States. People from England, Germany, and Sweden, for example, made up a large number of these immigrants, but people from other countries came as well.

- What motivated immigrants in the colonial period to come to the United States?

Reasons for Immigration Some came seeking political and religious freedom. Others sought to improve their economic standing and their way of life. The Africans came unwillingly, as slaves.

Areas of Settlement English settlement spread along the Atlantic Coast from Maine to Georgia and inland to the Appalachians. Within this area, other ethnic groups became concentrated in certain regions. For example, many Dutch settled in New York and New Jersey, many Germans in Pennsylvania, and many Scotch-Irish in the backcountry areas of the Carolinas. Most Africans came at first to the Chesapeake region, then spread through the South.

Difficulties They Faced Immigrants came into conflict with the Native Americans. They also had to overcome the challenge of building homes, farms, and a new way of life in an unfamiliar region.

Contributions The immigrants succeeded in establishing a culture much like the one they had left in Europe, yet heavily influenced by the geographic factors they encountered in North America. In addition to their language, people coming from England brought forms of government, religions, family and cultural traditions, and economic patterns from their home country. Other groups contributed customs from their home country. All worked to build a successful economy in North America.

Old Immigration

The old immigration covered the years from the establishment of the United States until around 1850. Most immigrants came from northern and western Europe, especially Ireland, Germany, and Scandinavia.

Reasons for Immigration Massive famine caused by failure of the potato crop drove millions of Irish immigrants to seek opportunity in the United States. Revolution in Germany caused many immigrants to seek peace and stability in America. Many people continued to arrive in search of better economic opportunity.

Areas of Settlement The Irish largely settled in cities in the Northeast. Some Germans also stayed in cities, but many moved west to start farms, as did a large number of Scandinavian immigrants.

Difficulties They Faced Irish and German Catholic immigrants often faced hostility on their arrival in the United States. Some Americans feared economic competition from the newcomers. Since at this time the nation was predominantly Protestant, resentment toward Catholics and Jews was also strong.

Contributions Irish workers helped build railroads and canals and labored in factories. Germans and Scandinavians brought, among other things, advanced farming techniques and new ideas on education such as kindergarten.

New Immigration

The New Immigration covered the time from roughly 1870 to 1924. This period was marked by a shift in sources of immigration to southern and eastern Europe, especially the nations of Italy, Poland, and Russia. In addition, substantial numbers of Japanese and Chinese arrived.

Reasons for Immigration Hope of greater economic opportunity prompted many of these immigrants to come to America. Some also came seeking political freedom. Other groups, such as Russian Jews, sought religious freedom.

Areas of Settlement Most of the new immigrants settled in cities, especially industrial centers and ports, and often were concentrated in **ghettos,** or urban

Geography in History

Organizing Information
During the colonial period, in what areas did most English immigrants settle? List two other examples of immigrant groups and the areas in which they settled.

1.

2.

Key Themes and Concepts

Immigration and Migration
"Old immigration" took place during the first half of the nineteenth century. People from northern and western Europe, Ireland, and Scandinavia, for example, made up a large number of these immigrants, but people came from other countries as well.

• What motivated immigrants in the colonial period to come to the United States?

Geography in History

Organizing Information
• Where did most Irish and German immigrants settle?

• What difficulties did these immigrant groups face?

Immigrants

Where they came from 1840–1860

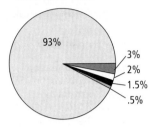

93%
3%
2%
1.5%
.5%

Where they came from 1880–1900

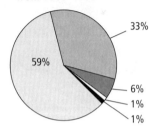

33%
59%
6%
1%
1%

☐ Northern and Western Europe

▨ Eastern and Southern Europe

▧ Americas

☐ Asia

■ All others

Source: *Historical Statistics of the United States*

Analyzing Documents

Interpret Data
Examine the pie charts, then answer the following questions.

- What percentage of immigrants between 1840 and 1860 came from northern and western Europe?

- How much did the percentage of immigrants from eastern and southern Europe increase from the period 1840 to 1860 to the period 1880 to 1900?

areas (usually poor) that are dominated by a single ethnic group. Asian immigrants tended to settle on the west coast, usually in California.

Difficulties They Faced Adjusting to life in the United States could cause strains in immigrant families. At school, immigrant children learned not only English but American tastes and customs. Immigrant parents often feared that their children were losing their religious and cultural heritage.

In addition, the growing numbers of new immigrants produced reactions of fear and hostility among many native-born Americans whose ancestors had come from very different backgrounds. Newcomers faced discrimination in jobs and housing. (As low-wage workers, they also competed against other minority groups, such as African Americans.) Popular pressure to limit immigration increased. Political party bosses often arranged assistance for newly arriving immigrants and in return expected those immigrants to show their gratitude by supporting that political party in elections.

Contributions The new immigrants found an abundance of jobs in the nation's expanding industries. Yet the steady stream of incoming workers to fill such jobs kept wages low. Young Italian and Jewish girls worked in the sweatshops of the garment industry. Poles and Slavs labored in the coal mines and steel mills of Pennsylvania and the Midwest. Chinese workers helped build the transcontinental railroad. These immigrants aided America's economic expansion and contributed to the nation's rich cultural diversity.

Reaction Against Immigration

The flood of immigration in the late 1800s brought with it a new wave of **nativism.** This was the belief that native-born Americans and their ways of life were superior to immigrants and their ways of life. In the late 1800s, descendants of the old immigrants were often among the nativists protesting the arrival of new immigrants.

Nativists believed that immigrant languages, religions, and traditions would have a negative impact on American society. Nativist workers believed that the many new immigrants competing for jobs kept wages low. A series of downturns in the economy added to fears that immigrants would take jobs from native-born Americans. These immigrants were generally unskilled laborers.

Immigrants thus often met with prejudice and discrimination. Jokes and stereotypes about the newcomers were common. Nativists also tried to influence legislation against immigrants. Key developments in this area are included in the chart on the following page.

Immigrants and American Society

Over the years, sociologists and others who studied immigration developed different theories on how immigrants were absorbed into the larger society.

"Melting Pot" Theory According to this theory, people from various cultures have met in the United States to form a new American culture. The contributions of individual groups are not easily distinguished. The resulting culture is more important than its parts.

Assimilation/Americanization According to this theory, immigrants disappeared into an already established American culture. They gave up older languages and customs and became Americanized, adopting the appearances and attitudes of the larger society in order to be accepted. Immigrants from Africa and Asia, who looked least like Americans of European ancestry, had the hardest time becoming assimilated.

Reaction Against Immigration

- **Know-Nothing Party:** The party's members worked during the 1850s to limit the voting strength of immigrants, keep Catholics out of public office, and require a lengthy residence before citizenship. Also known as the American party, the Know-Nothing party achieved none of these goals and died out by the late 1850s.

- **Chinese Exclusion Act of 1882:** Some native-born Americans labelled immigration from Asia a "yellow peril." Under pressure from California, which had already barred the Chinese from owning property or working at certain jobs, Congress passed this law sharply limiting Chinese immigration.

- **"Gentlemen's Agreement":** In 1907 President Roosevelt reached an informal agreement with Japan under which that nation nearly halted the emigration of its people to the United States.

- **Literacy Tests:** In 1917 Congress enacted a law barring any immigrant who could not read or write.

- **Emergency Quota Act of 1921:** This law sharply limited the number of immigrants to the United States each year to about 350,000.

- **National Origins Act of 1924:** This law further reduced immigration and biased it in favor of those from northern and western Europe.

Analyzing Documents

Relate Patterns of Change and Continuity
Examine the chart, then answer the following questions.

- How influential was the Know-Nothing party?
- What prompted Congress to pass the Chinese Exclusion Act of 1882?
- Which laws restricted the number of immigrants to the United States each year?
- Why are the laws examples of nativism?

Preparing for the Exam

Which sociological theory argues that different immigrant groups can live side-by-side without losing their distinctive characters?

Pluralism This theory recognizes that groups do not always lose their distinctive characters. They can live side by side, with each group contributing in different ways to society. This approach is sometimes called the salad bowl theory, since groups, like different vegetables in a salad, remain identifiable but create a new, larger whole.

The American West in the Late 1800s

In 1893, Frederick Jackson Turner wrote in his paper "The Significance of the Frontier in American History" that the frontier, "and the advance of American settlement westward, explain American development." Turner claimed life in the West had given rise to inventiveness, independence, and unique American customs. (While other historians would argue instead that other factors, such as the nation's European heritage or economic abundance, were the key influences, Turner's thesis has had lasting influence.) In 1890, the government had announced that the West was closed. Industrialization had aided the settling of the West.

The American West, 1862–1896

Analyzing Documents

Interpret Data
Examine the timeline, then answer the following questions.

- How many years passed between the Homestead Act and the Battle of Wounded Knee?
- Which event occurred first: the Battle of Little Bighorn or the passage of the Dawes Act?

Native Americans and Westward Expansion

The westward expansion of the late 1800s continued to create problems for the Native Americans who stood in its path. By the 1840s, only scattered groups of Native Americans still lived in the East. Most lived west of the Mississippi on lands that few whites wanted. The California gold rush, the building of the transcontinental railroad, and the discovery of rich farmland in the Great Plains changed this situation. Now white people began to move onto Native American lands in the West.

Government

The Dawes Act was aimed at breaking up Native American tribes and reservations. It offered Native Americans who gave up tribal ways the deeds to their land and United States citizenship after 25 years.

- Was the Dawes Act fair to Native Americans?

- Did Native Americans support it?

Turning Point

Why can the decline of the Plains Indians can be traced to the following events?

- the Homestead Act

- the mass killing of buffalo

- the transcontinental railroad

Analyzing Documents

Identify Causes and Effects
American expansion onto Native American lands led to many wars and the near destruction of western Native American nations. The table outlines the struggle experienced by one tribe, the Sioux. Examine the chart, then answer the following questions.

- What caused the first Sioux War in 1865?

- How did the federal government respond to Sitting Bull's defeat of General Custer?

- How many Sioux were killed by American soldiers at the Massacre of Wounded Knee?

Indian Wars The Native Americans fought back. From the 1850s to 1890, a series of wars raged in the West. Gradually the Native Americans were forced to accept treaties that crowded them into smaller and smaller areas of land called **reservations.** Native American resistance was weakened by the greater numbers of whites with superior technology, and divisions among Native American peoples that did not permit a unified resistance. The defeat of the Sioux at Wounded Knee, South Dakota, in 1890 is usually considered the end of the Indian wars.

Sitting Bull

Changing Government Policies In victory, the federal government continued to display little understanding or respect for Native American cultures and values. Native Americans were given reservation land that rarely could produce adequate crops or support game for the people living on it. Reservations were located in sparsely populated areas of the west. Further, in 1887, Congress passed the **Dawes Act,** aimed at Americanizing the Native Americans. It proposed to break up tribes and reservations and to grant land directly to Native Americans as individuals and families. Native Americans who abandoned tribal ways would be granted deeds to their land and United States citizenship. Relatively few Native Americans accepted the terms of the Dawes Act. By 1900, the effect of these government policies had greatly reduced the size of the Native American population and had made them among the poorest Americans.

The Sioux Wars

1865	Federal government decides to build a road through Sioux territory. Sioux warriors resist violently, sparking Red Cloud's War.
1867	Red Cloud's War ends. Sioux agree to live on reservation in Dakota Territory.
1875	Federal government allows miners to search for gold on Sioux reservation. Second Sioux War begins. Chief Sitting Bull leads many Sioux off the reservation.
1876	At the Battle of the Little Bighorn, Sitting Bull's warriors destroy General Custer's army. In response, federal government sends more troops to the region. Most Sioux agree to move to reservations.
1890	At the Massacre of Wounded Knee, American soldiers open fire on unarmed Sioux, killing 200.

The Economy of the West

An **Agricultural Revolution** with new technologies helped people who moved onto Native American lands exploit the wealth of the West. Railroads brought people and carried western crops and products to eastern markets. Barbed wire aided the growth of both farming and ranching. Steel plows cut tough prairie soil. Windmills pulled water to the surface of dry western lands. Mechanical reapers and farm tools allowed a smaller number of workers to plant and harvest larger crops.

The riches of the West, like the land itself, took many forms. In the Rocky Mountains, miners dug millions of dollars in gold, silver, copper, lead, and zinc ore. In the Great Plains, ranchers turned cattle raising into big business, as cowhands moved huge herds across the open ranges to rail lines. Farmers, too, were attracted to the Great Plains because of its rich topsoil and overcame heat, blizzards, droughts, insects, and occasional conflicts with ranchers to raise crops. Many settled lands claimed under the Homestead Act and later built huge farms. (Through the Homestead Act, as well as government land grants and other aid to large railroad companies, the federal government played a significant role in encouraging development of the resources of the West.) By the late 1800s, American farmers were raising enough to feed the nation and still export wheat and other crops. Mechanization of agriculture caused an increase in production.

Spurred by the expansion of mining, ranching, and farming, cities like Omaha, Denver, and San Francisco became some of the fastest-growing in the nation.

Farmers, Populists, and Politics

Farmers gained more influence and power through two organizations: the Grange and the Populist party.

The Grange Many farmers facing the hardships and isolation of rural life joined the Grange. This organization, founded in 1867, was originally meant to develop social ties. However, poor economic conditions made farmers aware that railroad companies, which often stored farmers' crops and carried them to market, had great control over their livelihoods. To win back some of this control, the Grange began to press for political changes to limit the power of the railroads. Pressure from the Grange and other groups led to the state laws regulating railroads that were upheld in *Munn* v. *Illinois* and to the federal law creating the Interstate Commerce Commission.

The Populist Party Farmers and many factory workers realized that the best hope of winning more reforms was the formation of a new political party. In 1891, they founded the Populist Party, which had among its goals a graduated income tax, direct election of United States senators, government ownership of railroads, telegraphs, and telephones, and an eight hour day.

Courtesy of the Library of Congress

William McKinley

William Jennings Bryan

The new party had strong grassroots support—support directly from the people rather than established political figures. Populist candidates soon made strong showings in elections for state legislatures and for the United States Congress. Many of the ideas and goals of the Populists eventually became laws.

The Election of 1896 The Populists made their strongest showing in the election of 1896, the first election to follow an economic depression that had begun in 1893. The chief Populist issue in the campaign was **free silver.** The free coinage of silver would produce cheap money, or currency inflated in value that would make it easier for farmers to pay off debts. William Jennings Bryan, who ran on both the Populist and Democratic tickets, argued tirelessly for this idea. Republican candidate William McKinley had the support of big business, which contributed heavily to his campaign. McKinley claimed the nation's economy was sound and opposed free silver.

McKinley won the election by a fair margin. The nation's economy meanwhile improved, and the Populists disappeared as a political party. Yet, as has happened with other minor parties in American history, some of the Populists' ideas were later adopted by the other political parties.

The defeat of the Populists symbolized the great changes that had swept the nation since the Civil War. The economy had changed from agrarian to industrial. The United States was becoming a nation of cities rather than farms and villages. The West was closing and its influence coming to end. New immigrants were creating a new, complex, pluralistic culture in America. By 1900, the United States was entering both a new century and a modern age.

Reading Strategy

Reinforcing Main Ideas
• What changes did the outcome of the election of 1896 symbolize in the United States?

Preparing for the Exam

During the election of 1896, the chief Populist party issue was free silver. Populist candidate William Jennings Bryan believed that the free coinage of silver would make it easier for farmers to pay off debts.

• Why do you think Republican candidate William McKinley opposed the idea of free silver?

Some Late 19th Century Inventions That Changed American Life

DATE	INVENTION	IMPACT ON CULTURE
1857	passenger elevator	multi-story buildings could be built and by 1885 the first skyscraper was built in Chicago; escalators followed in 1891
1867	barbed wire	allowed farmers to fence in the formerly open prairies
1873	Levi Strauss creates blue jeans, known as "Levi's"	heavy duty farm clothing was quickly successful and continued into the twenty-first century as a fashion garment
1874	first structural steel bridge	steel from the Carnegie Mills used in a triple arch design that spanned the Mississippi River at St. Louis, opened the way for other bridges
1876	telephone	increased speed and ease of communication for business, political, and social needs, aided in organization for farm groups and others
1879	earliest incandescent lights	before the end of the century, offices, homes, factories, and farms were affected by availability of longer hours of light
1892	first gas powered car and first gas powered tractor	earliest efforts at "horseless carriages" and farm equipment without animal helped spur further growth

Multiple Choice

Directions: Review the Test-Taking Strategies section of this book. Then answer the following questions, drawn from actual Regents examinations. For each statement or question, choose the *number* of the word or expression that, of those given, best completes the statement or answers the question.

1   The literacy tests and poll taxes used in the Southern states after 1870 were designed to
    (1) ensure that only well-informed people voted
    (2) prevent African Americans from voting
    (3) provide an alternative to citizenship tests
    (4) promote advances in public education

2   President Abraham Lincoln's post-Civil War plan for reconstruction of the South was based on the theory that the former Confederate states
    (1) should be treated as conquered territories
    (2) could be readmitted to the Union only by Congress
    (3) had never actually left the Union
    (4) must grant full equality to all people

3   During Reconstruction, what was a belief of the Radical Republicans?
    (1) The former Confederate states should be brought back into the Union quickly.
    (2) Reconstruction should force political and social reform in Southern states.
    (3) The North and the South should take equal responsibility for causing the Civil War.
    (4) The people who were freed from slavery should be denied equal civil rights.

4   One similarity between the Know-Nothings and the Ku Klux Klan is that both
    (1) opposed the spread of communism
    (2) exposed abuses in big business and government
    (3) believed the problems of society were caused by the growth of labor unions
    (4) fostered resentment against minority groups in American society

5   The most long-lasting victory for civil rights achieved during Reconstruction was the
    (1) ratification of the thirteenth, fourteenth, and fifteenth amendments to the Constitution
    (2) establishment of a strong two-party political system in the South
    (3) increased prominence given to the Office of the President
    (4) passage of Black Codes throughout the South

6   The solid South refers to the political situation in the post-Reconstruction South where
    (1) most eligible voters supported the Prohibition party
    (2) people who were freed from slavery held most government posts
    (3) the Democratic party was dominant
    (4) civil rights issues were strongly supported

7   Which statement best describes a major economic trend in the United States during the period from 1865 to 1900?
    (1) Many business practices were developed to eliminate competition.
    (2) Workers determined working conditions and factory output.
    (3) The gross national product decreased steadily.
    (4) Basic industries were taken over by the government.

8 An important result of industrialization in the United States was a growth in the

(1) influence of small family-owned businesses

(2) idea of socialism as the main political philosophy

(3) power of large corporations

(4) political power of small farmers

9 The Interstate Commerce Act, Sherman Antitrust Act, and Clayton Antitrust Act were attempts to limit

(1) business competition

(2) labor unions

(3) monopolies

(4) tariffs

10 Which factor that contributed to the economic growth of the United States in the period from 1865 to 1920 aroused the most opposition?

(1) growth of rapid transportation

(2) existence of democratic government

(3) mechanization of agriculture

(4) liberal immigration policies

11 Between 1865 and 1900, an issue that dominated national politics in the United States was

(1) slavery

(2) the rise of big business

(3) sectionalism

(4) environmental protection

12 During the second half of the nineteenth century, a major goal of new types of business organizations was to

(1) introduce safer and less expensive products to consumers

(2) consolidate the manufacture and distribution of products

(3) support the large number of government regulations

(4) compete successfully with Japanese imports

Base your answers to questions 13 and 14 on the chart below and on your knowledge of social studies.

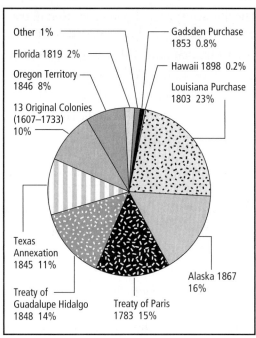

American Territorial Growth
(as a percentage of present United States territory)

Other 1%
Florida 1819 2%
Oregon Territory 1846 8%
13 Original Colonies (1607–1733) 10%
Texas Annexation 1845 11%
Treaty of Guadalupe Hidalgo 1848 14%
Treaty of Paris 1783 15%
Gadsden Purchase 1853 0.8%
Hawaii 1898 0.2%
Louisiana Purchase 1803 23%
Alaska 1867 16%

13 Which territorial gain accounted for the largest increase in United States land growth?

(1) Treaty of Guadalupe Hidalgo

(2) Texas Annexation

(3) Louisiana Purchase

(4) purchase of Alaska

14 Which policy is best illustrated by the chart?

(1) isolationism

(2) manifest destiny

(3) containment

(4) globalization

15 "[Buffalo hunters] have done more in the last two years, and will do more in the next year, to settle the . . . Indian question than the entire regular army has done in the last thirty years. . . . For the sake of peace let them kill, skin, and sell until the buffalo are destroyed."

—General Philip Sheridan

What was the result of the process described in this quotation?

(1) Native Americans were granted farmland under the Homestead Act.

(2) The disappearance of their economic base helped drive Native Americans onto reservations.

(3) Many Native Americans moved to eastern cities to work in factories.

(4) Most Native Americans migrated to Canada to find new ways to earn a living.

16 "I am tired of fighting. . . . Hear me, my chiefs. I am tired. My heart is sick and sad. From where the sun now stands, I shall fight no more forever!"

—Chief Joseph, 1877

In this statement, Chief Joseph of the Nez Percé expressed his reluctant acceptance of a government policy of

(1) placing Native American tribes on reservations

(2) requiring Native Americans to settle west of the Mississippi River

(3) granting immediate citizenship to Native Americans

(4) forcing Native Americans to assimilate into American culture

Base your answer to question 17 on the graph below and on your knowledge of social studies.

Farm and Non-farm Workers 1860–1900

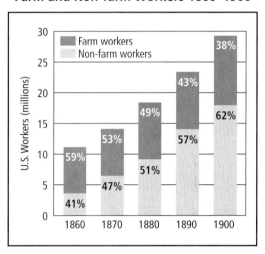

17 Which development contributed most to the trends shown in this graph?

(1) industrialization

(2) westward migration

(3) commercial revolution

(4) trade restrictions

18 A pioneer wanting to settle in the West in the 1870s would have benefited most from the

(1) Homestead Act

(2) Sherman Antitrust Act

(3) Interstate Commerce Act

(4) Agricultural Adjustment Act

19 Unlike other minorities in the United States, Native Americans have some of their rights guaranteed by

(1) the Emancipation Proclamation

(2) treaties with the federal government

(3) the Declaration of Independence

(4) black codes

Questions for Regents Practice

20 A belief in Manifest Destiny, the passage of the Dawes Act, and the completion of the transcontinental railroad are most closely associated with the

(1) rise of big business

(2) growth of the labor movement

(3) abolitionist movement

(4) expansion and settlement of the West

21 Which factor was most critical to the building of the transcontinental railroads after the Civil War?

(1) government ownership of the railroads

(2) capital investments by labor unions

(3) land and money provided by the federal government

(4) willingness of Native Americans to leave tribal lands

22 During the late 1800s, the growing of cash crops by an increasingly large number of farmers resulted in

(1) greater isolation of farmers from American economic life

(2) a shift from self-sufficiency to commercial farming

(3) less food available for export

(4) general economic prosperity for all farmers

23 As the United States became industrialized, an important effect of mechanization and the division of labor was that

(1) smaller industries had difficulty maintaining their competitiveness

(2) the price of most manufactured goods increased

(3) the demand to improve transportation systems decreased

(4) pools and trusts became less efficient forms of business organization

24 In the late 1800s, most strikes by unions were unsuccessful mainly because

(1) unions were generally considered to be unconstitutional

(2) government usually supported business instead of workers

(3) strikes had never been used before in labor disputes

(4) strikers failed to use militant tactics

25 The poll tax, the literacy test, and the actions of the Ku Klux Klan were all attempts to limit the effectiveness of

(1) the fourteenth and fifteenth amendments

(2) the Supreme Court's decision in *Brown v. Board of Education*

(3) civil rights legislation passed in all states after the Civil War

(4) immigration laws such as the Chinese Exclusion Act

26 The Rockefeller Foundation, Carnegie Hall, and the Morgan Library illustrate various ways that entrepreneurs and their descendants have

(1) suppressed the growth of labor unions

(2) supported philanthropic activities to benefit society

(3) applied scientific discoveries to industry

(4) attempted to undermine the United States economic system

27 The major reason the United States placed few restrictions on immigration during the early 1800s was that

(1) few Europeans wished to give up their economic security

(2) little opposition to immigration existed

(3) the growing economy needed a steady supply of cheap labor

(4) most immigrants spoke English and thus needed little or no education

Directions: Write a well-organized essay that includes an introduction, several paragraphs addressing the task below, and a conclusion.

Theme: **Industrialization**

> The growth of industry in the nineteenth century had a major impact on many aspects of American society.

Task:

> Identify any *three* aspects of American society and for *each*.
>
> - Use specific examples to discuss how the growth of industry had an impact on that aspect of society.
> - Evaluate whether the role of industrialization had a positive or a negative effect and explain your reasoning using specific historic examples.

You may use any examples from your study of industrialization in the United States. Some suggestions you might wish to consider include: rise of organized labor, government involvement in the economy, status of the farmer, urbanization, or the role of women.

You are *not* limited to these suggestions.

Guidelines:

In your essay, be sure to:
- Develop all aspects of the task
- Support the theme with relevant facts, examples, and details
- Use a logical and clear plan of organization, including an introduction and a conclusion that are beyond a simple restatement of the theme

In developing your answer, be sure to keep this general definition in mind:

> <u>discuss</u> means "to make observations about something using facts, reasoning, and argument; to present in some detail"

Document-Based Question

In developing your answers, be sure to keep this general definition in mind:

> <u>discuss</u> means "to make observations about something using facts, reasoning, and argument; to present in some detail"

This question is based on the accompanying documents. The question is designed to test your ability to work with historical documents. Some of the documents have been edited for the purposes of the question. As you analyze the documents, take into account the source of each document and any point of view that may be presented in the document.

Historical Context:

> Extensive railroad construction in the 1800s transformed the United States by linking sections of the nation. This transformation had both positive and negative effects.

Task: Using information from the documents and your knowledge of United States history, answer the questions that follow each document in Part A. Your answers to the questions will help you write the Part B essay, in which you will be asked to:

> - Discuss the positive and negative effects of railroads in the United States during the 1800s

Part A: Short Answer Questions

Directions: Analyze the documents and answer the short-answer questions that follow each document in the space provided.

Document #1

> For half a century after Lewis and Clark's expedition, the Great Plains aroused little interest in the young nation. The plains were too dry for agriculture, people said. They were barren, forever a wasteland at the center of the continent. These ideas began to change in the years leading up to the Civil War. As the railroads were built westward, Americans realized how wrong they had been about the plains. Settlers in Kansas found no desert, but millions of acres of fertile soil. Cattlemen saw an open range for millions of cattle, a land of opportunity larger than even the Lone Star State. Of course, the plains were already inhabited by buffalo and Indians. But these meant little to the newcomers. Civilization, they believed, demanded that both be swept away and the land turned to "useful" purposes. How this came about is one of the saddest chapters in our history. . . .
>
> **Source: Albert Marrin, *Cowboys, Indians, and Gunfighters*, Atheneum**

1. According to this passage, how did the use of the railroads change people's opinions about the Great Plains?

_____

_____

Document #2

> It was with a shock of abhorrence, therefore, that they discovered in 1871 the presence of railroad surveyors running a line through the valley of the Yellowstone. With Sitting Bull's approval, the young warriors immediately began a campaign of harassment, first letting the intruders know that they were not wanted there, and then driving them away. The reason the surveyors had come into this area was that the owners of the Northern Pacific Railroad had decided to change its route, abandoning the line through previously ceded lands and invading unceded lands without any consultation with the Indians. In 1872, the surveyors accompanied by a small military force came back to the Yellowstone country, and again Sitting Bull's followers drove them away. . .
>
> **Source: Dee Brown, *Hear That Lonesome Whistle Blow*, Henry Holt and Co.**

2. According to this document, why were Native American Indians hostile to the surveyors?

_____

_____

Document #3

3. What does this illustration show about the effect of the railroads on the buffalo herds?

_____

_____

_____

_____

Document #4

If nineteenth-century Monterey County owed much to the coming of the railroads, Santa Cruz County owed everything, for railroads constructed during the 1870s tied together the isolated communities along the north coast of Monterey Bay and launched an era of unparalleled development. . . .

Between 1875 and 1880 the Chinese built three separate railroads, laid forty-two miles of track, and drilled 2.6 miles of tunnels to stitch Santa Cruz County together and attach it permanently to the world beyond the Santa Cruz Mountains. The Chinese contributed not only their muscle and sweat, but their lives. At least fifty Chinese were killed in accidents while building those railroads. For every mile of railroad, one Chinese died. . . .

Chinese railroad workers on the Santa Cruz Railroad worked six ten-hour days a week and were paid one dollar a day. Two dollars per week was deducted from their pay for food, while expenses such as clothing and recreation chipped away at the remaining four dollars so that they averaged three dollars per week profit. . . .

**Source: Sandy Lydon, *Chinese Gold: The Chinese in the Monterey Bay Region,*
Capitola Book Company**

4. (a) According to this document, how did railroad development help Monterey and Santa Cruz counties?

_____

_____

(b) Based on this document, state one working condition the Chinese experienced as they built the railroads.

_____

_____

Document #5

Rich Farming Lands!
For Sale VERY CHEAP by the
Union Pacific Railroad Company

The Best Investment! No Fluctuations!
Always Improving in Value.
The Wealth of the Country is made by the advance
in Real Estate.
NOW IS THE TIME!
MILLIONS OF ACRES

Of the finest lands on the Continent, in Eastern
Nebraska, now for sale, Many of them never before
in Market, at prices that Defy Competition.

FIVE AND TEN YEARS' CREDIT GIVEN, WITH
INTEREST AT SIX PER CENT.

The Land Grant Bonds of the Company taken at par
for lands. ⟶ Full particulars given, new Guide with
new Maps mailed free.

THE PIONEER

A handsome illustrated paper, containing the
Homestead Law, sent free to all parts of the world.
Address

O.F. DAVIS,
Land Commissioner U.P.R.R.,
Omaha, Neb.

—nineteenth-century broadside (adapted)

---

5. According to the suggestions in this advertisement, how did railroads encourage settlement of the West?

_____

_____

_____

_____

Document #6

. . . That year (1877) there came a series of tumultuous strikes by railroad workers in a dozen cities; they shook the nation as no labor conflict in its history had done.

It began with wage cuts on railroad after railroad, in tense situations of already low wages ($1.75 a day for brakemen working twelve hours), scheming and profiteering by the railroad companies, deaths and injuries among the workers—loss of hands, feet, fingers, the crushing of men between cars.

At the Baltimore & Ohio station in Martinsburg, West Virginia, workers determined to fight the wage cut went on strike, uncoupled the engines, ran them into the roundhouse, and announced no more trains would leave Martinsburg until the 10 percent cut [in pay] was canceled. A crowd of support gathered, too many for the local police to disperse. B. & O. officials asked the governor for military protection, and he sent in militia. A train tried to get through, protected by the militia, and a striker, trying to derail it, exchanged gunfire with a militiaman attempting to stop him. The striker was shot in his thigh and his arm. His arm was amputated later that day, and nine days later he died.

Six hundred freight trains now jammed the yards at Martinsburg. The West Virginia governor applied to newly elected President Rutherford Hayes for federal troops, saying the state militia was insufficient. In fact, the militia was not totally reliable, being composed of many railroad workers. Much of the U.S. Army was tied up in Indian battles in the West. Congress had not appropriated money for the army yet, but J. P. Morgan, August Belmont, and other bankers now offered to lend money to pay army officers (but no enlisted men). Federal troops arrived in Martinsburg, and the freight cars began to move. . . .

Source: Howard Zinn, *A People's History of the United States*, Harper Collins Publishers

6. According to this passage, why did the railroad workers go on strike in 1877?

_____

_____

_____

_____

Document #7

The policy which has been pursued has given us [the United States] the most efficient railway service and the lowest rates known in the world; but its recognized benefits have been attained at the cost of the most unwarranted discriminations, and its effect has been to build up the strong at the expense of the weak, to give the large dealer an advantage over the small trader, to make capital count for more than individual credit and enterprise, to concentrate business at great commercial centers, to necessitate combinations and aggregations of capital, to foster monopoly, to encourage the growth and extend the influence of corporate power, and to throw the control of the commerce of the country more and more into the hands of the few. . . .

Source: United States Senate, Select Committee on Interstate Commerce, 1886

7. According to this document, how did the railroad owners engage in unfair business practices?

_____

_____

_____

_____

Document #8

We believe that the time has come when the railroad corporations will either own the people or the people must own the railroads; and, should the government enter upon the work of owning and managing all railroads, we should favor an amendment to the Constitution by which all persons engaged in the government service shall be placed under a civil service regulation of the most rigid character, so as to prevent the increase of the power of the national administration by the use of such additional government employees. . . . Transportation, being a means of exchange and a public necessity, the government should own and operate the railroads in the interest of the people. . . .

Source: Populist Party Platform, 1892

8. According to the Populist Party platform, why should the government own the railroads?

_____

_____

_____

_____

Document-Based Question

Part B

Essay

Directions: Write a well-organized essay that includes an introduction, several paragraphs, and a conclusion. Use evidence from at least **five** documents in the body of the essay. Support your response with relevant facts, examples, and details. Include additional outside information.

Historical Context:

Extensive railroad construction in the 1800s transformed the United States by linking sections of the nation. This transformation had both positive and negative effects.

Task:

Using information from the documents and your knowledge of United States history, write an essay in which you

> • Discuss the positive and negative effects of railroads in the United States during the 1800s

Guidelines:

In your essay, be sure to:
- Address all aspects of the task by accurately analyzing and interpreting at least *five* documents
- Incorporate information from the documents in the body of the essay
- Incorporate relevant outside information
- Support the theme with relevant facts, examples, and details
- Use a logical and clear plan of organization
- Introduce the theme by establishing a framework that is beyond a simple restatement of the *Task* or *Historical Context* and conclude with a summation of the theme

The Progressive Movement:
Responses to the Challenges Brought About by Industrialization and Urbanization

Section 1: **Reform in America**

Section 2: **The Rise of American Power**

Unit Overview

Between the end of the Civil War and the turn of the twentieth century, the United States became a more industrialized and urbanized nation. These changes brought many benefits to society, but they created problems as well. In this unit, you will review how Americans responded to change, both at home and overseas, in the years from 1900 to 1920. This period is called the Progressive Era. The term comes from the word "progress" and indicates that Americans were reacting to problems by working for reform.

Some key questions to help you focus on the Progressive Era include:

- What were the pressures for reform that led to the Progressive movement?
- Who were the Progressives? What were their goals?
- How successful were the Progressives in meeting their goals?
- What were the causes of increased international involvement of the United States from 1890 to 1920?
- What were the effects of this involvement on the United States and other peoples around the world?

Reform in America

Section Overview

From the 1890s to 1920, a reform movement swept the nation as many people focused their energies on domestic reform, on improving conditions within the United States. The Progressive movement was made up of groups and individuals who worked to change the negative effects of industrialization and urbanization in the United States. Three Progressive presidents—Theodore Roosevelt, William Howard Taft, and Woodrow Wilson—implemented bold domestic reform programs at the national level.

The
Big Idea

The Progressive Era was a period of reform movements during which:

• Progressives promoted political, economic, and social reform.

• reforms were made at the city, state, and national levels.

• Progressive presidents championed reform nationwide.

• Progressive reforms laid the groundwork for future success.

Key Themes and Concepts

As you review this section, take special note of the following key themes and concepts:

Reform Movements What conditions stirred Progressive reformers to action?

Diversity How did women and African Americans work for their own rights during the Progressive Era, and how successful were they?

Environment What environmental protections began in the Progressive Era?

Government What role did the government play in Progressive reform?

Civic Values In what ways were democratic values expanded by the Progressives?

Culture and Intellectual Life What social and moral changes did Progressives promote, and by what means?

Science and Technology What role did science and technology play in both creating and solving the problems the Progressives confronted?

Key People

As you review this section, be sure you understand the significance of these key people:

Upton Sinclair	Margaret Sanger	Theodore Roosevelt
Jacob Riis	Booker T. Washington	Gifford Pinchot
Jane Addams	W.E.B. Du Bois	John Muir
Lincoln Steffens	Marcus Garvey	William Howard Taft
Carrie Chapman Catt	Ida B. Wells-Barnett	Woodrow Wilson
Alice Paul	Robert M. La Follette	

Key Terms

Progressive Era	Square Deal
muckrakers	consumer protection
prohibition	trust-busting
suffrage	conservation
initiative	New Nationalism
referendum	New Freedom
recall	graduated income tax
direct primary	Federal Reserve System
direct election of senators	

Key Supreme Court Cases

As you review this section, be sure you understand the significance of these key Supreme Court cases:

Lochner v. *New York* (1905)
Muller v. *Oregon* (1908)
Northern Securities Co. v. *United States* (1904)

Pressures for Progressive Reform

By 1900, the United States was a rich and powerful nation. Industrialization, urbanization, and immigration had transformed the nation into a major world economy. The changes in American life, however, also brought problems. The Progressives' call for reform, which led to a period of time known as the **Progressive Era,** was a reaction to:

- powerful monopolies restricting competition and controlling prices.
- labor unrest and violence.
- unhealthy and unsafe living and working conditions.
- increasing gap between living standards of the rich and the poor.
- urban poverty, crime, congestion, and poor sanitation.
- political corruption and lack of government responsiveness.
- abuse of the nation's natural resources.

Reform During the Progressive Era, 1901–1916

Effects of Business Practices

The corporate world grew increasingly wealthy and more powerful. Industrial leaders believed that economic success demonstrated fitness to lead, that Social Darwinism explained why some were rich and others were poor. Those who

Preparing for the Exam

Historical Continuity and Change
Identify the similarities and differences among the five periods of American reform movements listed below.

- Birth of reform tradition in first half of 19th century.

- The Grange Movement and the Populist Party in the late 19th century.

- Progressive movement in the early 20th century.

- New Deal reforms of the 1930s.

- Civil Rights movements of the 1960s.

Analyzing Documents

Using and Interpreting Evidence
Using the information in this section and the timeline, answer the following questions.

- During whose presidency was the Supreme Court case *Lochner* v. *New York* (1905) decided?

- Which event on the timeline involved the creation of an organization that worked for the rights of African Americans?

- How did Sinclair's *The Jungle* lead to reform?

Geographic Reasoning
Some urban problems persist over time, while others arise as society develops. Evaluate the relationship between human activities and the environment.

- Consider concerns in urban areas, such as waste disposal, water and air pollution, energy usage, and congestion.

- Consider which urban problems at the beginning of the 20th century continue to be problems today.

- Consider what new urban problems exist at the start of the 21st century.

Preparing for the Exam

Government
Two landmark Supreme Court cases that dealt with state laws limiting the number of working hours were *Lochner* v. *New York* (1905) and *Muller* v. *Oregon* (1908).

"There is no reasonable ground for interfering with the liberty of a person or the right of free contract by determining the hours of labor . . . Clean and wholesome bread does not depend upon whether the baker works but ten hours per day or only sixty hours per week. . . ."
—*Lochner* v. *New York* (1905)

- What seems to be the position of the Court on Progressive reform?

- How do the decisions in *Lochner* and in *Miller* differ?

- How does the Court's action compare with the Supreme Court's decisions during the New Deal?

succeeded earned their position, and those who failed deserved their failure. Social Darwinists believed that the government should not intervene in this process, a belief consistent with the ideas of laissez faire economics.

Conditions for Industrial Workers

Working conditions for factory workers continued to be harsh. Many laborers worked 60-hour weeks on machinery, often in unsafe, unhealthy conditions. Getting hurt on the job often resulted in the worker being fired. Workers earned low wages, and women and children were paid even less than male workers. Workers had little security because their employers could fire them at any time.

Soon, workers grew less tolerant of these terrible working conditions. Some tried to organize labor unions, but employers often fired those who did. Strikes were met with armed attacks from factory security guards and sometimes even federal troops.

Life for the Urban Poor

The gap between living standards of the rich and the poor increased widely during this period. This gap was most apparent in the cities. As the rich grew richer, building lavish townhouses in relatively safe and clean neighborhoods, the poor grew even poorer. They lived in urban slums characterized by poverty, crime, congestion, and poor sanitation. Housing in the cities was segregated by social and economic status, by race, and often by ethnic background.

An elevated train in New York City

Mixed Response of Government at All Levels

Government at all levels remained relatively unresponsive to the impact of industrialization and urbanization. Industries were unrestrained by federal and many state governments; the courts most often failed to support fair standards of business. The laissez faire philosophy prevailed, and so did political corruption at all levels of government. The public received little help from its elected representatives.

Several United States Supreme Court rulings provide examples of the mixed response of the federal government in the struggle for improved working conditions:

- In *Lochner* v. *New York* (1905), the Supreme Court ruled that a New York law limiting bakers' hours was unconstitutional because it interfered with the contract between employer and employee.
- In *Muller* v. *Oregon* (1908), the Court let stand an Oregon law limiting women to a ten-hour work day, ruling that the law was justified because it protected women's health. The effect of laws like this, however, was to keep women out of better paying jobs.

Who Were the Progressives?

The Progressives set out to tackle the problems of their era. They did not form one single group. The Progressive movement was made up of many different movements, and the Progressives were many different kinds of Americans. Their commitment and their success varied from person to person and from cause to cause. They did have some things in common, however.

Characteristics

The Progressives were influenced by the Populists but differed from them. While the Populists lived in the country or in small towns, the Progressives were largely city dwellers. Most of the Populists were farmers, who focused on farm problems. The Progressives tended to be educated professionals—doctors, lawyers, social workers, clergy, and teachers—with a wide range of concerns. The Progressive movement demonstrated the rising power and influence of America's middle class.

Beliefs and Goals

Like all reformers, the Progressives were optimists. They believed that abuses of power by government and business could be ended. They believed that new developments in technology and science could be used to improve the basic institutions of American society—business, government, education, and family life. Progressives believed in capitalism and were concerned about the growth of socialism as a more radical reaction to the effects of industrialization. Progressives wanted to bypass party politics, which they saw as corrupt, but they had faith that a strong government could and should correct abuses and protect rights.

Not all Americans were Progressives or agreed with Progressive goals. Many business and political leaders opposed business regulation. They accepted the Social Darwinists' view that the vast differences in wealth and power in American society were the result of scientific forces that could not be changed. Many workers and farmers did not benefit from Progressive reform, nor did most African Americans, Asian immigrants, and Native Americans.

Factors Aiding the Movement

Many Progressives worked with national voluntary organizations, which grew rapidly in the 1890s. The movement was centered in cities at a time when more of the population was living in cities. This helped communication among Progressives, as did the expanding telephone and telegraph systems. The availability of inexpensive mass-circulation magazines and newspapers also helped spread Progressive ideas. Finally, the Progressives were aided by an improved economy. The first decade of the twentieth century brought prosperity. Industrial profits, wages, and employment all rose; farmers thrived. The result was an optimistic climate and the financial resources to support reform.

Progress Toward Social and Economic Reform and Consumer Protection

A wide variety of reform movements developed from the 1890s to the 1920s.

The Muckrakers and Reform

Muckrakers helped bring reform issues to the attention of the public. Most were journalists and writers, but others were artists and photographers. Muckrakers investigated and exposed corruption and injustice through articles in mass-circulation magazines. They also wrote novels dramatizing situations that demanded reform.

Geography in History

Throughout history, the middle class has developed with the growth of cities built around trade, commerce, and industry.

Collect evidence to evaluate the geographic, historic, and economic role of the middle class in America's history.

Reading Strategy

Organizing Information
- Identify the major reform movements of the Progressive Era.

- Compare and contrast the characteristics of each reform movement using the categories below.

Causes:

Goals:

Leadership:

Influence:

Degree of success achieved:

Key Themes and Concepts

Culture and Intellectual Life
Media has played an investigative role at various times in United States history. Newspaper, radio, and television journalists provide a different view in order to balance that of governments, corporations, and other sources of power.

The muckraking tradition continued long after the Progressive Era. The publication by *The New York Times* of the Pentagon Papers and the reporting of the Watergate scandal by Bob Woodward and Carl Bernstein in *The Washington Post* are two late twentieth-century examples of the muckraking tradition.

Preparing for the Exam

- What are some current examples of investigative reporting on government or corporations using television or the Internet?

- What is the difference between investigative reporting and sensationalism in the media?

- What has been the effect of the Internet and twenty four hour cable news on journalism?

Reading Strategy

Analyzing Cause and Effect
Use the text and the chart above to answer this question.

- What effect did the work of each muckraker have on Progressive reform?

In 1906, the work of the muckrakers resulted in the passage of the Pure Food and Drug Act and the Meat Inspection Act—the first two acts of consumer protection legislation. The federal government passed these laws after it became clear that the unsanitary conditions exposed by Upton Sinclair's novel *The Jungle* were based on fact.

As time passed, the muckrakers' influence declined, partly because readers tired of their sensationalism. Nevertheless, their tradition has continued to the present day.

Progressive Era Muckrakers

Muckraker	Book/Article	Subject of Exposé
Frank Norris	*The Octopus* (1901)	monopolistic railroad practices in California
Ida Tarbell	*History of the Standard Oil Company* (1904)	ruthless practices of Standard Oil Company
Lincoln Steffens	*The Shame of the Cities* (1906)	political corruption in city government
Jacob Riis	*How the Other Half Lives* (1890)	conditions of the poor in New York's tenements
Upton Sinclair	*The Jungle* (1906)	dangerous and unsanitary conditions in meatpacking industry

Other Areas of Concern

Other people and groups also worked to bring Progressive reforms to American society.

Problems of Poverty Attempts to end the poverty, crowding, and disease in American cities began before 1900. Once the germ theory of disease was accepted, cities put more effort into improving water and sewage systems. A well-known urban reformer was Jacob Riis, who used writings and photographs to show the need for better housing for the poor. Some Protestant church leaders became part of the Social Gospel movement, which worked to help poor city dwellers. One goal of urban reformers was building codes that would require safer, better-lighted, better-ventilated, and more sanitary tenements.

Social Settlement Movement One early group of Progressive urban reformers was the settlement-house workers. Settlement houses, located in working-class slums, offered people—especially immigrants—education, child care, social activities, and help in finding jobs. Well-known settlement houses included Hull House in Chicago, founded by Jane Addams, and the Henry Street Settlement in New York City, founded by Lillian Wald.

The Peace Movement Addams and Wald were among the Americans who led peace groups, such as the Woman's Peace Party, in the period before and during World War I. Support of pacifism—the policy of opposition to war and fighting—weakened with America's entry into World War I in 1917 but was later revived. Pacifist Jeannette Rankin, the first woman elected to Congress (1916), voted against the entry of the United States entry into World War I (and World War II as well). For her pacifist efforts, Jane Addams won the Nobel Peace Prize in 1931.

Temperance and Prohibition The temperance movement, which opposed the use of alcoholic beverages, began in the 1820s. Over the years, its chief goal became **prohibition**—outlawing the manufacture and sale of alcoholic beverages. Under the leadership of Frances Willard, the Woman's Christian Temperance Union (WCTU), founded in 1874, was a strong advocate of prohibition. Its members included many Populists and Progressives. It joined with the Anti-Saloon League, and the two groups sought moral reform through prohibition. They believed that consuming alcohol was damaging to society and that through prohibition, problems of poverty and disease could be eased, family life improved, and the national economy made more productive. The temperance crusade led to national prohibition with the adoption of the **Eighteenth Amendment,** which banned the manufacture, sale, and transportation of alcoholic beverages in the United States as of 1920.

Child Labor The National Child Labor Committee was formed in 1904 to rouse public opinion against child labor. The committee recognized the courts' opposition to child labor legislation as expressed in the Supreme Court's "freedom to contract" verdict in *Lochner* v. *New York* (1905) but successfully lobbied the federal government to create a Federal Children's Bureau (1912) to investigate child labor and pressured most states to set minimum wages and maximum hours for children. As a result of state laws and compulsory school attendance, by 1920 11.3 percent of children ages 10 to 15 were working, down from 18.2 percent in 1900.

Women's Rights

Women were involved in all aspects of social reform, but **suffrage** for women continued to be the main goal of the women's rights movement in the Progressive Era. Women who had experienced success in other reform activities wanted to be able to vote. Furthermore, many suffragists thought that the women's vote would serve to correct various social problems.

Women's Suffrage Movement The women's suffrage movement began as part of a broader drive for women's rights in 1848 at Seneca Falls, New York. The intellectual leader was Elizabeth Cady Stanton. Susan B. Anthony provided the driving leadership. In the 1860s, the women's suffrage movement split over its tactics and goals. The National Woman Suffrage Association was led by Stanton and Anthony. The more conservative American Woman Suffrage Organization was headed by Lucy Stone, Henry Blackwell, and Julia Ward Howe. In 1890, the groups reunited to form the National American Woman Suffrage Association (NAWSA) with Stanton as president.

Stanton died in 1902, and Anthony died in 1906, without achieving the objective of their life work. However, the Progressive spirit gave the movement a new surge. In the early 1900s, leadership of NAWSA and the campaign passed to Carrie Chapman Catt, who devised the strategy that was to secure women the vote. She concentrated on achieving the vote for women by a constitutional amendment while coordinating the national effort with a state-by-state movement to put more pressure on Congress and build grassroots support for ratification when the time came. NAWSA swelled to two million members.

Preparing for the Exam

• What are several different tactics that women used in their fight for the right to vote?

• Why was passage of the 14th and 15th Amendments considered by some leaders to be a setback for the movement?

• What 20th century event contributed to the success of the women's suffrage movement? How?

Geography in History

• Why is it significant that this map is dated 1920?

• In what region of the nation did women first receive the right to vote?

• In what regions did they have partial suffrage?

• What relationship is there between the pattern of suffrage and the pattern of migration and settlement of the states?

• What might explain that pattern?

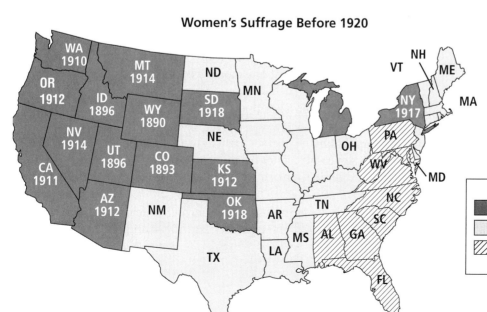

Women's Suffrage Before 1920

KEY
- Equal Suffrage (date voted)
- Partial Women's Suffrage
- No Statewide Women's Suffrage

Civic Values
*"The right of citizens of
the United States to vote shall
not be denied or abridged by the
United States or by any state on
account of sex."*
—Section 1, Nineteenth
Amendment

- Whose rights does this
  amendment protect?

- What are the other
  important steps in U.S.
  history in the extension of
  the right to vote?

Diversity
A far-reaching debate
among African Americans
over goals and tactics took
place between Booker T.
Washington and W.E.B.
Du Bois.

*". . . agitation of questions of
social equality is of the extremest
folly, and . . . progress in the
enjoyment of all privileges that
will come to us must be the result
of severe and constant struggle
rather than artificial forcing."*
—Booker T. Washington

*"I am resolved to be quiet and
law abiding, but to refuse to
cringe in body or soul, to resent
deliberate insult, and to assert
my just rights in the face of
wanton aggression."*
—W.E.B. Du Bois

- Based on the two
  quotes, what belief do
  Washington and Du Bois
  share?

- What differences of
  opinion do they have?

Alice Paul led the more militant Congressional Union until she was expelled from NAWSA. She then formed the National Woman's Party. Paul alienated many women by her use of militant tactics and her campaigning against Woodrow Wilson for reelection in 1916. In the end, it was the highly visible activity of women during World War I that brought them the final public support needed. In 1920, the Nineteenth Amendment was ratified, giving women the right to vote.

Education for Women Another sign of women's progress was the growth of educational opportunities. Among women's colleges founded in the late 1800s were Vassar (1861), Wellesley (1870), and Smith (1871). State universities set up under the Morrill Act of 1862 were coeducational. By the early 1900s, one third of those attending college were women.

The Fight for Birth Control The women's movement also included a campaign for family planning through birth control. This campaign was led by Margaret Sanger, who began her work as a nurse caring for poor immigrant women in New York City. The American Birth Control League founded by Sanger later became the Planned Parenthood Federation. Sanger's movement was very controversial. She was arrested several times for sending information about contraception through the mail.

The Rights of African Americans

The decades following the Civil War were a difficult time for African Americans. Laws prevented them from exercising their right to vote. In *Plessy* v. *Ferguson* (1896), the Supreme Court upheld the Jim Crow laws, which required segregated—"separate but equal"—public facilities for African Americans and whites. Lynchings by white mobs killed hundreds of African Americans.

Key African American leaders who worked to secure their people's rights are described below.

- Booker T. Washington, a former slave and founder of Tuskegee Institute, urged African Americans to get vocational training in order to establish themselves economically. This strategy, he believed, would increase their self-esteem and earn them respect from white society. Washington's policy, called accommodation, was expressed in an 1895 speech known as the Atlanta Compromise.

- W.E.B. Du Bois, a Harvard-educated professor, shared Washington's view of the importance of education but rejected accommodation. He felt that African Americans should protest unfair treatment and receive a broad, liberal education, rather than a vocational one. In 1905, Du Bois founded the Niagara Movement to work for equal rights. More successful was the National Association for the Advancement of Colored People (NAACP), started in 1909 by a group of reformers that included Du Bois and Jane Addams. The NAACP successfully used lawsuits as a weapon on behalf of civil rights.

- Marcus Garvey founded the Universal Negro Improvement Association, an African American nationalist and separatist group, in 1914. The group wanted a separate African American economy and urged African Americans to emigrate to Africa. Many of Garvey's ideas influenced the Black Power Movement of the 1960s.

- Ida B. Wells-Barnett was a journalist who launched a lifelong national crusade against lynching in the 1890s. She was also a suffragist and one of the founders of the NAACP.

Rights of Others Facing Discrimination

In 1913, a group of American Jews established the Anti-Defamation League, an agency of the Jewish service organization B'nai B'rith ("Sons of the Covenant"), which had been founded in 1843. The Anti-Defamation League worked mainly to combat defamation, or libel and slander, directed against Jews. Later, its program was broadened to aim at securing the civil liberties of all Americans.

Progressivism and Government Action

During the Progressive Era, political reform took place at all levels of government—city, state, and national.

Reform of City Government

Given the Progressives' urban, middle-class roots, it is not surprising that they first concentrated their efforts on the governments of the cities in which they lived and in which they were influential citizens. They attacked political machines where they controlled government at the city and state levels, condemning practices such as accepting bribes in return for favors. In the 1890s, Americans interested in good government worked to elect reformist mayors. Success in doing so, however, did not always ensure permanent improvement. Progressives had to change not only the leader, but also the way city government worked.

Two new types of city government are associated with the Progressive movement. They were popular in small and medium-sized cities. In the city commissioner plan, the city is run by a group of commissioners, rather than by a mayor and city council. In the city manager plan, the city council hires a professional city manager to run the various municipal departments.

Progressives Respond to Urban Problems

While some Progressives concentrated not only on making city governments more efficient and less corrupt, architects and city planners tried to improve the appearance of cities by constructing large, elaborate libraries, museums, and other public buildings. Progressive engineers recognized that the sudden and rapid growth of cities called for redesigning and improving needed city services such as sanitation, street lighting, and the water system. Still others worked to regulate these and other utilities or even turn them into publicly owned facilities.

Reform of State Government

Progressives also acted to limit the power of boss-controlled political machines and powerful business interests at the state level. Progressives recognized that states exercised control over many of their cities. Extension of reform to the state, even the national level, was necessary to protect any gains made at the municipal level.

Progressive reforms often proved difficult to enforce, meeting opposition from business interests and the courts. Thus, changes in the way state governments worked were also part of the Progressive program. These changes, aimed at increasing citizen participation in government, included the following:

- The secret, or Australian, ballot lessens the chance of intimidation because it prevents party bosses (and anyone else) from knowing how people vote.
- The **initiative** is a system that allows voters to petition the legislature to consider a proposed law.
- In a **referendum,** voters, not the legislature, decide whether a given bill or constitutional amendment should be passed.

Reading Strategy

Organizing Information
To help you understand the various reforms at the city, state, and federal levels:

- Create a chart that outlines the major reforms made at each level.
- Find evidence to identify the most influential factors for and against reform at each governmental level.

Key Themes and Concepts

Government
- Which do you consider the most important of the changes to increase citizen participation in government? Why?

- Has direct election stopped undue influence on U.S. senators?

- How have initiative and referendum been used by a special interest group?

- How has the direct primary changed the way in which we select a president?

- **Recall** is a form of petition used by voters to force elected officials out of office.
- A **direct primary** allows voters, rather than party leaders, to select the candidates who will run for office. In recent years the number of state convention delegates elected by a direct primary has increased to the point that the party's presidential nominee is known well before the national convention is held.
- Ratified in 1913, the Seventeenth Amendment replaced election of U.S. Senators by state legislatures with direct election of senators by the people of each state. Progressives had labeled the Senate the Millionaire's Club, serving the business and political interests who controlled state legislatures.

Remember that the secret ballot, initiative, referendum, and **direct election of senators** were all parts of the Populist party program. Adoption of these reforms offers an example of how third parties can influence major parties.

State Social, Economic, and Environmental Reforms

Wisconsin, under Governor Robert M. La Follette, was the model for Progressive reform. The State passed laws to regulate railroads, lobbying, and banking. It also started civil service reforms, shifted more of the tax burden to the wealthy and to corporations, required employers to compensate workers injured on the job, and provided for factory inspections.

Several other states passed laws like those of Wisconsin. In 1912 Massachusetts became the first state to pass a minimum wage law. Leading Progressive governors included Hiram Johnson of California, who reformed the railroad industry, and Theodore Roosevelt of New York. As governor of New York (1899–1900), Roosevelt, a friend of Jacob Riis and other Progressives, was concerned about social and economic reform. He supported the creation of the New York State Tenement Commission to investigate New York City tenements. He also worked to eliminate sweatshop factory conditions which forced women and children to work long hours for very low pay in dangerous conditions.

The Presidents of the Progressive Era

1901	1906	1908	1913	1914	1915
McKinley shot; Theodore Roosevelt succeeded as President	Square Deal	William Howard Taft elected President	16th, 17th Amendments ratified	Federal Trade Commission Act passed; Clayton Anti-trust Act passed	New Freedom

1900 | 1903 | 1906 | 1909 | 1912 | 1915 | 1918

1904	1906	1912	1916
Theodore Roosevelt elected President	Meat Inspection Act passed	T. Roosevelt forms Progressive Party; Woodrow Wilson elected President	Woodrow Wilson reelected President

Theodore Roosevelt and the Square Deal

The first three Presidents of this century—Theodore Roosevelt, William Howard Taft, and Woodrow Wilson—are known as the Progressive Presidents. Roosevelt, elected Vice President in 1900, became President when President William McKinley was assassinated in 1901. He was elected in his own right in 1904.

Roosevelt saw his job as one of stewardship—leading the nation in the public interest, like a manager or supervisor. He believed that the President had any powers not specifically denied to the executive in the Constitution. Roosevelt's administration is often known as the **Square Deal** because of the many reforms made during his presidency.

Consumer Protection

Although basically conservative, Roosevelt did not hesitate to use his presidential power to deal directly with social and economic problems. Recognizing the need to protect public health and safety, he influenced the 1906 passage of the Pure Food and Drug Act and the Meat Inspection Act.

Regulating Business

Strengthening Railroad Legislation Under pressure from Roosevelt, in 1903 Congress passed the Elkins Act, followed in 1906 by the Hepburn Act. The objective of both was to strengthen the Interstate Commerce Commission (ICC) and allow it to set railroad shipping rates. Also, the ICC's powers were expanded to include regulation of pipelines, ferries, bridges, and terminals. Some complained because the act allowed railroads to appeal to the courts. However, Roosevelt was often willing to compromise on details to make a larger point—in this case the right of government to regulate business.

Trust-Busting Roosevelt saw a difference between "good trusts," which were to be subject only to regulation, and "bad trusts," which were to be dissolved. The actions he took against big business earned him a reputation as someone who would do trust-busting. In 1903, Roosevelt convinced Congress to form the Bureau of Corporations within the Department of Commerce and Labor. He used the bureau to pressure corporations through investigations and publicity about their activities.

The Northern Securities Case By the end of the 1800s, the Northern Securities Company controlled the railroad system in the Pacific Northwest. In 1901, the Justice Department began prosecution of Northern Securities under the Sherman Antitrust Act. The case was eventually appealed to the Supreme Court. In its ruling in *Northern Securities Co.* v. *United States* (1904), the Supreme Court upheld the judgment against the company and ordered the company to be dissolved.

The "Beef Trust" Another government action using the Sherman Antitrust Act was directed against a group of meatpackers known as the "beef trust." This prosecution, too, was upheld by the Supreme Court, in *Swift & Co.* v. *United States* (1905). This decision gave the government broader powers under the Constitution's interstate commerce clause than the Court's ruling in the landmark case, *United States* v. *E.C. Knight Company* (1895).

Preparing for the Exam

When writing **an essay** on the cause and effects of the Pure Food and Drug Act, how would you include these **supportive facts and examples?**

• laissez-faire, muckrakers, *The Jungle*, Meat Inspection Act, patent medicines, truth in labeling, product recalls, salmonella, e-coli

Analyzing Documents

Examine the cartoon, then answer the following questions.

• Who are the men at the desks?

• What place is pictured?

• Who do the large figures represent?

• Which constitutional amendment was the result of concern over the problem that is depicted in this cartoon?

Labor Conditions

Roosevelt also achieved important reforms in working conditions.

The Anthracite Coal Strike In 1902, when Pennsylvania coal mine owners refused to negotiate with striking workers, Roosevelt threatened to send the army to take over the mines. The mine owners then agreed to arbitration, and the United Mine Workers, under John Mitchell, won shorter hours and higher wages but not recognition of their union. For the first time federal government in a labor dispute did not intervene solely on the side of management.

Employers' Liability One Progressive goal was to make employers assume more liability, or responsibility, for their workers. The Employers Liability Act of 1906 provided accident insurance for workers on interstate railroads and in Washington, D.C.

Working Hours Another Progressive goal was to limit workers' hours on the job. As you read above, in *Lochner* v. *New York* (1905) and *Muller* v. *Oregon* (1908), there were inconsistent results in conflicts between the rights of individuals and the rights of businesses.

Conservation

As a naturalist, Theodore Roosevelt was interested in conservation, or protecting the nation's environment and its wilderness lands. His policies were influenced by the conservationists Gifford Pinchot and John Muir.

Before Roosevelt, the government's land policy put land in the private hands of homesteaders, railroads, and colleges. Roosevelt shifted this policy and kept some land under federal government protection. This was the philosophy of John Muir, a founder of the Sierra Club, who was also instrumental in the creation of Yosemite National Park.

Key Themes and Concepts

Environment
- How did Roosevelt's land policy differ from that of earlier presidents?

- What was the end result of Roosevelt's land policy by the time he left office?

- Roosevelt used the Forest Reserve Act of 1891 to place national forests under the control of the U.S. Forest Service, headed by conservationist Gifford Pinchot. A total of about 150 million acres of public lands was placed under the protection of the federal government. When Roosevelt left office, he had tripled the amount of land set aside for the public as national forests, national parks, wildlife refuges, and national monuments.
- The National (Newlands) Reclamation Act of 1902 set aside money from the sale of public lands to build dams and irrigation systems in the West.
- In 1908, Roosevelt called a national Conservation Congress, attended by hundreds of naturalists and conservationists as well as by 44 governors.

Progressivism Under Taft

After Roosevelt declined to run for a third term, William Howard Taft succeeded him in 1909. Taft began his presidency with the support of Roosevelt and the Progressive wing of the Republican Party.

Reforms Under Taft

Under Taft, the Justice Department brought twice as many suits against big business as it had under Roosevelt. One of the most important cases involved the Supreme Court's ruling in *Standard Oil Co. of New Jersey* v. *United States* (1911) held that the monopoly should be dissolved. But it also applied the so-called "rule of reason" to the Sherman Antitrust Act. There was a difference, said the Court, between "reasonable" and "unreasonable" business combinations. Size alone did not mean that a company was "unreasonable."

The Taft era witnessed other reforms, too. The Mann-Elkins Act of 1910 gave the ICC the power to regulate communication by telephone and telegraph. In 1913, the Sixteenth Amendment was ratified, authorizing Congress to impose an income tax.

Problems for Taft

Taft, who was not as politically able as Roosevelt, soon ran into problems that split the Republican Party into a Taft faction and a Progressive faction. Like other Progressives, Taft wanted to lower tariffs, but he was unable to stand up to the Republican Congress that raised them with the Payne-Aldrich Act of 1909. Taft angered Progressives by calling the law "the best bill that the Republican party ever passed."

Taft ran into more trouble the following year when he dismissed Forest Service head Gifford Pinchot—a favorite of Progressive conservationists. Taft's secretary of the interior, Richard A. Ballinger, had allowed a group of business people to obtain several million acres of Alaskan public lands. Pinchot protested the action, and Taft fired him. Ballinger was identified with mining, lumbering, and ranching interests that wanted to develop the land for personal profit. They were supported by many senators from western states.

Woodrow Wilson and the New Freedom

In 1912, Theodore Roosevelt challenged Taft for the Republican presidential nomination. When the nomination went to Taft, Roosevelt ran as the candidate of a third party, the Progressive or Bull Moose Party. Woodrow Wilson was the Democratic candidate, and Eugene Debs ran on the Socialist ticket.

Roosevelt offered what he called the **New Nationalism,** while Wilson called his program the **New Freedom.** Both were Progressive philosophies. Roosevelt, however, accepted social legislation and business regulation. The more traditional Wilson aimed for a return to competition in the marketplace with enforcement of antitrust laws. Wilson won the election of 1912 by a landslide of electoral votes, although he received only 41 percent of the popular vote. In 1916, he was reelected into office in an even closer race.

Two Major Financial Reforms

In 1913, Wilson secured passage of the Underwood Tariff Act, which lowered tariffs for the first time since the Civil War. The law, a reaction to unequal distribution of income, included a progressive or **graduated income tax**—one that taxed larger incomes at a higher rate (6 percent) than it did lower ones (1 percent). Ratification of the Sixteenth Amendment in 1913 made this new income tax possible.

Also in 1913, the **Federal Reserve System** was created to provide economic stability by strengthening federal control over the money supply. This national banking system is divided into 12 districts, each with a Federal Reserve bank. The government could now (1) issue a new, sound currency—Federal Reserve notes; (2) control the amount of money in circulation and set interest rates; and (3) shift money from one bank to another as needed. The Federal Reserve Board lowers interest rates to stimulate consumer spending in times of recession or raises interest rates to control inflation.

Business Regulation

Wilson also achieved two important business regulations. The Federal Trade Commission Act of 1914 aimed to prevent unfair competition. It created a commission to investigate such practices as false advertising and mislabeling.

Reading Strategy

Gathering and Using Supporting Evidence
Income tax supporters argued that:

- excise taxes were regressive, falling hardest on the less affluent.

- newly made industrial fortunes were now taxable.

- a more steady and reliable source of income for the nation was now available.

- revenue lost through lowering tariffs was now replaceable.

Gather and evaluate evidence in support of each argument.

Preparing for the Exam

Established in 1913, the Federal Reserve System created the first central banking system since the Second Bank of the United States. Twelve banks, rather than just one, exercised monetary controls.

- Who proposed the first national bank of the United States?

- Why was the Second Bank of the United States terminated?

- What is the primary role of the Federal Reserve System?

- What methods does it use to accomplish its goals?

Federal Progressive Era Legislation

Date	Legislation	Purpose
1890	Sherman Antitrust Act	Outlawed monopolies and practices that result in restraint of trade, such as price fixing
1902	National (Newlands) Reclamation Act	Created to plan and develop irrigation projects
1903	Department of Commerce and Labor	Concerned with national issues of business, industry and labor; included Bureau of Corporations
1903	Elkins Act	Increased powers of Interstate Commerce Commission; declared rebates illegal
1905	United States Forest Service	Established to manage and protect the nation's water and timber resources
1906	Hepburn Act	Gave ICC greater power to investigate railroads and control rates
1906	Pure Food and Drug Act	Outlawed interstate transportation of impure or diluted foods and the deliberate mislabeling of foods and drugs
1906	Meat Inspection Act	Required federal inspection of meat processing to ensure sanitary conditions
1910	Mann-Elkins Act	Extended powers of ICC to include regulation of communication
1913	Department of Labor	Made cabinet department separate from Department of Commerce
1913	16th Amendment	Passed by Congress in 1909; ratified in 1913; gave Congress power to levy an income tax
1913	17th Amendment	Passed by Congress in 1912; ratified in 1913; provided for the direct election of senators
1913	Underwood Tariff Act	Lowered tariffs and created first graduated income tax
1913	Federal Reserve Act	Created a federal banking system to ensure national financial stability
1914	Federal Trade Commission Act	Created to prevent unfair competition, it had the power to investigate monopolies and stop false and misleading advertising
1914	Clayton Antitrust Act	Passed to restore business competition; strengthened Sherman Antitrust Act by making some specific practices of monopolies illegal
1916	National Park Service	Created to take over the administration of the nation's parks
1919	18th Amendment	Passed by Congress in 1917, ratified in 1919; prohibited manufacture, transport, and sale of liquor (repealed in 1933)
1920	19th Amendment	Passed by Congress in 1919; ratified in 1920; women gained the right to vote
1920	Women's Bureau	Created within the Department of Labor to promote the status of working women

The Clayton Antitrust Act of 1914 strengthened the government's power to control business practices that threatened competition. Among other things, the act prohibited companies from price fixing and from buying stocks in competing firms. The Clayton Antitrust Act tried to end the practice of using antitrust laws against unions, but later Supreme Court decisions undercut this provision. Later in the twentieth century, federal prosecutions of alleged violations of antitrust laws continued against corporations such as AT&T and Microsoft.

Other Reforms Under Wilson

- The Adamson Act (1916) set an eight-hour day for workers on railroads in interstate commerce.
- The Federal Farm Loan Act (1916) made low-interest loans available to farmers.
- The Keating-Owen Child Labor Act (1916) tried to outlaw child labor, but the Supreme Court ruled the law unconstitutional in the case of *Hammer* v. *Dagenhart* (1918).
- Ratification in 1919 of the Eighteenth Amendment prohibited the manufacture, sale, or transportation of liquor.
- Ratification of the Nineteenth Amendment in 1920 gave women the right to vote.

End of the Progressive Era

The Progressive Era came to an end when the United States entered World War I. During the war, American priorities shifted to the war effort, and in the 1920s, the trend shifted away from reform and toward acceptance of society as it was.

The Rise of American Power

Section Overview

The changes in the United States that led to Progressive reform at home also influenced American expansion overseas. From 1865–1920, a newly industrialized United States moved beyond the borders of North America to become an imperialist power on a global scale. Presidential power was a central issue, as was the shift in traditional foreign policy. Presidents Theodore Roosevelt and Woodrow Wilson dominated foreign policy as the nation involved itself in an interdependent world. Americans debated their motivations, their policies, and their effects on people at home and abroad.

Key Themes and Concepts

As you review this section, take special note of the following key themes and concepts:

Places and Regions How did America's industrialization increase pressures for overseas expansion?

Constitutional Principles How did reactions to the Russian Revolution and World War I result in the restriction of some people's civil rights in the United States?

Change How did the United States change its traditional foreign policy in the early years of the twentieth century? In what ways did the nation continue policies of the past?

Presidential Decisions and Actions How did actions of Presidents Theodore Roosevelt and Woodrow Wilson increase both the power of the United States and the power of the presidency?

Key People

As you review this section, be sure you understand the significance of these key people:

Frederick Jackson Turner
Henry Cabot Lodge
Matthew Perry

Theodore Roosevelt
William Howard Taft
Woodrow Wilson

Key Terms

Open Door Policy
jingoism
imperialism
Roosevelt Corollary
dollar diplomacy

Fourteen Points
self-determination
Treaty of Versailles
League of Nations
reparations

The Big Idea

Between 1865 and 1920:

- the United States became a world power.
- U.S. territory was acquired by military conquest, treaty, purchase, and annexation.
- industrial and commercial expansion motivated expansion.
- the United States moved away from its traditional foreign policy.
- the transition to a world power increased feelings of nationalism in the nation, but it also caused debate and division.

As you review this section, be sure you understand the significance of this key Supreme Court case:

Schenck v. *United States* (1919)

Emerging Global Involvement

In the late 1800s and early 1900s, American expansion was in many ways a resumption of the expansionist drive that had been halted by the Civil War. A number of factors led the United States into greater global involvement in the late 1800s.

New Technology

Improvements in transportation and communication technology shortened distances around the world. At the same time, other inventions accelerated industrial growth. Railroads connected factories and farms to Atlantic and Pacific ports, from which steamships carried goods to Europe, Latin America, and Asia. Communication was faster and easier thanks to the telegraph, telephone, and transatlantic cable. Communications technology quickly provided information on international markets and on events in other nations that might affect the United States. The world was becoming more interdependent.

Drive for Markets and Raw Materials

Economics linked the domestic and foreign policy goals of the United States. Business leaders wanted raw materials from abroad. Both business leaders and farmers also wanted overseas markets. Overseas markets could provide economic stability, especially when, as in the 1890s, domestic consumption could not absorb the nation's output. At the same time, international competition increased as European nations, Japan, and the United States sought raw materials and markets. Foreign trade increased dramatically. High U.S. tariffs played a role in revolutions in Hawaii and in Cuba.

United States Expansion, 1803–1867

Date	Territory	How Acquired
1803	Louisiana Purchase	purchased from France
1819	Florida	occupation, followed by treaty with Spain
1845	Texas	annexation by joint resolution of Congress
1846	Oregon Country	agreement with Great Britain
1848	Mexican Cession	Mexican War/treaty with Mexico
1853	Gadsden Purchase	purchase from Mexico
1867	Alaska	purchase from Russia
1867	Midway	annexation

Growth of Naval Power

The U.S. Navy began to expand in the 1880s, building steel-hulled warships with steam engines and the latest in weapons. Behind this growth was the urging of expansionists like Alfred T. Mahan, who argued that as foreign trade grew, a nation needed a strong navy to protect shipping routes. The navy, in turn, needed bases at which to refuel and restock supplies.

Manifest Destiny and the Closing of the Frontier

As you will recall, the idea of Manifest Destiny took hold in the United States in the mid-1800s. Manifest Destiny is the idea that the United States had a divine mission to expand in order to spread the ideals of freedom and democracy.

Value of United States Exports, 1870–1920

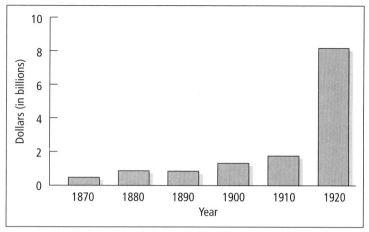

Source: Historical Statistics of the United States, Colonial Times to 1970

Analyzing Documents

Bar graphs help you to compare quantities over a period of time. Based on the graph to the left, answer the following questions.

- What was the value of United States foreign trade

  in 1870?

  in 1900?

  in 1920?

- What are possible explanations of the changes on the chart?

- What evidence supports your explanations?

This belief was fueled by historian Frederick Jackson Turner's frontier thesis. In a famous 1893 essay, Turner argued that the existence of a frontier throughout our history had been vital in shaping the American character. By 1893, Turner noted, that frontier no longer existed, an argument supported by the 1890 census. Some people interpreted this development to mean that Americans needed new frontiers beyond the current borders.

Social Darwinism

Closely tied to Manifest Destiny was the idea that the American way of life was so superior that the United States was obliged to carry its benefits to other peoples. Few wondered whether these peoples wanted American "benefits," or recognized that this notion implied that other peoples and their ways of life were inferior. The belief in Anglo-Saxon superiority was a form of Social Darwinism. According to Social Darwinists, the law of nature resulted in the survival of superior people. Similarly, the same law led to the survival of superior nations, which are meant to dominate inferior nations. Few questioned the fact that no scientific evidence supported this theory.

The Missionary Spirit

Another motive for expansion was the missionary spirit. It lay behind attempts to introduce Christianity and "civilization" to others, particularly in China, where the movement was strongest. The missionary impulse did result in certain improvements, such as the building of schools and hospitals. However, it also fostered a paternalistic view—one that saw the United States as a parent supervising weaker, less "developed" peoples. Underlying Manifest Destiny, Social Darwinism, and the missionary movement were nationalism, racism, and a strong sense of cultural superiority.

The United States as a World Power: Asia and the Pacific

The role of the United States in Asia expanded because of the establishment of trade with China and Japan and the acquisition of Hawaii, Pacific bases, and the Philippines.

China

American trade with China began in the 1780s through the port of Canton. By the late 1800s, however, Americans were afraid that their economic opportunities in

"The policy of the United States is to seek a solution which may bring about permanent safety and peace to China, preserve Chinese territorial and administrative entity, protect all rights guaranteed to friendly powers by treaty and international law, and safeguard for the world the principle of equal and impartial trade with all parts of the Chinese Empire."
—**2nd Open Door Note, 1900**

- Explain how the geographical and historical circumstances affected the issuing of this policy statement.

- Analyze the wording for evidence that it was in American self-interest to call for the preservation of Chinese territorial and administrative integrity.

Preparing for the Exam

Stimulus Based Question
Examine the timeline to the right, then answer the following questions.

- Which event occurred first—Roosevelt's use of "Big Stick diplomacy" or the Spanish-American War?

- Which events are examples of use of force?

- What other methods of carrying out foreign policy are suggested?

China might be limited. Throughout the nineteenth century, China had been subjected to imperialistic demands by Japan, Germany, Russia, Great Britain, and France. Each nation gained a sphere of influence—a region in which it had exclusive trade, mining, or other economic rights.

Open Door Policy In 1899, Secretary of State John Hay tried to ensure economic opportunity for the United States. He asked the European powers to keep an "open door" to China. He wanted to ensure through his Open Door Policy that the United States would have fair access to the Chinese market. The European powers, however, met his request with a cool response.

The Boxer Rebellion In 1900, a secret patriotic Chinese society called the Boxers attacked missionaries, diplomats, and other foreigners in China in what is known as the Boxer Rebellion. The Boxers were revolting against the Manchu Dynasty and against the intervention of Western powers in China. The Western powers, including the United States, sent troops to restore order. Fearing that rival nations would take even more Chinese land, Hay expanded the Open Door Policy to mean that the current boundaries of China should be preserved.

American Imperialism, 1867–1914

1867		1889	1900	1906	1914
Alaska purchased		Samoa agreement signed	"Big Stick diplomacy"; Boxer Rebellion	U.S. troops restore order in Cuba	Panama Canal opens

1860	1870	1880	1890	1900	1910	1920

	1880s	1899	1898	1904	1910
	U.S. trade abroad increases	Open Door Policy	Spanish-American War; Hawaii annexed	Roosevelt Corollary established	"Dollar diplomacy"

Japan

Japan had developed into a major economic power after 1854, the year Commodore Matthew Perry ended Japan's isolation by negotiating a treaty opening two Japanese ports to ships from the United States. Unlike China, Japan carried out a far-reaching modernization program making it a major economic power by 1900.

From 1900 to 1941, a key aim of American policy in Asia became protecting American economic, political, and territorial interests by providing the balance of power to restrict Japanese expansion.

- Japan displayed its growing strength by defeating Russia in the Russo-Japanese War of 1904–1905. President Theodore Roosevelt mediated the Treaty of Portsmouth in an effort to protect American possessions and interests in Asia. It was understood that Japan could remain in Manchuria and annex Korea. Japanese anger at the terms of the Treaty increased tensions between the two nations.

- United States agreement to the Japanese takeover of Korea was formalized in the 1905 Taft-Katsura Agreement. In return, Japan would not threaten the Philippines.

- United States–Japanese relations experienced a setback when, in 1906, the San Francisco schools placed Asian children in separate classes. The Japanese government condemned this segregation. In 1907, President Theodore Roosevelt achieved a compromise with Japanese officials called the Gentlemen's Agreement. This agreement ended school segregation in San Francisco but also restricted Japanese immigration to the United States.

- In 1908 the two nations also entered into the Root-Takahira Agreement in which the United States recognized Japan's interest in Manchuria, while the Japanese agreed to uphold the Open Door Policy and support China's *independence and integrity*. They each agreed to maintain the *status quo*, meaning no attempt would be made to seize the other's possessions.

Hawaii

From the beginning of the nineteenth century, Americans – traders, whalers, missionaries – came to the Hawaii. Descendents of some of the missionaries developed important business interests there, namely sugar plantations. In 1887, the United States gained the right to establish a naval base at Pearl Harbor. By the 1890s Americans dominated the islands politically, economically, and militarily. But, until the 1890s, Hawaii remained an independent country ruled by a monarch.

Then, in 1890 a tariff law eliminated the favored status given in 1875 to Hawaiian sugar imports. The new law allowed all sugar to enter the United States duty free but gave sugar cane producers in the United States an incentive that encouraged the industry at home. This meant that Americans would be more likely to buy domestic sugar rather than Hawaiian sugar, and American planters in Hawaii would lose money.

At the same time, Americans in Hawaii feared Hawaiian nationalism led since 1891 by Queen Liliuokalani. Challenged both economically and politically, in 1893 American planters carried out a successful revolution against the Hawaiian ruler. They were aided by the chief United States diplomat to Hawaii and by American marines.

Against the wishes of the Hawaiian people, the American sugar growers asked that the United States annex Hawaii so that their sugar would be considered domestic and not foreign. But President Grover Cleveland opposed expansion by force. Hawaii remained in the hands of the American sugar interests as the independent Republic of Hawaii with Sanford B. Dole as president.

Not until 1898 during the Spanish-American War did it become a United States possession. It then became important as a military and commercial link to the Philippines and the rest of East Asia. Annexation was accomplished by a joint resolution of Congress rather than a treaty.

Samoa

In 1878, the United States gained the rights to a naval station at Pago Pago in the Samoan Islands. The port was also used by Germany and Great Britain. Samoa was situated in the Pacific on the trade route to Australia. Conflicts arose among the three nations. In 1899, Germany and the United States divided Samoa.

Imperialism: The Spanish-American War

In 1898, the United States began to acquire new territories, making it an imperial power. Most of these territorial gains resulted from the Spanish-American War.

Underlying Causes of the Spanish-American War

There were several underlying causes of the war between Spain and the United States.

Economic United States business interests had invested $50 million in Cuba. Almost all of Cuba's sugar was exported to the United States. In 1894, the United States placed a high protective tariff on Cuban sugar, which had previously entered the nation duty free. Growers in Cuba lost millions because their sugar was no longer competitively priced. The result was economic chaos, which, combined with resentment of Spanish rule, set off a Cuban revolution against Spain in 1895. The revolution further endangered American investments.

Humanitarian Many Americans sympathized with the Cuban revolution and were appalled by the tactics of the Spanish military commander, Valeriano Weyler. He imprisoned hundreds of thousands of Cuban civilians in camps, where about 30 percent of them died from disease and starvation.

Expansionist American expansionists—including Theodore Roosevelt, Senator Henry Cabot Lodge, and Secretary of State John Hay—recognized that war offered an opportunity to seize territory from Spain, a weak nation.

Immediate Causes of the Spanish-American War

In addition to the underlying causes of the Spanish-American War, several immediate events aroused Americans' emotions. These fed a growing **jingoism**— a super patriotism and demand for aggressive actions—that created a warlike mood.

Yellow Journalism In the late 1890s, two of the most famous American publishers, William Randolph Hearst of the *New York Morning Journal* and Joseph Pulitzer of the *New York World*, were battling for readers in a circulation war. Both newspapers printed the most sensational stories and pictures they could find about the horrors of the Cuban revolution. The stories often exaggerated and distorted events for emotional effect. This kind of sensationalism is called "yellow journalism."

The de Lôme Letter A personal letter written by the Spanish minister to the United States, Enrique Dupuy de Lôme, was printed in the *New York Journal* in February 1898. De Lôme's unfavorable comments—he called President McKinley "weak and catering to the rabble"—made it hard for the president and other political leaders to withstand demands for war.

Sinking of the *Maine* Less than a week after publication of the de Lôme letter, the United States battleship *Maine* exploded and sank in the harbor of Havana, Cuba, killing 266 Americans. The public blamed Spain, although a later investigation was never able to determine the cause of the explosion nor assign responsibility.

Fighting the Spanish-American War

In April 1898, despite Spain's agreement to an armistice with Cuba, McKinley asked Congress to declare war. Congress complied. It also approved the Teller Amendment, which promised that the United States would not annex Cuba.

The war lasted four months, with fighting in both the Caribbean Sea and the Pacific Ocean. Of the 2,446 Americans who lost their lives, fewer than 400 were killed in combat; the rest died from infection and disease.

The Results of the Spanish-American War

In December 1898 the terms of the Treaty of Paris negotiated with Spain:

- granted Cuba its independence.
- gave the Philippines to the United States in return for $20 million.
- ceded Puerto Rico and Guam to the United States.

For the United States, the Treaty of Paris of 1898:

- led to the acquisition of many former Spanish territories that formed the basis of an American empire.
- set off a national debate among imperialists and anti-imperialists.
- increased American involvement in Latin America and Asia as the nation sought to protect its new lands.

The Spanish-American War

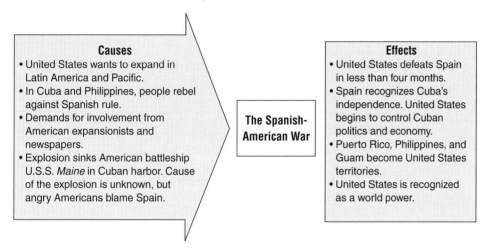

Causes
- United States wants to expand in Latin America and Pacific.
- In Cuba and Philippines, people rebel against Spanish rule.
- Demands for involvement from American expansionists and newspapers.
- Explosion sinks American battleship U.S.S. *Maine* in Cuban harbor. Cause of the explosion is unknown, but angry Americans blame Spain.

The Spanish-American War

Effects
- United States defeats Spain in less than four months.
- Spain recognizes Cuba's independence. United States begins to control Cuban politics and economy.
- Puerto Rico, Philippines, and Guam become United States territories.
- United States is recognized as a world power.

With a quick victory in the Spanish-American War, the United States established itself as a new world power.

Analyzing Documents

Examine the graphic organizer, then answer the following questions.

- Which are the *basic* causes of the war?
- Which are the *immediate* causes of the war?
- Which effects were long term?
- How was the War a turning point in United States history?

Imperialism: The Great Debate

Ratification of the Treaty of Paris set off a great debate in the United States. As with all treaties, it had to be approved by a two-thirds vote of the Senate. The fundamental question was whether the United States should pursue imperialism— the policy of expanding a nation's power by foreign acquisitions.

Debating Imperialism

Americans in both political parties, in all regions, and from all social classes could be found on either side of the debate. Progressives were also divided. Imperialists included Theodore Roosevelt, Senator Henry Cabot Lodge, and Alfred T. Mahan. Among the anti-imperialists were Andrew Carnegie, Mark Twain, Jane Addams, William Jennings Bryan, Booker T. Washington, and former Presidents Grover Cleveland and Benjamin Harrison.

Analyzing Documents

Differing Points of View
"It has been a splendid little war; begun with the highest motives, carried out with magnificent intelligence and spirit."
—*Secretary of State John Hay, 1898*

- How is this description of a war unusual?
- Why would anti-imperialists and pacifists object to this description?

The American Empire During the Progressive Era, 1898–1917

Date	Territory	How Acquired
1898	Hawaii	annexation after 1893 revolution
1898	Puerto Rico	gained from Spain after war
1898	Guam	gained from Spain after war
1898	Philippines	gained from Spain after war
1899	Samoa	treaty with Great Britain
1899	Wake Island	annexation
1903	Panama Canal Zone	treaty with Panama
1917	Virgin Islands	purchased from Denmark

Reading Strategy

Making Generalizations
Self-interest is what determines a nation's foreign policy. Often that self-interest is mixed with idealism and nationalism.

Summarize the major reasons for the expansionism of the United States in the 1890s and early 1900s.

- Which reasons were based on self-interest, idealism, nationalism?

- How did the Hawaiians and Filipinos show their nationalism by their reactions to American actions and attitudes?

Geography in History

1898: Guantanamo Bay in Cuba was site of first U.S. troop landing in Spanish-American War.

1901: Platt Amendment gave U.S. right to lease area "for use as coaling or naval station only."

1903: U.S.-Cuba Treaty continues lease of this first U.S. overseas naval base.

1934: Treaty is renegotiated. Can be broken only by "mutual consent" or U.S. abandonment.

2002: Under President G. W. Bush, part of base is used as a detention camp for "enemy combatants." Releases 532 by 2009.

2009: President Obama orders detention camp to be closed within one year but faces Congressional opposition to relocation in U.S., national security issues and problems with transfers to other nations.

2017: 45 detainees remain. President Trump indicates he will keep Guantanamo detention camp open.

Acquiring the Philippines by Annexation and War

In February 1899, President McKinley secured Senate approval of the Treaty of Paris by a one vote margin. That January, Emilio Aguinaldo, who had been fighting the Spanish for Philippine independence, resisted annexation by the United States and declared the Philippines a republic. A bitter United States-Filipino war followed, lasting from 1899 until 1902. More than 4,000 Americans and some 16,000 Filipinos were killed in this war. An additional 200,000 Filipinos died from starvation and disease. Atrocities were committed by both sides. At the end of the war, the Philippines were under American control.

The Constitution and the Territories

Imperialism was supported by the Supreme Court from 1901 to 1904, with decisions in the Insular Cases. The Court ruled that the Constitution applied only in those territories that Congress decided would be incorporated into the United States. The Court also held that people in annexed territories did not automatically have the rights of United States citizens. Congress would make that decision, based on the status given to a territorial possession.

Imperialists' Point of View	Anti-Imperialists' Point of View
The United States needs colonies to compete economically.	Supporting an empire would be a financial burden.
To be a true world power, the United States needs colonies and naval bases.	The United States should concentrate its energies on solving problems at home.
It is the American destiny to expand, and its duty to care for poor, weak peoples.	Nonwhite people cannot be assimilated into American society.
To abandon territories makes the United States appear cowardly before the world.	An empire would involve the United States in more wars.
It is only honorable to keep land that Americans lost their lives to obtain.	It is a violation of democratic principles to annex land and not offer its people the same rights as those of U.S. citizens.

Governing the Territories

The United States set up different means of governing its new territories.

- **Hawaii** was made a territory in 1900, its first step to statehood in 1959.

- In 1916, the Jones Act promised the Philippines independence, but the law did not name a date. In 1934, the **Philippines** was promised independence in ten years. This promise was delayed because of World War II but was honored in 1946.

- The Foraker Act of 1900 provided for a Puerto Rican legislature elected by the people with a governor and council appointed by the American president. Puerto Ricans received United States citizenship in 1917. In 1952, the island became a commonwealth. This status gives **Puerto Rico** many rights of a state excluding sending representatives to Congress.

- U.S. troops remained in **Cuba** until 1902. American troops were sent to Cuba twice between 1902 and 1922. Cuban independence was limited by the Platt Amendment (1901), which remained part of the Cuban constitution until 1934. The amendment (1) required that the United States approve treaties between Cuba and other nations, (2) gave the United States the right to lease naval bases in Cuba, and (3) allowed the United States to intervene in Cuba to preserve order or peace.

United States Expansion, 1857–1903

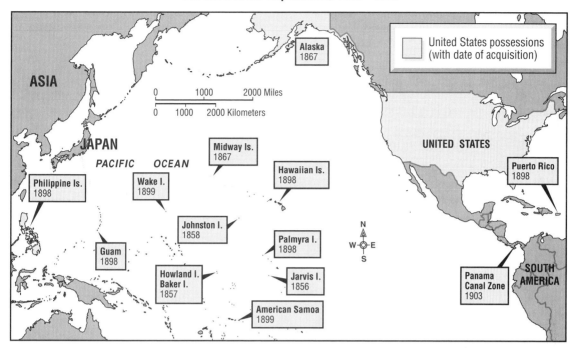

United States possessions (with date of acquisition)

ASIA

JAPAN

PACIFIC OCEAN

Alaska 1867

UNITED STATES

Midway Is. 1867

Hawaiian Is. 1898

Wake I. 1899

Philippine Is. 1898

Johnston I. 1858

Guam 1898

Palmyra I. 1898

Howland I. Baker I. 1857

Jarvis I. 1856

American Samoa 1899

Puerto Rico 1898

Panama Canal Zone 1903

SOUTH AMERICA

0   1000   2000 Miles
0   1000   2000 Kilometers

N W E S

America as a World Power: Latin America

Having acquired an empire, the United States found itself increasingly involved around the globe as it protected its new territories and interests. Of particular interest to the United States was Latin America.

Expanding the Monroe Doctrine

The Monroe Doctrine of 1823 warned foreign powers to stay out of the Western Hemisphere. For several decades, the relatively weak United States seldom enforced the doctrine. It was used, however, to support the American annexation of Texas as well as the Mexican War. It was also used at the end of the Civil War against France, which had set up a puppet government in Mexico and refused to give in to American demands to withdraw. France withdrew only after the United States massed troops along the Mexican border.

The Venezuelan Border Dispute In 1895, the United States had an opportunity to reaffirm and expand the Monroe Doctrine. Great Britain and Venezuela were involved in a quarrel over the boundary between Venezuela and British Guiana (now Guyana). The United States offered to arbitrate, or help settle, the dispute. When Great Britain refused arbitration, the United States claimed that the British were violating the Monroe Doctrine and forced them to negotiate by threatening war. Secretary of State Richard Olney, in the Olney Interpretation of the Monroe Doctrine, claimed, "Today, the United States is practically sovereign of this continent."

The Roosevelt Corollary President Theodore Roosevelt, further reinforced, even reinterpreted, the Monroe Doctrine. Economic problems in Venezuela and the Dominican Republic led to threats of European intervention. In both cases, the United States stepped in to restore order. Roosevelt explained American policy in a 1904 message to Congress. If a nation in the Western Hemisphere is guilty of consistently behaving wrongly, he said, the Monroe Doctrine requires that the United States step in and act "as an international police power." This policy is known as the Roosevelt Corollary to the Monroe Doctrine.

Geography in History

Based on the map above and the text, answer the following questions.

- Which United States acquisition was closest to Japan?

- Under what circumstances did the United States acquire the Philippines?

- What was particularly controversial about these circumstances?

- What were the strategic and economic interests of the U.S. that influenced the expansion shown on the map?

The "Big Stick" Policy With the Roosevelt Corollary to the Monroe Doctrine as its justification, the United States intervened often in Latin American affairs usually to maintain economic stability in order to protect American investments and prevent European involvement in the Hemisphere.

There are several examples of "Big Stick" foreign policy by the United States in the first decades of the 1900s.

- The United States occupied Nicaragua with troops from 1912 until 1933. It also maintained a military occupation of Haiti (1915–1934) and the Dominican Republic (1916–1924).

- The Dominican Republic had trouble paying its debts to European nations. When the Europeans threatened force, the United States took over Dominican finances, supervising them between 1905 and 1941. Haiti was supervised between 1916 and 1941 as was Nicaragua from 1911–1924.

Dollar Diplomacy President Taft's foreign policy approach was known as dollar diplomacy. This meant that the United States could help maintain orderly societies in other countries by increasing American investment in foreign economies. These investments tended to increase American intervention in foreign affairs.

Intervention in Mexico During the Mexican Revolution, President Wilson intervened in Mexico's affairs in order to protect huge U.S. investments there. He also believed in moral diplomacy—conducting foreign affairs in terms of judgments about right and wrong. In 1913, after Victoriano Huerta overthrew the Mexican president and had him murdered, Wilson refused to recognize Huerta's government. The next year, the U.S. Navy seized the port of Vera Cruz to prevent a German ship from landing its cargo of arms for Huerta. Wilson also sent a force into northern Mexico in 1916 in an attempt to capture Pancho Villa, a Mexican rebel whose border raid into New Mexico in 1916 led to American deaths.

Latin American Reaction The actions of the United States were met with protests from the Latin American nations. Cuba, Colombia, and other nations expressed their objections in strongly nationalistic language. The attitude of the United States left a heritage of distrust that persists today.

The Good Neighbor Policy Only under Presidents Herbert Hoover (1929–1933) and Franklin D. Roosevelt (1933–1945) did the United States try to improve its relations with Latin America. Roosevelt backed what came to be called the "good neighbor policy." This meant less emphasis on intervention and more on cooperation. However, American economic dominance of the region continued.

The Panama Canal Since the mid-1850s, the advantages of building a canal across the isthmus, or narrow piece of land connecting North and South America, were well recognized. The growth of United States commerce as well as the expansion of its navy increased pressure to be able to move navy and merchant ships quickly between the Atlantic and Pacific Oceans. The Spanish-American War and the management of the newly acquired empire heightened interest in the project.

Under Theodore Roosevelt, the United States settled on a route across Panama, which was part of Colombia. When Colombia seemed reluctant to agree to financial terms, Roosevelt encouraged Panamanians to revolt and declare their independence. The United States quickly negotiated a treaty with the new nation of Panama, which gave the United States a 99-year renewable lease on a ten-mile-wide strip of land, the Panama Canal Zone, across Panama.

Begun in 1904, building the canal was a mammoth task. Yellow fever and malaria caused delays as did the difficulty of moving more than 250 million cubic yards of soil. However, workers made the remarkable achievement of completing the canal ahead of schedule and under budget. The canal opened to traffic in 1914.

Responding to Panamanian demonstrations in 1979, the United States turned the Canal Zone over to the nation of Panama but continued to run the canal jointly with Panama. On December 31, 1999, the Canal itself was returned to Panama. By 2000, the Canal had less strategic and economic value because many commercial and naval ships were too large to pass through the locks.

The United States and World War I

World War I began in Europe in 1914 and lasted until 1918. The United States did not enter the war until 1917. The financial and human costs of this devastating conflict were enormous.

Causes of World War I

There were several factors that led to the outbreak of war in Europe.

Nationalism Strong nationalistic competition had developed among France, Great Britain, Russia, Austria-Hungary, and Germany, especially after the unification of Germany in 1871. There was also ethnic unrest within nations. For instance, the Czechs and Slovaks wanted to free themselves from Austro-Hungarian control.

Imperialism Several nations were involved in keen competition for markets and colonies throughout the world.

The Alliance System As national and imperial goals conflicted, two groups of nations organized against each other in an effort to maintain a balance of power. The Triple Alliance consisted of Germany, Austria-Hungary, and Italy. The Triple Entente was made up of France, Russia, and Great Britain. If fighting were to break out, members of either alliance were pledged to help each other. When the war began, Italy did not join with the Triple Alliance and in 1915 became a part of the Triple Entente.

Militarism The early 1900s witnessed a continual buildup of armies and navies. Germany, for instance, tripled naval construction in order to challenge Great Britain's control of the seas.

Preparing for the Exam

Before understanding how the United States became involved in World War I, it is important to review the basic causes of that war which began in 1914.

What is an example to support each of the causes of World War I?

Nationalism:

Industrialism:

Imperialism:

Alliances:

Militarism:

The United States and World War I

1910	1911	1912	1913	1914	1915	1916	1917	1918	1919	1920

1913 Civil war erupts in Mexico

1915 Germans sink *Lusitania*

1917 U.S. enters war; Espionage Act passed

1919 Senate rejects Treaty of Versailles

1914 War begins in Europe

1916 Germany suspends submarine attacks

1918 Fourteen Points announced; Germany surrenders

United States Entry into World War I

War broke out in Europe in July 1914, after the heir to the Austro-Hungarian throne was assassinated. Because of the alliance system, most major European nations soon joined the conflict. The United States was officially neutral. In 1917, however, the United States was drawn into the war. There were several reasons for this.

Cultural and Ethnic Links Few Americans were truly neutral. Some sympathized with the Central Powers, dominated by Germany and Austria-Hungary. These included German-Americans because of ties to Germany and Irish-Americans because of anti-British feeling. The majority of Americans, however, favored the Allies, or the Triple Entente nations. Americans had long-standing cultural ties with Great Britain. Many also felt loyalty to our first ally, France.

Geography in History

Stimulus Based Question Examine the map at right, then answer the following questions.

- Which nations were the Allied Powers?

- Which were the Central Powers?

- Which nations remained neutral?

How did geographic location influence a nation's choice of sides?

Europe During World War I: 1914–1918

Economic Ties United States links to the Allies were economic as well as cultural. A British blockade of the North Sea effectively ended American exports to Germany, which dropped in value from about $345 million in 1914 to $29 million in 1916. Meanwhile, the value of trade with the Allies increased fourfold. American business and agriculture benefited from this trade, much of it financed by U.S. government loans to the Allies, totaling more than $2 billion by 1917.

Most Americans did not believe that trade with or loans to the Allies violated the nation's neutrality. In fact, President Wilson and his closest advisers were in favor of the Allies. However, even in the 1916 election for president, Wilson continued to proclaim American neutrality, campaigning on the slogan "He kept us out of war."

Propaganda Aided by their control of the transatlantic cable, the Allies conducted an effective propaganda campaign in the United States. They pictured the war as one of civilized, democratic nations against the barbaric monarchy of Germany.

Freedom of the Seas and German Submarine Warfare In 1915, determined to use its submarines to stop trade between the Allies and the United States and to break the British blockade, Germany announced a war zone around Great Britain. The German U-boats would sink enemy ships in the war zone. To avoid attack by error, neutral nations and their citizens should avoid the zone. Because a submarine is very vulnerable when surfaced, Germany ignored international law that required that a warship to stop and identify itself, then board a merchant or passenger ship and remove its crew and passengers before sinking it.

Germany's attempt to destroy the British blockade by attacking Allied ships was the single most important reason for American entrance into the war. Wilson insisted that America as a neutral nation had the right to trade with nations at war and to send its civilians on ships into war zones. He was defending the principle of freedom of the seas. This is the right of all nations to unrestricted travel in international waters in times of peace, except when limits are placed by international agreements, and the right of neutral nations to trade and its citizens to travel during war as well. The United States defense of this principle was a factor in the undeclared war with France in 1798, the Barbary Wars (1801–1805), the War of 1812, and World War I.

NOTICE!

TRAVELLERS intending to embark on the Atlantic voyage are reminded that a state of war exists between Germany and her allies and GreatBritian and her allies; that the zone of war includes the waters adjacent to the British Isles; that, in accordance with formal notice given by the Imperial German Government, vessels flying the flag of Great Britian, or of any of her allies, are liable to destruction in those waters and that travellers sailing in the war zone on ships cf Great Britian cr her allies do so at their own risk.

IMPERIAL GERMAN EMBASSY,
WASHINGTON, D. C., APRIL 22, 1915.

CUNARD

EUROPE VIA LIVERPOOL

LUSITANIA

Fastest and Largest Steamer now in Atlantic Service Sails
SATURDAY, MAY 1, 10 A. M.
Transylvania - Fri., May 7, 5P.M.
Orduna. - - - Tues., May 18, 10 A.M.
Tuscania, - - - Fri., May 21, 5 P.M.
LUSITANIA, - Sat., May 29, 10 A.M.
Transylvania, - - 5 P.M.

Events of 1917 Lead to War A series of events early in 1917 finally led to America's entry into World War I.

- On February 1, Germany announced a policy of unrestricted submarine warfare. It warned it would attack without warning all vessels headed for Allied ports. The main reason for Germany's decision was that the war was at a stalemate. Germany knew that its move would probably bring the United States into the war. However, Germany believed its U-boats, or submarines, could break the blockade and defeat the Allies before the United States could get troops to the battlefields.

- Two days later, the United States broke diplomatic relations with Germany. Tension and suspicion increased with the Zimmermann note of March 1. This was a message from the German foreign secretary, Arthur Zimmermann, to the German minister in Mexico. It urged a German military alliance with the Mexicans, promising them support in regaining their "lost territories" in the southwestern United States. When the message was made public, Americans reacted angrily.

- Five U.S. merchant ships were sunk by the Germans in March.

- Also in March, the Russian Revolution overthrew the czar. It appeared that more democratic forces would take control in Russia, so that if the United States went to war, it would be joining an alliance of democratic nations.

Role of the United States in the War

Preparedness The United States entered World War I on the side of the Allies in April 1917. But earlier, in 1916, passage of the National Defense Act and the Navy Act began the expansion of the armed forces. The 1916 Revenue Act was also passed to pay for military expansion.

The Draft Issue Even before the entrance of the United States into World War I, the question of how to raise an army was being debated. Those favoring the draft saw it as being fair and democratic, with all Americans serving together. Those opposed to the draft—who preferred that military service be voluntary—viewed the draft as an example of the rich and educated exercising power over the poor, the working class, and immigrants. In May 1917, Congress passed the Selective Service Act, which established a draft. Eventually all males between the ages of 18 and 45 had to register. The constitutionality of the draft was challenged but upheld by the Supreme Court.

American Expeditionary Force By the end of the war, 4.8 million Americans had served in the armed forces, 2.8 million of them draftees. Eventually, over 2 million Americans served in France in a separate command, the American Expeditionary Force, led by General John J. Pershing.

The United States supplied fresh troops to a war in which both sides were exhausted by years of trench warfare. Neither side had moved more than a few miles, but casualties were in the millions. The entry of the United States tipped the scale in favor of the Allies. The United States lost about 51,000 men, far fewer than the millions lost by other nations.

Costs of the War for the Allies

Money Spent

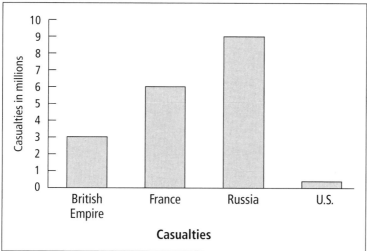

Casualties

Source: V.J. Esposito, A Concise History of World War I

Analyzing Documents

Examine the graphs, then answer the questions that follow.

- Approximately how many casualties did Russia suffer in the war?

- Approximately how much money did the United States spend on the war?

Mobilizing the Economy To get the nation's economy geared up for war, certain economic operations were centralized and concentrated through a series of government agencies. Relying on the broad wartime powers of the president, Wilson used the Council of National Defense to oversee these agencies. Government control over the American economy increased during World War I. For the first time, the government entered fields such as housing and labor relations. It also supervised various public utilities, including the telephone and telegraph. About 16 percent of male workers went into the military, and their jobs were filled by women and African Americans.

Patriotism To President Wilson, World War I was a crusade. He believed that the Allies were fighting the war to end all wars, a war to make the world "safe for democracy." These idealistic goals helped make Wilson the Allies' moral leader. They also helped mobilize the American people to support the first conflict the United States had ever fought outside the Western Hemisphere. The nation geared up for the war with patriotic enthusiasm.

A propaganda campaign organized by the Committee on Public Information encouraged patriotism. Songs, posters, and pamphlets attacked Germany, urged the purchase of Liberty Bonds, and encouraged the conservation of resources.

Reading Strategy

Organizing Information Suppose you were a member of Congress in 1917. You must decide whether the United States should go to war against Germany and the other Central Powers.

- Based on the information from this section, which events would influence your decision?

- How important to your decision is the policy of *Freedom of the Seas*?

Patriotism was accompanied by an outbreak of anti-German and anti-immigrant hysteria. Americans burned German books, banned the teaching of German in some schools, and renamed sauerkraut "liberty cabbage."

A Liberty Bond poster. *Courtesy of The Library of Congress*

Wartime Constitutional Issues

War Opposition Many well-known Americans were against the United States entering the war, including Progressives such as Robert La Follette and Jane Addams. The vote to declare war followed intense Congressional debate. But once committed to the war effort, the nation's social climate was one of patriotism and nativism. These emotions sometimes led to actions that restricted some people's civil rights, usually in the name of national security. In addition to those of German background and immigrants in general, socialists pacifists, and in fact anyone questioning the war, became suspect as possible traitors. Nativism was expressed in a 1917 law passed over Wilson's veto that required a literacy test for immigrants. Its objective was to restrict immigration from Southern and Eastern Europe. It turned out that most could read and write, if not in English, then in the language of their homeland.

The Espionage and Sedition Acts Two broadly worded acts served to control and punish those who opposed the war effort. The Espionage Act of 1917 made it a crime to interfere with the draft and allowed the postmaster general to bar "treasonous" materials from the mail. The Sedition Act of 1918 made it a crime to speak or publish anything "disloyal, profane . . . or abusive" about the government, Constitution, flag, or military services of the United States.

Under these acts, the government prosecuted more than 2,000 Americans and sent 1,500 of them to jail. Pacifists, socialists, and others seen as extremists suffered the most. A special target was the Industrial Workers of the World (IWW), a radical union active in the West. Its leaders were arrested, its strikes broken up, and many of its members interned.

Schenck v. United States In 1919, the Supreme Court ruled that free speech could be restricted during wartime in the landmark case *Schenck v. United States*. In a unanimous decision, Justice Oliver Wendell Holmes wrote, "Free speech would not protect a man falsely shouting "fire" in a theater and causing a panic." Holmes went on to say that Congress has the right to prevent words that would cause "a clear and present danger." That same year, the Court upheld the Sedition Act,

Analyzing Documents

In wartime (particularly during the Civil War, World War I, and World War II), civil liberties were restricted. The Red Scare and McCarthyism that followed each of the world wars also led to violations of certain civil liberties.

"Words can be weapons. . . . The question . . . is whether the words used are used in such circumstances and are of such nature as to create a clear and present danger that will bring about the substantial evils that Congress has a right to prevent."
—Schenck v. United States (1919)

- According to this Supreme Court ruling, under what circumstances was it constitutional to restrict freedom of speech?

- What is the meaning of "to create a clear and present danger" as it is used in the Court decision?

but in that decision the minority expressed concern that freedom of expression was endangered.

The Red Scare 1918–1919 In November of 1917, a second revolution, this time by Bolsheviks, or communists, took place in Russia. The communist system was openly hostile to American values and beliefs, such as capitalism, private ownership of property, and certain freedoms. By 1918, an intense fear of communism swept the United States, and many Americans began to call for the imprisonment or exile of communists in the United States, even though the number of American communists was very small. Fear and distrust of foreigners resulted in targeting of socialists, anarchists, labor leaders, immigrants and others seen as dissidents.

The Search for Peace and Arms Control

World War I ended in November 1918 with an Allied victory. The United States, particularly President Wilson, played a major role in the peacemaking process.

The Fourteen Points

Wilson had first suggested his own peace proposals in January 1918. His Fourteen Points included the following:

- Open, not secret, diplomacy
- Freedom of the seas
- Removal of trade barriers
- Arms reduction
- **Self-determination** of peoples—that is, letting various national groups make their own political decisions
- An "association of nations" to guarantee political independence and territorial integrity

Wilson and the Treaty of Versailles

The Fourteen Points became the basis for the peace negotiations held at Versailles, France, beginning in January 1919. Wilson led the American delegation, thus becoming the first president of the United States to leave American soil while in office. Other Allied leaders included Georges Clemenceau of France, David Lloyd George of Great Britain, and Vittorio Orlando of Italy.

European nations, who had suffered far more than the United States, were cool to Wilson's plans. They wanted to be repaid for some of their losses, and some had made secret wartime deals involving territorial changes and money settlements that contradicted provisions of the Fourteen Points.

The most important agreement reached at Versailles was the treaty with Germany, the Treaty of Versailles. According to its provisions, Germany had to do the following:

- Accept complete responsibility for causing the war
- Pay huge **reparations** to the Allies
- Give up its military forces
- Cede lands to the new nations of Poland and Czechoslovakia
- Give up its overseas colonies

Wilson opposed many of the provisions of the Versailles Treaty and treaties with the other Central Powers. However, he was willing to compromise because the treaties provided for a new world organization, the **League of Nations.** The League, Wilson believed, would correct any problems caused by the peace treaties.

Key Themes and Concepts

Government
- Were Wilson's Fourteen Points a realistic basis for the peace treaty written at Versailles?

- Why did the Senate refuse to ratify the Treaty of Versailles?

- Was the failure to approve the Treaty of Versailles a turning back or a temporary halt in United States foreign policy?

The League of Nations

The United States Senate had to approve the Versailles Treaty that included the League of Nations, and there Wilson met with opposition. Wilson had angered Republicans by excluding them from the American delegation to the Versailles Conference. Yet Republicans had a majority of seats in the Senate. Wilson and the chairman of the Senate Foreign Relations Committee, Henry Cabot Lodge, distrusted and disliked each other. This mutual hostility was a factor in their failure to compromise.

Preparing for the Exam

Examine the cartoon, then answer the following questions.

- Who is the man in the cartoon?

- What does the child represent?

- Who does the man want the child to play with?

- Why does the child want to play by himself?

- What is the point of view of the cartoonist?

- How does the cartoonist's point of view affect the document as a reliable source of evidence?

THE CHILD WHO WANTED TO PLAY BY HIMSELF.
President Wilson: "Now come along and enjoy yourself with the other nice children. I promised that you'd be the life and soul of the party."

Isolationists in the Senate worried that joining the League of Nations would involve the United States in future foreign wars. They feared, for instance, that the United States might be obligated to furnish troops to defend member nations.

Wilson stubbornly refused to allow any but the most minor changes in the Treaty of Versailles. He became increasingly moralistic and uncompromising.

When Wilson went on a speaking tour to gain popular support for the treaty, he collapsed and then suffered a stroke. His illness thereafter prevented him from playing an active role in the treaty debate. The Senate voted several times on the Treaty of Versailles but always defeated it. The United States made a separate peace with Germany, and never did join the League. Fundamentally, the nation had voted to retain its traditional foreign policy of preferring nonintervention and of acting alone when it did choose to play a role.

The Peace Movement: Women's International League for Peace and Freedom

Although the United States failed to join the League of Nations, there was still great concern in the United States about keeping the peace. During the Paris Peace Conference, for example, many American women met with others from around the world to form the Women's International League for Peace and Freedom. Jeannette Rankin, a prominent American pacifist, and reformer Jane Addams were among this group. Addams was voted the first president of the league.

The Women's International League for Peace and Freedom opposed peace terms that would create additional hostility among nations. The organization opposed the Treaty of Versailles for that reason, suggesting that its legacy would only be more war. Peace organizations wanted disarmament, arms control, and neutrality.

Reparations and War Debts

In 1914, the United States had been a debtor nation, meaning that it owed more money to foreign nations than they owed to the United States. After World War I, the United States became the world's leading creditor nation, meaning that other countries owed more to the United States than it owed them. The nation was also the world's leading industrial producer, exporter, and financier. These changes were due in large part to money from the payment of war debts owed this nation by the former Allies.

During World War I, the European Allies borrowed a great deal of money from the United States in order to buy war supplies from American manufacturers. After the war, these debts became a source of conflict. European nations argued that their debts should be canceled because, while the United States had contributed money, Europe had paid a heavy price in lives. Nevertheless, the United States insisted on repayment.

A factor that made repayment difficult was U.S. protectionist policy. High American tariffs limited European trade with the United States and thus reduced earnings that might have been used to pay off war debts. These tariffs also led to retaliation by 26 nations, which raised their own tariff rates.

One step aimed at making repayment easier was the Dawes Plan, adopted in 1924. Under this plan, the United States lent funds to Germany so that it could make war reparations—money it owed to the European Allies as payment for economic losses during the war. The Allies would, in turn, use the funds to make payments on the war debts they owed the United States, as the diagram shows.

Steps Toward Peace and Arms Control

In 1921, President Warren G. Harding hosted the Washington Naval Conference. The United States, Great Britain, France, Italy, and Japan agreed to set limits on the number of warships each nation could build. They also pledged to keep the peace in Asia and to protect the independence of China. The conference, however, failed to establish any means of enforcement.

In 1928, 15 nations met in Paris to sign the Kellogg-Briand Pact, which outlawed war except in self-defense. Enforcement provisions were missing from the pact, which 60 nations eventually signed.

Although the United States never joined the League of Nations or the World Court, it did send observers to League meetings. American judges also served on the World Court, which was based in Geneva, Switzerland.

Postwar Loans and Debts

U.S. loans
$ to Germany

Germany pays reparations to Allies

Allies pay war debts to U.S.

Preparing for the Exam

The history of United States foreign policy can be viewed as a sequence of stages listed below.

- What is always the objective of a nation's foreign policy?

- What are the patterns of continuity and of change in U.S. foreign policy?

1776–1823
Protecting national independence

1824–1897
Fulfilling Manifest Destiny

1898–1918
Emerging global involvement

1919–1940
Limiting international involvement

1941 to the present
Accepting world leadership

Questions for Regents Practice

Multiple Choice

Directions: Review the Test-Taking Strategies section of this book. Then answer the following questions, drawn from actual Regents examinations. For each statement or question, choose the *number* of the word or expression that, of those given, best completes the statement or answers the question.

1   In the late 1800s, which reason led the United States to give greater attention to the world beyond its borders?

(1) fear of revolution in Latin America

(2) fear of Russian expansion in Alaska

(3) interest in finding places to settle surplus population

(4) interest in obtaining markets for surplus goods

2   The United States government economic policy shifted away from laissez faire in the early 1900s. The main reason for this shift was the desire to

(1) increase government ownership of major industries

(2) make the United States more competitive with foreign economies

(3) coordinate the economy for a war effort

(4) reduce the abuses of big business

3   "Third parties in the United States are not . . . especially important in their own right, but only in terms of their influence on the major parties." Which is the most valid conclusion to be drawn from this quotation?

(1) The contribution of third parties has been insignificant in American history.

(2) The ideas of third parties have often been adopted by the two major parties.

(3) Third-party leaders have often become the candidates of the major parties.

(4) Third parties have failed to become important because they have been unable to develop new ideas.

4   Which is the most valid conclusion to be drawn from a study of the role of the Populist, Progressive, and Prohibition Parties in United States history?

(1) Coalition government is a practical idea for United States society.

(2) Improvements for racial minorities are often initiated by third parties.

(3) Third-party platforms are often important in helping to bring about change.

(4) Voters are most greatly influenced by the religious beliefs they hold.

5   In the United States, the term *muckraker* has been used to describe authors whose writings deal mainly with

(1) criticizing the government's social welfare policies

(2) publicizing constitutional issues relating to minorities' rights

(3) advancing the cause of socialism

(4) exposing social conditions in need of reform

6   Which event of the early 1900s is evidence that Upton Sinclair's novel *The Jungle* had an important impact on the United States?

(1) adoption of reform in public education

(2) passage of legislation limiting immigration

(3) adoption of the Eighteenth Amendment establishing Prohibition

(4) passage of legislation requiring federal inspection of meat

7   "All forms of life developed from earlier forms. In every case the fittest survived and the weak died out. It is the same for people and nations." This passage expresses a view most often found in

(1) fundamentalism

(2) Social Darwinism

(3) liberalism

(4) utopian socialism

8   Jacob Riis's photographs and the settlement house movement led by Jane Addams drew attention to the needs of the

(1) former slaves immediately after the Civil War

(2) farmers in the 1880s and 1890s

(3) urban poor in the late nineteenth and early twentieth centuries

(4) Japanese and Chinese laborers in the late 1800s

9   "In the period between the Civil War and World War I, often the first American to greet the sea-weary immigrants when they walked down the gangplank into the United States was a member of the local political machine. This considerate politician helped the immigrant through customs, got him a job, and lent him a few dollars until payday."

The process described in the quotation was a major benefit to the immigrant and to the nation because political machines

(1) encouraged new citizens to vote according to issues, not party labels

(2) helped provide a supply of cheap and willing labor for industry

(3) assisted the social, economic, and political assimilation of immigrants into the community

(4) helped to ensure honest government

10   Western territories were among the first to adopt laws granting political rights to women because the

(1) Native American heritage of matriarchy served as an example to territorial governors

(2) strongest women's rights movements began in the West

(3) settlers brought a tradition of women's suffrage to American homesteads

(4) hardships of pioneer life encouraged men and women to share responsibilities

11   A major purpose of the Federal Reserve System is to

(1) deal with the trade deficit through tariffs and quotas

(2) control the minimum wage

(3) establish the federal budget

(4) regulate interest rates and the money supply

12   The views of W.E.B. Du Bois clashed with those of Booker T. Washington because Du Bois insisted that African Americans should

(1) seek immediate equality of all types and resist any form of second-class citizenship

(2) pursue a policy of gradual integration

(3) accept racial segregation laws because they were constitutional

(4) learn a trade before pursuing political equality

13   Theodore Roosevelt's New Nationalism and Woodrow Wilson's New Freedom were designed primarily to

(1) increase the power and influence of the United States in foreign affairs

(2) reduce the role of government in the economy

(3) help the United States solve problems caused by industrialization

(4) protect the constitutional rights of religious and racial minorities

14 Which statement reflects a foreign policy view held by both President James Monroe and President Theodore Roosevelt?

(1) Revolutionary movements in Western Europe must be stopped.

(2) Close economic ties with Asia must be maintained.

(3) Noninvolvement in world affairs is the wisest policy for the United States.

(4) United States influence in Latin America must be accepted by other countries.

Base your answers to questions 15 and 16 on the excerpt from the Progressive Party platform of 1912 below and on your knowledge of United States history.

"We of the Progressive Party here dedicate ourselves to the fulfillment of the duty laid upon us by our fathers to maintain the government of the people, by the people, and for the people whose foundations they laid. . . .

"To destroy this invisible government, to dissolve the unholy alliance between corrupt business and corrupt politics is the first task of statesmanship of the day."

15 The phrase "invisible government" refers to the power exerted by

(1) the president's Cabinet

(2) the Supreme Court

(3) pressure groups

(4) minority parties in Congress

16 The phrase "government of the people, by the people, and for the people" has been previously stated in the

(1) Declaration of Independence

(2) Bill of Rights

(3) preamble to the Constitution

(4) Gettysburg Address

17 Which pair of terms represents two major causes of imperialism in the Nineteenth Century?

(1) industrialism and communism

(2) communism and fascism

(3) nationalism and industrialism

(4) collectivism and missionary zeal

18 "The Constitution rides behind
And the Big Stick rides before
(Which is the rule of precedent
In the reign of Theodore)."

This rhyme from the early 1900s suggests that President Theodore Roosevelt

(1) relied heavily on the advice of his Cabinet and Congress

(2) failed to make adequate use of executive power

(3) developed strong foreign policies but neglected domestic needs

(4) ignored democratic principles in carrying out foreign policy

19 During the late nineteenth century, some United States newspapers printed exaggerated accounts of Spanish cruelty in Cuba. These reports helped to bring about the Spanish-American War primarily by

(1) arousing public anger against Spain

(2) provoking the anger of the business community

(3) alienating the Spanish government

(4) encouraging the formation of Spanish revolutionary groups

20 In the late nineteenth and early twentieth Centuries, United States intervention in Latin America was motivated mainly by the United States desire to

(1) suppress Latin American movements for national independence

(2) reduce the influence of communism

(3) ensure the safety of its growing investments in the area

(4) counteract Spain's economic dominance of the area

21 The main reason the United States developed the Open Door Policy was to

(1) allow the United States to expand its trade with China

(2) demonstrate the positive features of democracy to Chinese leaders

(3) aid the Chinese nationalists in their struggle with the Chinese communists

(4) encourage Chinese workers to come to the United States

22 The "clear and present danger" ruling in the Supreme Court case *Schenck* v. *United States* (1919) confirmed the idea that

(1) prayer in public schools is unconstitutional

(2) racism in the United States is illegal

(3) interstate commerce can be regulated by state governments

(4) constitutional rights are not absolute

23 The main objective of President Woodrow Wilson's Fourteen Points was to

(1) establish a military alliance with European nations

(2) punish Germany for causing World War I

(3) provide for a just and lasting peace

(4) encourage open immigration in industrial nations

24 "Why, by interweaving our destiny with that of any part of Europe, entangle our peace and prosperity in the toils of European ambition, rivalship, interest, humor, or caprice?"

Which action by the United States best reflects the philosophy expressed in this quotation?

(1) passage of legislation restricting immigration

(2) rejection of the Treaty of Versailles

(3) enactment of the Lend-Lease Act

(4) approval of the United Nations Charter

25 "The chief opponents of the Versailles Treaty were dead men: Washington, Jefferson, and Madison."

This statement suggests that opposition in the United States to the Versailles Treaty was based on the

(1) rejection of Woodrow Wilson's Fourteen Points

(2) fear that the treaty would violate the tradition of noninvolvement

(3) belief that the treaty was too harsh on the Central Powers

(4) unhappiness of citizens with United States participation in World War I

26 The greatest contribution of the United States to world peace during the period between World War I and World War II was

(1) support of the League of Nations

(2) support of the disarmament movement

(3) membership in the World Court

(4) adoption of free trade

Thematic Essay Question

Directions: Write a well-organized essay that includes an introduction, several paragraphs addressing the task below, and a conclusion.

Theme: **Foreign Policy**

> The primary aim of a nation's foreign policy is the self-interest of that nation. Throughout United States history, certain foreign policy actions have led to debate over whether they were in the national interest.

Task:

> From your study of United States history, identify *two* foreign policy actions that have led to debate over whether they were in the national interest.
> For *each* foreign policy action identified:
>
> - Discuss the historical circumstances that led the United States to take a specific foreign policy action
> - Describe the foreign policy action that was taken
> - Describe the opposing viewpoints about the role of national self-interest in that action
> - Evaluate whether the action taken succeeded in promoting the national self-interest

You may use any major controversial foreign policy action from your study of United States history. Some suggestions you might wish to consider include: War of 1812; Mexican War (1846–1848); acquisition of the Philippines (1898–1902); Roosevelt Corollary to the Monroe Doctrine (1904); Treaty of Versailles (1919); Lend-Lease Act (1941); Vietnam War; Persian Gulf Crisis (1990–1991).

You are not limited to these suggestions.

Guidelines:

In your essay, be sure to
- Develop all aspects of the task
- Support the theme with relevant facts, examples, and details
- Use a logical and clear plan of organization, including an introduction and a conclusion that are beyond a simple restatement of the theme.

In developing your answer, be sure to keep these general definitions in mind:

(a) **describe means "to illustrate something in words or tell about it"**
(b) **discuss means "to make observations about something using facts, reasoning, and arguments; to present in some detail"**
(c) **evaluate means "to examine and judge the significance, worth, or condition of; to determine the value of"**

Document-Based Question

In developing your answers, be sure to keep this general definition in mind:

> discuss means "to make observations about something using facts, reasoning, and argument; to present in some detail.

This question is based on the accompanying documents. The question is designed to test your ability to work with historical documents. Some of the documents have been edited for the purposes of the question. As you analyze the documents, take into account the source of each document and any point of view that may be presented in the document.

Historical Context:

As the United States transformed into an industrialized nation, the effects of this massive change were felt at all levels of society. Industrialization had long-term social, economic, and political effects on American society.

Task: Using information from the documents and your knowledge of United States history and government, answer the questions that follow each document in Part A. Your answers to the questions will help you write the Part B essay in which you will be asked to:

> • Discuss the social, economic, and political reactions to industrialization and urbanization in the United States from 1890 to 1920

Part A: Short Answer

Document #1

> *Today three-fourths of [New York's] people live in tenements. . . . The gang is the ripe fruit of tenement-house growth. It was born there, endowed with a heritage of instinctive hostility to restraint by a generation that sacrificed home to freedom, or left its country for its country's good. . . . New York's tough represents the essence of reaction against the old and the new oppression, nursed in the rank soil of its slums.*
>
> — Jacob Riis, *How the Other Half Lives*, 1890

1. According to Jacob Riis, what problems developed as a result of urbanization?

_____

_____

Document-Based Question

Document #2

> *I insist that the true object of all true education is not to make men carpenters, it is to make carpenters men. . . .*
> *The Talented Tenth of the Negro race must be made leaders of thought and missionaries of culture among their people.*
> *No others can do this work and Negro colleges must train men for it.*
>
> **— W.E.B. Du Bois**

2. According to Du Bois, what should be the role of well-educated African Americans in society?

_____

_____

_____

Document #3

Reform	Before the Reform	After the Reform
Primary	Party leaders pick candidates for state and local offices	Voters select party's candidates
Initiative	Only members of state legislatures can introduce bills	Votes can put bills before state legislatures
Referendum	Only legislators pass laws	Voters can vote on bills directly
Recall	Only courts or legislatures can remove corrupt officials	Voters can remove elected officials from office

3. State one way in which Progressive legislation granted citizens greater participation in state governments.

_____

_____

_____

Document #4

> It shall be unlawful for any person engaged in commerce . . . to discriminate in price between different purchasers of commodities of like grade and quality . . . where the effect of such discrimination may be substantially to lessen competition or tend to create a monopoly. . . .
>
> No person engaged in commerce . . . shall acquire . . . the whole or any part of the stock . . . where in any line of commerce or in any activity affecting commerce in any section of the country, the effect of such acquisition may be substantially to lessen competition, or to tend to create a monopoly.
>
> — Clayton Antitrust Act

4. What effect did the Clayton Antitrust Act have on monopolies such as Standard Oil?

_____

_____

_____

Document #5

Value of United States Exports, 1870–1920

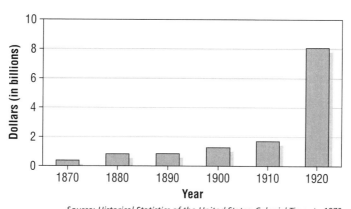

Source: *Historical Statistics of the United States, Colonial Times to 1970*

5. Based on this graph and your knowledge of United States history, how did industrialization affect the activity of American businesses in international markets?

_____

_____

_____

Document-Based Question

Part B

Essay

Directions: Write a well-organized essay that includes an introduction, several paragraphs, and a conclusion. Use evidence from *at least **three*** documents in your essay. Support your response with relevant facts, examples, and details. Include additional outside information.

Historical Context:

As the United States transformed into an industrialized nation, the effects of this massive change were felt at all levels of society. Industrialization had long-term social, economic, and political effects on American society.

Task:

Using information from the documents and your knowledge of United States history and government, write an essay in which you:

> - Discuss the social, economic, and political reactions to industrialization and urbanization in the United States from 1890 to 1920

Guidelines:

In your essay, be sure to

- Address all aspects of the task.
- Develop all aspects of the task
- Incorporate information from *at least **three*** documents
- Incorporate relevant outside information
- Support the theme with relevant facts, examples, and details
- Use a logical and clear plan of organization, including an introduction and conclusion that are beyond a restatement of the theme.

At Home and Abroad:
Prosperity and Depression, 1917–1940

Section 1: **War and Prosperity: 1917–1929**

Section 2: **The Great Depression**

Unit Overview

During the 1920s and 1930s, the United States completed the transition to a modern, urban, industrial nation. In the 1920s, the United States experienced sharp differences in income levels and shifts in cultural values, which created tensions in society and raised issues of civil liberties. At the end of that decade, the nation and the world plunged into a severe economic depression. President Franklin D. Roosevelt's New Deal programs in the 1930s attempted to overcome the effects of the Great Depression in the United States.

Some key questions to help you focus on America between the wars include:

• What tensions developed between the people who were a part of the traditional rural culture and those who were members of the new, urban-based society in the 1920s?

• What were the causes of the Great Depression, and how did that event affect the American people and their institutions?

War and Prosperity: 1917–1929

Section Overview

The 1920s were a time of many changes in the economic and social aspects of life in the United States. Following World War I, the United States struggled to return to what President Harding called "normalcy." However, the impact of the war, the new age of consumerism, the automobile, and the growth of the suburbs contributed to the creation of a different and new national lifestyle.

While transportation and communications technology served to unite the nation, a clash of values between the new urban-centered life and the legacy of the traditional rural life caused uneasiness and conflict. In addition, all Americans did not share in the good times. Beneath the surface was an economy with structural flaws that brought the Roaring Twenties to an abrupt end with the stock market crash in October 1929.

Key Themes and Concepts

As you review this section, take special note of the following key themes and concepts:

Diversity How did World War I affect women and minorities?

Factors of Production Were the 1920s a period of business boom or false prosperity?

Culture and Intellectual Life What social changes caused a clash of values during the twenties?

Science and Technology In the 1920s, how did new technology lead to social, economic, and political changes?

Citizenship In the 1920s, why were the civil liberties of socialists, anarchists, labor leaders, foreigners, Catholics, and African Americans threatened?

Key Terms

Great Migration	flapper	Eighteenth
normalcy	Harlem Renaissance	Amendment
mass consumption	Jazz Age	Twenty-first
assembly line	Red Scare	Amendment
consumer goods	quotas	Scopes Trial

Key People

As you review this section, take special note of the following key people:

Warren G. Harding	Ernest Hemingway	Sinclair Lewis
Calvin Coolidge	Langston Hughes	A. Mitchell Palmer
Henry Ford	Zora Neale Hurston	Nicola Sacco
F. Scott Fitzgerald	Edward K. "Duke" Ellington	Bartolomeo Vanzetti

The Impact and Aftermath of War

World War I triggered a number of important changes in American society, most notably for some women and for many immigrants and African Americans. Some changes were subtle and gradual while others were immediate and dramatic.

The Twenties

1920	1921	1922	1923	1924	1925	1926	1927	1928	1929	1930

1921 Emergency Quota Act passed; Washington Conference began

1924 Teapot Dome Scandal indictments; National Origins Act; Coolidge elected president

1926 U.S. Marines oversee Nicaragua elections

1928 U.S. signs Kellogg-Briand Pact

1920 Warren G. Harding elected president

1923 Calvin Coolidge succeeds Harding

1925 Scopes Trial

1927 Sacco and Vanzetti executed

1929 Stock Market crash

Preparing for the Exam

Based on the timeline:

- What event on the timeline is an example of a clash of values?

Effects on Women and Minorities

As many men went off to fight in Europe, the roles and responsibilities of women were affected. Their family responsibilities increased. They contributed to the war effort as volunteers. Some women went to work in male-dominated fields, such as weapons factories. Many women served overseas with the Red Cross and the Salvation Army. Most, however, worked in traditionally female jobs, for which there was an increased demand. Only about five percent of the women entering the wartime workforce were new to work outside the home. At war's end, with the return of male workers, women were expected to quit their jobs or return to more traditional female work. Between 1910 and 1920, only 500,000 more women were added to the workforce.

The war had harsh consequences for immigrant families. Further immigration to the United States came to a halt. About 18 percent of the American troops were foreign-born. Yet, many immigrant families already in the country faced fierce social and job discrimination in an antiforeign climate whipped up by the war.

Most African American civil rights leaders supported World War I, and some 400,000 African American troops served in it. African American soldiers were assigned to segregated units and often worked as laborers. Discrimination was common.

Preparing for the Exam

Examine the graphic below and use your knowledge of social studies to answer the following questions.

- What was the impact of post World War I conditions on different groups in American society?

- How did American business respond to the post World War I economic slowdown?

- Did any of these conditions exist after World War II? If so, what actions were taken in the late 1940s and 1950s?

After World War I

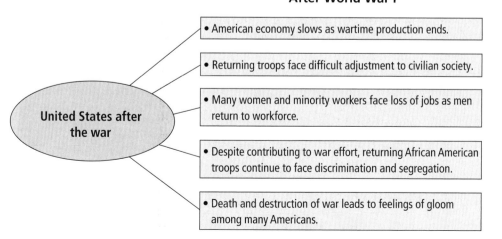

- American economy slows as wartime production ends.
- Returning troops face difficult adjustment to civilian society.
- Many women and minority workers face loss of jobs as men return to workforce.
- Despite contributing to war effort, returning African American troops continue to face discrimination and segregation.
- Death and destruction of war leads to feelings of gloom among many Americans.

United States after the war

After World War I, many Americans faced a difficult adjustment to peacetime life.

Geography
in History

- Who participated in the Great Migration to the North from 1910 to 1930 and again in the 1940s?

- What were the causes of it?

- What were the effects of it?

Election of 1920

Republican Warren G. Harding 76% of electoral vote

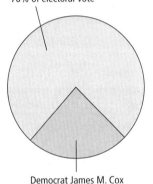

Democrat James M. Cox 24% of electoral vote

Analyzing
Documents

Interpreting Evidence

"America's present need is not heroics, but healing, not nostrums [remedies] but normalcy, not revolution but restoration, not surgery but serenity."
—Warren G. Harding

Examine the pie graph and the quotation.

- How does the pie graph support the statement that the 1920 election was a landslide in favor of "normalcy"?

Where they saw combat, African American soldiers served with distinction. Several African American regiments fighting alongside of French troops were honored by that nation. Many returning African American soldiers questioned why the liberties and freedoms they had fought to preserve in Europe were denied them in their own country.

Migration to the North

World War I accelerated the migration of African Americans to northern cities. This migration began after the Civil War. From about 1910 to 1920, southern agricultural jobs were lost to floods and to crop damage. About 500,000 African Americans moved from the South to jobs in the industrial North. Meanwhile in the North, workers were needed to meet war production goals. The flow of immigrant labor was ended by the fighting, creating an additional need for workers to replace those in uniform.

After the war, this **Great Migration** continued. Between 1910 and 1930 and again in the 1940s, almost two million African Americans left the South. Although they were usually able to improve their economic situation, they were still faced with discrimination and segregation. Competition for jobs and housing produced racial tensions that at times led to individual violence and to riots.

The "Return to Normalcy," 1918–1921

After World War I, disillusioned Americans wanted to return to the traditional foreign policy of isolationism. The 1920 landslide election of Republican President Warren G. Harding and Vice President Calvin Coolidge represented the desire of many Americans to remove themselves from the pressures of world politics and the idealistic goals of the Progressives. While Progressivism continued, it was at a slower pace and reforms took place largely at the state and local levels.

The 1920s: Business Boom or False Prosperity?

For many Americans, postwar life did return to **normalcy.** Yet beneath the surface, troubling political and economic problems had begun to develop.

Greed and Scandal Under Harding

Harding was an Ohio newspaper publisher with little experience in politics. Historians credit him for pardoning socialist Eugene V. Debs (who had been jailed for opposing the war) and for supporting antilynching legislation. Harding appointed some dedicated people to office, including Charles Evans Hughes as secretary of state.

However, the president also gave political jobs to members of the so-called Ohio Gang, corrupt associates who took advantage of him. After Harding's death in 1923, the public learned of several scandals during his administration.

- *Theft:* The head of the Veterans Bureau was convicted of selling hospital supplies for his own profit. He was imprisoned and fined.
- *Fraud:* The Alien Property Custodian was imprisoned for selling former German property for private profit.
- *The Teapot Dome Scandal:* Secretary of the Interior Albert Fall was convicted of accepting bribes from two oil executives in exchange for allowing them to lease government-owned petroleum reserves. One of the oil fields was at Teapot Dome, Wyoming.

Under Coolidge, Prosperity for Some

Calvin Coolidge became president when Harding died in office in 1923. In the 1924 election, Coolidge was returned to office. Coolidge is best known for his laissez-faire approach to the economy and his strong commitment to business interests. Coolidge retained financier Andrew Mellon as secretary of the treasury. Mellon acted on the philosophy that government's role was to serve business.

Recession The end of World War I was followed by a recession caused by the shift from a wartime to a peacetime economy. Production, farm income, and exports fell. Unemployment rose, reaching 11.7 percent in 1921. For farmers, in particular, hardship continued throughout the decade.

Calvin Coolidge

Election of 1924

Republican Calvin Coolidge
72% of electoral vote

Democrat
John W. Davis
26% of electoral vote

Progressive Party
Robert M. La Follette
2% of electoral vote

Recovery In other sectors of the economy, however, a period of economic recovery had begun by 1923, when Coolidge became President. The years between 1923 and 1929 were seen as a time of booming business. The Gross National Product (GNP) rose 40 percent. Per capita income went up 30 percent. With little inflation, actual purchasing power—and therefore the standard of living—increased. At the time, few people questioned this Coolidge prosperity.

Pro-Business Policies Some groups, especially big corporations and the wealthy, benefited greatly from Coolidge prosperity. For example:

- businesses and the wealthiest citizens were helped by tax laws that reduced personal income tax rates, particularly for upper income groups, removed most excise taxes, and lowered corporate income taxes.

- the government reduced the national debt and balanced the budget by raising tariffs and demanding repayment of war debts.

- tariff rates were raised in a return to protectionism. Republicans argued that higher tariffs would limit foreign imports, thus protecting United States industry and agriculture from foreign competition, but the actual effect was to weaken the world economy.

- regulatory agencies such as the Federal Reserve Board, the Federal Trade Commission, and the Interstate Commerce Commission were staffed with people who saw their role as assisting business rather than regulating it.

- a relaxed attitude toward corporate mergers was supported by the executive branch and by the Supreme Court. By 1929, about 1,300 corporations produced three fourths of all American manufactured goods, and 200 companies owned half the nation's wealth.

Economic Boom Bypasses Others

Coolidge prosperity was not for everyone. Key segments of the population failed to share in the general rise in living standards.

Labor Strikes had dropped sharply during World War I, mainly because the Wilson government supported collective bargaining in return for a no-strike pledge. Membership in the American Federation of Labor grew, and wages for war industry employees rose sharply. However, inflation wiped out any real gains in buying power.

Preparing for the Exam

Economics in History
Use economic indicators to analyze the state of the economy in the 1920s.

The **Gross National Product** (GNP) is the total value of all goods and services produced in one year.

Per Capita Income means income per individual; it is based on the national income divided by the population.

- Analyze how the government economic policies of the 1920s affected the GNP and PCI.

Reading Strategy

Reading for Evidence
What evidence is presented in the text to support the following statement?

"Important segments of the population failed to share in the general rise in living standards."

Factors of Production
The term used to describe the resources used to make all goods and services is the *factors of production*. The three factors of production are land, labor, and capital.

- *Land* refers to all natural resources needed to produce goods and services. Land includes coal, water, or farmland.

- *Labor* is the paid effort that a person devotes to a task. Labor can include the medical aid provided by a doctor as well as the tasks performed by an assembly-line worker.

- *Capital* is any human-made resource used to produce other goods and services. Physical capital includes factory buildings and tools, while human capital includes workers' knowledge and experience.

The 1920s saw a reversal of any union gains. Strikes in the steel, mining, and railroad industries failed, in part because the government used not only troops to end the strikes but also injunctions, which are court orders that prohibit specified actions. The Supreme Court also ruled against child labor laws and against minimum wages for women and children. In addition, some companies began to offer health and life insurance in hopes of lessening workers' interest in unions. The strategy often worked. Membership in labor unions fell from a high of about 5 million in 1921 to under 3.5 million in 1929.

While the labor movement weakened in the 1920s, conditions improved for many workers. After 1923, unemployment averaged 5 percent or less. Worker productivity rose over 40 percent. In general, however, real wages for workers increased only slightly during this period, boosted primarily by wages of workers in the new industries such as communications and automobile manufacturing. This situation meant that they could not afford to buy many of the new consumer goods.

Farmers The only farmers to benefit from Coolidge prosperity were those involved in large commercial operations. Small farmers were hurt by a combination of factors.

- Farmers expanded production during World War I in response to rising prices and the demand for food. They added to their acreage and bought more farm machinery.
- New machinery and new farm techniques increased farmers' crop yield per acre.
- After the war, when European farms began producing again, American farmers were growing too much. With overproduction the prices of both farm products and farmland decreased dramatically.
- Net farm income fell 50 percent during the 1920s. As farm income fell, many farmers lost their land when they could not make their mortgage payments. As a result, the number of farmers declined, too. By 1930, only about 20 percent of the labor force made a living by farming.

Native Americans During the 1920s, Native Americans had the highest unemployment rate of any group and the shortest average life span. Most lived on reservations, without the basics, such as heat and running water.

African Americans African Americans who migrated to the North enjoyed a higher standard of living than in the South. However, they still earned less than white workers and experienced a higher rate of unemployment.

Stock Market Speculation
The economic recovery helped produce a surge of investment in the stock market. Optimistic business and government leaders saw no end to the boom. They encouraged everyone to play the bull market—that is, the rising stock market. Some families invested their life savings. The profits rolled in—for a while.

Yet the new wealth flowed from a stock market with a deeply flawed structure. Many stocks were traded on margin. This meant that buyers could purchase stocks by making only small down payments in cash—sometimes as low as 5 percent of the value of the stocks. They borrowed the rest from brokers and counted on their profits to repay the loans. The system worked as long as the profits continued.

Mass Consumption

The 1920s were a time of mass consumption—huge quantities of manufactured goods were available, and many people had more money to spend on them.

The Effects of New Industries on American Life

The Automobile Industry:
1. stimulated the steel, rubber, paint, glass, and oil industries
2. accelerated a middle-class move to the suburbs that fueled a real estate boom
3. led to an increase in highways and a decline in railroad construction and use
4. caused tractors to replace horses on farms
5. increased social equality as low prices made cars available to Americans at almost all income levels
6. stimulated installment buying
7. contributed to growing sophistication of advertising techniques
8. expanded cities into larger urban areas
9. stimulated development of services such as gas stations, motels, supermarkets, and shopping malls
10. gave greater independence to women and teenagers, changing family life

The Electrical Industry:
1. changed homes, businesses, and cities through electric lights
2. helped double business productivity through electric power
3. transformed life and leisure with electric-powered durable goods such as washing machines, stoves, vacuum cleaners, refrigerators, and irons
4. stimulated installment buying
5. connected people and eased rural isolation through the telephone

Radio and Motion Pictures:
1. helped erase regional differences and homogenize American culture
2. increased people's expectations, often unrealistically
3. helped end rural isolation
4. helped popularize ragtime and jazz
5. provided an outlet for advertising
6. increased interest in politics and spectator sports
7. created nationally known celebrities—stars of radio, sports, and movies

Role of Technology

Technology, combined with new marketing strategies, best explains the transformation of American society in the 1920s. Led by Henry Ford and the automobile industry, mass production and the moving **assembly line** resulted in uniform products produced at lower costs.

These new technologies made possible a consumer-oriented economy, one in which more goods, costing less, were available to more Americans. Encouraged by a boom in advertising, families spent a smaller portion of their income on necessities and a larger proportion on new **consumer goods** such as appliances, radios, and ready-to-wear clothing. Often these goods were purchased over time through installment buying.

Growing Cultural Homogenization

The new technology also made American culture more homogeneous, or uniform. Americans from one coast to the other tended to use the same products, wear the same styles, see the same movies, and listen to the same music. Regional and class differences were blurred, and individualism became less important than conformity.

Cars on a city street

Source: *Courtesy of the Library of Congress*

Suburban Growth

With over half the population living in places with populations of more than 2,500 people, the United States in the 1920s was an urban rather than a rural nation for the first time in its history. Only the Great Depression ended the building boom that was part of this growth. The automobile made it possible to draw people to suburbs that grew even faster than cities. New regional, political, and economic units developed, resulting in the present-day conflict between urban and suburban needs, priorities, and values.

Shifting Cultural Values

During the 1920s, American society experienced a struggle with social change as it became an urban, industrial nation. Changes in lifestyle, values, morals, and manners increased tension and conflict. Wealth, possessions, having fun, and sexual freedom—ideas influenced by the psychology of Sigmund Freud—were the new values.

Leisure With a shorter work week and with more paid vacation, Americans had more leisure time. Movies such as *The Ten Commandments* and the first movie with sound, *The Jazz Singer*, drew millions of people a week to theaters during the 1920s. Americans idolized Charlie Chaplin and other movie stars. They also admired sports figures, such as Babe Ruth. After his 1927 solo transatlantic flight, Charles Lindbergh became an overnight hero. Listening to the radio and to records were two other popular pastimes. Games such as bridge, crossword puzzles, and the board game of mah-jongg swept the country.

The popular image of young women in the 1920s was the **flapper,** a young, pretty woman with bobbed hair and raised hemlines. She drank alcohol, she smoked, and she thought for herself.

Analyzing Documents

- What information from the graph helps you to gain a more complete picture of the effect of the automobile industry in the 1920s?

Passenger Car Sales, 1920–1929

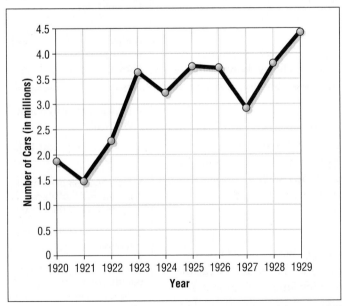

Source: *Historical Statistics of the United States, Colonial Times to 1970*

The flapper was featured in movies, magazines, advertising, and novels, such as those of F. Scott Fitzgerald. The flapper was an expression of women's new sense of independence, a statement of change, even rebellion. As such, the flapper represented another example in the debate over traditional versus modern values that was dividing the nation.

Literature The conflict and concern created by changing American values also saw expression in literature. American writers of the 1920s protested the effects of technology and mass consumption. They criticized the business mentality, the conformity of the times, and the preoccupation with material things. Some writers, such as Ernest Hemingway, became expatriates, leaving the United States to settle in Europe. Often called the Lost Generation, these writers of the twenties produced some of the most enduring works of American literature.

Harlem Renaissance One of the most influential cultural movements of the 1920s was the Harlem Renaissance, led by a group of African American writers in the New York City neighborhood of Harlem. These creative intellectual figures—mainly well-educated members of the middle class—felt alienated from the society of the 1920s. In their works they called for action against bigotry and expressed pride in African American culture and identity. Outstanding literary figures of the Harlem Renaissance include W.E.B. Du Bois, **Langston Hughes,** Zora Neale Hurston, and Alain Locke.

The Great Depression of the 1930s ended the Harlem Renaissance, cutting the sales of books and literary magazines. However, during the civil rights movement of the 1960s, the writers of the Harlem Renaissance and their works attracted renewed interest.

African American artists, musicians, and dancers also participated in the Harlem Renaissance. Black musicians in the South blended elements of African, European, and American music to create the distinctive sounds of jazz and the blues. This music was carried all over the country and abroad.

Edward K. "Duke" Ellington is one of the towering figures in jazz. Ellington recorded and composed music, performed on the piano, and conducted his own orchestra until his death in 1974. Bessie Smith, known as the "Empress of the Blues," was one of the most popular singers of the 1920s. This new music, to which people danced such daring new steps as the Charleston, became so popular that the period of the 1920s is often called the **Jazz Age.**

Leading Writers of the 1920s

Willa Cather	novelist	*My Antonía*
F. Scott Fitzgerald	novelist	*The Great Gatsby*
Ernest Hemingway	novelist	*A Farewell to Arms*
Langston Hughes	poet, novelist	*The Weary Blues*
Zora Neale Hurston	novelist, folklorist	*Their Eyes Were Watching God*
Sinclair Lewis	novelist	*Main Street, Babbitt*
Eugene O'Neill	playwright	*Desire Under the Elms*
Edith Wharton	novelist	*The Age of Innocence*

Women's Changing Roles

The conflict between modern and traditional values in the 1920s also found expression in the contradictory roles of women.

Women in the Workforce Throughout the 1920s, the number of women in the workforce increased steadily. By 1930, 10.7 million women were working outside the home, making up 22 percent of the workforce. Most working women were single, widowed, or divorced. While, by 1930, about one in six married women worked—more than ever before—90 percent continued to remain at home.

By 1930, women earned 40 percent of the bachelor degrees awarded. Many of them became teachers, nurses, and social workers, traditional female occupations. Fewer than 20 percent worked in the better-paying skilled factory jobs. Changes in technology and scientific management created opportunities for women in white-collar and service industry jobs. These low-paying, low-status, and low-mobility-occupations included work as secretaries, salespeople, telephone operators, and beauticians. Because these jobs were labeled "female only," even in hard times, women were able to be hired for these and other new occupations.

One important gain for working women was the creation in 1920 of the Women's Bureau, part of the federal Department of Labor. It tried to improve working conditions for women from inside the government and provided data about working women.

Involvement in Politics In 1920, women voted in a national election for the first time. However, their vote did not have a distinctive effect on the outcome. Women did not vote in large numbers, nor did they vote as a bloc. To encourage women to play a greater part in politics, the National American Woman Suffrage Association reorganized itself as the nonpartisan League of Women Voters.

Health, Rights, and Working Conditions The divisions of the 1920s were reflected in the fate of two pieces of legislation. Encouraged by women reformers, Congress passed the Sheppard-Towner Act in 1921. With the aim of reducing infant mortality, the law provided for public health centers where women could learn about nutrition and health care. The program came to an end in 1929, largely because of opposition from the American Medical Association.

An equal rights amendment to the Constitution, proposed by Alice Paul in 1923, led to bitter disagreement among women. Many feminists supported it, but other feminists opposed it because they believed it would do away with special laws protecting female workers.

Daily Life Contrary to the image of the flapper, women were still restricted by economic, political, and social limits. In some ways, technology made life easier in the 1920s, especially for middle class women. With electric washing machines, vacuum cleaners, stoves, and refrigerators, household chores did not require so much time, and there was less need for servants. On the other hand, the typical homemaker now was expected to handle almost all the household tasks herself and to meet higher standards of cleanliness.

Emphasis on Wife Rather Than Mother The role of the woman as wife received increased importance. Women did have more choices in life. Families changed during this period, and divorce and family planning became more acceptable. However, divorce laws continued to favor men, and wives were expected to stay at home rather than work outside the home. Family size decreased; only 20 percent of women who married during the 1920s had five or more children. The family, which in earlier times had been a producing unit,

Key Themes and Concepts

Diversity
In the 1920s women were workers, flappers, wives, mothers, voters, students, and housewives. In what ways were their lives different from the lives of women during the following periods in history?

- the first half of the nineteenth century
- the second half of the nineteenth century
- the Progressive Era
- World War I
- the Great Depression
- World War II
- the 1950s
- the 1960s and 1970s
- today

growing and processing much of its food, was now a consuming unit. Marketing and advertising appeals flooded the media, encouraging consumers to buy more goods.

Constitutional and Legal Issues

Major constitutional and legal issues divided Americans in the 1920s. Many issues reflected the struggle between modern and traditional values and showed how international affairs affected domestic policies and attitudes. For some Americans, these tensions took the form of nativism, racism, and intolerance of differences in religion and politics.

Threats to Civil Liberties

In the 1920s, the Red Scare and the Ku Klux Klan exploited fears about people who were considered un-American, often threatening their civil liberties.

The Red Scare 1918–1919 The imposition of stern measures to suppress dissent after World War I in a crusade against internal enemies was known as the Red Scare. It was fueled by the November 1917 Bolshevik Revolution, an uprising of Communists in Russia. In the United States, Communists made up only one half of one percent of the population, but many of them were targeted by the crackdown, as were various other groups viewed as un-American. Among them were socialists, anarchists, labor leaders, and foreigners.

The Red Scare was led by Attorney General A. Mitchell Palmer. It was sparked by several events that took place after the war ended. Race riots erupted in more than 25 cities. In Boston, a series of labor strikes climaxed with a walkout by the police. Several unexplained bombings added to the hysteria. All these events were seen as part of a Communist conspiracy.

The attorney general ordered the first so-called Palmer Raids late in 1919. In 33 cities, police without warrants raided the headquarters of Communists and other organizations. Eventually they arrested more than 4,000 people, holding them without charges and denying them legal counsel. Some 560 aliens were deported. Palmer's extreme actions and statements soon turned the public against him. However, the Red Scare had lingering effects, discouraging many Americans from speaking their minds freely in open debate, thus squelching their constitutional right to freedom of speech.

Sacco and Vanzetti Closely linked to the Red Scare was the case of Nicola Sacco and Bartolomeo Vanzetti. These two Italian immigrants—admitted anarchists— were convicted of murder in 1921 in connection with a Massachusetts robbery. Many people questioned the evidence against Sacco and Vanzetti, concluding that the two men were convicted more for their beliefs and their Italian origin than for a crime. In spite of mass demonstrations and appeals, the two men were executed in 1927. The governor of Massachusetts eventually cleared the two men in 1977, some 50 years later.

The Ku Klux Klan Antiforeign attitudes encouraged a revival of the Ku Klux Klan. The first organization, active during Reconstruction, had died out in the late 1800s. A reorganized Klan, formed in 1915, grew slowly until 1920. In that year, it added 100,000 members. The Klan of the 1920s targeted not only African Americans but also Catholics, Jews, and immigrants. To the Klan, the only true Americans were white, Protestant, and American-born. In 1925, membership peaked at two million.

Preparing for the Exam

- What are the similarities and differences in concern about foreigners and foreign ideas during these events in U.S. history? Consider the historical context and the identity of the foreigners.

- Does historical evidence support adding or eliminating any event?

- 1790s: Alien and Sedition Acts

- 1840s: nativism and the Know-Nothings

- 1882 and 1907: Chinese Exclusion Act and Gentlemen's Agreement

- 1917–1918: suppression of dissent during World War I

- 1920s: Ku Klux Klan, Sacco and Vanzetti case, National Origins Quota Acts

- 1940s: internment of Japanese Americans during World War II

- 1950s: McCarthyism

Immigrants at Ellis Island

Restrictions on Immigration

The nativism expressed in the Red Scare, the Sacco-Vanzetti case, and the new Klan was also evident in 1920s immigration legislation. Immigration had resumed after World War I, but there was less of a need for workers. In the post-war recession, immigrants were seen as taking jobs from returning soldiers and somehow threatening American values. The nativist climate led to the Immigration Act of 1924. This act established a system of national **quotas,** which limited the number of immigrants from each country. These quotas deliberately kept the totals for eastern and southern Europe low and excluded all immigration from Asia.

Immigration to the United States, 1921 and 1926

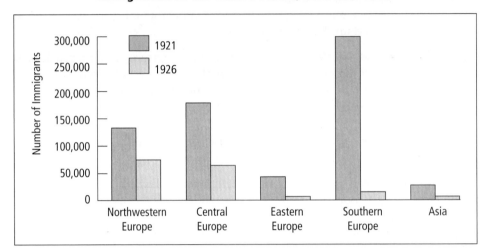

Key Themes and Concepts

Immigration and Migration
During the 1920s, immigration from the western hemisphere was not limited. Large numbers of Mexicans moved into southwestern cities and Puerto Ricans moved into New York City, most in search of economic opportunities.

- What are the most dramatic changes pictured on the chart at right?

- What changes were made to immigration laws in the 1920s? Why?

Preparing for the Exam

- Why did Prohibition turn out to be unenforceable?

- Why is the reaction to the Eighteenth Amendment often compared to the reaction to the 1850 Fugitive Slave Law?

Prohibition

Both the rebirth of the Klan and the movement to restrict immigration reflected the struggle in the 1920s between what some saw as old, rural American values and the new values of a changing urban, industrialized culture. However, the clash between these two sets of values did not divide on the basis of where one lived.

For example, the temperance movement working for Prohibition, a ban on the sale and consumption of alcoholic beverages, was not confined to rural America, though it received much support there. The **Eighteenth Amendment**, allowing Prohibition, became part of the Constitution in 1919. Congress passed the Volstead Act to implement Prohibition, but the law turned out to be unenforceable. Most Americans were simply unwilling to accept a total ban on alcohol. Furthermore, it stimulated crime, encouraging smuggling and bootlegging, the illegal manufacture and sale of alcoholic beverages. In 1933, the **Twenty-first Amendment** ending Prohibition was ratified.

The Scopes Trial

The 1925 Scopes Trial, held in Dayton, Tennessee, received nationwide attention because it pitted the scientific ideas of Darwinian evolution against the Protestant fundamentalist view of biblical creationism. John Scopes, a biology teacher, had deliberately violated a state law forbidding anyone to teach the theory of evolution. Scopes was represented by a famous trial lawyer, Clarence Darrow. The prosecution relied on the assistance of William Jennings Bryan, a three-time presidential candidate and firm believer in fundamentalist Christianity. Although Scopes was convicted and fined $100, Bryan's confused testimony weakened fundamentalist arguments.

The Great Depression

Section Overview

The 1930s were dominated by the Great Depression. Worldwide in scope, the Great Depression affected virtually every aspect of American life. With roots in unregulated stock market speculation, a flawed banking system, and the overproduction of goods, the Great Depression was triggered by the stock market crash in 1929. Banks failed, and many people lost their life savings. The losses shut down businesses, producing widespread unemployment, homelessness, and hunger.

President Herbert Hoover's response to the Great Depression proved ineffective. In 1933, President Franklin D. Roosevelt's New Deal launched ambitious programs of relief, recovery, and reform. The New Deal dramatically increased the role and responsibility of government in American social and economic life and strengthened the power of the presidency. The entry of the United States into World War II in 1941 put a final end to the nation's worst economic collapse. Today, the Great Depression remains the benchmark against which an economic crisis is measured.

Key Themes and Concepts

As you review this section, take special note of the following key themes and concepts:

Factors of Production What were the causes of the Great Depression?

Economic Systems Which New Deal actions were intended to reform the United States economic system?

Government How did the New Deal change the nineteenth-century role of government in the United States?

Culture and Intellectual Life How did the depression affect daily life and culture in America?

Diversity How did the New Deal affect organized labor, minorities, and women?

Key Terms

Great Stock Market Crash	Bonus Army
speculation	Hoovervilles
on margin	Dust Bowl
Great Depression	New Deal
overproduction	bank holiday
underconsumption	collective bargaining
distribution of wealth	court-packing proposal
"trickle down" economics	

The Big Idea

In the 1930s:

- fundamental weaknesses in the national and world economies caused the stock market crash and the Great Depression that followed.

- the Great Depression dominated every aspect of political, social, and economic life of the 1930s.

- President Herbert Hoover's efforts toward economic recovery did not succeed.

- President Franklin Roosevelt's New Deal worked for relief, recovery, and reform.

- the New Deal was based on the belief that government had a responsibility for the social and economic well-being of its citizens.

- President Franklin Roosevelt's New Deal provided relief but only limited recovery, and left a legacy of economic and social reform laws.

Key People

As you review this section, take special note of the following key people:

Herbert Hoover

Eleanor Roosevelt

John Steinbeck

John L. Lewis

Franklin Delano Roosevelt

Mary McLeod Bethune

Frances Perkins

John Maynard Keynes

Harry Hopkins

Huey Long

Key Supreme Court Cases

As you review this section, take special note of the following key Supreme Court case:

Schechter Poultry Corporation v. *United States (1935)*

The Great Depression

1929 Stock market crash; Great Depression begins	1933 New Deal begins; drought on Great Plains; FDIC created	1935 Passed Wagner Act; Social Security Act	1939 *The Wizard of Oz* becomes popular movie	1941 U.S. enters WW II

1929	1931	1933	1935	1937	1939	1941

1932 Jobless veterans march on Washington; F.D. Roosevelt elected president	1934 Indian Reorganization Act passed; SEC created	1938 *War of the Worlds* broadcast; Wages and Hours Act passes	1940 FDR elected to third term

Analyzing Documents

According to the timeline:

- which event on the timeline resulted in a migration of farmers?

- which was a law passed to benefit workers?

- which act was passed to provide a "safety net"?

- which acts were passed to provide banking and investment reform?

The Great Stock Market Crash

The end of the prosperity of the 1920s was marked by a series of plunges in the United States stock market in the fall of 1929 known as the Great Stock Market Crash. Throughout the 1920s, the stock market had grown on **speculation** by people who bought **on margin,** and, in fact, owned only a small portion of their stocks. Many could not meet margin calls, demands to put up the money to cover their loans. The result was panic selling. On October 29 (Black Tuesday) alone, stock values fell $14 billion. They dropped lower and lower in the weeks months, and years that followed, reaching bottom in July 1932. By then the market had fallen 89 percent from its September 1929 high point.

The stock market crash triggered the start of the **Great Depression.** It shattered the national sense of optimism and confidence of the 1920s. The crash dramatically exposed the fact that the national economy had serious weaknesses.

Causes of the Great Depression

The Great Depression was caused by an unsound economy—**overproduction** and **underconsumption,** overexpansion of credit, and fragile corporate structures—combined with ineffective government action. The growing interdependence of international trade and banking made the effects even more damaging.

Reading Strategy

Meaning of Words as Used in a Text
Underconsumption or overproduction means that people buy fewer goods than are produced. In other words, supply is greater than demand.

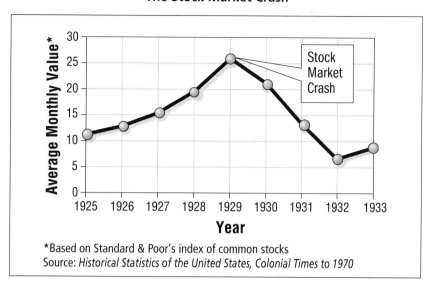

The Stock Market Crash

Stock Market Crash

*Based on Standard & Poor's index of common stocks
Source: *Historical Statistics of the United States, Colonial Times to 1970*

Preparing for the Exam

Stimulus Based Question
Based on the graph and your knowledge of social studies, answer the following questions.

• When did the stock market crash occur?

• In what year did stock prices reach their lowest point?

• What role did speculation play in the crash?

• What is the relationship of the stock market crash to the Great Depression?

Weaknesses in the Overall Economy

Weaknesses in the economy had existed before 1929 and were expanding.

• The agricultural sector had been depressed throughout the 1920s, with a worldwide drop in prices.

• Unemployment plagued the railroad, coal, and textile industries well before 1929.

• Speculation in real estate and the resulting building boom had declined.

• The number of bank failures was rising as farmers, people speculating in stocks, and consumers buying on credit could not repay their loans.

• As early as the summer of 1929, the economy showed signs of underconsumption. Inventories of unsold goods began to accumulate in warehouses as consumer demand slowed.

Unequal Distribution of Income

Contributing to underconsumption and to the weakness of the economy was an unequal distribution of wealth.

• In the 1920s, at a time that a family needed an annual income of $2500 to have a modest standard of living, over 60 percent of American families lived on only $2000 per year—just enough to cover basic needs. Some 40 percent of all families had an income of less than $1,500, which put them below the poverty line. At the same time, the 24,000 richest families in the nation had a total income *three times as large* as the total income of the 6 million poorest families. In short, while 1 percent of the population owned 59 percent of the nation's wealth, 87 percent of the population owned only 10 percent of the wealth.

Income Distribution in the United States, 1929

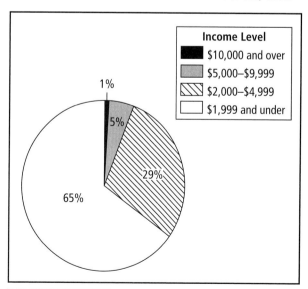

Income Level
■ $10,000 and over
▨ $5,000–$9,999
▨ $2,000–$4,999
□ $1,999 and under

1%
5%
29%
65%

How does the pie graph support the statement that underconsumption contributed to the weaknesses in the economy that led to the depression?

- As a result, the economy was dependent on the spending of a very small portion of the population. These wealthy people spent their money on luxury goods and on investments. This type of spending was greatly affected by the stock market crash.
- The wealthy, not the great mass of the population, had benefited from increased output per worker. With the increased output, production costs had dropped and corporate profits had risen, but overall, wages were stagnant or had increased only slightly. Often workers could not buy what they produced. As a result, demand dropped. As the economy weakened, this non-purchasing group grew in size and became less and less able to buy even the necessities of life.

Excessive Buying on Credit

Excessive buying on credit was one result of these low and unequally distributed wages. The abundance of new products, the sense that these good times would never end, and the availability of easy credit encouraged people to spend money beyond their means. As the economy slowed, people bought less in order to pay their installment loans and home mortgages. This underconsumption led to decreased production and a rise in unemployment.

Weak Corporate Structure

The stock market crash set off the collapse of the nation's business structure. Business consolidations of the 1920s resulted in a few large companies in each industry. Holding companies controlled the stock of many different corporations and depended on the earnings of the various companies they held. This was a very fragile system, because when one company collapsed, it affected—in a domino fashion—the rest of the holding company.

Weak Banking Structure

Some 6,000 banks failed in the 1920s. Many were rural banks that failed when farmers were unable to repay loans. Large banks were also vulnerable because they held inadequate reserves, investing too much in the stock market and making risky loans.

Inadequate Government Policies

Actions by the federal government contributed to the depression.

- Stock market speculation was unregulated by the government.
- Tax policies that favored the wealthy resulted in further uneven distribution of income.
- The consolidation of corporations was not challenged under antitrust laws.
- The Federal Reserve Board allowed a low discount rate—the interest charged to member banks. This policy led to stock speculation. The board then raised interest rates in 1931, discouraging spending at just the time when spending would have helped the economy.

Weak International Economy

The world's economies were affected by the collapse triggered by the crash of the United States stock market. Many European economies had never fully recovered from World War I, and the international economy depended heavily on the economy of the United States.

Foreign nations owed the United States money from World War I that they could repay only after the United States bought their goods and made foreign investments and loans. In June 1930, Congress passed the Hawley-Smoot Act, raising tariffs on agricultural and manufactured goods to the highest levels in

American history. High American tariffs kept out goods from overseas and led to high foreign tariffs. Americans invested at home rather than abroad.

When the economy slowed, the United States made even fewer foreign investments and had less money to lend. This meant that foreign nations had less money to buy American goods and often defaulted on loans. The international nature of the banking system can be seen by the fact that banks in both Europe and the United States failed as a result of defaults on loans.

Some Economic Changes Between 1928 and 1932
(Figures in millions unless otherwise noted)

	1928	1929	1930	1931	1932
A. United States exports (merchandise)	$5,030	$5,157	$3,781	$2,378	$1,576
B. Spending for new housing	$4,195	$3,040	$1,570	$1,320	$485
C. Farm spending for lime and fertilizer	$318	$300	$297	$202	$118
D. Federal spending	$2,933	$3,127	$3,320	$3,578	$4,659
E. Cash receipts from farming	$10,991	$11,312	$9,055	$6,331	$4,748
F. Lumber production (billions of board ft.)	36.8	38.7	29.4	20	13.5
G. Unemployment (in thousands)	2,080	1,550	4,340	8,020	12,060
H. Average weekly earnings of production workers in manufacturing (actual dollars)	$24.97	$25.03	$23.25	$20.87	$17.05

Analyzing Documents

Interpreting Evidence
Examine the chart and then answer the following questions.

- How much did spending for new housing change between 1928 and 1932?

- What does the drop in U.S. exports indicate about the nature of the depression?

- How much did unemployment increase between 1928 and 1932?

- Based on this chart, which year was the economy in its most serious state?

Hoover's Response to the Great Depression, 1929–1933

Herbert Hoover was the president who first had to deal with the deepening depression. Hoover took office in 1929, after serving as Coolidge's secretary of commerce. Like Harding and Coolidge, he believed that the federal government should assist business and limit regulation of it. An engineer by training, Hoover was a good businessman, a self-made millionaire, and a humanitarian. During and after World War I, he had an international reputation as a leader of a successful relief effort to aid starving Europeans and to help Europe recover economically.

Hoover's Economic Plan

In order to improve economic conditions, Hoover:

- tried to restore confidence in the American economy with such statements as "Prosperity is just around the corner."

- altered his view that government should not become directly involved in the economy. He promoted programs that aided businesses, on the theory that as businesses recovered, economic benefits would **trickle down** to the workers and consumers.

- allowed the organization of the Reconstruction Finance Corporation (1932) to lend money to railroads, mortgage and insurance companies, and banks on the verge of bankruptcy.

- set a precedent for Franklin Roosevelt's New Deal when in 1932 the Emergency Relief Construction Act provided for federal works projects to create jobs and stimulate the economy.

- obtained voluntary agreements from businesses not to lower wages or prices. However, as companies increasingly faced collapse, they often could not honor these promises.

- halted the payment of war debts by European nations.

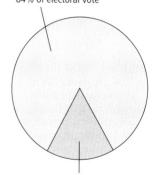

Election of 1928

Republican Herbert C. Hoover
84% of electoral vote

Democrat Alfred E. Smith
16% of electoral vote

"Our Republican leaders tell us economic laws . . . cause panics which no one could prevent. But while they prate of [chatter about] economic laws, men and women are starving . . . I pledge you, I pledge myself, to a new deal for the American people."
—F. D. Roosevelt, 1932

"The urgent question today is the prompt balancing of the budget. When that is accomplished, I propose to support adequate measures for relief of distress and unemployment."
—Herbert Hoover, 1932

Both of these statements were made during the 1932 presidential campaign.

- Which speech has a greater sense of urgency?

- Which man is more optimistic? Why?

- What is the clearest difference in their approach to the Great Depression?

Reading
Strategy

Multiple Causes and Effects
- Evaluate the causes of unemployment during the Great Depression and the multiples effects on individuals, other people, businesses and organizations.

Failure of Hoover's Program

Despite these efforts, Hoover's refusal to provide direct relief damaged his image as the nation's leader. Also damaging was his insistence, in the face of worsening conditions, that the economy was actually improving.

In the summer of 1932, thousands of unemployed World War I veterans and their families set up camps in Washington, D.C. to demand early payment of the bonus due to them for their war service. When the bill was defeated by Congress, many of the **Bonus Army,** as they were called, refused to leave town. Hoover insisted that the veterans were influenced by Communists and other agitators. He called out the army to break up the Bonus Army's camps and disperse the veterans. The newspaper photographs showing tanks and tear gas being used against war veterans destroyed Hoover's remaining popularity as well as his reelection campaign.

Herbert Hoover took many steps to use the power of the federal government to stop the growing depression. In the end, his efforts were too little. It was not until 1932 that he changed some of his views, agreeing to increase federal spending to fight the depression. At the same time, he remained opposed to direct relief for the homeless and unemployed and supported raising taxes to balance the federal budget. Historians still debate whether he should be praised for the efforts he did make or condemned for not going far enough. Hoover's ability to act was limited by his inability to grasp the depth and breadth of the economic crisis and by his beliefs. For example:

- He had great faith in the American economic system, insisting that the forces of the market would eventually set the economy right again.

- He believed in volunteerism and private relief efforts rather than governmental action to solve problems of society.

- He believed in self-help and opposed direct relief on the grounds that it would destroy people's **"rugged individualism."**

The Human Impact of the Great Depression

The Great Depression had a profound effect on all Americans.

Unemployment

By 1932, some 12 million people—25 percent of the American labor force—were unemployed. The human toll was seen in long "bread lines" at soup kitchens. Relief efforts by organizations such as the Red Cross were limited, because voluntary contributions slowed down. As banks failed, people lost their savings; as companies failed, people lost their jobs as well.

African Americans and unskilled workers were the first to experience unemployment. In 1931, African American unemployment was estimated as 30 to 60 percent greater than white unemployment. Women were criticized for working while men could not find jobs. In truth, female occupations, usually in service sectors such as nursing and clerical work, were less affected than positions in manufacturing that were usually given to men. Family life was disrupted as parents looked for ways to stretch what money the family had. Families moved in with relatives. Marriages were postponed. The birth rate dropped, as did college enrollment.

Urban Life

In many cities, families who had lost their homes lived in unheated shacks they had built of cardboard, tin, or crates. These communities became known as **Hoovervilles.** Some people slept under old newspapers called "Hoover blankets."

Unemployment, 1929–1940 (in millions)

- Millions of People (y-axis: 2, 4, 6, 8, 10, 12, 14)
- Years (x-axis): 1929 1930 1931 1932 1933 1934 1935 1936 1937 1938 1939 1940

Annotations on graph:
- Hoover loses bid for second term
- FDR takes office
- World War II starts in Europe
- Stock market crash
- FDR reelected
- Economic downturn begins

Analyzing Documents

Based on the graph, what was the relationship between the unemployment rate and Hoover's defeat in the election of 1932?

Others slept in city parks. People selling apples and shoelaces on the street became a common sight. Cases of malnutrition, tuberculosis, and typhoid increased, as did deaths from starvation and suicide. Parents often went hungry to give what food they had to their children.

Rural Life

With more people unable to buy food, farmers' already depressed income dropped by one half. Farm foreclosure sales grew in number. The farmers' desperate situation only worsened in the 1930s with years of drought in parts of Texas, Oklahoma, Kansas, Colorado, and New Mexico, a region that became known as the **Dust Bowl.** The drought, combined with poor farming methods, resulted in the loss of the topsoil, which was whipped into giant dust storms that swept across the Great Plains. Devastation in the Dust Bowl created a group of migrant farmers called "Okies" who moved to California in search of work. Their sufferings were made famous in John Steinbeck's novel *The Grapes of Wrath.* In 1935, the New Deal passed the **Soil Conservation Act** to help the region.

The Culture of the Great Depression

The sufferings of people during the Great Depression changed the popular culture of the 1930s, as people sought inexpensive and escapist leisure activities.

Spectator sports, especially baseball, remained popular, but fewer people could afford to attend. Instead, they played miniature golf, softball, pinball machines, the new board game Monopoly®, or they read comic books. Dick Tracy was one of the most popular comic strips of the decade.

Geography in History

Human Activities and the Environment
Starting in the late 1800s, farmers using steel plows cut through the thick grasses that covered the Great Plains. They grew wheat in areas too dry to grow corn. After World War I, when farm prices dropped, farmers responded by overfarming—clearing more land and growing more wheat. The 1930s were a decade of drought. For seven years, winds blew the top soil, no longer protected by the grass cover, east from New Mexico, Texas, Oklahoma, Colorado, and Kansas to the Atlantic and beyond. Sixty percent lost their farms.

- How do the problems of farmers in the 1920s and 1930s compare with farmers' problems of the the 1880s, the 1950s, the 1980s, and today?

A bread line

Reading Strategy

Formulating Questions
Reread the section about the culture of the Great Depression, then answer the following questions.

- What forms of entertainment were most popular during the Great Depression?

- Why were these forms of entertainment so popular?

- How did the tone of popular entertainment (such as movies and radio) differ from that of art and literature?

About one third of the nation's movie theaters closed during the depression, but each week as many as 90 million people turned out to see Hollywood films. Movies of the 1930s often dealt with issues other than the grim realities of depression life. Depression-era movies included *King Kong, Gone With the Wind,* and *The Wizard of Oz,* as well as cowboy adventures, serials, musicals, comedies, and Walt Disney cartoons starring characters such as Mickey Mouse.

Radio, offered the comedy of George Burns and Gracie Allen or Jack Benny, as well as soap operas, news, sports, serials, and music. Radio was to the 1930s what television is today—an influential, unifying means of communication. Some popular books, including detective stories, helped to distract readers from the burdens of Depression life.

However, most literature, photography, and paintings of the 1930s reflected the poverty and despair of the times. The photographs of Walker Evans and Margaret Bourke-White revealed the suffering of the people. Bourke-White's work appeared in *Life* magazine, which for decades depicted American life in pictures. Government programs provided work for artists, writers, and actors through theater and art projects. Artists painted murals on public buildings. Writers wrote histories and guidebooks about various regions. Actors appeared in plays funded by the Federal Theater Project. Dancers performed, and orchestras played.

Some novels, such as those of John Dos Passos or **John Steinbeck,** protested the life of the 1930s. William Faulkner set his novels in the South from after the Civil War through the Great Depression. **Langston Hughes** continued to celebrate racial pride in his writings about working class African Americans while condemning segregation and discrimination.

Jazz, created by Louis Armstrong, **Duke Ellington,** and other musicians dominated the music of the 1930s. It was the age of swing, a form of jazz played by the big bands such as those of Glenn Miller and Benny Goodman. George Gershwin, Irving Berlin, Cole Porter, and Jerome Kern made the musical a popular form of theater.

Franklin Delano Roosevelt

> "I pledge you, I pledge myself, to a new deal
> for the American people."
>
> —*Franklin Delano Roosevelt*

In 1932, Franklin Delano Roosevelt was elected the thirty-second president. He was educated at Harvard University and the School of Law at Columbia University. He served as a Democrat in the New York State legislature, as assistant secretary of the navy under Woodrow Wilson, and as governor of New York before being elected president. He served as president throughout the rest of the depression and most of World War II, until his death in 1945.

Restoring Public Confidence

Franklin Roosevelt is ranked by historians as one of the greatest presidents in American history. He inspired support and confidence in people. He was a master politician—intelligent, energetic, self-confident, charming, and optimistic. He had been tested by polio, which had left him in a wheelchair but made him tougher, more patient, and more compassionate.

Roosevelt, popularly called FDR, was also a master communicator. He held press conferences and effectively used the radio for "fireside chats" with the American

Election of 1932

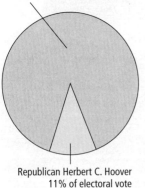

Democrat Franklin D. Roosevelt
89% of electoral vote

Republican Herbert C. Hoover
11% of electoral vote

public. He involved the public emotionally in his explanations of what he was doing to solve the nation's economic problems. He was able to convince people that he had confidence in himself and in the nation as well as genuine concern for the people.

FDR was controversial. While many respected and even loved him, others saw him as taking on almost dictatorial powers for himself and for the government. His attempt to make major changes in the Supreme Court is one example of controversy in his administration.

Another is his decision to break the so-called unwritten Constitution and run for a third term in 1940. Roosevelt ran for and was elected to a fourth term in 1944. He died in office in 1945. In 1951, the Twenty-second Amendment was added to the Constitution, limiting a president to two terms in office. Some saw it as a reaction against Roosevelt.

Preparing to Lead the Nation

In the months between his election and his inauguration, Roosevelt surrounded himself with a group of formal and informal advisers. His cabinet members included Postmaster James Farley, Secretary of State Cordell Hull, and the first woman to hold a Cabinet post, Frances Perkins, as secretary of labor. FDR's informal advisers, known as the "brain trust," were a group of intellectuals and lawyers, several of whom were Columbia University professors. They favored reform and strongly influenced Roosevelt's administration. The most well-known brain trust member was social worker Harry Hopkins.

Analyzing Documents

The two cartoons offer two points of view on FDR and the New Deal.

- Which cartoonist supports FDR's policies and which one opposes them?

- What is your evidence?

Old Reliable

Source: Berryman, Graff Collection Apr. 12, 1938

Alphabet Agencies Dance to FDR's Tune

FDR's Eyes and Ears: Eleanor Roosevelt

Another major influence on Roosevelt was his wife, Eleanor Roosevelt. She was a humanitarian, active on behalf of women and minorities, especially African Americans. As First Lady, she became an important political figure in the nation. Through her travels, she served as the president's eyes and ears, but what he heard and saw was filtered through her progressive views and sensitivity to the plight of others. She helped to mold policy in several ways: through intervention with her husband on behalf of social reform; through her syndicated newspaper column; and through her travels and speeches around the nation. After Franklin Roosevelt's death in 1945, Eleanor Roosevelt became a leader in the issue of human rights, playing a key role in the creation of the 1948 Universal Declaration of Human Rights.

The New Deal in Action: Relief, Recovery, Reform

Roosevelt's program to combat the problems caused by the depression was called the New Deal. The programs of the New Deal had the following goals:

- relief for those people who were suffering
- recovery for the economy, so it could grow again
- reform measures to avoid future depressions

Relief Legislation of the New Deal

Congress passed a wide range of relief legislation as part of the New Deal.

Emergency Banking Act, 1933 Roosevelt's first act as president was to close the nation's banks by declaring a **bank holiday** in order to stop the collapse of the national banking system. The time was used to assure the public that it could have confidence in the banks once they reopened. The law required the examination of banks to ensure that only financially sound banks were operating. In the same month, Roosevelt began to take the United States off of the gold standard.

Federal Emergency Relief Act (FERA), 1933 Between 1933 and 1935, some $500,000 was provided for distribution by states and cities for direct relief and work projects for hungry, homeless, and unemployed people.

Public Works Administration (PWA), 1933 Operating from 1933 until 1939, the PWA provided jobs through construction projects, such as bridges, housing, hospitals, schools, and aircraft carriers. The PWA also moved government money into the economy. It was hoped that this "pump priming" would create jobs, revive production, and lead to more consumer spending.

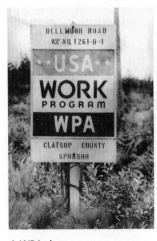

A WPA sign

Civilian Conservation Corps (CCC), 1933 Between 1933 and 1942, the CCC provided work for 2.5 million young men ages 18 to 25 conserving natural resources. Only 8,000 young women joined the CCC.

Works Progress Administration (WPA), 1935 From 1935 until 1943, the WPA provided jobs for 25 percent of adult Americans. The agency was created to replace direct relief with public works projects. The WPA spent more government money than any other program. While WPA workers built roads, bridges, airports, public buildings, playgrounds, and golf courses, the program also offered work to writers, artists, musicians, scholars, and actors. Critics attacked the cultural work projects in particular. Others criticized the WPA for being inequitable. With WPA employment limited to one member of a family, only women who were heads of households were eligible for WPA jobs. However, the WPA provided jobs for over 8.5 million people who left a legacy in books, works of art, and public buildings, bridges, tunnels, and stadiums still in use.

Recovery Legislation of the New Deal

Congress also passed a wide range of recovery legislation as part of the New Deal.

Some Major New Deal Programs

Program	Initials	Begun	Purpose
Civilian Conservation Corps	CCC	1933	provided jobs to young men to plant trees, build bridges and parks, and set up flood control projects
Tennessee Valley Authority	TVA	1933	built dams to prevent flooding and to provide cheap electric power to seven southern states through regional planning; set up schools and health centers
Federal Emergency Relief Administration	FERA	1933	gave money to states and cities for aid to the unemployed and needy
Agricultural Adjustment Administration	AAA	1933	paid farmers not to grow certain crops; between 1933 and 1937 farm prices doubled; first AAA declared unconstitutional in 1936
National Recovery Administration	NRA	1933	enforced codes that regulated wages, prices, and working conditions; in 1935, Supreme Court ruled law unconstitutional
Public Works Administration	PWA	1933	built ports, schools, aircraft carriers, and other large scale public work projects
Federal Deposit Insurance Corporation	FDIC	1933	insured savings accounts in banks approved by government; part of Glass-Steagall Banking Act that also separated commercial and investment banking
Securities Exchange Act	SEC	1934	set up Securities and Exchange Commission to oversee stock market and stock advisors
Rural Electrification Administration	REA	1935	loaned money to extend electricity to rural farmers
Works Progress Administration	WPA	1935	employed men and women to build hospitals, schools, parks, and airports; employed artists, writers, and musicians
Social Security Act	SSA	1935	set up a system of insurance for elderly, unemployed, and disabled; later added benefits for surviving spouses and children
National Labor Relations Act (Wagner Act)	NLRA	1935	gave labor right to form unions, and to collective bargaining; set up a Board (NLRB) to monitor elections, and enforce law
Fair Labor Standards Act (Wages and Hours Act)	FLSA	1938	set a minimum wage and a maximum work week and banned child labor in businesses in interstate commerce

Reading Strategy

Organizing Information
Organize the information on the chart to categorize those programs that provided for:

1. Relief
2. Recovery
3. Reform

National Industrial Recovery Act, 1933 The National Recovery Administration (NRA) had the authority to work with businesses to help them recover. The NRA set "codes of fair competition" within industries to maintain prices, minimum wages, and maximum hours. The public was encouraged to buy from companies that followed the NRA codes. The NRA was not popular, however. Some consumers complained that the NRA plan raised prices. Companies opposed the provisions giving unions the right to organize. Small companies felt at a disadvantage compared to larger companies. The NIRA was declared unconstitutional in 1935.

Home Owners Loan Corporation (HOLC), 1933 This agency was created to help homeowners save their houses from foreclosure. It provided funds to pay off mortgages and financed over one million new long-term mortgages at lower, fixed-interest rates.

First Agricultural Adjustment Act (AAA), 1933 The aim of the AAA was to raise farmers' income by cutting the amount of surplus crops and livestock. In that way, farmers would be able to sell their crops at the same prices of the years 1909–1914, a time when farm prices were high. The government paid farmers for reducing the number of acres they planted. The plan was financed through a processing tax on companies that made the wheat, corn, cotton, hogs, milk, and

Preparing for the Exam

The purpose of agricultural price supports is to keep the prices of farm products at a reasonable and stable level. By paying farmers to reduce the number of acres they plant, the government helps reduce the supply of farm products. When demand stays the same for the reduced supply, prices will rise.

- Does this type of a program still exist today?
- If so, in what form?

tobacco into consumer products. Large farmers, rather than small farmers and tenant farmers, benefited from the AAA. The public was outraged at the destruction of crops and animals in order to keep production down. However, farm prices did increase. Although the AAA was declared unconstitutional in 1936, the principle of farm price supports had been established. The AAA was replaced with a law that encouraged using soil conservation methods.

Federal Housing Administration (FHA), 1934 The FHA was created by the National Housing Act to insure bank mortgages. These mortgages were often for 20 to 30 years and at down payments of only 10 percent.

Second Agricultural Adjustment Act (AAA), 1938 The second AAA was passed in response to a drop in farm prices in 1938. The government paid farmers to store portions of overproduced crops until the price reached the level of prices from 1909 to 1914. In spite of New Deal efforts, America's farmers did not regain prosperity until the 1940s, when World War II brought increased demand for food.

Reform Legislation of the New Deal

Congress also passed a wide range of reform legislation as part of the New Deal.

Glass-Steagall Banking Act, 1933 This banking act aimed at restoring and maintaining stability in the national economy. It created the Federal Deposit Insurance Corporation (FDIC), which guaranteed individual bank deposits up to $5,000, an amount that had increased up to $100,000 by 2008. In 2009, Congress temporarily raised the insurance coverage for a depositor per bank up to $250,000. The Glass-Steagall Act separated investment banks from commercial ones, prohibiting commercial banks from involvement in securities markets. In 1999 Congress repealed this portion of the law. The Glass-Steagall Act also increased the powers of the Federal Reserve Board so that it had more control over speculation on credit.

Securities Exchange Act, 1934 Created to promote economic stability, the Securities and Exchange Commission (SEC), has the authority to regulate stock exchanges and investment advisers. SEC powers included the right to bring action against those found practicing fraud. The SEC could require financial information about stocks and bonds before they were sold.

Social Security Act, 1935 The 1935 Social Security Act was a combination of public assistance and insurance. The law had three main parts: (1) It provided old-age insurance, paid by a tax on both the employer and employee while the employee was working. The worker and employer, not the government, funded this part of social security. (2) It provided unemployment insurance for workers, paid by employers. (3) It gave assistance to dependent children and to the elderly, ill, and handicapped.

National Labor Relations Act (Wagner Act), 1935 The Wagner Act, named for its author, New York Senator Robert Wagner, guaranteed labor the right to form unions and to practice **collective bargaining.** It created the National Labor Relations Board (NLRB) to ensure that elections to select unions were conducted fairly. The NLRB could also halt practices such as blacklisting, made illegal by this law.

Fair Labor Standards Act, 1938 This law, also called the Wages and Hours Act, set a minimum wage (originally 25 cents per hour) and a maximum work week (originally 44 hours) for workers in industries involved in interstate commerce. The law also banned child labor in interstate commerce. It is one of many examples of New Deal legislation passed using the power given to Congress to regulate interstate commerce.

Key Themes and Concepts

Government

"Every qualified person shall be entitled to receive, with respect to the period beginning on the date he attains the age of sixty-five . . . an old-age benefit. . . ."
—Social Security Act, 1935

- What was the reason for the Social Security Act?

- How was it funded?

- What are current concerns and proposals regarding social security?

Analyzing Documents

"Employees shall have the right of self-organization, to form, join, or assist labor organizations, to bargain collectively through representatives of their own choosing. . . ."
—National Labor Relations Act (Wagner Act) July 5, 1935

- Why was this act called the "Magna Carta of Labor"?

- What were some of the obstacles that organized labor faced prior to this act?

The New Deal and Organized Labor

Roosevelt was interested in helping workers primarily through social legislation, such as social security. He also wanted to work cooperatively with business, as seen in the NRA legislation. When the NRA was ruled unconstitutional, and with it the part that ensured labor the right to form unions, Roosevelt turned to the Wagner Act as a means of aiding labor. By 1935, he had turned away from business and saw organized labor unions as a force in society that would balance the power of big business.

This pro-labor attitude of the New Deal resulted in an increase in union membership of more than 1.5 million members between 1933 and 1935. After the Wagner Act became law in 1935, membership grew another 3 million. By 1938, it had reached 7 million organized workers. These gains took place during a split within organized labor over how to unionize workers.

The American Federation of Labor (AFL), whose craft unions of skilled workers had dominated the labor movement since 1886, was challenged for control by a new union organized by industry. These new unions organized all workers, skilled and unskilled, in a given industry, such as textiles, coal, steel, and automobiles, much like the old Knights of Labor. But unlike the Knights, the industrial unions concentrated on "bread and butter" issues of wages, hours, and working conditions. Led by John L. Lewis, head of the United Mine Workers, the new industrial unions formed the Committee for Industrial Organization (CIO) within the AFL. In 1937 the CIO became a separate union, the Congress of Industrial Organizations (CIO).

In addition to the way it organized workers, the CIO differed from the AFL because its members included women, African Americans, and immigrants from southern and eastern Europe. These groups made up a large percentage of the unskilled work force that comprised the CIO unions. Despite their differences, the two organizations merged in 1955 to form the powerful AFL-CIO.

The 1930s were marked by a series of bitter strikes as the CIO attempted to unionize large industries, including the steel and automobile industries. Union workers demanded that companies enter into collective bargaining. Often police and company-paid guards used force against strikers. The workers made effective use of the sit down strike, a tactic in which they remained in the plant but refused to work until their demands were met.

The New Deal's Effects on Minorities and Women

The New Deal legislation affected Native Americans, African Americans, Latinos, and women in a variety of ways.

Native Americans and the New Deal

In 1924, Native Americans were finally granted citizenship by Congress. However, Native Americans continued to suffer under the government policy of forced assimilation enacted in 1887 by the Dawes Act. It aimed at breaking up the tribal structure of Native American life and forcing Native Americans to become landowning farmers. The Native Americans lost an additional 90 million acres of land between 1887 and 1934.

Under Roosevelt and the New Deal, government policy changed to one of tribal restoration. The 1934 Indian Reorganization Act, also called the Wheeler-Howard Act, was passed largely through the efforts of Roosevelt's commissioner of Indian affairs, John Collier. The bill's aim was to restore tribal self-government as well as

---

Analyzing Documents

Primary Sources

"They picked me up about eight different times and threw me on my back on the concrete. While I was on the ground they kicked me in the face, head, and other parts of my body . . . I never raised a hand."
—Walter Reuther, 1937 Ford Motor Company strike

- Did the Wagner Act resolve problems between management and labor?

- What is your evidence?

Preparing for the Exam

Native Americans and the New Deal
- How did the Indian Reorganization Act of 1934 compare to the Dawes Act of 1887 in terms of goals and Native Americans' reactions?

Native American languages, customs, and religious freedom. Another New Deal program provided for the education of Native American children under the Bureau of Indian Affairs.

Reading Strategy

Organizing Information
The New Deal affected various groups in different ways. To help you understand how different people were affected by the New Deal, create a chart showing the impact of the New Deal on:

• African Americans.

• Latinos.

• women.

African Americans and the New Deal

African Americans were not a well-organized interest group in the 1930s. Therefore, they benefited less from the New Deal than did other groups. Roosevelt was not a strong advocate of civil rights, in part because he did not want to alienate southern Democrats in Congress, whose votes he needed to pass New Deal legislation. He did not support African American efforts to abolish the poll tax or to pass an antilynching law. Lynchings, in fact, increased during the 1930s.

However, within the New Deal programs, Eleanor Roosevelt and Harry Hopkins gave strong support to African Americans. As many as 50 African Americans were appointed to posts in various New Deal agencies. The most influential among them was Mary McLeod Bethune, who served in the National Youth Administration. While African Americans protested discrimination within New Deal programs, some 40 percent of the nation's African Americans received help through a New Deal program. Many moved from the Republican Party to the Democratic Party during the New Deal.

Latinos and the New Deal

Many Latinos worked in agriculture and were hit particularly hard by the depression. "Okies" fleeing the Dust Bowl competed with Mexicans and Mexican Americans for migrant farmwork in California. While the New Deal provided relief for these workers, the government's policy was to stop immigration and return to Mexico any unemployed noncitizens.

Women and the New Deal

Like African Americans, women were not an organized group during the 1930s. As you have read, women experienced less unemployment during this period, because they worked in low-paying female-only jobs less affected by the depression. Single women and female heads of families made up a large portion of the female workforce. Women earned about 50 cents for every dollar a man was paid, and they were often expected to give up jobs to male heads of families. The belief that the proper work for women was that of a wife and mother remained strong. Many New Deal programs simply would not hire women.

While women made little progress in the workplace, the New Deal did help women in government. Eleanor Roosevelt, Frances Perkins, and Mary McLeod Bethune were only a few of the women visibly active in the New Deal administration. More women also ran for and won political office although they were still far outnumbered by men.

The 1936 Election Mandate

In his first term, Roosevelt won the support of large numbers of Americans. Popular belief in him and in his New Deal program that seemed to offer something to everyone translated into votes. Roosevelt carefully built what is known as the New Deal coalition, a voting bloc that embraced the solid Democratic South, new immigrant workers, the big cities, African Americans who had previously voted Republican, organized labor, the elderly, and farmers who usually voted Republican.

This coalition emerged in the 1936 election, when Roosevelt was reelected to a second term. Roosevelt received a mandate, or a clear endorsement, from the electorate, carrying all but two states. This shift in the two-party system was to dominate American politics over the next generation.

Stages of the New Deal

1. 1933–early 1935: New Deal legislation dealt with relief and recovery. Much of this legislation was passed in the "First Hundred Days" after FDR took office in March 1933. The 1934 Congressional elections increased the size of the Democratic majority in each house, which helped the New Deal legislative effort.
2. 1935 and early 1936: Often called the "Second Hundred Days" or the "Second New Deal," this period's legislation focused more on social reform.
3. 1936 election: This year is considered the high point of the New Deal.
4. 1937–1938: A recession led to a new collapse in the weak economy that had just been starting to improve. The recession was due in part to New Deal cutbacks in spending after the 1936 election.
5. 1938: By 1938 the New Deal had ended due to increased opposition in Congress and preoccupation with the danger of world war. Unemployment did not improve significantly until World War II created jobs in the production of war goods.

Analyzing Documents

Examine the chart at left, then answer the following questions.

- What was the significance of the "First Hundred Days"?

- What is meant by the term *Second New Deal*, and what did it accomplish?

- Why did the economy weaken in 1937 and 1938?

- What ultimately caused the unemployment rate to improve?

New Deal Generates Controversy

Roosevelt and his New Deal mobilized the government and the nation to fight the effects of the Great Depression. His program for relief, recovery, and reform provoked controversy. Criticisms came from those who felt that it was too radical or went too far as well as from those who felt its programs were too conservative or did not go far enough.

FDR's Policy Strategies

Roosevelt was a pragmatist. That means he did not come to office committed to a single theory or set of beliefs but rather was a man of action, interested in whatever worked to solve a problem. In short, he was an experimenter. The New Deal showed his willingness to make choices based on trial and error in order to solve problems.

FDR was influenced by Populist and Progressive philosophies of using the government to solve social and economic problems. He also used ideas of the Hoover administration and lessons learned in mobilizing the nation to fight World War I. The strategies used by the New Deal included:

- passing relief measures that involved the federal government in the nation's economy to a greater degree than ever before. This direct governmental action was justified by using the commerce and elastic clauses of the Constitution.

- taking fiscal action to stimulate the economy and lower unemployment by lowering taxes and increasing government spending.

- assuming responsibility for the general welfare by protecting people against risks that they could not handle on their own.

- increasing the regulatory role of the federal government over banks, businesses, and the stock exchange.

- adopting deficit spending as an economic means of reviving the economy. This policy was based on the theories of economist John Maynard Keynes, who argued that the government must spend huge amounts of money to encourage production levels and purchasing power to increase. This policy, Keynes argued, would result in economic recovery.

Preparing for the Exam

Compare the New Deal to other reform movements, such as Progressivism and the Great Society.

- Do they too appear to have stages?

Use the chart and your
knowledge of social studies
to answer the following
questions.

- What is the definition of
  a *budget deficit*?

- In what year was the
  budget deficit the
  largest?

- What caused this increase
  in the budget deficit?

- On what New Deal pro-
  grams were these funds
  spent?

Federal Income and Spending, 1928–1940

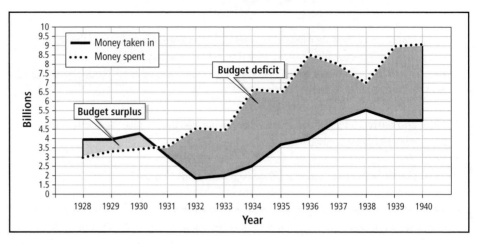

Constitutional Issues

Supreme Court Reaction

Throughout the New Deal, the Supreme Court majority practiced judicial restraint, narrowly interpreting the interstate commerce clause and striking down many of FDR's programs, which were based on a broad interpretation of that part of the Constitution. In a series of decisions, the Court ruled that several key New Deal laws were unconstitutional.

Supreme Court and the NRA The National Recovery Act (NRA) was declared unconstitutional in *Schechter Poultry Corporation* v. *United States* (1935). The Court ruled that the law illegally gave Congress power to regulate intrastate commerce (or commerce within a single state) and violated the separation of powers by giving the legislative powers to the executive branch.

Supreme Court and the AAA In *United States* v. *Butler* (1936), the Supreme Court struck down the Agricultural Adjustment Act (AAA) on the grounds that agriculture was a local, not an interstate, matter under the provisions of the Tenth Amendment.

Tennessee Valley Authority (TVA), 1933: Model Yardstick or Creeping Socialism?

The federally funded TVA provided jobs, cheap electricity, and flood control to poor rural areas of seven states through dam construction on the Tennessee River and its tributaries. The TVA was made possible through the efforts of Republican Senator George Norris of Nebraska. The TVA was praised as a bold experiment in government intervention to meet regional needs. It was attacked as "creeping socialism."

FDR's "Court-Packing" Proposal: Failure and Success

Supreme Court opposition to FDR's programs continued with the Court consistently vetoing New Deal legislation. Franklin Roosevelt asked Congress to approve a law that would permit the president to increase the number of judges from nine to fifteen if the judges refused to retire at the age of 70.

The Judicial Reorganization Bill—or the **"court-packing" plan,** as its opponents called it—was intended to make the Supreme Court approve the New Deal laws. It never became law because it would have threatened the separation of powers and the system of checks and balances. The Supreme Court did not void another New Deal law and Roosevelt eventually appointed seven Supreme Court justices.

Key Themes and Concepts

Constitutional Principles
The Supreme Court's ruling in *Schechter Poultry* v. *United States* (1935) declared the NRA unconstitutional. This decision was based in part on a narrow definition of the interstate commerce clause. It also considered this law a violation of separation of powers.

- Review *Gibbons* v. *Ogden* (1824) regarding interpretation of the interstate commerce clause.

- Review *Marbury* v. *Madison* regarding separation of powers.

- When else has the interstate commerce clause produced controversy?

- What is meant by separation of powers?

THE INGENIOUS QUARTERBACK!

The Third Term Controversy

Several constitutional questions were raised during the New Deal years, among them the third term controversy when, in 1940, President Roosevelt challenged the unwritten constitution, winning both a third and a fourth term (1944). In 1951, the Twenty-second Amendment, setting a two-term limit for president, was ratified. Historians debate whether the amendment was solely a political reaction against Roosevelt and whether it makes a president a "lame duck" from the moment of the second inauguration.

Political Opposition

In his first two terms, Roosevelt's strongest opposition was from big business. In 1934, a group of conservative Democratic and Republican business owners and politicians, including former presidential candidate Al Smith, formed the American Liberty League. It claimed that Roosevelt was exercising too much power as president. It attacked the New Deal because its programs were being financed through deficit spending. The group expressed fear that the American free enterprise system was being destroyed.

Radical groups such as the Communist Party also offered alternatives to the New Deal but failed to gain any major public support. At its peak in 1938, the Communist Party of the United States of America had only 55,000 members, and its 1936 presidential candidate won only 80,000 votes. Meanwhile, the pro-Nazi German-American Bund became active, as did the Black Shirts, fascists who supported the views of Italian dictator Benito Mussolini.

Using the table below and the text, answer the following questions.

- Who are some specific people who voiced the criticisms shown in the graphic summary?

- What evidence is there to support each of these positions?

Compare these positions with these comments about FDR and the New Deal:

"…A hundred years from now, when historians look back at it, they will say that old things didn't work. What ran through the New Deal was finding a way to make them work."
—Gardiner C. Means government financial advisor, New Deal

"Roosevelt is the only President we ever had that thought the Constitution belonged to the pore [poor] man too…"
—George Dobbin, Mill worker 1939

- Identify and analyze evidence of bias in statements critical of or supportive of FDR and the New Deal.

The Socialist Party in America drew some rising support, although some members began to vote for Roosevelt. The party was led by Eugene Debs and Norman Thomas, the party's presidential candidate. Unlike the Communist Party, the Socialists believed in the use of democratic means to make changes in the American economic structure.

As frustration grew in the face of the prolonged depression, various individuals entered the political scene, each criticizing the New Deal and often offering simplistic solutions to the economic crisis. These men were called "homegrown demagogues" because their philosophies did not come from a foreign nation and because they appealed to people's emotions and prejudice. These demagogues included:

- Francis E. Townsend, who created a financially impossible plan to provide government pensions for the elderly.
- Father Charles E. Coughlin, a Catholic priest who blamed business owners, especially Jewish ones, for the economic crisis.
- **Huey Long**, a powerful United States senator from Louisiana, who proposed that income and inheritance taxes on the wealthy be used to give each American a $2,500 income, a car, and a college education. Long was assassinated in 1935.

Critics of the New Deal

Women and African Americans	Progressives and Socialists	Republicans and other political opponents
New Deal programs offered more opportunities to white men than to women and minorities. Women and African Americans were paid less for the same work.	New Deal programs were not doing enough to solve the nation's problems. More should have been done to distribute the nation's wealth among all Americans.	Government was becoming too powerful. The Constitution was threatened. FDR was like a dictator. New Deal taxes on the wealthy were unfair. New Deal programs were too much like socialism.

Evaluating the New Deal

Most historians agree on the following assessment of the New Deal:

- World War II was largely responsible for ending the Great Depression. The New Deal improved but did not solve unemployment, the farm crisis, or underconsumption.
- Nevertheless, the New Deal did help people cope with the effects of the Great Depression while preventing economic and social disaster.
- The New Deal restored confidence in government while it brought more power to the presidency and the federal government.
- The government assumed a role and a responsibility in more aspects of the economic and social life of its citizens.
- The New Deal preserved the free-enterprise system, instituting reforms to provide stability and encourage growth.
- The deficit spending of the New Deal raised the national debt.

Multiple Choice

Directions: Review the Test-Taking Strategies section of this book. Then answer the following questions, drawn from actual Regents examinations. For each statement or question, choose the *number* of the word or expression that, of those given, best completes the statement or answers the question.

1 Which was a major problem faced by United States farmers in both the 1890s and 1920s?

(1) lagging technology

(2) lack of tariff protection

(3) overproduction of basic staples

(4) inflationary currency

2 In which respect were the decades of the 1920s and the 1960s in the United States most similar?

(1) organized militancy by ethnic minorities

(2) public concern with pollution of the environment

(3) widespread government activity dealing with social issues

(4) significant changes in manners and morals

3 What was the one similarity between the Red Scare following World War I and the Cold War following World War II?

(1) Fear of communism led to the suppression of the civil liberties of some Americans.

(2) Large numbers of Russian revolutionaries settled in the United States.

(3) Congressional investigations proved that the federal government was heavily infiltrated by Communist spies.

(4) Renewed fighting between wartime enemies was a constant threat.

4 Which is most commonly associated with the presidencies of Ulysses S. Grant and Warren G. Harding?

(1) depression in business

(2) corruption of public officials

(3) humanitarian reforms

(4) territorial expansion

5 In the United States, the widespread disregard of the fugitive slave laws and of Prohibition laws most clearly indicated that

(1) strongly held values are difficult to regulate

(2) the federal government is generally unable to enforce its own laws

(3) little respect is given to the legal system

(4) the judicial system is too lenient in its treatment of offenders

6 A major reason for the isolationist trend in the United States following World War I was

(1) a desire to continue the reforms of the Progressives

(2) the public's desire to end most trade with other nations

(3) the failure of the United States to gain new territory

(4) a disillusionment over the failure to achieve United States goals in the postwar world

7 The "boom" years of the 1920s were characterized by

(1) a decrease in both agricultural surpluses and farm foreclosures

(2) limited investment capital and declining numbers of workers in the labor force

(3) widespread use of the automobile and an increase in buying

(4) increased regulation of the marketplace by both federal and state governments

8   The racial segregation and poverty experienced by African Americans in the South during the 1920s led them to

(1) move to the North in great numbers to find factory jobs

(2) join with whites in strong national movements to protest unjust laws

(3) evolve their own strong labor movement

(4) support federal programs that gave them their own farmland

9   The Harlem Renaissance of the 1920s was a period when African Americans

(1) left the United States in large numbers to settle in Nigeria

(2) created noteworthy works of art and literature

(3) migrated to the West in search of land and jobs

(4) used civil disobedience to fight segregation in the armed forces

10   In the 1920s, the Sacco and Vanzetti case, the Red Scare, and the activities of the Ku Klux Klan all represented

(1) threats to civil liberties

(2) victories over discrimination and persecution

(3) support for the Prohibition movement

(4) greater social freedom for Americans

11   The conviction of John Scopes in 1925 for teaching about evolution supported the ideas of those Americans who

(1) believed in religious freedom and the separation of church and state

(2) hoped to lessen the differences between rural and urban lifestyles

(3) wanted to promote traditional fundamentalist values

(4) favored the changes resulting from the new technology of the 1920s

12   One important cause of the Great Depression in the United States was that by the end of the 1920s

(1) the government controlled almost every aspect of the economy

(2) tariffs were so low that foreign products had forced many United States companies out of business

(3) investors were too cautious and put their money only into government bonds

(4) factories and farms were able to produce far more than buyers could afford to purchase

13   President Herbert Hoover's refusal to provide funds for the unemployed during the Depression was based on his belief that

(1) the unemployment problem was not serious

(2) workers would not accept government assistance

(3) labor unions should provide for the unemployed

(4) federal relief programs would destroy individual initiative

14   Which is a valid conclusion based on a study of the presidencies of Thomas Jefferson and Franklin D. Roosevelt?

(1) Strong third parties develop when the two major parties ignore popular demands.

(2) Presidential success depends mainly on a sympathetic Supreme Court.

(3) Economic crisis can force a president to suspend basic civil liberties.

(4) A president's political program may change in the face of current needs.

15   The rapid, worldwide spread of the Great Depression of the 1930s was evidence of

(1) the failure of government job programs

(2) global financial interdependence

(3) a shortage of American factories making consumer goods

(4) the negative effects of unrestricted immigration

16 Which New Deal reforms most directly targeted the basic problem of the victims of the Dust Bowl?

(1) guaranteeing workers the right to organize and bargain collectively

(2) regulating the sale of stocks and bonds

(3) providing farmers low-cost loans and parity payments

(4) raising individual and corporate income tax rates

17 Deficit spending by the federal government as a means of reviving the economy is based on the idea that

(1) purchasing power will increase and economic growth will be stimulated

(2) only the national government can operate businesses efficiently

(3) the national government should turn its revenue over to the states

(4) lower interest rates will encourage investment

18 The main purpose of the New Deal measures such as the Securities and Exchange Commission (SEC) and the Federal Deposit Insurance Corporation (FDIC) was to

(1) provide immediate employment opportunities

(2) develop rules to limit speculation and safeguard savings

(3) enable the federal government to take over failing industries

(4) assure a guaranteed income for American families

19 During President Franklin D. Roosevelt's administration, which situation was viewed by critics as a threat to the principle of separation of powers?

(1) changing the date of the presidential inauguration

(2) congressional support of banking legislation

(3) proposing the expansion of Supreme Court membership

(4) passage of Social Security legislation

20 "Section 202. (a) Every qualified individual shall be entitled to receive . . . on the date he attains the age of sixty-five . . . and ending on the date of his death, an old-age benefit. . . ."

A major purpose of this section of federal legislation was to

(1) guarantee an annual income to experienced employees

(2) assure adequate medical care for the elderly

(3) reward workers for their support of the union movement

(4) provide economic assistance to retired workers

21 The popularity of escapist novels and movies during the Great Depression is evidence that

(1) the Great Depression was not really a time of economic distress

(2) popular culture is shaped by economic and social conditions

(3) American society did not try to solve the problems of the Great Depression

(4) the greatest employment opportunities for the average person in the 1930s were in the field of entertainment

22 A major effect of the National Labor Relations Act (Wagner Act, 1935) was that labor unions
(1) were soon controlled by large corporations
(2) experienced increasing difficulty in gaining new members
(3) obtained the right to bargain collectively
(4) lost the right to strike

23 The effectiveness of the New Deal in ending the Great Depression is difficult to measure because
(1) President Franklin D. Roosevelt died during his fourth term
(2) United States involvement in World War II rapidly accelerated economic growth
(3) the Supreme Court declared most New Deal laws unconstitutional
(4) later presidents failed to support most New Deal reforms

24 Many opponents of New Deal programs claimed that these programs violated the American tradition of
(1) welfare capitalism
(2) governmental regulation of business
(3) collective bargaining
(4) individual responsibility

25 A lasting result of the New Deal in the United States has been the
(1) reduction of the national debt
(2) control of stock prices by the federal government
(3) joint effort of business and labor to strengthen the presidency
(4) assumption by the federal government of greater responsibility for the nation's well-being

26 The process of collective bargaining is best described as
(1) meetings of joint congressional committees to achieve compromise on different versions of a proposed law
(2) diplomatic strategies used to make treaties between two nations
(3) discussions between labor union leaders and management to agree on a contract for workers
(4) negotiations between a multinational company and a nation with which the company wishes to do business

27 Which generalization most accurately describes the literary works of Langston Hughes, Sinclair Lewis, and John Steinbeck?
(1) Politics and art seldom mix well.
(2) The best literature concerns the lives of the wealthy.
(3) Literature often reflects the times in which it is created.
(4) Traditional American themes are the most popular.

28 An immediate result of the Supreme Court decision in *Schechter Poultry* v. *United States* was that
(1) some aspects of the New Deal were declared unconstitutional
(2) state governments took over relief agencies
(3) Congress was forced to abandon efforts to improve the economy
(4) the constitutional authority of the president was greatly expanded

Thematic Essay Question

Directions: Write a well-organized essay that includes an introduction, several paragraphs addressing the task below, and a conclusion.

Theme: **Reform Movements**

> Throughout United States history, there have been times when movements or programs have developed in response to demands for political, economic, or social reform.

Task:

> From your study of United States history, identify *two* movements or programs that developed in response to demands for reform. For *each* movement or program identified:
>
> - State one problem that led to the movement or program
> - Describe a specific reform advocated by the movement or program to deal with the problem
> - Discuss the tactics or means used by supporters of the movement or program to achieve the specific reform
> - Evaluate the extent to which the movement or program reform was successful

You may use any major reform movement or program from your study of United States history. Some suggestions you might wish to consider include: abolitionist movement (1830–1865); temperance movement (1830–1933); women's movement (1848–1920); Progressivism (1900–1920); New Deal (1933–1945); Great Society (1960s); Native American movement (1960–present).

You are not limited to these suggestions.

Guidelines:

> **In your essay, be sure to**
> - Develop all aspects of the task
> - Support the theme with relevant facts, examples, and details
> - Use a logical and clear plan of organization, including an introduction and a conclusion that are beyond a simple restatement of the theme

In developing your answer, be sure to keep these general definitions in mind:

(a) <u>describe</u> means "to illustrate something in words or tell about it"

(b) <u>discuss</u> means "to make observations about something using facts, reasoning, and argument; to present in some detail"

(c) <u>evaluate</u> means "to examine and judge the significance, worth, or condition of; to determine the value of"

Document-Based Question

In developing your answers, be sure to keep this general definition in mind:

discuss means "to make observations about something using
facts, reasoning, and argument; to present in some detail"

This question is based on the accompanying documents. The question is designed to test your ability to work with historical documents. Some of the documents have been edited for the purposes of the question. As you analyze the documents, take into account the source of each document and any point of view that may be presented in the document.

Historical Context:

The federal government responded quite differently to the prosperity of the 1920s and the Great Depression that followed. Roosevelt's New Deal was not only a decisive plan to combat the Depression, but it also marked a new direction in the role of government in managing the economy—a role that is still being debated today.

Task:

Using information from the documents and your knowledge of United States history and government, answer the questions that follow each document in Part A. Your answers to the questions will help you write the Part B essay in which you will be asked to

- Discuss the response of the United States government to the Great Depression. In your essay, include a discussion of how this response can be considered a turning point in the role of the federal government in managing the economy

Part A: Short Answer

Document #1

" . . . we must have tax reform. The method of raising tax revenue ought not to impede the transaction of business; it ought to encourage it. I am opposed to extremely high taxes, . . . because they are bad for the country, and because they are wrong. We cannot finance the country through any system of injustice, even if we attempt to inflict it on the rich. . . . The wise and judicious course to follow in taxation and economic legislation is not to destroy those already who have secured success, but to create conditions under which everyone will have a better chance to be successful."

—Calvin Coolidge, *Inaugural Address*, March 4, 1925

1. According to this quote, how did Calvin Coolidge feel about the role of government in managing business?

_____

_____

Document #2

Economic Impact of the Great Depression

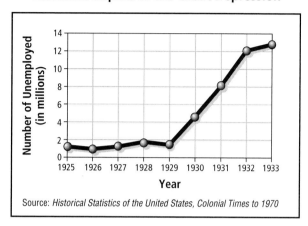

Source: *Historical Statistics of the United States, Colonial Times to 1970*

2. Based on the chart above, what effect did the stock market crash of 1929 have on the overall economy of the United States?

_____

_____

_____

Document #3

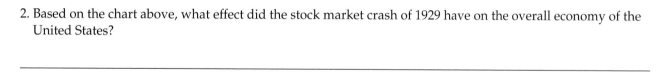

"I have recounted to you in other speeches, and it is a matter of general information, that for at least two years after the crash, the only efforts by the [Hoover] administration to cope with the distress of unemployment were to deny its existence."

—Franklin D. Roosevelt, 1932

3. Based on this quote that Roosevelt made during the 1932 presidential campaign, how did Roosevelt evaluate the efforts made by the Hoover administration to resolve the nation's economic problems?

_____

_____

_____

Document-Based Question

"So, first of all, let me assert my firm belief that the only thing we have to fear is fear itself—nameless, unreasoning, unjustified terror which paralyzes needed efforts to convert retreat into advance. In every dark hour of our national life a leadership of frankness and vigor has met with that understanding and support of the people themselves which is essential to victory. I am convinced that you will again give that support to leadership in these critical days.

In such a spirit on my part and on yours we face our common difficulties. They concern, thank God, only material things. Values have shrunken to fantastic levels; taxes have risen; our ability to pay has fallen; government of all kinds is faced by serious curtailment of income; the means of exchange are frozen in the currents of trade; the withered leaves of industrial enterprise lie on every side; farmers find no markets for their produce; the savings of many years in thousands of families are gone.

More important, a host of unemployed citizens face the grim problem of existence, and an equally great number toil with little return. Only a foolish optimist can deny the dark realities of the moment."

—**Franklin D. Roosevelt, *First Inaugural Address*, March 4, 1933**

4. In this excerpt from FDR's first inaugural speech, how did he attempt to win the support of the American people for his leadership during the economic crisis of the Great Depression?

_____

_____

_____

Document #5

5. According to the above cartoon, how did some Americans view the New Deal?

_____

_____

_____

Document-Based Question

Part B

Essay

Directions: Write a well-organized essay that includes an introduction, several paragraphs, and a conclusion. Use evidence from *at least **three*** documents in your essay. Support your response with relevant facts, examples, and details. Include additional outside information.

Historical Context:

The federal government responded quite differently to the prosperity of the 1920s and the Great Depression that followed. Roosevelt's New Deal was not only a decisive plan to combat the Depression, but it also marked a new direction in the role of government in managing the economy—a role that is still being debated today.

Task: Using information from the documents and your knowledge of United States history and government, write an essay in which you

- Discuss the response of the United States government to the Great Depression.
- Include a discussion of how this response can be considered a turning point in the role of the federal government in managing the economy.

Guidelines:

In your essay, be sure to
- Develop all aspects of the task
- Incorporate information from *at least **three*** documents
- Incorporate relevant outside information
- Support the theme with relevant facts, examples, and details
- Use a logical and clear plan of organization, including an introduction and a conclusion that are beyond a restatement of the theme

The United States in an Age of Global Crisis
Responsibility and Cooperation

Unit Overview

This unit covers the time period from 1933 to 1960, a period that included the Great Depression, World War II, and the Cold War. This unit focuses on American foreign policy and how it affected life in the United States during those years.

Some of the key questions about the history of the United States during this period include:

- What caused the United States to change its foreign policy from isolationism and neutrality to a growing commitment to global involvement?

- Why did the world go to war from 1939 until 1945? How and when did the United States become involved in the conflict? How did the Allies strategize to end the war? How did World War II affect the lives of Americans on the home front?

- Why did the United States and the Soviet Union change from being allies in World War II to enemies during the Cold War?

- How did the United States try to stop the spread of communism in Europe and Asia? How did the desire to halt the spread of communism lead the United States into war in Korea? What effects did the fear of communism have within the United States?

Peace in Peril, 1933–1950

Section Overview

In the 1930s, great changes were happening in Europe and Asia. Totalitarian regimes rose to power in Germany, Italy, and Japan, threatening the freedom of nations on their borders. In 1939, the German invasion of Poland launched World War II, which quickly engulfed Europe and much of Asia. The United States, still embracing isolationism, tried to maintain neutrality, but the 1941 Japanese bombing of Pearl Harbor drew the nation into the conflict. Four more years of bloody fighting in Europe and Asia left millions of soldiers and civilians dead and hundreds of cities damaged or destroyed. The United States suffered relatively light losses in comparison to other nations, and it emerged as a world leader with a growing commitment to international involvement.

Key Themes and Concepts

As you review this section, take special note of the following key themes and concepts:

Presidential Decisions and Actions How did Presidents Roosevelt and Truman influence the events and outcomes of World War II?

Foreign Policy How did world events change American foreign policy from one of isolationism to a growing commitment to global involvement?

Diversity How did World War II change the lives of women, African Americans, and Japanese Americans?

Key People

Franklin D. Roosevelt	Robert Oppenheimer
Adolf Hitler	Harry S. Truman
Benito Mussolini	Joseph Stalin
Francisco Franco	Winston Churchill

Key Terms

totalitarian	Allies	Rosie the Riveter
fascism	Axis Powers	Nisei
appeasement	Manhattan Project	WRA camps
Lend-Lease Act	Holocaust	

In the 1920s and 1930s, the United States pursued a policy of neutrality and isolationism. In order to understand the reasons for this policy, we must examine the lingering impact of World War I.

Isolationist Sentiment After World War I

The United States had been reluctant to enter World War I. Fighting had begun in Europe in 1914, and the United States stayed out of the war until 1917. Between April 1917, when the United States formally declared war, and Germany's surrender in November 1918, some 48,000 American soldiers were killed in battle, 2,900 were declared missing in action, and 56,000 soldiers died of disease. These losses were far less than those of the European nations, some of which had lost millions of soldiers and civilians. Nevertheless, the American losses were great enough to cause Americans to take a close look at the reasons for the entry of the United States into the war and at the nation's foreign policy.

Isolation and Neutrality

Isolationism and neutrality are similar foreign policies, but an important difference exists between them. Isolationism is a national foreign policy of remaining apart from political or economic entanglements with other countries. Strict isolationists do not support any type of contact with other countries, including economic ties or trade activities.

When a country chooses a policy of neutrality, it deliberately takes no side in a dispute or controversy. Countries following this path are often referred to as being nonaligned or noninvolved. Neutral nations do not limit their trading activities with other nations, unless a trading partnership would limit that country's ability to stay politically noninvolved.

Events Preceding American Involvement in World War II

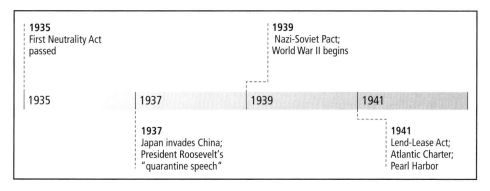

1935
First Neutrality Act passed

1939
Nazi-Soviet Pact; World War II begins

1935 — 1937 — 1939 — 1941

1937
Japan invades China; President Roosevelt's "quarantine speech"

1941
Lend-Lease Act; Atlantic Charter; Pearl Harbor

Historical Roots of Isolationism and Neutrality

The roots of isolationist and neutralistic sentiments in the United States can be traced to the late eighteenth and early nineteenth centuries.

Precedents Set by George Washington As president, George Washington set the precedent of American neutrality—but not isolationism. He knew that trade was necessary for the new nation, but that alliances might force it into war.

In 1793, Washington issued his Proclamation of Neutrality, making it clear that the United States would not offer aid during the French Revolution. In his farewell address of 1796, Washington warned the nation to avoid "entangling alliances," or political commitments to other nations, although he supported economic ties to other countries.

Monroe Doctrine The Monroe Doctrine reinforced the neutrality of the United States toward Europe. In 1823, President Monroe stated that the United States would not interfere in European affairs. He also warned European powers to remain out of the affairs of nations in the Western Hemisphere.

Geography in History

- How did the United States' location relative to Europe and Asia contribute to isolationist sentiment before and after World War I?

Preparing for the Exam

Many questions on the exam will require you to distinguish between similar concepts and terms.

- What is the difference between isolationism and neutrality?

Reading Strategy

Reinforcing Main Ideas
- How did the Monroe Doctrine contribute to isolationist and neutralistic sentiments in the United States prior to World War II?

Isolationism in the 1930s

In 1934, when the United States was trying to recover from the worst economic depression in its history, Senator Gerald Nye led an investigation into the reasons the United States entered World War I. The committee concluded that the United States had gone to war at the encouragement of financiers and armament makers, eager for profits. As a result of this investigation, many Americans supported a return to isolationism.

In 1935, the Senate refused to allow the United States to join the World Court. That same year, Congress passed the first of a series of neutrality acts, which prevented Americans from making loans to nations at war. Any sales of goods to such nations were strictly on a **"cash and carry"** basis. In 1937, President Roosevelt made his famous quarantine speech, in which he stated that the United States would attempt to quarantine the warring nation "patients" in order to protect the rest of the world.

Presidential Election of 1940 In 1940, President Franklin D. Roosevelt faced a challenge no other president had faced. He had helped the nation to survive the worst depression in its history while watching the rise of dictators in Europe and Asia. Roosevelt was at the end of his second term as president of the United States. Since the precedent set by President George Washington, no president had served more than two terms. This practice was not set by law at that time but was considered a respected tradition. Roosevelt surprised the nation by campaigning for and accepting the Democratic Party's nomination for a third term. He ran against Republican Wendell L. Wilkie, who appealed to many voters but not to anywhere near enough to defeat the popular F.D. Roosevelt. For the first time in the nation's history, a president was elected to a third term. (F.D. Roosevelt was elected to a fourth term in 1944, making more presidential history.) It was not until 1951, when the Twenty-second Amendment to the U.S. Constitution was passed, that American presidents were limited to a total of two terms or ten years of service as president.

Events Leading to World War II

The rise of totalitarian governments in Germany and Italy in the 1930s set the stage for World War II.

The Rise of Totalitarian Governments

In totalitarian governments, one political party has complete control over the government and bans all other parties. Totalitarian governments rely on terror to suppress individual rights and silence opposition.

In Germany and Italy, totalitarian governments were established based on the philosophy of **fascism.** Fascism places the importance of the nation above all else, and individual rights and freedoms are lost. Nazi Germany (led by Adolf Hitler) and fascist Italy (led by Benito Mussolini) were two fascist governments characterized by extreme nationalism, racism, and militarism (desire to go to war).

Hitler and Mussolini provided military assistance to Francisco Franco, a fascist leader in Spain who was attempting to overthrow the republican government. The devastating Spanish Civil War that erupted in 1936 became a "dress rehearsal" for World War II. The war in Spain was a testing ground for new weapons and military strategies that were used in World War II.

In the United States, opinions about support for the Spanish Civil War were divided. Some Americans traveled to Spain to fight for the republican cause. The United States government, however, continued to pursue a policy of neutrality.

Key Themes and Concepts

Foreign Policy
The Neutrality Acts of the 1930's reflect the efforts of Congress to avoid the foreign policy mistakes that led the country into World War I. The Neutrality Acts passed in 1935, 1936, and 1937 declared that the United States would withhold weapons and loans of money from all nations at war and that U.S. citizens who traveled on ships belonging to nations at war did so at their own risk. The acts also required that nonmilitary goods sold to nations at war be paid for in cash and transported by the purchaser.

• What events in the nation's history caused the government to be wary of Americans' involvement in ocean trade and travel?

Preparing for the Exam

One way to remember the meaning of the term *totalitarianism* is from the word *total*: totalitarian governments have total control over every aspect of life. They suppress all individual rights and silence all opposition with threats. Fascism places the importance of the nation above individual rights.

• What is the relationship between totalitarianism and fascism?

Congress passed a resolution forbidding the export of arms to either side in 1937. Franco won the Spanish Civil War in 1939, established a fascist government, and remained leader of Spain until his death in 1975.

Major World Events, 1918–1941

Year	Event	Year	Event
• 1918	Germany surrenders. World War I is concluded.	• 1935	Italy invades Ethiopia. The United States passes the first Neutrality Act.
• 1919	Germany signs the Treaty of Versailles. The United States refuses to approve the Treaty of Versailles.	• 1936	Hitler reoccupies the Rhineland. The German/Italian Axis is formed. The Spanish Civil War begins (ending in 1939). The United States passes the second Neutrality Act. The United States votes for nonintervention at the Pan-American Conference.
• 1921	Great Britain, France, and Japan attend the Washington Naval Conference on limiting arms. The conference produces the Four Power and Nine Power treaties.	• 1937	Japan invades China. Japan sinks an American gunboat in Chinese waters. The United States passes the third Neutrality Act, including a "cash and carry" plan.
• 1922	Benito Mussolini becomes Italy's fascist dictator. The USSR is officially formed, following the communist victory in the Russian Revolution.	• 1938	Germany annexes Austria (the *Anschluss*). Hitler demands the Sudetenland of Czechoslovakia. Great Britain, France, and Germany sign the Munich Pact, giving in to Hitler's demands.
• 1923	Adolf Hitler writes *Mein Kampf* in prison.	• 1939	A German/Soviet nonaggression pact is signed. Japanese and American relations are deadlocked. The United States Senate refuses to grant aid to Great Britain or France. Hitler invades Poland, marking the beginning of World War II.
• 1924	In the USSR, Lenin dies. Stalin continues his rise to power.		
• 1928	The Kellogg-Briand Pact outlawing war is signed by 62 nations. The pact contains no method of enforcement.	• 1940	Germany occupies Norway, Denmark, the Netherlands, Belgium, Luxembourg, and France. Germany attacks Great Britain. Japan joins the Axis Powers. President Roosevelt arranges to supply destroyers to Great Britain. Congress passes the Selective Training and Service Act, the first peacetime draft in United States history.
• 1929	The most serious economic depression in history begins, continuing through the 1930s.		
• 1930	Japan occupies Manchuria.		
• 1932	Japan seizes Shanghai. The United States issues the Stimson Doctrine, condemning Japanese aggression against Manchuria.	• 1941	Germany invades the USSR. The United States passes the Lend-Lease Act, granting aid to countries whose defense was seen as critical to the defense of the United States. President Roosevelt and Prime Minister Churchill agree to the Atlantic Charter. Japan attacks the United States at Pearl Harbor. The United States enters World War II.
• 1933	Hitler assumes power in Germany. Japan announces its withdrawal from the League of Nations. President Roosevelt announces the Good Neighbor Policy in Latin America. The USSR is formally recognized by the United States. Nazi Germany begins operation of the first concentration camp at Dachau, near Munich.		

Analyzing Documents

Make Inferences and Draw Conclusions
Examine the chart then answer these questions.

• How might dissatisfaction with the outcome of World War I and economic depression have contributed to the rise of dictators in Italy and Germany?

• Which events described in the chart represent actions of appeasement on the part of France and Great Britain?

Major World Events, 1918–1941

The chart "Major World Events, 1918–1941" summarizes the major events between the end of World War I and the entry of the United States into World War II. As you review the chart, look for relationships between events in order to understand how certain events caused others that occurred later.

Some events in the chart are so significant that they require further discussion.

1938 Munich Agreement With this agreement, Great Britain and France allowed Germany to annex the Sudetenland, a region of Czechoslovakia with a large German-speaking population. Hitler convinced the British prime minister Neville Chamberlain and the French premier Édouard Daladier that Germany would make no further territorial demands in Czechoslovakia after annexing the Sudetenland. When Chamberlain returned to Great Britain with this agreement, he told the world that he had achieved "peace for our time." Six months later, however, Hitler seized the rest of Czechoslovakia.

Key Themes and Concepts

Foreign Policy
President Roosevelt explained the Lend-Lease Act to the American people through the use of a simple comparison:

If your neighbor's house is on fire, you don't sell him a hose. You lend it to him and take it back after the fire is out.

• How did the Lend-Lease Act lead to greater U.S. involvement in the war?

Key Themes and Concepts

Science and Technology
• How did advances in aviation technology contribute to changes in American isolationist sentiments?

Great Britain and France had resorted to the policy of **appeasement,** which means to agree to the demands of a potential enemy in order to keep the peace. Hitler demonstrated by his action that he could not be permanently appeased, and the world learned a costly lesson.

Lend-Lease Act Although the United States was officially committed to a policy of neutrality, President Roosevelt soon found a way around the Neutrality Acts to provide aid, including warships, to Great Britain. In 1941, Roosevelt convinced Congress to pass the **Lend-Lease Act,** which allowed the United States to sell or lend war materials to "any country whose defense the President deems vital to the defense of the United States." Roosevelt said that the nation would become the "arsenal of democracy," supplying arms to those who were fighting for freedom.

Japan's Attack on Pearl Harbor The United States did not enter World War II until 1941. President Roosevelt had promised that the United States would not fight in a war in which the country was not directly involved. However, on December 7, 1941, Japanese war planes attacked the U.S. Navy fleet at Pearl Harbor, Hawaii. Roosevelt called the attack a day that would "live in infamy," a day that Americans would never forget. This surprise attack shattered the American belief that the Atlantic and Pacific Oceans would safely isolate the United States from fighting in Europe and Asia. The attack on Pearl Harbor fueled American nationalism and patriotism. The day after the attack, Congress agreed to President Roosevelt's request to declare war on Japan. As a nation recently recovering from its worst economic depression in its history, the United States financed a great part of its involvement in World War II with the sale of government war bonds.

World War II in Review

World War II began in 1939, when German forces invaded Poland. The United States entered the war two years later, after the Japanese attacked Pearl Harbor. War in Europe ended in May 1945, and fighting in the Pacific ended on August 14, 1945, when the Japanese surrender brought World War II to a conclusion.

Major Powers

The war pitted 26 nations united together as the **Allies** against eight **Axis Powers.** The major powers among the Allies were Great Britain, the Soviet Union, and the United States. Germany, Italy, and Japan were the major Axis nations. Leaders of the major powers are listed below.

Leaders During World War II

Allies	
• Great Britain	Winston Churchill, Prime Minister
• USSR	Joseph Stalin, Communist dictator
• United States	Franklin D. Roosevelt, President until his death in April 1945
	Harry S. Truman, President following Roosevelt's death
	Dwight D. Eisenhower, Supreme Commander of Allied troops in Europe
	Douglas MacArthur, Commander of the Allied troops in the Pacific
• France	Charles de Gaulle, leader of the Free French during the Nazi occupation

Axis Powers	
• Germany	Adolf Hitler, leader of the National Socialist German Workers' Party (Nazis), known as "Der Führer" ("The Leader")
• Italy	Benito Mussolini, Fascist dictator known as "Il Duce" ("The Leader")
• Japan	Emperor Hirohito
	Tojo Hideki, General and Prime Minister

Major Events

World War II was fought primarily in two major regions: Europe and North Africa, and in the Pacific. Major military engagements and turning points in World War II are presented on the next two pages.

Europe During World War II

Major Events of World War II

- **1939** Germany invades Poland with a rapid attack by armored vehicles supported by airplanes. This is known as a blitzkrieg, or "lightning war."

- **1940** Denmark, Norway, Belgium, the Netherlands, and much of northern France fall to Nazi invasion. Battle of Britain—months of terrifying air raids by Germany against Great Britain known as the blitz.

- **1941** Germany invades the Soviet Union. The siege of Leningrad begins and lasts 17 months. Japan attacks Pearl Harbor, Hawaii. The United States enters the war.

- **1941–1942** Japan seizes the Philippines, Burma, Singapore, the Dutch East Indies, and French Indochina. Japan continues to press southward toward Australia.

- **1942** Battle of Midway in the Pacific. The United States regains naval superiority in the Pacific.

- **1942–1943** Battle of Stalingrad. German troops are forced to surrender after thousands have been killed. This battle marks a turning point in the East and allows Russian soldiers to begin to move west.

- **1943** In North Africa, Allied troops defeat Axis armies for control of the Mediterranean Sea and the Suez Canal.

- **June 6, 1944** Allied invasions of Normandy, France, across the English Channel. This was the largest such invasion in history, involving over 150,000 soldiers. This invasion was known by the code name Operation Overlord and the D-Day Invasion.

- **1944–1945** Bitter fighting in the Pacific (for example at Leyte, Iwo Jima, and Okinawa) costs thousands of American lives.

- **December 1944** Battle of the Bulge. A surprisingly strong response by German troops slows the movement of Allied forces eastward to Germany.

- **April 12, 1945** Franklin Roosevelt dies unexpectedly from a cerebral hemorrhage.

- **April 1945** Allied troops from the East and West meet at the Elbe River in Germany. Hitler commits suicide.

- **May 8, 1945** The end of war in Europe, celebrated as V-E Day (Victory in Europe).

- **August 6, 1945** The United States drops an atomic bomb on the Japanese city of Hiroshima.

- **August 9, 1945** The United States drops an atomic bomb on the Japanese city of Nagasaki.

- **August 14, 1945** Hirohito announces Japan's defeat to the Japanese people.

- **September 2, 1945** Japan formally surrenders.

Analyzing Documents

Recognize and Interpret Examine the timeline. Then answer the following questions.

- What was the significance of the Battle of Midway?

- Which ended first, the war in Europe or the war in the Pacific?

Turning Point

Why is the Battle of Midway considered a turning point in World War II?

World War II in the Pacific

Wartime Diplomacy

During the war, leaders of the Allied nations met in a series of conferences to discuss wartime strategies and plans for the postwar world. Key meetings are described below.

Atlantic Charter Meeting, 1941 Roosevelt and Churchill met on battleships in the North Atlantic to agree on certain principles for building a lasting peace and establishing free governments in the world. The document containing these agreements was called the Atlantic Charter.

Casablanca, 1943 Roosevelt met with Churchill to plan "victory on all fronts." They used the term "unconditional surrender" to describe the anticipated victory.

Cairo, 1943 Roosevelt, Churchill, and Chiang Kai-shek of China discussed the Normandy invasion.

Tehran Conference, 1943 Roosevelt and Churchill met with Stalin to discuss war strategy and plans for the postwar world.

Yalta, 1945 Roosevelt, Churchill, and Stalin outlined the division of postwar Germany into spheres of influence and planned for the trials of war criminals. The Soviet Union promised to enter the war against Japan.

Potsdam Conference, 1945 Allied leaders (with Truman now replacing Roosevelt) warned Japan to surrender to prevent utter destruction.

Reading Strategy

Analyzing Cause and Effect
At Yalta, Roosevelt, Churchill, and Stalin agreed to split Germany into four zones, each under the control of one of the major Allies. Stalin promised to allow elections in the nations his army liberated from the Germans in Eastern Europe. Stalin did not fulfill this promise.

• How did the agreements at Yalta set the stage for the problems that later arose during the Cold War?

The Atomic Bomb

In an effort to bring the war to a speedy conclusion and to prevent further destruction and loss of life, Allied leaders decided to embark on an atomic research project.

The Manhattan Project In the spring of 1943, a group of scientists from the United States, Canada, Great Britain, and other European countries began work on the top-secret atomic research program known as the **Manhattan Project.** The research was done primarily at Los Alamos, New Mexico, under the direction of Dr. Robert Oppenheimer. Many scientists involved in the project were refugees from Hitler's Germany. By July 1945, the first atomic bomb was tested in New Mexico. The success of this project enabled the United States to determine the ultimate use of the new weapon.

The Bombings of Hiroshima and Nagasaki Within days after the first atomic test, Allied leaders warned Japan to surrender or face "prompt and utter destruction." Since no surrender occurred, President Truman made the decision to drop atomic bombs on the Japanese cities of Hiroshima and Nagasaki. The bombs killed more than 100,000 Japanese instantly, and thousands more died later from radiation sickness. For a time after World War II, the United States held a monopoly on atomic weapons. The world had entered the atomic age. A controversial issue that resulted from World War II was the morality of nuclear warfare. The topic continues to be debated in the twenty-first century.

Japan Surrenders Within days of the devastating bombings of Hiroshima and Nagasaki, Japan formally surrendered, and World War II came to an end. Following Japan's surrender, the United States occupied Japan under the leadership of General Douglas MacArthur. A new constitutional monarchy introduced democratic reforms which included a democratic constitution dictated by MacArthur. Emperor Hirohito retained his throne, but only as a figurehead.

Turning Point

Several alternatives were considered before dropping the atomic bombs on Hiroshima and Nagasaki, Japan. The final decision rested with President Truman who made the decision to use the bombs to end the war as quickly as possible and thereby save American lives.

- Why might the dropping of the atomic bombs be considered a turning point in American history?

Casualties in World War II

Country	Military Dead	Military Wounded	Civilian Dead
Great Britain	373,000	475,000	93,000
France	213,000	400,000	108,000
Soviet Union	11,000,000	14,102,000	7,000,000
United States	292,000	671,000	*
Germany	3,500,000	5,000,000	780,000
Italy	242,000	66,000	153,000
Japan	1,300,000	4,000,000	672,000

All figures are estimates   * Very small number of civilian dead

Analyzing Documents

Evaluate Evidence
Study the chart at left, then answer the following question.

- Which country had the greatest number of military casualties during World War II?

Individuals, Groups, Institutions
During the Holocaust, individuals were singled out for persecution because of their membership in a group. Institutions were developed, and individuals were put in place within those institutions to carry out the atrocities of the Holocaust. Genocide is the deliberate murder of an entire people.

List two other examples of genocide in the twentieth century.

1.

2.

The Holocaust

When Adolf Hitler rose to power in Germany, he did so by finding a scapegoat, someone to blame for Germany's problems after World War I. By appealing to anti-Semitism, feelings of hatred against Jewish people, Hitler encouraged the Germans to turn viciously on all Jewish citizens.

The "Final Solution"

Early in his rise to power, Hitler had seized Jewish property, homes, and businesses and barred Jews from many jobs. At the Wannsee Conference of 1942, the Nazis set as a primary goal the total extermination, or genocide, of all Jews under their domination. This effort was to be kept secret from the German people and from the rest of the world. Hitler's plan to eliminate the Jews was known to the Nazis as the Final Solution.

The Horror of Concentration Camps

In the 1930s, the Nazis began to build concentration camps to isolate Jews and other groups from society and provide slave labor for industry. As Hitler's conquest of Europe continued, the camps became factories of death. More than six million Jews were killed in the camps as were another four million people—dissenters, Gypsies, homosexuals, the mentally and physically handicapped, Protestant ministers, and Catholic priests. Today, concentration camp names such as Auschwitz, Treblinka, and Dachau stand as memorials to the incredible human suffering and death of this time, a period now called the **Holocaust.**

The United States and other nations failed to take strong action to rescue Jews from Nazi Germany before World War II. In 1939, the *St. Louis*, a passenger ship carrying more than 900 Jewish refugees, left Europe for Cuba, but when they arrived, most of the refugees were denied permission to land there. The refugees were also denied permission to enter the United States, and the ship was forced to return to Europe. Most of the ship's passengers eventually were killed in the Holocaust.

After war broke out, the Allies still failed to speak out forcefully against the treatment of Jews or to make direct attempts to stop the genocide. Only toward the end of the war did the United States create the War Refugee Board to provide aid for Holocaust survivors.

War Crimes Trials

As a result of the Potsdam Conference, a final chapter to the Holocaust occurred in Nuremberg, Germany, in 1945 and 1946. At that time an international military court tried 24 high-level Nazis for atrocities committed during World War II. By finding former Nazis guilty of "crimes against humanity," a precedent was established that soldiers, officers, and national leaders could be held responsible for such brutal actions. Escaped Nazis who were found after the end of the war—even decades later—were also brought to trial for war-related crimes.

Among the most infamous Nazis who were tried and convicted was Adolf Eichmann. He was captured in Argentina in 1960 and tried in Israel for the torture and deaths of millions of Jews. Eichmann was convicted of crimes against humanity and was hanged in 1962. Klaus Barbie, known as the "Butcher of Lyon" (France), was also apprehended and tried in 1987 for his wartime brutality against Jews.

War crime trials in Japan led to the execution of former premier Tojo and six other war leaders. About 4,000 other Japanese war criminals were also convicted and received prison sentences.

Reading Strategy

Draw Conclusions
• What important legal precedent was set at the Nuremberg trials?

American Patriotism

After the United States entered the war, the nation moved to full-scale wartime production and mobilization of the armed forces. Americans rallied behind the war effort.

With the exception of the attack on Pearl Harbor and battles on several Pacific islands, World War II was not fought on American soil. Nonetheless, America's coastal areas and large cities held blackout drills in case of attack. Americans supported the war effort by rationing food, gasoline, and other necessities and luxuries. During World War II, the federal government used rationing to provide more resources for the military. Rationing means that the availability of many consumer goods was very limited. Government campaigns encouraged Americans to have "meatless Tuesdays," and many Americans planted "victory gardens" to increase the food supply. Hollywood entertainers made special presentations to persuade citizens to buy war bonds to help the government finance the war.

The Role of American Women

World War II brought dramatic changes to the lives of American women in the military and in the civilian workforce.

In the Military During the war, more than 200,000 women joined the military services. Women served in separate units from men, such as the Women's Army Corps (WAC), and performed vital military duties. They operated radios and repaired planes and vehicles. They were also assigned, along with men, to clerical duties.

In the Civilian Workforce When millions of men joined the military, employment opportunities opened up to women. Many women took jobs that had once been open to men only. More than five million women eventually worked in factories devoted to wartime production, although their pay never came close to equaling men's pay. One song about a woman named Rosie the Riveter became popular during the war years because it captured the sense of duty and patriotism felt by millions of women. The term **"Rosie the Riveter"** became a slang term for all women who worked in wartime factories.

Women factory workers

Preparing for the Exam

- What trend emerged following World War II in regard to women's participation in the labor force?

Reading Strategy

Predicting Content
- How might the experiences of African Americans during World War II have contributed to the rise of the civil rights movement during the 1950s?

Resulting Change Women's wartime work resulted in important changes in employment and lifestyle, even after the war. Before the war, most employed American women were young and unmarried. During the war, large numbers of married women and mothers who had never worked outside the home took jobs. This trend continued after the war. Although many women willingly returned to the roles of wife and mother at the end of the war, thousands more remained in the workforce, which improved their standard of living.

The entry of women into the paid workforce during World War II marked the beginning of a long-term trend. Women continued to enter the workforce throughout the rest of the century. New issues became important. For example, child care became important during the war years, and it remains an important issue today.

African Americans

The experiences of African Americans during the war years provided the foundation of the civil rights movement of the 1950s and 1960s.

In the Military Nearly one million African American men and women served in the military during World War II. Military units were segregated, and initially, African American soldiers were limited to support roles. Once the war went on, these soldiers soon saw combat, and many became distinguished themselves. One example of such heroism were the Tuskegee Airmen, the first black military pilots. These 994 fighter pilots were some of the most decorated fliers of the war effort, but they fought two wars, one overseas against a foreign enemy and the other against racism at home. In 1948, President Truman showed his support for civil rights by issuing Executive Order 9981, which led to the end of racial segregation in the military.

At Home In the 1940s, many southern African Americans began moving to northern cities in search of economic opportunity and freedom from discrimination. However, they met discrimination in the North. Race riots broke out in Detroit and New York City in the summer of 1943. Membership in civil rights organizations grew as African Americans struggled against discrimination.

African Americans experienced gains during the war years. Politically, their migration north had made them a significant voting bloc in urban areas. Economically, new jobs in war industries brought many African Americans the chance to earn more than they ever had before. Despite these gains, African Americans experienced discrimination and inequality in salaries in the workplace. The black press urged that the struggle for freedom be fought on two fronts—overseas and at home as well.

Japanese Americans

Thousands of Japanese Americans faced hardship and economic losses after the attack on Pearl Harbor.

Immigration to America Immigrants from Japan began arriving in the United States in the early 1900s. These immigrants settled mainly on the west coast of the United States. By 1941, thousands of Americans of Japanese descent, called **Nisei,** had been born in the United States and were American citizens. Many had never been to Japan, and many had no desire to go there.

Wartime Relocation Authority (WRA) After the Japanese attack on Pearl Harbor, many Americans feared that Japanese Americans presented a threat to national security. Anti-Japanese sentiment grew, and in 1942 President Roosevelt issued Executive Order 9066, establishing military zones for the imprisonment of

Japanese Americans. More than 100,000 people of Japanese descent were forced to leave their homes and move to **WRA camps,** hastily constructed military-style barracks ringed with barbed wire and guarded by troops.

Ansel Adams

High-school recess period, Manzanar Relocation Center, CA

Preparing for the Exam

Analyze Point of View
"It is a fact that the Japanese navy has been reconnoitering [investigating] the Pacific Coast. . . . It is [a] fact that communication takes place between the enemy at sea and enemy agents on land."

• Would the writer of this excerpt have supported the Supreme Court's decision in *Korematsu v. United States?*

• Explain your answer.

Korematsu **v.** *United States* In the 1944 landmark case *Korematsu* v. *United States*, the Supreme Court upheld the forced evacuation as a reasonable wartime emergency measure. However, no acts of Japanese-American sabotage or treason were ever identified, and thousands of Nisei fought honorably in the war. Almost 50 years after World War II, the United States government admitted that the wartime relocation program had been unjust. In 1988, Congress voted to pay $20,000 to each of the approximately 60,000 surviving Americans who had been interned. The first payments were made in 1990, and the government also issued a formal apology.

Nisei Soldiers Despite the injustices endured by Japanese Americans, thousands proved their loyalty by serving in the U.S. armed forces, primarily in Europe. The 442nd Regimental Combat Team, made up entirely of Japanese Americans, won more medals for bravery than any other unit of its size in the war.

Demobilization

During the war, American factories, geared up for wartime production, had helped the nation recover from the Great Depression. Now the challenge was to convert from a wartime to a peacetime society. The United States underwent a period of demobilization, or the movement from a military to a civilian status. The United States armed forces reduced from 12 million members to 1.5 million. Factories that had made planes and tanks now began producing consumer goods. It also meant ensuring that the nation would not slip back into depression.

Truman's Legislative Program During President Truman's administration, legislation was passed to deal with different issues raised by demobilization. Truman's legislative program aimed at promoting full employment, a higher

Key Themes and Concepts

Diversity
The Korematsu Case shared a similarity with *Plessy* v. *Ferguson* (1896) in that specific groups were being targeted by the government based on race or ethnicity.

Preparing for the Exam

Which groups were targeted by each case?

• Korematsu v. United States

• Plessy v. Ferguson

minimum wage, greater unemployment compensation for workers without jobs, housing assistance, and other items was known as the **Fair Deal,** a play on words from Franklin Roosevelt's New Deal.

Servicemen's Readjustment Act of 1944 (The GI Bill of Rights) This act authorized billions of dollars to pay for veterans' benefits, such as college education, medical treatment, unemployment insurance, and home and business loans. The GI Bill made it possible for more people to attend college and buy homes than ever before.

Employment Act of 1946 This act made full employment a national goal and set up a Council of Economic Advisors to guide the president on economic matters.

An End to Price Controls Wartime legislation had put controls on the prices of most goods. In 1946, the government moved to end most such controls. However, the end of controls coupled with a tax cut caused a rapid increase in inflation. For example, food prices soared 25 percent in just two years.

The Taft-Hartley Act Workers' wages could not keep up with inflation after the war. Major strikes were held as unions pushed for higher wages. Antiunion feelings grew and led Congress to pass the Taft-Hartley Act over Truman's veto. The act:

- provided an 80-day "cooling-off" period through which the president could delay a strike that threatened national welfare.
- barred the closed shop, under which workers had to belong to a union before being hired.
- allowed states to pass "right-to-work laws," which said workers could take jobs and not have to join a union.
- banned union contributions to political campaigns.
- required union leaders to swear they were not communists.

National Security Concerns

During Truman's administration, the National Security Act of 1947 was passed. This created the National Military Establishment, which later became the Department of Defense. The act also created the Central Intelligence Agency to oversee intelligence gathering activities. Truman also issued an executive order banning discrimination in the armed forces.

The Baby Boom

In addition to problems caused by converting to a peacetime economy, the nation also experienced the largest population explosion in its history. The economic hardships of the Great Depression that had encouraged smaller families were gone. Families grew larger. This "baby boom" led to the expansion of many public services, especially schools. The rapid growth in personal income in the decade after World War II also contributed to an expansion of the middle class. You will learn more about the long-term effects of the baby boom in the next unit.

The Election of 1948

Many voters had become dissatisfied with Truman's presidency because of inflation, strikes, Truman's actions on civil rights, and the developing cold war. Polls predicted that the Republican candidate, Governor Thomas Dewey of New York, would defeat Truman easily in the 1948 presidential election. Yet Truman pulled off one of the greatest upsets in American political history by winning reelection. He then attempted to build on this victory by proposing a program called the Fair Deal that aimed to extend reforms started under FDR's New Deal.

Preparing for the Exam

The Taft-Hartley Act of 1947 was a setback for organized labor. It gave the president the power to delay (through court injunction) any strike that took place within an industry that the President deemed important to the nation's health or safety.

- Identify one or two industries that would be considered important to the nation's health or safety.

Key Themes and Concepts

Change
- How did the prosperity of the 1940s and 1950s influence the nation's population growth rate?

Peace with Problems, 1945–1960

Section Overview

The end of World War II brought the desire to prevent such devastation from ever happening again. The United Nations was established to help nations find peaceful solutions to conflicts. Meanwhile, the uneasy wartime alliance between the United States and the Soviet Union dissolved as the Cold War took hold. As communism spread through the efforts of the Soviet Union and later China, the United States worked to strengthen its influence in Western Europe and Asia by providing economic aid and building strategic alliances. A growing anxiety about the spread of communism led the United States to become more deeply involved in global affairs, while also fearing a communist influence at home.

Key Themes and Concepts

As you review this section, take special note of the following key themes and concepts:

Change Why did the United States and the Soviet Union change from being allies in World War II to enemies during the Cold War?

Foreign Policy How did the United States use economic aid to build its influence in Europe and Asia?

Constitutional Principles How did the fear of communism lead to the violations of some people's civil rights in the United States?

Key People

Eleanor Roosevelt	Douglas MacArthur
George C. Marshall	Alger Hiss
Mao Zedong	Joseph McCarthy
Chiang Kai-shek	Ethel and Julius Rosenberg

Key Terms

containment	NATO
"iron curtain"	Warsaw Pact
Truman Doctrine	38th parallel
Marshall Plan	HUAC
Cold War	

The United States emerged from World War II as the world's greatest military power. Compared to other nations, it had suffered relatively little physical destruction. For a short time, the United States held a monopoly on the ability to use nuclear power. After World War II, the United States was aware of its strength as a nation and its responsibility to preserve world peace.

The Big Idea

The post-World War II hostilities between the United States and the Soviet Union are together known as the Cold War.

The Cold War:

- lasted from about 1946 to 1991.

- was brought about by competition between the United States and the Soviet Union for power and influence in the world.

- consisted of political and economic conflict and military tensions throughout the globe.

Analyzing Documents

identify and evaluate data
Review the timeline, then answer the following questions.

- How long did the Korean War last?

- In what year was NATO formed?

1945		1949		1953	
World War II ends		NATO formed		Cease-fire in Korea	

| 1945 | 1947 | 1949 | 1951 | 1953 | 1955 |

	1947		1950		1954
	Marshall Plan; Truman Doctrine		Korean War begins; Rosenbergs arrested		McCarthy censured by Senate

The United Nations

American foreign policy changed dramatically as a result of World War II. Even before the conclusion of the war, the United States began planning for an international peacekeeping organization. Plans were made at the Yalta Conference for a United Nations Conference to be held in San Francisco in April 1945. The Soviet Union, under the leadership of Joseph Stalin, agreed to participate in planning the new organization which would be known as the United Nations. The United States Senate approved the United Nations Charter by a vote of 82 to 2.

Organization of the United Nations

The structure of the United Nations (UN) includes a General Assembly of all its members and a Security Council of 15 members. The Security Council consists of ten rotating member nations and five permanent members. (The original permanent members were the United States, Great Britain, the Soviet Union, China, and France. After the breakup of the Soviet Union, the Russian Federation became a permanent member.)

The General Assembly serves as a forum for world leaders to speak on a variety of concerns. Although the UN has become militarily involved in a number of world crises, most of its members would agree that its greatest accomplishments have been in fighting hunger and disease and in promoting education. The headquarters of the United Nations is in New York City.

Reading Strategy

Organizing Information
- Who are the five permanent members of the United Nations Security Council?

1.

2.

3.

4.

5.

The United Nations

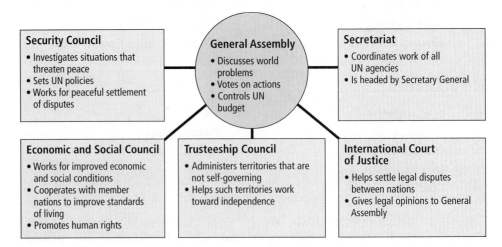

Security Council
- Investigates situations that threaten peace
- Sets UN policies
- Works for peaceful settlement of disputes

General Assembly
- Discusses world problems
- Votes on actions
- Controls UN budget

Secretariat
- Coordinates work of all UN agencies
- Is headed by Secretary General

Economic and Social Council
- Works for improved economic and social conditions
- Cooperates with member nations to improve standards of living
- Promotes human rights

Trusteeship Council
- Administers territories that are not self-governing
- Helps such territories work toward independence

International Court of Justice
- Helps settle legal disputes between nations
- Gives legal opinions to General Assembly

Analyzing Documents

Study the chart, then answer the following questions.

- Which branch of the United Nations would help two countries resolve a legal dispute?

- Which branch sets UN policies?

Universal Declaration of Human Rights In 1946, President Truman appointed former first lady Eleanor Roosevelt as a United Nations delegate, the only woman in the American delegation. The committee that Eleanor Roosevelt led authored the Universal Declaration of Human Rights, a proclamation that is still part of the guiding philosophy of the UN today. In the postwar years, people all over the world were especially eager to have an international organization succeed at defining human rights for all people.

Containment as a Foreign Policy

American foreign policy after World War II was influenced by two factors: the willingness of the United States to become involved in international peacekeeping efforts and its determination to prevent the spread of communism.

Growing Distrust of the Soviet Union

In 1939, Germany and the Soviet Union had signed a nonaggression treaty, but after Germany violated the pact, the Soviet Union sought a new alliance to protect itself from Germany. The United States then allied with the Soviet Union throughout World War II. Although they were allies, American and Soviet leaders did not fully trust one another. After the war, it became apparent that the only common goal shared by the United States and the Soviet Union was the defeat of the Axis powers.

After World War II, the Soviet Union was viewed as a grave threat to the security of the noncommunist world. In defeating Nazi Germany, the Soviets had moved troops into the nations of Eastern Europe. After the war, the Soviet Union actively supported communist governments in those nations.

The United States, which had emerged as a superpower nation, took on the task of limiting communist expansion—a policy known as **containment.** The goal of containment was to confine communism to the area in which it already existed—the Soviet Union and the Eastern European nations. American presidential power increased during this time period as the United States sought to carry out this policy.

Following are key foreign policy developments related to the containment of communism immediately after World War II.

Reading Strategy

Reinforcing Main Ideas
Containment of communism to the areas where it already existed was a central tenant of American foreign policy during the Cold War.

- How did communism spread to Eastern Europe?

- What had Stalin promised at Yalta in regards to Eastern Europe?

Analyzing Documents

Make Inferences and Draw Conclusions
Examine the cartoon at left, then answer the following questions.

- What major world event has recently ended?

- Describe the buildings below the climber.

- Why is the climber named "Europe"?

- What is the importance of the climber's rope?

- What does the caption mean?

In one or two sentences, write a summary of the idea this cartoon is conveying.

The Way Back

Churchill's "Iron Curtain" Speech

In his 1946 speech at Westminster College in Fulton, Missouri, Prime Minister Winston Churchill of Great Britain cautioned the world about the threat of communist expansion. He warned that "from Stettin in the Baltic to Trieste in the Adriatic, an iron curtain has descended across the Continent." Churchill's phrase "iron curtain" drew a clear picture of the postwar world. There had come to be recognizable division between the free Western Europe and the communist Eastern Europe.

The Truman Doctrine

Before World War II, Great Britain had been a powerful force in the Mediterranean. The tremendous losses and expense of World War II, however, weakened Great Britain's influence there. The Soviet Union, which had long been striving for access to the Mediterranean Sea by way of the Turkish straits, sought to extend its influence in the area.

The Soviets supported communist rebels in their attempt to topple the government of Greece. This led the United States to try to contain the spread of communism in the Mediterranean region. On March 12, 1947, President Truman asked Congress for $400 million in aid to Turkey and Greece. He called on the United States to support free people in resisting control by armed minorities or outside pressures. Truman believed that the failure of the United States to act at this time would endanger both the nation and the free world.

Congress approved Truman's request. By 1950, more than $660 million had been spent in aid to Turkey and Greece. This policy of economic and military aid became known as the **Truman Doctrine.** It represents a major step in the evolution of American foreign policy further away from isolationism and neutrality.

The Marshall Plan

World War II left much of Europe in ruins. Major cities and industrial centers were destroyed. Survivors of the war struggled to find food, shelter, and clothing. Dissatisfaction with such conditions grew rapidly. In many war-torn countries, the Communist Party seemed to offer solutions to such problems.

To prevent the spread of communist influence in Europe, General George C. Marshall, secretary of state under President Truman, announced a new economic-aid program called the **Marshall Plan.** In a speech delivered on June 5, 1947, Marshall announced that the United States was against "hunger, poverty, desperation, and chaos." Between 1948 and 1952, about $13 billion in economic aid was allocated by the Republican-dominated Congress for the rebuilding of Europe under the Marshall Plan. The largest amount went to Great Britain, France, Italy, and West Germany.

This aid enabled Western Europe to begin consumer production once more and to build prosperous economies. Both Western Europe and the United States felt that with stabilized and improving economies, communist expansion would be halted.

The Beginning of the Cold War: Germany 1948–1949

At the end of World War II, Germany was divided into four zones of occupation controlled by Great Britain, France, the Soviet Union, and the United States. Berlin, the capital of Germany, was located in the Russian sector. However, the city was divided into four sections, each controlled by one of the four Allies. Disagreements during this period of occupation marked the beginning of the Cold War, a period of tension between the United States and the Soviet Union from the end of World War II to 1991.

Geography in History

Stalin wanted control of the Dardanelles, a narrow strait in Turkey, because it would give Soviet ports on the Black Sea access to the Mediterranean.

- How does this fact relate to the Truman Doctrine?

Analyzing Documents

Evaluate Causes and Effects

"In these circumstances, it is clear that the main element of any United States policy toward the Soviet Union must be that of a long-term, patient but firm and vigilant containment of Russian expansive tendencies."
—American diplomat George Kennan, July 1947

- In what ways were the Truman Doctrine and the Marshall Plan examples of "long-term, patient but firm and vigilant" containment of communism?

The Berlin Blockade The United States, France, and Great Britain cooperated in governing the western sectors of Germany. Unable to reach agreement with the Soviet Union over the eventual unification of Germany, the three western powers decided to unify their zones without the Soviet zone. In 1949, the Federal Republic of Germany, commonly known as West Germany, was established. The Soviets opposed the establishment of this separate government. Prior to that on June 24, 1948, the Soviets had cut off all access to West Berlin by blockading the roads leading to the city, all of which had to go through the Soviet-controlled sector of Germany. The Soviets hoped that the blockade would force the western powers out of Berlin.

The Berlin Airlift The United States, Great Britain, and France would not back down. Recognizing that West Berlin could not get supplies by road anymore, the western powers began an airlift of food, clothing, coal, medicine, and other necessities to the city. Almost a year later, on May 12, 1949, the Soviets recognized their defeat in the area and ended the blockade. Shortly afterward, the Soviets announced the formation of the German Democratic Republic, commonly known as East Germany. In 1955, West Germany was given full sovereignty. The West had learned once again that although World War II was over, its struggle against aggressor nations was not.

Point Four Program

The United States recognized that the Soviet Union's expansionist aims were targeted not only at Europe but at developing nations of the world as well. In 1950, Congress approved President Truman's Point Four Program, which provided nearly $400 million for technical development programs in Latin America, Asia, and Africa. The Point Four Program was designed to modernize and strengthen the economies of developing nations and thereby discourage the growth of communism.

The North Atlantic Treaty Organization

The United States and other Western European nations also fought the spread of communism by forming alliances. In April 1949, the United States and 11 other western nations signed a collective security agreement called the North Atlantic Treaty. This agreement bound the participating nations to act together for their common defense. Members pledged that an attack on any one of them would be considered an attack on all of them. This is known as a system of mutual defense. Defense arrangements were coordinated through the North Atlantic Treaty Organization **(NATO)**. The Soviets later formed an opposing alliance with seven Eastern European nations under the **Warsaw Pact.**

In 1949, President Truman announced that the Soviet Union had successfully exploded an atomic bomb. Fearing the power that this gave the Soviets, the United States worked to strengthen its influence in the world by committing several billion dollars in assistance to countries in Western Europe and elsewhere.

European Cooperation

In order to rebuild and strengthen their economies after the war, Western European nations made ever-increasing efforts at economic cooperation. In 1951, the European Coal and Steel Community formed to enable six European nations to set prices and regulate the coal and steel industries. By 1957, the scope of economic cooperation had broadened to include efforts to improve transportation and eliminate tariff barriers within Europe. Those same six nations signed a treaty in 1957 to form the European Economic Community (EEC), also known as the Common Market. As economic cooperation continued to broaden, this organization later transformed into the European Union (EU) that exists today.

Reading Strategy

Organizing Information Who controlled the four zones of occupation in Germany following World War II?

1.

2.

3.

4.

- In which zone was the capital Berlin located?

- Which zones were combined to form West Germany?

- How did the Soviets attempt to take control of Berlin?

Key Themes and Concepts

Foreign Policy NATO represented the principle of mutual military assistance or collective security. By joining NATO, the United States dropped its opposition to military treaties with Europe for the first time since the Monroe Doctrine. As a member of NATO the United States became actively involved in European affairs. This is an example of the United States using the Cold War Policy of containment.

The Cold War in Europe

Analyzing Documents

Geographic reasoning
After losing more than 20 million people during the war and suffering widespread destruction, the Soviet Union was determined to rebuild in ways that would protect its own interests. One way was to establish satellite nations, countries subject to Soviet domination, on the western borders of the Soviet Union.

• How does this map illustrate the Soviet Union's desire to protect itself from non-communist rivals?

The European Union has experienced many changes in recent years. The European Parliament, the legislative branch of the EU, now has the power to approve or reject the EU's budget. In 1999, eleven member states began using a common currency called the euro. The EU continues to grapple with such key issues as increasing employment opportunities for citizens in all member nations. The EU today has 15 member states and is preparing for the admission of new members from eastern and southern Europe.

Containment in Asia

During World War II, the United States had been an ally of China and an enemy of Japan. After World War II, the United States reversed its political alliances in Asia. With its new constitutional democracy, Japan became an American ally. Meanwhile, a communist takeover in China made the United States increasingly suspicious of and hostile to that nation.

Communist Victory in China

In the 1930s, China had plunged into civil war. Mao Zedong, leader of the communist forces in China, sought to defeat the nationalist regime of Chiang Kai-shek. In 1949, the communist forces defeated the nationalists and renamed the now communist-led country the People's Republic of China. Chiang Kai-shek and the nationalists fled to the island of Taiwan.

Reading Strategy

Analyzing Cause And Effect
• How might the victory of the communists in the Chinese civil war in 1949 have contributed to United States involvement in the Korean War in 1950?

The United States was alarmed by this development because it feared that communism would spread beyond China. Because the United States had overseen the initial rebuilding of postwar Japan and had helped put a new constitutional democracy in place, it did not want to see communism spread to Japan. Support for Japan was now seen as a way of offsetting communist China's influence in Asia.

The Korean War

During World War II, Korea had been occupied by Japan. At the end of the war, Korea was divided along the **38th parallel,** or line of latitude. The northern zone was under the influence of the Soviet Union, and the southern zone was controlled by the United States. By 1948, the southern zone had elected an anticommunist government headed by Syngman Rhee and was now called the Republic of Korea. In the northern zone, now named the Democratic People's Republic of Korea, a communist government ruled.

Fighting Begins North Korea invaded South Korea in 1950 in an attempt to unify the country. President Truman responded to this invasion by committing American troops to major involvement in the Korean conflict.

MacArthur in Command General Douglas MacArthur, a World War II hero, was sent to command the United States military in Korea. Troops from the United States, along with small numbers of soldiers from other UN member nations, were soon involved in battles as fierce as those of World War II. A particularly devastating loss came at the Yalu River, when Chinese forces entered the conflict and pushed UN troops south. By the middle of 1951, the war had reached a stalemate. Fighting continued, but neither side was able to advance successfully.

Disagreement over the objectives and military strategies of the Korean War caused a major conflict between President Truman and General MacArthur. Although Truman was a civilian, the Constitution makes the president the commander in chief of the armed forces. When General MacArthur disagreed with Truman publicly about the conduct of the war, the President recalled him to the United States and dismissed him from command.

Reading Strategy

Organizing Information
- Who fought on the side of communist North Korea during the Korean War?
- Who fought on the side of anticommunist South Korea during the Korean War?

President Harry Truman (left) and General Douglas MacArthur

Hostilities End Although truce talks began in June 1951, no resolution was reached before the American presidential election of 1952. During that campaign the Republican candidate, World War II hero Dwight D. Eisenhower, promised that if he were elected president he would go to Korea to aid in the peace negotiations. Eisenhower won the election and did keep his campaign promise, but a truce or cease-fire was not officially signed until July 27, 1953.

The war in Korea lasted for more than three years and cost more than $15 billion. Approximately 34,000 Americans and one million Koreans and Chinese died in the conflict. At the end of the Korean War, Korea remained a divided nation and has continued in that political situation into the twenty-first century.

New Directions The policy of containment took a different course with American involvement in the Korean conflict. Early containment efforts focused primarily on economic aid programs. With the Korean War, the United States now showed

Key Themes and Concepts

Civic Values
The Korean War caused enormous frustration at home. When the truce was signed in 1953, Korea remained divided at almost exactly the same place as before the war, near the 38th parallel. Americans wondered why more than 54,000 of their soldiers had been killed and 113,000 wounded for such limited results. Why would some Americans wonder if their government was serious about stopping communism?

Key Themes
and Concepts

Foreign Policy
• In what way did the
Korean War mark a
change in the U.S. policy
of containment?

its willingness to undertake military action to contain communism if it was necessary. American experiences in Korea were a warning of future global confrontations between democratic and communist opponents.

The Cold War at Home

Even as the United States defended democratic freedoms worldwide, sometimes those same freedoms were in danger at home. The spreading of communism to China and the apparent growing strength of the Soviet Union led some Americans to fear that communism could spread to the United States. This fear led some Americans to take actions that violated the civil rights of others.

Many Americans charged that communist agents were trying to subvert, or destroy, the American political system. Other Americans responded that the actions of anticommunists were more subversive of American values and more dangerous to the nation.

Looking for Communists

The fear of communism in the United States had its roots in the period before World War II. Anticommunist activity began in the 1930s.

HUAC In 1938, the House Un-American Activities Committee (HUAC) was formed as a temporary investigative unit to look into communist activity in the United States. HUAC operated for more than 30 years. Its well-publicized probe of the movie industry in the 1940s and 1950s led to the blacklisting, or cutting off from employment, of many actors, writers, and directors.

Reading
      Strategy

Reinforcing Main Ideas
Americans' fears of
communism resulted from
the fact that communists
were openly hostile to
American beliefs and values
such as capitalism, private
ownership of land and
business, and First Amendment freedoms.

• What other foreign
and domestic events
contributed to Americans'
fears of the spread of
communism?

J. Edgar Hoover, director of the Federal Bureau of Investigation, often aided HUAC investigations. Critics argued that Hoover conducted anticommunist activities that often violated the civil rights of Americans.

The Smith Act In 1940, Congress passed the Smith Act, which made it illegal for anyone to advocate "overthrowing . . . any government in the United States by force" or to "affiliate" with groups that called for such action.

In the 1951 landmark case of *Dennis* v. *United States,* the Supreme Court upheld the Smith Act. Eugene Dennis, general secretary of the Communist Party in the United States, and ten others were convicted of advocating the violent overthrow of the government.

Two court decisions in 1957 weakened the intent of the Smith Act. In *Watkins* v. *United States,* the court ruled the HUAC could not punish witnesses who refused to cooperate with its investigations. In *Yates* v. *United States,* the court ruled that the Smith Act applied only to those who teach or advocate direct "action" to overthrow government, not to those who merely advocate it in principle.

The Loyalty Program In 1947, President Truman fueled anticommunist feelings by ordering a Loyalty Review Board to conduct security checks on thousands of government employees. Those whose loyalty was considered doubtful were dismissed.

In the early 1950s, Robert Oppenheimer, who had led the research to develop the atomic bomb, voiced his opposition to building the new, more destructive hydrogen bomb. This action and his past association with others whose loyalty was being questioned led to a government hearing about his own loyalty. He was determined to be a "loyal citizen," but his security clearance was removed, and he was barred from future government research.

The Hiss Case The Alger Hiss case led many Americans to believe that there was a reason to fear that there were communists in the government. In 1948, Alger Hiss, a former adviser to President Roosevelt, was charged with having been a Communist spy during the 1930s. Whittaker Chambers, a former Communist party member, made these charges, which Hiss denied. A congressional committee investigated them.

A young Republican committee member from California, Richard Nixon, believed that Hiss was guilty. Nixon's pursuit of the case and Hiss's eventual conviction on perjury charges made Nixon a national figure. The conviction also added weight to Republican charges that Roosevelt and Truman had not been alert enough to the dangers of communism.

McCarthyism

Against this political background, Senator Joseph McCarthy of Wisconsin began his own hunt for communists. In 1950, McCarthy charged he had a list of State Department employees known to be communists. Over the next four years, McCarthy went on to charge that many other people and government agencies had been corrupted by communism. He used the term "infiltrated" to describe how the people he accused had secretly obtained government positions.

McCarthy made bold accusations without any evidence. This tactic became known as "McCarthyism." He ruined the reputations of many people he carelessly accused of being communists. Meanwhile, the Rosenberg case and congressional legislation helped win public support for McCarthy's actions.

The Rosenberg Case In 1950, Ethel and Julius Rosenberg and Morton Sobell were charged with giving atomic secrets to the Soviets during World War II. After a highly controversial trial, they were convicted of espionage. The Rosenbergs were sentenced to death and Sobell to prison. The Rosenbergs were executed in 1953.

Congressional Legislation In the same year the Rosenbergs were arrested, Congress passed the McCarran Internal Security Act. The law aimed at limiting the actions of anyone the government considered a threat to United States security. The McCarran-Walter Act of 1952 restricted the immigration of persons from communist-dominated nations in Asia and southern and central Europe. President Truman vetoed the bill, but Congress passed it over his veto.

McCarthy's Fall In 1954, McCarthy charged that even the army was full of communists. He held televised investigations into these charges. For the first time, millions of Americans saw McCarthy's bullying tactics for themselves. His public support quickly faded, and in December 1954, the Senate censured, or denounced, him for "conduct unbecoming a member." The fall of McCarthy ended the red scare of the 1950s, although anticommunist attitudes lingered as the Cold War continued to drag on. During this time the tactics of Senator McCarthy were criticized because he violated important constitutional liberties. The term McCarthyism has come to mean the use of methods of investigation and accusation that are regarded as unfair, in order to suppress opposition.

Preparing for the Exam

- What was the outcome of the Alger Hiss case and what was its significance?

Key Themes and Concepts

Constitutional Principles Although many people knew that Senator McCarthy's claims were exaggerated at best, he was still able to gain power and ruin the lives of many people.

- How did McCarthy contribute to the suppression of free speech and open, honest debate?

Preparing for the Exam

McCarthyism during the 1950s had many similarities to the Red Scare following World War I.

- How were the actions of Attorney General A. Mitchell Palmer and McCarthy similar?

Questions for Regents Practice

Multiple Choice

Directions: Review the Test-Taking Strategies section of this book. Then answer the following questions, drawn from actual Regents examinations. For each statement or question, choose the *number* of the word or expression that, of those given, best completes the statement or answers the question.

1 United States senators who opposed the Treaty of Versailles objected mainly to

   (1) United States membership in the League of Nations

   (2) payment of reparations by Germany to the Allied nations

   (3) the transfer of Germany's colonial possessions to the League of Nations

   (4) the creation of new and independent nations in Eastern Europe

2 A major reason for the United States neutrality in the 1930s was the nation's

   (1) belief in the domino theory

   (2) disillusionment resulting from World War I

   (3) strong approval of political conditions in Europe

   (4) military and naval superiority

3 At the outbreak of both World War I and World War II in Europe, public opinion in the United States generally favored

   (1) remaining neutral

   (2) entering the war on the side of the Allies

   (3) invading Europe in order to acquire territory

   (4) settling the conflict through an international peace organization

4 Isolationism as a foreign policy is more difficult to achieve in the twentieth century than in prior times mainly because

   (1) the increase in the world's population has forced people to live more closely together

   (2) there are more sovereign nations today than in the past

   (3) modern technology had made nations more interdependent

   (4) public opinion on issues is more easily disregarded

5 The appeasement policy followed by Western European leaders in the late 1930s was based primarily on the belief that war could be avoided by

   (1) satisfying Hitler's desire for territorial expansion

   (2) encouraging communist expansion into Nazi Germany

   (3) limiting the development of Germany's armed forces

   (4) appealing to the League of Nations for international cooperation

6 Which event led directly to United States entry into World War II?

   (1) invasion of Poland by Germany and Russia

   (2) attack on France by Italy

   (3) sinking of the *Lusitania* by Germany

   (4) attack on Pearl Harbor by Japan

Base your answer to question 7 on the announcement below and on your knowledge of social studies.

> **WESTERN DEFENSE COMMAND AND FOURTH ARMY WARTIME CIVIL CONTROL ADMINISTRATION**
>
> **Presidio of San Francisco, California April 1, 1942**
>
> **INSTRUCTIONS TO ALL PERSONS OF**
>
> # JAPANESE
> ### ANCESTRY
>
> **Living in the Following Area:**
>
> All that portion of the City and County of San Francisco, State of California, lying generally west of the north-south line established by Junipero Serra Boulevard, Worcester Avenue, and Nineteenth Avenue and lying generally north of the east-west line established by California Street, to the intersection of Market Street, and thence on Market Street to San Francisco Bay.
>
> All Japanese persons, both alien and non-alien, will be evacuated from the above designated area by 12:00 o'clock noon Tuesday, April 7, 1942.

7 During World War II, the action required by this announcement was based largely on

(1) racial prejudice

(2) a labor shortage

(3) the needs for skilled workers in defense industries

(4) a desire to protect Japanese Americans from military attack

8 The rulings of the Supreme Court in *Dred Scott* v. *Sanford* (1857), *Plessy* v. *Ferguson* (1896), and *Korematsu* v. *United States* (1944) all demonstrate that the Supreme Court has

(1) continued to extend voting rights to minorities

(2) protected itself from internal dissent

(3) sometimes failed to protect the rights of minorities

(4) often imposed restrictions on free speech during wartime

9 An important effect of World War II on United States foreign policy was a

(1) refusal to become involved in world affairs

(2) smaller role for the president in foreign policy and national security issues

(3) stronger commitment to collective security and world leadership

(4) willingness to intervene only when the national economy is involved

10 After World War II, the United States was better able than its allies to adjust its economy from wartime to peacetime because the United States

(1) possessed nuclear weapons

(2) raised tariffs on imports

(3) had collected its war debts from the Allies

(4) had suffered no widespread wartime destruction

11 What was a major effect of World War II on women and minorities in the United States?

(1) They were drafted into the military.

(2) They had new opportunities in the workforce.

(3) They received equal voting rights for the first time.

(4) They were granted equal pay for equal work.

Questions for Regents Practice

Base your answers to questions 12 and 13 on the speakers' conversation below and on your knowledge of social studies.

Speaker A: "We must provide arms to the legitimate governments of Greece and Turkey if they are to defeat Soviet-sponsored subversion."

Speaker B: "The first priority is to help rebuild the postwar economies of European countries so that democratic governments can survive."

Speaker C: "Our main goal is to create a system of collective security agreements to deal with any military threats."

Speaker D: "We must continue to build both our nuclear and our conventional arsenals if we are to have any hope of world peace."

12 The central concern of all the speakers is
 (1) the containment of communism
 (2) the defeat of the Axis Powers in World War II
 (3) a ban on the proliferation of nuclear weapons
 (4) the support of United Nations peacekeeping efforts

13 These speakers' statements would most likely have been made during the presidential administration of
 (1) Franklin D. Roosevelt
 (2) Harry S. Truman
 (3) John F. Kennedy
 (4) Richard M. Nixon

14 "Wilson Orders Controls on U.S. Industry to Fight War Against Germany"

"FDR OK's Destroyer Deal with England to Fight Sub Threat"

"Truman Orders Airlift of Supplies to Berlin"

Which generalization about governmental power in the United States is supported by these headlines?
 (1) Important presidential decisions usually follow the results of public opinion polls.
 (2) Presidential actions during international crises have increased executive power.
 (3) Foreign policy is ultimately determined by Congress's power to allocate funds.
 (4) Presidential power to act in wartime cannot be exercised without bipartisan support.

15 The Truman Doctrine and the Eisenhower Doctrine were United States foreign policies concerning
 (1) the international balance of payments
 (2) the containment of communism
 (3) worldwide environmental pollution
 (4) nuclear disarmament

16 The North Atlantic Treaty Organization (NATO) and the Truman Doctrine were attempts to carry out a United States foreign policy of
 (1) brinkmanship
 (2) containment
 (3) appeasement
 (4) neutrality

17 After World War II, relations between the Soviet Union and the United States were marked by

(1) conflicts where the superpowers supported opposing sides, but did not confront each other directly

(2) refusal to negotiate on any issues

(3) slow but steady decreases in military forces and armaments

(4) reliance on international peace organizations to resolve disputes

18 The Red Scare and McCarthyism were similar in that both

(1) advocated the development of the arts and sciences

(2) supported United States foreign aid programs

(3) encouraged nativist ideas

(4) promoted economic development

19 The NATO alliance, Truman Doctrine, and Marshall Plan were all attempts to

(1) contain the spread of communism

(2) give military assistance to China

(3) defend United Nations peacekeeping forces

(4) bring peace to the Middle East

20 During the 1950s, Senator Joseph McCarthy held congressional hearings to expose suspected

(1) Nazis

(2) members of organized crime

(3) terrorists

(4) communists

21 The Cold War developed after World War II as a result of

(1) a decrease in arms production

(2) the collapse of the United Nations

(3) Japan's new economic growth

(4) tension between the superpowers

22 The need for an international peacekeeping organization after World War II resulted in the development of the

(1) Red Cross

(2) League of Nations

(3) United Nations

(4) Alliance for Progress

23 "We Americans live in a world we can no longer dominate, but from which we cannot isolate ourselves." The author of this quotation is saying that the United States should

(1) become less dependent on foreign nations

(2) realize that it is no longer a world power

(3) recognize important changes in international relations

(4) increase its economic and military strength

24 What was a major goal of United States foreign policy in Europe after 1945?

(1) development of nuclear weapons for World War II Allies of the United States

(2) liberation of nations under the control of the Soviet Union

(3) military support for nationalist movements within individual European nations

(4) promotion of international cooperation through political and economic agreements

25 In its dependence upon members to enforce human rights declarations, the United Nations most closely resembles the

(1) Soviet Union under Joseph Stalin

(2) United States under the federal Constitution

(3) United States under the Articles of Confederation

(4) Japanese government before World War II

Thematic Essay Question

Directions: Write a well-organized essay that includes an introduction, several paragraphs addressing the task below, and a conclusion.

Theme: **Foreign Policy**

The primary aim of a nation's foreign policy is the self-interest of that nation. Throughout United States history, certain foreign policy actions have led to debate over whether they were in the national interest.

Task:

- Identify *three* different foreign policies that have been followed by the United States.
- Discuss a specific application of that policy by the United States.
- Include in your discussion one reason the United States applied that policy and one result of the application of that policy.

You may use any example from your study of United States foreign policy actions during the twentieth century. Some suggestions you might wish to consider include: isolationism, containment, formation of military alliances, reliance upon international alliances, and nonrecognition.

You are *not* limited to these suggestions.

Guidelines:

In your essay, be sure to

- Develop all aspects of the task
- Support the theme with relevant facts, examples, and details
- Use a logical and clear plan of organization, including an introduction and a conclusion that are beyond a restatement of the theme

In developing your answer, be sure to keep this general definition in mind:

discuss **means "to make observations about something using facts, reasoning, and argument; to present in some detail"**

Document-Based Question

In developing your answers, be sure to keep this general definition in mind:

> discuss means "to make observations about something using facts, reasoning, and argument; to present in some detail.

This question is based on the accompanying documents. The question is designed to test your ability to work with historical documents. Some of the documents have been edited for the purposes of the question. As you analyze the documents, take into account the source of each document and any point of view that may be presented in the document.

Historical Context:

> World events after 1939 drew the United States into greater international involvement. These events forced the United States to abandon its isolationist foreign policy in favor of more active global involvement.

Task: Using information from the documents and your knowledge of United States history and government, answer the questions that follow each document in Part A. Your answers to the questions will help you write the Part B essay in which you will be asked to:

> * Discuss how the need for military security and the protection of democratic ideals have shaped American foreign policy since 1939

Document-Based Question

Document #1

> "Yesterday, December 7, 1941, a date which will live in infamy, the United States of America was suddenly and deliberately attacked by naval and air forces of the Empire of Japan.
>
> "The attack yesterday on the Hawaiian Islands has caused severe damage to American naval and military forces. Very many American lives have been lost. In addition, American ships have been reported torpedoed on the high seas between San Francisco and Honolulu.
>
> "As Commander in Chief of the Army and Navy I have directed that all measures be taken for our defense. . . . I believe I interpret the will of the Congress and of the people when I assert that we will not only defend ourselves to the uttermost but will make very certain that this form of treachery shall never endanger us again.
>
> "I ask that the Congress declare that, since the unprovoked and dastardly attack by Japan on Sunday, December 7, a state of war has existed between the United States and the Japanese Empire."
>
> —Franklin D. Roosevelt, *Address to Congress*, December 8, 1941

1. Why did President Roosevelt believe that the attack on Pearl Harbor justified the United States officially declaring war on Japan?

_____

_____

_____

Document #2

2. This cartoon represents Roosevelt, Stalin, and Churchill at the Yalta Conference. What does their activity in this cartoon say about their accomplishments at Yalta?

_____

_____

Document #3

> "[The Soviet Union] cannot be easily defeated or discouraged by a single victory on the part of its opponents . . . but only by intelligent long-range policies . . . no less steady in their purpose . . . than those of the Soviet Union itself. In these circumstances, it is clear that the main element of any United States policy toward the Soviet Union must be that of a long-term, patient but firm and vigilant containment of Russian expansive tendencies."
>
> **—Foreign service officer George Kennan, July 1947**

3. What foreign policy position did Kennan believe the United States should take toward the Soviet Union?

_____

_____

_____

Document #4

> "The Parties agree that an armed attack against one or more of them in Europe or North America shall be considered an attack against them all and consequently they agree that, if such an armed attack occurs, each of them, in exercise of the right of individual or collective self-defense. . . will assist the Party or Parties so attacked by taking . . . such action as it deems necessary, including the use of armed force, to restore and maintain the security of the North Atlantic area."
>
> **—The North Atlantic Treaty, April 4, 1949**

4. How did joining NATO demonstrate the long-term commitment of the United States to international involvement?

_____

_____

_____

_____

Document #5

> "I believe that it must be the policy of the United States to support free peoples who are resisting attempted subjugation [takeover] by armed minorities or by outside pressures. . . . I believe that our help should be primarily through economic and financial aid, which is essential to economic stability and orderly political processes. . . .
>
> "I therefore ask the Congress to provide authority for assistance to Greece and Turkey in the amount of $400,000,000. . . .
>
> "The free peoples of the world look to us for support in maintaining their freedoms. If we falter in our leadership, we may endanger the peace of the world—and we shall surely endanger the welfare of our own nation. Great responsibilities have been placed upon us by the swift movement of events. I am confident that the Congress will face these responsibilities squarely."
>
> **—President Harry S. Truman,** *Address Before a Joint Session of Congress,* **March 12, 1947**

5. Based on this quote, why did President Truman believe that the United States should help Greece and Turkey in their fight against a communist takeover?

_____

_____

Document #6

Berlin Airlift Statistics, 1948–1949					
		Cargo (short tons)			
	Flights	Total	Food	Coal	Other
USA	189,963	1,783,573	296,319	1,421,119	66,135
UK	87,841	541,937	240,386	164,911	136,640
France	424	896	unknown	unknown	unknown
Total	278,228	2,326,406			

6. How does the chart above demonstrate the commitment that the United States made to prevent the Soviet Union from crippling West Berlin in the blockade of 1948–1949?

_____

_____

Document #7

> "Our purpose in the Persian Gulf remains constant: to drive Iraq out of Kuwait, to restore Kuwait's legitimate government, and to ensure the stability and security of this critical region. Let me make clear what I mean by the region's stability and security. . . . We seek a Persian Gulf where conflict is no longer the rule, where the strong are neither tempted nor able to intimidate the weak.
>
> "Most Americans know instinctively why we are in the Gulf. They know we had to stop [Iraqi leader] Saddam [Hussein] now, not later. . . .They know we must make sure that control of the world's oil resources does not fall into his hands, only to finance further aggression. They know that we need to build a new, enduring peace, based not on arms races and confrontation but on shared principles and the rule of law."
>
> **—President George Bush, _State of the Union Address_, January 29, 1991**

7. According to this quote, why did President Bush believe that American involvement in the Persian Gulf War was necessary?

_____

_____

Part B

Essay

Directions: Write a well-organized essay that includes an introduction, several paragraphs, and a conclusion. Use evidence from *at least **four*** documents in the body of the essay. Support your response with relevant facts, examples, and details. Include additional outside information.

Historical Context:

World events after 1939 drew the United States into greater international involvement. These events forced the United States to abandon its isolationist foreign policy in favor of more active global involvement.

Task: Using information from the documents and your knowledge of United States history and government, write an essay in which you:

> • Discuss how the need for military security and the protection of democratic ideals have shaped American foreign policy since 1939

Guidelines:

In your essay, be sure to

• Develop all aspects of the task
• Incorporate information from *at least **four*** documents
• Incorporate relevant outside information
• Support the theme with relevant facts, examples, and details
• Use a logical and clear plan of organization, including an introduction and conclusion that are beyond a restatement of the theme

The World in Uncertain Times, 1950–the Present

Unit Overview

The foreign policies that began after World War II continued to shape America's response to events abroad for decades. The policy of containment, begun under President Truman, eventually led the United States into its longest war, one that caused deep splits within American society.

During the period from the 1950s to the present, life changed at home for Americans. An expanding civil rights movement, a major constitutional crisis, new technologies, and a changing economic picture are some of the highlights of these years.

Some key questions to help you focus on this time period include:

- How did the foreign policy concerns of the United States become more global in scope?
- What were the goals and the achievements of the Civil Rights Movement?
- How did the war in Vietnam affect American society?
- How did relations of the United States with the Soviet Union change under Presidents Reagan and Bush?
- Why is September 11, 2001, considered a major turning point in United States history?
- What are some of the major challenges that the nation will face in years to come?

Containment Abroad and Consensus at Home: 1945–1960

Section Overview

During the 1950s, the Cold War intensified and spread to new locations around the world. Meanwhile, the new economic prosperity allowed many Americans to enjoy greater wealth and leisure than their parents had. At the same time, the Civil Rights Movement intensified as African Americans demanded justice and equality.

Key Themes and Concepts

As you review this section, take special note of the following key themes and concepts:

Foreign Policy How did tensions between the United States and the Soviet Union increase and decrease during Eisenhower's presidency?

Citizenship How did African Americans begin to organize the Civil Rights Movement?

Economic Systems Who benefited from the "Eisenhower prosperity," and who did not?

Key People

Dwight D. Eisenhower	Jackie Robinson
Nikita Khrushchev	Rosa Parks
Fidel Castro	Martin Luther King, Jr.

Key Terms

balance of power	domino theory
brinkmanship	Eisenhower Doctrine
arms race	suburbanization
Sputnik	Civil Rights Movement

Key Supreme Court Cases

Brown v. Board of Education of Topeka, Kansas (1954)

The Cold War Continues

The United States emerged from World War II as the strongest nation in the world. It controlled the atomic bomb, and its economy was undamaged by the destruction of war. The Soviet Union, however, quickly became America's chief rival. By 1949, it too had the atomic bomb. It had also taken control of most of the nations of Eastern Europe and was seeking to extend its influence elsewhere.

President Harry S. Truman began the policy of containment after the war in an attempt to limit the spread of communism. As the United States and the Soviet

Union—the two world superpowers—attempted to maintain a **balance of power,** a cold war developed.

The Cold War, 1950–1960

1950	1953	1956	1960
Korean War begins	Korean War ends	Suez crisis begins; Hungarian revolt	U-2 shot down over USSR

| 1950 | 1952 | 1954 | 1956 | 1958 | 1960 |

1952	1955	1959
Dwight D. Eisenhower elected president	Summit conference in Geneva	Castro wins power in Cuba

Analyzing Documents

Interpret Data
Examine the timeline, then answer the following questions.

- Did the Korean War begin before or after Eisenhower became president?

- Which events on the timeline took place in Europe?

Eisenhower's Foreign Policy

As President, Dwight D. Eisenhower continued Truman's basic policy of containment. However, he and his secretary of state John Foster Dulles introduced some new ideas.

Massive Retaliation Eisenhower worried that defense spending would bankrupt the nation. Yet he feared that the Soviets might see cutbacks in military spending as a sign of weakness.

Eisenhower and Dulles instead devised a "new look" for the nation's defense. The United States would rely more heavily on air power and nuclear weapons than on ground troops. Dulles announced a policy of massive retaliation. This meant that the United States would consider the use of nuclear weapons to halt aggression if it believed the nation's interests were threatened.

Dulles further stated that the nation must be ready to go "to the brink of war" in order to preserve world peace. This policy of **brinkmanship** greatly increased world tensions during the 1950s.

The Arms Race The United States and the Soviet Union began an arms race, stockpiling nuclear and nonnuclear weapons. The United States exploded a hydrogen bomb in 1952, and the Soviets tested one a year later. Both nations rushed to develop missiles capable of carrying nuclear weapons. The balance of power became a balance of terror.

In 1953, Eisenhower announced the Atoms for Peace Plan at the United Nations. The plan called for United Nations supervision of a world search to find peaceful uses for nuclear technology. The Soviet Union refused to participate. Americans were encouraged to build fallout shelters in homes, schools and public buildings to enable survival in the case of nuclear attack.

In 1957, the Soviets launched a satellite, **Sputnik,** into orbit around the earth. The arms race then became a space race as the United States rushed to launch its own satellites, some for military purposes.

Turning Point

- Why would the Soviet launch of Sputnik cause the federal government to increase spending on the study of math and science in schools?

Foreign Policy in Asia

Asia became a major area of concern for United States foreign policy. The Communist victory in China in 1949 raised fears of further Communist expansion. The war in Korea, even though it ended in what was basically a draw in 1953, added to these fears.

The Domino Theory As Communists took control of the governments of China and, later, some nations of Southeast Asia, American worries about Communist expansion increased. Eisenhower stated that the United States must resist further aggression in the region and explained what came to be known as the domino theory. The nations of Asia, he said, were like a row of dominoes standing on end. If one fell to communism, the rest were sure to follow.

SEATO One way to resist aggression, Dulles claimed, was through alliances. To mirror the formation of NATO in Europe, Dulles in 1954 pushed for the creation of the Southeast Asia Treaty Organization (SEATO). Its original members—Pakistan, Thailand, the Philippines, Australia, New Zealand, Great Britain, and the United States—pledged to meet any "common danger" from Communist aggression.

Foreign Policy in the Middle East

The Middle East was the scene of several outbreaks of trouble during the Eisenhower administration.

Iran In 1954, the prime minister of Iran tried to nationalize that country's foreign-owned oil industry. The United States, through the Central Intelligence Agency, secretly arranged the overthrow of the prime minister's government and the restoration of the shah to the throne of Iran. This action helped secure America's supply of oil at the time but caused problems for the nation in years to come.

Egypt Gamal Abdel Nasser, president of Egypt, had counted on economic support from the Soviet Union and the United States to build a huge dam at Aswan on the Nile River. Nasser's friendliness to the Soviet Union led the United States to withdraw its support. Nasser then nationalized the Suez Canal, which was run by a British and French company. He planned to use revenues from the canal to pay for the dam.

Great Britain and France, joined by Israel, sent troops to seize the canal. Fearing that fighting would spread through the region, both the United States and the Soviet Union supported a United Nations resolution condemning the attack. Great Britain, France, and Israel withdrew, and the canal remained under Egyptian control.

The Eisenhower Doctrine Troubles in the Middle East led Congress to adopt what became known as the Eisenhower Doctrine in 1957. The United States pledged to help any Middle Eastern nation resist Communist aggression.

Lebanon In 1958, the Eisenhower Doctrine was tested when the governments of Lebanon and Jordan asked for help. The United States sent marines to Lebanon, and Great Britain sent troops to Jordan to help restore political calm in those nations.

Foreign Policy in Latin America

Troubles also flared up closer to home during Eisenhower's time in office. Three instances are especially notable.

Guatemala The CIA staged a successful covert operation in Guatemala in 1954. It arranged a revolt that toppled a government considered to be too friendly to Communists.

Nixon's Tour In 1958, Vice President Richard Nixon went on a goodwill tour of Latin America. In Peru and Venezuela, however, angry mobs surrounded his limousine, throwing rocks and eggs at it. This event revealed the strong anti-American feelings that had built up in Latin America in response to repeated interventions in the region by the United States.

Cuba In 1956, Fidel Castro began a revolt against the government of Cuban dictator Fulgencio Batista. When the revolt ended with Castro's victory in 1959, the United States quickly recognized the new government.

Castro, however, soon adopted policies that angered the Eisenhower administration. He limited civil liberties and imprisoned political opponents. He also nationalized key industries and turned to the Soviet Union for aid.

Large numbers of Cubans fled Castro's rule, with many settling in southern Florida. Some worked actively to end Castro's rule. Meanwhile, they became one more immigrant group that contributed to the richness of the American multicultural experience.

Changing Relations With the Soviet Union

Tensions between the United States and the Soviet Union rose and fell during Eisenhower's time in office.

New Soviet Leadership Joseph Stalin, leader of the Soviet Union since the 1920s, died in 1953. In time, Nikita Khrushchev took over as the head of the Soviet government. This change marked a temporary easing of Cold War tensions as the Soviets began to focus more on improving conditions within their nation.

Peaceful Coexistence Relations between the superpowers gradually improved. In 1955, the leaders of the United States, the Soviet Union, Great Britain, and France held the first summit meeting since World War II in Geneva, Switzerland. The superpower leaders began talks on disarmament that, in time, led to a suspension of nuclear testing.

Poland and Hungary In 1956, riots by Polish workers won concessions from the Communist Polish government. Inspired by this, students and workers in Hungary began demonstrations that fall that ended with the Soviet Union sending tanks and troops to bring that nation firmly back under Communist control. The suppression of the Hungarian revolt cooled relations between the United States and the Soviet Union.

Camp David Relations improved again by 1959. Khrushchev visited the United States, and he and Eisenhower held lengthy talks at Camp David, the presidential retreat near Washington, D.C. The spirit of goodwill that grew at these talks encouraged the leaders to announce another summit meeting in Paris in 1960.

The U-2 Incident The Paris summit proved a disaster. Shortly before it opened, the Soviet military shot down an American U-2 aircraft deep in Soviet territory. The pilot admitted that he had been spying on Soviet military bases.

Eisenhower said that he had approved the U-2 flights and promised to suspend them. Khrushchev denounced the United States and demanded an apology. Eisenhower refused, and the summit collapsed before it really started.

In summary, Eisenhower's foreign policy was primarily a continuation of Truman's containment policy. Many of the events of the 1950s can be compared to kettles ready to boil over in the 1960s. In later years, the Eisenhower administration was criticized by some as not being aware enough of the struggles of developing nations and of their desires to end colonial rule.

Reading Strategy

Analyzing Cause and Effect
- Why did the policies of Fidel Castro anger the Eisenhower administration?

Key Themes and Concepts

Foreign Policy
Relations between the United States and the Soviet Union changed several times during the 1950s. Following the death of Soviet leader Joseph Stalin in 1953, the new Soviet leader Nikita Khrushchev focused more on improving conditions within his nation. This eased Cold War tensions.

- What event rekindled the Cold War in 1956?

Turning Point

- Why is the U-2 incident considered a turning point in U.S.-Soviet relations?

An Improving Economy at Home

When Dwight Eisenhower became president in 1953, he was the first Republican president since 1933—the year Herbert Hoover left office during one of the worst years of the Great Depression. Since that time, Democrats Franklin D. Roosevelt and Harry S. Truman had called for New Deal and New Society policies that had vastly increased both the federal government's spending and its role in society.

Eisenhower's Economic Policies

Eisenhower had a deep dislike for strong centralized government. In addition, he generally believed policies that were good for big business were good for the nation as a whole.

Eisenhower's Domestic Policies Eisenhower attempted to cut back on the federal government's size and power. He reduced spending for defense and foreign aid.

Eisenhower did recognize that many social programs begun under the New Deal were very popular. He extended some of these and, in some cases, started new programs. The Social Security program was expanded to include seven million more people, and a new cabinet post, the Department of Health, Education, and Welfare, was created.

The Farm Problem Conditions on the nation's farms pulled Eisenhower between his desire to cut government spending and his wish to extend some social programs. Farm production had been increasing while prices for agricultural products had been declining. During the twentieth century the number of farms and the number of Americans employed in agriculture decreased significantly. At the same time, individual farm sizes were increasing.

Farmers had been receiving payments from the federal government to make up for changes in market conditions. Eisenhower's secretary of agriculture wanted to be able to cut such payments. Farmers protested, and in 1956, Congress approved a new program that paid farmers for not planting crops. Both types of payments are called subsidies, or direct payments by a government to private individuals.

"Eisenhower Prosperity" and Consumer Spending

Despite the problems noted above, the American people commonly prospered during the 1950s. There were several reasons for this.

- During World War II, Americans had worked hard and generally earned good wages. Because of rationing and shortages, however, they could usually spend their money only on basic necessities.
- By war's end, Americans had accumulated huge amounts of capital—wealth in the form of money or property. They were ready to spend this capital on consumer goods.
- By the 1950s, wartime price controls were over, and factories had converted from the production of military supplies to the production of consumer goods.

New Homes The postwar years saw the start of a **"baby boom."** The growth in family size, the accumulation of capital, and the availability of government loans to veterans brought a rapid increase in home building.

Suburbs Much new home building was done in areas surrounding major cities (urban areas). These areas are called suburbs. The suburbs offered limited jobs and services for their residents, most of whom worked in the cities. The suburbs grew rapidly. Levittown, New York, for example, became a symbol of **suburbanization,** with some 17,000 tract houses built in four years. By the 1960s, almost a third of all Americans lived in suburbs.

Key Themes and Concepts

Presidential Decisions and Actions
President Eisenhower believed that what was good for business benefited the United States as a whole. He attempted to limit the federal government's power but expanded several social programs, including Social Security.

- Why did farm conditions present a problem for Eisenhower?

- How did Congress resolve the problem?

Reading Strategy

Reinforcing Main Ideas
- How did the growth of suburbs contribute to the decline of many cities?

Refrigerator-Freezers!

THE FINAL FROST BARRIER!

IT'S HERE!
A FROST-PROOF
FOOD FREEZER!
NO FROST!
NO FROST-LOCKED
FOODS!
NO DEFROSTING!

You'll feel like a queen . . .
- Trim Upright Freezer with award-winning Sheer Look and embossed white-bright Lacework Styling.
- Takes so little floor space—only 32 inches wide—yet this 16 cu. ft. Frost-Proof Imperial Freezer shown, stores 560 lbs. of food.

- Serve family meals in minutes. Be always ready for guests.
- Shop once a week. Enjoy bulk buying that cuts food bills.
- Cook and bake in quantity. Enjoy "free" days.
- Freeze leftovers, like stew, turkey, cake, enjoy them weeks later.
- Have fun freezing your own fruits and vegetables; fish and game, too.

DESIGNED WITH YOU IN MIND!

GM Built and Backed by General Motors

Analyzing Documents

Interpret Evidence
Examine the advertisement, then answer the questions.

- What product is the advertisement promoting?

- Who is the advertisement targeting? What clues lead you to this conclusion?

- What does this advertisement suggest about the U.S. economy at the time?

- How is this advertisement similar to ads you see today? How is it different?

The growth of suburbs contributed to the decline of many cities. As people moved out of cities to suburbs, fewer taxpayers remained to help pay for essential services. At the same time, a greater concentration of poorer people in the cities increased the demand for many social services.

Automobiles Cars made the growth of suburbs possible, and suburbs increased the demand for cars. Since public transportation systems grew more slowly than suburbs, people in suburbs relied increasingly on their cars. Increased demand for automobiles benefited many areas of the nation's economy. Factories turned out the steel, glass, and rubber that went into new cars. Refineries also produced oil and gas that powered them.

Reading Strategy

Formulating Questions
The increase in demand for cars benefited many industries, such as the steel and oil industries. Increased automobile ownership also made it possible for people to live in suburbs without public transportation, because the government provided funding for an extensive highway network.

- What were some of the negative consequences of this increased reliance on cars?

The federal government stepped into the transportation picture with passage of the Federal Highway Act of 1956 (sometimes known as the Interstate Highway Act). This provided funding for what became a 44,000-mile network of interstate highways.

A Nation on the Move This new network of highways encouraged Americans to move from central cities to suburbs. They also moved to new areas of the country. Many people moved from the industrialized but decaying cities of the Northeast and the Midwest and from the farms of the Midwest to the Sun Belt. This was the name given to the states of the South and the West—including Florida, Texas, Arizona, and California—that experienced a faster than average population growth beginning in the postwar years.

The sun and warm climate of these states enticed both retirees and businesses that wished to relocate. As this region grew, it attracted more industry and prompted both population and job loss in what came to be called the Rust Belt. This region

Geography in History

Analyze Changing Connections
In which areas of the United States did the population grow most quickly during in the 1950s? Give examples of three states that experienced rapid growth.

1.

2.

3.

included the states of the Northeast (including New York and Massachusetts) and the Midwest (including Ohio and Michigan).

Homes With Television Sets, 1948–1960

Analyzing Documents

Interpret Data
• Examine the bar graph at right. Between which two years did the number of homes with television sets increase most dramatically?

Source: *Statistical Abstract of the United States*

Television After limited broadcasting in 1939, national broadcasting began in 1946. Television became the leading form of popular entertainment, and its growth, both as a source of amusement and a tool for learning, has continued to the present day. The use of television has also become extremely important in political campaigns.

A Renewed Struggle for Civil Rights

Turning Point

• Why is it considered a turning point in the struggle for civil rights when Jackie Robinson joined the Brooklyn Dodgers?

Since the period of Reconstruction after the Civil War, African Americans faced discrimination, especially in southern states. Jim Crow laws limited the freedoms of African Americans. For generations, white southerners continued to maintain economic, social, and political control over the South.

Beginnings of Change

Until well into the twentieth century, much of the South was segregated, or separated by race. Although such segregation was less apparent in the North, African Americans were generally restricted to poorer neighborhoods and lower-paying jobs. Although African Americans fought for change, until the 1950s their gains were limited.

Not until 1947, for example, were African Americans permitted to play on major league baseball teams in this country. In that year, Jackie Robinson joined the Brooklyn Dodgers. This was one sign that public attitudes on segregation were beginning to change.

Reading Strategy

Organizing Information
The struggle to secure African American civil rights required the efforts of countless dedicated activists, organizers, and political leaders. What are two changes that President Truman made that had an impact on civil rights?

1.

2.

Truman's Policies on Civil Rights President Truman appointed a presidential commission on civil rights in 1946. Based on its report, Truman called for the establishment of a fair employment practices commission. Congress, however, failed to act on the idea.

Using his powers as commander in chief, Truman issued Executive Order 9981 banning segregation in the armed forces. He also strengthened the Justice Department's civil rights division, which aided blacks who challenged segregation in the courts.

Civil Rights Milestones 1947–1957

1947: Jackie Robinson became first African American to play in major league baseball.

1948: Truman ordered end to segregation in armed forces.

1954: Supreme Court issued *Brown* v. *Board of Education* ruling, stating that segregated schools were unconstitutional.

1955–1956: Montgomery bus boycott protested segregation on city buses; Supreme Court ruled bus segregation unconstitutional.

1957: Eisenhower used National Guard to enforce desegregation of schools in Little Rock, Arkansas.

Civil Rights and the Courts

In the 1950s, the Supreme Court made several important decisions concerning the civil rights of African Americans.

The Warren Court In 1953, a vacancy occurred on the Supreme Court. President Eisenhower then appointed Earl Warren, former governor of California, as chief justice. Warren presided over the Supreme Court until 1969. During that period, the Court reached a number of decisions that deeply affected many areas of American life. Among the most far-reaching of the Warren Court's decisions were those dealing with civil rights for African Americans.

Brown v. Board of Education Only a year after he became chief justice, Warren presided over the court as it reached a landmark decision in *Brown* v. *Board of Education of Topeka, Kansas* (1954). The Supreme Court actually combined five cases related to overturning state laws that allowed for school segregation in Kansas, Delaware, South Carolina, Virginia, and also in Washington, D.C. There were nearly 200 plaintiffs, including Oliver Brown for whom the case was named. Linda Brown, a young African American student, requested the right to attend a local all-white school in her Topeka neighborhood, rather than attend an all-black school that was further away.

The 1896 *Plessy* v. *Ferguson* decision had held that separate but equal public facilities were legal. Schools were such public facilities, and Brown was refused admittance to the all-white school.

The National Association for the Advancement of Colored People (NAACP) joined the case and appealed it all the way to the Supreme Court. In a unanimous decision, the Court reversed its ruling in *Plessy* v. *Ferguson* and held that in the field of public education, "the doctrine of separate but equal has no place."

Little Rock Although the Brown case opened the door for desegregation, integration did not follow immediately. Many Americans were shocked by the decision. In the South, whites began campaigns of "massive resistance" to public school desegregation.

Key Themes and Concepts

Constitutional Principles
Brown v. *Board of Education of Topeka, Kansas (1954)* established that facilities separated by race were unequal. The decision reversed *Plessy* v. *Ferguson* (1896) and made integration of schools possible.

- How did the governor of Arkansas respond to *Brown* v. *Board of Education of Topeka, Kansas*?

Key Themes and Concepts

Government
President Eisenhower was acting in his role as Commander in Chief when he sent troops to Little Rock.

Although the Supreme Court had ordered that school integration go forward "with all deliberate speed," many school systems openly defied the ruling. In 1957, the governor of Arkansas ordered the state's National Guard to prevent nine African American students from attending Central High School in Little Rock.

Major Civil Rights Protests, 1954–1965

Year	Event	Outcome
1954	*Brown v. Board of Education*	Supreme Court ruled that separate educational facilities for whites and African Americans are inherently unequal.
1955–1956	Montgomery Bus Boycott	Alabama bus company was forced to desegregate its buses. Martin Luther King, Jr., emerged as an important civil rights leader.
1961	Freedom Rides	Interstate Commerce Commission banned segregation in interstate transportation.
1963	James Meredith sues University of Mississippi for admission	Supreme Court upheld Meredith's right to enter the all-white institution.
1963	Protest marches in Birmingham, Alabama	Violence against peaceful demonstrators shocked the nation. Under pressure, Birmingham desegregated public facilities.
1963	March on Washington	More than 200,000 people demonstrated in an impressive display of support for civil rights.
1965	Selma March (Alabama)	State troopers attacked marchers. President Johnson used federal force to protect route from Selma to Montgomery and thousands joined march. On the 50th anniversary of the March (2015) President and Mrs. Obama led lawmakers and civil rights activists in a march in the same location. In a speech that day the President said that "our march is not yet finished" and cited the need for the full restoration of the Voting Rights Act which has been weakened in some states.

Analyzing Documents

Connect Historical Developments
The table outlines some of the major civil rights protests from 1954 to 1965.

- Which protest led to the rise of Dr. Martin Luther King, Jr., as an important civil rights leader?

- Which three key protests occurred in Alabama?

Key Themes and Concepts

Individuals, Groups, Institutions
African Americans began to take direct action to end segregation following *Brown v. Board of Education* (1954). Boycotts of schools, lunch counters, and buses, for example, began.

- How did the actions of Rosa Parks and Martin Luther King, Jr., change attitudes toward segregation?

President Eisenhower was reluctant to step in, but the governor's defiance was a direct challenge to the Constitution. Eisenhower placed the Arkansas National Guard under federal control and then used it to enforce integration. When President Eisenhower sent federal troops, he acted in his presidential role as Commander in Chief. At the end of the school year, Governor Orval Faubus continued his defiance by ordering all city high schools closed for the following year. The tactic failed, however, and in 1959 the first racially integrated class graduated from Central High School.

African American Activism

Public facilities of all kinds were segregated in the South—schools, movie theaters, lunch counters, drinking fountains, restrooms, buses, and trains. Rather than wait for court rulings to end segregation, in the 1950s, African Americans began to organize the **Civil Rights Movement.**

The Montgomery Bus Boycott In Montgomery, Alabama, in 1955, an African American seamstress named **Rosa Parks** refused to give up her seat to a white man and move to the back of the bus, as was required by law. She was arrested for violating the law, and her action inspired a boycott of the city's buses.

Martin Luther King, Jr., a young Baptist minister, emerged as a leader of the protest. King had studied the nonviolent methods of Mohandas Gandhi and Henry David Thoreau. His dynamic speaking style drew the attention and support of large numbers of people.

The boycott lasted 381 days. In the end, the Supreme Court ruled that segregation of public buses was illegal. Although Parks had not planned her action that day, her stand against injustice led the way for others.

Civil Rights Legislation

Congress also made some moves to ensure civil rights for African Americans. In August 1957, it passed the first civil rights act since Reconstruction. The bill created a permanent commission for civil rights and increased federal efforts to ensure blacks the right to vote. Another bill in 1960 further strengthened voting rights.

Although these bills had only limited effectiveness, they did mark the beginning of change. Martin Luther King, Jr., once remarked that it was impossible to legislate what was in a person's heart, but that laws can restrain the heartless. During this time some southern Senators attempted to delay passage of civil rights legislation by using a filibuster. This is an effort by one or more senators to speak continuously on the floor of the Senate until support for their view can be gained or until the Senate leaders decide to delay the proposed bill. Filibusters may last several weeks and can be ended only by a special vote called cloture which can close debate.

Some Landmark Cases of Earl Warren Supreme Court 1953–1969

Landmark Case	Date	Court Decision	Constitutional Basis
Brown v. Board of Ed.	1954	Public school segregation unconstitutional	Equal Protection Clause
Heart of Atlanta v. United States	1964	Upheld 1964 Civil Rights Act prohibiting discrimination in public accomodations	Interstate Commerce Clause Equal Protection Clause
Mapp v. Ohio	1961	Evidence from "unreasonable search and seizures" excluded from trial	Exclusionary Rule "essential" to 4th amendment right
Gideon v. Wainwright	1963	In state and federal criminal cases all defendants have right to counsel	6th amendment applies to states via 14th amendment
Escobedo v. Illinois	1964	Right to counsel when taken into custody; request for attorney must be honored	6th amendment; exclusionary rule applies to "illegal" confessions
Miranda v. Arizona	1966	Must be advised of right to remain silent and right to counsel	5th amendment protection against self-incrimination
Griswold v. Connecticut	1965	Unconstitutional to criminalize using or counseling use of contraception	Marital privacy right in 3rd, 4th, 9th amendments; due process
Baker v. Carr	1962	Court has right to hear apportionment cases	Representation is equal protection not political issue
Reynolds v. Sims	1964	State legislative districts must be equal in population	"one person, one vote" equal protection clause
Engel v. Vitale	1962	Government sponsored public school prayer unconstitutional	Establishment clause of 1st amendment
N.Y. Times Co. v. Sullivan	1964	Statements about public officials not libel unless made with "actual malice"	1st amendment freedom of press and speech
Tinker v. Des Moines School District	1969	Upheld symbolic student speech when no evidence of threat to school discipline	1st amendment free speech applies via 14th amendment

Directions: Identify some Supreme Court cases since 1975 that indicate current Constitutional positions on the fundamental issues cited above.

Decade of Change: 1960s

The Big Idea

The 1960s were a tumultuous era in American society. During this period:

- the struggle for civil rights continued.

- the women's rights movement organized.

- other groups, including Native Americans, struggled for equality.

- New Frontier and Great Society programs expanded upon the New Deal of the 1930s.

- the Cold War affected foreign policy in Latin America.

Section Overview

In the early 1960s, the continuing pressure of African American civil rights groups, plus growing public sympathy, forced the passage of new legislation. Women, Latino Americans, Native Americans, and disabled Americans adapted civil rights tactics to achieve their own goals of equality. Meanwhile, the cold war tensions between the United States and the Soviet Union continued, as the two nations came into conflict in Germany and Cuba. So much fear was created by Cold War tensions that average citizens built bomb shelters in their backyards or basements. Local communities erected model shelters to serve as examples of how to prepare for an attack.

Key Themes and Concepts

As you review this section, take special note of the following key themes and concepts:

Citizenship How did the African American Civil Rights Movement inspire others to struggle to achieve greater equality?

Government How did Presidents Kennedy and Johnson continue and expand upon traditions from the New Deal of the 1930s?

Foreign Policy How did the antagonism between the United States and the Soviet Union bring the two nations to the brink of war?

Key People

James Meredith

Medgar Evers

Betty Friedan

John F. Kennedy

Lyndon B. Johnson

Malcolm X

Cesar Chavez

Key Terms

civil disobedience

Civil Rights Act of 1964

Voting Rights Act of 1965

Equal Rights Amendment

affirmative action

United Farm Workers

American Indian Movement

mainstreaming

Americans with Disabilities
 Act of 1990

New Frontier

Great Society

Cuban Missile Crisis

Berlin Wall

Key Supreme Court Cases

Heart of Atlanta Motel v. *United States* (1964)
Roe v. *Wade* (1973)
Regents of the University of California v. *Bakke* (1979)

For additional cases, see the Landmark Supreme Court Cases chart in the Reference Section.

The 1960s

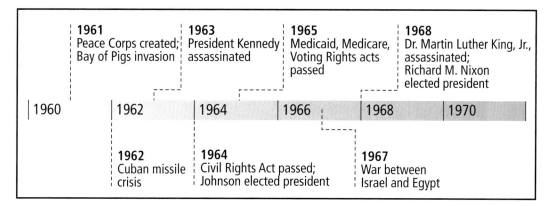

1961 Peace Corps created; Bay of Pigs invasion	**1963** President Kennedy assassinated
1965 Medicaid, Medicare, Voting Rights acts passed	**1968** Dr. Martin Luther King, Jr., assassinated; Richard M. Nixon elected president

1960 1962 1964 1966 1968 1970

1962 Cuban missile crisis

1964 Civil Rights Act passed; Johnson elected president

1967 War between Israel and Egypt

The Struggle for Civil Rights Continues

During the 1960s, the struggle of African Americans to win equality before the law grew more intense. In their fight, African Americans were seeking to overcome a heritage of racism that had been a part of American thought and tradition for more than 300 years.

By the 1960s, however, many African Americans were working together for the common goal of justice and equality. The successes they gained would deeply affect many parts of American society.

African Americans Organize

African Americans formed a number of different groups that used a variety of approaches in the attempt to achieve justice and equality. In the early 1960s, many groups followed the nonviolent methods introduced by Dr. Martin Luther King, Jr., and the Southern Christian Leadership Conference (SCLC), an organization of clergy who shifted the leadership of the Civil Rights Movement to the South.

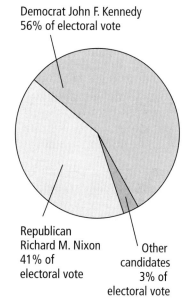

Election of 1960

Democrat John F. Kennedy 56% of electoral vote

Republican Richard M. Nixon 41% of electoral vote

Other candidates 3% of electoral vote

Many civil rights activists used a form of protest called **civil disobedience.** This means the deliberate breaking of a law to show a belief that the law is unjust. For example, they attempted to use segregated facilities at interstate train stations and bus depots. Usually they were arrested for such acts; often they were beaten.

Major African American Organizations

Organization	Date of Founding	Background
National Association for the Advancement of Colored People (NAACP)	1909	Organized by black and white progressives; W. E. B. Du Bois an early leader; favored court challenges to segregation; appealed primarily to the professional and college-educated
National Urban League	1910	Began as the Urban League; devoted to empowering African Americans to enter the economic and social mainstream, and to secure economic self-reliance, equality, power, and civil rights
The Nation of Islam	1930	Known as Black Muslims, founded as a black separatist religious group; became the voice of black nationalism in the 1960s; Muhammad Ali converted in 1964; Malcolm X, a leading spokesperson, assassinated in 1965
Congress of Racial Equality (CORE)	1942	Became best known for the "freedom rides" of the 1960s, efforts to desegregate interstate transportation
Southern Christian Leadership Conference (SCLC)	1957	Founded by Martin Luther King, Jr., to encourage nonviolent passive resistance; organized black Christian churches
Student Nonviolent Coordinating Committee (SNCC)	1960	In early days, used nonviolent civil disobedience in sit-ins and boycotts; later supported the idea of "black power" put forward by Stokely Carmichael

Key Themes and Concepts

Power

In 1966 Huey Newton and Bobby Seale organized the Black Panther Party for Self Defense. A goal was to defend African Americans from discriminatory police tactics. The radical positions of some factions of the Party prevented it from becoming one of the major African American organizations of the era.

Preparing for the Exam

Fifty years later (2016) African Americans are still struggling with discriminatory practices by police. Baltimore, Maryland and Ferguson, Missouri have been the site of riots against police.

- Why do you think this has happened?

James Meredith The push to integrate education continued. In 1962, James Meredith, an African American Air Force veteran, made headlines when he tried to enroll at the all-white University of Mississippi. The governor of the state personally tried to stop Meredith from enrolling. Riots broke out, and federal marshals and the National Guard were called up. Although he had to overcome continued harassment, Meredith did finally enter and eventually graduate from the university.

Greensboro Practicing civil disobedience, demonstrators protested such discrimination as segregated lunch counters and buses. Sit-ins at lunch counters—the 1960s version of fast-food restaurants—began at Greensboro, North Carolina, in 1960. There, a group of African Americans sat at a "whites only" lunch counter and refused to leave until served. As such protests became popular, some sympathetic whites often joined the sit-ins.

Birmingham In 1963, Dr. Martin Luther King, Jr., and the SCLC began a campaign to bring integration to Birmingham, Alabama, which many considered to be the most segregated city in the South. At a protest march, police used dogs and fire hoses to break up the marchers and arrested more than 2,000 people. One of those jailed was King, who then wrote his famous "Letter from a Birmingham Jail," in which he defended his methods of nonviolent civil disobedience and restated the need for direct action to end segregation.

Television cameras had brought the scenes of violence in Birmingham to people across the country. This helped build support for the growing civil rights movement. In Birmingham, the protests eventually resulted in the desegregation of city facilities.

Medgar Evers White reaction to African American protests sometimes turned deadly. Medgar Evers, field secretary of the NAACP, had been working to desegregate Jackson, Mississippi. In June 1963, Evers was murdered by a sniper outside his home.

The March on Washington

Turning Point

As civil rights were changing during this time period, so too were rights for accused persons as a result of decisions of the Supreme Court.

See pages A-10 and A-11 for court cases that expanded the rights of accused persons during this time period.

• How did the Mapp, Gideon, and Miranda cases expand rights for accused persons?

University of Alabama Also in June 1963, Governor George Wallace of Alabama vowed to stop two African American students from registering at the state university. Pressure from President Kennedy and the later arrival of the National Guard forced Wallace to back down. The two students enrolled peacefully.

The March on Washington The growing civil rights movement moved President Kennedy to deliver a televised speech to the nation in June 1963 on the need to guarantee the civil rights of African Americans. This marked the first speech by a president specifically on this issue. Eight days later, he sent the most comprehensive civil rights bill in the nation's history to Congress.

Civil rights groups organized a huge march on Washington, D.C., in August 1963, to show support for the bill. At the march, Dr. Martin Luther King, Jr., delivered his famous "I have a dream" speech to a crowd of more than 200,000 participants. In the speech, he eloquently expressed his hopes for a unified America.

Not all Americans shared King's dream, however. Just a few weeks after the March on Washington, white terrorists bombed an African American church in Birmingham, killing four young girls.

Johnson and the Civil Rights Act After the assassination of John F. Kennedy in November 1963, the new president, Lyndon Johnson, recognized the urgency of pushing forward with civil rights legislation. Johnson worked tirelessly for the passage of the bill, and in July 1964, he signed the **Civil Rights Act of 1964,** the most sweeping civil rights law in American history. The bill called for:

Turning Point

• Why is the Civil Rights Act of 1964 considered a turning point in the struggle for civil rights?

• protection of voting rights for all Americans.
• opening of public facilities (restaurants, hotels, stores, restrooms) to people of all races.
• a commission to protect equal job opportunities for all Americans.

Passage of the Civil Rights Act came just months after ratification of the Twenty-fourth Amendment to the Constitution, which abolished the poll tax in federal elections. A poll tax was a fee that had to be paid before a person could vote. The poll tax had prevented poorer Americans—including many African Americans—from exercising their legal right to vote.

The Civil Rights Act of 1964 outlawed race discrimination in public accommodations, including motels that refused rooms to African Americans. In the landmark Supreme Court case *Heart of Atlanta Motel* v. *United States* (1964), racial segregation of private facilities engaged in interstate commerce was found unconstitutional. Title VIII of the Civil Rights Act of 1968, also known as the **Fair Housing Act,** prohibits discrimination in the sale, rental, or financing of dwellings based on race, color, national origin, sex, or familial status.

The Voting Rights Act of 1965 Many southern states continued to resist civil rights legislation and Supreme Court rulings. Southern resistance to civil rights laws angered Johnson. He proposed new legislation, which was passed as the Voting Rights Act of 1965. This bill:

- put an end to literacy tests—tests of a person's ability to read and write that had often been misused to bar African American voters.
- authorized federal examiners to register voters in areas suspected of denying African Americans the right to vote.
- directed the attorney general of the United States to take legal action against states that continued to use poll taxes in state elections.

Changes in the Civil Rights Movement The summer of 1964 was known as "Freedom Summer" for its many demonstrations, protests, voter registration drives, and the March on Washington. Freedom Summer and the passage of the Voting Rights Act a year later marked highpoints of the Civil Rights Movement.

By the mid-1960s, some civil rights activists became frustrated that the new legislation had not improved conditions enough. Some demanded "Black Power," stressing that African Americans should take total control of the political and economic aspects of their lives. Some advocated the use of violence. Meanwhile, more moderate leaders continued to call for nonviolent methods of protest. These splits weakened the effectiveness of the Civil Rights Movement.

A new, more militant leader, **Malcolm X,** began to attract a following from African Americans who were frustrated by the pace of the Civil Rights Movement. Malcolm X spoke against integration, instead promoting black nationalism, a belief in the separate identity and racial unity of the African American community. A member of the separatist group Nation of Islam until 1964, Malcolm X broke with that group to form his own religious organization, called Muslim Mosque, Inc. After a pilgrimage to the Muslim holy city of Mecca in Saudi Arabia, during which he saw millions of Muslims of all races worshipping peacefully together, he changed his views about integration and began to work toward a more unified civil rights movement. He had made enemies, though, and in February 1965, he was assassinated at a New York City rally.

In 1964 and 1965, frustration at the discrimination in housing, education, and employment boiled over into riots in New York City, Rochester, and the Watts neighborhood of Los Angeles. In Watts alone, 34 people were killed, and more than a thousand were injured.

The federal government set up the Kerner Commission to investigate the cause of the rioting. It concluded that the riots were a result of the anger that had been building in many of America's inner cities.

Reading Strategy

Organizing Information
In the space below, list three provisions of the Voting Rights Act of 1965. Which do you think is the most significant? Why?

1.

2.

3.

Key Themes and Concepts

Individuals, Groups, Institutions
In the 1960s, many African Americans felt that they should take more control over the political and economic conditions in their lives. A new leader named Malcolm X emerged and began to attract attention from more militant individuals.

- How were Malcolm X's beliefs different from those of Martin Luther King, Jr.?

Assassinations Dr. Martin Luther King, Jr., had been awarded the Nobel Peace Prize in 1964 "for the furtherance of brotherhood among men." He remained a leading speaker for African American rights, even as splits developed in the Civil Rights Movement.

As a supporter of the underprivileged and the needy, King went to Memphis, Tennessee, in April 1968 to back a sanitation workers' strike. There he was shot and killed by a white assassin. The death of the leading spokesperson for nonviolence set off new rounds of rioting in American cities.

Just two months after King's death, Senator Robert F. Kennedy, brother of the late president and now a presidential candidate committed to civil rights, was assassinated. The shock of these deaths and the increasing urban violence made the goals of King and the Kennedys seem far off to many Americans.

The Women's Rights Movement

Like African Americans, women had long been denied equal rights in the United States. The successes of the African American Civil Rights Movement in the 1960s highlighted the need for organized action by women to achieve similar goals.

Past Successes, New Goals
The women's rights movement was not just a product of the 1960s. The struggle for equality had been a long one. Some of the key events in the struggle are listed below.

1848   The Seneca Falls Convention marked the beginning of the organized women's rights movement in this nation.

1870   Passage of the Fifteenth Amendment granted the vote to African American men but not to any women. Susan B. Anthony arranged to have a women's suffrage amendment introduced in Congress. It was defeated there, but Anthony and others continued the fight.

1920   Ratification of the Nineteenth Amendment gave women the right to vote.

1940s   Thousands of women took jobs in war-related industries.

By the 1960s, women had exercised the right to vote for 40 years, yet women still had not achieved equal status with men economically and socially. Women's groups renewed demands for a variety of goals including more job opportunities, equality of pay with men, and an end to discrimination based on sex.

Presidents Kennedy and Johnson appointed no women to major posts in their administrations. Yet in those years, fundamental changes occurred.

- More and more women entered fields that men had traditionally dominated, such as law, medicine, engineering, and the sciences.
- In 1963, **Betty Friedan** wrote ***The Feminine Mystique,*** a book arguing that society had forced American women out of the job market and back into the home after World War II. The book was influential because it energized a new women's rights movement. Friedan said that not all women were content with the role of homemaker and that more job opportunities should be open to women.
- Title VII of the Civil Rights Act of 1964 barred job discrimination on the basis of sex as well as race.
- The National Organization for Women (NOW) formed in 1966 to push for legislation guaranteeing equality for women.

Turning Point

- Why is the assassination of Martin Luther King, Jr., in 1968 considered a turning point in history?

Reading Strategy

Organizing Information
- List five important events of the women's rights movement of the 1960s and early 1970s.
- Which event do you consider to be the most significant? Why?

Analyzing Documents

Interpret Data
- According to the line graph below, between which years did the number of women working outside the home first exceed 50 percent?

Women Working Outside the Home, 1955–1990

Source: *Statistical Abstract of the United States*

- Congress approved the **Equal Rights Amendment** (ERA) in 1972 and sent it to the states for ratification. This proposed amendment has never been ratified. The amendment stated "equality of rights under the law shall not be denied or abridged by the United States or any state on account of sex."
- The Equal Opportunity Act of 1972 (Equal Pay Act) required employers to pay equal wages for equal work.
- Title IX of the Educational Amendments Act of 1972 gave female college athletes the right to the same financial support as male athletes.

In the landmark case of *Roe* v. *Wade* (1973), the Supreme Court ruled that a woman's right to terminate a pregnancy is constitutionally protected. Laws making abortion a crime were overturned because they violated a woman's right to privacy; the Supreme Court held that the states could only limit abortion after the first six months of pregnancy. Challenges to the decision in *Roe* v. *Wade* have continued for decades afterward.

Median Income of Men and Women, 1950–1975

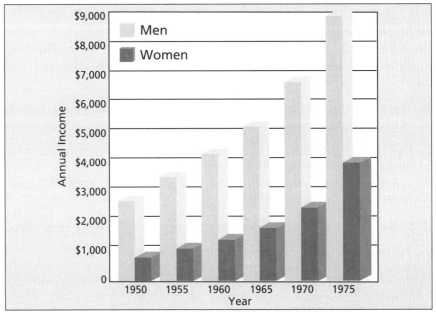

Source: *Statistical Abstract of the United States*

Analyzing Documents

Interpret Data
Examine the bar graph at right, then answer the questions.

- During the period 1950–1975, did the gap between men's and women's incomes appear to be widening or narrowing?

- What might explain this trend?

Affirmative Action Some of the laws guaranteeing equal opportunities for women, African Americans, and other minority groups called for affirmative action. This meant taking positive steps to eliminate the effects of past discrimination in hiring. In practice, it often meant giving preference to members of such groups when hiring workers or accepting applicants to schools. These affirmative action programs were begun during the Johnson administration of the 1960s.

Women's Rights Vocabulary The term *feminism* refers to the belief that women should have the same economic, social, and political rights as men. The women's rights movement is sometimes called the feminist movement.

The term *sexism* refers to beliefs or practices that discriminate against a person on the basis of sex. The women's movement directed its efforts at removing sexist terminology, practices, and literature from American business and education.

Adapted from The New Yorker

"Founding Fathers? How come no Founding Mothers?"

Analyzing Documents

Evaluate Evidence
Examine the cartoon at left, which features a painting by John Trumbull that shows the signing of the Declaration of Independence.

• What criticism about this painting are the two characters giving?

The term *glass ceiling* was used to describe a mid-level position to which women might be promoted in many jobs but which allowed women to see upper-level, better-paying positions that were held by men and were not open to women. This type of unspoken discrimination occurred in all types of employment and can still be found today.

Setbacks for the Women's Rights Movement

Not all Americans supported the women's rights movement. Some argued that women already had equal rights. Others claimed that those goals undermined "traditional" values. In 1971, President Nixon vetoed a bill that would have provided for a national system of day care for the children of working mothers. His reason for vetoing the bill was that he believed that the family rather than the government should be responsible for the care of children.

Reading Strategy

Formulating Questions
• Why might some women support the women's rights movement of the 1960s, while others might oppose it?

Critics also charged that affirmative action programs were a kind of reverse discrimination, in which white males lost chances at jobs to less-qualified women and members of minority groups. In 1979, the Supreme Court ruled in *Regents of the University of California* v. *Bakke* that the school used racial quotas when deciding on applicants to medical school. This meant that Allan Bakke was rejected admission to the medical school in favor of less-qualified applicants. The Court ruled that Bakke had been denied equal protection under the Fourteenth Amendment. It nevertheless found that other affirmative action programs may be constitutional.

The proposed ERA generated tremendous controversy. Opponents claimed that the women's rights movement had led to rising divorce rates, increasing numbers of abortions, and the growing acceptance and recognition of homosexuality—all threats to traditional values, said critics. Ratification of the ERA, they argued, would cause still more problems for American society. By the 1982 deadline, the ERA was three states short of ratification and thus was defeated.

Preparing for the Exam

• Why did the proposed Equal Rights Amendment cause controversy?

In the late 1980s and 1990s, women's groups began to demand legal protection against physical and mental abuse directed toward both women and children. Lawsuits began to occur to protest sexual harassment, especially in the workplace.

Other Groups Struggle for Their Rights

In addition to the African American and women's civil rights movements, Latinos, Native Americans, and disabled Americans fought for equality and justice.

Latino Victories in the 1960s

Latino Victories

Labor
- Under leadership of Cesar Chavez, United Farm Workers union made important financial, health, and safety gains for farm workers.

Politics
- Voters elected Texans Henry Gonzalez and Eligio de la Garza to the House of Representatives. Joseph Montoya of New Mexico was elected to the Senate.

Civil Rights
- Mexican American Legal Defense and Education Fund helped Mexican Americans gain civil rights and encouraged Mexican American students to become lawyers.

Latinos began to organize against discrimination in the 1960s.

Analyzing Documents

Identify Causes and Effects
- According to the graphic organizer at right, how did Latinos gain political strength at a national level in the 1960s?

Turning Point

The 1966 case of *Miranda v. Arizona* established the rights of the accused prior to questioning. The accused must be informed that he or she may remain silent and has the right to a lawyer.

- Why was it important for an accused person to be told that he or she had the right to a lawyer?

Latinos

Latinos—people whose family origins are in the Spanish-speaking nations of Latin America—have often been denied equal opportunities in employment, education, and housing. The largest group of Latinos is Mexican Americans, often known as Chicanos.

By the early 1960s, large numbers of Chicanos were employed as farm workers, often migrants. They faced problems of discrimination, poor pay, and hazardous working conditions. In 1962, a Chicano named Cesar Chavez emerged as a labor leader, starting a union for migrant farm workers, a union that became the **United Farm Workers.** Chavez's work was especially helpful to grape and lettuce pickers in their struggle for higher wages and better working conditions. Chavez's efforts at boycotts of grapes and lettuce increased public support for the goals of farm workers.

Chavez, like Dr. Martin Luther King, Jr., believed in nonviolent methods. Chavez continued to serve as spokesperson for farm workers until his death in 1993. He helped raise the self-esteem of the nation's growing Latino population by making their contributions to the American economy and culture more visible.

Native Americans

In the twentieth century, some conditions for Native Americans had improved. They were granted full citizenship in 1924. Franklin Roosevelt's Indian Reorganization Act of 1934 (Wheeler-Howard Act), known as the Indian New Deal, revised earlier government policies to rebuild tribes and promote tribal cultures. As the circumstances of the Native Americans improved, their population began to increase.

Nevertheless, conditions remained poor for many Native Americans. The per capita income of Native Americans was well below the poverty level. Rates of alcoholism and suicide were the highest of any ethnic group in the United States. Unemployment rates were far higher than the national average, and the high-school dropout rate was near 50 percent.

Native Americans Organize In the early 1950s, Congress had enacted legislation to lessen government control over reservations, but this led to the loss of property

Key Themes and Concepts

Government
- How did the federal government change its policies toward Native Americans in the early 1900s? What were the effects of these changes?

by many Native Americans and forced some onto welfare. During the Johnson administration, the government tried to improve conditions by starting new programs to raise the standard of housing and to provide medical facilities, educational institutions, and vocational training.

Native Americans began demanding greater responsibility in making decisions that affected their lives. Native Americans took inspiration from the African American Civil Rights Movement. They began to call for "Red Power" and formed the **American Indian Movement** (AIM) to further their goals.

In 1969, a group of militant Native Americans seized Alcatraz Island in San Francisco Bay with the demand that it be turned into an Indian cultural center. In 1972, members of AIM occupied the Bureau of Indian Affairs in Washington, D. C., demanding rights and property they said were guaranteed to them under earlier treaties. In 1973, AIM members occupied the reservation village of Wounded Knee, South Dakota, site of the last battle in the Indian wars of the 1800s. The takeover lasted two months, with the militants demanding changes in policies toward Native Americans.

Although these actions did not always achieve Native Americans' goals, the agitation did draw attention to their problems. Throughout the 1970s, court decisions tried to remedy earlier treaty violations. By 1989, Native Americans had been awarded more than $80 million as compensation for lost land.

In addition, government policies changed again. The Indian Self-Determination and Education Assistance Act of 1975 gave Native Americans more control over reservations. Also, the post of Assistant Secretary of the Interior for Indian Affairs was created in 1975 to protect Native American interests.

New York State and Native Americans Some major court cases involving Native American rights have taken place in New York State. For example, in *County of Oneida* v. *Oneida Indian Nation of New York State* (1985), the Supreme Court ruled that Native Americans had a right to sue to enforce their original land rights. The Court further stated that New York's purchase of 872 acres from the Oneida Indians in 1795 was illegal, because it was neither witnessed by federal agents nor approved by Congress. Both these steps were required under the federal Indian Trade and Non-Intercourse Act of 1793. Such court decisions have encouraged other Native American groups in New York State and across the nation to sue for return of lost lands.

More recent controversies have arisen in northern New York regarding the St. Regis Indian Reservation, or Akwesasne Mohawk Reservation as it is also known. Violence erupted on the 14,000-acre reservation, which stretches into southern Canada, in the spring of 1990. At issue was gambling on the reservation. The incident involved questions of which Native American group controlled reservation policy as well as the role New York State has in dealing with the reservation.

Disabled Americans

Americans with disabilities have endured a long struggle to gain their full rights in American society. In the nation's early years, care of the handicapped was usually left to their families, often resulting in the neglect or abuse. Reformers began to work for change in the early 1800s. For example, in Massachusetts, Dorothea Dix led a campaign to improve conditions for mentally ill people, resulting in the founding of more than 30 state institutions to care for them.

Preparing for the Exam

• What problems did Native Americans face in the 1960s and 1970s?

• How did they draw attention to their plight?

Key Themes and Concepts

Constitutional Principles
The Supreme Court case *County of Oneida* v. *Oneida Indian Nation of New York State* (1985) established that Native American tribes had the right to sue state governments to reclaim their tribal lands.

• Why is *County of Oneida* v. *Oneida Indian Nation of New York State* important in the struggle for Native American equality?

Reading Strategy

Reinforcing Main Ideas
• How has the view of people with handicaps changed from the nation's early years to today?

Key Themes and Concepts

Diversity
- What is the purpose behind the practice of mainstreaming?

Justice
In October 2010 new Federal legislation known as Rosa's Law replaced the phrase "mentally retarded" with "intellectual disabilities" in health, education, and labor policy.

Educational opportunities for hearing-impaired students were gradually widened. Gallaudet College in Washington, D.C., was founded in 1857, and today that institution is internationally recognized for its educational programs for hearing-impaired students. In the late 1980s, its students successfully demonstrated to win the appointment of a hearing-impaired person as president of the college. In New York State, the National Technical Institute for the Deaf at the Rochester Institute of Technology is another school for the hearing impaired whose programs have won wide recognition. The school provides deaf students with college training in technical and scientific fields.

Educational opportunities were also widened for visually-impaired students. In 1829, the Perkins School for the Blind opened in Boston and quickly became a model for schools elsewhere. Although such schools still exist and serve important functions, many visually-impaired students today attend regular schools under a practice called **mainstreaming.** The idea behind mainstreaming is to bring handicapped students out of the isolation of special schools and into the "mainstream" of student life.

New Programs for People With Disabilities The federal government has been especially active in setting out new programs and policies for people with disabilities.

- President Kennedy established the Presidential Commission on Mental Retardation to study and highlight the problems of the mentally handicapped individuals in American society.

- President Kennedy also backed the establishment of the Special Olympics to provide both a showcase and encouragement for athletes with handicapping conditions.

- The Rehabilitation Act of 1973, Section 504, barred discrimination against people with disabilities in any programs, activities, and facilities that were supported by federal funds.

- The Education for All Handicapped Children Act of 1975 ensured a free, appropriate education for children with disabilities, including special education and related services.

- The **Americans With Disabilities Act of 1990** prohibited discrimination in employment, public accommodation, transportation, state and local government services, and telecommunications. Benefits of the act included greater accessibility to public buildings and transportation for people who use wheelchairs and the availability of electronic devices to allow hearing-impaired people to use telephones and enjoy movies.

Reading Strategy

Analyzing Cause and Effect
- How did the Americans With Disabilities Act (1990) change the lives of people with handicaps?

Activism by disabled veterans, especially from the Vietnam War, drew increased attention to the needs of people with disabilities. Celebrities have also taken up the cause of working for increased congressional funding of medical research. Some examples include the late Elizabeth Taylor for AIDS research, the late Christopher Reeve for spinal cord injuries research, and Michael J. Fox for Parkinson's disease research.

Schools began to mainstream students with disabilities into regular classrooms. Students who previously might have attended special schools with other students with similar disabilities have begun to attend regular public schools in a major attempt at deinstitutionalization. These efforts are known as programs of inclusion.

The New Frontier and the Great Society

Not all legislation on domestic issues during the 1960s concerned civil rights. President Kennedy's programs, known as the New Frontier, and President Johnson's, known as the Great Society, continued and expanded upon traditions begun during Franklin Roosevelt's New Deal of the 1930s.

Kennedy's New Frontier

- *The Space Program* Following the successful launch of a Soviet cosmonaut, the first man in space, in 1961, President Kennedy committed the nation to a space program with the goal of landing a person on the moon by the end of the 1960s. In 1962 John Glenn became the first person to orbit the earth. In July 1969, six years after Kennedy's death, astronaut Neil Armstrong stepped onto the moon's surface. That effort cost some $25.4 billion.

- *The Peace Corps* This program sent thousands of American volunteers to developing nations where they trained local people in technical, educational, and health programs. The Peace Corps program was intended to improve economic conditions and offset the growth of communism. The program is still in existence.

Johnson's Great Society

- *The VISTA Program* The Volunteers in Service to America (VISTA) program was meant as a domestic Peace Corps, aiding poor citizens in rural and impoverished areas.

- *The Office of Economic Opportunity* Set up in 1964, this was the directing agency in President Johnson's War on Poverty. Its branches included Project Head Start (to provide education for preschoolers from low-income families), Project Upward Bound (to assist high-school students from low-income families to attend college), and the Job Corps (to provide vocational training for high-school dropouts.)

President Kennedy and Vice President Johnson

- *The Elementary and Secondary Education Act* This 1965 measure provided more than $1 billion in federal aid to education, with the greatest share going to school districts with large numbers of students from low-income families. Sections of the bill required that schools accepting the money be integrated.

- *Medicare* Amendments to the Social Security Act provided health insurance and some types of health care to those over the age of 65. A Medicaid program provided states with funds to help the needy who were not covered by Medicare.

- *Department of Housing and Urban Development* This cabinet post was meant to oversee federal efforts to improve housing and aid economic development of cities. Its first head, Robert C. Weaver, was the first African American to hold a cabinet post.

- *Food Stamp Program* With the Food Stamp Act of 1964, Johnson continued a program of assistance for low-income families to purchase food, which had originally begun in 1939 and existed until 1943. Kennedy issued the first executive order for Food Stamps in 1961. That was replaced and increased by the Act of 1964. In the decades following, various adjustments were made to the program (FSP). By August 2008, an all-time non-disaster high of 29 million Americans per month were part of the program. In October 2008, the name of the program was changed to Supplemental Nutrition Assistance Program (SNAP).

Preparing for the Exam

On the examination, you will need to understand the major domestic programs of the 1960s.

In the space below, give two provisions of President Kennedy's "New Frontier" program and the reasons for these provisions.

1.

2.

Key Themes and Concepts

Government
Johnson's domestic programs are an example of the concept of change. He often referred to his efforts as the **War on Poverty**. Today, 50 years later, Medicare is changing as it struggles to meet the needs of the growing senior citizen population.

Foreign Policy in the 1960s

United States foreign policy under Kennedy and Johnson continued Truman's cold war policy of containment of communism. In Section 3, you will review how this policy led the nation into the **Vietnam War.** In this section, you will see how cold war concerns affected other aspects of the United States foreign policy in the 1960s.

A History of Involvement

As you remember, the United States has been deeply involved in the affairs of Latin America since early in its history. Latin American nations often resented such intervention, and United States policies have left a legacy of anger and hostility.

Some of the key events in United States-Latin American relations are listed on the next page. For additional discussion of these events, see Unit 3, Section 2.

Kennedy and Latin America

Some of President Kennedy's most significant foreign policy decisions involved Latin America.

The Alliance for Progress Kennedy hoped to improve relations with Latin America and stop the spread of communism there through the Alliance for Progress, which pledged $20 billion to help economic development in the region. However, funds often went to aid repressive governments simply because they were anticommunist.

The Bay of Pigs After President Kennedy took office, he approved a CIA plan to overthrow Fidel Castro, the Communist leader of Cuba. The plan called for Cuban exiles—supplied with U.S. arms, material, and training—to invade Cuba and set off a popular uprising against Castro. The invasion took place on April 17, 1961, at a location called the Bay of Pigs, about 90 miles from Havana. No uprising followed, and Castro's troops quickly crushed the invading forces, to the embarrassment of Kennedy and the United States government.

Key Developments in United States-Latin American Relations

The Monroe Doctrine	In 1823, President Monroe warned the nations of Europe not to interfere with the nations of the Western Hemisphere, thus assuming the role of protector of the Western Hemisphere. However, this policy earned the United States a negative image in much of Latin America.
Spanish-American War (1898)	Victory in a war with Spain brought the United States an overseas empire. It also increased the nation's role in Latin America by giving it possession of Puerto Rico and much control over the government of Cuba.
Panama Canal (1901–1914)	The United States gained control over land where it wanted to build a canal by interfering in the internal affairs of Colombia. As a result, the United States made many enemies in Latin America.
Roosevelt Corollary (1904)	Under this addition to the Monroe Doctrine, President Theodore Roosevelt claimed the United States had the right to intervene in the affairs of Latin American nations guilty of "chronic wrongdoing."
"Dollar Diplomacy" (early 1900s)	President Taft planned to increase U.S. influence in Latin America through economic investment backed by military force.
"Good Neighbor" Policy (1933)	President Franklin Roosevelt made an effort to improve relations with Latin America by stressing increased cooperation.

The Cuban Missile Crisis Fearing another U.S. invasion attempt, Castro agreed to a Soviet plan to base nuclear missiles aimed at the United States in Cuba. Kennedy learned of the plan while the bases were under construction. On October 22, 1962, he announced a naval blockade or quarantine of Cuba and demanded that the Soviets withdraw the missiles. The Cuban Missile Crisis brought the United States and the Soviet Union to the brink of war, but the Soviets backed down and withdrew their missiles.

Kennedy had clearly demonstrated that the United States would not tolerate a Soviet presence in the Western Hemisphere just 90 miles from its shores. By doing so, Kennedy also helped the nation recover some of the prestige it had lost in the failed Bay of Pigs invasion.

U.S. Soviet Tensions, 1961–1963

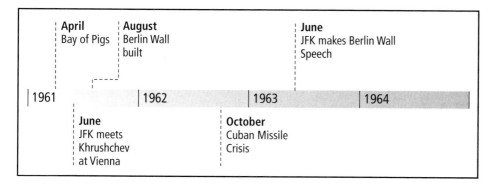

In 1963, the United States, Soviet Union, and Great Britain signed a **Nuclear Test Ban Treaty** in which they agreed not to test nuclear weapons in the air, in outer space, or under the sea. Underground testing was permitted.

Kennedy and Berlin

Since World War II, the division of Germany into a Communist East Germany and a democratic West Germany had added to cold war tensions. President Kennedy and Soviet Premier Nikita Khrushchev met in Austria in June 1961 to discuss relations between the United States and the Soviet Union. Khrushchev thought that the Bay of Pigs disaster revealed American weakness, and he tried to threaten Kennedy into removing NATO troops from Europe. Instead, Kennedy increased U.S. military and financial commitment to West Germany.

Response to the American moves came in August 1961 when the East German government built a wall between East and West Berlin. The **Berlin Wall** was meant to stop the flood of East Germans escaping to freedom in the West and quickly became a symbol of tyranny. In June 1963, Kennedy visited West Berlin, renewing the American commitment to defend that city and Western Europe. In a famous speech, he said that he and all people who wanted freedom were citizens of Berlin.

The Berlin Wall stood as a strong cold war symbol until 1989. In that year, political change sweeping through Eastern Europe led East Germany to tear down the wall. By October 1990, the rapid political changes in the region had led to the reunification of the two Germanys as a single nation for the first time since the end of World War II.

Impact of Kennedy's Death Kennedy's energetic voice for world democracy, and his multilingual wife, Jacqueline, helped to make friends for the United States in many areas of the world. His tragic and unexpected assassination in November 1963 caused an outpouring of grief from around the world, as dozens of foreign heads of state came hurriedly to Washington, D.C., for Kennedy's funeral.

Turning Point

• Why is the Cuban missile crisis of 1962 considered a turning point in U.S.-Soviet relations?

Analyzing Documents

Interpret Data
Examine the timeline then answer these questions.

• How many years passed between the fall of the Berlin Wall and the reunification of Germany?

• Which event occurred first: the meeting between President Kennedy and Soviet Premier Khrushchev, or the building of the Berlin Wall?

Limits of Power: Turmoil at Home and Abroad: 1965–1972

The Big Idea

Fears of Communist expansion in Southeast Asia led to the United States' involvement in the Vietnam War. During this period:

- President Johnson escalated the war.

- student protests became part of the anti-war movement.

- the political and social upheaval of the 1960s divided Americans.

- President Nixon oversaw a cease fire agreement that allowed for U.S. withdrawal from Vietnam.

Section Overview

The fear of Communist expansion led the United States to become increasingly involved in Southeast Asia. This involvement led to the Vietnam War—the longest war in United States history. As the war dragged on, American support began to erode. The combination of negative public opinion and the inability of the military to achieve clear-cut victory led to a gradual withdrawal from the war. Meanwhile, great social and cultural changes were taking place in many parts of American society.

Key Themes and Concepts

As you review this section, take special note of the following key themes and concepts:

Foreign Policy Why did the United States become involved in Vietnam?

Presidential Decisions and Actions How did the decisions made by Presidents Johnson and Nixon affect how the Vietnam War was conducted?

Change What social and cultural changes developed in the 1960s?

Constitutional Principles How did Congress limit the power of the President in wartime?

Key People

Lyndon B. Johnson   Richard Nixon   Henry Kissinger

Key Terms

Gulf of Tonkin Resolution   Vietnamization
hawks   War Powers Act
doves

Fear of Communist expansion led the United States to become deeply involved in Southeast Asia. Review the chart on the next page to learn about the growing involvement of the United States in this region.

Unrest in Asia, 1945–1960

Date	Event
September 1945	World War II ended in Asia; Ho Chi Minh, a member of the Communist party since 1920, proclaimed the Democratic Republic of Vietnam.
1946–1949	France, which had controlled Vietnam since the nineteenth century, appointed a "puppet leader" named Bao Dai, who was ineffective against the power of Ho Chi Minh.
1949	Mao Zedong declared the (Communist) People's Republic of China; recognized the Vietnamese government of Ho Chi Minh in 1950.
1950–1953	United States fought in the Korean War and provided the French with financial aid in their struggle to hang onto Vietnam.
1953–1954	President Eisenhower debated how far the United States should go in backing the French.
1954	The forces of Ho Chi Minh defeated the French at Dienbienphu; Geneva Accords divided Vietnam at the 17th parallel; North and South Vietnam agreed to hold elections in 1956 to reunite the country; the United States joined with seven Asian and European nations in the Southeast Asia Treaty Organization (SEATO), an anticommunist pact which extended protection to Vietnam.
1955	United States under President Eisenhower increased aid to South Vietnam.
1956	South Vietnamese President Ngo Dinh Diem, fearing the popularity of Ho Chi Minh, refused to hold elections scheduled under the Geneva Accords.
1960	Ho Chi Minh recognized the Vietcong, Communist guerrillas in South Vietnam, as the National Liberation Front (NLF) of Vietnam; President Kennedy sent Vice President Johnson to study the crisis in Vietnam.

Kennedy and Vietnam

President Kennedy shared Eisenhower's belief in the domino theory. He, therefore, continued to support the Diem regime. By 1963, the number of United States "advisers" in South Vietnam totaled about 17,000. That year, 489 Americans died in the fighting in Vietnam.

Debate Over Involvement

American advisers urged Diem to adopt reforms to broaden his support. Diem, however, brutally suppressed all opponents and ruled as a dictator. On November 2, 1963, the South Vietnamese military overthrew Diem, with the knowledge and approval of the United States. Around the same time, the White House announced that it intended to withdraw all United States military personnel from Vietnam by 1965. Kennedy was unable to keep this promise because he was assassinated.

Geographic Reasoning
Laos shares a long border with North Vietnam. During the Vietnam War, the dense jungle terrain made it difficult for U.S. and South Vietnamese forces to cut off the supply lines that ran between Laos and North Vietnam.

• How might this role as supplier have had an impact on Laos later in the war?

Key Themes and Concepts

Presidential Decisions and Actions
Without a formal declaration of war by Congress, Presidents Eisenhower, Kennedy, and Johnson all sent U.S. military forces to Vietnam.

• What authorized these presidents to take these actions?

Key Themes and Concepts

Foreign Policy
In 1964, Congress passed the Gulf of Tonkin Resolution. The resolution, which empowered the President to "repel an armed attack against the forces of the United States," was used to escalate U.S. bombings in North Vietnam.

• What obstacles did U.S. troops fighting in Vietnam face?

Johnson and Escalation

Under the Constitution, only Congress can declare war. However, by 1964, three presidents—Eisenhower, Kennedy, and Johnson—had sent United States aid and troops into Vietnam. Each did so by acting as the commander in chief of the nation's military forces.

The Tonkin Gulf Resolution

On August 4, 1964, President Johnson escalated the war dramatically. He announced on television that American destroyers had been the victim of an unprovoked attack by North Vietnamese gun boats. (It later appeared that the ships might have been protecting South Vietnamese boats headed into North Vietnamese waters.) The next day, Johnson asked Congress for the authority to order air strikes against North Vietnam. With only two dissenting votes, Congress passed the **Gulf of Tonkin Resolution.** The resolution empowered "the President, as commander in chief, to take all necessary measures to repel any armed attack against the forces of the United States and to prevent further aggression." Johnson used the resolution to justify expansion of the war. By April 1965, U.S. planes regularly bombed North Vietnam.

A Guerrilla War At first, United States military leaders expected that the nation's superior technology would guarantee victory. However, they soon found themselves bogged down in a guerrilla war fought in the jungles of Southeast Asia. The enemy did not wear uniforms, and no clear battlefront emerged. Thousands of Vietnamese casualties occurred each month as the United States dropped more bombs on Vietnam, an area about twice the size of New York State, than it had used on Nazi Germany during the heaviest months of fighting during World War II.

Reasons for War The massive commitment in Vietnam raised questions in the minds of many Americans about why the United States got involved in Vietnam and why it stayed there. The administration argued that the United States was involved in Vietnam to prevent the fall of Vietnam to communism, to stop the rise of aggressor governments, and to protect the nation's position as a superpower and defender of democracy. However, as the war dragged on, many Americans began to question these motives.

Resistance to the War

By late 1965, an antiwar movement had begun to take shape in the United States.

Hawks and Doves In Congress, there were differences of opinion concerning the war. Some stood solidly behind the president and argued in favor of victory at any cost. These members were known as hawks. Those who favored immediate withdrawal and an end to the war were known as doves.

Student Protests College campuses became centers of political protest against the war. The University of California, Berkeley campus, became a leader in anti-Vietnam War protests. The name *Berkeley* became synonymous with the activities of the protest movement. Students organized a new form of protest called teach-ins, or meetings in which speakers, usually promoting unconditional American withdrawal from Vietnam, held study sessions and rallies.

The strongest antiwar group in the 1960s was Students for a Democratic Society (SDS), founded in 1960. SDS was antiestablishment, or against big business and government. It led demonstrations, sit-ins, draft-card burnings, and protests against universities with "pro-establishment" regulations. By 1969, the organization had collapsed into a number of splinter groups. However, SDS's legacy of protest against authority remained a strong force into the 1970s.

Protest Marches People of all ages joined in protest marches against the war. The first huge march took place in Washington, D.C., in 1965. In 1967, some 300,000 Americans marched in New York City. That same year, another 50,000 tried to shut down the Pentagon.

Draft Resisters In 1967, former Olympic boxing light heavy-weight gold medal winner, Muhammad Ali (Cassius Clay) refused to take the oath of induction into the army after being drafted. He was found guilty of draft evasion but remained free on appeal until 1971, when the Supreme Court overturned his case. By 1968, about 10,000 draft resisters, people unwilling to serve in the military after being drafted, had fled the country for Canada. The nation's youth became increasingly divided as some chose to fight for the United States in Vietnam, while others sought deferments to go to college. A large number of minorities, who could not afford the cost of college, responded to the draft and went to Vietnam. The attitude of American youth became increasingly hostile toward the Johnson administration and all war-related issues. In 1968, Lyndon Johnson announced his decision not to run for a second term as president. This was largely due to his low popularity ratings as a result of his Vietnam War policies.

Preparing for the Exam

On the examination, you will need to have a thorough understanding of U.S. foreign policy.

List three reasons President Johnson's administration used to justify U.S. involvement in Vietnam.

1.

2.

3.

Key Themes and Concepts

Reform Movements
College campuses became centers of the antiwar movement in the United States. Students organized teach-ins and other protests aimed at getting the Johnson administration to end U.S. involvement in Vietnam. Protest marches featuring people of all ages took place in major cities.

• In what different ways did young people respond to the draft?

The 1960s—Political and Social Upheaval

Some political analysts who studied the events of 1968 believed the nation had survived one of the biggest tests to its political institutions since the Civil War. The 1960s had been shaped by two movements: the Civil Rights Movement and the antiwar movement. The political turmoil of the decade helped produce great social upheaval, especially among the nation's youth.

Cultural Changes

Some young people became disillusioned with traditional American values. For the first time in United States history, thousands of Americans flaunted the use of illegal drugs, often popularized in rock music.

Many young Americans referred to themselves as hippies or flower children. They claimed to be searching for a freer, simpler way of life. Communal living attracted thousands of youths who adopted lifestyles foreign to older Americans. Some spoke of a generation gap between youth and people over 30.

The Civil Rights Movement and the Vietnam War also divided Americans. The assassinations of Robert Kennedy and Dr. Martin Luther King, Jr., heightened emotions.

Reading Strategy

Reinforcing Main Ideas
Identify three events that occurred during 1968 that caused that year to be associated with political and social upheaval.

Key Events of 1968

Month	Event
January	• North Vietnam launched the Tet (New Year's) offensive, using Soviet-made jets and weapons for the first time.
March	• Eugene McCarthy, a peace candidate and leading "dove," won the Democratic presidential primary in New Hampshire. • Robert Kennedy announced his candidacy for the presidency. • President Johnson announced that he would not seek reelection and that he would devote the remainder of his term to trying to end the war. The war had hurt his popularity with voters.
April	• American forces in Vietnam reached 549,000; combat deaths climbed to 22,951. • North Vietnam announced its willingness to enter into peace talks. • An assassin claimed the life of Dr. Martin Luther King, Jr.
May	• Preliminary peace talks with the North Vietnamese began, but serious negotiations would not take place for several years.
June	• An assassin claimed the life of Robert Kennedy shortly after his victory in the California Democratic presidential primary.
August	• The Democratic National Convention nominated Hubert Humphrey amid the worst political rioting and demonstrations any convention had ever experienced; Humphrey (Johnson's Vice President) inherited a divided party and sought election in a divided nation. • The Republican National Convention nominated Richard Nixon, whose only serious challenger was Ronald Reagan. • The American Independent party nominated Governor George Wallace of Alabama, showing that a third party could attract white-backlash voters who opposed the Civil Rights Movement.
November	• Nixon won the 1968 election with 43.4% of the popular vote; Humphrey claimed 42.7%; Wallace took 13.5%.

Nixon and Vietnam

By 1969, President Nixon faced a national crisis. The Vietnam War had turned into the nation's most costly war. American support for the war was at an all-time low.

Winding Down the War

Nixon did not bring an end to the war right away. In fact, for a time, he widened American military activities, attacking North Vietnamese supply routes out of Laos and Cambodia. This expansion of the war in Indochina caused increased human and financial losses for the United States.

Vietnamization Nixon called for Vietnamization of the war, or a takeover of the ground fighting by Vietnamese soldiers. Both Kennedy and Johnson had favored this approach, but neither had been able to make it work. While Nixon promoted Vietnamization, he also bombed neighboring Cambodia, which he claimed served as a base for North Vietnamese guerrillas.

The bombings triggered a large student protest at Kent State University in Ohio. By the time the National Guard broke up the demonstration, four students lay dead and nine others wounded. More and more Americans were questioning the role of the United States in Vietnam, yet President Nixon increased bombing raids on North Vietnam throughout 1970.

Peace With Honor Henry Kissinger, Nixon's chief foreign policy adviser, met in Paris with North Vietnamese officials seeking an end to the war. For several years, negotiations remained deadlocked. Finally, on January 15, 1973, Nixon announced that "peace with honor" had been reached and that a cease-fire would soon take effect.

Key Themes and Concepts

Presidential Decisions and Actions
• What impact did President Nixon's decision to bomb Cambodia have on student protests?

The War Powers Act

The War Powers Act, passed over President Nixon's veto in 1973, gave Congress more power in dealing with international conflicts.

• The President can send troops overseas, but must inform Congress within 48 hours.

• Troops may not stay overseas more than 60 days without the approval of Congress.

• Congress has the power to force the President to bring troops home.

The War Powers Act

In November 1973, Congress passed the War Powers Act over Nixon's veto. This law helped reverse the precedent set by the Gulf of Tonkin Resolution, which gave the President sweeping powers in Vietnam. The War Powers Act included the following provisions:

• The President had to notify Congress within 48 hours of sending troops into a foreign country. At that time, the President would have to give Congress a full accounting of the decision.

• The President had to bring the troops home within 60 days unless both houses voted for them to stay.

Reading Strategy

Problem Solving
• Why do you think Congress passed the War Powers Act over President Nixon's veto?

For the examination, it will be important to understand the significance of historical events, not just the dates of and participants in those events.

- Overall, was the Vietnam War a success or a failure? Why?

- What enduring lessons were learned from the war?

- How has the Vietnam War continued to be remembered in American society?

Vietnam and Limits on United States Power

When the United States finally withdrew from Vietnam, the North Vietnamese overran South Vietnam. For two years, the United States poured billions of dollars of aid into South Vietnam. However, on April 30, 1975, the government in Saigon collapsed. Bitterness over the war persisted. When the president asked for funds to evacuate the South Vietnamese who had helped the United States, Congress refused. In the end, some 100,000 people fled the country.

The United States had tried for 20 years to guarantee freedom to the people of South Vietnam. However, the United States ultimately could not count its efforts as a success. In the conflict, some 58,000 Americans died, and another 300,000 were wounded. The United States spent over $150 billion on the war effort. Not only did Vietnam fall to communism, but so did its neighbors Cambodia (Kampuchea) and Laos. Throughout the late 1970s and 1980s, the United States sought to understand the Vietnam experience. It was the subject of films, books, and national monuments such as the Vietnam Veterans Memorial in Washington, D.C.

Conclusions Drawn from U.S. Involvement in Vietnam

The following is a list of conclusions drawn from the Vietnam War era.

- The American political system acted in response to a variety of public pressures.
- Modern war technology was not always powerful enough if an opponent is armed with a determined spirit of nationalism.
- Successful military efforts required a well-prepared and supportive public. (Compare, for example, the differing experiences in Vietnam and World War II.)
- The United States was committed to a foreign policy that supported the global nature of United States involvement in foreign affairs.
- The United States questioned its role as a police officer to the world.
- The President of the United States should learn from the lessons of Vietnam when foreign policies are considered that could cause loss of American lives as well as great financial cost.

The Trend Toward Conservatism: 1972–1985

Section Overview

After the upheaval of the 1960s, Richard Nixon tried to take the nation into a new direction, but the Watergate affair led to his resignation. His successors, Gerald Ford and Jimmy Carter, struggled with lingering economic troubles. In the 1980s, conservatives Ronald Reagan and George Bush came to power. After the cold war ended, the United States struggled to determine its new role in international relations.

Key Themes and Concepts

As you review this section, take special note of the following key themes and concepts:

Presidential Decisions and Actions How did President Nixon shape a new policy toward China and the Soviet Union?

Economic Systems How did economic problems of the 1970s present unique challenges to the Nixon, Ford, and Carter administrations?

Key People

Mao Zedong

Warren Burger

Gerald Ford

Jimmy Carter

Ronald Reagan

Mikhail Gorbachev

Key Terms

détente

Watergate affair

stagflation

Camp David Accords

supply-side economics

"Star Wars"

Iran-Contra affair

Key Supreme Court Cases

Engel v. *Vitale* (1962) *

Gideon v. *Wainwright* (1963) *

Miranda v. *Arizona* (1966)

Tinker v. *Des Moines Community School District* (1969)

New York Times v. *United States* (1971) *

Roe v. *Wade* (1973)

United States v. *Nixon* (1974)

New Jersey v. *T.L.O.* (1985) *

The Big Idea

Beginning in the early 1970s, conservatism replaced liberalism in American politics. During this period:

• President Nixon opened diplomatic relations with China and shaped a policy of détente toward the Soviet Union.

• President Ford pardoned President Nixon following his resignation over the Watergate affair.

• President Reagan supported a domestic program of New Federalism during the 1980s that was begun by President Nixon.

---

* For information on these cases, see the Landmark Supreme Court Cases chart in the Reference Section. Cases without the * appear both in the text and in the chart in the Reference Section.

An Era of Conservatism, 1972–1990

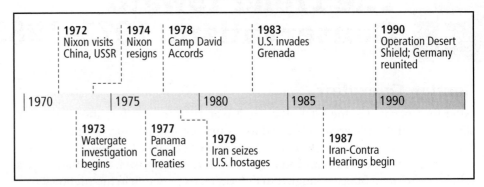

| 1972 Nixon visits China, USSR | 1974 Nixon resigns | 1978 Camp David Accords | 1983 U.S. invades Grenada | 1990 Operation Desert Shield; Germany reunited |

1970 | 1975 | 1980 | 1985 | 1990

1973 Watergate investigation begins | 1977 Panama Canal Treaties | 1979 Iran seizes U.S. hostages | 1987 Iran-Contra Hearings begin

From Cold War to Détente

Although President Nixon's main foreign policy objective was ending the Vietnam War, he had other foreign policy interests as well.

Nixon Doctrine

In 1969, Nixon announced what became known as the Nixon Doctrine. This doctrine stated that the United States would no longer provide direct military protection in Asia. Even though the Vietnam War was not yet concluded, the president promised Americans that there would be no more Vietnams for the United States.

A New Policy Toward China

President Nixon also adopted a new foreign policy toward China. The United States had not had diplomatic relations with the People's Republic since the 1949 Communist revolution.

Presidential Visit In 1971, Nixon stunned Americans by announcing that he had accepted an invitation to visit China. On February 21, 1972, Nixon arrived in China. National Security Adviser Henry Kissinger accompanied the president on his peace mission.

Opening the Door After more than 20 years of hostility, President Nixon and Chinese leaders Mao Zedong and Premier Zhou Enlai agreed to open the door to normal diplomatic relations. Nixon's visit cleared the way for economic and cultural exchanges. American manufacturers, for example, now had a new market for their products. By following a policy toward China that was separate from the Soviet Union, Nixon underscored the splits that had occurred within communism. This visit ultimately reduced tensions between the United States and China.

A New Policy Toward the Soviet Union

Nixon balanced his openness with China by looking for ways to ease tensions with the Soviet Union, China's Communist rival.

Détente Nixon and Kissinger shaped a policy called détente. The goal of détente was to bring about a warming in the cold war. In contrast to President Truman's policy of containment, President Nixon's policy of détente was designed to prevent open conflict.

During the Nixon administration, the foreign policy of the United States was shaped by *Realpolitik,* a political philosophy favored by Kissinger. The meaning of *Realpolitik* is power politics. Therefore, in its dealings with China and the Soviet Union, the United States made its decisions based on what it needed to maintain its own strength—regardless of world opinion.

Turning Point

- Why is President Nixon's visit to China considered a turning point in U.S. foreign policy?

Key Themes and Concepts

Foreign Policy
- As secretary of state, Henry Kissinger favored the political philosophy of *Realpolitik.* In your own words, how would you define *Realpolitik*?

President Nixon underscored his willingness to pursue détente by visiting the Soviet Union in May 1972. He was the first president since World War II to make such a journey.

SALT While in Moscow, Nixon opened what became known as the Strategic Arms Limitations Talks (SALT). These talks led to a 1972 agreement called the SALT Agreement. The agreement set limits on the number of defensive missile sites and strategic offensive missiles each nation would keep.

Nixon's Domestic Policies

```
                                    ┌──────────────────────────────────┐
                                    │ • Try to slow inflation          │
                                    └──────────────────────────────────┘

                                    ┌──────────────────────────────────┐
   ┌─────────────────────┐          │ • Decrease support for Great     │
   │                     │          │   Society social programs        │
   │  Nixon's Policies   │          └──────────────────────────────────┘
   │                     │
   └─────────────────────┘          ┌──────────────────────────────────┐
                                    │ • Strengthen law and order,      │
                                    │   discourage protests            │
                                    └──────────────────────────────────┘

                                    ┌──────────────────────────────────┐
                                    │ • Move slowly on civil rights,   │
                                    │   appoint conservative justices  │
                                    │   to Supreme Court               │
                                    └──────────────────────────────────┘
```

Analyzing Documents

Analyze Evidence
Based on the graphic organizer at left and your knowledge of social studies, would you characterize Nixon as a conservative or a liberal president? Provide two reasons to justify your answer.

1.

2.

Nixon's Domestic Policies

President Nixon was mainly interested in foreign affairs. He knew that he faced a Congress controlled by a Democratic majority. Because of the system of checks and balances, Nixon realized that it would be almost impossible to push Republican policies through Congress. Therefore, he limited his domestic policy goals.

Nixon's Domestic Initiatives

In 1970, the Occupational Safety and Health Administration (OSHA) was created to ensure safe and healthful working conditions for all working Americans. OSHA assisted states in providing research, information, education, and training in the field of occupational safety and health.

The Environmental Protection Agency (EPA), established in 1970, coordinated federal programs to combat pollution and protect the environment.

The Clean Air Act of 1970 was a major comprehensive federal law addressing topics related to air pollution. It was amended in 1977 to set new goals since many parts of the country did not meet the standards set by the 1970 act. It was amended again in 1990 to address problems such as acid rain, ground level ozone, stratospheric ozone depletion, and air toxins.

On July 12, 1973, President Nixon united several existing federal drug agencies into the Drug Enforcement Administration (DEA), which enforced federal drug laws and conducted investigations of illegal drugs overseas.

In 1974, the Energy Reorganization Act created the Nuclear Regulatory Commission to regulate the nuclear power industry and the Energy Research and Development Administration to manage the nuclear weapon, nuclear reactor, and energy development programs of the federal government. In 1977, under President Carter, the Department of Energy was established. Today, the department ensures energy security and safety.

Preparing for the Exam

- What did Nixon intend to accomplish with his policy of New Federalism?

- To what previous presidential policy was he reacting?

Key Themes and Concepts

Constitutional Principles
- Did these landmark Supreme Court cases provide more protection for individual rights or less protection?

- *Gideon* v. *Wainwright* (1963), *Escobedo* v. *Illinois* (1964), and *Miranda* v. *Arizona* (1966) increased the rights of individuals who were accused of a crime.

Key Themes and Concepts

Science and Technology
- Why was it significant that an American was the first person to set foot on the moon?

Key Themes and Concepts

Change
- How did passage of the Twenty-sixth Amendment affect the number of voters in the United States?

- Would you say that this amendment made the United States more democratic or less democratic?

New Federalism

Like Eisenhower, Nixon wanted to reduce the role of the federal government and turn over more activities to the states. Nixon called this policy the New Federalism. He criticized Johnson's Great Society as too costly and tried to reduce involvement of the federal government in social welfare programs. To achieve this goal, Nixon instituted revenue sharing, a policy in which the federal government gave part of its income to the states to spend on social welfare as they saw fit.

Curbing Inflation

The Vietnam War had helped trigger inflation, which was one of Nixon's biggest domestic problems. During the 1968 election, Nixon had promised to end inflation and balance the budget. By the time he took office, prices were rising faster than they had in 20 years. Unemployment was rising too. At the same time, the nation's gross national product (GNP) was declining. To bring the economy under control, Nixon implemented a 90-day wage-price freeze in August 1971. He was the first president to impose mandatory wage-price controls in peacetime.

Nixon and the Supreme Court

Each President hopes to influence the decisions of the Supreme Court through the appointment of justices. However, the appointees do not always rule as a President might expect. For example, President Eisenhower regretted his appointment of Earl Warren to the Supreme Court, because Warren made many liberal decisions that opposed Eisenhower's conservative political views.

Nixon Appointees In 1969, Warren retired, and Nixon appointed Warren Burger as chief justice. During his administration, Nixon also had the opportunity to appoint three other justices. Nixon's appointees were all strict constructionists, believing that Congress and the President have only those powers specifically given to them by the Constitution. The "Nixon Court," however, did not overturn many of the liberal rulings of the 1960s, as Nixon had expected.

Other Domestic Events Under Nixon

Advances in the space program, an increase in the electorate, and additional rights movements occurred in the 1970s.

The Space Program

In 1969, American astronaut Neil Armstrong became the first person to walk on the moon. The triumph of seeing Armstrong plant a United States flag on the moon's surface marked a bright spot in an otherwise troubled decade.

The Twenty-sixth Amendment

In 1971, the Twenty-sixth Amendment to the Constitution was ratified. This amendment extended the vote to people ages 18 and older. By lowering the voting age from 21 to 18, this amendment added almost 12 million new voters to the American electorate. The ratification of this amendment has been seen as a result of the participation of the United States in the Vietnam War, where thousands of Americans between the ages of 18 and 21 died.

Women's Rights Movement

In the 1970s, more and more women enrolled in schools of law, medicine, engineering, and business, fields that had been traditionally reserved for men. However, full-time working women in 1971 were paid only 59 percent as much as men. Many of them also did not hold positions equal to their talents. As you read in Section 2, the Equal Rights Amendment failed to win ratification.

Consumer Rights Movement

A strong consumer rights movement also developed in the early 1970s to address abuses by major American industries. The movement was led by Ralph Nader, a young Washington lawyer who organized a protest in the 1960s against the automotive industry. Nader attracted a number of young volunteers, known as "Nader's Raiders," to his cause. They championed environmental and consumer protection.

The Watergate Affair

In 1972, the Republicans nominated Nixon for reelection. The Democrats selected George McGovern. President Nixon claimed credit for bringing down inflation and scoring foreign policy triumphs abroad. He swept to victory, carrying the largest popular majority in United States history. Yet less than two years later, Nixon resigned from office.

- **What happened** an illegal break-in to wiretap phones in the Democratic Party headquarters with electronic surveillance equipment
- **Where** Watergate Towers, an apartment complex in Washington, D.C.
- **When** June 17, 1972
- **Who** the Committee to Reelect the President, acting with the knowledge of several high-level Nixon advisers
- **Why** to secure information to undermine the Democratic campaign against Nixon

The Cover-Up

Police captured the "burglars," who carried evidence linking them to the White House. Nixon did not know about the plan until after it happened. However, he then ordered a cover-up, which was a crime under federal law.

The Investigation Reporters from the *Washington Post* probed into the case, now known as the **Watergate affair,** but their reports did not hinder Nixon's reelection. Then in 1973, the Senate set up a committee to look into "illegal, improper, or unethical activities" in the 1972 election. For more than a year, the Senate committee came closer and closer to implicating President Nixon.

Resignation of Agnew While the Watergate hearings were under way, the Justice Department charged Vice President Spiro Agnew with income tax evasion. Agnew resigned, and Nixon appointed Gerald R. Ford, the minority leader in the House of Representatives, as Vice President.

The Tapes In mid-1973, the Senate committee learned that the White House had kept tape recordings of key conversations between Nixon and his top aides. Nixon refused to turn over the tapes. During the summer, the committee opened the hearings to television. The televised proceedings had the appeal of a soap opera as millions of Americans watched.

Nixon Resignation The situation ended when the Supreme Court ordered Nixon to surrender the tapes in its ruling in *United States* v. *Richard Nixon.* Based on evidence in the tapes, the House Judiciary Committee began voting on articles of impeachment against the president. To avoid impeachment, Nixon resigned on August 9, 1974, becoming the first President to do so. On noon of that day, Gerald Ford took the oath of office.

Gerald Ford became the first nonelected president. To fill the office of Vice President, Ford named Nelson Rockefeller, the former governor of New York.

Key Themes and Concepts

Reform Movements
The consumer rights movement of the 1960s, led by Ralph Nader, achieved important reforms, such as improved safety features in U.S.-built automobiles.

- What earlier movement in American history championed the cause of improving products available to the American people?

Reading Strategy

Reinforcing Main Ideas
The Watergate affair was a serious scandal that brought down a president.

- What was the reason behind the Watergate break-in?
- What was Nixon's role?
- How did Nixon's involvement in the Watergate affair lead to his resignation?
- How did the Watergate affair prove that the system of checks and balances works?

Key Themes and Concepts

Change
The 25th Amendment passed in 1967 established the procedure for Gerald Ford to become President.

Why was this necessary?

From 1974 until 1977, the United States had both a President and Vice President who had not been elected to their offices but had been appointed. Such a situation had not occurred before and has not occurred since.

Turning Point

- Why is the Watergate affair considered a turning point in U.S. history?

Significance of Watergate

Although Nixon was never charged with any specific crimes, President Ford pardoned him. Ford hoped to end what he called "our long national nightmare." Many of Nixon's advisers, however, were found guilty of crimes and sentenced to prison. The incident showed, as Ford put it, that "the Constitution works." The system of checks and balances had stopped Nixon from placing the presidency above the law. However, one impact of the Watergate Scandal was a decline in the public's trust in government.

The Ford Administration

Many people called Nixon's administration the "Imperial Presidency" because of his disregard of the Constitution. Ford tried to rebuild the image of the President. However, the Watergate affair had disillusioned many Americans.

Ford's Domestic Policies

From the start, President Ford faced a number of domestic problems.

- *Nixon's Pardon* Many Americans questioned Ford's decision to pardon Nixon when so many of his advisers stood trial and were convicted and jailed.

- *Amnesty Plan* Ford stirred bitter debate when he offered amnesty to thousands of young men who avoided military service in Vietnam by violating draft laws, fleeing the country, or deserting the military.

- *Inflation* In 1973, the Organization of Petroleum Exporting Countries (OPEC) placed an oil embargo on the United States for its support of Israel. The price of oil and gasoline more than doubled, setting off a new round of inflation. Temporary rationing of gasoline and federal incentives to research energy alternatives helped ease shortages. Even so, Americans remained highly dependent on foreign oil. Inflation topped 10 percent, and the nation entered into its worst recession since World War II.

Key Themes and Concepts

Presidential Decisions and Actions
Following a Senate investigation into the Watergate affair, President Nixon resigned on August 9, 1974. Vice President Gerald Ford became the first non-elected president in U.S. history. Although President Nixon was never charged with any crime, President Ford issued a pardon to him.

- Why do you think President Ford pardoned President Nixon?

Analyzing Documents

Interpret Data
Based on the chart and your knowledge of social studies, answer the following questions.

- What happened to fuel prices in 1973 and 1974?

- What caused the change in fuel prices in those years?

- How might the change in fuel prices and in all consumer item prices be related?

Rate of Inflation, 1968–1976

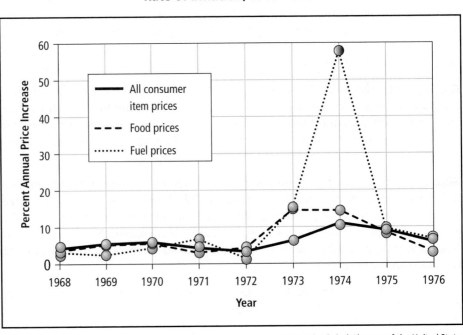

Source: *Statistical Abstract of the United States*

Ford's Foreign Policies

Henry Kissinger continued working with the Ford administration. Kissinger helped:

- negotiate a cease-fire agreement between Egypt and Israel, thus ending the 1973 Yom Kippur War and OPEC oil embargo.
- continue the policy of détente with the Soviet Union, including the sale of tons of grain to the Soviets and a hookup of Soviet and American space capsules.
- oversee the end of the Vietnam War, including the withdrawal of the last American personnel from Saigon in 1975.

The Election of 1976

The nation's bicentennial (200th anniversary) in 1976 gave the Ford presidency a boost. However, it was not enough to help Ford completely shake off his negative association with the Nixon years. He lost a close election to the Democratic candidate, James (Jimmy) Earl Carter, former governor of Georgia.

The Carter Administration

Jimmy Carter won the 1976 election, in part, because of his appeal to the American sense of honesty and integrity. He stated a desire to return to basic American "down home" values. He wanted to prove that an "outsider" could make government more responsive to the people. However, Carter's unfamiliarity with Washington politics proved a disadvantage. First Lady Rosalynn Carter became his most trusted adviser.

Carter's Domestic Policies

Carter's presidency was made more difficult by changes that had taken place within Congress because of Watergate. Newly elected members tended to question every executive act.

"Stagflation" President Carter ran into the same economic woes as Ford—inflation coupled with rising unemployment. The problems were worsened by many welfare programs that increased the cost of government. With the economy apparently stalled in place, economists coined a new term, stagflation, to describe the situation. (The term referred to the stagnation of the economy and simultaneous inflation of prices.)

Energy Problem As the world's leading industrial power, the United States was also the world's leading consumer of energy. By the late 1970s, the nation had to import more than 40 percent of its oil. OPEC kept prices high, and American dollars flowed out of the country, worsening the trade deficit—the situation in which a nation buys more foreign goods than it exports abroad. In 1977, President Carter spoke to the American people about the energy crisis. He presented a national energy plan based on ten principles including conservation, environmental protection, and the development of new conventional or alternative sources of energy.

Corporate Bailouts Some American corporations were hard hit by stagflation and the decline in purchasing power at home. Foreign imports undersold some American goods, especially automobiles. The Chrysler Corporation and Lockheed Aircraft faced possible bankruptcy. Fearing the effect of massive layoffs on the economy, the federal government authorized huge loans to both corporations to keep them in business.

Environmental Problems Acid rain, created by toxic air pollution, continued to threaten forests, lakes, and wildlife in the United States. President Nixon had

Election of 1976

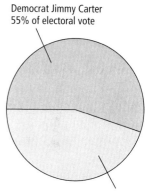

Democrat Jimmy Carter 55% of electoral vote

Republican Gerald R. Ford 45% of electoral vote

Key Themes and Concepts

Environment
In the 1970s, the United States faced a number of environmental problems.

- What steps did Nixon and Carter take to resolve some of these problems?

- Do any of these problems persist today? If so, which ones?

taken steps to end harmful industrial pollution by creating the Environmental Protection Agency. Carter supported environmental programs as well, but inflation and energy shortages prevented him from undertaking ambitious programs to protect the environment. Coal polluted the air, but the nation needed coal to offset oil shortages. The nation needed to clean up the air, but emission devices for cars and factories pushed up prices.

Nuclear Energy Carter supported nuclear energy as an alternative to coal and oil. However, in 1979, an accident occurred at the Three Mile Island nuclear plant near Harrisburg, Pennsylvania. Although the problem was brought under control, the incident highlighted the hazards of the nuclear power industry, which by the late 1970s supplied about 4 percent of the nation's energy.

Carter's Foreign Policy

During his presidency, Carter faced a number of foreign-policy challenges.

Helsinki Accords In 1975, the United States and other nations signed the Helsinki Accords, promising to respect basic human rights. Carter believed that the United States should withhold aid from nations that violated human rights.

Camp David Accords In 1977, Egyptian President Anwar el-Sadat surprised the world by visiting Israeli Prime Minister Menachem Begin. President Carter seized the opportunity for bringing peace to the Middle East by inviting the two leaders to Camp David, the president's retreat in Maryland. There, Sadat and Begin hammered out the terms for a peace treaty known as the Camp David Accords. The two leaders signed the treaty in 1979. Other Arab nations, however, still refused to recognize Israel.

Key Themes and Concepts

Presidential Decisions and Actions
As you know from your study of United States history, all events are influenced by decisions, actions, and outcomes of earlier times.

- How was Carter's presidency influenced by the shadow of Nixon's presidency?

President Carter announces the results of the Camp David Accords to a Joint Session of Congress

Panama Canal Treaties In 1977, President Carter signed two treaties promising to turn over control of the Panama Canal to Panama in 1999. The treaties aroused bitter debate, but the Senate narrowly ratified them in 1978.

Problems With Détente In June 1979, Carter met with Soviet leader Leonid Brezhnev to negotiate the SALT II Treaty. However, a Soviet invasion of Afghanistan later that year ended détente. Carter cut off grain shipments to the Soviet Union and boycotted the 1980 summer Olympic games held in Moscow. Carter's tough line spurred debate at home.

Hostage Crisis The biggest foreign policy crisis for Carter came in Iran. In 1979, a revolution led by Islamic fundamentalists toppled the pro-American shah, Reza Pahlavi. The shah, suffering from terminal cancer, requested treatment in the United States, and Carter agreed. Islamic rebels struck back by seizing the United States embassy in Teheran and holding more than 50 Americans hostage.

The 1980 Election

During the 1980 presidential campaign, President Carter was haunted by the continuing hostage crisis, persistent energy shortages, and lingering inflation. The conservative Republican candidate, former California governor Ronald Reagan, promised Americans a "new beginning" and a restoration of confidence at home and abroad. Reagan swept to victory, and on the day of his inauguration, Iran released the hostages after more than a year of captivity.

Reagan and the Challenges of the 1980s

A former actor, Reagan appealed to many Americans with his references to the "good old days" and his patriotic speeches. He used his prepared speeches to promote a conservative approach to government and the economy. He targeted inflation as his top priority and argued that big government was the cause of inflation. "In the present crisis," said Reagan, "government is not the solution to our problem; government is the problem."

Reagan's First-Term Domestic Policies

During his first term in office, President Reagan supported a domestic program backed by both Eisenhower and Nixon. Like his Republican predecessors, he supported New Federalism, a policy that turned over federal control of some social welfare programs to the states.

Supply-Side Economics Reagan called for cuts in taxes on businesses and individuals, especially those with large incomes. The president believed that they would reinvest in more businesses. These businesses would hire more workers and increase the supply of goods and services. Reagan argued that supply-side economics, or the trickle down theory, would end inflation without increasing the national debt. His ideas later became known as Reaganomics.

Balanced Budget Reagan tried to balance the budget by reducing many social welfare programs. He also made sharp cuts in the Environmental Protection Agency. Despite such efforts, however, the national debt climbed throughout Reagan's presidency.

"Star Wars" Reagan felt national security rested on defense and made every effort to fight off cuts in the military budget. He pushed for increased spending on missiles, ships, and bombers. He also asked for funding for the Strategic Defense Initiative (SDI), a massive satellite shield designed to intercept and destroy incoming Soviet missiles. SDI became popularly known as "Star Wars."

President Reagan charts budget deficits

Farm Aid In the 1980s, farmers experienced their worst economic problems since the Great Depression. A worldwide recession made it impossible for farmers to sell their surpluses—and to repay their loans. The Reagan administration responded by paying farmers not to plant millions of

Election of 1980

Republican Ronald Reagan
91% of electoral vote

Democrat Jimmy Carter
9% of electoral vote

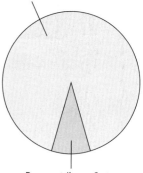

Preparing for the Exam

- What reasons led the American people to elect Ronald Reagan as president in 1980?

acres of land to reduce the supply and raise prices. However, prices did not rise, and the national debt grew. Rising farm costs caused reduced profits.

Immigration In an effort to cut down on the number of undocumented workers living in the United States, Congress passed the 1986 Immigration Reform and Control Act, which forbade employers from hiring illegal immigrants. This new legislation did not solve the problem of the thousands of people who enter the United States illegally every year. These immigrants often work in sweatshop type factories, live in substandard housing, and are paid very low wages.

Analyzing Documents

Interpret Data
Use the graph and your knowledge of social studies to answer the following questions.

• From 1982 to 1995, where did the largest group of immigrants to the United States come from?

• How is this different than the origin of most immigrants in the nineteenth century?

Origin of Immigrants, 1982–1995

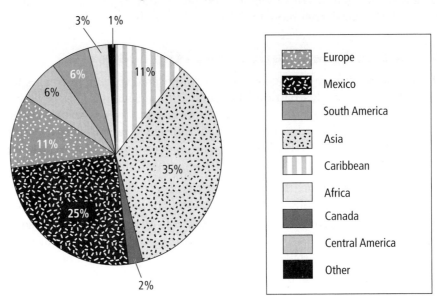

Europe
Mexico
South America
Asia
Caribbean
Africa
Canada
Central America
Other

Source: Statistical Abstract of the United States

Reagan's First-Term Foreign Policy

President Reagan adopted a tough stand toward communism, describing the Soviet Union as an "evil empire."

Questioning Détente Reagan's attitude hardened toward communism in December 1981, when the Polish government cracked down on Solidarity, an independent labor party. The president called for economic sanctions to force the communist-backed government to end martial law. A renewal of détente did not take place until Reagan's second term.

Intervention in Central America Reagan believed that unstable economic conditions opened the door to communism. He asked for aid to Latin American groups fighting Communist takeovers and approved limited military intervention in some nations.

Reading Strategy

Analyzing Cause and Effect
• What factors contributed to United States military interventions in El Salvador, Nicaragua, and Grenada?

• *El Salvador* Reagan sent arms and military advisers to El Salvador to back anticommunist forces in a civil war. He also pressured the government to hold democratic elections.
• *Nicaragua* In 1979, Marxist guerrillas called the Sandinistas overthrew anticommunist dictator Anastasio Somoza. Because the Sandinistas accepted aid from Cuba and the Soviet Union, Reagan approved aid to the contras, rebels seeking to oust the Sandinistas. Actions by the CIA to help the contras angered Congress, and it cut off aid to the contras in 1987.

- *Grenada* In October 1983, a rebellion in the Caribbean island nation of Grenada raised fears that it might become a Communist base in the Caribbean. To prevent such a possibility, Reagan ordered a surprise United States invasion.

Turmoil in the Middle East Religious conflicts in the Middle East increased tensions in an already unstable region. An international peacekeeping force went into Lebanon to try to end bloody fighting between Christians and Muslims. In October 1983, U.S. marines became the target of terrorists when a bomb-laden truck drove into their barracks, killing more than 300 people. In 1984, Reagan admitted the peacekeeping effort had failed and withdrew American troops.

Terrorism Global concern was raised by an increase in terrorism, random acts of violence to promote a political cause. In some countries, Islamic fundamentalists engaged in terrorism against those believed to be enemies of Islam. Charges of terrorism were also leveled against the Soviets in September, 1983, when they shot down a South Korean airliner that strayed into their air space, killing 269 people.

The Election of 1984
In the presidential election of 1984, Walter Mondale won the Democratic nomination over several contenders including Jesse Jackson, an influential African American minister. Mondale selected Representative Geraldine Ferraro as his running mate. President Reagan campaigned for reelection, with George Bush as his running mate. Reagan won the election and became the first president since Eisenhower to serve two full terms in office.

Reagan's Second-Term Domestic Policy
Reagan, nicknamed the Great Communicator by some journalists, used his charm and persuasive talents to convince many Americans to support a plan aimed at creating a balanced budget by the early 1990s.

Reagan and his supporters promised to make deep cuts in federal programs. Only a few select programs, such as Social Security and defense, were to be spared. Reagan also called for simplification of tax laws and tax cuts for about 60 percent of Americans. It was believed that tax cuts would encourage economic growth. Some people charged that the cuts favored the rich. In fact, by the late 1980s, wealth was more unevenly distributed than at any time since the end of World War II.

Trade Imbalance Despite drastic actions by the federal government, the national debt climbed. This was due, in part, to a huge trade imbalance, a situation in which a nation imports more goods than it exports. At the start of Reagan's second term, the trade deficit approached $150 billion.

Reagan's Second-Term Foreign Policy
President Reagan redirected his foreign policy to meet changes taking place in the Soviet Union. However, an issue that arose out of the United States dealings in the Middle East and Latin America took up much of his attention.

The Iran-Contra Affair In 1986, the American public learned that several top presidential aides had sold weapons to Iran in exchange for Iranian help in freeing American hostages held in Lebanon. The money from the sale of arms was then channeled to Nicaragua to support the contras.

Reagan had vowed never to bargain with terrorists or kidnappers. Also, Congress had banned aid to the contras. A congressional committee cleared the president of any wrongdoing in the Iran-Contra affair and concluded that the actions had been illegally undertaken at the direction of Colonel Oliver North and members of the CIA.

Preparing for the Exam
Terrorism is random acts of violence that promote a political cause. Terrorist acts raised global concern during the 1980s.

- Why do you think terrorists bombed an American marine barracks in Lebanon in 1983?
- What effect did this bombing have on Reagan's policy in Lebanon?

Election of 1984

Republican Ronald Reagan 98% of electoral vote

Democrat Walter Mondale 2% of electoral vote

Key Themes and Concepts

Presidential Decisions and Actions
President Reagan supported the policy of New Federalism that had been begun by President Nixon. New Federalism turned over government control of some social programs to the states. As part of New Federalism, Reagan also supported tax cuts for businesses, a balanced federal budget, and increased spending for national defense.

- Why do you think President Reagan supported New Federalism?

Key Themes and Concepts

Presidential Decisions and Actions
Later in 2007, George W. Bush (43) commuted Libby's sentence of 30 months in jail, stating that the sentence was too harsh. Libby avoided any jail time.

• Why might this have happened?

In March 2007, Lewis "Scooter" Libby, former Chief of Staff to Vice President Cheney was convicted of lying and obstruction of justice. He was the highest ranking White House official convicted in a government scandal since the Iran-Contra affair during the Reagan administration.

Renewal of Détente In 1985, Mikhail Gorbachev became the new charismatic leader of the Soviet Union. Gorbachev criticized Reagan's policy of "Star Wars" and called for a renewal of détente.

Gorbachev helped further relations by announcing his new policies of *glasnost* and *perestroika*. Glasnost called for greater openness, including increased political freedom in the Soviet Union and Eastern Europe. Perestroika allowed a measure of free enterprise to improve economic conditions within the Soviet Union.

Arms Reductions In 1987, the United States and Soviet Union reached an agreement to eliminate short-range and medium-range land-based missiles.

The End of the Cold War

Causes		Results
• Anticommunist movements gained force in Eastern Europe. • Soviet leader Mikhail Gorbachev encouraged Eastern European leaders to adopt more open policies.		• Reform leaders came to power after free elections in Poland and Czechoslovakia. • New governments took charge in Bulgaria, Hungary, Romania, and Albania. • Berlin Wall fell, East and West Germany were reunified. • Soviet Union broke apart.

Preparing for the Exam

• How did Soviet leader Mikhail Gorbachev work to improve relations with the United States?

Troubles Elsewhere Troubles over other foreign policy issues were not so easily resolved. These included the following.

• *Continuing Terrorism* Terrorists continued to claim some American lives. In 1985, for example, Palestinian terrorists killed an American passenger aboard an Italian cruise ship, the *Achille Lauro*. In 1988, a bomb destroyed a Pan Am jet over Scotland.

• *Battling the Drug Trade* First Lady Nancy Reagan launched an antidrug campaign with the slogan, "Just say no!"

• *Ending Apartheid* Many people demanded that Americans divest, or get rid of, investments in South Africa to protest that nation's policy of apartheid, or strict racial segregation and discrimination. In 1986, Congress overrode Reagan's veto and imposed strict economic sanctions against South Africa until it ended apartheid.

Key Themes and Concepts

Economic Systems
• How did Americans protest South Africa's policy of apartheid?

Approaching and Beginning the 21st Century

Section Overview

In 1988 George H.W. Bush (41), a conservative Republican from Texas defeated the Democratic candidate, Michael Dukakis for the presidency. After serving one term, President Bush was defeated by Arkansas Governor Bill Clinton. President Clinton served from 1993 until President Bush's son George W. Bush (43) was inaugurated in 2001 after he defeated President Clinton's Vice President Al Gore in the race for the White House.

Key Themes and Concepts

Conflict What domestic and international conflicts caused problems for the United States during this time?

Culture How did values of other cultures clash with values of the United States?

Power In what ways did the United States government use its power at home and abroad?

The George H. W. Bush (41) Administration

Domestic Events

Economic Troubles During the election campaign, Bush had promised voters no new taxes. However, as the budget deficit mounted, President Bush was forced to break this promise in 1990. By 1992, an economic recession caused increased layoffs and rising unemployment.

Savings and Loan Scandal In 1990, the misuse of funds by savings and loan institutions surfaced. American taxpayers paid hundreds of billions of dollars to bail out the savings and loan industry.

Supreme Court Appointments President Bush appointed two new justices to the Supreme Court: David Souter in 1990 and Clarence Thomas in 1991. Thomas was confirmed by the Senate after controversial hearings in which he was charged with sexual harassment by Anita Hill, a former employee.

Events Abroad

End of the Cold War In November 1989, the world watched in amazement as Germans tore down the Berlin Wall—a symbolic reminder of the division between the communist and democratic worlds. Throughout the winter of 1990, Communist governments in Eastern Europe crumbled. In 1990, Gorbachev received the Nobel Peace Prize for relaxing control over former Soviet satellites. In October of that year, East and West Germany were formally reunited. A failed coup by hard-line Communist leaders in 1991 led to the dissolution of the Soviet Union and the 1992 formation of a Commonwealth of Independent States.

Invasion of Panama As President, Bush continued Reagan's war on drugs. He ordered United States troops into Panama to capture General Manuel Noriega, the dictator of Panama, and return him to the United States to face drug charges. In 1992, Noriega was sentenced to serve 40 years in federal prison.

The Big Idea

During the time approaching and beginning the 21st century:

- President George H.W. Bush (41) served during the end of the Cold War.

- President Clinton promoted many ambitious domestic programs during the 1990s.

- President Clinton became the second president to experience an impeachment trial.

- President George W. Bush (43) led the nation in the War on Terrorism following the attacks of September 11, 2001.

- Barack Obama, the first African American president, was inaugurated on January 20, 2009.

Key Themes and Concepts

Foreign Policy
The end of the Cold War eventually led to the growth of NATO with the additions of Eastern European countries such as Poland and Hungary.

Persian Gulf War In August 1990, Iraqi leader Saddam Hussein invaded the oil-rich nation of Kuwait. President Bush responded by sending United States troops into Saudi Arabia, with the agreement of Saudi leaders. The United Nations condemned Iraq's actions and approved economic sanctions against Iraq. The UN also authorized a joint military buildup in Saudi Arabia, called Operation Desert Shield. The United States involvement reflected its longterm commitment to protecting oil resources.

Operation Desert Shield became **Operation Desert Storm** in January 1991 when the United States with a troop force of over 500,000 (the largest American military commitment since Vietnam) and Allied troops from a number of other nations began a total air assault on Iraq. By the end of February, Bush ordered a cease-fire, and Iraq accepted all UN demands to end the Persian Gulf War. More than 300 Allied lives were lost. The Iraqi death toll was estimated at 100,000.

Bosnia and the Balkans The end of the Bush administration was marked by the outbreak of violence in the Balkans. In 1991, Slovenia and Croatia declared their independence from Yugoslavia, and fighting broke out throughout the area. Millions became refugees during the fighting. Bosnian Serbs, led by Slobodan Milosevic, carried out ethnic cleansing, or genocidal warfare, killing thousands of innocent civilians.

The 1992 Election

In the 1992 presidential election, George Bush ran as the Republican candidate with Dan Quayle as his running mate. The Democrats selected Arkansas governor Bill Clinton as their candidate, with Al Gore as his running mate. Texas billionaire Ross Perot, an independent challenger, also entered the race. Perot ran as a candidate from what he called the Independent Party. In 1996 he ran again as a candidate of the Reform Party. These political parties are known as "Third Parties" because the United States has traditionally had a two-party system. The ideas of third party candidates are often incorporated into the platforms of the major parties, although sometimes that doesn't happen until later elections. Third party candidates are often blamed for taking votes from the two major party candidates. This was especially true in the election of 2000. The major issues of the campaign concerned the state of the American economy. In the election, Clinton made Bosnia an issue and promised to take strong action there.

Clinton carried 32 states with a total of 370 electoral votes. Although Perot did not earn any electoral votes, he received over 19 million popular votes. Women, African Americans, and Latino Americans were elected to Congress in record high numbers in 1992.

The Bill Clinton Administration

Domestic Issues

Health-Care Reform In 1993, President Clinton presented to Congress a health-care reform plan that would ensure health insurance for all Americans. Critics of the plan complained it was too expensive, complex, and would limit choice in health care. In 1994, Congress rejected Clinton's plan. Since the 1990s, the primary issue concerning health care in the United States has been the increasing cost of medical insurance. In the twenty-first century, growing numbers of Americans have been unable to afford health care insurance.

Social Security It became clear that the Social Security program, begun during the Great Depression, would run into trouble because of changing demographics. The number of recipients is increasing rapidly due to longer life spans and the

Election of 1992

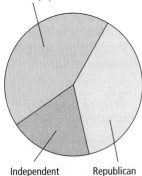

Democrat Bill Clinton
43% of popular vote

Independent Ross Perot 19% of popular vote

Republican George Bush 38% of popular vote

Preparing for the Exam

• Was Bill Clinton's victory in the 1992 presidential election decisive? Why or why not?

aging baby boomer generation. Several plans to fund Social Security have been considered, but no plan has been agreed upon.

Supreme Court Appointees With his nominations of Ruth Bader Ginsburg and Stephen Breyer, President Clinton became the first Democratic president in 26 years to name a Supreme Court justice.

The 1994 Congressional Elections In 1994, Republicans took majority control of Congress for the first time in 40 years.

The 1996 and 1998 Elections At the end of 1995, disagreements between Republicans and President Clinton over the budget led to a shutdown of the federal government. During the 1996 presidential campaign, Clinton focused public attention on the Republicans' role in the shutdown. He also adopted several Republican issues by signing welfare reform into law and supporting a balanced budget. Clinton easily won reelection. Republicans maintained their congressional majority after both elections, but Democrats gained five House seats in 1998.

Scandal and Impeachment Some of President Clinton's activities were the subject of investigations, including the Whitewater affair, which accused him and his wife Hillary Rodham Clinton of involvement with an illegal real estate scheme in Arkansas. The Clintons were never formally charged.

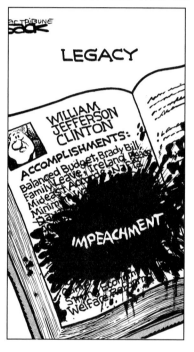

In 1998, a special prosecutor accused President Clinton of several offenses, including lying under oath about his relationship with a White House intern. On December 19, 1998, the House impeached President Clinton on charges of perjury and obstruction of justice. The Senate acquitted President Clinton two months later. This was similar to President Andrew Johnson's impeachment trial in 1868. Both presidents went through the impeachment process and both won acquittals in the Senate. There was a major difference between the impact of the impeachment on each president. President Andrew Johnson lost power in Washington, whereas President Clinton has remained an extremely popular political figure.

Economic Prosperity In the 1990s, the United States enjoyed the longest period of economic growth in its history.

Foreign Issues

The Middle East and Africa The Arab-Israeli conflict has long focused attention on the Middle East. Since 1948, Arabs and Israelis have waged four wars. In 1993, the Palestine Liberation Organization and Israel agreed to a measure of Palestinian self-government. However, incidents of violence slowed the peace process. President Clinton continued to try to achieve peace in the Middle East by hosting the Camp David Summit for Israeli and Palestinian leaders. It did not produce lasting peaceful results. U.S. troops were also sent to Somalia to try to resolve war caused food shortages.

The Former Yugoslavia Tensions between ethnic groups in the former Yugoslavia led to war in Bosnia in the early 1990s. The United States helped win

Key Themes and Concepts

Government
How did the 1994 Congressional elections shift the balance of power in Congress?

Analyzing Documents

Interpret Data
Stimulus-Based Question

Examine the cartoon, then answer the questions.

- What does the black spot stand for?

- What is the meaning of the title of the cartoon?

- What is the opinion that this cartoon is trying to convey?

- Why is this event an example of Checks and Balances?

Key Themes and Concepts

Presidential Decisions and Actions
In the early 1990s, war erupted in the Balkans as the former Yugoslavia fell into a bitter civil war.

- How did President Clinton handle tensions between ethnic groups in the former Yugoslavia in the 1990s?

- What gave President Clinton the authority to take this action?

Key Themes and Concepts

Economic Systems
By the 1990s, the economies of many nations had become more interdependent.

- Name two organizations or agreements designed to improve trade among member nations.

- To which of these does the United States belong?

an agreement between the two sides in 1995. In 1998, violence erupted in Kosovo, where Serbian forces massacred ethnic Albanian civilians. A brief bombing campaign by NATO forced the Serbs to withdraw. Many Serbian leaders then were arrested for war crimes and tried.

Latin America In 1994, President Clinton ordered U.S. troops to lead a multinational force in Haiti to restore a legitimate government after years of dictatorships and unrest. During the rest of the decade, millions of dollars in aid was pledged to Haiti by many countries but little has been sent due to the continuing lack of a stable government in that area.

Global Economy In 1992, the United States, Canada, and Mexico signed the **North American Free Trade Agreement (NAFTA)** in an effort to break down trade barriers among the three nations. American trade in Europe continued to be strong, despite the formation of the **European Union,** a trade organization designed to break down trade barriers within Europe. The **General Agreement on Trade and Tariffs (GATT)** was formed in 1945 to encourage international trade. In 1995 the World Trade Organization was formed from GATT and included other nations as well. These organizations are an example of globalization or global interdependence.

Historic Appointment In late 1996 at the beginning of his second term in office, President Clinton nominated Madeleine K. Albright to be Secretary of State. After being unanimously confirmed by the U.S. Senate, she was sworn in as the 64th Secretary of State in January 1997. Secretary Albright was the first female secretary of state. Since then two women have held that position, Condoleezza Rice in the Bush (43) administration and Hillary Rodham Clinton in the Obama administration.

The 2000 Election

In the 2000 presidential election, Texas Governor George W. Bush ran as the Republican candidate against the Democrat, Vice President Al Gore. In one of the closest presidential races in history, Florida emerged as the key state because its electoral votes could decide the winner. The Florida vote was so close that a recount of ballots was ordered by law. The election ended when the Supreme Court ruled to discontinue the recounts. Although Gore won the popular vote, Bush won the electoral vote. The election marked the first time the Supreme Court intervened in a presidential election.

The presidential election of 2000 was also the first election since the Hayes/Tilden election of 1876 where the winner of the popular vote—Tilden in 1876 and Gore in 2000—did not win the electoral vote.

This election also popularized the term **Swing State,** which is a term used for a state in which the voters are almost evenly divided between major parties. Candidates and political experts acknowledge that either major party candidate could win the popular vote and therefore that state's electoral votes. Swing states such as Florida, Ohio, and Michigan were also crucial to the elections of 2004 and 2008.

The George W. Bush (43) Administration

Domestic Issues

Taxes and the Economy President Bush attempted a tax cut and rebates to taxpayers earlier in his administration and in 2008 taxpayers received rebate checks of $300 to $1200. Since 2007, the economy has shown signs of a possible recession, especially in the housing market as thousands of homeowners struggled to meet mortgage payments and others faced bank foreclosures. In 2007, Congress

Election of 2000

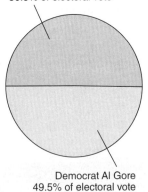

Republican George W. Bush 50.5% of electoral vote

Democrat Al Gore 49.5% of electoral vote

approved an increase in the minimum wage from $5.15 to $5.85 with an increase to $7.25 by 2009. The Federal Reserve Board has lowered its interest rate several times, including a drop of .75 percent, the largest in the history of the Federal Reserve Board. By early spring 2009, the Federal Reserve interest rate was actually at a record breaking 0 percent. All of these actions were an effort to reverse the threat of a recession. By late 2008, the recession was being described as the worst economic downturn since the Great Depression of the 1930s.

Educational Reform On January 8, 2002, President Bush signed into law a major educational reform bill called No Child Left Behind. The plan called for increased student and teacher accountability and targeted funds for improving schools. Critics said that it did not accomplish what it needed to do to improve American education.

Mass Acts of Violence In 2007, following several years of mass acts of violence in schools and on college campuses, the most deadly shooting rampage in United States history took place, with 33 students, including the killer, dead at Virginia Tech in Blacksburg, Virginia. Later in 2007, a sniper in an Omaha, Nebraska shopping mall killed eight, while in February 2008, another gunman killed five students as well as himself at Northern Illinois University. Each incident of this type of violence renewed the debate among Americans about gun control.

Immigration Issues The Bush administration had to deal with several issues relating to immigration, some of which became more serious after the attacks of September 11, 2001. The Real ID Act of 2005 strengthened security requirements at U.S. borders and gave the Director of Homeland Security additional powers. Several proposals were introduced in both houses of Congress to increase border patrols and protection, restrict illegal immigration, and strengthen anti-terrorism laws. There was also extensive discussion over funding bills to construct a wall along the U.S. border between Mexico and the United States. This produced mixed reactions on both sides of the border.

It is estimated that illegal immigrants in the United States today number more than ten million. Immigration was a discussion topic among the 2008 presidential candidates.

Social Security President Bush wanted to make Social Security reform a primary agenda item. The president's plan to allow younger workers to choose private accounts for a portion of their Social Security contributions drew praise as well as criticism. The president also tried to reform the Medicare program. A major concern with these programs is that the number of Americans eligible for them is growing. There is an increasing senior citizen population due to the aging of the, "baby boom" generation. At the same time there are fewer workers contributing to the system, due to declining American birth rates of the 1970's and 1980's. Some suggest a solution would be to raise the age of eligibility.

Election 2004 In November 2004, George W. Bush, the Republican incumbent won a close race against challenger, Massachusetts Senator and Vietnam War veteran, John Kerry. The popular vote was Bush, 62,040,606 (51%) to Kerry's 59,028,109 (48%). The state of Ohio ultimately gave the president the needed Electoral votes to win, 286 to 251.

Vice President Dick Cheney continued for a second term. Dr. Condoleezza Rice, former National Security Advisor, became the first African American woman to hold the position of Secretary of State. Within the first few months of being appointed Secretary of State, Rice made trips to Europe, the Middle East, and parts of Asia.

Key Themes and Concepts

Economics
The term "outsourcing" has been used in the last decade to describe the strategy of American businesses sending work to foreign countries to save money in production costs. This benefits the foreign countries but hurts workers in the United States and causes a rise in American unemployment.

• Can you suggest something that the U.S. government might do to discourage "outsourcing"?

Election of 2004

Republican George W. Bush
53% of electoral vote

Democrat John Kerry
47% of electoral vote

On September 11, 2001 the United States suffered the worst attack on American soil in U.S. history. Al Qaeda, a terrorist organization led by Osama bin Laden, caused the deaths of almost 3,000 people, primarily U.S. citizens. Two passenger planes were hijacked and flown into the high rise buildings known as the World Trade Center in New York City. At the same time, another plane flew into the Pentagon in Washington, D.C. A fourth plane was unable to attack its intended target as heroic passengers attempted to overtake the hijackers but crashed into farmland in Shanksville, PA, killing all aboard.

The passage of the USA Patriot Act of 2001 and the creation of the Department of Homeland Security reflect the determination of the United States government to prevent future terrorist attacks. See page 309 for additional information on this topic.

Key Themes and Concepts

Presidential Decisions and Actions
- How did President Bush's actions during the war in Iraq demonstrate his use of presidential power?

The Congressional elections of 2006 were a major upset for both President Bush and the majority Republican Party. Democrats took control of both the House of Representatives and the Senate. Nancy Pelosi, a representative from California, was elected by her party to be the first female Speaker of the House of Representatives. This made Speaker Pelosi the highest ranking woman in the history of the United States government. According to the Constitution, the Speaker of the House is second only to the Vice President in succession to the Presidency.

Foreign Issues

September 11, 2001 and Resulting Events President Bush focused largely on foreign policy after the September 11, 2001, attacks on the World Trade Center in New York City and the Pentagon in Washington, D.C. The president called the attacks "acts of war" and committed the country to a campaign against terrorists. American forces attacked military sites and terrorists training camps in Afghanistan. A major goal of this campaign was to aid in the overthrow of the Taliban rule and to find and bring to justice the al Qaeda leader, Osama bin Laden. Bush urged Americans not to "expect one battle but a lengthy campaign unlike any other we have ever seen."

The Middle East Problems between the Israelis and Palestinians continued with repeated incidents of suicide bombers and cross border attacks by both sides. Attempts were made by the United States to develop compromise solutions but episodes of violence delayed peace keeping efforts.

In November 2004, Yasir Arafat, the leader of the Palestine Liberation Organization and recipient of the Nobel Peace Prize, died at 75 after an almost 50-year struggle to gain a permanent homeland for the Palestinian people. In November 2007, President Bush hosted a Middle East Peace Conference in Annapolis, Maryland, which brought together Israeli Prime Minister Ehud Olmert and Palestinian President Mahmound Abbas, as well as representatives from 49 other countries. The leaders agreed to work on details of a peace treaty. The area continues to be troubled with violence and disagreeing factions.

War in Iraq In late 2002 and early 2003, the Bush administration warned Saddam Hussein to eliminate Iraq's weapons of mass destruction (WMD). Hussein claimed not to have any WMD. The United Nations sent an inspection team, which reported little success finding these weapons. The United States worked to gain United Nations support for an invasion of Iraq. Failing to gain this support, a small number of countries led by the United States and Great Britain attacked Iraq in March 2003. This action strained foreign relations with France, Germany and Russia. This campaign is known as **Operation Iraqi Freedom.** More than 200,000 American troops were sent to the area. For the first time, the United States military allowed reporters to be "embedded" with the troops. By the end of the War in 2011 over 170 journalists had been killed. Bush prematurely declared an official end to the war on May 1, 2003 using the words "Mission Accomplished."

In July 2003, both sons of Saddam Hussein were killed in a shootout with U.S. forces in Mosul, Iraq. Hussein escaped capture until December 2003. An Iraqi Governing Council was established during 2003 with the goal of making Iraq an independent, democratic nation. American casualties continued to rise as the military met resistance. President Bush defended the war on the grounds that a brutal dictator who had terrorist links and was hiding WMD was removed. Given the rising loss of human lives and financial costs to the United States, and the failure to find WMD, critics questioned the Bush administration's activites in Iraq and its long term plan for the country.

During 2004, President Bush and Secretary of Defense Donald Rumsfeld faced serious questions about the treatment of Iraqi prisoners after reports disclosed abuse by American troops. Some soldiers were found guilty and sentenced to prison terms. In January 2005, with American and Coalition Forces' support, the new Iraqi government held its first democratic elections under extremely tight security. Insurgents who opposed the new government and the American presence in Iraq continued violent attacks on both military and civilians in Baghdad and elsewhere. In 2006, President Bush replaced the Secretary of Defense Rumsfeld with Robert Gates, who agreed to continue in that position in President Obama's administration. Early in 2007, the Bush administration was forced to answer questions about the poor treatment of many returning wounded soldiers. At the end of 2007, several Army leaders were dismissed from their jobs as a result of the conditions at Walter Reed Medical Center in Washington.

Although the new Iraqi government made some progress at establishing democracy, the two most powerful Islamic sects, the Shiites and the Sunnis, continued to have difficulties working together. The trial of Saddam Hussein concluded with his being found guilty of multiple murders. He was hanged on December 30, 2006. By 2007, the violent actions of the insurgents moved Iraq into a civil war. Daily violence and loss of life increased as American and coalition troops tried to maintain order. With these events, President Bush's popularity ratings with the American public declined to the lowest levels of his presidency. There was growing antiwar pressure from mainstream Americans as the number of Americans dead and wounded continued to grow. Early in 2007, Great Britain, America's strongest ally in the Iraqi war, began to withdraw its troops from Iraq.

Despite the attempts of Congress to limit the increase of troops in Iraq, President Bush announced a new strategy called a "Surge" in which American troop strength increased to over 160,000. This plan was an effort to control the number of suicide bombers, car bombs, and roadside attacks by Iraqi insurgents that had caused thousands of Iraqi deaths. The Surge did meet with some success, but American war deaths in 2007 increased to their highest level since 2003. The estimates of the cost of the war in Iraq vary widely, but the cost is currently believed to be more than $800 billion. Over 5,000 American servicemen and women have been killed in Iraq and thousands more have been seriously wounded.

Afghanistan Following the Soviet occupation of Afghanistan from 1979 until the end of the 1980s, millions of Afghans fled their country and Afghan fighters fought a resistance movement to force the Soviets to leave. In the 1990s, a reactionary, extremist Islamic fundamentalist group known as the **Taliban** took over the Afghan government and imposed strict, conservative laws on the population. Women were forced to wear traditional coverings and to remain primarily in their homes. In 2001, NATO forces led by the United States forced the Taliban from power. Many of the surviving Taliban fled across the border into Pakistan where they continued to launch attacks across the border. In 2006, President Bush visited the area under very heavy security to emphasize the desire of the United States to cooperate with that part of Asia. In 2007, Vice President Cheney visited Afghanistan, and suicide bombers attempted to attack the secured compound where the vice president was staying. Osama bin Laden, the head of the terrorist group al Qaeda, responsible for the September 11, 2001 attacks, was killed by United States special forces on May 1, 2011. Continued American involvement in Afghanistan is considered crucial to American goals and interests in that part of Asia. By the spring of 2016 over 2300 U.S. service members have

Key Themes and Concepts

Justice
Hussein's trial demonstrated the principle that leaders can be held accountable for crimes against humanity.

Key Themes and Concepts

Power
With the 2011 death of bin Laden and some other al Qaeda leaders, the terrorist organization has lost some of its power. The anti-democratic Taliban exists as an extremist Islamic force in Afghanistan and Pakistan. The United States military in the area continues to try to destroy the influence of both organizations. A stable democratic government without the opportunity for terrorism in both countries is a goal of U.S. foreign policy.

• Identify other places in the world, at other times in history, where the United States has tried to support stable democratic governments.

Preparing for the Exam

Remember that current topics like Afghanistan and the Taliban, who continue to be a threat to western ideas in that country, are valid topics for both multiple choice and essay questions.

- Why do western nations like the United States continue to oppose the goals of the Taliban?

died as a result of the war in Afghanistan. As in the case of the war in Iraq, estimates of total cost vary widely. In 2013 the cost of the war in Afghanistan is estimated by some sources to be over $690 billion in total spending.

North Korea In 2007, relations improved between the United States and North Korea. For the first time in five years, U.S. representatives visited North Korea. North Korea agreed to dismantle its nuclear production facilities and to allow international inspectors to visit the country. This was in exchange for a multi-million dollar aid package. The Bush administration also agreed to begin the process of removing North Korea from its list of nations sponsoring terrorism.

Iran American foreign policy toward Iran continued to be a difficult problem. Iranian President Mahmoud Ahmadinejad spoke in New York City at Columbia University in September 2007 as well as at the United Nations. The ability of Iran to produce nuclear weapons is of primary concern to the United States. President Bush repeatedly took a hard line position against this possibility.

Pakistan During the years after 9/11, Pakistani President Pervez Musharraf generally supported the United States in its efforts in the war on terror. In the fall of 2007, former Pakistani leader Benazir Bhutto returned to Pakistan after eight years of exile. This return was followed by political upheaval and the death of Bhutto at a campaign rally. In 2008 when elections were held, Musharraf's party lost and a new coalition government was formed. It will be crucial to American efforts in this area that favorable diplomatic relations continue with the new government.

Africa Early in 2008, President Bush and the First Lady made a visit to several African nations. Throughout the Bush presidency, aid to Africa was a major goal, with funds being directed to the widespread problem of AIDS there. The civil war in Kenya caused thousands of deaths, and the situation of starvation and mass murders in Darfur has drawn world wide attention.

Cuba The relationship between the United States and Cuba, the island nation ninety miles from southern Florida, has been troubled since 1959, when Fidel Castro became the Communist leader. On February 19, 2008, Castro announced that he would step down from the Cuban presidency and that he would be succeeded by his brother Raul.

Kosovo Since the Clinton administration, the United States has been part of a United Nations peace keeping force in Kosovo, a province of Serbia in the Balkan peninsula. On February 17, 2008, Kosovo declared its independence from Serbia. The following day, the United States, along with several other Western nations, formally recognized the new nation. Russia, in a move suggestive of the Cold War days, sided with Serbia and stated that Kosovo's declaration was a violation of international law.

The 2008 Election

Early in 2007, several candidates entered the race for the presidency. Some of these candidacies were particularly historic because they represented "firsts" in American history. New York Senator Hillary Clinton was both the first former First Lady and the first female from a major political party (Democratic) to run for President. Illinois Senator Barack Obama, also a Democrat, was the first African American to be considered a serious presidential candidate from a major party. Obama won in Iowa and Clinton won in New Hampshire for the Democrats, setting the stage for weeks of continuing debates and campaign travel for both.

Key Themes and Concepts

Foreign Policy
- How would the United States and Cuba each benefit from an improved relationship?

- In December 2014 President Obama announced that the United States and Cuban President Raul Castro would begin the process of restoring formal diplomatic relations between the two countries. This will eventually include increased trade and travel opportunities for Americans and Cubans.

- In the spring of 2016 President Obama visited Cuba and met with President Raul Castro. It was the first time an American President had visited Cuba since the 1920's.

Arizona Senator John McCain, the Republican front runner, took a strong lead over his opponents. In February 2008, Ralph Nader announced that he would run again for president as a third party candidate. In the 2000 election, when Nader ran as a third party candidate, he was blamed for taking votes from the Democratic candidate.

Throughout the spring of 2008, Hillary Clinton and Barack Obama, each won primaries. The candidates attracted different groups of voters, and each continued to build large numbers of delegate votes. As the primary season continued, Senator Clinton gradually fell behind both in convention delegates and in campaign money raised. Many sources, ranging from party officials to politicians to the media, urged her to leave the race. Senator Obama stated that Clinton had worked hard and should stay in the race as long as she wanted to do so. Senator Clinton refused to quit, stayed on the primary ballot, and continued to win states until the very last day of the primaries, June 3, 2008. That evening, Obama clinched the Democratic nomination. Both candidates congratulated each other on their success at bringing so many new voters into the political process. Their candidacies drew thousands of new voters representing several groups, such as younger voters, African Americans, and Hispanics. The increase in eligible Democratic voters concerned the Republican party leadership as they tried to retain control of the White House despite declining popular support for President George W. Bush (43).

Barack Obama became the Democratic candidate for president and he selected Senator Joseph Biden of Delaware as his vice presidential running mate. Senator McCain surprised many people with his choice of Sarah Palin, Governor of Alaska, to be his vice-presidential running mate. While Democratic candidate Biden brought many years of experience in the Senate, including time as Chairman of the Senate Foreign Relations committee, Palin brought executive experience as a state governor to the Republican ticket.

The election results were clear by the evening of Election Day on November 4, 2008. John McCain conceded the election to Barack Obama. The Obama ticket received over 67,000,000 votes to McCain's 58,000,000-plus votes. Ralph Nader took in around 700,000 votes and did not have enough voters to earn one electoral vote. Obama earned 365 electoral votes compared to McCain's 173. The results of the races for the Senate and the House of Representatives also favored the Democrats, and for the first time in a number of years, Democrats controlled both the legislative and executives branches of government.

The Barack Obama Administration

When President Barack Obama, First Lady Michelle Obama, and their two young daughters moved into the White House following his inauguration on January 20, 2009, they made American history. They were the first African American family to serve in this role.

Domestic Issues

The Economy President Obama took office as the United States faced its most serious economic crisis since the Great Depression of the 1930s. The President came into office knowing that an enormous economic stimulus plan would be necessary to solve this crisis. Some major banks had failed and other companies, primarily the massive AIG Insurance company, needed billions of dollars of American taxpayer money, known as "bail out" money to prevent them from collapsing. About $700 billion in what is known as TARP money, or the Troubled

Turning Point

- For what reasons could the election of 2008 be considered a turning point in United States political history?

Election of 2008

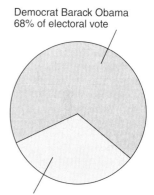

Democrat Barack Obama 68% of electoral vote

Republican John McCain 32% of electoral vote

President Barack Obama

Asset Relief Program, was used to help banks that were in danger of failing. The unemployment rate in some parts of the United States was at its highest rate in almost 25 years, between eight and ten percent. Ben Bernanke, the Chairman of the Federal Reserve Board, was called to Capitol Hill several times to explain the policies that the Fed was implementing to remedy the crisis. There has been general support for the President's efforts to keep the three major American automotive companies, General Motors, Ford, and Chrysler, economically afloat. The difference with the money being lent to the auto industry is that it is being paid back to the taxpayers through the government. Other major billion dollar spending plans have received more criticism. A major sticking point with the bailout funds has been the discovery by the White House, Congress, and the public that millions of dollars of taxpayer money went to pay bonuses for executives at failing companies. It is believed that other financial incentives may be required to restore the economic foundations of the United States.

The Economy and Civil Rights The first act that President Obama signed into law was the Lilly Ledbetter Fair Pay Act of 2009 (January 29, 2009). This law was the result of an original suit filed by Lilly Ledbetter, a Production Supervisor at a Goodyear Tire factory, over pay discrimination in 1998. After years of disputes in the courts, the Supreme Court ruled in 2007 in a 5 to 4 decision that too much time had passed between the discrimination and the filing of the suit. An attempt at an Act to correct the situation in the future was defeated by a Republican majority in 2007. After President Obama's election in 2008, Congress quickly passed a new 2009 version of the Fair Pay Act named for Ms. Ledbetter and ending the issues of timing for filing a pay discrimination suit.

Health Care In March 2010 President Obama made history by signing the Health Care Reform Bill. Health care reform had been a major goal of the President and the Democratic Party. The bill passed with a narrow margin over fierce Republican opposition. The law will be phased in over several years and has provisions to forbid insurance companies to deny health care coverage to applicants, to extend coverage to young adults until they are 26 if living at home and to eventually require all Americans to obtain health care insurance. By February of 2016 Republicans have tried over 60 times to repeal the law, also known as the Affordable Care Law, but so far have been unsuccessful.

2010 Congressional Elections President Obama, a Democrat, had the good fortune to be working with a Democratic majority in both the Senate and the House of Representatives during his first two years in office. In November 2010 a Republican majority retook control of the House with Representative John Boehner of Ohio being chosen as the new Speaker of the House. Nancy Pelosi, the former Speaker, became the Minority Leader. The Senate lost some seats to Republicans but retained a Democratic majority. These Republican gains were seen as a protest against various Obama policies such as conduct of the wars in Iraq and Afghanistan, the failure to significantly reduce the deficit, consistently high unemployment, the Health Care Reform Bill and the failure to adopt immigration reform. A factor in some of the Congressional elections has been the development of a third party known as The Tea Party. The Tea Party's name is a reference to the Boston Tea Party protest by colonists against British taxation before the American Revolution. Today the word "Tea" according to some also stands for "taxed enough already". A major plank in the Tea Party platform is the reduction of taxes at all levels. The base of the Tea Party comes from the most conservative members of the Republican Party. More moderate members of the Republican Party expressed concerns about the 2012 Presidential election and the negative or divisive impact of the Tea Party.

Other Domestic Issues:

- President Obama visited schools nationwide to stress his interest in educational reform. Millions of dollars of the government stimulus plan were marked for use by the states to improve education.

- Another domestic need that will receive stimulus dollars is the repair of the American infrastructure. High-speed rail lines may be an improvement for New York State, while some states have refused funds to construct high speed rail lines considered unnecessary given the size of the U.S. deficit.

- During the spring of 2013 a bipartisan Senate committee made significant progress on the possible passage of new immigration legislation. If passed, this legislation will deal with the increasing numbers of illegal aliens living in the United States as well as the large number of children of these immigrants.

- One major issue that the Obama administration is facing is the Social Security program. The growing number of retiring and aging "baby boomers" has caused concern that funding for Social Security and Medicare, the government medical assistance program, will be inadequate.

- In 2014 and 2015 several African Americans encountered incidents of deadly violence by police officers. These well documented and publicized events caused reactions from peaceful protests and requests for equal treatment under the law to street riots in areas as diverse as Missouri, Maryland, and New York.

The 2012 Election

As an incumbent, President Barrack Obama did not face any opposition for the Democratic presidential nomination. Mitt Romney, a former governor of Massachusetts, earned the Republican nomination and selected Congressman Paul Ryan of Wisconsin to be his running mate for Vice President. President Obama won the election and took the oath of office for his second term as President in January 2013.

Foreign Issues

President Obama made his first European trip as president in March 2009. One of his major Cabinet appointments was that of his former rival, Hillary Rodham Clinton, to be Secretary of State. This appointment received Senate support due to her extensive background and knowledge of foreign affairs. She made official visits to Japan, China, the Middle East, Europe, Southeast Asia and Latin America and is considered one of the most traveled Secretaries of State in United States history. Secretary Clinton was a vital part of the Obama administration overseas. She announced in the fall of 2012 that she would resign her position in January of 2013. Senator John Kerry, a former presidential candidate in 2004 and a Vietnam war veteran was appointed Secretary of State.

Wars in Iraq and Afghanistan President Obama announced plans to "draw down," or to withdraw, troops from Iraq. By October 2011 the U.S. troop strength in Iraq decreased to less than 39,000. The war in Iraq was declared officially over in December 2011. Simultaneously the number of American troops in Afghanistan increased to around 100,000. This was the first time that U.S. troop strength in Afghanistan exceeded that in Iraq. The war in Afghanistan has drawn increased American attention, as the once-defeated Taliban continue their battle to regain power. Through the spring of 2017, American losses have continued in Afghanistan. The United States position is that the Afghan government must be helped in its effort to maintain stability against both the Taliban and terrorist organizations such as al Qaeda and Isis.

Election of 2012

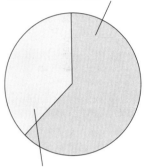

Democrat Barack Obama 62% of electoral vote

Republican Mitt Romney 38% of electoral vote

US Secretary of State John Kerry (2nd-R) and Jordanian Foreign Minister Nasser Judeh (R) listen to a briefing by Zaatari refugee camp manager Kilian Kleinschmidt (L, across from Kerry) at the refugee camp near the Jordanian city of Mafraq on July 18, 2013. Kerry visited the sprawling Zaatari camp home to tens of thousands of Syrian refugees to see at first-hand the tragedy of the conflict. Kerry first overflew the vast camp by helicopter, surveying hundreds of tents and trailers lined up on the desert sand about 20 kms (12.4 miles) from the Syrian border.

The Middle East Secretary of State Clinton returned frequently to the Middle East indicating that the Obama administration takes the issues in the area seriously. Obama and Clinton have both been clear in the American support of Israel. Early in 2013 the new Secretary of State John Kerry traveled to the Middle East, including Israel, to reaffirm the support of the United States. The spring of 2011 was termed the Arab Spring due to the political uprisings against established and often dictatorial governments in Egypt, Yemen, Bahrain, Libya, Syria, and elsewhere. As part of a NATO mission, the United States participated in attacks on Libya to assist rebels in removing long-time dictator Moammar Gadhafi. In October 2012 a terrorist attack occurred against the United States mission in Benghazi, Libya which killed the United States Ambassador and three other Americans. The surprise attack caused a series of Congressional investigations concerning the issue of how well the United States could defend itself in dangerous foreign locations. President Obama and Secretary of State Clinton have been accused of covering up information about the attack although no information has been uncovered to prove these charges. The attack has become a cause for increased partisan politics in Washington.

The Syrian civil war has drawn international attention due to the loss of thousands of lives, including thousands of civilians, women, and children. The United Nations estimates that by the end of 2015 there had been over 250,000 deaths in Syria. There are also estimated to be almost 11 million refugees who have fled the fighting. These refugees are seeking safety in nearby Middle Eastern countries, Turkey, North Africa and also European nations. President Obama has pledged the United States to accept about 10,00 refugees. As of the spring of 2016, 1300 had been accepted into the United States. The admission of Syrian refugees to the United States has become a controversial topic due to the concern of many Americans of the possibility that terrorists may use this opportunity to enter the United States. The Syrian government has been accused by some nations of using chemical warfare against its own citizens.

At the same time as the US involvement in Iraq was ending and the Syrian civil war was escalating, a new extremely violent terrorist group, ISIS was becoming active in the Middle East. ISIS is a group claiming to be the Islamic State of Iraq and Syria (also ISIL, Islamic State of Iraq and Levant, the geographic area). This terrorist group is responsible for numerous public, violent executions of Westerners as well as thousands of others who disagree with their practices. One of their tactics is to recruit new members from foreign countries using social media. This has occurred in the United States and in European countries, which in turn has enabled violent terrorist acts in Paris, France and Brussels, Belgium. In 2015 ISIS/ISIL has been called Daesh (pronounced "dash"). Daesh standards for the Arabic words, or phrase for the Islamic State of Iraq and the Levant, the eastern part of the Mediterranean area. The use of the term Daesh is seen by some Western countries, as a way to challenge the legitimacy of ISIL since the term is not seen favorably by ISIS/ISIL. The goal of ISIS is to create a hard line Islamic state that includes both Syrian and Iraqi territory.

North Korea Since 2013 North Korea's Communist leader, Kim Jong Un, has continued to increase tensions with threats of the use of nuclear power against the United States and South Korea. North Korea claimed early in 2016 to have successfully tested a hydrogen bomb. This action was condemned by the United Nations Security Council with the threat of new sanctions against North Korea.

Domestic Issues/Second Term

Continued Acts of Mass Violence In December 2012 a lone gunman attacked an elementary school in Newtown, Connecticut, causing the deaths of 20 young children and six educators. In the months following, the President and others in government have increased their efforts to limit the sale of guns, especially assault rifles. Little progress has been made as the National Rifle Association, a very powerful lobbyist group, continues to exert public pressure, claiming that their 2nd Amendment rights to gun ownership are being or will be denied.

In June 2016 over 100 people were shot, including 49 deaths, in a gay bar in Orlando, Florida. The shooter was a native born American with self-proclaimed ties to ISIS. This attack is the largest mass shooting in United States history.

Gay Rights By spring 2015, thirty-seven states legalized gay marriage, including New York State. For this reason and related issues, a bill signed into law in 1996 by President Clinton called the Defense of Marriage Act (DOMA) was brought before the Supreme Court. The Court ruled that DOMA is unconstitutional. The ruling stated that if a state provides for legal same-sex marriages, the federal government must recognize these marriages as legal too. This opens the door for equal treatment in economic, medical, legal, and social issues. In June 2015 the Supreme Court in *Obergefell* v. *Hodges* ruled that same sex marriages were legal in all fifty states.

Immigration Reform A major goal of the Obama administration has been immigration reform. Some efforts have not been successful, but there is recognition by both political parties that there must be new attempts at solutions to the number of people trying to immigrate to the United States both legally and illegally, and also the large number of illegal aliens already living in this country. The children born in the United States to illegal aliens have attracted particular attention due to their large numbers and the fact that many are graduating from colleges and universities and trying to enter the job market. A bipartisan group of Senators, known as the Gang of Eight, made some progress on this national goal, but no new legislation has been passed.

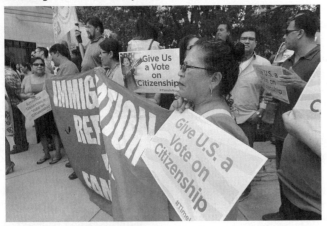

In July 2013, dozens of protesters came out 2016 for an immigration reform rally in Bakersfield, California.

During part of 2014 the United States experienced a swelling of numbers of unaccompanied minors/children from Guatemala, Honduras, El Salvador, and Mexico. This put an increased strain on relations with Mexico and the other countries and on social services and educational facilities in the southern border states in the United States. By some estimates the number was four times the number of illegal immigrants from 2012.

Scandals President Obama has dealt with damaging situations to his administration. The Internal Revenue Service (IRS) investigated a number of groups requesting tax exempt status. Certain groups appear to have been targeted based on their names or associations, for example, groups connected with the Tea Party Movement The President has denounced these activities as illegal and unacceptable. The Attorney General's office wiretapped the Associated Press. The National Security Administration (NSA) has also been criticized for spying on selected Americans. The Department of Veterans Affairs has been investigated for inadequate medical care for veterans across the country.

The Supreme Court In February 2016, Associate Justice of the Supreme Court Antonin Scalia died unexpectedly of natural causes. The topic of choosing his successor was almost immediately the cause of partisan conflict in Washington. President Obama was president until January 20, 2017 and one of his executive duties was the appointment of justices to the Supreme Court. The Senate has the constitutional responsibility to ultimately vote on the nominee. The Republican leadership in the Senate quickly announced that it would not hold hearings or meet with any nominee, nor vote on any nominee but would wait until a new President was elected. In March 2016 President Obama announced a nominee for the Supreme Court, Merrick Garland a Chief Judge in the U.S. Court of the Appeals in Washington. The Republiican majority Senate prevented Judge Garland from moving forward in the confirmation process.

2014 Congressional Elections The Republican Party regained control of both Houses of Congress. There are more Republicans serving in Congress than there have been in fifty years. Since President Obama is a Democrat, he had more difficulty trying to enact his goals for his second term.

2016 Presidential Election

By the spring of 2015 both the Democrat and Republican Parties were beginning to identify candidates for the Presidential election of 2016. One of the earliest announced Democratic candidates was Hillary Rodham Clinton, former Senator from New York State, former Secretary of State, and also former First Lady. In the 2016 Democratic primary races, Senator Bernie Sanders of Vermont was a strong challenger to Secretary Clinton. Sanders and Clinton participated in a series of debates which highlighted both their similarities (concern with immigration reform, equal pay for women, environmental issues) and their differences (Sanders' dislike of big banks and big business, Clinton's depth of foreign policy experience). Senator Sanders attracted an especially large number of young and first time voters. He said that he started a "Movement" and a revolution for changes in government. Clinton was the first female candidate for President from a major party. As the Democratic nominee Hillary Clinton chose Senator Tim Kaine of Virginia as her running mate and candidate for Vice President.

The Republican Party had seventeen potential nominees in Iowa in February 2016 with some very familiar names, like Jeb Bush (son of a President (Bush 41) and brother of one (Bush 43). During the months that followed, a number of debates occurred across the country and the field narrowed with one political newcomer gaining a majority of delegates. Donald J. Trump, a New York self-proclaimed billionaire, businessman, land developer, and reality TV show figure, surprised the Republican Party by attracting thousands of supporters across the United States. Trump became famous for his outspoken and negative opinions towards Mexicans, immigration, women, the handicapped, some veterans, and Muslims. Many long time conservative Republicans expressed concerns that Trump should not be allowed the opportunity to become the voice of the party. By mid-May 2016 with more state primaries still to be completed, Mr. Trump earned enough votes to cause the remaining contenders to suspend their campaigns. Trump clinched the nomination at the Republican Convention in Cleveland, Ohio in July. Donald Trump chose Mike Pence, the Governor of Indiana to be his Vice Presidential running mate.

After a close and hard fought campaign, Democrat Hillary Rodham Clinton won the Popular vote with 65,853,516 votes cast (48.5%). Republican Donald J. Trump won the presidency by winning the Electoral vote with 306 votes (56.9%) over Clinton's 232 votes.

The Donald J. Trump Administration

President Trump made a number of campaign pledges to voters. As of late spring 2017, his chief accomplishment has been the nomination and eventual approval of U.S. Court of Appeals Judge Neil Gorsuch to the United States Supreme Court. The Court had been functioning with only eight justices for more than a year.

Foreign Issues

Early in his administration, President Trump authorized an American air strike on a Syrian air base believed to have been used in chemical warfare against Syrian civilians. North Korea has continued to test missiles that threaten allies such as Japan and South Korea. United States naval presence in the Pacific has been increased. President Trump took his first overseas trip as President. He visited Saudi Arabia, Israel, Vatican City and Brussels, Belgium for a NATO meeting and Sicily, Italy for a G 7 meeting. (The G 7 nations are the most industrialized nations in the world and were formed as a group in 1975). In early June 2017, President Trump announced that the United States would withdraw from the Paris Agreement of 2016.

Domestic Issues

A campaign pledge of President Trump was to repeal the Affordable Care Act (known as Obamacare). By late spring the President has been unsuccessful in getting a majority of Congress to repeal and replace it.

President Trump also had a campaign promise of having Mexico pay for a large, new wall separating the two countries. Mexico has refused to pay for such a wall and its construction continues to be controversial.

Candidate Trump promised to enact a ban against Muslims entering the United States. Early in his Presidency he signed an Executive Order blocking immigration from six Muslim majority nations. Lower courts halted the travel ban, but the Supreme Court upheld the partial limitation of immigrants from six countries and agreed to hear the case in the fall session of the Court.

Election of 2016

Democrat Hillary Clinton
43% of electoral vote

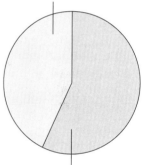

Republican Donald J. Trump
57% of electoral vote

Toward a Postindustrial Society: Living in a Global Age

Section Overview

The United States began as a nation of farmers. Today it is one of the leading economic and political powers in the world. Because of the advanced technology of the postindustrial age, the world has become what some call a "global village." Because of increased interdependence, major events in one part of the world have an impact upon the rest of the world.

Key Themes and Concepts

As you review this section, take special note of the following key themes and concepts:

Change What effects do technological change have on American society?

Places and Regions How does the United States play a unique role in helping resolve conflicts in other regions of the world?

Environment How are concerns about the environment being addressed by activist groups?

Interdependence How has the emergence of a global economy strengthened the interdependence of nations?

Key Terms

alternative energy sources
Internet

multinational corporations
Earth Day

Rapid Pace of Change

Every generation since the Civil War has experienced the effects of the Industrial Revolution. However, the pace of technological change has picked up dramatically since World War II. Today, the United States is moving into a postindustrial age. That is, the American economy no longer rests on the development of new factories and heavy industries, such as the production of steel or coal. Instead, because of technological changes, service-related industries now occupy a larger sector of the economy.

Technology—What Is It?

Technology is the application of scientific knowledge to commerce and industry. To appreciate the effect of technological change, think of the following situations out of the past.

• Abraham Lincoln, president during the Civil War, never called generals on the telephone and never listened to battle reports on the radio.

• Franklin Roosevelt, president during World War II, never had a speech transmitted by satellite to Europe and never watched a program on television.

• John F. Kennedy, president in the early 1960s, never wrote a speech on a computer and never ate a snack cooked in a microwave.

- All recent presidents have supported the American space program, but none has yet traveled into space. It is difficult even to imagine the changes that await future presidents.

The Post-World War II Era

Since the end of World War II, a number of forces have had a great impact upon the economy and upon the lifestyles of Americans.

Scarce Energy Sources Scarce oil supplies have led scientists to research **alternative energy sources,** such as solar power and wind power. There are already communities in New York State that are utilizing and benefiting from wind power. Other communities in the state as well as nationally are giving serious study to the possibility of developing this natural resource. Recently horizontal hydraulic fracturing/hydrofracking (fracking), drilling with millions of gallons of pressurized water for natural gas, has become very controversial in New York State. Nuclear power is being used in some parts of the world. However, the hazards associated with nuclear energy, such as the storage of nuclear waste, are also controversial.

Use of New Materials Inventions, such as synthetic plastic, since World War II have replaced wood and steel in many jobs. In some cases, these new materials are lighter and more durable than traditional materials.

Computer Usage The prevalent use of computers in American homes and businesses since the 1980s has revolutionized record keeping and the storage of information. Advocates of computers praise their ability to process and store large volumes of information. Critics charge that computers have increased the chances for the invasion of privacy as people access private records without permission, particularly as **Internet** use becomes increasingly widespread. The introduction of automation and computers is considered a cause of job losses in manufacturing industries. Social media such as Facebook® now connects millions of people globally. The speed at which videos, such as those posted to YouTube®, can be shared with countless numbers of worldwide viewers has introduced the new phrase "going viral" into the language of pop culture.

Security Concerns The global increase in acts of terrorism, especially the attacks on the Pentagon and the World Trade towers, made some Americans fear that they were not safe. In response, the government took a number of measures. Airport security was tightened, as was security at bridges, tunnels, nuclear power plants, courthouses, and other vulnerable places. **The Patriot Act** of 2001 gave sweeping new powers to government agencies, which in some cases limited the privacy of American citizens. In a controversial act the Senate allowed most portions of the Patriot Act to expire in June 2015. To coordinate federal government efforts, the **Homeland Security Act** created a new Cabinet-level department, **Homeland Security.** Its job was to coordinate the efforts of more than 40 federal agencies fighting terror. These agencies include the CIA, FBI, and the National Guard. In 2002, President Bush and Congress created the independent, bipartisan National Commission on Terrorist Attacks on the United States. After extensive hearings by the Commission, a detailed report was released in the summer of 2004. One of its major recommendations was to unify the United States Intelligence community under the leadership of a new National Intelligence Director.

Growth of Multinational Corporations Since the 1800s, the organization of American businesses has changed from single ownership and partnerships to corporations. In the post-World War II period, many corporations have become multinational corporations, or businesses with bases of operation in many nations.

Key Themes and Concepts

Change
The United States faced a rapid pace of change during the Industrial Revolution, but that pace increased dramatically after World War II.

- How did the American economy change after World War II?

Key Themes and Concepts

Science and Technology
Bill Gates, as founder of Microsoft, became one of the world's richest individuals. Huge fortunes have been made and lost in the computer industry in the last fifteen years. Bill and his wife Melinda administer the charitable Gates Foundation that has given millions of dollars in aid for education and medical research, among other causes.

Technology
Information Technology is a term that describes the wider use of computers and telecommunications equipment that can save, send, and utilize data. The term also can describe a college major or be a job description.

- Identify three factors that might limit a person's use of technology.

Change
Changes in technology frequently have an impact on the availability of certain jobs. For example, early telephones did not have a dial or push buttons to make a phone call. Instead, a caller placed a call through an operator, who made the phone connections at a switchboard. Once technology improved and direct dialing became available, the need for operators decreased.

- In the 1990s and early 2000s, what impact did technological improvements have on agricultural job opportunities?

Preparing for the Exam

How have Americans' lifestyles been influenced by each of the following since the end of World War II?

- average family size
- longer life spans
- expansion of public education

Analyzing Documents

Stimulus Based Question
Use the chart at right to answer the following questions.

- Between 1994 and 2050, which group of Americans is expected to grow most rapidly?
- Which group of Americans is expected to be a smaller proportion of the U.S. population?
- Which group is expected to remain the same proportion of the overall population?

In the United States during the twentieth century and since the beginning of the twenty-first century, federal prosecutions of corporations such as Standard Oil, AT&T, and Microsoft were based on alleged violations of antitrust laws. There has also been reduced competition in the airline industry, which has ultimately hurt the consumer.

Job Opportunities The greatest increases in jobs in the early 2000s promise to be in the service fields. The largest declines will occur in agricultural employment. Technological advances have made it possible for fewer farmers to produce more food, which will continue to reduce the need for agricultural labor.

New Lifestyles and Longer Life Spans American attitudes toward family size and divorce have changed since the 1950s. Average family size has declined. After years of expansion, many school districts throughout the nation, including New York, experienced declining school enrollments in the 1980s. Divorce rates first rose and then remained constant. This created the largest number of single-parent households in the nation's history. At the same time, health-care improvements resulting from new technologies, such as laser surgery and organ transplants, have increased average life spans. This has increased the number of older Americans, who in recent years have organized to protect their rights and improve their lives. Social scientists use the term "the graying of America" to describe the aging of the nation's population.

Expansion of Public Education Access to free public education has helped many Americans improve their standard of living. As individuals complete higher levels of education, they have the chance to secure better-paying jobs and more desirable housing. Thus, education helps further social mobility.

Increasingly Diverse Population If current trends continue, it is projected that the population of the United States will grow increasingly diverse over the next half century. More of the newest immigrants to the United States come from Asian and Latin American countries, compared with earlier waves of immigration that came from Europe.

The Changing Ethnic Composition of the United States

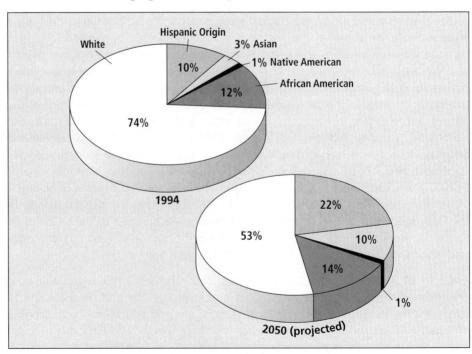

Source: *Statistical Abstract of the United States*

Dealing With the AIDS Crisis Since the 1980s, medical researchers have gathered more information about preventing AIDS, or Acquired Immune Deficiency Syndrome. Even so, AIDS has spread through some sectors of the American population at an alarming rate. Without a known cure, scientists and public health officials have tried to increase public awareness and prevention of the disease.

Helping the Homeless Not everyone enjoyed the prosperity of the post-World War II years. President Johnson's Great Society programs in the 1960s tried to reduce poverty in the United States. However, cuts in social programs and high unemployment have caused a significant rise in the number of Americans living below the poverty line. Local communities and private charitable organizations have tried to provide relief, but homelessness remains a serious concern.

Gun Control The issue of gun control continues to be hotly debated. Urban violence, as well as a number of highly publicized school shootings, have caused millions of Americans to reconsider attitudes toward and the availability of guns in this nation. In January 2011 Arizona Congressional Representative Gabby Giffords was severely wounded but survived an assassination attempt at a public gathering of her constituents. Six people in attendance died from gunshots fired by the assassin. Early in 2012 Representative Giffords resigned her seat in Congress to continue to work on her recovery.

The National Rifle Association continues to be one of the strongest lobbying groups in the United States and remains committed to the rights of gun owners. This topic will continue to be a controversial one for years to come. Random gun violence in workplaces, shopping malls, universities, and even health care facilities continues to be a serious problem.

Right to Life Issues The United States continues to be a very divided society on the topics of abortion and the right to life/the right to die. In March 2005, President Bush and Congress took unprecedented actions by involving themselves in the case of Terri Schiavo. Schiavo was a terminally ill Florida woman whose right to die had been debated in the Florida courts for many years. Ultimately the decisions of the Florida courts were upheld. This allowed her husband to authorize the removal of a feeding tube which led to her death after a fourteen-year period in which she had been medically determined to be in a persistent vegetative state.

The United States and Contemporary World Problems

International Terrorism

Although the attack on New York and Washington, D.C., on September 11, 2001, was aimed at one nation, it mobilized government leaders all over the world. The attacks showed how terrorism has expanded its global reach and has affected the security and stability of all nations.

As the war in Iraq fueled anti-Western attitudes in 2004, terrorists caused almost 200 deaths in a railroad bombing in Spain. Other areas of the world heightened their efforts at limiting the ability of terrorist groups to share information, money, weapons, and personnel. The terrorist group ISIS is described on page 306.

Population Growth

Although most developed nations have experienced a decline in their birthrates, the developing nations have an overpopulation problem. Millions of people suffer from malnutrition, living only a marginal existence. Foreign aid from the United States has become of vital economic importance in combating world hunger.

Preparing for the Exam

Every ten years since 1790, the United States has conducted a census to count all citizens. In 2010 over 134 million forms were sent at the cost of over $14,000,000.

- Given the topics on this page and elsewhere in this Unit, what kinds of decisions might the government make based on the statistics it learns from the census?

The 2010 census indicated that New York State has lost population again since the last census. New York lost two Congressional seats and is being redistricted. Will this change impact representation in the Senate?

Preparing for the Exam

Be sure to review the Landmark Supreme Court Cases *Roe v. Wade* (1973) and *Planned Parenthood of Southeastern Pennsylvania v. Casey* (1992) on page A-12 with regard to abortion rights and also *Cruzan v. Director, Missouri Department of Health* (1990) with regard to end-of-life decisions.

Key Themes and Concepts

Interdependence
The concept of a global community means that the United States can not isolate itself from problems in other countries. Population growth in developing nations and environmental concerns in nations with essential ecosystems are two issues that affect the entire world.

- Why should the destruction of tropical rain forests be a concern to people in other nations, including the United States?

Reading Strategy

Organizing Information
List three ways that environmental activists have raised public awareness about environmental issues.

1.

2.

3.

Environmental Concerns

Because of increased interdependence, an environmental problem in one nation frequently raises global concerns. One example is the destruction of the Brazilian tropical rain forests.

Environmental Activists Many groups have organized to reduce and clean up pollution on the land, in the water, and in the air. Other activist groups work to save endangered species of animals.

Recycling efforts have been organized to reuse paper, glass, plastic, and aluminum. Community organizers have opposed plans to convert vacant lands into dumpsites. Communities have studied the effects of industrial pollution on the groundwater that people drink. In response to public pressure, the federal government has enacted laws requiring automobile manufacturers to put antipollution devices on their cars. Since the first **Earth Day** celebration in 1970, the American people, along with the rest of the world, have begun to realize their obligation to protect the environment for future generations. In 2007, former Vice President Al Gore won a Nobel Peace Prize for his efforts to increase public understanding of issues related to global warming. This followed his widely viewed documentary film, "An Inconvenient Truth." The phrase "going green" has come to mean the conscious efforts of Americans to conserve energy in all aspects of daily life. Presidents Clinton, Bush (43), and Obama have all directed efforts within the White House itself to increase energy efficiency. Efforts that extend from the First Family to all American families include activities such as recycling, installation of energy efficient light bulbs, the use of solar power where possible, appropriate conservation of heating and cooling sources, and other individual initiatives.

Natural Disasters In December 2004, a tsunami, or a giant destructive wave, caused more than 200,000 deaths and left as many as 5,000,000 homeless in parts of Southeast Asia, the Indian subcontinent and East Africa. It was the worst natural disaster in modern history, and the international community joined together in a massive outpouring of financial aid. President Bush committed the United States to $350 million in aid and millions more were donated by Americans directly to private relief agencies. The president also requested his father, former President George H.W. Bush, and former President Bill Clinton to work together to draw attention to the extent of disaster damage in the stricken areas.

In 2005, one of the worst hurricane seasons in United States history occurred. Hurricane Katrina caused major flooding in New Orleans, Louisiana, and along the Gulf Coast states of Mississippi and Alabama. About 2,000 people died, thousands of homes were destroyed, and thousands of people were evacuated. Millions of dollars in property damage occurred throughout the area. Businesses, schools, hospitals, hotels, and stores were forced to close. Media coverage of the hurricane exposed the misery in the area, especially the poverty of large numbers of African Americans. The Bush administration had to defend the slow and inadequate response of the Federal government led by FEMA, the Federal Emergency Management Agency. In November 2007, Congress passed the $23 billion Water Resource Bill, with $3.5 billion specifically earmarked for areas destroyed by Hurricane Katrina. This bill was the first bill passed by Congress after a veto by President Bush (43). In 2007, other natural disasters included tornadoes, snow and ice storms, and high winds that caused over 100 deaths.

Wildfires were so extensive in California that at one point over one half million residents were evacuated.

Flooded neighborhoods in the aftermath of Hurricane Katrina

In February 2010 Haiti and Chile both experienced major earthquakes. The United States sent aid in both cases. It was especially involved with the disaster in Haiti where there was estimated to be 220,000 deaths and over 1.2 million displaced persons.

In April 2010 a fire and explosion at a British Petroleum (BP) oil rig in the Gulf of Mexico off the coast of Louisiana cost eleven workers their lives and began the worst oil spill disaster in United States history. The spill ultimately impacted the coastline and wildlife of Louisiana, Mississippi, Alabama, and part of Florida. It took months before technicians were able to cap the pipeline that continued to leak oil in massive quantities into the Gulf. Environmental damage to wetlands, beaches, and wildlife was catastrophic. BP set up a claims fund for those impacted but large numbers of American citizens and businesses remained without sufficient funds to return to life as they knew it prior to the disaster.

In March 2011 Japan experienced a major earthquake that was immediately followed by a massive tsunami that caused thousands of deaths and the total destruction of some cities and towns in coastal areas. These events were the direct cause of radiation leaks at nuclear power plants in the impacted areas. These events attracted both worldwide humanitarian aid, including from the U.S. Navy, as well as concern over the possibilities of a potential nuclear disaster of grave proportions. International nuclear experts offered assistance to the overwhelmed Japanese. Two years later debris from the tsunami was still washing ashore in the Pacific Northwest.

The largest hurricane since Katrina occurred in the fall of 2012. Superstorm Sandy caused the deaths of 285 people in seven countries from the Caribbean to Canada and damages were estimated at over $50 billion dollars. At the worst of the storm there were an estimated 7,500,000 people without power. Particularly hard hit were the New Jersey and New York shorelines where thousands of homes were damaged and many just washed into the ocean. Congress was criticized for taking weeks to provide federal assistance.

Key Themes and Concepts

Environment
The winter of 2011–2012 brought record breaking warmth, very early and then very late snowfalls and a very early, severe tornado season. The tornado season of 2013 also began with a level 5 tornado (the highest level that is currently recognized) in Moore, Oklahoma killing 24 people including 9 children. Millions of dollars of damage occurred in just minutes while schools, houses, and businesses were leveled to the ground. January through May 2014 was the coldest year in the United States since records have been kept.

The winter of 2014–15 was colder and snowier in the Northeast than previous recent winters, but the following winters have been milder than normal.

• How do these fluctuations in weather cause problems?

International Efforts on the Environment
In November 2016, about 150 countries agreed to the Paris Agreement of the United Nations Convention on Climate Change. These nations recognized the need to strengthen the global response to the threat of climate change by making efforts to limit global temperature rise. The goal is to limit and decrease greenhouse gas emissions.

Questions for Regents Practice

Multiple Choice

Directions: Review the Test-Taking Strategies section of this book. Then answer the following questions, drawn from actual Regents examinations. For each statement or question, choose the *number* of the word or expression that, of those given, best completes the statement or answers the question.

1 The quotations below are from two United States Supreme Court decisions.

I. "Separation of the races does not place a badge of inferiority upon one group over another, thus it is not a violation of the 14th amendment." (1896)

II. "To separate [children in grade school and high school] from others of similar age and qualifications solely because of their race generates a feeling of inferiority as to their status . . . that may affect their hearts and minds in a way unlikely ever to be undone." (1954)

The difference in opinion between these two rulings best shows

(1) a change in judicial philosophy and public attitudes

(2) the persistent efforts of the major political parties to increase equal opportunity

(3) a recognition that democracy depends on economic equality for all citizens

(4) the refusal of the Supreme Court to deal with controversial issues

2 The successful launching of *Sputnik* by the Soviet Union in 1957 signaled the beginning of

(1) American fears that the Soviets had achieved technological superiority

(2) the Cold War with the United States

(3) Soviet aggression in Afghanistan and China

(4) disarmament discussions between the superpowers

3 Which development contributed most to the expansion of suburbs since the 1950s?

(1) construction of interstate highways

(2) invention of the computer

(3) completion of transcontinental railroads

(4) development of jet aircraft

4 When President Dwight D. Eisenhower sent federal troops to Little Rock, Arkansas, during the 1957 school integration crisis, he was exercising his constitutional power as

(1) chief legislator

(2) commander in chief

(3) chief diplomat

(4) head of state

5 Which is a valid conclusion based on United States involvement in the Korean War?

(1) The policy of containment was applied in Asia as well as in Europe.

(2) United Nations economic sanctions are more effective than military action.

(3) The American people will support United States participation in any war, whether declared or undeclared.

(4) United States cooperation with a wartime ally ends when the war ends.

6 What was the significance of the use of federal marshals to protect African American students in Little Rock, Arkansas, in 1957?

(1) It was the first time martial law had been declared in the United States.

(2) It led to federal takeover of many southern public schools.

(3) It strengthened control of education by state governments.

(4) It showed that the federal government would enforce court decisions on integration.

7 "We conclude that in the field of public education the doctrine of 'separate but equal' has no place. Separate educational facilities are inherently unequal."

This quotation expresses the Supreme Court decision in the case of

(1) *Plessy* v. *Ferguson*

(2) *Engel* v. *Vitale*

(3) *Tinker* v. *Des Moines Independent Community School District*

(4) *Brown* v. *Board of Education of Topeka, Kansas*

8 The Supreme Court under Chief Justice Earl Warren had a major impact on the United States in that this Court

(1) became involved in foreign affairs by reviewing the constitutionality of treaties

(2) weakened the judiciary by refusing to deal with controversial issues

(3) supported the idea that states could nullify acts of Congress

(4) followed a policy of judicial activism, leading to broad changes in American society

9 Segregation in public schools was declared unconstitutional because it violated the

(1) reserved powers provision

(2) due process of law provision

(3) principle of equal protection under the law

(4) principle of a clear and present danger

10 One similarity between the laws being challenged in the United States Supreme Court cases of *Plessy* v. *Ferguson* (1896) and *Korematsu* v. *United States* (1944) is that

(1) specific groups of people were being targeted based on race or ethnicity

(2) state laws were declared unconstitutional

(3) immigrants were relocated to prison camps

(4) federal laws segregating public transportation were upheld

11 Which list of wars that involved the United States is in the correct chronological order?

(1) Vietnam War → War on Terrorism → Korean War → World War II

(2) Korean War → World War II → Vietnam War → War on Terrorism

(3) World War II → Vietnam War → War on Terrorism → Korean War

(4) World War II → Korean War → Vietnam War → War on Terrorism

12 The women's movement was strengthened in the 1960s chiefly because

(1) women became increasingly dissatisfied with their status and their roles in society

(2) women were angered by the failure of the voters to elect them to Congress

(3) job discrimination against women and minorities was eliminated

(4) the radical liberation movements of the 1950s had failed

13 "And so my fellow Americans—ask not what your country can do for you—ask what you can do for your country."

When President John F. Kennedy made this statement, he was encouraging the American people to develop

(1) a personal commitment to work for national ideals

(2) an awareness of environmental hazards

(3) a concern for national defense

(4) an appreciation for the contributions of immigrants to American society

14 Which statement about the Cuban missile crisis (1962) is most accurate?

(1) The crisis showed that the United States and the Soviet Union could agree on total disarmament.

(2) The crisis brought the two major world powers very close to war.

(3) The United States wanted to establish missile sites in Cuban territory.

(4) The Communist government in Cuba was overthrown.

15 President Lyndon B. Johnson's Great Society was an effort to solve the problem of

(1) poverty

(2) drug trafficking

(3) overpopulation

(4) illegal immigration

16 One similarity between the actions of Presidents Franklin D. Roosevelt and Lyndon B. Johnson is that both

(1) led the United States to victory in war

(2) expanded the role of government in citizens' lives

(3) vetoed legislation on the issue of rights for minorities

(4) achieved a balanced federal budget during their terms in office

17 "Four Students Killed at Kent State University"

"Gulf of Tonkin Resolution Passed"

"Radical Protesters Disrupt Democratic Convention in Chicago"

These headlines relate to which event in United States history?

(1) Civil War

(2) World War II

(3) Vietnam War

(4) Persian Gulf War

18 During the Vietnam War, serious questions were raised in the United States concerning the

(1) authority of the Supreme Court in regard to national security

(2) extent of the President's powers as commander in chief

(3) loyalty of United States military leaders

(4) role of the North Atlantic Treaty Organization (NATO) in international peacekeeping

19 A major long-term effect of the Vietnam War has been

(1) an end to Communist governments in Asia

(2) a change in United States foreign policy from containment to imperialism

(3) a reluctance to commit United States troops for extended military action abroad

(4) a continued boycott of trade with Asia

20 The outcome of the Watergate scandal reinforced the principle that

(1) national security takes precedence over freedom of the press

(2) the power of executive privilege is greater than the rule of law

(3) the law applies equally to all citizens, including government officials

(4) impeached government officials are immune from criminal prosecution

21 The Camp David accords promoted by President Jimmy Carter were significant because they represented

(1) the first peace agreement between Israel and an Arab nation

(2) the establishment of a worldwide human rights policy

(3) a lasting arms-reduction treaty

(4) the end of the Vietnam War

22 The "trickle down" economic theory of President Herbert Hoover and the "supply side" economic policies under President Ronald Reagan were based on the idea that

(1) balanced budgets are essential to economic success

(2) the federal government needs to assume more responsibility for solving economic problems

(3) economic growth depends on making increased amounts of capital available to businesses

(4) economic stability is the responsibility of federal monetary agencies

23 The North American Free Trade Agreement (NAFTA) between the United States, Mexico, and Canada is meant to

(1) increase commerce and eliminate tariffs

(2) encourage lower labor costs

(3) raise environmental standards

(4) allow citizens to move freely from one nation to another

24 **"Clinton Offers Economic Aid to Russia"**

"U.S. Sends Peacekeeping Troops to Bosnia"

"U.S. Airlifts Food and Medicine to Somalia"

These headlines illustrate that United States foreign policy during the 1990s stressed

(1) containment

(2) collective security

(3) global involvement

(4) neutrality

25 How does the present-day United States economy differ from the nation's economy in 1900?

(1) Immigrants are no longer a source of labor.

(2) Today's government plays a less active role in the economy.

(3) The United States is less dependent on oil imports.

(4) The growth of service industries is greater today.

Thematic Essay Question

Directions: Write a well-organized essay that includes an introduction, several paragraphs addressing the task below, and a conclusion.

Theme: **Technological Change**

> Many aspects of United States society have been greatly affected by technological changes.

Task:

> Identify *three* aspects of United States society that have been affected by technological change since the beginning of the twentieth century, and for *each*
>
> - Explain how that aspect was affected by a specific technological change
> - Discuss the extent to which the impact of the change was positive or negative

You may use any example from your study of the United States in the twentieth century. Some suggestions you might wish to consider include: environment, politics, agriculture, urbanization, individual rights, or cultural pluralism.

You are not limited to these suggestions.

Guidelines:

In your essay, be sure to
- Develop all aspects of the task
- Support the theme with relevant facts, examples, and details
- Use a logical and clear plan of organization, including an introduction and a conclusion that are beyond a simple restatement of the theme

In developing your answer, be sure to keep these general definitions in mind:

(a) <u>explain</u> means "to make plain or clear; render understandable or intelligible"
(b) <u>discuss</u> means "to make observations about something using facts, reasoning, and argument; to present in some detail"

Document-Based Question

In developing your answers, be sure to keep this general definition in mind:

> <u>discuss</u> means "to make observations about something using facts, reasoning, and argument; to present in some detail"

This question is based on the accompanying documents. The question is designed to test your ability to work with historical documents. Some of these documents have been edited for the purposes of this question. As you analyze the documents, take into account the source of each document and any point of view that may be presented in the document.

Historical Context:

> The Preamble to the United States Constitution reads: "We the people of the United States, in order to form a more perfect union, establish justice, insure domestic tranquility, provide for the common defense, promote the general welfare, and secure the blessings of liberty to ourselves and our posterity, do ordain and establish this Constitution for the United States.

Task: Using the information from the documents and your knowledge of United States history and government, answer the questions that follow each document in Part A. Your answers to the questions will help you write the Part B essay, in which you will be asked to

> • Discuss whether the American government, since 1950, has achieved the goals for our nation established in the Preamble to the United States Constitution.

Document-Based Question

Document #1

Selected Events in African American Civil Rights History (1950s–1960s)

	1954 Supreme Court rules in *Brown* v. *Board of Education of Topeka, Kansas*	1960 Sit-ins by African Americans begin at "whites only" lunch counters	1964 Riots by African Americans occur over discrimination in housing, education, and employment	1965 President Lyndon B. Johnson signs the Voting Rights Act of 1965

1950	1952	1954	1956	1958	1960	1962	1964	1966	1968

	1955–56 The actions of Rosa Parks inspire the Montgomery, Alabama bus boycott, resulting in a Supreme Court ruling	1963 Dr. Martin Luther King Jr. delivers his "I have a dream" speech	1968 Dr. Martin Luther King Jr. is assassinated

1. What do the events in the time line suggest about the process of achieving "the blessings of liberty" for African Americans during the 1950s and 1960s?

_____

_____

_____

_____

Document #2

> "One thing became clear: that in the black movement I had been fighting for someone else's oppression, and now there was a way that I could fight for my own freedom, and I was going to be much stronger than I ever was."
> —**Cathy Cade, women's rights activist**

2. What experience motivated Cathy Cade to work for the delivery of the "blessings of liberty" to women?

_____

_____

_____

_____

Document #3

Selected Great Society Legislation, 1964–1966

Legislation	Purpose
Economic Opportunity Act, 1964	Created to combat causes of poverty, such as illiteracy and unemployment
Volunteers in Service to America (VISTA), 1964	Sent volunteers to help people in poor communities and set up community action programs to give the poor a voice in defining local housing, health, and education policies
Medicare, 1965	Provided hospital and low-cost medical insurance for most Americans aged 65 and older
Medicaid, 1965	Provided low-cost health insurance for low-income Americans of any age who could not afford private health insurance
Elementary and Secondary Education Act of 1965	Provided education aid to states based on the number of children from low-income households
Department of Housing and Urban Development (HUD), 1965	Established to oversee the nation's housing needs and to develop and rehabilitate urban communities. HUD also provided money for rent subsidies and low-income housing.
Water Quality Act, 1965 Clean Water Restoration Act, 1965	Established water and air quality standards and provided funding for environmental research
National Traffic and Motor Vehicle Safety Act, 1966	Established safety standards for all vehicles to protect consumers.

3. How did Lyndon Johnson's Great Society "promote the general welfare"?

_____

_____

_____

_____

Document-Based Question

Document #4

4. What opinion does this cartoon express about how the American government should "provide for the common defense"?

_____

_____

_____

_____

Document #5

> *"Nixon acts as if the kids had it coming. But shooting into a crowd of students, that is violence. They say it could happen again if the [National] Guard is threatened. They consider stones threat enough to kill children. I think the violence comes from the government."*
>
> **—Mother of Jeffrey Glenn Miller,**
> **a student killed at Kent State University, quoted in *Life* magazine, May 15, 1970**

5. What opinion did this speaker have about the actions of the National Guard at Kent State University?

_____

_____

_____

_____

6. Who did this speaker blame for the events at Kent State?

_____

_____

_____

_____

Document #6

> *"He told me they didn't fire those shots to scare the students off. He told me they fired those shots because they knew the students were coming after them, coming for their guns. People are calling my husband a murderer; my husband is not a murderer. He was afraid."*
>
> **—Wife of a member of the National Guard, quoted in *Newsweek* magazine, May 18, 1970**

7. What opinion did this speaker have about the actions of the National Guard at Kent State University?

_____

_____

_____

Document-Based Question

Part B
Essay

Directions: Write a well-organized essay that includes an introduction, several paragraphs, and a conclusion. Use evidence from *at least four* of the documents in your essay. Support your response with relevant facts, examples, and details. Include additional outside information.

Historical Context:

The Preamble to the United States Constitution reads: "We the people of the United States, in order to form a more perfect union, establish justice, insure domestic tranquility, provide for the common defense, promote the general welfare, and secure the blessings of liberty to ourselves and our posterity, do ordain and establish this Constitution for the United States."

Task: Using the information from the documents and your knowledge of United States history and government, write an essay in which you

> • Discuss whether the American government, since 1950, has achieved the goals established for our nation in the Preamble to the United States Constitution

Guidelines:

In your essay, be sure to
- Develop all aspects of the task
- Incorporate information from *at least four* of the documents
- Incorporate relevant outside information
- Support the theme with relevant facts, examples, and details
- Use a logical and clear plan of organization, including an introduction and a conclusion that are beyond a restatement of the theme

Presidents of the United States

George Washington **(1732–1799)** *Years in office: 1789–1797* *Federalist* *Vice President: John Adams*	• Commanded the Continental army during the American Revolution • President of the Constitutional Convention • Set precedents that were followed by other presidents, such as forming a cabinet • Strengthened new government through support of Hamilton's financial policies and use of force against the Whiskey Rebellion • Kept peace through Proclamation of Neutrality and Jay Treaty • Set basis of U.S. foreign policy in his Farewell Address
John Adams **(1735–1826)** *Years in office: 1797–1801* *Federalist* *Vice President: Thomas Jefferson*	• American Revolution leader who protested Stamp Act • Helped draft Declaration of Independence • President during times of war in Europe • Alien and Sedition Acts contributed to his unpopularity and the fall of his party
Thomas Jefferson **(1743–1826)** *Years in office: 1801–1809* *Democratic-Republican* *Vice President: Aaron Burr,* *George Clinton*	• Major author of the Declaration of Independence • Opposed Federalists • Favored limited, decentralized government • Opposed Hamilton's financial plan and Alien and Sedition Acts • Negotiated the Louisiana Purchase from France, which doubled the size of the nation
James Madison **(1751–1836)** *Years in office: 1809–1817* *Democratic-Republican* *Vice President: George Clinton,* *Elbridge Gerry*	• Called the "Father of the Constitution" • One author of the Virginia Plan; his journals provide a record of events at the Constitutional Convention • Wrote 29 of *The Federalist Papers* • Proposed the Bill of Rights to Congress • Gained popularity after the War of 1812
James Monroe **(1758–1831)** *Years in office: 1817–1825* *Democratic-Republican* *Vice President: Daniel Tompkins*	• Established U.S. foreign policy in the Western Hemisphere with the Monroe Doctrine • Settled boundaries with Canada (1818) • Acquired Florida (1819) • President during this "Era of Good Feelings" • Supported and signed Missouri Compromise (1820)
John Quincy Adams **(1767–1848)** *Years in office: 1825–1829* *Democratic-Republican* *Vice President: John Calhoun*	• Became president after election was decided in the House of Representatives • Secretary of State under James Monroe • After leaving office as president, served in House of Representatives; only president to do so

Andrew Jackson **(1767–1845)** *Years in office: 1829–1837* *Democrat* *Vice President: John Calhoun,* *Martin Van Buren*	• Hero of Battle of New Orleans (War of 1812) • Opposed Calhoun and nullification of 1828 and 1832 tariffs • Vetoed rechartering of Second National Bank • Supported Indian Removal Act • Associated with Jacksonian Democracy—the start of mass politics and nominating conventions • Used "spoils system" to give jobs to supporters
Martin Van Buren **(1782–1862)** *Years in office: 1837–1841* *Democrat* *Vice President: Richard Johnson*	• First New Yorker to become president • Served as vice president to Jackson • Opposed Texas annexation because slavery issue divided his party • Presidency weakened by economic crisis of the Panic of 1837 • Had major role in creating the Democratic Party from the Democratic-Republicans and the nation's second party system—the Democrats versus the Whigs
William Henry Harrison **(1774–1841)** *Years in office: 1841* *Whig* *Vice President: John Tyler*	• While governor of Indiana Territory, led military actions against Native Americans in the Battle of Tippecanoe (1811) • Elected as first Whig candidate on the slogan "Tippecanoe and Tyler Too" • First president to die in office; served only one month
John Tyler **(1790–1862)** *Years in office: 1841–1845* *Whig* *Vice President: none*	• First vice president to come into presidency on death of president, called "His Accidency" • Texas annexed by congressional vote largely because of his influence • His pro South and pro states rights positions resulted in his expulsion from the Whig Party by its pro nationalism leaders
James K. Polk **(1795–1849)** *Years in office: 1845–1849* *Democrat* *Vice President: George Dallas*	• Foreign policy aimed at fulfilling goal of Manifest Destiny • With slogan "54' 40 or fight!" campaigned for all of Oregon country, settled for Oregon Treaty (1846) with Great Britain, dividing region at 49th parallel • Supported Tyler's annexation of Texas and favored acquisition of California • Led nation in Mexican War, 1846–1848 • The Treaty of Guadalupe Hidalgo gave the United States the Mexican Cession, which included California
Zachary Taylor **(1784–1850)** *Years in office: 1849–1850* *Whig* *Vice President: Millard Fillmore*	• West Point graduate and military hero of Mexican War, known as "Old Rough and Ready" • A Virginian, a slave owner, and a nationalist—he opposed secession • Died in office after 16 months as president
Millard Fillmore **(1800–1874)** *Years in office: 1850–1853* *Whig* *Vice President: none*	• New Yorker by birth, became president on death of Taylor • Negotiated passage of the Compromise of 1850 • Supported enforcement of the Fugitive Slave Law and opposed secessionists angering both Northerners and Southerners • Failure of Compromise of 1850 marked end for Whig Party • In 1856, lost as presidential candidate of the Know-Nothing Party
Franklin Pierce **(1804–1869)** *Years in office: 1853–1857* *Democrat* *Vice President: William King*	• New Englander who supported Kansas-Nebraska Act • Gadsden Purchase ratified during his presidency • Trade treaty with Japan became effective during his administration, due to the efforts of Commodore Matthew Perry

James Buchanan **(1791–1868)** *Years in office: 1857–1861* *Democrat* *Vice President: John Breckinridge*	• In office when *Dred Scott* v. *Sanford* decision was issued and John Brown's raid at Harper's Ferry occurred • Took no action in response to the secession of South Carolina and six other states, claiming he lacked the power to act
Abraham Lincoln **(1809–1865)** *Years in office: 1861–1865* *Republican* *Vice President: Hannibal Hamlin,* *Andrew Johnson*	• Became nationally known as result of Lincoln-Douglas debates in 1858 • First Republican to be elected president • Used war powers of the presidency during Civil War to achieve his goal of preserving the nation • Issued Emancipation Proclamation; gave Gettysburg Address • Assassinated before he could act on his plans for reconstruction
Andrew Johnson **(1808–1875)** *Years in office: 1865–1869* *Democrat* *Vice President: none*	• Impeached by House after bitter disagreements with Congress over Reconstruction; acquitted by a single vote in Senate • Thirteenth and Fourteenth Amendments ratified during his presidency
Ulysses S. Grant **(1822–1885)** *Years in office: 1869–1877* *Republican* *Vice President: Schuyler Colfax,* *Henry Wilson*	• Civil War military leader who served as General-in-Chief of the Union army • Transcontinental railroad completed and Fifteenth Amendment ratified during his presidency • Crédit Mobilier and the Whiskey Ring scandals marred his presidency
Rutherford B. Hayes **(1822–1893)** *Years in office: 1877–1881* *Republican* *Vice President: William Wheeler*	• Election decided through compromise, preventing a constitutional crisis after a dispute over electoral votes • Federal troops removed from the South, marking the end of Reconstruction
James A. Garfield **(1831–1881)** *Years in office: 1881* *Republican* *Vice President: Chester A. Arthur*	• Assassinated after four months in office
Chester A. Arthur **(1830–1886)** *Years in office: 1881–1885* *Republican* *Vice President: none*	• Vetoed Chinese Exclusion Act (1882) but signed another act reducing the Chinese immigration ban to ten years • Supported Pendleton Act (1883) that enacted civil service reform • Worked to reform American restrictive tariffs
Grover Cleveland **(1837–1908)** *Years in office: 1885–1889;* *1893–1897* *Democrat* *Vice President: Thomas* *Hendricks, Adlai Stevenson*	• Expanded the civil service • Only president to serve two nonconsecutive terms • Served as governor of New York • In second term confronted major depression that began with Panic of 1893 • An anti-imperialist, he opposed annexation of Hawaii • In 1894, sent federal troops to end Pullman Strike

Benjamin Harrison **(1833–1901)** *Years in office: 1889–1893* *Republican* *Vice President: Levi Morton*	• Elected president with most electoral but not popular votes • Supported Sherman Antitrust Act • Encouraged conservation of forest reserves • Favored U.S. expansion in the Pacific Ocean and building of a canal in Central America • Expanded U.S. Navy
William McKinley **(1843–1901)** *Years in office: 1897–1901* *Republican* *Vice President: Garret Hobart,* *Theodore Roosevelt*	• President during a period of expansionism marked by Spanish-American War • A high tariff and the Gold Standard Act passed during his administration • Annexed Hawaii • Open Door Policy issued by his secretary of state • Assassinated in 1901
Theodore Roosevelt **(1858–1919)** *Years in office: 1901–1909* *Republican* *Vice President: Charles Fairbanks*	• Progressive governor of New York (1899–1900) • Presidential programs called the Square Deal • Known as a trustbuster, conservationist, reformer, and nationalist • Used the power of presidency to regulate economic affairs of the nation and to expand its role in Asia and the Caribbean • Issued the Roosevelt Corollary to the Monroe Doctrine
William Howard Taft **(1857–1903)** *Years in office: 1909–1913* *Republican* *Vice President: James Sherman*	• Policy of "dollar diplomacy" gave diplomatic and military support to U.S. business investments in Latin America • Continued Progressive Era policies of business regulation, but his conservative tariff and conservation policies split the party
Woodrow Wilson **(1856–1924)** *Years in office: 1913–1921* *Democrat* *Vice President: Thomas Marshall*	• Progressive Era president whose program was known as New Freedom • Reform regulation included Clayton Antitrust Act, Federal Reserve System, Federal Trade Commission Act, and Underwood Tariff Act (which lowered rates) • Led the nation during World War I • Supported the Treaty of Versailles and League of Nations, which the Senate failed to approve
Warren G. Harding **(1865–1923)** *Years in office: 1921–1923* *Republican* *Vice President: Calvin Coolidge*	• Led nation into "Roaring Twenties" on a call for "normalcy" • Administration known for corruption and scandals, including the Teapot Dome Scandal • Opened Washington Conference on Naval Disarmament in 1921, although he opposed internationalism
Calvin Coolidge **(1872–1933)** *Years in office: 1923–1929* *Republican* *Vice President: Charles Dawes*	• Presidency marked by conservative, laissez-faire attitudes toward business, stating that "after all, the chief business of the American people is business" • Presided over "Coolidge prosperity" • Kellogg-Briand Pact signed during his administration • Immigration Act (1924), setting national quotas, passed during his presidency
Herbert Hoover **(1874–1964)** *Years in office: 1929–1933* *Republican* *Vice President: Charles Curtis*	• Used government resources against the Great Depression without success • Supported loans through Reconstruction Finance Corporation • Opposed direct relief • Used federal troops against the World War I veterans' "Bonus Army"

Franklin D. Roosevelt (1882–1945) *Years in office: 1933–1945* *Democrat* *Vice President: John Garner,* *Henry Wallace, Harry S. Truman*	• Led U.S. through Great Depression and World War II from which the nation emerged as world's leading economic, military, and political power • Increased government's role in and responsibility for economic, financial, and general welfare of nation through New Deal policies such as Social Security Act. • Expanded power of federal government with programs of Relief, Recovery, Reform, as well as by military and diplomatic conduct of the war • New Deal programs criticized as both inadequate and too extreme • Issued Japanese-American internment order; proposed "Court-packing" • Only president to serve more than two terms
Harry S. Truman (1884–1972) *Years in office: 1945–1953* *Democrat* *Vice President: Alben Barkley*	• Made decision to drop two atomic bombs on Japan in 1945 to end World War II • Began the policy of containment of communism with the Truman Doctrine • Supported economic recovery in Europe through the Marshall Plan • Continued the New Deal philosophy with his Fair Deal • Entered the Korean War during his presidency
Dwight D. Eisenhower (1890–1969) *Years in office: 1953–1961* *Republican* *Vice President: Richard M. Nixon*	• Commander of Allied forces in Europe during World War II • Issued Eisenhower Doctrine • Approved Saint Lawrence Seaway and 1956 Federal Highway Act • Sent troops to Little Rock, Arkansas, to support school desegregation • In office when Alaska and Hawaii became 49th and 50th states
John F. Kennedy (1917–1963) *Years in office: 1961–1963* *Democrat* *Vice President: Lyndon B. Johnson*	• Promoted the New Frontier program (which centered on containment), the Peace Corps, and the Alliance for Progress • Successfully resolved the Cuban missile crisis • Assassinated in 1963
Lyndon B. Johnson (1908–1973) *Years in office: 1963–1969* *Democrat* *Vice President: Hubert Humphrey*	• Promoted antipoverty programs and civil rights through his Great Society program • Used the Gulf of Tonkin Resolution to expand the Vietnam War • Division over his war policy led to his decision not to seek reelection • President during a period of active civil rights movements for African Americans and women
Richard M. Nixon (1913–1994) *Years in office: 1969–1974* *Republican* *Vice President: Spiro Agnew,* *Gerald R. Ford*	• Pursued a "Vietnamization" policy and increased bombing followed by a 1973 cease-fire in Vietnam • Relaxed relations with USSR and the People's Republic of China • Resigned as president because of Watergate affair
Gerald R. Ford (1913–2006) *Years in office: 1974–1977* *Republican* *Vice President: Nelson Rockefeller*	• Only president not to be elected by the American public; appointed as vice president under Nixon and succeeded to the presidency after Nixon's resignation • Pardoned Nixon, for which he was both criticized and praised • Worked to restore faith in government after Watergate crisis

Jimmy Carter **(1924–)** *Years in office: 1977–1981* *Democrat* *Vice President: Walter Mondale*	• Domestic problems included inflation and oil shortages • Supported international human rights and Panama Canal treaties • Opposed the Soviet invasion of Afghanistan • Facilitated the Camp David Accords, which led to peace between Egypt and Israel
Ronald Reagan **(1911–2004)** *Years in office: 1981–1989* *Republican* *Vice President: George H.W. Bush*	• Conservative viewpoint on issues such as abortion and prayer in school • Based his supply-side economic policy (or "Reaganomics") on the belief that government works against individual initiative • Presidency marked by trade and federal budget deficits • Arms control agreements signed with the USSR in 1985, 1986, and 1987 • Foreign policy aimed at keeping communism out of Latin America • Popularity damaged and foreign policy weakened by Iran-Contra scandal
George H.W. Bush **(1924–)** *Years in office: 1989–1993* *Republican* *Vice President: J. Danforth Quayle*	• Inherited budget deficit, savings and loan scandal, and legacy of Iran-Contra Affair from the Reagan administration • In office when Cold War ended, and communist governments in Eastern Europe and Soviet Union fell • Led the United States in the Persian Gulf War against Iraq
William (Bill) Clinton **(1946–)** *Years in office: 1993–2001* *Democrat* *Vice President: Albert Gore, Jr.*	• Domestic policies centered on health care and social security reform, as well as economic issues, such as reduction of the national deficit • Secured approval of NAFTA (North American Free Trade Agreement) • Backed NATO intervention against Serbia to stop "ethnic cleansing" • Impeached by the House of Representatives in 1998 on charges of perjury and obstruction of justice, but acquitted by the Senate
George W. Bush **(1946–)** *Years in office: 2001–2009* *Republican* *Vice President:* *Richard (Dick) B. Cheney*	• Took office after a close election in which a dispute over ballot recounts in Florida was decided by the Supreme Court in *Bush* v. *Gore* (2000) • Conservative domestic agenda included tax cuts, No Child Left Behind, creation of Department of Homeland Security, and attempts to privatize social security • After attacks of September 11, 2001, ordered U.S. forces into Afghanistan to defeat Taliban and al Qaeda extremists and into a war against Iraq • Left office with nation in major recession, and controversy that included Iraq War, treatment of prisoners, and balancing of liberty versus security in a democracy
Barack H. Obama **(1961–)** *Years in office: 2009–2017* *Democrat* *Vice President:* *Joseph (Joe) R. Biden, Jr.*	• First African American to be elected president; first president since Eisenhower to twice win at least 51 percent of the national popular vote • Led nation during most serious economic crisis since the Great Depression • Withdrew U.S. troops in Iraq and moved those in Afghanistan to a support mission • Legislation passed included Patient Protection and Affordable Health Care Act and American Recovery and Reinvestment Act
Donald J. Trump **(1946–)** *Years in office: 2017–* *Republican* *Vice President: Michael R. Pence*	• First person elected president without either military or government service; won electoral vote but lost popular vote

Landmark Supreme Court Cases

Every Supreme Court case deals with important **constitutional principles.**
Some cases have had such an enduring impact on United States history
and government that they require greater examination. The lasting
significance and central constitutional principles of 32 landmark
Supreme Court cases are outlined briefly in this section. For more
information about the meaning of the constitutional principles, review
Unit 2, Section 1, Part 4.

Year	Name of Case	Constitutional Principle	Why Decision is Important
1803	*Marbury* v. *Madison*	• Separation of Powers: Checks and Balances • The Judiciary	• Established the Supreme Court's right of *judicial review*—the right to determine the constitutionality of laws • Strengthened the judiciary in relation to other branches of government
1819	*McCulloch* v. *Maryland*	• Federalism: Federal Supremacy • National Power: *Necessary and Proper Clause* • the Judiciary	• Said no state could tax a federally chartered bank because *the power to tax involves the power to destroy* • Ruling established the principle of national supremacy—that the Constitution and federal laws overrule state laws when the two conflict • Expanded national power by supporting use of *necessary and proper* clause to carry out constitutional powers
1824	*Gibbons* v. *Ogden*	• Federalism: Federal Supremacy • Property Rights/ Economic Policy: Interstate Commerce • the Judiciary	• States may regulate only what is solely intrastate commerce (within a state) • Congress has power to regulate interstate commerce, including commerce that involved intrastate-interstate activity • Ruling established the basis of congressional regulation of interstate commerce
1832	*Worcester* v. *Georgia*	• Federalism • National Power • Separation of Powers • Equality • Rights of Ethnic/ Racial Groups	• The Constitution gives the federal, not state governments, exclusive jurisdiction over Native American nations • Treaties between the United States government and Native American nations are the *Supreme Law of the Land* • Therefore, Georgia laws taking jurisdiction of Cherokee people and land were void • President Andrew Jackson defied the ruling and the national policy of Indian Removal followed

Year	Name of Case	Constitutional Principle	Why Decision is Important
1857	*Dred Scott* v. *Sanford*	• the Judiciary • Equality • Civil Liberties • Rights of Ethnic/ Racial Groups	• Ruled that African Americans were not citizens (overturned by 14th Amendment) • Declared that enslaved people were property of owners • As property, protected by 5th amendment, enslaved people could be taken anywhere; therefore, Missouri Compromise was unconstitutional
1883	*Civil Rights Cases*	• Equality • National Power: Congress • Rights of Ethnic/ Racial Groups: 13th and 14th Amendments	• Declared 1875 Civil Rights Act unconstitutional • 14th Amendment prohibited states from discrimination, not individual actions in the private sector such as in theaters, hotels, and restaurants • Private discrimination was not a violation of the 13th Amendment, prohibition against slavery and *involuntary servitude*
1886	*Wabash, St. Louis & Pacific RR* v. *Illinois*	• Property Rights/ Economic Policy: Interstate Commerce • National Power • Federalism	• Invalidated state law setting railroad rates on the part of an interstate trip within state borders • By declaring it a federal power to regulate rates and by limiting state regulations, Court strengthened Constitution's interstate commerce clause • Ruling paved way for creation in 1887 of Interstate Commerce Commission
1895	*United States* v. *E.C. Knight Co.*	• National Power: Anti-Trust • the Judiciary • Federalism • Property Rights/ Economic Policy: Interstate Commerce	• While federal government did have the right to regulate some parts of economy, states, under the 10th Amendment, could regulate intrastate economic activities such as manufacturing • Refineries were *manufacturing operations*, not commerce; therefore, the Sherman Anti-Trust Act could not be applied to American Sugar Refining Co. although company controlled 90% of sugar processing in the nation
1895	*In Re Debs*	• National Power: Commerce Clause • Property Rights/ Economic Policy: Commerce Clause and Labor	• Ruled that federal government under commerce clause of Constitution had right to halt 1894 Pullman strike • Said strike hurt *general welfare* of nation by disrupting commerce and mail delivery

Year	Name of Case	Constitutional Principle	Why Decision is Important
1896	*Plessy* v. *Ferguson*	• Equality • Rights of Ethnic/Racial Groups 14th Amendment Equal Protection Clause • the Judiciary	• Upheld Louisiana law providing for *equal but separate accommodations for white and colored races* • Said law did not conflict with 13th or 14th Amendments, nor with commerce clause • 14th Amendment was not intended to enforce what Court called *social equality* • Provided legal justification for *separate but equal* segregation policy until overturned in 1954 by *Brown* v. *Board of Education*
1904	*Northern Securities Co.* v. *United States*	• National Power: Anti-Trust, Commerce Clause • Property Rights/Economic Policy	• Federal suit (part of T. Roosevelt's trust-busting) using Sherman Antitrust Act • Court ruled that the Northern Securities Company was formed only to eliminate competition and ordered it to be dissolved • Congress under commerce clause had authority to regulate any *conspiracy* to eliminate competition
1905	*Lochner* v. *New York*	• Property Rights/Economic Policy: Contracts • Civil Liberties: 14th Amendment	• Ruled that a New York law limiting bakers to 10-hour days and 60-hour weeks in order to protect public health was unconstitutional because it violated the *right and liberty of an individual to contract* • New York law went beyond *legitimate* police powers of a state
1908	*Muller* v. *Oregon*	• Civil Liberties: 14th Amendment • Federalism: 10th v. 14th Amendments • Equality • Rights of Women	• Upheld an Oregon law that limited women to a 10-hour work day in laundries or factories in order to protect women's health • Cited the physical differences between men and women when ruling that the need to protect women's health outweighed the liberty to make a contract that was upheld in *Lochner* v. *New York*
1919	*Schenck* v. *United States*	• Civil Liberties: Limited in Wartime • the Judiciary	• Established limits on free speech; right is not absolute but dependent on circumstances, i.e. person is not protected if falsely shouts fire in a crowded theatre • In this case, Court saw defendants' actions as a *clear and present danger* to security of the nation in wartime

Year	Name of Case	Constitutional Principle	Why Decision is Important
1935	*Schechter Poultry Corporation* v. *United States*	• Separation of Powers • Property Rights/ Economic Policy: Commerce Clause	• Placed limits on the ability of Congress to delegate legislative powers to president • By narrowly defining interstate commerce also restricted congressional powers to regulate commerce • Declared the New Deal's National Industrial Act unconstitutional
1944	*Korematsu* v. *United States*	• Civil Liberties: Equal Protection • Presidential Power in Wartime • Rights of Ethnic/ Racial Groups	• Upheld the power of the president in wartime to limit a group's civil liberties • Ruled that forcible relocation of Japanese Americans to Wartime Relocation Agency Camps during World War II was legal
1954	*Brown* v. *Board of Education*	• Equality: Equal Protection • Federalism • Rights of Ethnic/ Racial Groups	• In this school segregation case, Court overturned *Plessy* v. *Ferguson separate but equal* doctrine • Ruled that *separate educational facilities are inherently* (inseparably) *unequal* and violate the 14th Amendment's *equal protection* clause
1957	*Watkins* v. *United States*	• Criminal Procedures: Due Process • National Power: Congressional Investigations • Civil Liberties	• Congressional investigations must spell out their legislative purpose and jurisdiction • The Bill of Rights is applicable to congressional investigations • Watkins was within his rights to refuse to testify to matters beyond scope of House Committee on Un-American Activities
1961	*Mapp* v. *Ohio*	• Criminal Procedures: 4th Amendment • Civil Liberties: 14th Amendment	• Ruled that 4th and 14th Amendments protected citizen from illegal searches • Applied *exclusionary rule* to state courts, i.e. evidence obtained unconstitutionally—in this case without a search warrant—could not be used in federal or state courts
1962	*Baker* v. *Carr*	• Avenues of Representation: Voting Rights; Equal Protection • Federalism	• Court has jurisdiction over apportionment of seats in state legislatures • Overrepresentation of rural voters and under representation of urban voters was a violation of 14th Amendment's *equal protection* clause • Ruling led to other court cases that established *one person-one vote* concept

Year	Name of Case	Constitutional Principle	Why Decision is Important
1962	*Engel* v. *Vitale*	• Civil Liberties: Establishment Clause, 1st and 14th Amendments	• Reciting of an official prayer in the schools violated the 1st Amendment's *establishment of religion* clause, which was applied to the states by the 14th Amendment • Although students were not required to say the non-denominational prayer, its recitation in class put them under pressure
1963	*Gideon* v. *Wainwright*	• Civil Liberties • Criminal Procedures: 6th and 14th Amendments	• Ruled unanimously that the 6th Amendment right to an attorney, which was applied to the states by the 14th Amendment, required that a state provide lawyers for poor people accused of felony crimes, not just capital crimes
1964	*Heart of Atlanta Motel* v. *United States*	• National Power: Commerce Clause • Civil Liberties: Equal Protection Clause	• Upheld constitutionality of 1964 Civil Rights Act's use of Congressional interstate commerce powers to prohibit discrimination in private facilities whose operations affect interstate commerce
1966	*Miranda* v. *Arizona*	• Criminal Procedures: Due Process, Self-Incrimination • Civil Liberties: Equal Protection	• Established the requirement prior to questioning to inform those accused of crimes that they have the right to remain silent, the right to a lawyer, and that what they say can be used against them in court • Evidence obtained without this warning may not be used in court under the *exclusionary rule*
1969	*Tinker* v. *Des Moines Independent Community School District*	• Civil Liberties: 1st Amendment, Student Rights/Safe School Environment	• While recognizing the authority of schools *to prescribe and control conduct in the schools*, the court ruled that *neither students or teachers shed their constitutional rights to freedom of speech or expression at the schoolhouse gate* • Symbolic, silent expression of opinion in absence of any disorder (wearing of black armbands to protest Vietnam War) is protected under the 1st Amendment
1971	*New York Times Co.* v. *United States*	• Civil Liberties: Freedom of the Press • National Power	• Court narrowly upheld 1st Amendment right to Freedom of the Press • Ruled that government had not met the *heavy burden of prior restraint* i.e. not made a strong enough case to stop publication of *The Pentagon Papers* on the grounds that national security would be hurt

Year	Name of Case	Constitutional Principle	Why Decision is Important
1973	*Roe* v. *Wade*	• Civil Liberties: Right to Privacy • Rights of Women	• Declared state laws making abortions illegal to be unconstitutional while stating certain limits and conditions • Basis of decision was right to privacy, citing primarily the *due process* clause of 14th Amendment
1974	*United States* v. *Nixon*	• Separation of Powers: Due Process, Executive Power	• By 8-0 vote, Court ruled that Nixon had to turn over the Watergate Tapes to the Special Prosecutor. • No president was above the law; *executive privilege* (confidentiality) was not absolute • Separation of powers does not protect a president from judicial review of *executive privilege*, nor from the needs of the judicial process
1985	*New Jersey* v. *T.L.O.*	• Civil Liberties: 4th Amendment, Student Rights/ Safe School Environment	• Affirmed that 4th Amendment prohibition on *unreasonable searches and seizures* applied to school officials • But, necessity of maintaining discipline allowed for searches when there are *reasonable grounds* that the law or school rules have been broken compared to police requirement of *probable cause*
1990	*Cruzan* v. *Director Missouri Department of Health*	• Civil Liberties: Due Process	• Ruled that under *due process* clause, a competent person has the right to refuse life-sustaining treatment • Evidence of the wishes of an incompetent person must be *clear and convincing;* evidence not presented in this case • Cruzan's parents then gathered what Missouri Court agreed was *clear and convincing* evidence and the life support system was removed
1992	*Planned Parenthood of Southeastern Pennsylvania et al.* v. *Casey*	• Civil Liberties • Rights of Women	• Upheld *Roe* v. *Wade* decision • Determined that Pennsylvania law with provisions such as 24 hour waiting period and parental consent to a minor's abortion did not create *undue burden or substantial obstacles* to abortion • Struck down requirement of husband notification
1995	*Vernonia School District* v. *Acton*	• Civil Liberties: 4th Amendment, Student Rights/ Safe School Environment	• Ruled that a school's practice of testing athletes randomly for drug use did not violate their rights under 4th and 14th Amendments • Cited schools need to maintain student safety and fulfill its educational mission

Important People in United States History and Government

The following list highlights the key people other than presidents who are included in the New York State Core Curriculum for United States History and Government and therefore may be tested on the Regents Examinations. They represent the pluralism that is America.

Ansel Adams	• Photographer whose natural landscapes of the West are also a statement about the importance of the preservation of the wilderness
Samuel Adams	• American Revolutionary War leader who helped to organize the Sons of Liberty and the Massachusetts Committee of Correspondence • Signer of the Declaration of Independence
Jane Addams	• Progressive Era reformer in the social settlement house movement • Founder of Hull House, a Chicago settlement house • Cofounder of Women's International League for Peace and Freedom • Corecipient of the Nobel Peace Prize (1931) • Involved in organizing of the NAACP
Madeleine K. Albright	• Sworn in as the 64th and first female Secretary of State in January 1997, at the start of President Clinton's second term in office • Previously served as U.S. ambassador to the United Nations
Susan B. Anthony	• Women's rights leader from 1851 until her death in 1906 • Most active for women's suffrage, but also worked for women's property rights, rights of married women, temperance, and abolition
Yasir Arafat	• Palestinian leader involved in efforts to negotiate peace in the Middle East during President Clinton's administration • Led Palestinians during a number of violent clashes with Israel
Osama bin Laden	• Leader of al-Qaeda terrorist network; directed September 11, 2001, attacks against World Trade Center and Pentagon; killed in 2011
John Brown	• Extreme abolitionist who believed in use of violence to promote his cause • His antislavery group killed proslavery settlers at the Pottawatomie Creek Massacre; his raid of Harper's Ferry resulted in his trial and execution • Immortalized by Ralph Waldo Emerson in *John Brown's Body*
William Jennings Bryan	• Unsuccessful Democratic presidential candidate in 1896 and 1900 • Populist who supported farmers and free silver • Orator, religious fundamentalist (Scopes Trial), and anti-imperialist

John C. Calhoun	• Outspoken southern leader and advocate of states' rights • Favored nullification and the extension of slavery into the territories • Vice president under Presidents John Quincy Adams and Andrew Jackson; resigned over nullification issue • Secretary of state under President Tyler; successfully pressed for Texas annexation; opposed Mexican War and California statehood
Andrew Carnegie	• Industrialist and philanthropist who built Carnegie Steel Company • In an article, *The Gospel of Wealth* (1889) he defended Social Darwinism, but also stated that the rich had a duty to help the poor, and improve society in areas they deemed important
Rachel Carson	• Writer, scientist, and environmentalist whose book, *Silent Spring* (1962), identified the hazards of agricultural pesticides • Inspired the environmental movement and legislation
Fidel Castro	• Won Cuban revolution against dictator Batista; headed Cuba 1959–2008; limited civil liberties, and nationalized industries • Allied with Soviet Union in 1962 Cuban Missile Crisis • U.S. trade embargo against Cuba in place since 1962 eased in 2016
Willa Cather	• Pulitzer Prize winning writer about pioneers settling the frontier • Best known for *My Antonia* (1918) and *Death Comes to the Archbishop* (1927)
Cesar Chavez	• Latino leader of California farm workers from 1962 until his death in 1993 • Organized the United Farm Workers (UFW) to help migrant farm workers gain better pay and working conditions; used nonviolent tactics, boycotts, hunger strikes
Winston Churchill	• Prime minister of Great Britain during World War II
Hillary Rodham Clinton	• In 2000, became the first First Lady elected to U.S. Senate and first woman elected to statewide office from New York; reelected in 2006 • In 2008, ran unsuccessfully for Democratic Party presidential nomination • In 2009, became 67th Secretary of State • In 2016, first woman from a major party to run for president; lost electoral vote but won popular vote
Father Charles Coughlin	• Roman Catholic priest who used radio to attack FDR and New Deal and express pro-fascist, anti-semitic views
Eugene V. Debs	• Union organizer and Socialist presidential candidate in every election from the 1890s until World War I
Dorothea Dix	• Nineteenth-century reformer who revolutionized mental health reform
Stephen Douglas	• Illinois Senator whose Kansas-Nebraska Act included his idea of popular sovereignty, which increased sectional tensions • Lincoln-Douglas debates (1858) made Lincoln nationally known • Candidate of northern faction of Democratic party in 1860 election
Frederick Douglass	• Former slave, abolitionist, and lecturer; active in Underground Railroad • Supported Women's Suffrage, attended Seneca Falls Convention

W.E.B. Du Bois	• African American civil rights leader, historian, writer, and sociologist • Cofounder of Niagara Movement and of NAACP • Influenced Harlem Renaissance by publishing African Americans in *The Crisis* • Opposed Marcus Garvey's "back to Africa" movement and disagreed with Booker T. Washington by pressing for civil and political, not just economic, equality for African Americans
John Foster Dulles	• Secretary of state under President Dwight Eisenhower • Made famous the concept of brinkmanship, a foreign policy that brought the United States just to the brink of war
Edward K. "Duke" Ellington	• Songwriter, band leader, jazz composer, pianist, and a leading figure of the Harlem Renaissance • Famous songs include "Take the A Train" and "Mood Indigo"
Medgar Evers	• African American activist and NAACP field secretary • Murdered in Mississippi in 1963 by a sniper outside his house
F. Scott Fitzgerald	• Novelist whose works reflect climate of the "roaring twenties" • Novels include *The Great Gatsby* and *Tender Is the Night*
Henry Ford	• Industrialist who headed Ford Motor Company • His innovative production methods reduced the cost of producing cars, making it possible for the average person to own an automobile
Benjamin Franklin	• Philadelphia statesman, diplomat, scientist, and writer in revolutionary period • Drafted the 1754 Albany Plan of Union • Member of Second Continental Congress; served on committee to write the Declaration of Independence, which he signed • Helped persuade France to sign the 1778 Treaty of Alliance against England and helped negotiate the Treaty of Paris of 1783, ending American Revolution; delegate to Constitutional Convention
Betty Friedan	• Women's rights activist whose book, *The Feminine Mystique* (1963), encouraged women to find their own identity outside marriage • Helped found National Organization for Women (1966) and National Women's Political Caucus (1971)
William Lloyd Garrison	• Abolitionist editor of *The Liberator*, published 1831–1865 demanding immediate end to slavery; a leader of American Anti-Slavery Society
Marcus Garvey	• African American nationalist leader who advocated pride and self-help as a means of empowerment • Founder of the Universal Negro Improvement Association, a nationalist and separatist group that wanted a separate black economy and urged African Americans to emigrate to Africa • Ideas influenced the 1960s Black Power movement

Bill Gates	• In 1975 co-founded Microsoft with vision of "a computer on every desk and in every home;" believed "personal computers would change the world" • Philanthropist committed to improving education and public health
Samuel Gompers	• Organizer and president of American Federation of Labor, a craft union for skilled workers; stressed issues such as wages and hours
Albert A. Gore, Jr.	• Vice President of the United States (1993–2001); won popular vote but lost electoral vote in 2000 election that went to Supreme Court in *Bush* v. *Gore*. • Shared 2007 Nobel Peace Prize with U.N. Intergovernmental Panel on Climate Change. His film on global warming, *An Inconvenient Truth*, won an Academy Award.
Alexander Hamilton	• New York delegate at Constitutional Convention who worked for a strong central government • Wrote 51 of *The Federalist Papers* supporting ratifying the Constitution • First secretary of the treasury; promoted U.S. economic development
William Randolph Hearst	• Newspaper publisher whose yellow journalism style helped create public pressure for the Spanish-American War
Ernest Hemingway	• Novelist whose writings expressed conflict and concern created by changing American values; 1954 Nobel Prize for Literature winner
Patrick Henry	• Leader in the American Revolution in Virginia • Member of Continental Congress; supporter of independence • Led movement for addition of the Bill of Rights to the Constitution
Langston Hughes	• An influential poet, playwright, and novelist of the Harlem Renaissance • Works celebrated hope, pride, and cultural heritage of working class African Americans while protesting Jim Crow and segregation.
Saddam Hussein	• Long-time Iraqi dictator who invaded Kuwait causing Persian Gulf war • Removed from power in 2003 during Iraq War and hanged in 2006
Chiang Kai-shek	• Leader of the Chinese Nationalists in civil war; when defeated by Mao Zedong in 1949 left China and established a government in Taiwan
Robert Kennedy	• U.S. Attorney General (1961–1963); assassinated in 1968 while seeking Democratic presidential nomination
Martin Luther King, Jr.	• Civil rights leader who advocated civil disobedience and nonviolent demonstrations to achieve change • Founded Southern Christian Leadership Conference, led Montgomery, Alabama bus boycott, and Selma to Mongomery voting rights march • Gave "I Have a Dream" speech; won Nobel Peace Prize • Assassinated in 1968

Henry Kissinger	• Secretary of state under Presidents Nixon and Ford • Deeply involved in foreign policy in Vietnam, China, the Soviet Union, and the Middle East
Robert La Follette	• Governor of Wisconsin whose program, the "Wisconsin Idea," became the model for progressive reform • Served as United States senator and Progressive leader • Ran for President as the Progressive Party candidate in 1924
John L. Lewis	• President of United Mine Workers of America from 1920–1960; led UMWA in 1925 Anthracite Coal Strike • A founder of the Congress of Industrial Organizations (CIO), he worked to organize workers by industry leading to a split in the 1930s between American Federation of Labor and the CIO
Meriwether Lewis and William Clark	• Explorers who led the 1804–1806 expedition to survey lands included in the Louisiana Purchase; documented the land, plants, animals, and other natural resources from Missouri to Oregon
Sinclair Lewis	• Novelist whose work *Main Street* attacked middle class values • First American to win Nobel Prize for Literature (1930)
John Locke	• British Enlightenment writer whose ideas influenced the Declaration of Independence, state constitutions, and the United States Constitution • Believed that people are born free with certain natural rights, including the rights to life, liberty, and property, and must consent to be governed
Henry Cabot Lodge	• Massachusetts Republican senator whose support of American imperialism and of a powerful navy strongly influenced Theodore Roosevelt • Led successful fight against ratification of the Treaty of Versailles and entry of the United States into the League of Nations • Served as a U.S. representative to Washington Conference
Huey Long	• Populist governor of Louisiana and U.S. senator • Proposed that income and inheritance taxes on the wealthy be used to give each American a $2,500 income, a car, and a college education • Planned to challenge FDR for president, but was assassinated in 1935
Douglas MacArthur	• Led U.S. troops in the Pacific in World War II • Commander of U.S. occupation forces in Japan after World War II • Relieved of command by Truman after publicly disagreeing with him about the conduct of the Korean War
Malcolm X	• Leader of the 1960s Black Power movement; assassinated in 1965
Horace Mann	• Nineteenth century educator; helped create tax-based, nonsectarian public schools as well as better teacher-training institutions
George C. Marshall	• Army chief of staff during World War II and secretary of state under President Truman; promoted the Marshall Plan, which assisted the economic recovery of Europe after World War II

John Marshall	• Chief Justice of the United States (1801–1835) • Established prestige of the Supreme Court and strengthened power of federal government in cases such as *Marbury* v. *Madison* (1803), *McCulloch* v. *Maryland* (1819), and *Gibbons* v. *Ogden* (1824) • First stated the right of judicial review in *Marbury* v. *Madison* (1803)
Thurgood Marshall	• African American attorney who argued *Brown* v. *Board of Education* before the Supreme Court in 1954 and was appointed to that Court in 1967—the first African American to serve on the Supreme Court
Cotton Mather	• New England Puritan associated with the concept of the Puritan work ethic (meaning that hard work is its own reward) and an appreciation of thrift and industry • Supported the Salem witch trials
Joseph R. McCarthy	• Republican Senator of the late 1940s and early 1950s who led a campaign to root out suspected Communists in American life • The term *McCarthyism* came to be associated with an era of government investigation of the private lives of many in public service and in the entertainment industry
Baron de Montesquieu	• French Enlightenment philosopher who admired the British system of republican government • Influence is seen in separation of powers and in the checks and balances provisions in the Constitution
John Muir	• Naturalist, conservationist, and writer; influenced President Theodore Roosevelt to protect more land; founded the Sierra Club
Ralph Nader	• Consumer rights crusader; wrote *Unsafe at Any Speed* (1965) to expose the lack of safety standards for cars • Third party presidential candidate (1996, 2000, 2004, 2008)
Frank Norris	• Naturalist writer whose 1901 novel, *The Octopus*, told of the struggle between the railroad and California wheat growers
Robert Oppenheimer	• Physicist who led the American effort to build the first atomic bomb
Thomas Paine	• English-born writer and political philosopher whose influential pamphlet *Common Sense* (1776) pressed for independence from Great Britain
Rosa Parks	• African American civil rights activist whose 1955 refusal to give up her seat to a white person led to the Montgomery, Alabama, bus boycott and helped launch the civil rights movement
Frances Perkins	• Social reformer and political leader • Named secretary of labor under President Franklin D. Roosevelt in 1933, becoming the first woman to serve in a cabinet position

H. Ross Perot	• Third-party candidate and billionaire businessman who challenged George Bush and Bill Clinton for the presidency in 1992 with new ideas about balancing the federal budget and about other economic issues
Matthew Perry	• Led 1853–1854 naval mission to open Japan to world trade and negotiated U.S. trading rights with Japan (Treaty of Kanagawa)
Gifford Pinchot	• Conservationist and politician who led the Division of Forestry of the Department of Agriculture under President Theodore Roosevelt • Dismissed by Taft after attacking the Secretary of the Interior for removing from federal protection about a million acres of land
Joseph Pulitzer	• Publisher of the *New York Journal*, whose "yellow journalism" helped provoke the Spanish-American War
Condoleezza Rice	• Second Secretary of State under President George W. Bush; first female African American to hold that position
Jacob Riis	• Journalist, photographer, and social reformer of the Progressive Era • Used writings and photographs to show the need for better housing for the poor, such as in his 1890 book *How the Other Half Lives*
Jackie Robinson	• Professional baseball player • Became the first African American to play in major league baseball when he joined the Brooklyn Dodgers in 1947
John D. Rockefeller	• Industrialist and philanthropist • Founder of the Standard Oil Company
Nelson A. Rockefeller	• Former governor of New York who was appointed Vice President by President Gerald Ford in 1974 • Only nonelected Vice President to serve with a nonelected President
Eleanor Roosevelt	• Political activist and First Lady • Early and long-time activist for rights for African Americans and women during the New Deal as First Lady and as political activist on her own • Played a key role in creation of United Nations Declaration on Human Rights (1948) and heading the UN Commission on Human Rights (1961) • Chaired the Presidential Commission on the Status of Women during the Kennedy Administration
Julius and Ethel Rosenberg	• Convicted and executed for treason in 1953 during the era of McCarthyism
Jean-Jacques Rousseau	• French Enlightenment philosopher • Influenced the Declaration of Independence with his arguments in support of government by the consent of the governed
Sacajawea	• Native American guide for part of the Lewis and Clark expedition • Honored in 2000 with her image on a dollar coin

Nicola Sacco and Bartolomeo Vanzetti	• Italian immigrants and anarchists executed for armed robbery and murder at the height of the antiradical, anti-immigrant feelings of the 1920s • Cleared by the Massachusetts governor in 1977, some 50 years later
Margaret Sanger	• Pioneering advocate of birth control • Organized first American birth control conference in 1921 • Founder of a birth-control lobbying group that became Planned Parenthood in 1942
Upton Sinclair	• Muckraking journalist of the Progressive Era • Influenced the passage of the 1906 Meat Inspection Act with his novel *The Jungle*, which deals with the exploitation of the poor and the factory conditions that led to contaminated meat
Adam Smith	• In *The Wealth of Nations* (1776), this Scottish political economist rejected mercantilism and advocated a free enterprise system, the basis of modern capitalism • Argued for free trade, the division of labor, competition, individual freedom, supply and demand, and *laissez-faire* as necessary for a sound economy
Alfred E. Smith	• Reform governor of New York and first Catholic to run for President • Lost to Hoover in the 1928 election, largely because voters did not want a Catholic President and because Smith favored repeal of the Eighteenth Amendment • Right-wing conservative Democrat who helped organized American Liberty League (1934) and opposed New Deal
Bessie Smith	• Harlem Renaissance blues singer known as the "Empress of the Blues" • Recorded with prominent jazz musicians, such as Louis Armstrong and Benny Goodman
Elizabeth Cady Stanton	• Leading crusader for women's rights; also for abolition and temperance • Began women's rights movement with Seneca Falls Convention in New York in 1848; wrote Declaration of Sentiments (1848) • With Susan B. Anthony, cofounded the National Woman Suffrage Association and coedited *Revolution*, a women's rights journal
Lincoln Steffens	• Muckraking journalist, editor, and reformer; wrote about corruption in government and business in his 1906 novel, *The Shame of the Cities*
John Steinbeck	• Author whose novels often deal with problems of the working class during the Great Depression • *The Grapes of Wrath* (Pulitzer Prize, 1939) describes the effect of the drought that created the Dust Bowl on a group of farmers forced to leave Oklahoma and work as migrant laborers in California
Harriet Beecher Stowe	• Writer whose emotional, controversial, and best-selling novel, *Uncle Tom's Cabin* (1852), focused attention on slavery and contributed to the start of the Civil War

Ida Tarbell	• Muckraking journalist whose *History of Standard Oil Company* exposed Rockefeller's unfair and often ruthless business practices
Norman Thomas	• Political leader, minister, and pacifist who ran six times as Socialist party candidate for President • Supporter of moderate social reforms, strongly anticommunist • Helped organize the American Civil Liberties Union and urged nuclear disarmament
Dr. Francis Townsend	• Opponent of the New Deal who promoted a financially impossible plan to provide government pensions for the elderly
Mark Twain	• Author and humorist of the late nineteenth and early twentieth centuries, famous, in part, for his homespun stories about life along the Mississippi River • Mark Twain was the pen name of Samuel L. Clemens
Voltaire	• French Enlightenment philosopher who praised British institutions and rights and influenced framers of the Constitution • Wrote against religious intolerance and persecution
Earl Warren	• Chief Justice of the United States (1953–1969) • Landmark cases such as *Brown* v. *Board of Education* (1954) and *Miranda* v. *Arizona* (1966) marked his tenure
Booker T. Washington	• African American educator, author, and leader • Founded Tuskegee Institute (1881) and wrote *Up from Slavery* (1901) • Urged vocational education and self-improvement rather than confrontation as the way for African Americans to gain racial equality
Ida Wells-Barnett	• African American journalist, suffragist, and reformer • Launched a national crusade against lynching in the 1890s • Cofounder of the NAACP and of the National Association of Colored Women
Edith Wharton	• 1920s novelist who expressed concern about old versus new values in books such as *The Age of Innocence* (Pulitzer Prize, 1921)
Mao Zedong	• Leader of the communist Chinese government from 1949 until 1976 • Met with President Nixon on Nixon's historic trip to China in 1972
John Peter Zenger	• German immigrant, printer and journalist • Tried for criminal libel for criticizing New York governor in his paper; jury found him not guilty on the grounds that he had printed the truth • His case was an early step in establishing freedom of the press

Glossary

A

abolitionist: a person seeking the legal end of slavery

acquit: to be found not guilty in a trial

affirmative action: steps taken to increase the representation of women and minorities, especially in jobs and higher education

AFL/CIO: influential labor union resulting from a merger between the American Federation of Labor and the Congress of Industrial Organizations in 1955

agrarian protest: demands by farmers for improvements in areas affecting agriculture, especially in the late 1800s

Agricultural/Agrarian Revolution: introduction of new farming methods in the 18th century that improved the quality and quantity of farm products and led to the Industrial Revolution

alien: a citizen of a foreign country

alliance: a group of nations mutually allied by treaty

Allies: the World War I alliance of Great Britain, France, Russia, and later the United States; also the World War II alliance of Great Britain, the United States, the Soviet Union, and other nations

al-Qaeda: world terrorist organization responsible for September 11, 2001, attacks on the World Trade Center and the Pentagon; led by Osama bin Laden

amendment: a change in or addition to a legal document, motion, bylaw, law, or constitution

American system: a plan offered by Henry Clay for internal improvements

annex: to attach new territory to an existing area, such as a country

Antifederalist: a person opposed to the Constitution during the ratification debate of 1787

anti-Semitism: prejudice against Jews

antitrust: opposed to practices and agreements that restrict trade, such as monopolies, price-fixing, and trusts

appeasement: the policy of giving in to an aggressor's demands in order to keep the peace

appellate jurisdiction: the authority of a court to review the decisions of inferior (lower) courts

Articles of Confederation: the first American constitution

assassination: the murder of a public figure

assembly line: a method of production in which automobiles or other items being manufactured move past workers and machines and are assembled piece by piece until completed

assimilation: the process of becoming part of another culture

assumption plan: part of Hamilton's financial plan; called for the new federal government to take over and pay off American Revolution war debts of Continental Congress and states

atomic age: a term used to describe period begun by the explosion of the first atomic bomb in 1945

B

baby boom: the rapid growth in the population of the United States between 1945 and 1964

balance of power: distribution of political and economic power that prevents any one nation from becoming too strong

balance of terror: a balance of power achieved when opposing sides possess nuclear weapons

balance of trade: the difference in value between a nation's imports and its exports

bank holiday: 1933 banking act that closed banks to prevent collapse of banking system; sound banks then reopened

bankruptcy: a court action to release a person or corporation from unpaid debts

belligerents: nations fighting a war, usually after a declaration of war

bicameral legislature: a lawmaking body composed of two houses

big business: corporations or monopolies seen as having too much control over a society and its economy

Big Stick diplomacy: foreign policy of President Theodore Roosevelt threatening intervention in Latin American nations to insure their stability

bill: a proposal presented to a legislative body for possible enactment as law

Bill of Attainder: an act of a legislature that finds a person guilty without a trial; prohibited by the Constitution

Bill of Rights: the first ten amendments to the U.S. Constitution, dealing mostly with civil rights

bipartisan: supported by two political parties

Black Codes: laws passed, especially by southern states after the Civil War, to control the actions and limit the rights of African Americans

blacklist: a list, circulated among employers, of people who will not be hired because of their views, beliefs, or actions

blitzkrieg: a sudden invasion or "lightning war," first practiced by Germany in World War II

blockade: the shutting off of a port to keep people or supplies from moving in or out

blue-collar worker: someone who holds an industrial or factory job

boycott: an organized refusal to buy or use a product or service, or to deal with a company or group of companies, as a protest or as a means to force them to take some action

brinkmanship: the policy of being willing to go "to the brink" of war to preserve peace

bureaucracy: a collective term for all of the workers who run the agencies that do the everyday business of government

cabinet: the group of officials who head government departments and advise the President

capitalism: the economic system based on private initiative, competition, profit, and the private ownership of the means of producing goods and services

carpetbagger: pejorative name for a Northerner who went to the South during Reconstruction

cash crops: crops grown for sale rather than for family consumption

census: gathering information on the nation's population; required by the U.S. Constitution every ten years to determine number of votes a state has in the House of Representatives and the Electoral College

checks and balances: the system set up by the U.S. Constitution in which each branch of the federal government has the power to limit the actions of the other branches

citizen: a person who by birth or naturalization owes loyalty to, and receives the protection of, a nation's government

citizenship: the duties, rights, and privileges of a citizen

civil disobedience: nonviolent protest against unjust laws

civil liberties: certain rights guaranteed to all citizens of a nation

civil rights: rights guaranteed to citizens by the U.S. Constitution and laws of the nation

civil service: government jobs for which appointments and promotions are now based on merit rather than on political patronage

closed shop: a workplace in which employees must be labor union members in order to be hired

coalition: an alliance of political groups

Cold War: the state of tension between the United States and the Soviet Union after World War II

collective bargaining: the process by which a union negotiates with management for a contract

collective security: a system in which member nations agree to take joint action to meet any threat or breach of international peace

colonialism: the practice under which a nation takes control of other lands for its economic, military, or other use

colony: a settlement of people in a distant land who are ruled by a government of their native land

commerce clause: Article I, Section 8, Clause 3 of the U.S. Constitution, which gives Congress the power to regulate interstate and foreign trade

committee system: method under which members of the legislative branch form into smaller groups to facilitate such business as considering proposed legislation and holding investigations

communism: the economic system based on the collective ownership of property and the means of production, with all individuals expected to contribute to society according to their abilities and to receive from it according to their needs

compromise: the resolution of conflict in which concessions are made by all parties to achieve a common goal

concentration camp: a place where political opponents or other "enemies" of a nation are forcibly confined, especially those established by Nazi Germany before and during World War II

concurrent powers: powers shared by the national and state governments

confederation: an alliance of independent states

conference committee: a temporary joint committee of both houses of a legislature, created to reconcile differences between the two houses' version of a bill

conglomerate: a corporation that owns many different, unrelated businesses

Congress: the legislative, or lawmaking, branch of the United States government, made up of the Senate and the House of Representatives

consent of the governed: principle that says people are the source of the powers of government

conservation: the careful use or preserving of natural resources

conspicuous consumption: public enjoyment of costly possessions done in such a way as to emphasize the fact that one can afford such possessions

constitution: body of fundamental law, setting out the basic principles, structures, processes, and functions of a government and placing limits on its actions; the supreme law of the United States

constitutional: permissible under the Constitution

Constitutional Convention: formal meeting of state delegates in Philadelphia in 1787 at which the Constitution was written

consumer: person who spends money on goods and services

consumer goods: goods produced for use by individuals as opposed to use by businesses

consumerism: the practice of protecting consumers; also theory that increased consumption of goods is economically and personally beneficial.

consumer protection: measures to shield buyers of goods and services from unsafe products and unfair or illegal sales practices

containment: the U.S. policy after World War II of trying to keep the Soviet Union from expanding its area of influence and dominance

convict: to be found guilty in a trial

corporation: business owned by many investors that raises money by selling stocks or shares to those investors

court packing: Franklin Roosevelt's 1937 plan to add justices to the Supreme Court

credit: delayed payment for goods or services

creditor nation: a nation that is owed money by other nations

cultural diversity: many cultures existing in the same society

cultural pluralism: the idea that different cultures can exist side by side in the same society, all contributing to the society without losing their identities

culture: the way of life of a given people

custom: a habit or practice so established that it strongly influences social behavior

D

debtor nation: a nation that owes money to another nation or nations

Declaration of Independence: the 1776 document that stated Great Britain's North American colonies had become free and independent of the parent country

deficit: the amount by which money spent is greater than money received

deficit spending: government practice of spending more money than it takes in from taxes and other revenues

delegated powers: powers given by the Constitution to the national government and denied to state governments

demagogue: a person who gains political power by rousing the passions of the people

demobilization: the process by which a nation reconverts to peacetime status after a war or the threat of war

democracy: system of government in which supreme authority rests with the people, either directly or through elected representatives

Democratic Party: one of the modern political parties, descended from Jefferson's Democratic-Republican Party; also one of the oldest continuous political parties in the world

Democratic-Republican Party: one of the first political parties in the United States, led by Jefferson and other leaders who were opposed to the Federalists; also known as Jeffersonian Republicans

demography: the study of populations through statistics

depression: a long and severe decline in economic activity

détente: the easing of tension between nations

dictatorship: form of government in which the power to govern is held by one person or a small group

direct democracy: system of government in which the people participate directly in decision-making through the voting process

direct election of senators: system put into practice under the Seventeenth Amendment whereby the voters rather than the state legislatures elect members of the U.S. Senate

disarmament: reduction of a nation's armed forces or weapons of war

discrimination: policy or attitude that denies rights to people based on race, religion, sex, or other characteristics

disestablishment: depriving a state church of official support from the government, or never allowing a state church to be founded

diversity: variety

divestiture: a refusal to hold stock in companies that have operations in South Africa

division of powers: basic principle of federalism; the constitutional provisions by which governmental powers are divided between the national and the state governments

dollar diplomacy: President Taft's policy of encouraging United States investment in Latin America

domestic policy: everything a nation's government says and does in relation to internal matters

domino theory: the idea, prevalent during the Vietnam War, that if one Asian nation became Communist, neighboring nations would as well

due process of law: constitutional guarantee that government will not deprive any person of life, liberty, or property by any unfair, arbitrary, or unreasonable action

E

economic: pertaining to production, distribution, and use of wealth

economic nationalism: policies focused on improving the economy of one's own nation

economic programs: any policies set forward by a government that relate to the workings of its economy

elastic clause: Article I, Section 8, Clause 18 of the Constitution, which is the basis for the implied powers of Congress

Electoral College: an assembly elected by the voters that meets every four years to formally elect the President of the United States

electoral votes: number of votes each state and the District of Columbia can cast for president, equal to the number of senators plus representatives of each state, with 270 electoral votes needed to be elected president

electorate: all the persons entitled to vote in a given election

emancipation: the act of setting a person or people free

Emancipation Proclamation: the Presidential decree, effective January 1, 1863, that freed enslaved people in Confederate-held territory

embargo: government prohibition of trade with another nation or nation; also prohibition of ships leaving home ports. *See Embargo Act of 1807, United States embargo against Cuba*

empathy: the process of sharing and understanding the feelings or thoughts of another person

English Bill of Rights: the 1689 agreement between Parliament and William and Mary which established that representative government and the rule of law outweighed the power of any monarch

Enlightenment: Eighteenth-century movement that emphasized science and reason as key to improving society

entrepreneur: a person who organizes, operates, and assumes the risks of a business enterprise

environment: natural surroundings and all the things that make them up; also the social, cultural, and physical surroundings that affect behavior in a society

equal protection under the law: a clause in the Fourteenth Amendment requiring that states apply due process equally, without preference to an individual or group

espionage: spying

ethnic group: people of foreign birth or descent living in another country

European Economic Community: organization, also known as the Common Market, formed in 1957 to ease trade and travel among member European nations

European Union: the economic organization of European nations designed to increase the economic power of Europe in the world economy

excise tax: taxes levied on the production, transportation, sale, or consumption of goods or services

executive branch: part of a government that carries out its laws

executive power: the powers of the head of an executive branch of government to carry out the laws

executive privilege: the right claimed by presidents to withhold information from the legislative or judicial branches

expansionism: desire to enlarge the territory owned or controlled by one's nation

expatriate: a person who gives up her or his homeland to live in another country

expressed powers: those delegated powers of the national government that are given to it in so many words by the Constitution

F

farm output: total value of products produced by a nation's farms

fascism: political philosophy that calls for glorification of the state, a single party system with a strong ruler, and aggressive nationalism

federal government: the central or national government

federalism: a system of government in which authority is divided between national and state governments; the belief in or advocacy of such a system

Federalist: supporter of the Constitution in the ratification debate of 1787, favored a strong national government

Federalist Party: one of the first political parties in the United States, organized by those who favored the ratification of the Constitution

Federal Reserve System: the nation's central banking system, established in 1913; a system of 12 regional banks overseen by a central board

feminist movement: the struggle of women for equality

First Amendment: Bill of Rights' guarantee of freedom of religion, speech, press, assembly, and petition

fiscal policy: policies relating to a nation's finances

flapper: nickname for a young woman in the 1920s who declared her independence from traditional rules

foreign policy: the actions and stands that every nation takes in every aspect of its relationships with other countries; everything a nation's government says and does in world affairs

Fourteen Points: President Woodrow Wilson's proposal in 1918 for a postwar European peace

Fourteenth Amendment: Constitutional amendment that defines "citizen" to reverse Dred Scott decision; its due process and equal protection clauses are aimed at protecting basic rights

free enterprise: an economic system based on private ownership, individual enterprise, and competition

freedom of speech: the right of freedom of expression guaranteed to Americans by the First Amendment

freedom of the seas: right of merchant ships to travel in international waters during peace or war

frontier: the border of a country; as defined by the U.S. Bureau of the Census, the edge of settlement beyond which the land was occupied by two or fewer people per square mile

frontier thesis: idea set forth by historian Frederick Jackson Turner that the nation's frontier regions shaped its character and institutions

Fugitive Slave Law: part of the Compromise of 1850, the Fugitive Slave Law required all citizens to help catch runaway enslaved people

fundamentalist: one who believes that the Bible is the literal word of God

G

General Agreement on Tariffs and Trade (GATT): international agreement on reducing tariffs and expanding world trade (1947)

genocide: the systematic destruction of a race of people

Gentlemen's Agreement: informal agreement between the United States and Japan in 1907 to limit Japanese immigration to this country

Gettysburg Address: famous speech by President Abraham Lincoln on the meaning of the Civil War, given in November 1863 at the dedication of a national cemetery on the site of the Battle of Gettysburg

ghetto: area in which many members of some minority group live, to which they are restricted by economic pressure or social discrimination

Gilded Age: term used to describe the period from 1865 to 1900

glasnost: a period of "openness" in relations between the United States and the Soviet Union that began in the late 1980s

global interdependence: the idea that the nations of the world must rely on each other in many different ways, including trade, transportation, and communication

Glorious Revolution: the bloodless revolution in 1689 in which the English Parliament overthrew James II and replaced him with William and Mary

gold standard: a system in which a nation's currency is based on the value of gold

Good Neighbor Policy: Franklin D. Roosevelt's policy toward Latin America intended to strengthen relations with the nations of that region

government: the complex of offices, personnel, and processes by which a state is ruled, and by which its public policies are made and enforced

grandfather clause: laws passed in some southern states giving the right to vote only to people who had that right on January 1, 1867, and their descendants; intended to keep African Americans from voting

Grangers, The: organization of farmers founded for social reasons in 1867, which later campaigned for state regulation of railroads and other reforms

grass-roots support: political backing from ordinary citizens, especially from rural areas

Great Compromise: the plan for a two-house legislature adopted at the Constitutional Convention in 1787 that settled differences between large and small states over representation in Congress

Great Depression: period from 1929 to 1941 of severe worldwide economic downturn

Great Migration: migration of English Puritans to the Massachusetts Bay Colony beginning in the 1630s; also refers to the migration of African Americans from the South to the North in the early twentieth century

Great Society: the name given to President Johnson's domestic program in the 1960s

gross national product (GNP): the total value of all the goods and services produced in a nation in a year

guerrilla warfare: fighting by stealth and with small bands, which make surprise raids against stronger forces

H

habeas corpus: a writ of *habeas corpus* (produce the body) requires a person to be brought before a court to determine whether that person is being lawfully jailed

Harlem Renaissance: an African American cultural movement centered in New York City from the 1920s to the mid-1930s; focused on African American identity and pride through literature, art, music, dance, and philosophy

hemisphere: half of the Earth's surface

holding company: a company that gains control of other companies by buying their stock

Holocaust: name given to Nazi Germany's persecution of Jews before and during World War II; in this time, more than six million Jews died

Homestead Act: 1862 law that offered 160 acres of western land to settlers

House of Representatives: lower house of the U.S. Congress in which states are represented according to the size of their populations

humanitarian: one who is concerned with the welfare of all people

human rights: basic rights that should belong to all people including freedom of speech, religion, and the press

immigration: the movement of people into another nation in order to make a permanent home there

immigration laws: laws controlling the movement of people into a country

immigration quota: sets limits on numbers of people and/or their nation of origin to limit immigration from those nations

impeachment: the process by which the House of Representatives makes an accusation of wrongdoing against the President or other high federal officials

imperialism: policy by which one country takes control of another either directly or through economic or political dominance

implied powers: those delegated powers of the national government implied by (inferred from) the expressed powers; those powers "necessary and proper" to carry out the expressed powers

income tax: a tax levied on individual and corporate earnings permitted by 16th amendment (1913)

incumbent: person currently occupying a political office at the time of a new election

indemnities: money paid by a losing nation to a winning nation after a war

indentured servant: person who worked in the colonies for period of three to seven years in exchange for passage, food, housing, clothing; system resulting from labor shortage in colonies

independence: freedom from the control, influence, or support of other people or nations

Indian Removal Policy: under President Andrew Jackson, the policy of moving all Native Americans to lands west of the Mississippi River in the 1830s

individual rights: basic rights that belong to each person

industrialization: change from an agricultural society to one based on machine-made goods

inflation: an economic condition in which prices rise substantially over a significant period of time

injunction: a court order prohibiting a given action; used frequently against workers in nineteenth-century labor-management disputes

interchangeable parts: parts made exactly like each other, making the mass production of products on an assembly line possible

interdependence: a condition in which parties are reliant on each other

internal affairs: public or business matters within the boundaries of a country

internal improvements: roads, bridges, canals, and other similar projects funded by the national government

internationalism: the belief, held by some Americans in the 1930s, that the United States should aid the victims of international aggression

international law: the norms of behavior generally agreed to and followed by the nations of the world in their dealings with each other

internment camps: places of confinement, especially in wartime

interstate commerce: trade among the states

intervention: interference by one nation in the affairs of another

intrastate commerce: trade within the borders of a state

Iron Curtain: the line between Soviet-dominated Eastern Europe and the West, so-called because the Soviets and their satellite nations prevented the free passage of people, information, and ideas across their borders

isolationism: a policy of avoiding alliances and other types of involvement in the affairs of other nations

isthmus: a narrow strip or neck of land running from one larger land area to another

J

Japanese-American relocation: policy under which Americans of Japanese ancestry were confined during World War II

Jim Crow laws: laws in the Southern states in the nineteenth and twentieth centuries that forced the segregation of the races

jingoism: aggressive nationalism

joint resolution: legislative measure which must be passed by both houses and approved by the chief executive to become effective; similar to a bill, with the force of law, and often used for unusual or temporary circumstances

judicial activism: broad interpretation of the Constitution leading to court-directed change

judicial branch: part of the government that decides if laws are carried out fairly

judicial restraint: narrow interpretation of the Constitution

judicial review: power of the Supreme Court to determine the constitutionality of acts of the legislative and executive branches of the government

judiciary: judicial branch of a government, its system of courts

jurisdiction: power of a court to hear (to try and decide) a case

jury: a group of people who hear evidence in a legal case and give a decision based on that evidence

justice: fairness; trial and judgment according to established process of the law

K

Know-Nothing Party: common name for the American party, a nativist political organization formed in 1849

Korean War: conflict over the future of the Korean peninsula, fought between 1950 and 1953 and ending in a stalemate

Ku Klux Klan: secret society first formed in the South during Reconstruction to ensure white supremacy over blacks; re-formed in the 1920s to express opposition to Jews, Catholics, Bolsheviks, and others considered "un-American"

L

labor union: workers organized as a group to seek higher wages, improve working conditions, and obtain other benefits

laissez-faire: noninterference; has come to mean a policy by which the government minimizes its regulation of industry and the economy

landslide election: an election in which a victorious candidate gathers an overwhelming percentage of the total votes cast

law: rule recognized by a nation, state, or community as binding on its members

League of Nations: association of nations to protect the independence of member nations, proposed by President Wilson in his Fourteen Points and formed after World War I

legislative branch: the lawmaking agencies of a government

legislature: group of people with the power of making laws for a nation or state

less developed nations: nations that have not fully industrialized, usually Third World nations

lifespan: the lifetime of an individual

limited government: basic principle of the American system of government; belief that government is not all-powerful, and may only do those things the people have given it the power to do

Lincoln-Douglas debates: the series of political debates between Stephen Douglas and Abraham Lincoln during the Senate campaign of 1858, which catapulted Lincoln to the national spotlight

literacy: the ability to read and write

literacy test: test of a potential voter's ability to read and write; once used in several states to prevent African Americans and other minorities from voting; now outlawed

lobby: to attempt to influence legislation; also, groups that attempt to do so

lockout: during a labor dispute, the closing of a business (by locking the gates) to keep employees from entering

loose interpretation: a belief that the provisions of the Constitution, especially those granting power to the government, are to be construed in broad terms

Louisiana Purchase: purchase by the United States of the Louisiana Territory from France in 1803

lynch: to execute someone illegally, by hanging, burning, or other means

M

majority: at least one more than half (e.g., over 50 percent of the votes in an election)

Manhattan Project: secret American program during World War II to develop an atomic bomb

Manifest Destiny: a belief held in the first half of the nineteenth century that the United States had a mission to expand its borders to incorporate all land between the Atlantic and Pacific oceans

margin: a small part of the total price of a stock purchase deposited with a broker at the time of purchase with the promise to pay the full sum at a later date

Marshall Court: the Supreme Court during the tenure of John Marshall as chief justice, in which key decisions were made that strengthened the federal government's role in the nation's economic business

mass circulation: reaching a very large audience

mass production: rapid manufacture of large numbers of a product

Mayflower Compact: agreement signed by Pilgrims before landing at Plymouth

McCarthyism: the use of indiscriminate and unfounded accusations and sensationalist investigative methods to suppress political opponents portrayed as subversive; term taken from the name of Senator Joseph McCarthy, who carried out such practices

melting pot theory: the idea that different immigrant groups in the United States will lose their old identities and that a new American identity will emerge from the blending of cultures

mercantilism: economic theory that a nation's strength came from building up its gold supplies and expanding its trade

merger: a combining of two or more companies into a larger company

Mexican Cession: lands turned over to the United States after the Mexican War in what is now the states of California, Nevada, Utah, and parts of Wyoming, Colorado, Arizona, and New Mexico

Mexican War: conflict between the United States and Mexico from 1846 to 1848, ending with a victory for the United States

Middle Passage: transportation by force to European colonies in Western Hemisphere of Africans to be sold as enslaved people; name refers to second of three part transatlantic trade called Triangular Trade

migration: historically, a regular, deliberate movement of a group of people to specific locations

militarism: policy of building up strong military forces to prepare for war

minimum wage: the lowest wage that can be paid to certain workers as set by national or state law

minority: less than half

minority group: group within a nation that differs from most of the population in race, religion, national origin, and so on

minor party: one of the less widely supported political parties in a governmental system

missionary: one who attempts to spread the religious ideas of a faith in a foreign land

mobilization: a call-up of military forces, usually in preparation for war

monarchy: government headed by a single ruler, usually a king or queen

monetary policy: actions and positions taken by a government in regard to its system of money

monopoly: dominance in or control of a market for certain goods or services by a single company or combination of companies

Monroe Doctrine: policy statement of President James Monroe in 1823 warning nations of western Europe not to interfere with the newly independent nations of Latin America

moral diplomacy: a term describing President Woodrow Wilson's approach to foreign policy, which emphasized the use of negotiation and arbitration rather than force to settle international disputes

Mormons: members of the Church of Jesus Christ of Latter-day Saints; in the 1840s, thousands moved to Utah seeking freedom from religious persecution

muckraker: early twentieth-century American journalist who tried to improve society by exposing political corruption, health hazards, and other social problems

multilateral action: joint action taken by three or more nations

municipal government: the government of a city, town, or village

N

National Association for the Advancement of Colored People (NAACP): an organization founded in 1909 to fight for the rights of African Americans

national bank: bank chartered by the federal government

national government: in the United States, the federal government

nationalism: pride in or devotion to one's country

National Organization for Women (NOW): founded in 1966 to work for equal rights for women

national self interest: aim of all foreign policy

nativism: a belief in the superiority of the way of life of one's home country; in the United States, this was often associated with a desire to limit immigration

North Atlantic Treaty Organization (NATO): an alliance formed for mutual defense in 1949 under the North Atlantic Treaty, and now made up of 15 nations stretching from Canada to Turkey

naturalization: the process by which a citizen of one country becomes a citizen of another

natural rights: rights that all people are entitled to from birth

Nazism: belief in the policies of Adolf Hitler

necessary and proper clause: another name for the elastic clause, which is the basis of the implied powers of Congress

negotiation: talking over an issue by two or more parties with the aim of reaching a mutually agreeable settlement

neutrality: the policy of not taking sides in a dispute or a war

New Deal: name given to the programs of President Franklin D. Roosevelt

New Federalism: name given to the attempt to lessen the federal government's role in its dealings with states during the presidencies of Nixon and Reagan

New Freedom: name given to the programs of President Woodrow Wilson

New Frontier: name given to the programs of President John F. Kennedy

New Nationalism: plan under which Theodore Roosevelt ran for president in 1912

nominating convention: political gathering at which a party names candidates for office

noninvolvement: policy of taking no side in international disputes, neutrality

nonrecognition: refusal to establish formal diplomatic relations with the new government of a nation

normalcy: President Warren G. Harding's term for the return to peace after World War I

North American Free Trade Agreement (NAFTA): agreement calling for the removal of trade restrictions between the United States, Canada, and Mexico

nuclear freeze: a halt in the manufacture and deployment of nuclear weapons

nuclear power: energy produced from a controlled atomic reaction

nuclear waste: the byproducts of the production of nuclear power

nullification: a state's refusal to recognize a federal law

Nuremberg Trials: post-World War II trials in which German government and military figures were tried for crimes committed during the war

Open Door Policy: policy toward China set out by Secretary of State John Hay allowing any nation to trade in any other nation's sphere of influence

original jurisdiction: the court in which a case is heard firsthand

overproduction: a condition that exists when the supply of a product exceeds the demand for that product

pacifist: a person who is opposed to war and refuses to fight under any circumstances

pardon: a release from the punishment or legal consequences of a crime granted by a President or governor

parliament: the legislature of Great Britain

patent and copyright laws: laws giving rights to inventions, literary, musical, and artistic works to their creators

patriotism: love and support of one's nation

peaceful coexistence: phrase describing the aim of U.S.–Soviet relations during a time of improved relations between those nations in the 1950s

per capita income: income per person

perestroika: the restructuring of the Soviet Union's economy under Mikhail Gorbachev that began a move toward free enterprise

plantation: large estate farmed by many workers

political party: organized group that seeks to control government through the winning of elections and the holding of public office

political system: the way a nation is governed

poll tax: a tax that must be paid before one can vote, often used in Southern states to discourage or prevent blacks from voting and now banned in national elections by the Twenty-fourth Amendment

pool: method of ending competition used by railroads in the late 1800s in which they divided up business in given areas and fixed prices

popular sovereignty: basic principle of the American system of government that the people are the only source of any and all governmental power

popular vote: votes cast by the people for the electors representing candidates in presidential elections

Populist movement: political movement begun by farmers and members of labor unions in the late 1800s seeking to limit the power of big businesses and grant greater say in the governmental process to individuals

power: control, authority, right

preamble: an introduction to a speech or piece of writing

prejudice: unfavorable opinion about people who are of different religion, race, or nationality

President: the chief executive of a modern republic, especially of the United States

primary: election held before a general election in which voters choose their party's candidates for office

Progressive Era: the period from 1900–1920 that saw the greatest action by Progressive reformers

Progressive movement: reform movement that worked to correct abuses in American society

Prohibition: the period of 1920–1933 when the making and sale of liquor was illegal in the United States

propaganda: spreading of ideas or beliefs that help a particular cause and hurt an opposing cause

protectionism: belief in policies that favor the protection of domestically produced goods

protective tariff: tax on imports designed to discourage their sale and to favor the development of domestic industry

protectorate: a country under the protection and partial control of a stronger country

public opinion: those attitudes held by a significant number of persons on matters of government and politics; expressed group attitudes

purchasing power: the ability to buy goods and services; the value of what money could buy at one time compared to what the same amount could buy at another time

racial equality: a condition in which people are treated in the same manner by law and society regardless of their race

racism: belief that one race is superior to another

Radical Republicans: group of Republicans in Congress who wanted to protect the rights of people freed from slavery in the South and keep rich Southern planters from regaining political power

ratification: formal approval; final consent to the effectiveness of a constitution, constitutional amendment, or treaty

raw materials: natural substances before processing that will in some way increase their value or usefulness

recession: a decline in economic activity usually shorter and less severe than a depression

Reconstruction: the period of 1867–1877 when the federal government or local republican governments ruled the Southern states that had seceded

recovery: a restoring to a normal condition; one of the aims of FDR's New Deal

Red Scare: term used to describe periods in the 1920s and 1950s when American fear and suspicion of communism was at its height

reform: change for the better; one of the goals of FDR's New Deal

regulatory agencies: parts of the federal bureaucracy charged with overseeing different aspects of the nation's economy

religious freedom: the ability to worship as one chooses, guaranteed in this nation by the First Amendment

reparations: payments for losses a nation has suffered during a war

representation: condition of being acted and spoken for in government

representative government: system of government in which voters elect representatives to make laws for them

republic: nation in which voters choose representatives to govern them

Republican Party: one of the modern political parties, founded in 1854 in opposition to slavery

reservation: limited area set aside for Native Americans by the U.S. government

reserved powers: those powers held by the state in the American federal system

revenue: income

robber baron: terms used to describe large-scale entrepreneurs of the late 1800s

Roosevelt Corollary: expansion of the Monroe Doctrine announced by President Theodore Roosevelt in 1904 that claimed the United States had the right to intervene in Latin America to preserve law and order

rural: in or of the country

salad bowl theory: idea that people of different backgrounds can exist side by side in the United States, maintaining their identities while still contributing to the overall society

salutary neglect: manner in which England governed the American colonies in the late 1600s and early 1700s, marked by weak enforcement of laws regulating colonial trade

scalawag: white Southerner who supported Radical Republicans during Reconstruction

scarcity: too small a supply

secession: the act of formally withdrawing from membership in a group or organization; in the United States, the withdrawing of 11 southern states from the Union in 1861

sectionalism: strong sense of loyalty to a state or section instead of to the whole country

sedition: an attempt to incite a rebellion against a national government

segregation: separation of people of different races

Selective Service: the military draft name first used during World War I

self-determination: right of national groups to their own territories and their own forms of government

Senate: upper house of the U.S. Congress in which each state has two members

separate but equal: principle upheld in *Plessy* v. *Ferguson* (1896) in which the Supreme Court ruled that segregation of public facilities was legal

separation of church and state: principle set out in the First Amendment that the government shall take no actions to establish or interfere with the practice of religion

separation of powers: the principle that gives the powers of making, enforcing, and interpreting laws to separate legislative, executive, and judicial branches of government

settlement house: a private center providing social services for the poor in a needy neighborhood

sharecropper: farmer who works land owned by another and gives the landowner part of the harvest

sitdown strike: work stoppage in which employees refuse to leave the workplace and occupy it in an attempt to force their employer to come to terms

slavery: condition in which one person is the property of another; banned in this country by the Thirteenth Amendment

social contract theory: the idea that people agreed to give up some rights and powers to a government that would provide for their safety and well-being

Social Darwinism: the belief that the evolutionary idea of "survival of the fittest" applied to societies and businesses

socialism: economic and political system based on the public ownership of the means by which goods and services are produced, distributed, and exchanged

social reform: efforts to better conditions within a society

social security: programs of the federal government to provide economic assistance to the disabled, unemployed, poor, and aged

social welfare: programs to promote public well-being

sovereignty: absolute power of a state within its own territory

soviet: elected assembly in the Soviet Union; (Cap.) pertaining to the Soviet Union

speculator: person who invests in a risky business venture in hopes of making a large profit

spoils system: system or practice of giving appointed offices as rewards from the successful party in an election; name for the patronage system under President Andrew Jackson

Square Deal: name given to programs of President Theodore Roosevelt

stagflation: an economic condition characterized by both inflation and recession

states rights: idea that individual states had the right to limit the power of the federal government

stereotype: a fixed, oversimplified idea about a person or group

stock market: place where shares in corporations are traded

strict interpretation: a literal reading of the Constitution holding that the federal government has only those powers explicitly delegated to it in the Constitution

suburbs: smaller towns surrounding large cities

suffragists: people who campaigned for women's right to vote

summit meetings: conferences of the heads of two or more nations

supply-side economics: the theory that the government can best stimulate the economy by cutting taxes and encouraging investment in business

supremacy clause: Article VI, Section 2 of the Constitution, which makes that document and federal laws and treaties the "supreme law of the land"

Supreme Court: the highest federal court and the final interpreter of the Constitution

surplus goods: extra goods

swing state: in a presidential election year, a state that is not clearly for either a Democratic or Republican candidate; the popular vote of the state that determines the electoral vote may be a major factor in the outcome of an election

Taliban: a reactionary, extremist Islamic group that imposed strict conservative laws when it controlled the Afghan government in the 1990s and remains an opponent to westernization

tariff: tax placed on goods brought into a country

technology: practical application of knowledge

temperance movement: campaign against the sale or drinking of alcohol

tenant farming: system of farming in which a farmer rents land to farm from a landowner

territorial integrity: condition in which a nation's borders are guaranteed against disturbance by other nations

territory: a political division of the United States before it becomes a state; a large area of land

terrorism: the use of violence, intimidation, and coercion to achieve an end, to gain publicity for a cause, or to disrupt the normal functioning of society

Tet Offensive: 1968 attack by Viet Cong and North Vietnamese forces throughout South Vietnam; a turning point in the Vietnam War

third party: a political party formed in addition to the Democratic and Republican Parties, which usually promote a limited platform; historically, the two major parties have adopted some aspects of third parties' platforms

Third World: during the Cold War, nations in the modern world that professed not to be allied with the Soviet Union and its allies or the United States and its allies, especially the developing nations of Asia, Africa, and Latin America

three branches of government: the division of the powers of government into legislative, executive, and judicial functions

three-fifths compromise: compromise reached at the Constitutional Convention of 1787 whereby three-fifths of a state's population of enslaved people would be counted for both representation and taxation

totalitarian: form of government in which the power to rule embraces all matters of human concern

tradition: the handing down of beliefs, customs, and practices from generation to generation

Trail of Tears: the forced movement of the Cherokee in 1838–1839 to land west of the Mississippi River

transcontinental railroad: railway extending from coast to coast; completed in 1869

treaty: a formal agreement concluded between two or more countries

Treaty of Versailles: treaty marking the end of World War I that the U.S. Senate refused to ratify

triangular trade: trans-Atlantic trade among three regions; in particular in the seventeenth, eighteenth, and early nineteenth centuries with cash crops from colonies, manufactured goods from Europe, and enslaved people from West Africa

Triple Alliance: name of the alliance of Germany, Austria-Hungary, and Italy before World War I

Triple Entente: name of the alliance of Great Britain, France, and Russia before World War I

trust: group of corporations run by a single board of directors

trustbuster: person who wanted to break up some or all trusts

two-party system: political system in which the candidates of only two major parties have a reasonable chance of winning elections

unconstitutional: not permitted by the constitution of a nation

unilateral action: an action taken by one nation only

unitary government: form of government in which all of the powers are held in a single agency

universal suffrage: the right to vote is extended to all adults

unwritten constitution: a combination of executive and legislative actions and interpretations and judicial decisions, especially judicial review, as well as

customs and traditions such as development of political parties

urban: in or of the city

urbanization: process by which more of a nation's population becomes concentrated in its cities

venture capital: money invested in a new corporation or other business enterprise

veto: chief executive's power to reject a bill passed by a legislature

Vietnam War: nation's longest war; fought in Southeast Asia from the late 1950s to 1973

void: without legal force or effect

War of 1812: war between the United States and Great Britain

War Powers Act: law passed in 1973 requiring the President to seek congressional approval if troops are sent into action for longer than 60 days

weapons of mass destruction: WMD; devices used for large scale and total destruction, i.e. nuclear bombs, nerve gas, chemical warfare

Whig Party: one of the first political parties, standing for the limitation of executive power and the defense of liberty; by the 1850s had declined in power

white-collar worker: someone holding a job in business or in a profession

women's rights movement: the struggle of women for equality

work ethic: a belief that hard work is a virtuous end in itself

World War I: conflict between Allied Powers and Central Powers from 1914 to 1918

World War II: conflict between Allied and Axis nations from 1939 to 1945

Y

yellow dog contract: a contract between an employer and an employee in which the employee agrees not to join a union while employed; this is no longer legal

yellow journalism: sensational style of reporting used by some newspapers in the late 1800s

yellow peril: derogatory term implying that Asian peoples threatened the ways of life of white Americans

Index

La Follette, Robert M., 144, 181, A-17
laissez-faire, 106, 138
land
    after French and Indian War, 23
    Indian, 14, 74, 117–118, 271
    Louisiana Purchase and, 53–54
    use of, 7–8
land bridge, 5
Land Ordinance of 1785, 28
language, African, 19
Laos, 278, 281–282
Latin America
    foreign policy toward, 254, 274–275
    Monroe Doctrine and, 56
    Reagan and, 292–293
    United states and, 157–159
Latinos
    equal rights for, 270
    New Deal and, 202
Lawrence, Massachusetts, textile strike
    in, 110
laws, process of making, 37, 38
leaders, during World War II, 222
League of Nations, 165–167
League of Women Voters, 186
Lebanon, 254, 293
Lee, Richard Henry, 25
Lee, Robert E., 81–82
Ledbetter, Lilly. See Lilly Ledbetter Fair
    Pay Act.
legislation
    about national security, 239
    civil rights, 261
    in New Deal, 198–200
    in Progressive Era, 148
legislative branch, of U.S. Government,
    34, 36–38, 42
legislature, House of Burgesses as, 22
leisure, in 1920s, 184
Lend-Lease Act (1941), 219, 222
"Letter from a Birmingham Jail" (King),
    264
Levittown, New York, 256
Lewis, John L. (United Mine Workers), 201
Lewis, Meriwether, 76, A-17
Lewis, Sinclair, 185, A-17
Libby, Lewis "Scooter," 294
Liberator, The, 75, A-15
Liberty Bonds, in World War I, 163–164
life span, 308
lifestyle, 308
    after World War I, 179–180
    under Coolidge, 181
    geography and, 16–17
    of industrial workers, 138
    in 1920s, 186
    in 1960s, 280
    on plantations, 70–71
    in Progressive Era, 138
    in urban areas, 113–114

Lilly Ledbetter Fair Pay Act (2009). 304
limited government, 33
Lincoln, Abraham, 79, A-3
    in Civil War, 80–82
    Gettysburg Address by, 82
    Mexican cession and, 77
    Reconstruction plan of, 97
Lincoln-Douglas debates, 79
literacy tests, 100, 117, 164
literature
    in Great Depression, 196
    in 1920s, 185
Little Bighorn, battle of, 118
Little Rock, Arkansas, desegregation in,
    259–261
Lloyd George, David, 165
loans, after World War I, 167
lobbying, 49, 53
local government, 22
    reforms of, 143–144
location, 2
Lochner v. New York, 47, 50, 137–138,
    141, 146, A-9
Locke, Alain, 185
Locke, John, 20–21, 26, A-17
Lodge, Henry Cabot, 154, 155, A-17
Long, Huey, 206, A-17
loose construction, of Constitution (U.S.),
    46, 53
Louisiana Purchase, 53–54, 56, 76, 150
    slavery in, 77
Lowell mills, 68
loyalty program, under Truman, 238
Lusitania (ship), 160–161
lynchings, 142, 202

M

MacArthur, Douglas, 222, 225, 237, A-18
machines. See political machines
Madison, James, 52, 55, A-1
    at Constitutional Convention, 29
    Federalist Papers and, 32
    ratification and, 32
Madoff, Bernard, 305
Magna Carta, 20
Mahan, Alfred T., 150, 155
Maine (ship), 154
mainstreaming, 272
Malcolm X, 264, 266, A-18
Manchuria, 152
Manhattan Project, 225
Manifest Destiny, 6, 75, 150–151
Mann, Horace, 74, A-18
Mann-Elkins Act (1910), 147
manufacturing, 56, 68
Mao Zedong, 236, 277, 284, A-21
Mapp v. Ohio, 47, 261, A-10
Marbury v. Madison, 43, 47, 49,
    54, A-7

March on Washington
    King, Martin Luther and (1963),
        260, 265
    by veterans (1932), 190
margin trading, 182
market economy, 66–67
markets, global, 150
Marshall, George C., 234, A-18
Marshall, John, and Marshall Court,
    21, 43, 53, 54, 67, 73, A-18.
Marshall, Thurgood, A-18
Marshall Plan, 232, 234
Mason, George, 31, 32
Massachusetts, Mayflower Compact
    and, 22
Massachusetts Committee of
    Correspondence, 24
Massacre of Wounded Knee, 118
mass consumption, in 1920s, 183
massive retaliation policy, 253
mass politics, 71, 72
mass production, 102, 106
Mather, Cotton, 106, A-18
Mayflower Compact, 15, 22
McCain, John, 303–304
McCarran Internal Security Act (1953), 239
McCarthy, Eugene, 280
McCarthy, Joseph R., 239, A-18
McCulloch v. Maryland, 46, 47, 54, A-7
McGovern, George, 287
McKinley, William, 120, 144, 154, A-4
Meat Inspection Act (1906), 140, 144,
    145, 148
Medicaid, 263, 273
medical research, funding of, 272
Medicare, 263, 273, 305
medicine, in Civil War, 82
Mellon, Andrew, 181
melting pot theory, 116
mentally ill, reforms in care of, 74, 271
mercantilism, 24
Meredith, James, 260, 264
merger, 104–105
Mexican American Legal Defense and
    Education Fund, 270
Mexican Americans, 188, 202, 270
Mexican Cession, 77
Mexican War, 77
Mexico
    acquisitions from, 76–77
    civil war in, 160
    intervention in, 158
    NAFTA and, 298
middle class, 68, 113
Middle Colonies, settlers in, 16–17
Middle East, 254, 293, 297, 300–301, 305,
    306 See also Arab-Israeli wars, Camp
    David Accords
Middle Passage, 19
Midway, annexation of, 150

Midwest, 7

migration. 5, 69, 188 See also immigrants and immigration
  African American, 6, 104, 180, 228
  from industrial regions, 257–258
  westward movement and, 5, 6, 117–118

military. See also Armed forces; specific branches
  African Americans in, 228
  in Civil War, 81
  women in, 227–228

Miller, Glenn, 196

Million Mom March, 309

Milosevic, Slobodan, 296

mining, 119

minorities. See also specific groups
  New Deal and, 201–202, 206
  rights of, 48
  World War I and, 179

Miranda v. Arizona, 47, 261, 270, 286, A-11

missionaries, expansionism and, 151

Mississippi River region, 3, 54

Missouri Compromise, 77, 79

Mitchell, John, 146

Mondale, Walter, 293, A-6

money, Federal Reserve and, 147

monopolies, 104, 146

Monroe, James, 56, A-1

Monroe Doctrine, 56, 157–158, 219, 274
  Roosevelt Corollary to, 152, 157–158, 274

Montesquieu, Baron de, 21, A-18

Montgomery bus boycott, 259–261

Montoya, Joseph, 270

moon landing, 286

Morgan, J. Pierpont, 106

Mormons, 76

Morrill Land Grant Act, 81

motion pictures. See movies

Mott, Lucretia, 75

mountains. See specific mountains

movement, of early peoples, 5–7

movies, 183–184, 190, 196

muckrakers, 139–140

Muhammad Ali, 279

Muir, John, 146, A-18

Muller v. Oregon, 137–138, 146, A-9

Munich Agreement (1938), 221–222

municipal reforms, 143

Munn v. Illinois, 103, 107, 119

Musharraf, Pervez, 302

music, 19, 185, 196

musical theater, 196

Muslims. See also Islamic fundamentalists
  Black Muslims and, 266

Mussolini, Benito, 205, 220, 222

N

NAACP. See National Association for the Advancement of Colored People (NAACP)

Nader, Ralph, 287, 303, A-18

NAFTA. See North American Free Trade Agreement (NAFTA)

Nagasaki, bombing of, 225

Nasser, Gamal Abdel, 254

Nast, Thomas, 98

National American Woman Suffrage Association (NAWSA), 141, 186

National Association for the Advancement of Colored People (NAACP), 137, 142, 259, 264

national bank
  First, 51
  Second, 67, 72–73, 147

National Child Labor Committee, 141

National Commission on Terrorist Attacks, 309

national conventions, 39–40

national debt, 181

National Industrial Recovery Act (1933), 199

National Intelligence Director, 307

nationalism, 66, 152
  World War I and, 159–160

Nationalist Chinese, 236

National Labor Relations Act (Wagner Act, 1935), 190, 200

National Liberation Front (NLF), 277

National Origins Act (1924), 117

National Park Service, 137, 148

National Reclamation Act (1902), 148

National (Newlands) Reclamation Act (1902), 146

National Recovery Act (NRA), 199, 204

National Rifle Association, 309

national security
  after World War II, 230
  concerns about, 307
  legislation for, 239

National Security Act (1947), 230

Nation of Islam, 266

Native Americans, 5, 6, 13–15, 115
  as British allies, 26, 56
  citizenship, 48, 182, 201
  Dawes Act, 48, 117-118, 201
  equal rights for, 270–271
  Indian Reorganization Act and, 190, 201–202, 270
  land transfer before 1850, 74
  New Deal and, 201–202
  in 1920s, 182
  Removal Policy, 48, 73–74
  westward movement and, 6, 117–118

nativism, 116, 164, 187, 188

NATO. See North Atlantic Treaty Organization (NATO)

natural disasters, 310–311

natural law, 107

natural rights, 20, 24

Navigation Acts, 15, 24

navy, 150, 159. See also armed forces

Nazi Germany, 219–220
  Holocaust and, 226

Nazi-Soviet Pact, 219, 233

Negroponte, John, 307

Neutrality Acts of 1935, 1936, 1937, 220, 222

neutrality policy, 56
  after World War I, 219–220
  of Washington, George, 52, 219

New Deal, 189, 190, 196–206
  organized labor and, 201
  stages of, 203
  Supreme Court and, 204

New England
  economy in, 16, 17, 18, 56
  factory system in, 68
  settlement of, 5, 16, 17
  Town Meetings, 22

New Federalism, 286

New Freedom, 144, 147

New Frontier, 273

new immigration, 115–116

New Jersey Plan, 30

New Jersey v. T.L.O., 47, A-12

New Nationalism, 147

New Netherland, 15

New Orleans, 54, 310–311

New South, 104

newspapers, yellow journalism and, 154

New York City, 67–68
  terrorist attacks of September 11, 2001, 300

New York Morning Journal, 154

New York State
  constitution of, 29, 45
  federal government compared with, 46–50
  first state constitution in, 28
  Native Americans and, 271
  New Netherland as, 15

New York Times Co. v. United States, 47, 140, A-11

New York World, 154

Niagara Movement, 142

Nicaragua, 158, 179
  intervention in, 292
  Iran-Contra affair and, 293

Nineteenth Amendment, 45, 142, 148, 267

Ninth Amendment, 44

Nisei, 228–229

density of, 4
diversity of, 308
growth of, 111
of Native Americans, 13
urban and rural, 68, 112, 113
Populist party, 119–120
Porter, Cole, 196
potato famine, 69, 115
Potsdam Conference, (1945), 224
poverty, 140, 273, 309. *See also* poor
people
Powderly, Terence, 108
power(s)
of Congress, 36–37
in Constitution (U.S.), 33, 35
limits on, 282
presidential, 49
Powhatan, 14
Powhatan Confederacy, 14–15
prejudice, against immigrants, 116, 117
presidency
four-year term of, 31
path to, 40
two-term limit on, 52
president(s), 42. *See also specific
presidents*
election of, 39, 40, 41, 54, 71
list of, A-1–A-6
roles and powers of, 41, 49
press, freedom of, 22
primary elections, 39–40, 144
Proclamation of 1763, 23
Proclamation of Neutrality (1793), 52,
219
programs of inclusion, 272
Progressive Era, 135–136
American Empire during, 155
legislation during (list), 148
reforms in, 137–138
Roosevelt, Theodore, and, 144–146
Taft and, 146–147
Progressive party, of 1912, 144
Progressives
characteristics of, 139
government action and, 143–144
New Deal and, 206
voluntary organizations and, 139
Prohibition, 75, 140–141, 188
propaganda, in World War I, 161, 163
property rights, 21, 49
prosperity. *See also* Great Depression
in 1920s, 180–183
in 1990s, 297
Prosser, Gabriel, 71
protective tariffs, 52, 67, 167, 181
Protestantism, immigrants and, 69
protests
American Revolution and, 25
against taxation, 24
against Vietnam War, 279

public schools. *See also* education;
schools
expansion of, 308
reform of, 74
**Public Works Administration
(PWA, 1933),** 198–199
Puerto Rico and Puerto Ricans, 155–156,
188
Pulitzer, Joseph, 154, A-19
Pullman Strike, 105, 110
Pure Food and Drug Act (1906), 137, 140,
145, 148
Puritan work ethic, 106

Q

Quakers, 27
quarantine speech, 219, 220
Quayle, Dan, 296
quotas
on immigrants, 117, 188
racial, 269

R

race and racism
missionary movement and, 151
slavery and, 18–19
race riots, 228, 266
radicalism, 205
Radical Reconstruction, 97
Radical Republicans, 97
radio, 183, 190, 196
railroads, 67, 105, 119, 150
regulation of, 107–108, 119, 145
strikes against, 109
transcontinental, 81, 103
Rankin, Jeannette, 140, 167
ratification, of Constitution, 31–32
rationing, 227
raw materials, 150
Reagan, Nancy, 294
Reagan, Ronald, 291–294, A-6
domestic policies of, 291–293
foreign policy of, 292–294
Realpolitik, 284
recall, 144
recession, after World War I, 181
Reconstruction, 97–101
recovery legislation, in New Deal,
198–199
Red Cloud's War, 118
"Red Power," 271
Red Scare, (1918–1919), 47, 164, 165, 187,
239
referendum, 143
reform and reform movements. *See also*
civil rights movement; women's rights
movement; *specific reforms*
African American rights and, 142

for city and state government,
143–144
conservation movement and, 146
consumer rights movement as, 287
educational, 299
in 1800s, 74–75
Knights of Labor and, 108
muckrakers and, 139–140
in Progressive Era, 136–143
reform legislation, in New Deal, 200
*Regents of the University of California
v. Bakke,* 269
regions, 7–8
regulation, 107–108
after World War I, 181
of business, 145, 147–148
of communication, 147
of railroads, 119
Rehabilitation Act (1973), 272
relative location, 2
relief legislation, in New Deal, 198–200
religion. *See also specific religions*
disestablishment of churches and, 29
Great Awakening and, 24
of immigrants, 115
missionaries and, 151
as reason for colonial settlement, 16
Second Great Awakening and, 74
of slaves, 71
relocation, of Japanese Americans,
228–229
removal, of Indians, 73–74
reparations, after World War I, 167
representation, 19–20, 49
republic, 19–20
republican government, in states,
28–29
Republican Party, 99
New Deal and, 206
rise of, 79
Republicans. *See also* Democratic-
Republicans
of Jefferson and Madison, 54
Republic of Texas, 76–77
reservations (Indian), 118, 271
reserved powers, 35
resistance
by slaves, 19, 71
to Vietnam War, 279
restraint, 54
**reverse discrimination, affirmative action
as,** 269
revivalism, 74
revolts and rebellions
Shays' Rebellion, 28
by slaves, 19, 71
Whiskey Rebellion, 52
Revolutionary War. *See* American
Revolution

Acknowledgments

Photographs:

Every effort has been made to secure permission and provide appropriate credit for photographic material. The publisher deeply regrets any omission and pledges to correct errors called to its attention in subsequent editions. Unless otherwise acknowledged, all photographs are the property of Pearson Education, Inc. Photo locators denoted as follows: Top (T), Center (C), Bottom (B), Left (L), Right (R), Background (Bkgd)

Cover ©JustASC/Shutterstock; **i** (C) ©JustASC/Shutterstock; **xii** (C) Prints & Photographs Division, Library of Congress; **xxvi** Elliott Erwitt/©Magnum Photos; **11** Architect of the Capitol; **14** Steve Kelley/Creators Syndicate; **23** (T) Prints and Photographs Division, LC-USZC4-5315/Library of Congress; **83** Library of Congress; **95** W. P. Snyder/Library of Congress; **101** (R) Cheynes Studio/Library of Congress, (L) Cornelius M/. Battey/Library of Congress; **106** Library of Congress; **110** G. W. Peters/Library of Congress; **112** Frances Benjamin Johnston Collection/Library of Congress Prints and Photographs Division [LC-USZ62-1234]/Library of Congress; **118** Library of Congress; **119** (R, L) Library of Congress; **128** Library of Congress; **135** Library of Congress; **145** Library of Congress; **158** Louis Dalrymple/©The Granger Collection, NY; **161** Bettman/Corbis; **164** Library of Congress; **166** Stock Montage Inc.; **177** Lewis Wickes Hine/National Archives; **181** Library of Congress; **184** Library of Congress; **186** Getty Images; **188** Library of Congress; **195** National Archives; **197** (R) ©PARS International Corp., (L) Kennedy Berryman/©PARS International Corp.; **198** National Archives; **205** Clifford Kennedy Berryman/©PARS International Corp.; **215** National Archives; **217** J. Howard Miller/Produced by Westinghouse for the War Production Coordinating Committee/NARA Still Picture Branch [NWDNS-179-WP-1563]/National Archives; **227** Library of Congress; **229** Library of Congress; **233** D.R. Fitzpatrick (1947)/©The Granger Collection, NY; **237** Courtesy U. S. Army Corps of Engineers; **247** Ernest Howard Shepard/The Art Archive; **251** Warren K. Leffler/Library of Congress; **257** ©The Granger Collection, NY; **269** Dana Fradon/Cartoon Bank/ Conde Nast Publications; **273** National Archives; **290** Warren K. Leffler/Library of Congress Prints and Photographs Division [LC-DIG-ppmsca-09791]/Library of Congress; **291** Courtesy of the Ronald Reagan Presidential Foundation and Library/The White House; **297** Steve Sack/Creators Syndicate; **303** Pete Souza/The White House; **306** MANDEL NGAN/ AFP/Getty Images/Newscom; **308** Casey Christie/ZUMA Press/Newscom; **309** White House Photo/Alamy Stock Photo; **313** Petty Officer 2nd Class Kyle Niemi/U. S. Naval Academy; **322** The Herb Block Foundation. **Regents Exams: January 2017 7** N. C. Wyeth, U. S. Department of the Treasury, 1942; **7** Weimer Pursell, Office of Price Administration, 1943; **10** U. S. Department of Homeland Security (adapted); **11** U. S. Census Bureau (adapted); **22** Ray O. Evans, The Columbus Dispatch, February 10, 1937 (adapted); **August 2016 4** Bailey and Kennedy, The American Pageant, D. C. Heath and Company (adapted); **6** Jacob Riis, How the Other Half Lives, 1890; **7** Historical Statistics of the United States, U. S. Bureau of the Census; **8** U. S. National Archives & Records Administration; **10** Pat Oliphant, The Denver Post, December 29, 1967 (adapted); **15** The Digital Scriptorium, Duke University Libraries (adapted); **23** U. S. Census, 2000; **June 2016 6** John McCutcheon, Chicago Tribune, 1919 (adapted); **7** Farm Security Administration; Historical Statistics of the United States; **9** Marinship Corp., National Archives, 1942; Office of Wat Information 1943; **12** Jeff Stahler, The Columbus Dispatch, March 7, 2009 (adapted); **13** U.S. Department of Homeland Security (adapted); **18** J. S. Pughe, Puck, September 5, 1900 (adapted); **22** Tim Kane, Heritage Foundation, 2006 (adapted); **January 2016 05** U. S. Urban/Rural Population, 1850–1900; U.S. Bureau of the Census, **06** The Granger Collection, New York, **07** Library of Congress Prints and Photographs Division Washington, D.C. 20540, **08** Harris & Ewing, Washington, D.C. [Virginia Arnold holding Kaiser Wilson banner]. [Aug.?, 1917] Image. Retrieved from the Library of Congress, **11** Civilian Exclusion order; Western Historical Manuscript Collection, University of Missouri-St. Louis, **12** Published by Fawcett Books, **14** Copyright © 2009 The Record (Hackensack, NJ)/Jimmy Margulies, **15** ©Universal UClick. Used with permission., **20** Irving F. Ahlquist et al., United States History, Addison-Wesley, 1984 (adapted), **21** The Granger Collection, New York, **24** The Granger Collection, New York; **August 2015 07** World War II Poster Collection at Northwestern University Library/https://images.northwestern.edu/multiresimages/inu:dil-e099b32d-f48e-42b7-9219-e95ee3884114, **10** A 1973 Herblock Cartoon, © The Herb Block Foundation, **19** Robert A. Divine et al., America: Past and Present, Longman, 1999 (adapted), **21** From THE AMERICANS, Student Edition. Copyright © 1998 by McDougal Littell Inc. All rights reserved. Reprinted by permission of the publisher, Houghton Mifflin Harcourt Publishing Company.; **June 2015 04** Jacques W. Redway, F.R.G.S., The Redway School History (New York, NY: Silver, Burdett and Company, 1911) 241, **08** Robert A. Divine et al., America: Past and Present, Addison Wesley Longman, 1999, **18** Irving F. Ahlquist et al., United States History, Addison-Wesley, 1984, **20** © North Wind Picture Archives. All Rights Reserved, **24** The Granger Collection, New York.

This section contains the Regents Examination in United States History and Government that was given in New York State in January 2017.

Circle your answers to Part I on this exam and write your answers to the thematic essay and document-based essay questions on separate sheets of paper. Be sure to refer to the test-taking strategies in the front of this book as you prepare to answer the test questions.

Part I

Answer all questions in this part.

Directions (1–50): For each statement or question, record on your separate answer sheet the *number* of the word or expression that, of those given, best completes the statement or answers the question.

1 New England's geographic features most directly influenced the region's development of
 (1) industry
 (2) sugar mills
 (3) large plantations
 (4) tenant farming

2 • Colonists protest the Stamp Act.
 • Sons of Liberty groups are formed.
 • Crates of tea are thrown into Boston Harbor.
 • Parliament passes Coercive Acts.

 These events helped lead to the
 (1) French and Indian War
 (2) Revolutionary War
 (3) Whiskey Rebellion
 (4) War of 1812

3 Which heading best completes the partial outline below?

 I._____
   A. National government unable to levy direct taxes
   B. No single national currency
   C. Lack of an elected chief executive

 (1) Weaknesses of the Articles of Confederation
 (2) Strengths of the Continental Congress
 (3) Provisions of the United States Constitution
 (4) Influence of Treaties with European Governments

4 During the debate over ratification of the United States Constitution, Antifederalists argued that a bill of rights should be added to
 (1) preserve the interests of slaveholders
 (2) list the responsibilities of citizens
 (3) protect individual liberties
 (4) ensure federal supremacy

Base your answer to question 5 on the passage below and on your knowledge of social studies.

Congress shall make no law respecting an establishment of religion, or prohibiting the free exercise thereof; or abridging the freedom of speech, or of the press; or the right of the people peaceably to assemble, and to petition the Government for a redress of grievances.
—First amendment, United States Constitution

5 What is one impact of this amendment on American society?
 (1) Congress cannot mandate a national religion.
 (2) Religious groups cannot lobby Congress.
 (3) Members of the press cannot hold public office.
 (4) The Supreme Court cannot limit free speech during wartime.

6 The Supreme Court can influence the actions of the other two branches of the federal government by
 (1) vetoing legislation
 (2) pardoning criminals
 (3) exercising judicial review
 (4) impeaching the president

7 In 1790, the first census of the United States was taken in order to
 (1) create immigration quotas
 (2) determine each state's representation in Congress
 (3) establish the number of appointed federal judges
 (4) justify funding for public education

8 Which group benefited the most from the United States acquisition of the port of New Orleans?

(1) farmers in the Ohio River valley
(2) Native American Indians in the Southwest
(3) fur trappers in the Hudson River valley
(4) gold miners in northern California

9 A major reason for the issuance of the Monroe Doctrine (1823) was to

(1) improve trade relations with Asia
(2) gain new colonies in Latin America
(3) acquire land to build a canal in Central America
(4) limit European influence in the Western Hemisphere

10 A major reason for President Andrew Jackson's policy toward the Cherokee Nation was to

(1) provide Native American Indians with better farmland
(2) enforce the United States Supreme Court decision in *Worcester* v. *Georgia* (1832)
(3) obtain land from Native American Indians for white settlers
(4) gain the political support of Native American Indians

11 Which quotation best represents the idea of Manifest Destiny?

(1) "American interests are best served by strict isolationism."
(2) "The passage of protective tariffs will encourage industrial development."
(3) "Immigration is the key to the nation's economic growth."
(4) "The United States has a duty to spread American ideals westward."

12 . . ."We hold these truths to be self-evident: that all men and women are created equal; . . ."

—Seneca Falls Convention, 1848

Which document most influenced the authors of this statement?

(1) Mayflower Compact
(2) Albany Plan of Union
(3) Declaration of Independence
(4) Articles of Confederation

13 The Homestead Act (1862) encouraged the settlement of the West because it provided

(1) forty acres of land and a mule to formerly enslaved persons
(2) land to people who would live on it for at least five years
(3) mining claims for prospectors seeking gold and silver
(4) land to companies to build transcontinental railroads

14 What was one major result of the North's victory in the Civil War?

(1) The power of the Supreme Court was limited.
(2) Slave owners were compensated for their losses.
(3) The influence of corporations on government was reduced.
(4) The supremacy of the national government was upheld.

15 One way in which Andrew Carnegie and John D. Rockefeller are similar is that they both

(1) served in the United States Congress
(2) treated their workers with respect
(3) gave large sums of money to charitable causes
(4) made fortunes in the automobile industry

16 During the late 1800s, the use of child labor in United States factories was most opposed by

(1) parents   (3) labor unions
(2) nativists   (4) factory owners

17 In the late 1800s, an increased demand for raw materials and a desire for new markets contributed to the United States adopting a policy of

(1) imperialism   (3) collective security
(2) pacifism   (4) isolationism

18 ". . .You come to us and tell us that the great cities are in favor of the gold standard; we reply that the great cities rest upon our broad and fertile prairies. Burn down your cities and leave our farms, and your cities will spring up again as if by magic; but destroy our farms and the grass will grow in the streets of every city in the country. . . ."

— William Jennings Bryan, 1896

In the late 19th century, farmers attempted to address the issue raised by William Jennings Bryan by

(1) supporting the Populist Party
(2) demanding higher tariffs
(3) providing jobs for the unemployed
(4) lobbying Congress to cut income taxes

19 What was one result of the Supreme Court decision in *Plessy* v. *Ferguson* (1896)?

(1) Public schools were integrated nationwide.
(2) Civil rights for African Americans were strengthened.
(3) Northern states were forced to segregate public facilities.
(4) The "separate but equal" doctrine was established.

20 One major result of the Spanish-American War was that the United States

(1) formed an alliance with England
(2) gained recognition as a world power
(3) repealed the Monroe Doctrine
(4) decreased the size of its navy

21 A common goal of Lincoln Steffens, Frank Norris, and Ida Tarbell was to

(1) encourage government officials to decrease the regulation of business
(2) publicize the achievements of the captains of industry
(3) create a demand for new political parties to replace the two major parties
(4) increase public awareness of social, political, and economic problems

22 During the Progressive Era, direct primary elections were adopted to

(1) raise additional campaign funds for candidates
(2) increase the power of voters in the political process
(3) strengthen the role of political machines
(4) expand the power of the federal government

23 President Theodore Roosevelt was called a trustbuster because he

(1) directed the building of the Panama Canal
(2) encouraged conservation of natural resources
(3) supported legal action against business monopolies
(4) resigned from the Republican Party

24 What was President Woodrow Wilson's stated policy toward the warring nations of Europe prior to United States entry into World War I?

(1) neutrality   (3) internationalism
(2) containment   (4) dollar diplomacy

25 Which statement about the United States economy during the 1920s is true?

(1) Federal regulation of business was strengthened.
(2) The purchase of stocks steadily declined.
(3) Mass production increased the supply of consumer goods.
(4) Republican Party presidents supported unemployment insurance.

Base your answer to question 26 on the cartoon below and on your knowledge of social studies.

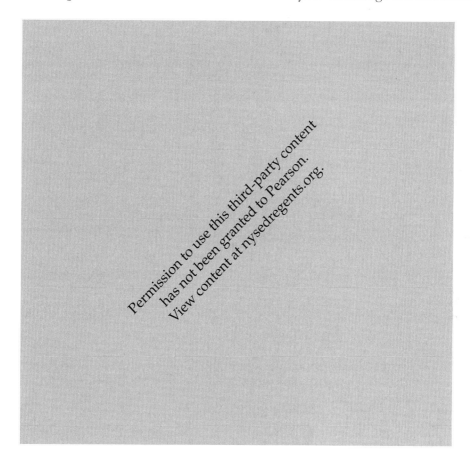

Permission to use this third-party content has not been granted to Pearson. View content at nysedregents.org.

26 This cartoon is portraying a situation that resulted from the
   (1) public rejection of the New Deal
   (2) economic downturn of the late 1920s
   (3) failure of the Civilian Conservation Corps
   (4) opposition to the Treaty of Versailles

27 President Franklin D. Roosevelt believed that declaring a bank holiday and creating the Federal Deposit Insurance Corporation (FDIC) would aid the nation's banking system by

(1) restricting foreign investments
(2) eliminating government regulation of banks
(3) restoring public confidence in banks
(4) granting tax relief

Base your answer to question 28 on the passage below and on your knowledge of social studies.

. . . I see one-third of a nation ill-housed, ill-clad, ill-nourished.

It is not in despair that I paint you that picture. I paint it for you in hope—because the Nation, seeing and understanding the injustice in it, proposes to paint it out. We are determined to make every American citizen the subject of his country's interest and concern; and we will never regard any faithful, law-abiding group within our borders as superfluous. The test of our progress is not whether we add more to the abundance of those who have much; it is whether we provide enough for those who have too little. . . .

—President Franklin D. Roosevelt, Second Inaugural Address, January 20, 1937

28 President Franklin D. Roosevelt addressed the situation described in this speech by

(1) reducing the influence of labor unions
(2) supporting programs to aid the poor and unemployed
(3) promoting the interests of big business
(4) adopting the trickle-down economic theory

29 The Neutrality Acts of 1935 and 1937 were enacted by Congress to

(1) help the United States recover from the Great Depression
(2) stop Nazi Germany from conquering Europe
(3) aid the Americans who fought in the Spanish Civil War
(4) prevent the United States from being drawn into another world war

30 "Yesterday, December 7, 1941—a date which will live in infamy—the United States of America was suddenly and deliberately attacked by naval and air forces of the Empire of Japan. . . ."

—President Franklin D. Roosevelt, Address to Congress, December 8, 1941

In this statement, President Roosevelt was addressing Congress about the

(1) sinking of merchant ships in the Atlantic Ocean
(2) D-Day invasion of France
(3) bombing of Pearl Harbor
(4) air raids on the Panama Canal

31 During World War II, the federal government was accused of violating constitutional rights by

(1) signing the Yalta Agreement
(2) implementing a draft to expand the armed forces
(3) relocating Japanese Americans to internment camps
(4) initiating the secret Manhattan Project

Base your answer to question 32 on the posters below and on your knowledge of social studies.

Source: N.C. Wyeth,
U.S. Department of the Treasury, 1942

Source: Weimer Pursell,
Office of Price Administration, 1943

32 These World War II posters encouraged Americans to

(1) demand higher wages
(2) enlist in the armed services
(3) purchase new automobiles
(4) support home-front war efforts

33 Which standard of justice was applied to Nazi leaders who were tried at Nuremberg after World War II?

(1) Military attacks on civilian populations are legal.
(2) Individuals can be held personally responsible for war crimes.
(3) Military officers are not accountable for crimes if they were obeying orders.
(4) Only the League of Nations can determine international law.

34 What was the purpose of the Berlin airlift?

(1) supplying West Berlin with necessities during the Soviet blockade
(2) helping defeat the German military
(3) assisting people trying to escape from East Berlin
(4) forcing the Soviet Union to end its occupation of East Germany

35 During the 1960s, members of the Student Nonviolent Coordinating Committee (SNCC) used sit-ins primarily to

(1) protest high college tuition costs
(2) promote passage of clean air laws
(3) support voting rights for 18-year-old citizens
(4) challenge racially segregated public facilities

36 What was a major result of the Cuban missile crisis of 1962?

(1) Fidel Castro was removed from power.
(2) Steps were taken to relax Cold War tensions.
(3) United Nations forces invaded Cuba.
(4) Trade between Cuba and the United States increased.

37 President Kennedy created the Peace Corps in the 1960s to

(1) fight revolutionaries in democratic nations with military force
(2) improve economic conditions in developing countries
(3) rebuild United States cities through urban renewal
(4) overthrow Soviet control in Eastern Europe

38 Which statement about the Vietnam War is an opinion?

(1) President Lyndon B. Johnson's escalation of the war was a mistake.
(2) United States forces withdrew from Vietnam during the presidency of Gerald Ford.
(3) Disagreement over the war divided the American public.
(4) The Vietnam War had been the longest military conflict in United States history.

39 The SALT I and SALT II agreements of the 1970s tried to improve Cold War relations between the United States and the Soviet Union by

(1) encouraging space exploration
(2) increasing cultural exchanges
(3) lowering barriers to trade
(4) limiting nuclear weapons

40 What was a major achievement of the presidency of Jimmy Carter?

(1) uniting East Germany and West Germany
(2) negotiating the peace accord between Egypt and Israel at Camp David
(3) ending United States dependence on imported oil
(4) rescuing United States hostages in Iran

41 President Ronald Reagan supported supply-side economics through reduced tax rates to

(1) encourage economic growth
(2) create more public-works jobs
(3) increase government regulation of business
(4) decrease defense spending

42 The North American Free Trade Agreement (NAFTA) and the General Agreement on Tariffs and Trade (GATT) were created primarily to

(1) support environmentalism
(2) maintain mutual defense
(3) improve public health worldwide
(4) promote economic interdependence

Base your answer to question 43 on the cartoon below and on your knowledge of social studies.

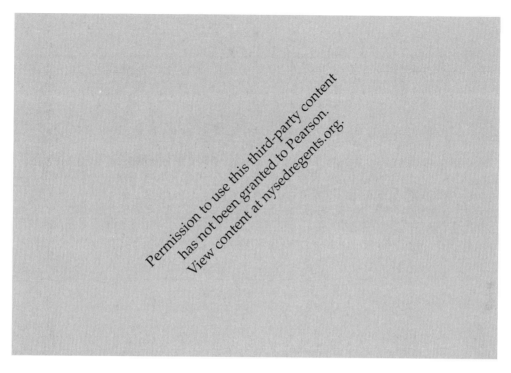

Permission to use this third-party content has not been granted to Pearson. View content at nysedregents.org.

43 This cartoon illustrates that actions taken during times of crisis have sometimes led to concerns about the functioning of

(1) federalism
(2) salutary neglect
(3) checks and balances
(4) bicameral legislatures

44 The decisions of the Supreme Court under Chief Justice John Marshall and under Chief Justice Earl Warren demonstrate that

(1) the Supreme Court can greatly influence economic and social change
(2) chief justices have little influence over the rest of the Supreme Court
(3) Supreme Court decisions must be approved by the president
(4) states can overturn decisions of the Supreme Court

45 ". . . Under a government which imprisons any unjustly, the true place for a just man is also a prison. . . ."

—Henry David Thoreau

Which leader's reform efforts reflect the idea in this statement by Thoreau?

(1) Booker T. Washington's support for vocational education
(2) Jane Addams's establishment of Hull House
(3) Rachel Carson's books about the environment
(4) Martin Luther King Jr.'s advocacy of civil disobedience

Base your answer to question 46 on the graph below and on your knowledge of social studies.

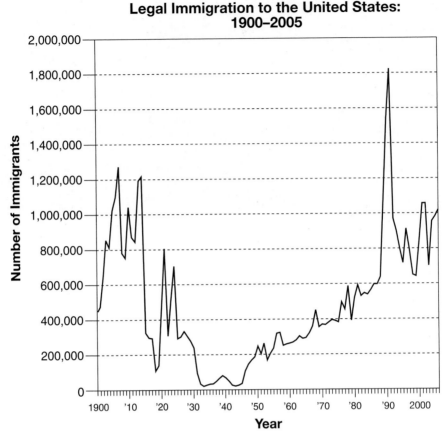

**Legal Immigration to the United States:
1900–2005**

Source: U. S. Department of Homeland Security (adapted)

46 Which statement is best supported by the information provided in this graph?

(1) Each year since 1950, immigration has increased.

(2) Quotas favored immigration from southern and eastern Europe.

(3) Immigration declined during world wars and economic hard times.

(4) Every year since 1920, at least one million people have come to the United States.

47 One way in which President Abraham Lincoln's suspension of habeas corpus (1861), the Espionage Act (1917), and the USA Patriot Act (2001) are similar is that these actions

(1) enforced international treaties

(2) expanded political cooperation

(3) encouraged economic development

(4) restricted civil liberties during wartime

48 The Harlem Renaissance was influenced by the

(1) migration of African Americans from the rural South to the urban North

(2) passage of federal laws outlawing racial discrimination in public facilities

(3) racial integration of the military during World War I

(4) use of affirmative action after World War II

Base your answers to questions 49 and 50 on the graph below and on your knowledge of social studies.

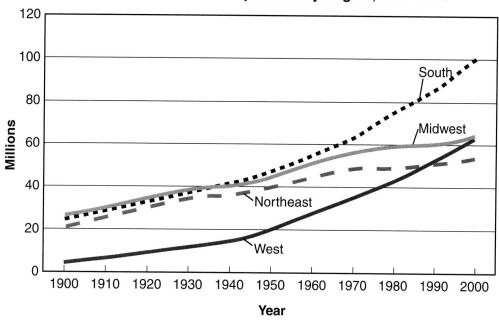

Total United States Population by Region, 1900–2000

Source: U.S. Census Bureau (adapted)

49 Which section of the country gained the most population in the years shown on the graph?

(1) South　　　　　　　　　(3) Northeast
(2) Midwest　　　　　　　　(4) West

50 What is one effect the population changes shown in the graph have had on national politics?

(1) reducing the number of senators from the Midwest
(2) increasing the representation of the South and West in Congress
(3) enhancing the chances for election of presidential candidates from the Northeast
(4) strengthening the Democratic Party's control of the South

This page left blank intentionally.

Answers to the essay questions are to be written in the separate essay booklet.

In developing your answer to Part II, be sure to keep these general definitions in mind:

    (a) <u>describe</u> means "to illustrate something in words or tell about it"

    (b) <u>discuss</u> means "to make observations about something using facts, reasoning, and argument; to present in some detail"

Part II

THEMATIC ESSAY QUESTION

Directions: Write a well-organized essay that includes an introduction, several paragraphs addressing the task below, and a conclusion.

Theme: Cultural and Intellectual Life—Influence of Mass Media

> Since the earliest days of the nation, mass media have significantly influenced the political, economic, and social life of the United States and American society. These media include pamphlets, newspapers, books, magazines, posters, photographs, radio, films, and television.

Task:

> Select *two* examples in which mass media have influenced the United States and for *each*
>
> • Describe the historical circumstances surrounding the issue addressed by mass media
>
> • Discuss *positive **and/or*** *negative* effects of this use of mass media on the United States and/or American society

You may use any example in which mass media have influenced the political, economic, and/or social life of the United States. Some suggestions you might wish to consider include:

Common Sense—Thomas Paine
Uncle Tom's Cabin—Harriet Beecher Stowe
yellow journalism—William Randolph Hearst and Joseph Pulitzer
How the Other Half Lives—Jacob Riis
The Jungle—Upton Sinclair
fireside chats—President Franklin D. Roosevelt
photo journalism—civil rights protests
televised nightly newscasts—Vietnam War
Washington Post—investigation of the Nixon administration

You are *not* limited to these suggestions.

Guidelines:

    In your essay, be sure to
      • Develop all aspects of the task
      • Support the theme with relevant facts, examples, and details
      • Use a logical and clear plan of organization, including an introduction and a conclusion that are beyond a restatement of the theme

This page left blank intentionally.

NAME _____ SCHOOL _____

Part III

DOCUMENT-BASED QUESTION

This question is based on the accompanying documents. The question is designed to test your ability to work with historical documents. Some of these documents have been edited for the purposes of this question. As you analyze the documents, take into account the source of each document and any point of view that may be presented in the document. Keep in mind that the language used in a document may reflect the historical context of the time in which it was written.

Historical Context:

Throughout United States history, presidents have made proposals to deal with important issues facing the nation. Members of Congress have not always agreed with these proposals. The outcomes of these situations have affected the United States and American society. These issues have included **the Mexican-American War and President James K. Polk, Reconstruction and Presidents Abraham Lincoln and Andrew Johnson,** and **Supreme Court decisions and President Franklin D. Roosevelt.**

Task: Using the information from the documents and your knowledge of United States history, answer the questions that follow each document in Part A. Your answers to the questions will help you write the Part B essay in which you will be asked to

> Select *two* issues mentioned in the historical context and for *each*
> - Describe the president's position on the issue
> - Describe congressional opposition to the president's position
> - Discuss how the outcome of the situation influenced the United States and/or American society

In developing your answers to Part III, be sure to keep these general definitions in mind:

(a) <u>describe</u> means "to illustrate something in words or tell about it"

(b) <u>discuss</u> means "to make observations about something using facts, reasoning, and argument; to present in some detail"

Part A
Short-Answer Questions

Directions: Analyze the documents and answer the short-answer questions that follow each document in the space provided.

Document 1

> . . . The grievous wrongs perpetrated by Mexico upon our citizens throughout a long period of years remain unredressed [uncorrected], and solemn treaties pledging her public faith for this redress have been disregarded. A government either unable or unwilling to enforce the execution of such treaties fails to perform one of its plainest duties. . . .
>
> Instead of this, however, we have been exerting our best efforts to propitiate [gain] her good will. Upon the pretext that Texas, a nation as independent as herself, thought proper to unite its destinies with our own she has affected to believe that we have severed her rightful territory, and in official proclamations and manifestoes has repeatedly threatened to make war upon us for the purpose of reconquering Texas. In the meantime we have tried every effort at reconciliation. The cup of forbearance [patience] had been exhausted even before the recent information from the frontier of the Del Norte [Rio Grande]. But now, after reiterated menaces, Mexico has passed the boundary of the United States, has invaded our territory and shed American blood upon the American soil. She has proclaimed that hostilities have commenced, and that the two nations are now at war.
>
> As war exists, and, notwithstanding [despite] all our efforts to avoid it, exists by the act of Mexico herself, we are called upon by every consideration of duty and patriotism to vindicate [justify] with decision the honor, the rights, and the interests of our country. . . .

Source: President James K. Polk, Special Message to Congress on Mexican Relations, May 11, 1846

1 According to his message to Congress, what is **one** reason President James Polk supports war with Mexico? [1]

_____

_____

Score ☐

Document 2

. . . The prompt and overwhelming vote in Congress for war—174 to 14 in the House and 40 to 2 in the Senate—is deceptive. Aroused by the loss of American lives, all sections and all parties at first enthusiastically endorsed the conflict. Popular slogans were "Ho for the Halls of the Montezumas!" and "Mexico or Death!" But gradually considerable sentiment developed against fighting "Jimmy Polk's War," especially among the opposition Whig party and the antislavery men. One abolitionist Congressman denounced the conflict as "unholy, unrighteous, and damnable." The distinguished Whig orator, Senator [Thomas] Corwin of Ohio, declared in a memorable speech [February 11, 1847] that if he were a Mexican he would say to the Americans, "Have you not room in your own country to bury your dead men? If you come into mine, we will greet you with bloody hands; and welcome you to hospitable graves."

Abraham Lincoln, who entered the House as a Whig some months after the war began, joined the dissenters. Through his famous "spot resolutions," which caused him to be dubbed the "spotty Lincoln," he demanded to know the precise "spot" on American soil where the shooting had begun. Certainly Polk would have been much nearer the truth if he had said that "American blood has been shed on soil in dispute between the United States and Mexico"—soil to which Mexico perhaps had a better technical claim than the United States. . . .

Source: Thomas A. Bailey, *A Diplomatic History of the American People,* Prentice-Hall, 1974 (adapted)

2 According to Thomas A. Bailey, what was ***one*** reason members of Congress opposed war with Mexico? [1]

_____

_____

Score ☐

Document 3a

United States Acquisitions from Mexico, 1848

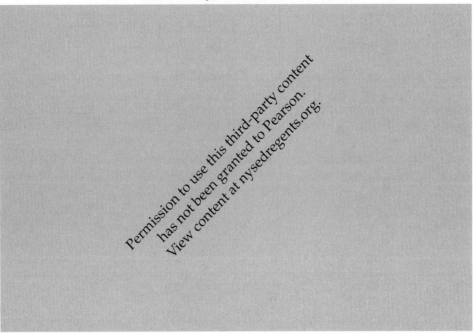

Document 3b

> . . . But Congress itself was split over the question of slavery, and California's statehood threatened that balance. Congress had once hoped that the issue of slavery's extension had been settled forever by the Missouri Compromise of 1820, which barred slavery in most of the West. But the defeat of Mexico—and the sudden acquisition of so many hundreds of thousands of square miles—had changed everything. . . .

Source: Geoffrey C. Ward et al., *The West: An Illustrated History,* Little, Brown and Company, 1996

3 Based on these documents, what were **two** effects of the Mexican-American War on the United States? [2]

(1) _____

_____

Score ☐

(2) _____

_____

Score ☐

Document 4a

. . . Abraham Lincoln believed the President should take the lead in peacemaking, and he was disposed to grant relatively mild conditions of peace. In 1863 he announced his willingness to pardon all rebels (except for certain of the leaders) who would lay down their arms and take an oath of future loyalty to the United States. He also proposed his "ten per cent plan" of reconstruction. According to this plan, ten per cent of the qualified voters (as of 1860) in a seceded state, upon taking the oath, could form a new state government and apply for readmission to the Union. They would have to accept the antislavery measures of Congress and the President, including the Emancipation Proclamation. Before the end of the war, the statemaking process had begun under Lincoln's plan in Louisiana, Arkansas, and Tennessee. . . .

Source: Richard N. Current, ed., *Reconstruction [1865–1877]*, Prentice-Hall, 1965

4a Based on this document, what was **one** proposal made by President Abraham Lincoln concerning the readmission of the South to the Union? [1]

Score

Document 4b

. . . Although Johnson thundered against the Confederate leaders and called for their personal punishment, he believed the states they represented were, in fact, still part of the Union and therefore guaranteed representation in Congress. Thus he desired their immediate restoration—not readmission, because in his view they'd never left. He preferred that this restoration take place after each state had ratified the Thirteenth Amendment abolishing slavery, but he wasn't inclined to insist on even this condition. Nor did he seek any safeguards for the freed people. . . .

Source: Hans L. Trefousse, "Andrew Johnson," in *"To the Best of My Ability": The American Presidents,* edited by James M. McPherson, DK Publishing, 2001

4b Based on this document, what was **one** position taken by President Andrew Johnson concerning the restoration of the South to the Union? [1]

Score

Document 5a

Selected Events from the Era of Reconstruction

1864	• Louisiana, Arkansas, and Tennessee established governments loyal to Union under Lincoln's plan • Wade-Davis Bill passed by Congress
1865	• Johnson tries to readmit rest of Confederate states to Union • Southern States enact Black Codes • Congress establishes Freedmen's Bureau • Congress reconvenes (December) and refuses to admit Southern representatives; creates Joint Committee on Reconstruction
1866	• Congress approves Fourteenth Amendment; most Southern states reject it
1867	• Military Reconstruction Act (and two supplementary acts) outlines congressional plan of Reconstruction • Tenure of Office Act and Command of the Army Act restrict presidential power • Southern states establish Reconstruction governments under congressional plan
1868	• Most Southern states readmitted to Union under congressional plan
1870	• Last Southern states readmitted to Union
1877	• Congressional Reconstruction ends

Source: Richard N. Current et al., *American History: A Survey,* Alfred A. Knopf, 1987 (adapted)

Document 5b

Congressional Reconstruction:
Radical Rule of the South

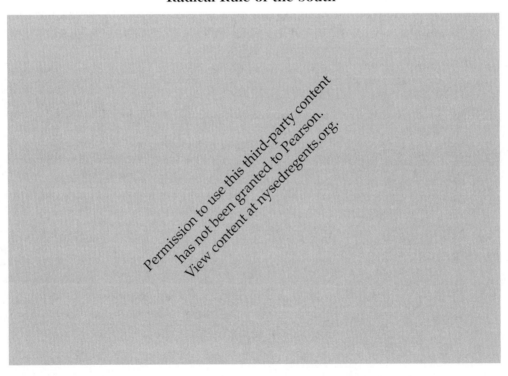

5 Based on this time line and map, identify **two** ways Congress dealt with Reconstruction. [2]

(1) _____

_____

Score ☐

(2) _____

_____

Score ☐

Document 6

The long ordeal of slavery came to an end in 1865 for 4 million African Americans. Suddenly the freedom they had longed for during two centuries of bondage was theirs. The world opened before them: they could freely visit loved ones, attend schools, or run for public office. Blacks soon realized, however, that chains other than slavery still held them. Penniless, they could not afford to buy farms; untrained, they could not move into better jobs. In the 1870s and 1880s they lost many of the privileges they had gained when freed, including the right to vote. Booker T. Washington grew to maturity in years when blacks experienced both the exhilaration of freedom and the humiliation of segregation. He proved in his early life that an ex-slave could prosper by hard work. When in his later years he saw the cords of prejudice tightening around his people, he responded in the best way he knew, advocating self-help in the face of prejudice and segregation. . . .

Source: J. William T. Youngs, "Beyond Emancipation," *American Realities: Historical Episodes,* Longman, 2001

6 According to J. William T. Youngs, what were **two** ways African Americans were affected by the end of slavery and by Reconstruction? [2]

(1) _____

_____

Score ☐

(2) _____

_____

Score ☐

Document 7a

Source: Ray O. Evans, *Columbus Dispatch,* February 10, 1937 (adapted)

7a Based on this political cartoon, why is President Franklin D. Roosevelt upset with the Supreme Court? [1]

_____

_____

Score ☐

Document 7b

President Franklin D. Roosevelt presented a proposal to encourage more cooperation between the three branches of government.

> . . . Last Thursday I described the American form of Government as a three horse team provided by the Constitution to the American people so that their field might be plowed. The three horses are, of course, the three branches of government—the Congress, the Executive and the Courts. Two of the horses are pulling in unison today; the third is not. Those who have intimated [suggested] that the President of the United States is trying to drive that team, overlook the simple fact that the President, as Chief Executive, is himself one of the three horses. . . .
>
> What is my proposal? It is simply this: whenever a Judge or Justice of any Federal Court has reached the age of seventy and does not avail himself of the opportunity to retire on a pension, a new member shall be appointed by the President then in office, with the approval, as required by the Constitution, of the Senate of the United States. . . .

Source: President Franklin D. Roosevelt, March 9, 1937

7b Based on this document, what is President Franklin D. Roosevelt's proposal regarding the Supreme Court? [1]

_____

_____

Score ☐

Document 8

THE JUDICIARY REFORM BILL

. . . [President Franklin D.] Roosevelt's "court-packing" proposal shocked many people, yet constitutionally Congress had the power to decide on the size of the Supreme Court. The President believed that since the Democrats had a majority, they would support him. Instead, however, the party split and many Democrats joined those who opposed the President. There were several reasons for the opposition. Perhaps the most important was that Roosevelt had "sprung" the plan upon his supporters without warning. Another was that, although Congress might be extremely annoyed by the Court, it could not bring itself to interfere with the separation of powers. And Congress, throughout its history, has reacted strongly against executive actions which it regarded as dictatorial. . . .

Source: Leonard F. James, *The Supreme Court In American Life,* Scott, Foresman and Company, 1964

8 According to Leonard F. James, what is **one** reason Congress opposed President Franklin D. Roosevelt's "court-packing" proposal? [1]

_____

_____

Score ☐

Document 9

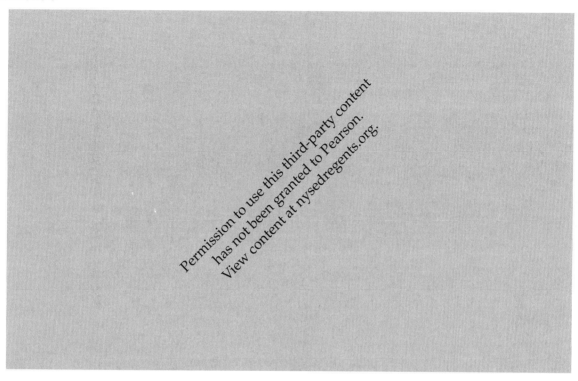

Permission to use this third-party content has not been granted to Pearson. View content at nysedregents.org.

9 According to William E. Leuchtenburg, what was **one** impact of President Franklin D. Roosevelt's attempt to pack the Supreme Court?   [1]

_____

_____

Score [   ]

Part B

Essay

Directions: Write a well-organized essay that includes an introduction, several paragraphs, and a conclusion. Use evidence from at *least four* documents in your essay. Support your response with relevant facts, examples, and details. Include additional outside information.

Historical Context:

Throughout United States history, presidents have made proposals to deal with important issues facing the nation. Members of Congress have not always agreed with these proposals. The outcomes of these situations have affected the United States and American society. These issues have included **the Mexican-American War and President James K. Polk, Reconstruction and Presidents Abraham Lincoln and Andrew Johnson,** and **Supreme Court decisions and President Franklin D. Roosevelt.**

Task: Using the information from the documents and your knowledge of United States history, write an essay in which you

> Select *two* issues mentioned in the historical context and for *each*
> - Describe the president's position on the issue
> - Describe congressional opposition to the president's position
> - Discuss how the outcome of the situation influenced the United States and/or American society

Guidelines:

In your essay, be sure to
- Develop all aspects of the task
- Incorporate information from *at least four* documents
- Incorporate relevant outside information
- Support the theme with relevant facts, examples, and details
- Use a logical and clear plan of organization, including an introduction and a conclusion that are beyond a restatement of the theme

Regents Examination – August 2016

This section contains the Regents Examination in United States History and Government that was given in New York State in August 2016.

Circle your answers to Part I on this exam and write your answers to the thematic essay and document-based essay questions on separate sheets of paper. Be sure to refer to the test-taking strategies in the front of this book as you prepare to answer the test questions.

Part I

Answer all questions in this part.

Directions (1–50): For each statement or question, record on your separate answer sheet the *number* of the word or expression that, of those given, best completes the statement or answers the question.

1 A major reason the American colonists of the 1600s chose to settle along the seacoast and rivers was so that they could

(1) export slaves
(2) carry out trade
(3) protect themselves from Native American Indians
(4) use water power to run factory machinery

2 Under the British system of mercantilism, the American colonies served primarily as a

(1) self-sufficient trading partner for other European nations
(2) market for British manufactured goods and a source of raw materials
(3) source of manpower for the British army and navy
(4) buffer to the expansion of French and Spanish colonies

3 Which heading best completes the partial outline below?

```
I. _____

    A. House of Burgesses
    B. Mayflower Compact
    C. New England town meetings
    D. Albany Plan of Union
```

(1) Early Colonial Documents
(2) Limits on Representative Government
(3) Contributions of the Enlightenment
(4) Foundations of American Democracy

4 The phrase "consent of the governed" refers to the

(1) source of the government's power
(2) need to create political parties
(3) commitment to use implied powers
(4) development of a federal system of government

5 One weakness of the Articles of Confederation was the inability of the central government to

(1) establish a postal system
(2) collect adequate taxes from the states
(3) control western lands
(4) admit new states to the Union

6 What was a result of the Great Compromise during the Constitutional Convention of 1787?

(1) creating a two-house legislature
(2) banning slavery in Southern states
(3) requiring that the president have a cabinet
(4) giving the Supreme Court the power to hear cases involving states

7 Based on the United States Constitution, the census helps to determine the number of

(1) presidential candidates
(2) members of congressional subcommittees
(3) electoral votes assigned to each state
(4) senators from each state

8 A primary reason the Antifederalists opposed ratification of the United States Constitution in 1787 was because the Constitution failed to

(1) include a bill of rights
(2) provide for a strong national defense
(3) restrict immigration
(4) extend voting rights to women

9 The power of judicial review was established when

(1) the original United States Constitution was adopted
(2) an amendment was added to the United States Constitution
(3) President Thomas Jefferson established the power in an executive order
(4) the Supreme Court issued its ruling in *Marbury* v. *Madison* (1803)

10 Which quotation is correctly paired with the document in which it is found?

(1) "…the right of the people to keep and bear arms, shall not be infringed."
— Washington's Farewell Address

(2) "We hold these truths to be self-evident, that all men are created equal…"
— Monroe Doctrine

(3) "Four score and seven years ago our fathers brought forth, upon this continent, a new nation…"
— Lincoln's Gettysburg Address

(4) "We the people of the United States, in order to form a more perfect union…"
— Declaration of Independence

11 During the 1790s, the primary goal of United States foreign policy was to

(1) preserve the nation's neutrality during European conflicts
(2) increase the nation's trade with Asia
(3) expand westward by signing new military alliances
(4) make the nation into a major colonial power

12 In *Gibbons* v. *Ogden* (1824), the Supreme Court strengthened the federal government's role in the national economy by

(1) outlawing the triangular trade
(2) banning states from issuing money
(3) upholding the power of Congress to regulate interstate commerce
(4) limiting the growth of corporations

13 One way in which Frederick Douglass, William Lloyd Garrison, and Sojourner Truth are similar is that they all supported the

(1) abolitionist movement
(2) passage of Black Codes
(3) nullification theory of States rights
(4) plantation system in the South

14 Abraham Lincoln's 1858 warning that "a house divided against itself cannot stand" referred to sectional differences over the

(1) treatment of Native American Indians
(2) issue of slavery
(3) funding for internal improvements
(4) treaties with European nations

15 What was a common goal of the 13th, 14th, and 15th amendments to the United States Constitution?

(1) punishing the South for seceding from the Union
(2) granting basic rights to formerly enslaved persons
(3) allowing the states to veto federal laws
(4) creating a "separate but equal" society

16 In the latter half of the 1800s, a large labor supply, an abundance of natural resources, and the construction of new railroads contributed most directly to the

(1) growth of American industry
(2) dependence on imported goods
(3) demand for limits on immigration
(4) rejection of high tariffs by the United States

17 In the late 1800s, many employers used black-listing to

(1) end the use of sweatshops
(2) discourage workers from joining labor unions
(3) restrict the use of open shops
(4) promote child labor reform

Base your answer to question 18 on the cartoon below and on your knowledge of social studies.

The Great American Cow

Source: Bailey and Kennedy, *The American Pageant*, D. C. Heath and Company (adapted)

18 Which statement most accurately describes the meaning of this 1896 cartoon?

(1) Western farmers have no market for their products.

(2) Grazing and water rights cause conflict in western states.

(3) Eastern businesses profit from western farming.

(4) Cattle and grain add little to the wealth of the United States.

19 Which heading best completes the partial outline below?

I. _____

  A. The United States claims the Hawaiian Islands.

  B. Puerto Rico becomes a United States territory.

  C. The United States fights an insurrection in the Philippine Islands.

  D. The United States Senate ratifies the Panama Canal treaty.

(1) Rise of American Imperialism

(2) Causes of World War I

(3) Enforcement of the Monroe Doctrine

(4) Trade Expansion in East Asia

20 Which statement best expresses President Theodore Roosevelt's philosophy on regulating big business?

(1) Regulation of big business should be left to the states.

(2) Any regulation of big business is undesirable.

(3) Abusive trusts should be broken up by a vigilant federal government.

(4) Government ownership of key industries will benefit consumers.

Base your answer to question 21 on the map below and on your knowledge of social studies.

Woman's Suffrage Before 1920

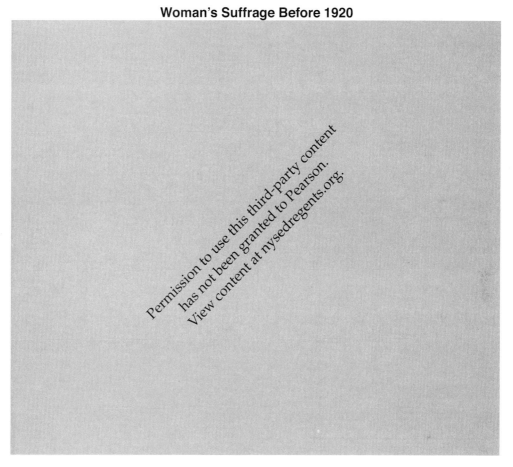

Permission to use this third-party content has not been granted to Pearson. View content at nysedregents.org.

21 Based on the map, which region of the United States demonstrated the most support for complete voting rights for women before 1919?

(1) New England   (3) South
(2) Midwest   (4) West

22 Upton Sinclair, Ida M. Tarbell, and Lincoln Steffens were considered muckrakers because they

(1) opposed railroad monopolies
(2) criticized the growing power of labor unions
(3) raised concerns about the negative effects of industrialization
(4) supported the need for reforms in education

23 In the 1920s, the passage of the Quota Acts and the trial of Sacco and Vanzetti illustrate that many Americans were

(1) intolerant of ethnic minorities
(2) committed to racial integration
(3) worried about foreign wars
(4) determined to increase immigration

Base your answer to question 24 on the photograph below and on your knowledge of social studies.

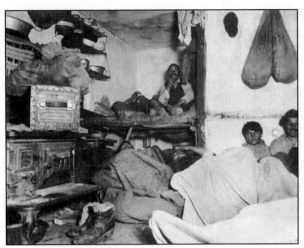

Source: Jacob Riis, *How the Other Half Lives,* 1890

24 One reason Jacob Riis published many photographs similar to this was to

(1) disprove claims of yellow journalists
(2) encourage government assistance for poor farmers
(3) promote the use of child labor
(4) increase public concern over tenement conditions

Base your answer to question 25 on the quotation below and on your knowledge of social studies.

…I pledge you, I pledge myself, to a new deal for the American people. Let us all here assembled constitute ourselves prophets of a new order of competence and of courage. This is more than a political campaign; it is a call to arms. Give me your help, not to win votes alone, but to win in this crusade to restore America to its own people.

—Franklin D. Roosevelt, Acceptance Speech, Democratic National Convention, 1932

25 In this statement, Franklin D. Roosevelt promised to

(1) build up the military
(2) reduce government interference in business
(3) end an isolationist foreign policy
(4) provide government assistance to combat the Great Depression

Base your answer to question 26 on the photograph below and on your knowledge of social studies.

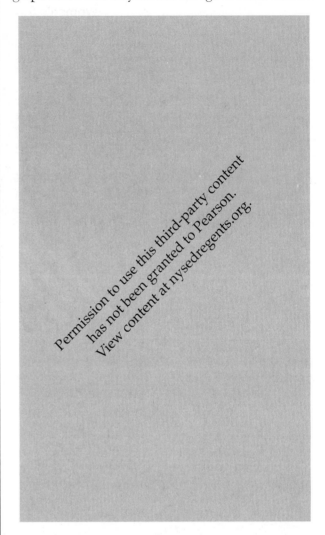

26 Which New Deal agency was created to provide employment for individuals such as the man in the photograph?

(1) Agricultural Adjustment Administration (AAA)
(2) Social Security Administration (SSA)
(3) Works Progress Administration (WPA)
(4) Federal Deposit Insurance Corporation (FDIC)

Base your answer to question 27 on the cartoon below and on your knowledge of social studies.

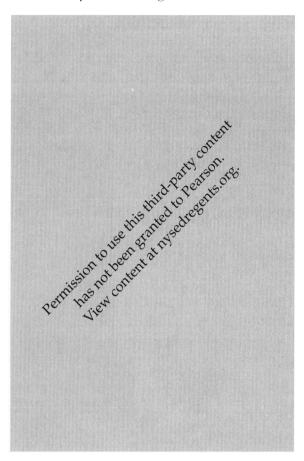

27 What is the main idea of this cartoon?

   (1) President Franklin D. Roosevelt wanted to end Supreme Court opposition to the New Deal.

   (2) Congress refused to pass New Deal legislation.

   (3) President Franklin D. Roosevelt had not faced any opposition to his New Deal.

   (4) Congress voted to increase the size of the Supreme Court.

Base your answer to question 28 on the graph below and on your knowledge of social studies.

Source: *Historical Statistics of the United States*, U.S. Bureau of the Census

28 Which conclusion about the United States economy during World War II is most clearly supported by the information in the graph?

   (1) Organized labor conducted frequent strikes during the war years.

   (2) The war led to improved economic conditions.

   (3) The Gross National Product (GNP) steadily declined during the war years.

   (4) Unemployment increased throughout the war.

29 One purpose of the GI Bill (Servicemen's Readjustment Act of 1944) was to

   (1) end racial segregation in the military

   (2) replace the draft with an all-volunteer military

   (3) maintain troop strength at World War II levels

   (4) give educational aid to returning veterans

Base your answers to questions 30 and 31 on the photograph below and on your knowledge of social studies.

**Members of the Mochida family await an evacuation
bus in Hayward, California, May 8, 1942.**

Source: U.S. National Archives & Records Administration

30 This photograph taken during World War II shows the

    (1) deportation of Japanese Americans to Japan
    (2) arrival of new Japanese immigrants in California
    (3) migration of Japanese American families to the East Coast
    (4) relocation of Japanese Americans to internment camps

31 The situation shown in this photograph was most directly the result of

    (1) legislation in California
    (2) a presidential executive order during World War II
    (3) a Supreme Court decision
    (4) a constitutional amendment

Base your answers to questions 32 and 33 on the map below and on your knowledge of social studies.

Berlin Airlift

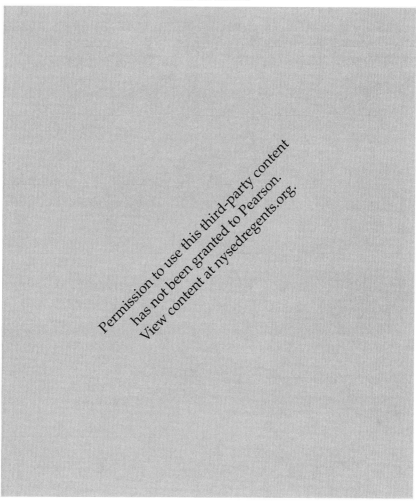

32 The situation shown on the map was primarily the result of the

 (1) continuing disagreement among wartime Allies about Germany's future
 (2) demand of Great Britain and France that Germany pay harsh reparations
 (3) desire to conduct war crimes trials for Nazi leaders
 (4) need to bring a unified Germany into the United Nations

33 The air corridors shown on the map were used during the airlift in 1948 and 1949 to

 (1) bomb the city of Berlin
 (2) fly combat troops into the Soviet sector
 (3) prevent a Soviet invasion of West Germany
 (4) overcome a Soviet blockade of Berlin in East Germany

Base your answer to question 34 on the statement below and on your knowledge of social studies.

…We may anticipate a state of affairs in which two Great Powers will each be in a position to put an end to the civilization and life of the other, though not without risking its own. We may be likened to two scorpions in a bottle, each capable of killing the other, but only at the risk of his own life….

— J. Robert Oppenheimer, 1953

34 In this statement, J. Robert Oppenheimer was referring to the

(1) benefits of neutrality
(2) dangers of the nuclear arms race
(3) failures of appeasement
(4) positive effects of atomic energy

35 Which event during the civil rights movement is most closely associated with President Dwight Eisenhower?

(1) granting permission for the March on Washington
(2) urging the Brooklyn Dodgers to sign Jackie Robinson
(3) supporting the sit-ins in Greensboro, North Carolina
(4) using federal troops to integrate schools in Little Rock, Arkansas

36 "No voting qualification or prerequisite to voting, or standard, practice, or procedure shall be imposed or applied by any State or political subdivision to deny or abridge the right of any citizen of the United States to vote on account of race or color."

— Section 2, Voting Rights Act of 1965

The specific goal stated in this section of the Voting Rights Act of 1965 was to

(1) expand the use of property qualifications
(2) establish voter qualifications such as literacy tests
(3) stop fraudulent voting in large cities
(4) remove barriers to voting based on racial background

Base your answer to question 37 on the cartoon below and on your knowledge of social studies.

HOT PURSUIT

Source: Pat Oliphant, *Denver Post*, December 29, 1967
(adapted)

37 What is the main idea of this 1967 cartoon?

(1) Desertion by United States soldiers was widespread.
(2) The domino theory no longer applied to Southeast Asia.
(3) The United States policy of expanding the war in Indochina would be filled with hazards.
(4) A bridge into Laos and Cambodia helped United States soldiers invade Asia.

38 A major goal of President Lyndon B. Johnson's Great Society program was to

(1) contain communism in Southeast Asia
(2) create a space program
(3) reduce poverty in the United States
(4) cut domestic programs to balance the budget

39 The presidency of Richard Nixon was weakened by his

(1) policies on the environment
(2) trip to the People's Republic of China
(3) foreign policy toward the Soviet Union
(4) involvement in the Watergate scandal

Base your answer to question 40 on the cartoon below and on your knowledge of social studies.

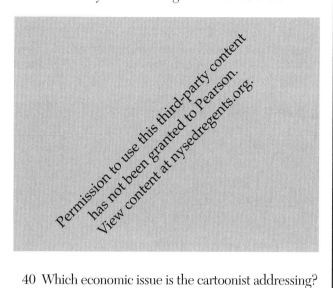

Permission to use this third-party content has not been granted to Pearson. View content at nysedregents.org.

40 Which economic issue is the cartoonist addressing?

(1) globalization
(2) high tariffs
(3) transportation costs
(4) quality of American cars

41 President George H. W. Bush's decisions to send military aid to Saudi Arabia in 1990 and to conduct the Persian Gulf War in 1991 were consistent with the United States

(1) long-term commitment to protecting oil resources
(2) determination to appease Saddam Hussein
(3) continued application of the Truman Doctrine
(4) goal of nuclear disarmament

42 **"Somalians Are Still Hungry and at War Despite Efforts of United States Troops"**

"United States Troops Help Reinstate Haitian President"

"United States and NATO Allies Use Air Strikes To Slow Ethnic Cleansing in Bosnia"

These 1990s headlines illustrate the efforts of the United States to

(1) support independence movements
(2) act as an international peacekeeper
(3) prevent the spread of communism
(4) protect United States business investments

43 Which United States foreign policy stated that European powers should no longer expect to establish colonies in the Western Hemisphere?

(1) Monroe Doctrine
(2) Dollar Diplomacy
(3) Good Neighbor Policy
(4) Alliance for Progress

44 Brinkmanship, the domino theory, and massive retaliation are elements of United States foreign policy associated with the

(1) Revolutionary War   (3) Cold War
(2) Civil War   (4) War on Terror

Base your answers to questions 45 and 46 on the speakers' statements below and on your knowledge of social studies.

Speaker A: United States expansion should not end when we reach the Pacific Coast.

Speaker B: The navy of the United States needs to increase in size to defend our overseas interests.

Speaker C: The United States must serve as the military protector of the Western Hemisphere.

Speaker D: The United States needs to avoid international commitments in order to protect our national interests.

45 Which speaker's statement best expresses the reason that many United States senators rejected the Treaty of Versailles after World War I?

(1) *A*   (3) *C*
(2) *B*   (4) *D*

46 Which president's decision demonstrated a commitment to the idea expressed by *Speaker A*?

(1) James K. Polk going to war with Mexico
(2) Abraham Lincoln signing the Homestead Act
(3) William McKinley annexing the Hawaiian Islands
(4) Woodrow Wilson sending troops to pursue Pancho Villa in Mexico

47 One way in which the elections of President Rutherford B. Hayes (1876) and President George W. Bush (2000) are similar is that in both instances the

(1) third-party candidate won electoral votes in several states

(2) winner of the electoral vote failed to win the popular vote

(3) eventual winner was selected by Congress

(4) elections were settled by a special prosecutor

48 The Federal Reserve System and the Securities and Exchange Commission (SEC) were both established to

(1) fund retirement pensions

(2) promote economic stability

(3) break up business monopolies

(4) create public jobs

49 Which principle was dealt with in the Supreme Court decisions in *Schenck* v. *United States* (1919) and *Tinker* v. *Des Moines* (1969)?

(1) States rights   (3) freedom of speech

(2) voting rights   (4) freedom of assembly

50 The war crimes trials of German military officials after World War II and of Saddam Hussein during the Iraq War (2003–2011) both demonstrate the principle that

(1) only nations are considered responsible for wartime actions

(2) international law may not be applied to national leaders

(3) protection of civil liberties depends on the circumstances at the time

(4) leaders can be held accountable for crimes against humanity

Answers to the essay questions are to be written in the separate essay booklet.

In developing your answer to Part II, be sure to keep these general definitions in mind:

   (a) <u>describe</u> means "to illustrate something in words or tell about it"

   (b) <u>discuss</u> means "to make observations about something using facts, reasoning, and argument; to present in some detail"

Part II

THEMATIC ESSAY QUESTION

Directions: Write a well-organized essay that includes an introduction, several paragraphs addressing the task below, and a conclusion.

Theme: Economic Policy

> Throughout United States history, the federal government has taken actions to strengthen or reform the nation's economy. These actions have had varying degrees of success.

Task:

> Select *two* federal government actions that have affected the United States economy and for *each*
>
> • Describe the historical circumstances that led to the government action
> • Discuss the extent to which the government action was successful in strengthening or reforming the United States economy

You may use any government action related to the economy from your study of United States history. Some suggestions you might wish to consider include creation of the Bank of the United States in 1790, passage of the Pacific Railway Act (transcontinental railroad) in 1862, passage of the Homestead Act in 1862, passage of the Sherman Antitrust Act in 1890, adoption of the income tax (16th) amendment in 1913, formation of the Tennessee Valley Authority in 1933, creation of the Social Security system in 1935, passage of the Interstate Highway Act in 1956, and ratification of the North American Free Trade Agreement (NAFTA) in 1993.

You are *not* limited to these suggestions.

Guidelines:

   In your essay, be sure to:
   • Develop all aspects of the task
   • Support the theme with relevant facts, examples, and details
   • Use a logical and clear plan of organization, including an introduction and a conclusion that are beyond a restatement of the theme

NAME _____ SCHOOL _____

Part III

DOCUMENT-BASED QUESTION

This question is based on the accompanying documents. The question is designed to test your ability to work with historical documents. Some of these documents have been edited for the purposes of this question. As you analyze the documents, take into account the source of each document and any point of view that may be presented in the document. Keep in mind that the language used in a document may reflect the historical context of the time in which it was written.

Historical Context:

> Large-scale migrations of Americans have occurred throughout United States history. These migrations have had economic, social, and political effects on the nation. These migrations include **the movement of settlers westward during the 1800s, the movement of African Americans to northern cities in the early 20th century,** and **the movement of people to the Sun Belt since World War II.**

Task: Using the information from the documents and your knowledge of United States history, answer the questions that follow each document in Part A. Your answers to the questions will help you write the Part B essay in which you will be asked to

> Choose **two** migrations mentioned in the historical context and for **each**
> - Describe the historical circumstances that led to the migration
> - Discuss the effects of this migration on the United States and/or on American society

In developing your answers to Part III, be sure to keep these general definitions in mind:

   (a) <u>describe</u> means "to illustrate something in words or tell about it"
   (b) <u>discuss</u> means "to make observations about something using facts, reasoning, and argument; to present in some detail"

Part A
Short-Answer Questions

Directions: Analyze the documents and answer the short-answer questions that follow each document in the space provided.

Document 1a

This 1869 poster advertised the different ways people could acquire land in Nebraska.

Source: The Digital Scriptorium, Duke University Libaries (adapted)

1a Based on this poster, state *one* reason people might choose to move west to Nebraska in 1869. [1]

_____

_____

Score

Document 1b

> The rich romantic place names of the big rolling land beyond the Mississippi echoed across the eastern United States. Broadsides [posters] in all the languages of Europe made the strange Indian names of the faraway country familiar to emigrants long before they reached New York en route to the free lands extending to the "shining mountains" and the Pacific. The slow march of settlement which had followed the Homestead Act of 1862 turned into a stampede during the 1870s and 1880s....
>
> The new settlers used different words to explain why they moved west, but beyond all their words was the old American vision of a better life beyond the far horizon. "We wanted to come to a new country," said Susan Frances Lomax, "so our children could grow up with the country. We were living on a good farm [in Mississippi]. My husband said he would live ten years longer by coming to a new country. You hardly ever saw a gray headed man. I did not want to come to Texas at all; I dreaded the Indians in those days.... It was a hard time on weman [women]; they staid [stayed] at home and did the work while the men were on their ponies hunting or looking after stock."...

Source: Dee Brown, *The American West*, Charles Scribner's Sons, 1994

1b According to Dee Brown, what was **one** reason settlers moved west of the Mississippi River during the 1870s and 1880s? [1]

_____

_____

Score

Document 2

...During the second half of the nineteenth century the direction of American expansion shifted from the countryside to the city. The West was popularly known as the land of wide-open spaces, but by the 1890s the typical westerner lived in an urban oasis like Omaha, Denver, or San Francisco. The American West included the fastest-growing cities in the nation, and by 1890 had become more heavily urban than any other region except the Northeast. When we think of the astounding growth of nineteenth-century American cities, most of us think of the flood of immigration from abroad; yet the single most important source of the expanding population of western cities came from the countryside. With the expansion of the commercial economy, farming and ranching became a significantly more capital-intensive [costly] business. After the Civil War a western settler needed an average of a thousand dollars to purchase land, the equipment necessary to work it, and the transportation to get the family there. Although railroads and land speculators continued to promote the West as a safety valve for the urban working class, as the "free range" disappeared and the number of tenant farmers and hired hands grew larger, it is more accurate to say that it was the cities that provided the safety valve for *rural discontent*. As one historian has put it, for every industrial worker who became a farmer, twenty farm boys moved to the city....

Source: Geoffrey C. Ward, *The West: An Illustrated History*, Little, Brown and Company, 1996

2 According to Geoffrey C. Ward, what was **one** way migration affected the American West? [1]

_____

_____

Score ☐

Document 3

...As settlers migrated westward [after the Civil War], federal troops systematically subdued Native American tribes and by successive treaties required that they reside on reservations isolated from American settlers. Eastern tribes were [earlier] forced to resettle west of the Mississippi by legal chicanery [trickery] and military force. The Cherokees of Georgia, for instance, were forcibly removed in 1837 and 1838, in a migration known as the "Trail of Tears." The post–Civil War years saw continued pressure on Native Americans, this time in the plains and mountain states. Despite armed resistance, Native Americans found themselves increasingly relegated [removed] to reservations on the least desirable western lands....

Source: Thomas Dublin, "Internal Migration," in Foner and Garraty, eds., *The Reader's Companion to American History*, Houghton Mifflin, 1991

3 According to Thomas Dublin, what was **one** effect of the westward migration of settlers on Native American Indians? [1]

_____

_____

Score ☐

Document 4a

This Langston Hughes poem, written in 1949, is about the migration of African Americans during the first half of the 20th century.

Document 4b

...From the early years of the twentieth century to well past its middle age, nearly every black family in the American South, which meant nearly every black family in America, had a decision to make. There were sharecroppers losing at settlement. Typists wanting to work in an office. Yard boys scared that a single gesture near the planter's wife could leave them hanging from an oak tree. They were all stuck in a caste system as hard and unyielding as the red Georgia clay, and they each had a decision before them. In this, they were not unlike anyone who ever longed to cross the Atlantic or the Rio Grande.

It was during the First World War that a silent pilgrimage took its first steps within the borders of this country. The fever rose without warning or notice or much in the way of understanding by those outside its reach. It would not end until the 1970s and would set into motion changes in the North and South that no one, not even the people doing the leaving, could have imagined at the start of it or dreamed would take nearly a lifetime to play out....

Source: Isabel Wilkerson, *The Warmth of Other Suns: The Epic Story of America's Great Migration,* Random House, 2010

4 Based on these documents, state *two* reasons for the migration of African Americans to the North and the West. [2]

(1)_____

_____

Score ☐

(2)_____

_____

Score ☐

Document 5

...During World War I and in the years just after, a new racial climate began to emerge. Blacks [African Americans] seemed more willing to express their opposition to racial oppression and to act against it. One reason was that the Great Migration increased the number of blacks in the North and West, where they were free to protest and to vote. Changes in employment also had an impact. In their traditional service jobs (servants, waiters, barbers), blacks served individual whites on a personal basis and therefore could not escape close white supervision. But now blacks were moving into factories with thousands of workers, where their relationship to white employers was much less personal. Under these conditions, blacks may have felt less controlled and freer to express themselves. Similarly, as black neighborhoods grew into ghettos, blacks had less contact with whites. For all the evils of the ghettos, they did create an environment in which black pride and self-expression could emerge. Also, many returning black soldiers were ready to claim their rights after having fought in what had supposedly been, after all, a war to make the world safe for democracy....

Source: Michael L. Levine, *African Americans and Civil Rights: From 1619 to the Present,* Oryx Press, 1996

5 According to Michael Levine, what was *one* effect of the Great Migration on African Americans? [1]

_____

_____

Score ⬜

Document 6

The [Great] migration of a million and a half African Americans from the South to the North between 1915 and 1930 initiated a new era in black—and American—political life. Once overwhelmingly southern, the African-American population would become national; once overwhelmingly rural and agricultural, it would become urban and industrial; once overwhelmingly subject to formal and informal repression, coercion, and exclusion, it would find precious new space for civic and political activism. The results would be seen not simply in the extension and reconstitution [rebuilding] of black communities, but also in the changing social and political face of the country as a whole. Many of the landmark political developments of twentieth-century America—electoral realignments, the New Deal, industrial unionism, the Great Society, and, of course, the battle for civil rights—would be difficult to imagine outside of this massive demographic shift that then continued, and accelerated, over the next three decades....

Source: Steven Hahn, "Epilogue: 'Up, You Mighty Race'," *A Nation Under Our Feet,* Belknap Press, 2003

6 According to Steven Hahn, what was **one** effect of the Great Migration on the United States? [1]

_____

_____

Score ☐

Document 7

Growth of the Sun Belt

...The trend became crystal clear in the next decade [the 1970s] when the South surpassed the West as a leading migration destination. People moving into the region outnumbered those leaving by 3.5 million during the 1970s, by 3 million in the 1980s, and by more than 2 million in the 1990s. Mostly they were coming from the same northern states that for half a century had been the prime destination for departing southerners. The Mid-Atlantic states suffered an actual population decline in the 1970s, as out-migrants exceeded in-migrants by almost 2 million. The East North Central states [IN, IL, MI, OH, WI] lost 1.3 million more people than they received through migration.

The turnaround seemed more abrupt than in fact it was. The South had been attracting people in growing numbers since World War II, and throughout the second phase of the exodus something of an exchange had been going on between North and South. Mostly blue-collar southerners had been going north, and mostly white-collar northerners had been coming south. The fast-developing economy of the postwar South had been the key. The building of new industries, military facilities, educational institutions, transportation systems, and urban infrastructure had attracted the services of engineers, managers, professors, technicians, and others with high-end skills. Equally important, the region had been attracting capital. Fortune 500 companies had been opening offices and branch plants and sometimes moving whole operations to Florida, Georgia, North Carolina, Texas, and Virginia, which were the key growth nodes [centers] of the new South....

Source: James N. Gregory, *The Southern Diaspora,* The University of North Carolina Press, 2005

7 According to James N. Gregory, what is *one* reason people moved to the Sun Belt after World War II? [1]

_____

_____

Score ☐

Document 8a

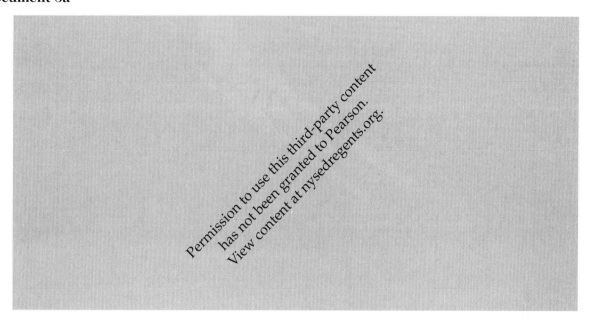

Permission to use this third-party content has not been granted to Pearson. View content at nysedregents.org.

Document 8b

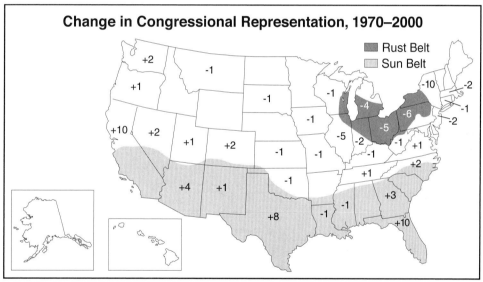

Change in Congressional Representation, 1970–2000

Rust Belt
Sun Belt

Source: U. S. Census, 2000

Note: Numbers in the map represent seats gained or lost in the House of Representatives.

8 Based on these documents, what is **one** effect of the population shift from the Rust Belt to the Sun Belt on congressional representation between 1970 and 2000? [1]

_____

_____

Score ☐

Document 9a

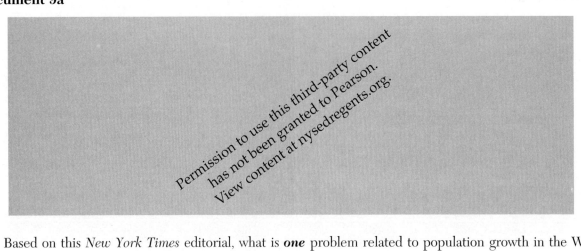

9a Based on this *New York Times* editorial, what is **one** problem related to population growth in the West? [1]

_____

_____

Score ☐

Document 9b

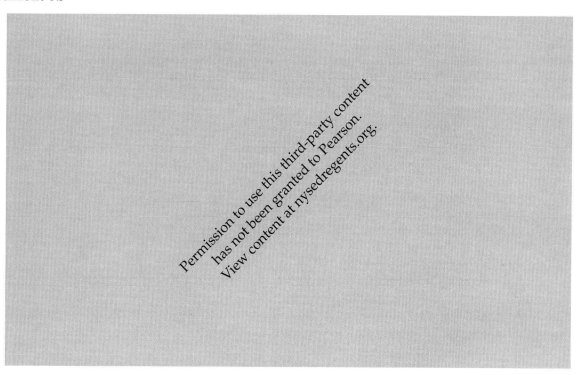

Permission to use this third-party content has not been granted to Pearson. View content at nysedregents.org.

9b According to Joel Kotkin, what is **one** way migration has contributed to economic growth in the Sun Belt? [1]

_____

_____

Score ☐

Part B
Essay

Directions: Write a well-organized essay that includes an introduction, several paragraphs, and a conclusion. Use evidence from *at least* **four** documents in your essay. Support your response with relevant facts, examples, and details. Include additional outside information.

Historical Context:

Large-scale migrations of Americans have occurred throughout United States history. These migrations have had economic, social, and political effects on the nation. These migrations include **the movement of settlers westward during the 1800s, the movement of African Americans to northern cities in the early 20th century,** and **the movement of people to the Sun Belt since World War II.**

Task: Using the information from the documents and your knowledge of United States history, write an essay in which you

> Choose *two* migrations mentioned in the historical context and for *each*
> - Describe the historical circumstances that led to the migration
> - Discuss the effects of this migration on the United States and/or on American society

Guidelines:

In your essay, be sure to
- Develop all aspects of the task
- Incorporate information from *at least* **four** documents
- Incorporate relevant outside information
- Support the theme with relevant facts, examples, and details
- Use a logical and clear plan of organization, including an introduction and a conclusion that are beyond a restatement of the theme

This section contains the Regents Examination in United States History and Government that was given in New York State in June 2016.

Circle your answers to Part I on this exam and write your answers to the thematic essay and document-based essay questions on separate sheets of paper. Be sure to refer to the test-taking strategies in the front of this book as you prepare to answer the test questions.

Part I

Answer all questions in this part.

Directions (1–50): For each statement or question, record on your separate answer sheet the *number* of the word or expression that, of those given, best completes the statement or answers the question.

1 Which geographic features had the most significant positive influence on settlement patterns and economic development in the British North American colonies?
   (1) rivers and harbors
   (2) mountains and plateaus
   (3) forests and deserts
   (4) prairies and lakes

2 The Erie Canal played a large role in the settlement of the Midwest because it provided a link between the Atlantic Ocean and the
   (1) Gulf of Mexico   (3) Missouri River
   (2) Great Lakes   (4) Pacific Ocean

3 During the 1600s and 1700s, the fundamental goal of British mercantilism was to
   (1) prohibit all exports of raw materials from the colonies
   (2) encourage economic competition with the American colonies
   (3) develop manufacturing within the colonies
   (4) maintain a favorable balance of trade for Great Britain with its colonies

4 The Proclamation of 1763 was issued by Great Britain after the French and Indian War primarily to
   (1) promote colonial settlement beyond the Appalachian Mountains
   (2) limit conflict between Native American Indians and colonial settlers
   (3) encourage colonial economic ties with France
   (4) force French settlers to leave British territory

Base your answer to question 5 on the passage below and on your knowledge of social studies.

…Small islands not capable of protecting themselves, are the proper objects for kingdoms to take under their care; but there is something very absurd, in supposing a continent to be perpetually governed by an island. In no instance hath nature made the satellite larger than its primary planet, and as England and America, with respect to each other, reverses the common order of nature, it is evident that they belong to different systems: England to Europe, America to itself….

— Thomas Paine, *Common Sense*

5 The argument presented in this passage was intended to
   (1) urge colonists to accept the Albany Plan of Union
   (2) provide a reason for ratification of the Constitution of the United States
   (3) convince American colonists to declare their independence
   (4) persuade France to aid the United States in the Revolutionary War

6 What was one effect of the Three-fifths Compromise?
   (1) Slave states gained additional congressional representation.
   (2) The number of justices on the Supreme Court was established.
   (3) Presidential appointments were assured easy confirmation.
   (4) A two-house legislature was created.

Base your answer to question 7 on the passage below and on your knowledge of social studies.

...No political truth is certainly of greater intrinsic [essential] value, or is stamped with the authority of more enlightened patrons of liberty, than that on which the objection is founded. The accumulation of all powers, legislative, executive, and judiciary, in the same hands, whether of one, a few, or many, and whether hereditary, self-appointed, or elective, may justly be pronounced the very definition of tyranny....

— James Madison, *The Federalist*, Number 47

7 Which constitutional principle was established to protect American citizens from the tyranny suggested in this quotation?

(1) due process of law
(2) States rights
(3) popular sovereignty
(4) separation of powers

Base your answer to question 8 on the passages below and on your knowledge of social studies.

Each state retains its sovereignty, freedom and independence, and every power, jurisdiction and right, which is not by this confederation expressly delegated to the United States, in Congress assembled.

— Article II, Articles of Confederation

The powers not delegated to the United States by the Constitution, nor prohibited by it to the states, are reserved to the states respectively, or to the people.

— 10th amendment, United States Constitution

8 The purpose of each of these provisions is to

(1) determine the division of power between state and central governments
(2) create a process for allowing amendments
(3) grant the central government power to control the states
(4) limit the power of the executive branch

9 **"President Jackson Vetoes Bill Rechartering Bank of United States"**
"Taney Court Overturns Missouri Compromise"
"Senate Approves NATO Treaty"

Which concept is best illustrated by these headlines?

(1) federalism
(2) direct democracy
(3) checks and balances
(4) westward expansion

10 What was a major demand of the Antifederalists during the debate over ratification of the United States Constitution?

(1) continuation of slavery
(2) right to habeas corpus
(3) inclusion of a bill of rights
(4) reduction in the number of representatives in Congress

11 Which headline would be considered an example of the unwritten constitution?

(1) **"President Nixon Vetoes War Powers Act"**
(2) **"Congress Approves President Reagan's Tax Cuts"**
(3) **"Congress Votes to Impeach President Bill Clinton"**
(4) **"President Obama Names Hillary Clinton to Cabinet"**

12 What was a common goal of the Proclamation of Neutrality (1793), the Embargo Act (1807), and the Monroe Doctrine (1823)?

(1) forcing Great Britain to grant independence to Canada
(2) avoiding conflicts with European nations
(3) providing wartime aid to European nations
(4) encouraging independence movements in Latin America

Base your answer to question 13 on the map below and on your knowledge of social studies.

Railroads in 1840 and 1860

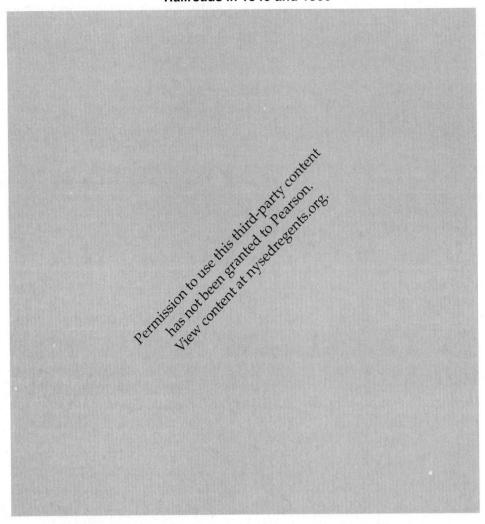

13 The information provided by the map best supports the conclusion that

(1) the South's transportation system was more efficient
(2) most railroads were owned and operated by the United States government
(3) the transcontinental railroad linked the West and the South
(4) the North had transportation advantages by the start of the Civil War

14 The Supreme Court decisions in *Marbury* v. *Madison* (1803), *McCulloch* v. *Maryland* (1819), and *Gibbons* v. *Ogden* (1824) are similar in that each resulted in the

(1) development of new political parties
(2) admission of new slave states
(3) strengthening of the power of the federal government
(4) expansion of the rights of corporations

15 The Missouri Compromise of 1820 and the Compromise of 1850 were attempts by the federal government to

(1) limit immigration from Europe
(2) reduce the conflict over slavery
(3) settle border disputes with Mexico
(4) control the migration of settlers to new western territories

16 The Homestead Act of 1862 was important to the expansion of the United States because it provided

(1) land for agricultural colleges
(2) assistance to sharecroppers in the South
(3) free land to settlers in the West
(4) land grants for construction of transcontinental railroads

17 After the Civil War, a significant cause of the conflict between President Andrew Johnson and the Radical Republicans in Congress was disagreement over

(1) the plans for restoring Southern states to the Union
(2) a proposal to repeal the Emancipation Proclamation
(3) reduction of the army and the navy to prewar levels
(4) congressional efforts to pay the Confederate war debt

18 In the late 1800s, which idea was used most often to justify the elimination of business competition?

(1) conservation   (3) Social Darwinism
(2) Manifest Destiny (4) populism

19 Poll taxes, literacy tests, and grandfather clauses were used in the South after 1890 to

(1) support the goals of the Freedmen's Bureau
(2) deny suffrage rights to African Americans
(3) undermine the "separate but equal" ruling of the Supreme Court
(4) enforce the amendments enacted during the Civil War and Reconstruction

20 The importance of *Northern Securities Co.* v. *United States* (1904) is that the Supreme Court

(1) used the Sherman Antitrust Act to break up a monopoly
(2) ruled child labor laws unconstitutional
(3) upheld the right of women to vote
(4) established regulations for the New York Stock Exchange

Base your answer to question 21 on the statement below and on your knowledge of social studies.

…the policy of the government of the United States is to seek a solution which may bring about permanent safety and peace to China, preserve Chinese territorial and administrative entity, protect all rights guaranteed to friendly powers by treaty and international law, and safeguard for the world the principle of equal and impartial trade with all parts of the Chinese Empire….

— Secretary of State John Hay, Circular Letter, July 3, 1900

21 This excerpt from John Hay's Circular Letter became part of the

(1) Open Door policy
(2) Roosevelt Corollary to the Monroe Doctrine
(3) policy of Dollar Diplomacy
(4) Kellogg-Briand Pact

22 In the early 1900s, Progressives succeeded in strengthening federal control over the money supply by

(1) passing the Clayton Antitrust Act
(2) creating the Federal Reserve System
(3) enacting the Underwood Tariff bill
(4) establishing the gold standard

23 What was the purpose of states adopting initiative, referendum, and recall during the Progressive Era?

(1) supporting new political parties
(2) increasing the power of voters over the political process
(3) reestablishing property qualifications for voting
(4) extending voting rights to immigrants

Base your answer to question 24 on the cartoon below and on your knowledge of social studies.

IF CAPITAL AND LABOR DON'T PULL TOGETHER

Source: John McCutcheon, *Chicago Tribune*, 1919 (adapted)

24 Which statement most accurately describes the main argument made in this 1919 cartoon?

(1) Labor and management have the same economic goals.
(2) The federal government should take ownership of major industries.
(3) Organized workers are more productive than nonunion workers.
(4) Disputes between labor and the leaders of business are hurting the economy.

25 Which action by Germany prompted the United States to enter World War I?

(1) attacking British shipping
(2) forming an alliance with Austria-Hungary
(3) resuming unrestricted submarine warfare
(4) invading France

26 The United States Supreme Court in *Schenck* v. *United States* (1919) ruled that freedom of speech may be limited during national emergencies when the speech

(1) threatens the principle of States rights
(2) conflicts with national economic policies
(3) interferes with a presidential campaign
(4) presents a clear and present danger to the nation

Base your answer to question 27 on the photograph below and on your knowledge of social studies.

Dust Bowl, 1936

Source: Farm Security Administration

27 The situation shown in this photograph occurred in which region?

(1) Ohio River valley   (3) Rocky Mountains
(2) Great Plains   (4) Northeast

Base your answer to question 28 on the chart below and on your knowledge of social studies.

Consumer spending (in billions) on selected items and total value of stock, 1929–1933

	1929	1933
Food	$19.5	$11.5
Housing	$11.5	$7.9
Clothing	$11.2	$5.4
Automobiles	$2.6	$0.8
Medical care	$2.9	$1.9
Philanthropy	$1.2	$0.8
Value of shares on the New York Stock Exchange	$89.7	$22.2

Source: *Historical Statistics of the United States*

28 Which conclusion is best supported by the information on the chart?

(1) Business advertising had succeeded in selling more products.
(2) Violence by labor had increased throughout the country.
(3) Economic conditions had become worse.
(4) The stock market had recovered in 1933.

Base your answer to question 29 on the passage below and on your knowledge of social studies.

…Of all the Nations of the world today we are in many ways most singularly blessed. Our closest neighbors are good neighbors. If there are remoter [distant] Nations that wish us not good but ill, they know that we are strong; they know that we can and will defend ourselves and defend our neighborhood.

We seek to dominate no other Nation. We ask no territorial expansion. We oppose imperialism. We desire reduction in world armaments….

— President Franklin D. Roosevelt,
Address at Chautauqua, NY, August 14, 1936

29 Which policy is President Franklin D. Roosevelt supporting in this speech?

(1) neutrality in foreign relations
(2) a growth in military spending
(3) an increase in foreign aid
(4) formation of military alliances

Base your answers to questions 30 through 32 on the cartoon below and on your knowledge of social studies.

Do We Want a Ventriloquist Act in the Supreme Court?

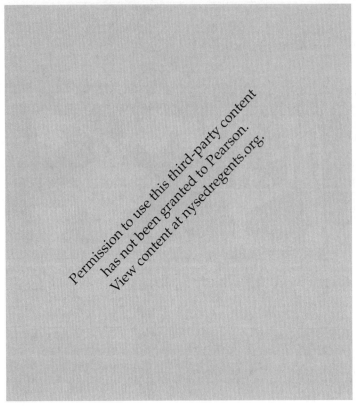

30 This 1937 cartoon is criticizing President Franklin D. Roosevelt's plan to

(1) reduce the number of federal courts
(2) impeach current Supreme Court justices
(3) give states the power to appoint Supreme Court justices
(4) increase the number of justices on the Supreme Court

31 One reason President Franklin D. Roosevelt proposed the plan shown in the cartoon was that the Supreme Court had

(1) challenged his right to run for a third term
(2) rejected several important Cabinet appointments
(3) ruled against laws to protect the rights of minorities
(4) declared parts of key New Deal programs unconstitutional

32 Many members of Congress opposed the plan shown in the cartoon because it would

(1) reduce the power of the president
(2) upset the system of checks and balances
(3) destroy the system of federalism
(4) cost too much to implement

Base your answer to question 33 on the photograph and poster below and on your knowledge of social studies.

Source: "Women workers chipping paint,"
Marinship Corp., National Archives, 1942

Source: Office of War Information, 1943

33 Photographs and posters showing scenes similar to these were used by the federal government to

(1) support the goal of equal pay for equal work
(2) discourage women from taking jobs from men with families
(3) recruit women to fill wartime manufacturing jobs
(4) encourage women to accept combat roles

34 The Servicemen's Readjustment Act of 1944 (GI Bill) was responsible for

(1) building United States military bases in allied countries throughout the world
(2) providing education and home loan benefits for soldiers returning from World War II
(3) maintaining the size of the active duty military at its pre–World War II level
(4) sending the United States economy into a post–World War II recession

35 President Harry Truman's decision to drop atomic bombs on Japan was based on the belief that the action would

(1) save American lives by avoiding an invasion of Japan
(2) force Germany and Italy to lay down their arms
(3) help create a military alliance with China
(4) persuade the Soviet Union to surrender

Base your answer to question 36 on the cartoon below and on your knowledge of social studies.

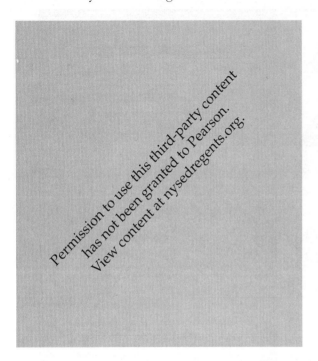

Permission to use this third-party content has not been granted to Pearson. View content at nysedregents.org.

36 Which United States effort is the Soviet Union responding to in this cartoon?

(1) a commitment to rebuild the League of Nations

(2) a plan to join with other nations to reduce military spending

(3) an effort to improve United States–Soviet relations

(4) an attempt to stabilize the economy of Western Europe

37 **"Greece Receives U.S. Aid to Fight Communists"**
"U.S. Military Airlifts Supplies to Berlin"
"U.S. Troops Sent to Defend South Vietnam"

These headlines best illustrate the United States commitment to a policy of

(1) détente   (3) containment
(2) isolationism   (4) imperialism

38 • Alger Hiss conviction
   • Rosenberg trial
   • McCarthy hearings

These post–World War II events are most closely associated with the fear of

(1) an increase in immigration from the Soviet Union

(2) labor conflicts in United States cities

(3) an expansion of communism into Cuba

(4) a communist threat inside the United States

39 The 1957 launch of *Sputnik* by the Soviet Union embarrassed the United States because it

(1) allowed the Soviets to place missiles in Turkey

(2) revealed that the Soviets had nuclear weapons

(3) appeared that the United States had failed to keep up in scientific achievement

(4) confirmed the United States use of U-2 spy planes

40 "…And so, my fellow Americans: ask not what your country can do for you—ask what you can do for your country.

My fellow citizens of the world: ask not what America will do for you, but what together we can do for the freedom of man.…"

— President John F. Kennedy, Inaugural Address,
January 20, 1961

President Kennedy sought to achieve the goal described in this speech through support for the formation of the

(1) Peace Corps

(2) World Bank

(3) Organization of American States (OAS)

(4) South East Asia Treaty Organization (SEATO)

Base your answer to question 41 on the poster below and on your knowledge of social studies.

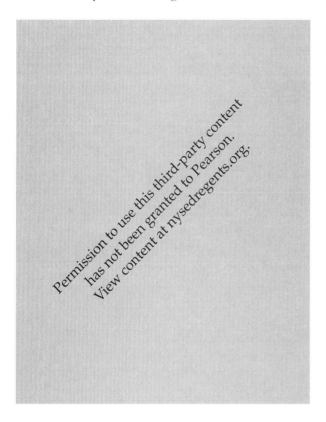

41 This poster from 1967 is an expression of
(1) support for the foreign policy of the president
(2) support for increased financing of environmental programs
(3) opposition to health care reform for seniors and the poor
(4) opposition to United States involvement in Vietnam

42 Which title best completes the partial outline below?

I. _____
   A. *Heart of Atlanta Motel* v. *United States* (1964)
   B. Voting Rights Act of 1965
   C. Fair Housing Act of 1968

(1) Latino Women Gain Equal Pay
(2) Civil Rights Movement Achieves Victories
(3) Native American Indians Regain Land Rights
(4) Persons With Disabilities Win Educational Opportunities

43 In *New York Times* v. *United States* (1971) and *United States* v. *Nixon* (1974), the Supreme Court placed limits on the
(1) authority of federal judges
(2) exercise of freedom of religion
(3) powers of the president
(4) right of Congress to declare war

44 Which statement accurately describes a result of the 1993 adoption of the North American Free Trade Agreement (NAFTA)?
(1) Tariff barriers were reduced between the three largest nations of North America.
(2) A single currency was created for the nations of North America.
(3) Immigration restrictions between North American nations were eliminated.
(4) The United States stopped importing oil from other North American nations.

Base your answer to question 45 on the cartoon below and on your knowledge of social studies.

Source: Jeff Stahler, *Columbus Dispatch*, March 7, 2009 (adapted)

45 Which situation related to the Great Recession in 2008 and 2009 is addressed in this cartoon?

(1) crisis in home foreclosures
(2) growth of federal budget deficits
(3) shortage of health care facilities
(4) decline in the financial stability of Social Security

46 **"Congress Passes Alien and Sedition Acts"**
"Lincoln Suspends Writ of Habeas Corpus"
"Roosevelt Authorizes Internment of Japanese Americans on West Coast"

Which conclusion is best supported by these headlines?

(1) Immigrants are a danger to the welfare of the United States.
(2) Perceived threats to national security sometimes result in limits on civil liberties.
(3) Foreign policy is greatly affected by domestic conflicts.
(4) The power of the federal government is weakened by risks to national security.

47 In the 1880s and the 1920s, low prices for United States agricultural products were the result of

(1) the overproduction of staple crops
(2) a shortage of usable farm land
(3) competition from cheaper imported goods
(4) inflationary monetary policies

48 One way in which the Progressive movement of the early 1900s and the women's rights movement of the 1960s are similar is that each resulted in

(1) restrictions on immigration
(2) limits on labor union activities
(3) passage of reform legislation
(4) a return to laissez-faire economic policies

49 One way in which President Franklin D. Roosevelt's New Deal and President Lyndon B. Johnson's Great Society are similar is that both programs

(1) made civil rights for African Americans a major goal
(2) drew wide support and few critics
(3) helped to end major depressions
(4) attempted to improve the lives of the poor and the aged

Base your answer to question 50 on the graph below and on your knowledge of social studies.

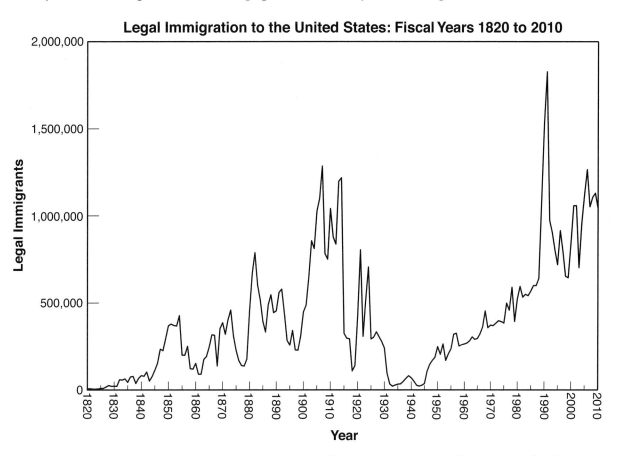

Legal Immigration to the United States: Fiscal Years 1820 to 2010

Source: U.S. Department of Homeland Security (adapted)

50 The low level of immigration between 1930 and 1945 is most directly related to
    (1) passage of the Chinese Exclusion Act
    (2) the Great Depression and World War II
    (3) the Cold War and the civil rights movement
    (4) improvements in living standards in Europe and Asia

This page left blank intentionally.

GO ON TO THE NEXT PAGE ⟹

Answers to the essay questions are to be written in the separate essay booklet.

In developing your answer to Part II, be sure to keep these general definitions in mind:

(a) <u>describe</u> means "to illustrate something in words or tell about it"

(b) <u>discuss</u> means "to make observations about something using facts, reasoning, and argument; to present in some detail"

Part II

THEMATIC ESSAY QUESTION

Directions: Write a well-organized essay that includes an introduction, several paragraphs addressing the task below, and a conclusion.

Theme: Reform Movements

> During the period from 1820 to 1933, individuals and groups participated in major reform movements to bring social, political, and economic changes to American society. These reform movements achieved varying degrees of success.

Task:

> Select *two* major reform movements during the period from 1820 to 1933 and for *each*
> • Describe the historical circumstances that led to the reform movement
> • Discuss the extent to which the movement achieved its goal

You may use any major reform movement during the period from 1820 to 1933. Suggestions you might wish to consider include the abolition movement, the woman's suffrage movement, the temperance movement (prohibition), the consumer protection movement, the labor movement, and the conservation movement.

You are *not* limited to these suggestions.

Guidelines:

In your essay, be sure to:
• Develop all aspects of the task
• Support the theme with relevant facts, examples, and details
• Use a logical and clear plan of organization, including an introduction and a conclusion that are beyond a restatement of the theme

NAME _____ SCHOOL _____

Part III

DOCUMENT-BASED QUESTION

This question is based on the accompanying documents. The question is designed to test your ability to work with historical documents. Some of these documents have been edited for the purposes of this question. As you analyze the documents, take into account the source of each document and any point of view that may be presented in the document. Keep in mind that the language used in a document may reflect the historical context of the time in which it was written.

Historical Context:

    Throughout the history of the United States, wars have been fought to protect national security and promote the national interest. These wars have affected the United States and American society in many different ways. These wars include the **Spanish-American War (1898)**, the **Korean War (1950–1953)**, and the **Persian Gulf War (1991)**.

Task: Using the information from the documents and your knowledge of United States history, answer the questions that follow each document in Part A. Your answers to the questions will help you write the Part B essay in which you will be asked to

---

Select *two* wars mentioned in the historical context and for *each*

- Describe the historical circumstances that led to United States involvement in the war
- Discuss the effects of the war on the United States and/or on American society

---

In developing your answers to Part III, be sure to keep these general definitions in mind:

    (a) <u>describe</u> means "to illustrate something in words or tell about it"

    (b) <u>discuss</u> means "to make observations about something using facts, reasoning, and argument; to present in some detail"

Part A
Short-Answer Questions

Directions: Analyze the documents and answer the short-answer questions that follow each document in the space provided.

Document 1

War Message to Congress

…The grounds for such intervention may be briefly summarized as follows:

First. In the cause of humanity and to put an end to the barbarities, bloodshed, starvation, and horrible miseries now existing there, and which the parties to the conflict are either unable or unwilling to stop or mitigate [lessen]. It is no answer to say this is all in another country, belonging to another nation, and is therefore none of our business. It is specially our duty, for it is right at our door.

Second. We owe it to our citizens in Cuba to afford them that protection and indemnity [security] for life and property which no government there can or will afford, and to that end to terminate the conditions that deprive them of legal protection.

Third. The right to intervene may be justified by the very serious injury to the commerce, trade, and business of our people and by the wanton [unlimited] destruction of property and devastation of the island.…

The issue is now with the Congress. It is a solemn responsibility. I have exhausted every effort to relieve the intolerable condition of affairs which is at our doors. Prepared to execute every obligation imposed upon me by the Constitution and the law, I await your action.…

Source: President William McKinley, Message to Congress, April 11, 1898

1 What are ***two*** reasons President William McKinley is asking Congress to declare war? [2]

(1)_____

_____

Score ☐

(2)_____

_____

Score ☐

Document 2a

Source: J. S. Pughe, *Puck*, September 5, 1900 (adapted)

Document 2b

...In the forcible annexation of the Philippines our nation neither adds to its strength nor secures broader opportunities for the American people.

Even if the principle of conquest were permissible under American public law, the conquest of territory so remote from our shores, inhabited by people who have no sympathy with our history or our customs, and who resent our attempt to overthrow their declaration of independence, would be a tax [burden] upon our military and naval strength the magnitude of which cannot now be determined.

Who can estimate in money and men the cost of subduing and keeping in subjection eight millions of people, six thousand miles away, scattered over twelve hundred islands and living under a tropical sun?...

Source: William Jennings Bryan, "Will It Pay?," Bryan et al., *Republic or Empire? The Philippine Question,* The Independence Company, 1899

2 Based on documents 2*a* and 2*b*, what are ***two*** ways the United States might be affected by the Spanish-American War? [2]

(1)_____

_____

Score ☐

(2)_____

_____

Score ☐

Document 3

...The transformation of America from a provincial to a world power began in the 1890s. When Theodore Roosevelt took office, the first and most important steps had already been taken. By going to war with Spain and keeping the Philippines in 1898, America had joined the more ambitious industrialized world powers. With the Platt Amendment in 1901, Congress declared to the world its continued independence from European colonial ambitions. In his presidency Roosevelt supported both the expansion that had taken place and the limitations Congress imposed upon it, and never envisioned any further American expansion. He regarded the taking of Panama as a fulfillment of the most direct American strategic interest, as a way of denying Europe a foothold in Central America, and at the same time assuring full mobility for a two-ocean navy....

Source: Richard H. Collin, *Theodore Roosevelt, Culture, Diplomacy, and Expansion: A New View of American Imperialism*, Louisiana State University Press, 1985

3 According to Richard Collin, what was ***one*** effect the Spanish-American War had on the United States? [1]

_____

_____

Score ☐

Document 4

> …Korea is a small country, thousands of miles away, but what is happening there is important to every American.
>
> On Sunday, June 25th, Communist forces attacked the Republic of Korea.
>
> This attack has made it clear, beyond all doubt, that the international Communist movement is willing to use armed invasion to conquer independent nations. An act of aggression such as this creates a very real danger to the security of all free nations.
>
> The attack upon Korea was an outright breach of the peace and a violation of the Charter of the United Nations. By their actions in Korea, Communist leaders have demonstrated their contempt for the basic moral principles on which the United Nations is founded. This is a direct challenge to the efforts of the free nations to build the kind of world in which men can live in freedom and peace.…
>
> Furthermore, the fact that Communist forces have invaded Korea is a warning that there may be similar acts of aggression in other parts of the world. The free nations must be on their guard, more than ever before, against this kind of sneak attack.…

Source: President Harry Truman, Radio and Television Address to the American People on the Situation in Korea, July 19, 1950

4 According to President Harry Truman, what is **one** reason the United States should be concerned about the situation in Korea? [1]

_____

_____

Score [ ]

Document 5

...And so the true brutality of the war never really penetrated the American cultural consciousness. An estimated 33,000 Americans died in it. Another 105,000 were wounded. The South Koreans lost 415,000 killed and had 429,000 wounded. Both the Chinese and North Koreans were exceptionally secretive about their casualties, but American officials put their losses at roughly 1.5 million men killed. The Korean War momentarily turned the Cold War hot, heightening the already considerable (and mounting) tensions between the United States and the Communist world and deepening the chasm between the United States and Communist forces asserting themselves in Asia. Those tensions and divisions between the two sides in the bipolar struggle [taking opposing positions] grew even more serious after American miscalculations brought China into the war. When it was all over and an armed truce ensued, both sides claimed victory, though the final division of the country was no different from the one that had existed when the war began. But the United States was not the same: its strategic vision of Asia had changed, and its domestic political equation had been greatly altered....

Source: David Halberstam, *The Coldest Winter: America and the Korean War*, Hyperion, 2007

5 According to David Halberstam, what were *two* effects the Korean War had on the United States? [2]

(1)_____

_____

Score ☐

(2)_____

_____

Score ☐

Document 6a

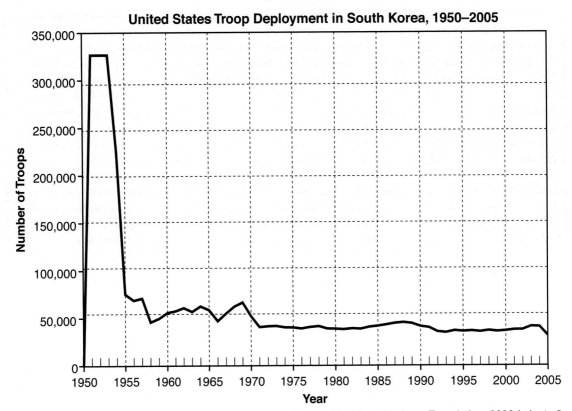

United States Troop Deployment in South Korea, 1950–2005

Source: Tim Kane, Heritage Foundation, 2006 (adapted)

Document 6b

...There is another subject that has to be addressed here today. When the guns fell silent, some asked what our forces in Korea had done for freedom, after all, for after all, the fighting began at the 38th parallel and ended at the 38th parallel. I submit to you today that looking back through the long lens of history, it is clear that the stand America took in Korea was indispensable to our ultimate victory in the cold war. Because we stood our ground in Korea, the Soviet Union drew a clear lesson that America would fight for freedom....

Because we have continued to stand with our democratic ally South Korea, with 37,000 American troops standing watch on the border today [2000], just as we have since 1953, we have kept the peace. And because of all that, there is now a chance for a different future on the Korean Peninsula....

Korea helped remind us of a few other lessons, too, that our people and all our rich diversity are our greatest strength, that a fully integrated military is our surest hope for victory, that our freedom and security depends on the freedom and security of others, and that we can never, ever, pull away from the rest of the world....

Source: President Bill Clinton, Remarks on the Observance of the 50th Anniversary of the Korean War,
June 25, 2000

6 Based on these documents, what were **two** effects the Korean War had on the United States? [2]

(1)_____

_____

Score ☐

(2)_____

_____

Score ☐

Document 7

Just two hours ago, allied air forces began an attack on military targets in Iraq and Kuwait. These attacks continue as I speak. Ground forces are not engaged.

This conflict started August 2nd when the dictator of Iraq invaded a small and helpless neighbor. Kuwait—a member of the Arab League and a member of the United Nations—was crushed; its people, brutalized. Five months ago, Saddam Hussein started this cruel war against Kuwait. Tonight, the battle has been joined....

Our objectives are clear: Saddam Hussein's forces will leave Kuwait. The legitimate government of Kuwait will be restored to its rightful place, and Kuwait will once again be free. Iraq will eventually comply with all relevant United Nations resolutions, and then, when peace is restored, it is our hope that Iraq will live as a peaceful and cooperative member of the family of nations, thus enhancing the security and stability of the Gulf....

President George H. W. Bush

Source: President George H. W. Bush, Address to the Nation Announcing Allied Military Action in the Persian Gulf, January 16, 1991 (adapted)

7 According to President George H. W. Bush, what is **one** reason the United States began air strikes in Iraq in January of 1991? [1]

_____

_____

Score

Document 8a

...As a result of servicewomen's performance during Operation Desert Storm, the last of the laws restricting women's service were lifted by the middle of the decade. In 1992, Congress repealed the restriction banning servicewomen from flying in aircraft engaged in combat missions. In 1993, they lifted the restriction banning women from serving aboard combat vessels. By the turn of this [21st] century, women comprised almost 14 percent of active military duty personnel and were reaching the highest levels of the military....

While issues of equal opportunity for women in the military still remained, the distance between the servicewomen of 1999 and the Army nurses of 1901 who served their country before they could even vote was staggering....

Source: Women in Military Service for America Memorial Foundation

Document 8b

Permission to use this third-party content has not been granted to Pearson. View content at nysedregents.org.

8 Based on these documents, what were **two** effects the Persian Gulf War had on American society? [2]

(1)_____

_____

Score [ ]

(2)_____

_____

Score [ ]

Document 9

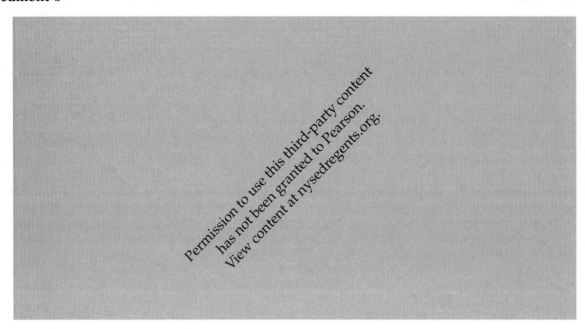

9 According to Thomas E. Ricks, what was **one** effect the 1991 Persian Gulf War had on the United States? [1]

_____

_____

Score [ ]

Part B
Essay

Directions: Write a well-organized essay that includes an introduction, several paragraphs, and a conclusion. Use evidence from *at least four* documents in your essay. Support your response with relevant facts, examples, and details. Include additional outside information.

Historical Context:

Throughout the history of the United States, wars have been fought to protect national security and promote the national interest. These wars have affected the United States and American society in many different ways. These wars include the ***Spanish-American War (1898)***, the ***Korean War (1950–1953)***, and the ***Persian Gulf War (1991)***.

Task: Using the information from the documents and your knowledge of United States history, write an essay in which you

> Select *two* wars mentioned in the historical context and for *each*
> - Describe the historical circumstances that led to United States involvement in the war
> - Discuss the effects of the war on the United States and/or on American society

Guidelines:

In your essay, be sure to

- Develop all aspects of the task
- Incorporate information from *at least four* documents
- Incorporate relevant outside information
- Support the theme with relevant facts, examples, and details
- Use a logical and clear plan of organization, including an introduction and a conclusion that are beyond a restatement of the theme

Regents Examination – January 2016

This section contains the Regents Examination in United States History and Government that was given in New York State in January 2016.

Circle your answers to Part I on this exam and write your answers to the thematic essay and document-based essay questions on separate sheets of paper. Be sure to refer to the test-taking strategies in the front of this book as you prepare to answer the test questions.

Part I

Answer all questions in this part.

Directions (1–50): For each statement or question, record on your separate answer sheet the *number* of the word or expression that, of those given, best completes the statement or answers the question.

1 Which geographic feature did the British government use in 1763 as a boundary to restrict the westward settlement of American colonists?

(1) St. Lawrence River
(2) Rocky Mountains
(3) Appalachian Mountains
(4) Mississippi River

2 Which heading best completes the partial outline below?

I. _____

   A. House of Burgesses
   B. Mayflower Compact
   C. New England town meetings

(1) British System of National Government in North America
(2) Colonial Responses to the Practice of Salutary Neglect
(3) British Attempts to Control Colonial Governments
(4) Colonial Efforts at Self-Government

3 During the colonial era, the British promoted the policy of mercantilism to

(1) control the commerce of their American colonies
(2) promote colonial trade with France and Spain
(3) ban all trade between the British colonies in North America
(4) restrict the importation of enslaved Africans

Base your answers to questions 4 and 5 on the passage below and on your knowledge of social studies.

…We hold these truths to be self-evident, that all men are created equal, that they are endowed by their Creator with certain unalienable rights, that among these are life, liberty, and the pursuit of happiness. That to secure these rights, governments are instituted among men, deriving their just powers from the consent of the governed,…

4 Which document includes this passage?

(1) Mayflower Compact
(2) Declaration of Independence
(3) Northwest Ordinance
(4) Monroe Doctrine

5 This passage suggests that the authority of government

(1) originates from the divine right of kings
(2) is based on a social contract meant to guarantee individual rights
(3) includes the power to seize private property for national defense
(4) is the source of all the natural rights of citizens

6 Which issue did the Virginia Plan, the New Jersey Plan, and the Great Compromise address at the Constitutional Convention (1787)?

(1) the power to regulate interstate commerce
(2) the number of justices on the Supreme Court
(3) a system for electing the president
(4) a method of determining state representation in Congress

7 Which headline is reporting the clearest example of the United States Constitution's system of checks and balances?

(1) **"Environmental Protection Agency Proposes Stricter Air Pollution Controls"**
(2) **"Supreme Court Rules on Arizona Immigration Law"**
(3) **"President Vetoes Defense Spending Bill"**
(4) **"California Passes Strict Gun Control Law"**

8 The Three-fifths Compromise adopted in the Constitution in 1787 had the effect of

(1) increasing the representation of southern states in Congress
(2) providing a method for ratifying amendments
(3) making possible the impeachment of the president
(4) allowing the use of the elastic clause in the legislative process

9 What was the major argument of those who opposed ratification of the United States Constitution?

(1) The states should not be forced to pay taxes to the federal government.
(2) The new constitution did not adequately protect individual liberties against abuse by the federal government.
(3) The judicial branch was granted more power than the legislative and executive branches.
(4) The federal government did not have enough power to defend the nation against foreign enemies.

10 Which foreign policy toward Europe did President George Washington recommend in his Farewell Address?

(1) military alliances   (3) imperialism
(2) internationalism   (4) neutrality

11 What was a primary goal of President Thomas Jefferson's 1803 decision to purchase the Louisiana Territory?

(1) studying Native American Indian societies
(2) mining gold and silver in California
(3) gaining control of the port of New Orleans
(4) securing access to the iron ore deposits near the Great Lakes

12 The case of *Marbury* v. *Madison* (1803) established the principle that

(1) the Supreme Court can declare federal laws unconstitutional
(2) the states have power over the federal government
(3) the president nominates federal judges
(4) Congress can override presidential vetoes

13 Which heading best completes the partial outline below?

I. _____

   A. Disputes over tariff rates
   B. Introduction of slavery into the territories
   C. Demands of abolitionists
   D. Disagreements over States rights

(1) Reasons for the American System
(2) Successes of Third Political Parties
(3) Causes of Sectionalism
(4) Justifications for Economic Reform

Base your answer to question 14 on the poster below and on your knowledge of social studies.

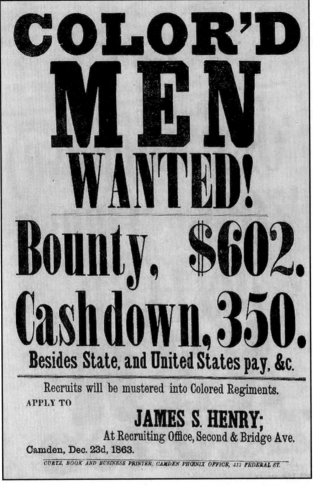

Source: Library of Congress

14 This 1863 poster is recruiting African Americans to help
  (1) defeat the Confederacy in the Civil War
  (2) assist in the efforts of the Underground Railroad
  (3) settle land in the South and in border states
  (4) enforce the terms of the Fugitive Slave Act

15 After the Civil War, many owners of large plantations in the South responded to the loss of enslaved labor by
  (1) hiring Irish immigrants to do the work of freedmen
  (2) selling their plantations to formerly enslaved persons
  (3) creating tenant farms and sharecropping
  (4) paying wages to farmworkers who had migrated from the North

16 The federal government responded to the railroad strikes of 1877 and the Pullman strike of 1894 by
  (1) using military force against the workers
  (2) requiring negotiation to resolve the disputes
  (3) maintaining a neutral position between labor and management
  (4) providing economic aid to striking workers

Base your answer to question 17 on the graph below and on your knowledge of social studies.

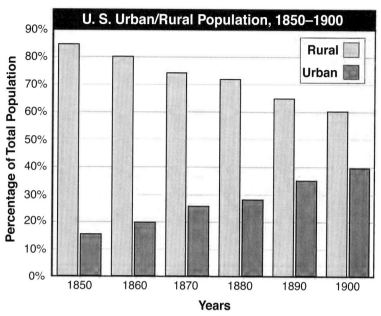

U. S. Urban/Rural Population, 1850–1900

Source: U.S. Bureau of the Census (adapted)

17 What was the primary cause of the trends shown on the graph?

   (1) closing of the western frontier

   (2) industrialization in the North and the Midwest

   (3) passage of the Homestead Act

   (4) completion of the transcontinental railroad

---

18 Few restrictions were placed on immigration to the United States in the late 19th century primarily because immigrants

   (1) would work for low wages

   (2) provided a rich source of investment capital

   (3) would add to the diversity of the population

   (4) faced little opposition from citizens

19 The "separate but equal" doctrine established by the Supreme Court in *Plessy* v. *Ferguson* (1896) upheld the legality of

   (1) woman's suffrage in state elections

   (2) the activities of the Ku Klux Klan

   (3) racial segregation in public facilities

   (4) restrictions on voting rights of African Americans

Base your answer to question 20 on the photographs below and on your knowledge of social studies.

Source: Nebraska State Historical Society, 1890

Source: Smithsonian Institution,
National Anthropological Archives

20 These photographs of 19th-century life on the Great Plains indicate that

(1) Native American Indians and white settlers used the same building materials for protection

(2) Native American Indians and white settlers adapted differently to the same environment

(3) white settlers learned farming practices from Native American Indians

(4) both Native American Indians and white settlers depended on the buffalo for survival

21 From 1870 to 1900, business leaders in the United States often attempted to increase productivity, maximize profits, and decrease costs by

(1) reducing competition through the formation of trusts

(2) increasing benefits for industrial workers

(3) supporting the passage of strict antitrust laws

(4) preventing foreign investment in the United States

22 Which proposal was most consistent with the goals of the American Federation of Labor under the leadership of Samuel Gompers?

(1) government ownership of the transportation and communication industries

(2) collective bargaining to reach agreements on wages and hours

(3) formation of a third political party to promote union policies

(4) organization of unskilled workers into one national union

Base your answers to questions 23 and 24 on the cartoon below and on your knowledge of social studies.

NO LACK OF BIG GAME
The President Seems to Have Scared Up Quite a Bunch of Octopi.

Source: Charles Bartholomew, *The Minneapolis Journal,*
April 13, 1903 (adapted)

23 Based on the information provided by the cartoon, President Theodore Roosevelt's goal was to

(1) persuade businesses to accept nationalization
(2) assist businesses in resisting interference by investors
(3) establish worker safety regulations in factories
(4) use federal power to control monopolies

24 Which act of Congress gave President Roosevelt the authority that he demonstrates in this cartoon?

(1) Meat Inspection Act
(2) Sherman Antitrust Act
(3) Underwood Tariff Act
(4) Pure Food and Drug Act

Base your answer to question 25 on the photograph below and on your knowledge of social studies.

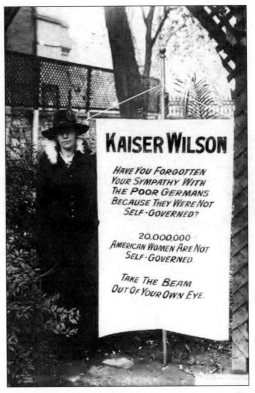

Source: Library of Congress

25 Which activity is illustrated in this photograph?

(1) picketing against United States involvement in World War I
(2) making a statement of support for the League of Nations
(3) protesting the nation's denial of woman's suffrage
(4) supporting punishment of Germany for causing World War I

26 The Federal Reserve Act of 1913 was passed in an attempt to

(1) increase United States exports
(2) safeguard the health of workers
(3) regulate the amount of money in circulation
(4) protect national forests from destruction

27 The Great Migration of African Americans between 1915 and 1930 was mainly a movement from

(1) cities to suburban developments
(2) northern farms to northern cities
(3) southern cities to free land in the West
(4) the rural South to northern cities

Base your answer to question 28 on the graph below and on your knowledge of social studies.

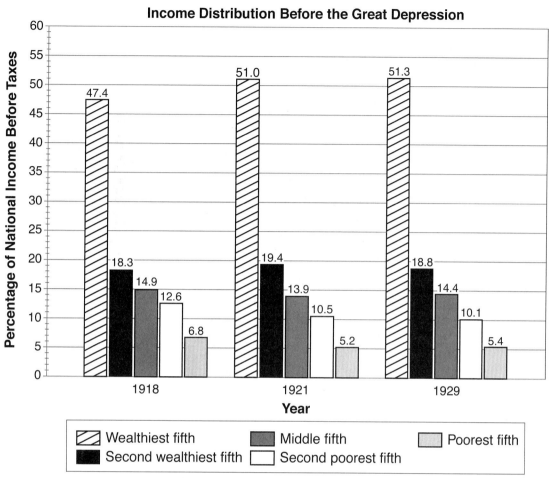

Income Distribution Before the Great Depression

Source: John M. Murrin et al., *Liberty, Equality, Power: A History of the American People,* Thomson Wadsworth, 2006 (adapted)

28 Which statement about the period from 1918 through 1929 is most clearly supported by information in the graph?

(1) The percentage of income controlled by the wealthiest Americans declined.
(2) The income gap between the wealthiest fifth and the rest of the population increased.
(3) The overall per capita income in the United States declined.
(4) The percentage of income controlled by the poor steadily increased.

29 Which New Deal agency had the creation of new jobs as its primary goal?

(1) Agricultural Adjustment Administration (AAA)
(2) Federal Deposit Insurance Corporation (FDIC)
(3) Securities and Exchange Commission (SEC)
(4) Works Progress Administration (WPA)

30 The Wagner Act (National Labor Relations Act) of 1935 helped organized labor by

(1) mandating government control over industry
(2) guaranteeing workers the right to collective bargaining
(3) banning the closed shop in the workplace
(4) requiring all workers to join unions

Base your answer to question 31 on the cartoon below and on your knowledge of social studies.

QUALIFYING TEST FOR SUPREME COURT JOBS

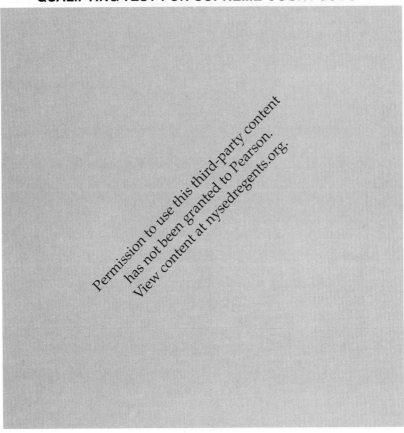

Permission to use this third-party content has not been granted to Pearson. View content at nysedregents.org.

31 The main idea of the cartoon is that President Franklin D. Roosevelt wanted to

(1) impeach justices who did not support him
(2) control the decisions of the Supreme Court
(3) create higher qualifications for justices
(4) encourage the Supreme Court to act more efficiently

32 In the mid–1930s, which action did the federal government take in an attempt to avoid the situations that drew the United States into World War I?

(1) passing the Neutrality Acts
(2) allowing only the United States Navy to deliver military goods overseas
(3) investing money in nations threatened by Germany
(4) forming a military alliance with the Soviet Union

33 The Lend-Lease Act of 1941 significantly changed United States policy toward nations involved in World War II because it

(1) supplied war materials to Allied nations without a declaration of war
(2) imposed a trade boycott on Germany and Japan
(3) authorized the seizure of British assets in the United States
(4) approved the appeasement policies of the French and British governments

Base your answer to question 34 on the public notice below and on your knowledge of social studies.

Civilian Exclusion Order No. 5
WESTERN DEFENSE COMMAND AND FOURTH ARMY
WARTIME CIVIL CONTROL ADMINISTRATION
Presidio of San Francisco, California
April 1, 1942

INSTRUCTIONS
TO ALL PERSONS OF
JAPANESE
ANCESTRY

Source: Western Historical Manuscript Collection, University of Missouri-St. Louis (adapted)

34 The instructions referred to in this public notice resulted in the

(1) deportation of most Japanese aliens to Japan
(2) protection of the homes and property of Japanese Americans
(3) removal of Japanese Americans to internment camps
(4) drafting of all young Japanese American men into the United States military

35 The scientists working on the Manhattan Project during World War II were responsible for

(1) designing weapons for the D-Day invasion
(2) building satellites to spy on the Axis nations
(3) creating materials for biological and chemical warfare
(4) developing the atomic bomb

Base your answer to question 36 on the passage below and on your knowledge of social studies.

...It is hereby declared to be the policy of the President that there shall be equality of treatment and opportunity for all persons in the armed services without regard to race, color, religion or national origin. This policy shall be put into effect as rapidly as possible, having due regard to the time required to effectuate [implement] any necessary changes without impairing efficiency or morale....

— Section 1, Executive Order 9981

36 The purpose of Executive Order 9981, issued by President Harry Truman, was to

(1) encourage women to join the armed services
(2) end racial segregation in the military
(3) ensure adequate manpower to fight the Korean War
(4) establish war crimes tribunals in Western Europe

Base your answers to questions 37 and 38 on the excerpt below and on your knowledge of social studies.

...The truth of the matter is that Europe's requirements for the next three or four years of foreign food and other essential products—principally from America—are so much greater than her present ability to pay that she must have substantial additional help, or face economic, social, and political deterioration of a very grave character....

— Secretary of State George Marshall, Remarks at Harvard University Commencement, June 5, 1947

37 In this excerpt, Secretary of State George Marshall is identifying the need to

(1) provide economic assistance to struggling European nations
(2) allow European workers to settle in the United States
(3) install democratic governments in the nations of Western Europe
(4) strengthen European military defenses

38 The situation in Europe described by Secretary of State George Marshall was the result of the

(1) failure of the United Nations to help people in need
(2) devastation caused by fighting in World War II
(3) construction of the Berlin Wall by the Soviet Union
(4) takeover of Greece and Turkey by communists

Base your answer to question 39 on the picture below and on your knowledge of social studies.

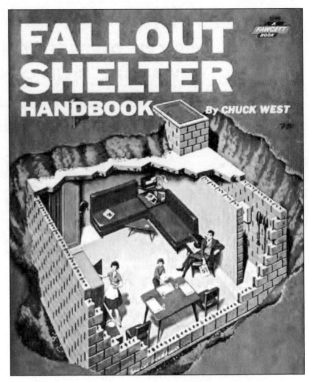

Source: Fawcett Publications (adapted)

39 The shelter pictured in this handbook was designed to help Americans survive

(1) global climate changes
(2) pandemic diseases
(3) natural disasters
(4) nuclear war

Base your answer to question 40 on the poem below and on your knowledge of social studies.

HARLEM

What happens to a dream deferred?

Does it dry up
like a raisin in the sun?
Or fester like a sore—
And then run?
Does it stink like rotten meat?
Or crust and sugar over—
like a syrupy sweet?

Maybe it just sags
like a heavy load.

Or does it explode?

— Langston Hughes, 1951 (adapted)

40 The "dream deferred" in this poem refers to the hopes African Americans had for

(1) social and political equality
(2) an independent African American nation
(3) access to affordable medical treatment
(4) separate public accommodations

41 One of the main effects of the passage of the Interstate Highway Act of 1956 was the expansion of

(1) ridership on long-distance passenger trains
(2) immigrant populations
(3) communities in the suburbs
(4) the airline industry

42 One way in which the Supreme Court decisions in *Mapp* v. *Ohio* (1961), *Gideon* v. *Wainwright* (1963), and *Miranda* v. *Arizona* (1966) are similar is that each resulted in

(1) more legal searches without warrants
(2) fewer gun control regulations
(3) additional limitations on religious freedom
(4) expanded rights for people accused of crimes

43 A major impact of the 24th amendment banning poll taxes and of the 1965 Voting Rights Act was the

(1) increase in the number of Jim Crow laws
(2) movement to create a new political party for Hispanics
(3) decrease in voting among African American women
(4) elimination of discriminatory voting practices against African Americans

Base your answer to question 44 on the cartoon below and on your knowledge of social studies.

Source: Jimmy Margulies, *The Record* (Hackensack, NJ), April 14, 2009

44 Which statement best expresses the cartoonist's point of view?

(1) Citizens sometimes fail to appreciate the tax-funded benefits provided by government.

(2) More social benefits programs are needed for older Americans.

(3) Older Americans reject tax-supported government assistance.

(4) The Tea Party movement lacks public support.

45 President George Washington's response to the Whiskey Rebellion (1794) and President Dwight Eisenhower's response to events at Little Rock High School (1957) show that the

(1) Supreme Court has often declared presidential actions unconstitutional

(2) federal supremacy clause of the Constitution is rarely enforced

(3) states have been successful in defying federal law

(4) president may use troops to enforce federal decisions

46 Which book title is accurately matched with the book's theme?

(1) *Uncle Tom's Cabin*—political machine corruption

(2) *The Jungle*—environmental conservation

(3) *How the Other Half Lives*—urban poverty

(4) *The Grapes of Wrath*—racial discrimination

47 **"Attorney General Palmer Orders Raids on Reported Communists"**

"Senator McCarthy Launches Investigation of Accused Traitors in State Department"

"Attorney General Ashcroft Authorizes Use of Wiretaps on Suspected Terrorists"

These headlines demonstrate the tension between

(1) States rights and federal control

(2) Democratic and Republican party platforms

(3) national security and individual liberties

(4) legislative authority and executive power

Base your answer to question 48 on the cartoon below and on your knowledge of social studies.

Source: Pat Oliphant, November 10, 2000

48 This cartoon was published in response to the

   (1) ratification of the 22nd amendment limiting presidential terms
   (2) influence of third-party candidates in presidential elections
   (3) decision of the Supreme Court establishing the "one man-one vote" principle
   (4) dispute over the presidential election between George W. Bush and Al Gore

Base your answer to question 49 on the cartoon below and on your knowledge of social studies.

Into the abyss

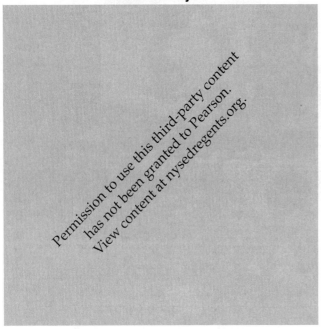

Permission to use this third-party content has not been granted to Pearson. View content at nysedregents.org.

49 The main idea of the cartoon is that President Barack Obama

(1) is determined to end President Lyndon B. Johnson's foreign policy commitments

(2) is better prepared than President Lyndon B. Johnson to lead the nation in war

(3) should learn from President Lyndon B. Johnson's failure in Vietnam

(4) should follow the advice of President Lyndon B. Johnson

50 "Hoover and Smith Campaign on Radio"

"Kennedy Passes Nixon in Polls After Televised Debate"

"Obama Raises Record Donations Using the Internet"

Which statement about the use of media in political campaigns is illustrated by these headlines?

(1) Media bias does not affect the ability of political leaders to communicate with voters.

(2) Political leaders adapt to new forms of media to communicate with voters.

(3) Electronic media are an ineffective way for political leaders to communicate with voters.

(4) Endorsements by the media have the greatest influence on voters.

Answers to the essay questions are to be written in the separate essay booklet.

In developing your answer to Part II, be sure to keep these general definitions in mind:
- (a) **describe** means "to illustrate something in words or tell about it"
- (b) **discuss** means "to make observations about something using facts, reasoning, and argument; to present in some detail"

Part II

THEMATIC ESSAY QUESTION

Directions: Write a well-organized essay that includes an introduction, several paragraphs addressing the task below, and a conclusion.

Theme: Foreign Policy—Latin America and the Caribbean

> During the 19th and 20th centuries, the foreign policy goals of the United States led to many diplomatic *and/or* military actions involving nations in Latin America and the Caribbean.

Task:

> Select *two* United States diplomatic *and/or* military actions involving nations in Latin America and the Caribbean and for *each*
> - Describe the historical circumstances that led to the United States action
> - Describe a goal the United States had in pursuing this action
> - Discuss the success *and/or* failure of the United States in achieving this goal

You may use any United States diplomatic and/or military action involving nations in Latin America and the Caribbean. Some suggestions you might wish to consider include issuance of the Monroe Doctrine in 1823, declaration of war against Mexico in 1846, declaration of war against Spain in 1898, acquisition of the Panama Canal Zone in 1903, Roosevelt Corollary to the Monroe Doctrine in 1904, announcement of the Good Neighbor Policy in 1933, naval blockade of Cuba in 1962, and adoption of the North American Free Trade Agreement (NAFTA) in 1994.

You are *not* limited to these suggestions.

Guidelines:

In your essay, be sure to:
- Develop all aspects of the task
- Support the theme with relevant facts, examples, and details
- Use a logical and clear plan of organization, including an introduction and a conclusion that are beyond a restatement of the theme

NAME _____ SCHOOL _____

Part III

DOCUMENT-BASED QUESTION

   This question is based on the accompanying documents. The question is designed to test your ability to work with historical documents. Some of these documents have been edited for the purposes of this question. As you analyze the documents, take into account the source of each document and any point of view that may be presented in the document. Keep in mind that the language used in a document may reflect the historical context of the time in which it was written.

Historical Context:

> In United States history, there have been conflicts between the three branches of government. Three issues that have led to conflict include **President Andrew Jackson's refusal to enforce a Supreme Court decision, the Senate's debate over the Treaty of Versailles negotiated by President Woodrow Wilson,** and **the investigation by Congress of President Richard Nixon's role in the Watergate affair.**

Task: Using the information from the documents and your knowledge of United States history, answer the questions that follow each document in Part A. Your answers to the questions will help you write the Part B essay in which you will be asked to

> Choose **two** of the issues mentioned in the historical context and for **each**
> - Describe the historical circumstances that led to the conflict between two branches of government
> - Discuss how the outcome of the conflict affected the United States *and/or* American society

In developing your answers to Part III, be sure to keep these general definitions in mind:
   (a) <u>describe</u> means "to illustrate something in words or tell about it"
   (b) <u>discuss</u> means "to make observations about something using facts, reasoning, and argument; to present in some detail"

Part A
Short-Answer Questions

Directions: Analyze the documents and answer the short-answer questions that follow each document in the space provided.

Document 1

...The Cherokees of Georgia, one of the most progressive tribes, attempted to consolidate their position there by setting up a state within a state. They were encouraged to do this by a series of treaties with the United States that recognized them as a nation capable of making peace and war, owning the land within its boundaries and "punishing its own citizens by its own laws." Georgia was bound, like any other state, to observe the treaties concluded by the federal government, but was obdurate [uncompromising] where the Cherokee treaties were concerned. It [Georgia] refused to recognize the Cherokees as an independent nation, and pressed them to sell their lands. They [the Cherokees] turned a deaf ear to this demand and asked for federal protection. In two major cases [*Cherokee Nation* v. *State of Georgia* (1831) and *Worcester* v. *Georgia* (1832)], the United States Supreme Court upheld the "rights" of the Cherokees against Georgia, only to have the state flout [ignore] each decision.

[President Andrew] Jackson supported Georgia. Whether or not he made the famous comment, "John Marshall has made his opinion, now let him enforce it," the Jacksonian policy was in full accord with the spirit of the remark. His first annual message [December 1829] asked Congress to set aside a region in the Far West to which the Indians might remove. Congress did so by a strict party vote, and the forced migration began, to continue through the decade of the eighteen-thirties....

Source: Glyndon G. Van Deusen, *The Jacksonian Era: 1828–1848,* Harper & Row, 1959

1a According to Glyndon G. Van Deusen, what was **one** reason the Cherokees asked for federal protection from the state of Georgia? [1]

_____

_____

Score [ ]

b According to Glyndon G. Van Deusen, what was **one** action taken by President Andrew Jackson that supported Georgia? [1]

_____

_____

Score [ ]

Document 2a

Effect of Policies Toward Native American Indians, 1830–1850

Source: Irving F. Ahlquist et al., *United States History,* Addison-Wesley, 1984 (adapted)

Document 2b

Source: Robert Lindneux, *Trail of Tears*

2 Based on these documents, what was **one** effect of President Andrew Jackson's policies toward Native American Indians? [1]

_____

_____

Score ▢

Document 3

...In the Indian Territory problems quickly developed among the new arrivals and Cherokees who had already settled, especially as reprisals were taken against the contingent [group] who had signed the Treaty of New Echota [1835 treaty with the Cherokees]. As these problems were resolved, the Cherokees proceeded to adapt to their new homeland, and they reestablished their own system of government, which was modeled on that of the United States....

This autonomy remained reasonably strong until the Civil War, when a faction of the Cherokees sided with the Confederacy. During Reconstruction they suffered a loss of self-government and, more importantly, their land base. Government annuities [payments] were reduced, and lands were sold to newly arrived tribes. Cessions of land continued during the later 19th century, and the federal government emerged as the major force for land cession under the Dawes Act of 1887, which divided up tribal lands. The establishment of the state of Oklahoma in 1907 increased pressure for land cessions. Many people of questionable Cherokee ancestry managed to get on the tribal rolls and participate in the allotment of these lands to individuals. By the early 1970s the western Cherokees had lost title to over 19 million acres of land....

Source: Trail of Tears Association

3 Based on this document, what is *one* impact of the federal government's policies toward the Cherokees? [1]

_____

_____

Score ☐

Document 4

...When, in 1919, President [Woodrow] Wilson sailed back home after his triumphant progress throughout Europe, he was the virtual author of the peace treaty. When the three government leaders — Lloyd George, Signor Orlando, Georges Clemenceau — saw him off they mimicked the joy and grief of disciples parting from an holy man.

By the way — and it's important to the developing plot — none of them liked him. But they all knew that the success of the infant League of Nations would depend a great deal on its care and feeding by the United States. They were confident, as Wilson was, that the Treaty would pass the United States Senate.

A little detail to which Europeans didn't pay much attention at the time, namely a firm clause in the constitution of the United States, ratified in 1787.* It laid down in article two, which is about the powers of the president — "He shall have power by and with the advice and consent of the Senate to make treaties, provided two thirds of the Senate present concur."...

Much worse for him and for the fate of the League of Nations, President Wilson was openly detested by the man who, in this cause, carried most weight in the Congress — the chairman of the Senate foreign relations committee — who would have and has today really the last word about whether to provide the necessary Senate consent to any foreign treaty....

Source: "A Plea to the Senate," *BBC News,* October 15, 1999 (adapted)

* The United States Constitution was actually ratified in 1788.

4 According to this *BBC News* article, what was **one** problem faced by President Woodrow Wilson in his efforts to gain Senate approval of the Treaty of Versailles? [1]

_____

_____

Score ☐

Document 5a

Interrupting the Ceremony

Source: Carey Orr, *Chicago Daily Tribune,* December 27, 1918 (adapted)

Document 5b

By United Press

WASHINGTON, March 20. — The Peace Treaty is now up to President Wilson.

The Senate washed its hands of the pact last night when by a vote of 49 to 35 it refused to ratify it, and by a vote of 47 to 37 voted to send it back to President Wilson with word that it could not be ratified. The question today was: "What will President Wilson do about it."

He can send it back to the Senate. In that case Senator Lodge and other Republicans, as well as some Democrats, declared that no action would be taken on it until after the issue of the treaty or no treaty is fought out in the coming campaign.

He can go to the American people in a "solemn referendum," as he said he would do in a letter to the Jackson Day dinner on the question of ratification of the pact as it is as nn [an] issue in the national campaign of 1920.

He can drop the treaty and begin negotiations with Germany for resuming the state of peace.

The general expectation among senators is that he will take the second course and ask the Democratic party to make the treaty the paramount issue in the campaign....

Source: *Columbia Evening Missourian,* March 20, 1920 (adapted)

5 Based on these documents, what was *one* outcome of the Senate debate over the Treaty of Versailles? [1]

_____

_____

Score ☐

Document 6

...The last chance of reversing that decision [the Senate's final vote on the Treaty of Versailles] lay in the election of the Democratic candidate, James Cox, to succeed [President Woodrow] Wilson in the White House. But in the November election, Cox was defeated, and Warren Harding, the Republican, became President. Before he was elected, some believed that Harding, too, wanted to see America in the League of Nations, but as soon as he took office he made clear he intended to keep the United States free of any such involvement with the rest of the world's troubles. Thus started the twenty years during which America isolated itself, twenty years for which the whole world, including, eventually, the Americans themselves, were to pay such a terrible price....

Source: George Scott, *The Rise and Fall of the League of Nations,* Macmillan Publishing Co., 1973

6 According to George Scott, what was **one** impact of the Senate's final vote on the Treaty of Versailles on United States foreign policy? [1]

_____

_____

Score [ ]

Document 7a

...By now, of course, Watergate has become part of our folklore: Five men wearing business suits and surgical gloves arrested in the middle of the night with illegal bugging devices at the Democratic Party headquarters in the Watergate building in Washington, D.C. The burglars turned out to be part of a wide-ranging political espionage and sabotage operation run by President [Richard] Nixon's top aides, one that triggered a massive White House cover-up directed by the president himself. After that cover-up unraveled, more than 70 people, including cabinet members and White House assistants, were convicted of criminal abuses of power; only a pardon by his presidential successor spared Nixon himself from becoming the first chief executive in history to be indicted for felonies committed in the Oval Office. In the words of Stanley Kutler, the scandal's leading historian, Watergate "consumed and convulsed the nation and tested the constitutional and political system as it had not been tested since the Civil War."...

Source: Mark Feldstein, "Watergate Revisited," *American Journalism Review,* August/September 2004

7a Based on this document, identify **one** event that led to the Watergate investigation.   [1]

_____

_____

Score [ ]

Document 7b

Trials and Tribulations > Overview

When Congress reconvened in January 1974, following its Christmas break, the House of Representatives compounded Nixon's legal troubles. On February 6, it authorized the Judiciary Committee to investigate grounds for the impeachment of President Nixon. This added to investigations already underway by Judge [John] Sirica and the grand jury, Special Prosecutor [Leon] Jaworski and the Justice Department, and the work done by the Senate select committee on Watergate....

The Aftermath > Overview

By May 9, 1974, the House Judiciary Committee began hearings on articles of impeachment. Judge Sirica turned over to the committee evidence gleaned against Nixon by the grand jury. Meanwhile, Jaworski appealed to the Supreme Court to force Nixon to surrender more tapes. On July 24, the Court handed down an 8-0 decision, laying bare the president's last line of defense.

In late July, the House committee drafted three articles of impeachment against Nixon:

- Obstructing the Watergate investigation
- Misuse of power and violating his oath of office
- Failure to comply with House subpoenas...

Source: "The Watergate Files," Gerald R. Ford Presidential Library & Museum

7b Based on this document, identify *one* action the legislative branch took during the Watergate investigation. [1]

Score ☐

Document 8

...The central issue raised by Watergate, finally, was not resolved. This was how to make American government, especially the President, more accountable to the people. A raft of legislation in 1973–74, including the War Powers Act of 1973, a law to regulate campaign financing and spending (1974), a Freedom of Information Act (1974), and a Congressional Budget and Impoundment Act (1974), tried to promote such accountability, but these laws for the most part failed to accomplish what they set out to do, largely because Presidents and other politicians figured out ways of evading them. As acts by subsequent Presidents made clear, White House high-handedness could and did happen again in the future....

Source: James T. Patterson, *Grand Expectations: The United States, 1945–1974,*
Oxford University Press, 1996 (adapted)

8 According to James T. Patterson, what is ***one*** impact of the Watergate investigation? [1]

_____

_____

Score ☐

Document 9

...The founders of this nation would have been stunned by the revelations of Watergate. But they would have been especially proud of the judiciary they had created. There was a trial judge who did not accept distortions of the truth. There was an appellate court that acted with decisiveness and dispatch to meet the first challenge by President Nixon opposing the release of the tapes. The same trial court and the same appellate court, without delay, decided that a crucial grand jury report should be transmitted to the House Judiciary Committee. And that trial court overruled the President's claim of executive privilege in response to a subpoena *duces tecum* [to produce evidence] in a situation involving criminal wrongdoing. The Supreme Court, in the interest of expediting [hastening] justice, bypassed the Court of Appeals and then boldly and with a minimum of delay laid to rest the troublesome problems that beset the nation....

From Watergate we learned what generations before us have known: our Constitution works. And during the Watergate years it was interpreted again so as to reaffirm that no one—absolutely no one—is above the law....

Source: Leon Jaworski, *The Right and the Power: The Prosecution of Watergate,* Pocket Books, 1977

9 According to Leon Jaworski, what is **one** impact of the Watergate investigation on the United States? [1]

_____

_____

Score ☐

Part B
Essay

Directions: Write a well-organized essay that includes an introduction, several paragraphs, and a conclusion. Use evidence from *at least four* documents in your essay. Support your response with relevant facts, examples, and details. Include additional outside information.

Historical Context:

In United States history, there have been conflicts between the three branches of government. Three issues that have led to conflict include **President Andrew Jackson's refusal to enforce a Supreme Court decision, the Senate's debate over the Treaty of Versailles negotiated by President Woodrow Wilson,** and **the investigation by Congress of President Richard Nixon's role in the Watergate affair.**

Task: Using the information from the documents and your knowledge of United States history, write an essay in which you

> Choose **two** of the issues mentioned in the historical context and for **each**
> - Describe the historical circumstances that led to the conflict between two branches of government
> - Discuss how the outcome of the conflict affected the United States *and/or* American society

Guidelines:

In your essay, be sure to
- Develop all aspects of the task
- Incorporate information from *at least four* documents
- Incorporate relevant outside information
- Support the theme with relevant facts, examples, and details
- Use a logical and clear plan of organization, including an introduction and a conclusion that are beyond a restatement of the theme

Regents Examination – August 2015

This section contains the Regents Examination in United States History and Government that was given in New York State in August 2015.

Circle your answers to Part I on this exam and write your answers to the thematic essay and document-based essay questions on separate sheets of paper. Be sure to refer to the test-taking strategies in the front of this book as you prepare to answer the test questions.

Part I

Answer all questions in this part.

Directions (1–50): For each statement or question, record on your separate answer sheet the *number* of the word or expression that, of those given, best completes the statement or answers the question.

Base your answer to question 1 on the map below and on your knowledge of social studies.

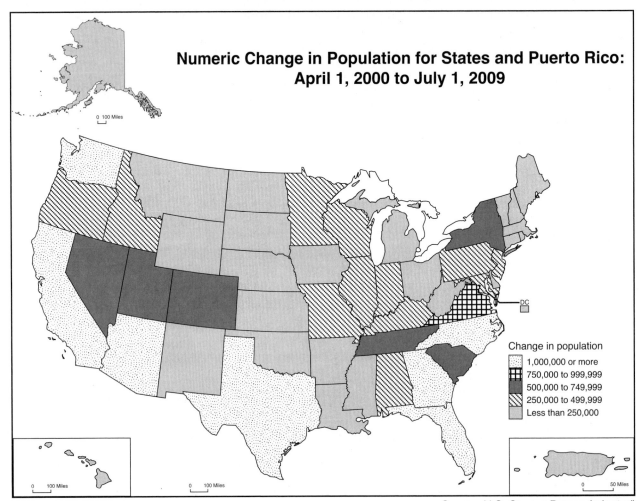

Numeric Change in Population for States and Puerto Rico: April 1, 2000 to July 1, 2009

Change in population
- 1,000,000 or more
- 750,000 to 999,999
- 500,000 to 749,999
- 250,000 to 499,999
- Less than 250,000

Source: U.S. Census Bureau (adapted)

1 Information such as that shown on the map is important to state governments because it is used to

(1) establish immigration quotas

(2) set Social Security taxation rates

(3) identify the best location for new military bases

(4) determine the number of seats each state will have in the House of Representatives

2 River systems were important to the development of the United States because they

(1) allowed Americans to travel easily between the east coast and the west coast
(2) prevented foreign invasion of United States territory
(3) provided routes for shipping agricultural and manufacturing products
(4) made the southeast the major destination for immigrants

Base your answer to question 3 on the passage below and on your knowledge of social studies.

…that to secure these rights, governments are instituted among men, deriving their just powers from the consent of the governed, —that whenever any form of government becomes destructive of these ends, it is the right of the people to alter or to abolish it, and to institute new government, …

— Declaration of Independence, 1776

3 This passage demonstrates that Thomas Jefferson was directly influenced by the

(1) ideas of John Locke
(2) goals of the Albany Plan of Union
(3) belief in the divine right of kings
(4) traditional separation of church and state

4 At the Constitutional Convention of 1787, supporters of the Virginia plan and supporters of the New Jersey plan differed over the method for

(1) determining congressional representation
(2) selecting the president's cabinet
(3) adopting the amendment process
(4) giving powers to the executive branch

5 Which provision of the original Constitution allows Congress to enact legislation that adapts to changing circumstances?

(1) due process
(2) elastic clause
(3) electoral college
(4) Three-fifths Compromise

Base your answer to question 6 on the passage below and on your knowledge of social studies.

Article 6. There shall be neither slavery nor involuntary servitude in the said territory, otherwise than in the punishment of crimes whereof the party shall have been duly convicted: Provided, always, that any person escaping into the same, from whom labor or service is lawfully claimed in any one of the original states, such fugitive may be lawfully reclaimed and conveyed to the person claiming his or her labor or service as aforesaid. …

— Northwest Ordinance, 1787

6 In which Supreme Court case did this provision of the Northwest Ordinance play an important part?

(1) *McCulloch* v. *Maryland (1819)*
(2) *Worcester* v. *Georgia (1832)*
(3) *Dred Scott* v. *Sanford (1857)*
(4) *Plessy* v. *Ferguson (1896)*

7 The *Federalist Papers*, written by Alexander Hamilton, John Jay, and James Madison, were intended to

(1) promote independence from Great Britain
(2) persuade voters to keep the Articles of Confederation
(3) win support for ratification of the Constitution
(4) endorse candidates running for Congress

8 Which provision of the Bill of Rights was influenced by the trial of John Peter Zenger?

(1) right to bear arms
(2) right to an attorney
(3) freedom of religion
(4) freedom of the press

9 The Preamble of the Constitution demonstrates that the writers believed that sovereignty belongs to the

(1) federal government   (3) president
(2) state governments   (4) people

10 **"Senate Rejects Supreme Court Nominee"**

"Supreme Court Declares National Recovery Act (NRA) Unconstitutional"

"Congress Overrides Truman Veto of Taft-Hartley Act"

Each of these headlines illustrates the use of

(1) reserved powers   (3) executive privilege

(2) checks and balances   (4) federal supremacy

11 During the presidency of George Washington, disagreements between Alexander Hamilton and Thomas Jefferson over the interpretation of the Constitution contributed to the

(1) impeachment of federal judges

(2) defeat of the Whiskey Rebellion

(3) formation of political parties

(4) elimination of the commerce clause

12 One reason President George Washington called for a policy of neutrality in the 1790s was to

(1) improve his popularity among Federalist voters

(2) avoid United States participation in European wars

(3) gain support for the development of a United States navy

(4) enforce the Treaty of Alliance with France

13 Which geographical consideration had the greatest influence on President Thomas Jefferson's decision to purchase the Louisiana Territory in 1803?

(1) Large gold reserves were located in the territory.

(2) The size of the territory would create a barrier to French influence.

(3) The Rocky Mountain region was an outlet for future population growth.

(4) Full control of the port of New Orleans on the Mississippi River would be established.

14 The Supreme Court decision in *Marbury* v. *Madison* (1803) strengthened the constitutional principle of separation of powers by

(1) defining the Court's role in impeachment trials

(2) clarifying the president's authority to veto bills passed by Congress

(3) denying states the right to sue the federal government

(4) establishing the Court's right to review the constitutionality of federal laws

15 One result of the War of 1812 was that the United States

(1) acquired French-held territory in southern Canada

(2) maintained its independence and its territory

(3) lost control of the Ohio River valley

(4) gained territory from Mexico

16 Which heading best completes the partial outline below?

I. _____

    A. Missouri Compromise

    B. Compromise of 1850

    C. Kansas-Nebraska Act

(1) Rise of Sectionalism

(2) Impact of Industrialization

(3) Examples of Religious Revivalism

(4) Events Leading to the Mexican War

17 The Homestead Act and grants of land to railroads were used to

(1) raise money to finance the federal government

(2) limit the influence of monopolies and trusts

(3) support the development of state universities

(4) encourage settlement of the West

18 What was one effect of the Industrial Revolution on United States agriculture in the late 1800s?

(1) a decrease in the size of farms

(2) a decrease in tenant farming and sharecropping

(3) an increase in agricultural imports

(4) an increase in productivity

19 As the Civil War ended, which action was supported by President Abraham Lincoln and the Radical Republicans?

(1) abolishing the institution of slavery by a constitutional amendment
(2) passing Black Codes to guarantee equality for formerly enslaved persons
(3) putting Confederate leaders on trial for war crimes
(4) ending the military occupation of the South immediately

20 In the late 1800s, which concept was used to justify the accumulation of great wealth and economic power?

(1) Manifest Destiny
(2) self-determination
(3) Social Darwinism
(4) conspicuous consumption

21 The Chinese Exclusion Act of 1882 and the Gentlemen's Agreement with Japan in 1907 both illustrate

(1) the role of nativism in the development of United States policies
(2) imperialist attitudes in foreign affairs
(3) restrictive trading policies toward Asian nations
(4) the influence of big business on foreign policy

22 President Theodore Roosevelt was called a trustbuster because he

(1) supported the building of the Panama Canal
(2) negotiated peace between Russia and Japan
(3) supported legal action against business monopolies
(4) protected public lands from environmental damage

23 President Theodore Roosevelt's commitment to the proverb, "Speak softly and carry a big stick; you will go far," was most clearly shown when he

(1) opposed consumer protection laws
(2) intervened in Latin American affairs
(3) promoted the conservation of natural resources
(4) conducted the Bull Moose campaign of 1912

24 Which heading best completes the partial outline below?

> I. _____
>
>   A. Direct election of senators
>   B. Federal income tax
>   C. National woman's suffrage

(1) Progressive Era Constitutional Amendments
(2) Steps to Promote Civil Rights
(3) Municipal and State Actions
(4) Changes During World War I

25 One way in which the Federal Trade Commission (1914) and the Clayton Antitrust Act (1914) are similar is that both

(1) helped to end child labor in factories
(2) attempted to correct abusive business practices
(3) advanced laissez-faire economic principles
(4) increased wages for factory workers

26 The Supreme Court decision in *Schenck* v. *United States* (1919) supported the position that during a national emergency

(1) internal migration may be restricted
(2) civil liberties of United States citizens may be limited
(3) Congress may take control of the economy
(4) minority groups may be segregated from the general population

27 During the 1920s, the Palmer raids, immigration quotas, and the trial of Sacco and Vanzetti resulted from

(1) racial prejudice against African Americans
(2) opposition to the Ku Klux Klan
(3) the fear that American values were threatened by radical ideas
(4) the need to strengthen national defense

28 Which factor led to agricultural overproduction and falling farm prices during the 1920s?

(1) decline in European demand after World War I
(2) lower tariffs enacted by Congress
(3) lack of access to cheap credit
(4) decreasing population in cities of the South

Base your answers to questions 29 and 30 on the photograph below and on your knowledge of social studies.

"Hooverville," Seattle, Washington

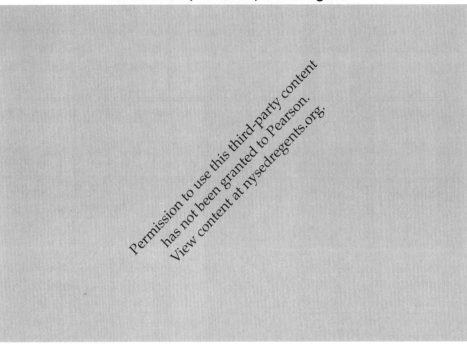

Permission to use this third-party content has not been granted to Pearson. View content at nysedregents.org.

29 What was the main reason for the emergence of "Hoovervilles" like the one shown in the photograph?

(1) Many Americans had lost jobs during the Great Depression.
(2) Thousands of homes had been destroyed by the effects of the Dust Bowl.
(3) Housing projects could not keep up with the demand for homes needed by the poor.
(4) Preparations for World War II had created a shortage of building materials.

30 The New Deal of President Franklin D. Roosevelt attempted to address the problem shown in the photograph by

(1) expanding the armed services
(2) using the police to evict "Hooverville" residents
(3) delivering food, water, and medical supplies to residents
(4) providing jobs and home loans to American workers

31 During the early 1930s, the main goal of the Bonus Army was to pressure the Hoover administration to

(1) strengthen the nation's defenses
(2) end the military draft
(3) bring American troops home from overseas
(4) support the early payment of money promised to veterans

32 Opponents of the New Deal criticized President Franklin D. Roosevelt for

(1) expanding the role and size of the federal government
(2) permitting banks to operate without government regulation
(3) weakening the executive branch
(4) reducing spending to balance the budget

Base your answers to questions 33 and 34 on the poster below and on your knowledge of social studies.

Source: Office of Price Administration, 1943

33 The poster indicates that rationing during World War II was a

(1) way of assuring that only the wealthy could buy certain products
(2) necessity caused by farm failures during the Great Depression
(3) program that was to be applied equally to all Americans
(4) policy to encourage small business owners

34 What was a major reason for wartime rationing?

(1) restricting lower-priced food imports
(2) ensuring that troops were adequately supplied
(3) providing jobs for the unemployed
(4) preventing currency deflation

35 The relocation of Japanese Americans from the West Coast during World War II occurred because

(1) most of them were not citizens of the United States
(2) they refused to serve in the United States military
(3) they were needed to work at inland defense industries
(4) military authorities considered them a threat to national security

Base your answers to questions 36 and 37 on the passage below and on your knowledge of social studies.

...We have agreed on common policies and plans for enforcing the unconditional surrender terms which we shall impose together on Nazi Germany after German armed resistance has been finally crushed. These terms will not be made known until the final defeat of Germany has been accomplished. Under the agreed plan, the forces of the three powers will each occupy a separate zone of Germany. Coordinated administration and control has been provided for under the plan through a central control commission consisting of the Supreme Commanders of the three powers with headquarters in Berlin. It has been agreed that France should be invited by the three powers, if she should so desire, to take over a zone of occupation, and to participate as a fourth member of the control commission. The limits of the French zone will be agreed by the four Governments concerned through their representatives on the European Advisory Commission. ...

— Joint Statement of President Franklin D. Roosevelt,
Prime Minister Winston Churchill, and
Marshal Joseph Stalin at Yalta, February 11, 1945

36 Based on this passage, a major purpose of the Yalta Conference was to

(1) prepare for control of Germany after World War II
(2) offer Germany generous terms of surrender to shorten the war
(3) rebuild German industries following the war
(4) prevent Germany's membership in the United Nations

37 The plan described in this passage contributed to the

(1) complete removal of United States troops from Germany
(2) authorization for Germany to join the Axis powers
(3) long-term division of Germany into two nations
(4) domination of Germany by France

38 Which action best illustrates the Cold War policy of containment?

(1) participating in the Nuremberg trials
(2) creating the North Atlantic Treaty Organization (NATO)
(3) encouraging scientific cooperation between the Allies
(4) recognizing the state of Israel in 1948

39 The Supreme Court under Chief Justice Earl Warren (1953–1969) is considered one of the most liberal in United States history because it

(1) worked effectively with lower courts
(2) gained the overwhelming support of the American people
(3) expanded the civil rights of various groups of people
(4) favored a strict interpretation of the Constitution

Base your answers to questions 40 and 41 on the cartoon below and on your knowledge of social studies.

"I'm Mrs. Edward M. Barnes. Where do I live?"

Source: Robert J. Day, *New Yorker*, 1954 (adapted)

40 Which characteristic of American life in the 1950s is illustrated in this cartoon?

　(1) growth of the elderly population
　(2) effects of suburbanization
　(3) decreasing use of automobiles
　(4) declining importance of the media

41 Which factor directly contributed to the post–World War II development of the community shown in the cartoon?

　(1) rise in the birth rate
　(2) decrease in school construction
　(3) decline in the availability of home loans
　(4) increase in the number of women in the labor force

Base your answers to questions 42 and 43 on the cartoon below and on your knowledge of social studies.

National Security Blanket

Source: Herblock, *Washington Post*, May 27, 1973
(adapted)

42 The main idea of this cartoon is that President Richard Nixon

    (1) refused to become involved in political activities
    (2) supported campaign finance reform
    (3) exercised presidential power to defend national interests
    (4) tried to use foreign policy issues to cover up illegal activities

43 Based on this cartoon, one effect of President Richard Nixon's actions on the United States was to

    (1) prove that the powers of presidents are unlimited
    (2) decrease the probability of impeachment for future presidents
    (3) weaken the public's trust in political leaders
    (4) demonstrate that the Supreme Court could not rule on presidential wrongdoing

44 Which statement most accurately explains why the War Powers Act (1973) was passed?

    (1) President Lyndon B. Johnson failed to send enough troops to South Vietnam.
    (2) President Richard Nixon negotiated a peace treaty with North Vietnam.
    (3) Congress wanted to reassert its right to authorize military action.
    (4) Military leaders demanded limits on presidential authority during wartime.

45 The 1972, 1979, and 1987 missile reduction agreements between the United States and the Soviet Union are examples of the foreign policy of

    (1) brinksmanship   (3) appeasement
    (2) détente   (4) neutrality

Base your answer to question 46 on the cartoon below and on your knowledge of social studies.

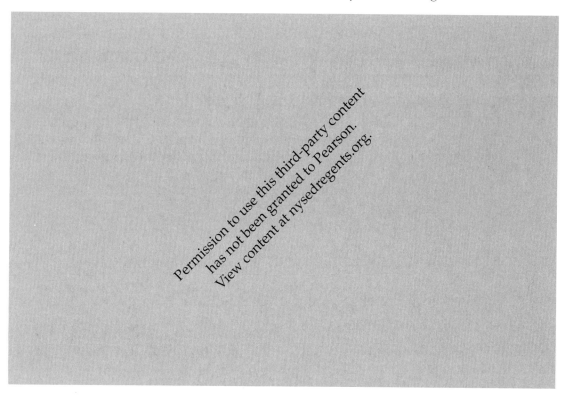

46 In this 2008 cartoon about a tax proposal by President George W. Bush, the cartoonist is implying that China anticipated

    (1) a more favorable balance of trade with the United States

    (2) greater difficulty in selling its products in the United States

    (3) the opening of new markets for Chinese goods in Europe

    (4) an increase in United States tariffs that could cause a recession in China

Base your answers to questions 47 and 48 on the cartoon below and on your knowledge of social studies.

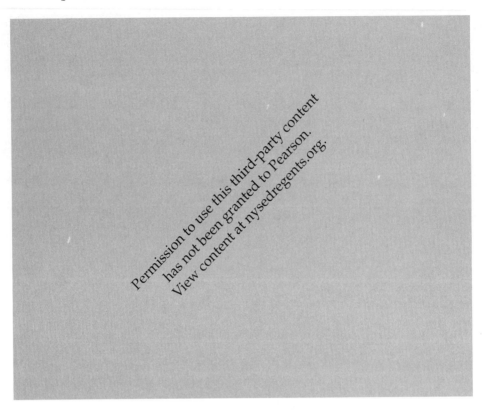

Permission to use this third-party content has not been granted to Pearson. View content at nysedregents.org.

47 Which statement most accurately expresses the cartoonist's point of view?

(1) Presidents have failed to learn the right lessons from past experiences in waging war.
(2) Victory in Vietnam inspired later presidents to become involved in wars.
(3) The Iraq and Afghanistan wars ended in quick victories for the United States.
(4) The military tactics used in Vietnam have been effective in Iraq and Afghanistan.

48 The cartoonist most likely refers to the war in Afghanistan as "Obama's Vietnam" because

(1) the war was begun during the administration of President Barack Obama
(2) the war ended soon after President Barack Obama took office
(3) President Barack Obama favored the reinstatement of the military draft
(4) President Barack Obama chose to continue military involvement in Afghanistan

49 **"President Carter Negotiates Camp David Accords"**
"President Reagan Sends Troops to Lebanon"
"President Bush Orders Operation Desert Storm"

Which United States foreign policy goal is most closely associated with these headlines?

(1) imperialism in Latin America
(2) globalization of trade
(3) stability in the Middle East
(4) delivery of humanitarian relief

50 During the Jacksonian Era, elections became more democratic when

(1) the poll tax was abolished
(2) states removed property qualifications for voting
(3) a women's rights amendment was ratified
(4) 18-year-old citizens were allowed to vote

Answers to the essay questions are to be written in the separate essay booklet.

In developing your answer to Part II, be sure to keep these general definitions in mind:
  (a) **describe** means "to illustrate something in words or tell about it"
  (b) **discuss** means "to make observations about something using facts, reasoning, and argument; to present in some detail"

Part II

THEMATIC ESSAY QUESTION

Directions: Write a well-organized essay that includes an introduction, several paragraphs addressing the task below, and a conclusion.

Theme: Foreign Policy

Throughout United States history, presidents have made foreign policy decisions that have been opposed by individuals and groups. These decisions have had an impact on both the United States and on other countries and regions.

Task:

Select *two* foreign policy decisions that have been opposed by individuals and groups and for *each*
- Describe the historical circumstances that led the president to make the decision
- Discuss why an individual and/or group opposed the decision
- Discuss the impact of this foreign policy decision on the United States and/or on another country or region

You may use any foreign policy decision that has been opposed by individuals and groups from your study of United States history. Some suggestions you might wish to consider include James K. Polk's decision to send troops to the Rio Grande (1846), William McKinley's decision to annex the Philippines (1898), Woodrow Wilson's support for the Treaty of Versailles (1919–1920), Franklin D. Roosevelt's aid to Great Britain before United States entry into World War II (1939–1941), Harry Truman's decision to defend South Korea (1950–1953), Lyndon B. Johnson's decision to send combat troops to South Vietnam (1965), and George W. Bush's decision to invade Iraq (2003).

You are *not* limited to these suggestions.

Guidelines:

In your essay, be sure to:
- Develop all aspects of the task
- Support the theme with relevant facts, examples, and details
- Use a logical and clear plan of organization, including an introduction and a conclusion that are beyond a restatement of the theme

This page left blank intentionally.

GO ON TO THE NEXT PAGE ⟹

NAME _____ SCHOOL _____

Part III

DOCUMENT-BASED QUESTION

This question is based on the accompanying documents. The question is designed to test your ability to work with historical documents. Some of these documents have been edited for the purposes of this question. As you analyze the documents, take into account the source of each document and any point of view that may be presented in the document. Keep in mind that the language used in a document may reflect the historical context of the time in which it was written.

Historical Context:

> Throughout the history of the United States, different groups have faced problems in American society. These groups have included **African Americans, industrial workers**, and **persons with disabilities**. Individuals, organizations, and governments have addressed problems faced by these groups.

Task: Using the information from the documents and your knowledge of United States history, answer the questions that follow each document in Part A. Your answers to the questions will help you write the Part B essay in which you will be asked to

> Choose **two** groups mentioned in the historical context and for **each**
> - Describe the historical circumstances surrounding a problem the group faced
> - Discuss how the problem was addressed by an individual, an organization, *and/or* a government

In developing your answers to Part III, be sure to keep these general definitions in mind:
   - (a) <u>describe</u> means "to illustrate something in words or tell about it"
   - (b) <u>discuss</u> means "to make observations about something using facts, reasoning, and argument; to present in some detail"

Part A
Short-Answer Questions

Directions: Analyze the documents and answer the short-answer questions that follow each document in the space provided.

Document 1

This excerpt is from a petition to Congress in 1871 by African Americans in Frankfort, Kentucky, seeking protection from the Ku Klux Klan.

> …We would respectfully state that life, liberty, and property are unprotected among the colored race [African Americans] of this State. Organized bands of desperate and lawless men, mainly composed of soldiers of the late rebel armies, armed, disciplined, and disguised, and bound by oath and secret obligations, have, by force, terror, and violence, subverted [undermined] all civil society among colored people; thus utterly rendering insecure the safety of persons and property, overthrowing all those rights which are the primary basis and objects of the Government, which are expressly guaranteed to us by the Constitution of the United States as amended [by the 13th, 14th, and 15th amendments]. …
>
> We would state that we have been law-abiding citizens, pay our taxes, and in many parts of the State our people have been driven from the polls, refused the right to vote; many have been slaughtered while attempting to vote. We ask, how long is this state of things to last? …

Source: Petition to the United States Congress, March 25, 1871,
Miscellaneous Documents of the United States Senate, 42nd Congress, 1st Session, 1871

1 According to this document, what was *one* problem faced by African Americans in Kentucky? [1]

_____

_____

Score [ ]

Document 2

...We want full manhood suffrage, and we want it now, henceforth and forever. ...

We want the laws enforced against rich as well as poor; against Capitalist as well as Laborer; against white as well as black. We are not more lawless than the white race, we are more often arrested, convicted and mobbed. We want justice even for criminals and outlaws. We want the Constitution of the country enforced. We want Congress to take charge of Congressional elections. We want the Fourteenth Amendment carried out to the letter and every State disfranchised* in Congress which attempts to disfranchise [deny voting rights to] its rightful voters. We want the Fifteenth Amendment enforced and no State allowed to base its franchise simply on color. ...

These are some of the chief things which we want. How shall we get them? By voting where we may vote, by persistent, unceasing agitation; by hammering at the truth, by sacrifice and work. ...

*The 14th amendment provides that states denying voting rights to male citizens will lose some representatives in Congress.

Source: W. E. B. Du Bois, Niagara Movement Address, 1906 (adapted)

2 According to this document, what is **one** demand made by W. E. B. Du Bois regarding the rights of African Americans? [1]

_____

_____

Score ☐

Document 3a

...Many of the issues of civil rights are very complex and most difficult. But about this there can and should be no argument. Every American citizen must have an equal right to vote. There is no reason which can excuse the denial of that right. There is no duty which weighs more heavily on us than the duty we have to ensure that right. ...

Every device of which human ingenuity is capable has been used to deny this right. The Negro [African American] citizen may go to register only to be told that the day is wrong, or the hour is late, or the official in charge is absent. And if he persists, and if he manages to present himself to the registrar, he may be disqualified because he did not spell out his middle name or because he abbreviated a word on the application.

And if he manages to fill out an application he is given a test. The registrar is the sole judge of whether he passes this test. He may be asked to recite the entire Constitution, or explain the most complex provisions of State law. And even a college degree cannot be used to prove that he can read and write. ...

Wednesday I will send to Congress a law designed to eliminate illegal barriers to the right to vote. ...

Source: President Lyndon B. Johnson, Special Message to the Congress: The American Promise, March 15, 1965

3a According to President Lyndon B. Johnson, what is **one** way African Americans are kept from voting? [1]

_____

_____

Score ☐

Document 3b

African American Voter Registration Before and After
Passage of the Voting Rights Act of 1965 (Percent Change)

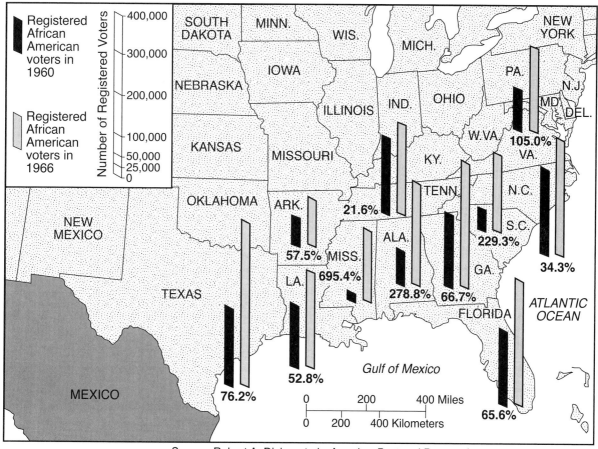

Source: Robert A. Divine et al., *America: Past and Present*, Longman, 1999 (adapted)

3b Based on this map, what was **one** effect of the Voting Rights Act of 1965? [1]

Score ☐

Document 4

This is an excerpt from the author's account of his visit to the Homestead, Pennsylvania, steel mill.

…"How long do you work?" I asked of a young man who stood at the furnace near me.

"Twelve hours," he replied. "The night set go on at six at night and come off at six in the morning. I go on at six and off at six."

"For how much pay?"

"Two dollars and a quarter."

"How much do those men get shovelling there in the rain?"

"One dollar and forty cents." (A cut has since taken place.)

"What proportion of the men get that pay?"

"Two-thirds of the whole plant, nearly two thousand. There are thirty-five hundred men in the mills. They get all prices, of course, from a dollar and forty cents up to the tonnage men, who get five and ten dollars per day when the mills run smooth."

"I suppose not many men make ten dollars per day."

"Well hardly." He smiled. "Of course the 'rollers' and the 'heaters' get the most, but there are only two 'rollers' to each mill, and three 'heaters,' and they are responsible for their product. The most of the men get under two dollars per day."

"And it is twelve hours' work without stop?"

"You bet! And then again you will see we only get this pay part of the time. The mills are liable to be shut down part of the year. They shut down part of the night sometimes, and of course we're docked. Then, again, the tendency of the proprietors is to cut down the tonnage men; that is, the 'rollers' and 'heaters' are now paid by the ton, but they'll some day be paid by the day, like the rest of us."

"You bet they will," said my guide, who seemed quite familiar with the facts. …

Source: Hamlin Garland, "Homestead and its Perilous Trades—Impressions of a Visit," *McClure's Magazine*, June 1894

4 According to Hamlin Garland, state **one** problem faced by workers in the Homestead steel mill. [1]

_____

_____

Score ☐

Document 5a

…We demand a reduction of the hours of labor which would give a due share of work and wages to the reserve army of labor [the unemployed] and eliminate many of the worst abuses of the industrial system now filling our poor houses and jails. The movement for the reduction of the hours of labor is contemporaneous with the introduction of labor saving machinery and has been the most faithful of all reformatory attempts of modern times, since it has clearly revealed the power of the working people to realize an improved industrial system and raises the hope that we may yet be able to stem the tide of economic, social and moral degradations, robbing those who work of four-fifths of their natural wages and keeping the whole of society within a few months of destitution. …

That the lives and limbs of the wage-workers shall be regarded as sacred as those of all others of our fellow human beings; that an injury or destruction of either by reason of negligence or maliciousness of another, shall not leave him without redress simply because he is a wage worker. We demand equality before the law, in fact as well as in theory. …

And by no means the least demand of the Trade Unions is for adequate wages. …

Source: Samuel Gompers, *What Does Labor Want?*, 1893

Document 5b

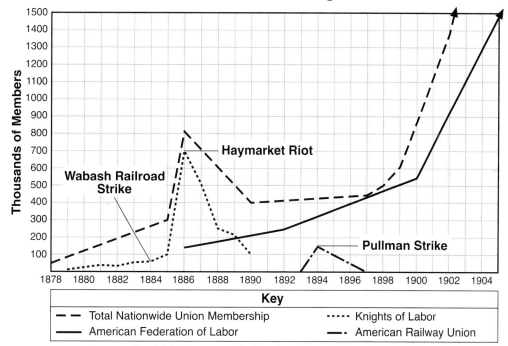

The Growth of Union Membership, 1878–1904

Source: Gerald A. Danzer et al., *The Americans*, McDougall Littell, 1998 (adapted)

5 Based on these documents, what were **two** ways workers tried to address their problems? [2]

(1)_____

_____

Score ☐

(2)_____

_____

Score ☐

Document 6a

This Act defines, as a part of our substantive [essential] law, the right of self-organization of employees in industry for the purpose of collective bargaining, and provides methods by which the Government can safeguard that legal right. It establishes a National Labor Relations Board to hear and determine cases in which it is charged that this legal right is abridged [diminished] or denied, and to hold fair elections to ascertain [determine] who are the chosen representatives of employees. ...

Source: President Franklin D. Roosevelt, Statement on Signing the National Labor Relations Act (Wagner Act),
July 5, 1935

Document 6b

...After many requests on my part the Congress passed a Fair Labor Standards Act, what we call the Wages and Hours Bill. That Act—applying to products in interstate commerce—ends child labor, sets a floor below wages [minimum wage] and a ceiling over hours of labor [maximum hours].

Except perhaps for the Social Security Act, it is the most far-reaching, the most far-sighted program for the benefit of workers ever adopted here or in any other country. Without question it starts us toward a better standard of living and increases purchasing power to buy the products of farm and factory. ...

Source: President Franklin D. Roosevelt, Fireside Chat, June 24, 1938

6 According to President Franklin D. Roosevelt, state **two** ways workers would benefit from legislation passed during his administration. [2]

(1)_____

_____

Score ☐

(2)_____

_____

Score ☐

Document 7

...What results from segregation [of the disabled] is social isolation. Physical and psychological separation, imprisonment in an institution or in a small, dilapidated apartment building, these are the realities for numerous disabled Americans. The psychic cost is incalculable. Enforced dependency and isolation crush the self-image, and combined with other architectural and transportation barriers may prove devastating. The individual cannot find work because the workplaces are inaccessible, employers discriminate against him, and no suitable transportation is available. Because he cannot find suitable work, he cannot afford decent housing. The barriers are inescapably intertwined [connected]. ...

Source: Frank Bowe, *Handicapping America: Barriers to Disabled People*, Harper & Row, 1978

7 According to Frank Bowe, what are **two** problems faced by persons with disabilities? [2]

(1)_____

_____

Score ☐

(2)_____

_____

Score ☐

Document 8

Selected Federal Legislation for Persons with Disabilities

Date Passed	Federal Legislation	Terms
1968	Architectural Barriers Act	Requires that buildings and facilities constructed with federal funding be accessible to people with physical disabilities.
1975	Education for All Handicapped Children Act	Requires that children with disabilities have the right to a public school education in an integrated (least restrictive) environment.
1982	Telecommunications for the Disabled Act	Requires that deaf and hard-of-hearing people have telephone access at important public places.

Source: Center for Assistive Technology and Environmental Access, 2001 (adapted)

8 Based on the information in this chart, state *two* ways federal legislation has helped persons with disabilities. [2]

(1)_____

_____

Score ☐

(2)_____

_____

Score ☐

Document 9

. . . [President Bill] Clinton diffused a controversy that had threatened to mar the dedication when he sided with disabled activists who demanded that a statue be added to the memorial showing FDR [President Franklin D. Roosevelt] in a wheelchair. On Clinton's recommendation, the Senate on Thursday night passed and sent to the House legislation to add the statue. . . .

But the biggest controversy arose over the decision by the FDR Memorial Commission to stick with 1978 statue designs that were in keeping with FDR's own reluctance to be seen publicly in a wheelchair. Roosevelt went to exhausting lengths not to appear disabled.

About two dozen demonstrators sat in wheelchairs, leaned on walkers, hobbled along with crutches or walked with white canes outside the memorial before the dedication. "We are no longer hiding our disabilities," said one of the group, Becky Ogle, 41, who is a double amputee and director of disabled outreach for the White House. "When I was a child growing up, the message to me was I am sick. Well, I am not sick. We are not victims. Attitude is the last barrier for us." . . .

Source: Doug Struck, "Clinton Dedicates Memorial, Urges Americans to Emulate FDR,"
Washington Post, May 3, 1997

9 Based on this document, how have the attitudes of the disabled changed since Franklin D. Roosevelt was president? [1]

Score ☐

Part B
Essay

Directions: Write a well-organized essay that includes an introduction, several paragraphs, and a conclusion. Use evidence from *at least four* documents in your essay. Support your response with relevant facts, examples, and details. Include additional outside information.

Historical Context:

Throughout the history of the United States, different groups have faced problems in American society. These groups have included **African Americans, industrial workers,** and **persons with disabilities**. Individuals, organizations, and governments have addressed problems faced by these groups.

Task: Using the information from the documents and your knowledge of United States history, write an essay in which you

Choose *two* groups mentioned in the historical context and for *each*

- Describe the historical circumstances surrounding a problem the group faced
- Discuss how the problem was addressed by an individual, an organization, *and/or* a government

Guidelines:

In your essay, be sure to

- Develop all aspects of the task
- Incorporate information from *at least four* documents
- Incorporate relevant outside information
- Support the theme with relevant facts, examples, and details
- Use a logical and clear plan of organization, including an introduction and a conclusion that are beyond a restatement of the theme

This section contains the Regents Examination in United States History and Government that was given in New York State in June 2015.

Circle your answers to Part I on this exam and write your answers to the thematic essay and document-based essay questions on separate sheets of paper. Be sure to refer to the test-taking strategies in the front of this book as you prepare to answer the test questions.

Part I

Answer all questions in this part.

Directions (1–50): For each statement or question, record on your separate answer sheet the *number* of the word or expression that, of those given, best completes the statement or answers the question.

Base your answer to question 1 on the cartoon below and on your knowledge of social studies.

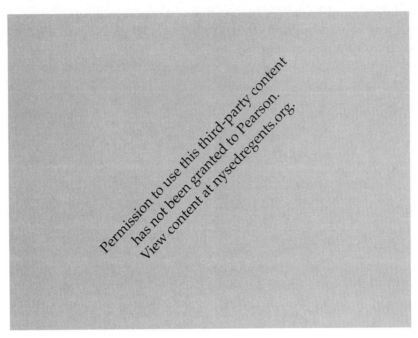

1 Which statement most accurately expresses the main idea of the cartoon?
 (1) Water pollution threatens public health.
 (2) Farmers fail to understand the water needs of cities.
 (3) Urban development has used all the water needed for farming.
 (4) Conflict is growing over the distribution of scarce water resources.

2 Which title best completes the partial outline below?

> I. _____
>
>   A. Virginia House of Burgesses
>   B. Mayflower Compact
>   C. New England town meetings

 (1) Developments in Colonial Self-Government
 (2) Colonial Efforts to Abandon British Rule
 (3) Attempts by Colonial Leaders to Form a National Government
 (4) Colonial Organizations Established by the British Parliament

3 One way that the British government carried out the policy of mercantilism was by
 (1) promoting free trade between its colonies and Europe
 (2) prohibiting the transatlantic trade in enslaved Africans
 (3) encouraging the development of colonial manufacturing and trade
 (4) requiring that most colonial trade occur within the British Empire

4 Thomas Jefferson incorporated John Locke's idea of the social contract theory in the Declaration of Independence because this idea

(1) justified the overthrow of a government that denied individual liberties
(2) considered economic rights more important than inalienable rights
(3) supported the divine right of kings
(4) called for a gradual change of government

Base your answer to question 5 on the passage below and on your knowledge of social studies.

…As to government matters, it is not in the power of Britain to do this continent justice: the business of it will soon be too weighty and intricate to be managed with any tolerable degree of convenience, by a power so distant from us, and so very ignorant of us; for if they cannot conquer us, they cannot govern us. To be always running three or four thousand miles with a tale or a petition, waiting four or five months for an answer, which, when obtained, requires five or six more to explain it in, will in a few years be looked upon as folly and childishness. There was a time when it was proper, and there is a proper time for it to cease.…

— Thomas Paine, *Common Sense*, 1776

5 What is the main argument Thomas Paine makes concerning the relationship between Great Britain and its American colonies?

(1) Britain wants to make America a part of the European continental system.
(2) America is too distant for Great Britain to govern effectively.
(3) America lacks representation in Parliament.
(4) American colonial leaders believe British officials want to use them to fight European wars.

6 At the Constitutional Convention of 1787, the Great Compromise between the large states and the small states resulted in

(1) the creation of a bicameral legislature
(2) a provision for equal protection of the laws
(3) a permanent solution to the slavery issue
(4) the guarantee of voting rights for all male property owners

7 The framework of government described in the Constitution of the United States (1787) most clearly shows the dissatisfaction of the founders with the

(1) Albany Plan of Union
(2) Northwest Ordinance
(3) Articles of Confederation
(4) Treaty of Paris

8 The term *federalism* is best defined as

(1) the process of amending a constitution
(2) the power of the courts to determine the constitutionality of laws
(3) a republican form of government with no hereditary ruler
(4) the division of power between the states and the national government

9 Which action is an example of the use of checks and balances?

(1) impeachment of President Bill Clinton
(2) choosing a vice presidential running mate by a presidential candidate
(3) election of the Speaker of the House by the majority party
(4) starting negotiations for a treaty by President George Washington

10 The Kentucky and Virginia Resolutions (1798) held that states could nullify the Alien and Sedition Acts because these laws

(1) repealed the Northwest Ordinance
(2) placed an unfair tax on whiskey made by western farmers
(3) violated the Constitution
(4) established limits on universal suffrage

11 The Supreme Court decision in *Marbury* v. *Madison* (1803) increased the power of the federal courts by

(1) increasing the number of judges
(2) enabling the president to overturn lower-court decisions
(3) establishing federal supremacy over state governments
(4) establishing the principle of judicial review

Base your answers to questions 12 and 13 on the map below and on your knowledge of social studies.

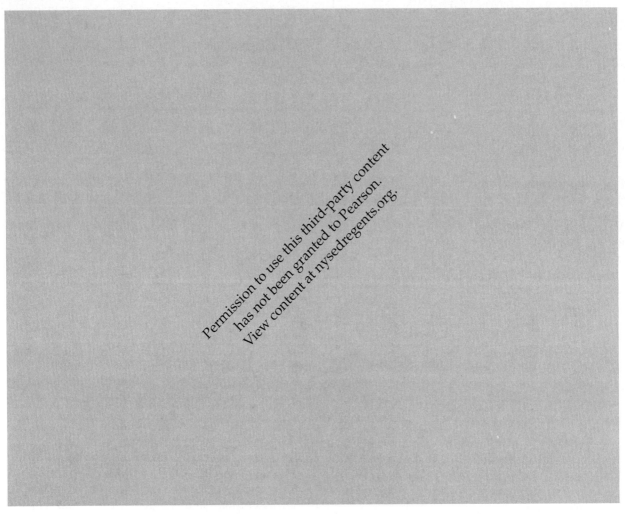

Permission to use this third-party content has not been granted to Pearson. View content at nysedregents.org.

12 Based on the map, the Erie Canal and Hudson River contributed directly to the

    (1) decisions to restrict immigration
    (2) rapid increase in population in upstate New York
    (3) settlement of New England
    (4) acquisition of land from Canada

13 Completion of the Erie Canal in 1825 encouraged the growth of the Midwest because it

    (1) linked the Great Lakes to the Atlantic Coast
    (2) helped force the removal of British forts in the Northwest Territory
    (3) stimulated development of cotton production in the Ohio River valley
    (4) increased trade with Asia

14 A major reason for President Thomas Jefferson's purchase of the Louisiana Territory was to

(1) eliminate Spanish control of California
(2) take possession of all of Florida
(3) give the United States control of the Mississippi River
(4) provide access to areas east of the Appalachian Mountains

15 What was one important geographic reason the United States was able to maintain a foreign policy of neutrality throughout most of the 19th century?

(1) The Atlantic Ocean provided a buffer from European interference.
(2) Extensive mountain ranges along the Pacific coastline prevented invasions.
(3) Scarce natural resources discouraged international trade.
(4) European immigrants had rapid communication with their homelands.

16 President Andrew Jackson used the spoils system to

(1) stop the westward expansion of slavery
(2) strengthen the military for national defense
(3) reward loyal political supporters
(4) destroy the Bank of the United States

17 After the Civil War, which development limited economic opportunities for African Americans in the South?

(1) creation of military districts
(2) establishment of the Freedmen's Bureau
(3) use of the sharecropping system
(4) ratification of the 14th amendment

18 During the 1870s, the Granger movement attracted the support of many western farmers because it proposed that

(1) the money supply should be deflated by removing paper currency from circulation
(2) shipping rates and grain storage fees charged by railroads should be regulated
(3) immigrants should be given land on the Great Plains
(4) the government should control the development of resources in the West

19 Literacy tests, grandfather clauses, and poll taxes were enacted by Southern States to

(1) limit the movement of African Americans
(2) restrict the voting rights of African Americans
(3) improve the social status of African Americans
(4) expand educational opportunities for African Americans

20 What was the primary goal of the Dawes Act of 1887 regarding Native American Indians?

(1) assimilating Native American Indians into mainstream American life
(2) increasing the size of Native American Indian reservations
(3) promoting Native American Indian languages and cultures
(4) strengthening Native American Indian tribal governments

21 During the late 19th century, businesses tried to maximize profits by

(1) eliminating tariffs
(2) supporting labor unions
(3) resisting laissez-faire policies
(4) creating monopolies

22 What was one major impact of industrialization in the United States?

(1) the disappearance of social class distinctions
(2) a rise in the standard of living
(3) an increase in the birth rate
(4) the elimination of urban tenements

23 What was one characteristic of American imperialism in the late 19th and early 20th centuries?

(1) avoiding involvement with nations in East Asia
(2) supporting independence movements in Africa
(3) rejecting the use of military force to gain colonies
(4) acquiring territory to promote economic and strategic interests

24 Which development was a result of the Progressive movement?

(1) Government increased its regulation of business practices.
(2) Women become less active in public life.
(3) The influence of the national government was reduced.
(4) Congress failed to balance the federal budget.

25 The Federal Reserve System was created to

(1) control the money supply
(2) stimulate trade with other nations
(3) regulate the stock market
(4) fund public works projects

26 What was the major cause of African American migration from the rural South to northern cities during World War I?

(1) offers of free public education
(2) availability of factory jobs
(3) desire to live in integrated neighborhoods
(4) opportunity to gain religious freedom

27 After World War I, a "return to normalcy" was most clearly demonstrated by

(1) opposition to joining the League of Nations
(2) ending farm subsidies under the Agricultural Adjustment Act
(3) reducing tariff rates on imported goods
(4) rejection of disarmament agreements

28 The term *Harlem Renaissance* best describes

(1) state and federal laws passed to end racial discrimination
(2) urban renewal efforts in New York City
(3) government programs to promote African American businesses
(4) a period of African American cultural achievements

29 In the 1920s, controversies over Prohibition, the National Origins Act, and the Scopes trial all reflected disagreement over the

(1) effects of demobilization
(2) cultural values of the American people
(3) role of the federal government in the economy
(4) influence of labor unions on American life

Base your answers to questions 30 and 31 on the passage below and on your knowledge of social studies.

...2. We propose to limit the amount any one man can earn in one year or inherit to $1 million to the person.

3. Now, by limiting the size of the fortunes and incomes of the big men, we will throw into the government Treasury the money and property from which we will care for the millions of people who have nothing; and with this money we will provide a home and the comforts of home, with such common conveniences as radio and automobile, for every family in America, free of debt....

— Senator Huey Long, 1935

30 Based on these statements by Senator Long, one reason for the suffering caused by the Great Depression was the
(1) failure of President Franklin D. Roosevelt to sign relief legislation
(2) overproduction of military equipment
(3) uneven distribution of income that favored the rich
(4) failure of labor unions to accept shorter work days

31 President Franklin D. Roosevelt responded to the circumstances described in this passage by
(1) renewing New Deal programs to help big business
(2) raising taxes to assure a balanced federal budget
(3) stressing free market economic principles
(4) increasing New Deal efforts for relief and reform

32 What was the primary motive behind President Franklin D. Roosevelt's 1937 proposal to add members to the Supreme Court?
(1) removal of Republican justices from the Court
(2) ending the Court's use of judicial review
(3) assuring United States neutrality at the start of World War II
(4) protection of New Deal programs from unfavorable Court decisions

33 Which trend in United States foreign policy is shown by the passage of the Neutrality Act of 1939, the destroyers for bases deal of 1940, and the Lend-Lease Act of 1941?
(1) withdrawal from overseas colonies
(2) expansion of trade with the Axis powers
(3) increase in support for the Allied powers
(4) reduction in war preparedness

34 The internment of Japanese Americans during World War II was initially authorized by
(1) a constitutional amendment
(2) an executive order of the president
(3) a proclamation by the governor of California
(4) a decision of the Supreme Court

Base your answers to questions 35 and 36 on the map below and on your knowledge of social studies.

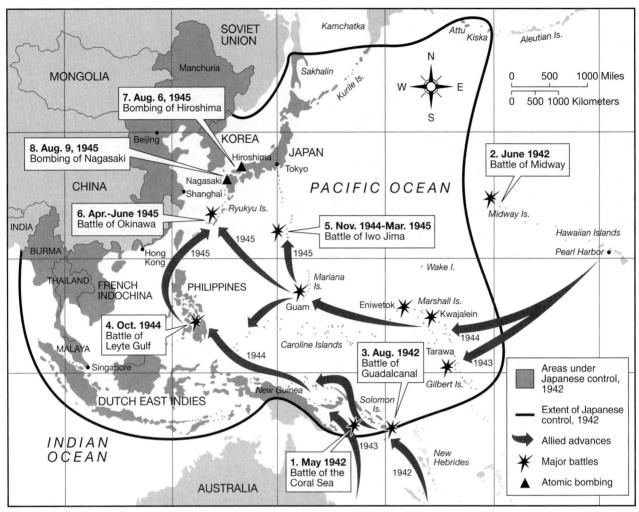

Source: Robert A. Divine et al., *America: Past and Present*, Addison Wesley Longman, 1999 (adapted)

35 What is the most accurate title for this map?

(1) American Imperialism in the 20th Century
(2) World War II in the Pacific
(3) Causes of World War II
(4) Creation of Wartime Alliances

36 The map shows that the Allied forces

(1) made slow but steady progress in defeating Japan
(2) conducted most of the battles north of the Hawaiian Islands
(3) maintained control of the Philippines from the beginning of the war
(4) had military support from the Soviet Union throughout the war

37 One reason the United States supported the creation of the United Nations was to

(1) determine blame for the start of World War II
(2) improve efforts to collect war debts
(3) maintain international peace
(4) promote the development of nuclear weapons

38 The announcement of the Truman Doctrine, the Berlin airlift, and the formation of the North Atlantic Treaty Organization (NATO) were actions taken by the United States to prevent the

(1) renewal of Nazi fascism in Germany, Italy, and Spain
(2) expansion of communism into Western Europe
(3) starvation of refugees from Eastern Europe
(4) start of an arms race between the United States and the Soviet Union

Base your answer to question 39 on the speech below and on your knowledge of social studies.

Good evening, my fellow citizens. This Government, as promised, has maintained the closest surveillance of the Soviet military build-up on the island of Cuba. Within the past week unmistakable evidence has established the fact that a series of offensive missile sites is now in preparation on that imprisoned island. The purposes of these bases can be none other than to provide a nuclear strike capability against the Western Hemisphere….

— President John F. Kennedy, Report to the American People, October 22, 1962

39 President John F. Kennedy reacted strongly to the situation described in this speech primarily because

(1) the United States feared an influx of Cuban refugees
(2) these missiles could threaten United States oil supplies in South America
(3) the location of Cuba would allow the United States little time to respond to an attack
(4) the United States and the Warsaw Pact nations had formed a military alliance

40 One criticism of the Warren Court's decisions in *Mapp* v. *Ohio* (1961), *Gideon* v. *Wainwright* (1963), and *Miranda* v. *Arizona* (1966) is that the Supreme Court

(1) limited police powers while expanding the rights of criminal defendants
(2) denied the first amendment rights of antiwar protestors and the press
(3) forced the desegregation of public transportation
(4) restricted the rights of students in public schools

41 During the 1960s, the foreign policy of President Lyndon B. Johnson was criticized because it

(1) failed to support the space program
(2) escalated the Vietnam War
(3) restricted overseas travel for American citizens
(4) eliminated economic aid to African nations

42 The decision of the Supreme Court in the case of *United States* v. *Nixon* (1974) stated that

(1) President Richard Nixon as commander in chief could extend the Vietnam War into Cambodia
(2) executive branch officials could be fired by the president without the Senate's approval
(3) executive privilege did not allow the president to withhold recordings that were related to the Watergate affair
(4) congressional approval of the War Powers Act of 1973 violated the separation of powers

Base your answers to questions 43 and 44 on the cartoon below and on your knowledge of social studies.

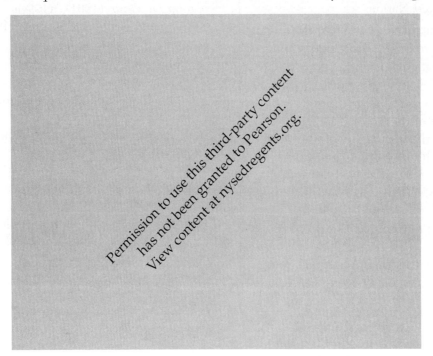

Permission to use this third-party content has not been granted to Pearson. View content at nysedregents.org.

43 Which statement most accurately expresses the point of view of the cartoonist?

(1) The United States should increase its imports from China.
(2) Many products made in the United States are sold in China.
(3) The American economy has become overly dependent on China.
(4) Many Americans have had to move to China to find work.

44 Many American corporations contributed to the problem shown in the cartoon by

(1) demanding that Congress increase export taxes
(2) establishing manufacturing facilities overseas
(3) paying workers lower wages to encourage them to retire
(4) lobbying the federal government to increase the minimum wage

Base your answer to question 45 on the cartoon below and on your knowledge of social studies.

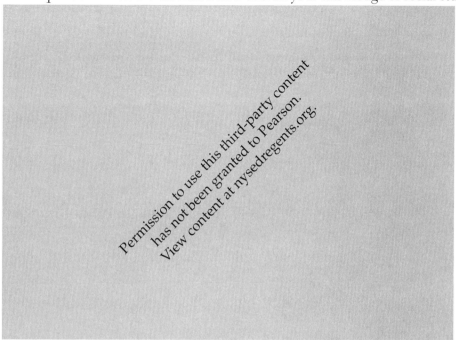

Permission to use this third-party content has not been granted to Pearson. View content at nysedregents.org.

45 What is considered a major cause of the problem shown in the cartoon?

(1) Employers pay higher Social Security taxes than employees pay.
(2) Most Americans want to end Social Security programs.
(3) Wealthy people pay the largest share of the Social Security taxes.
(4) The growing number of Social Security recipients are being supported by relatively fewer workers.

46 One important goal of the Monroe Doctrine (1823) was to

(1) reduce trade barriers between the United States and African nations
(2) establish United States colonies and naval bases in the Caribbean
(3) provide military assistance to help the Philippines gain independence from Spain
(4) prevent former colonial powers from taking over Latin American nations

47 The Strategic Arms Limitation Treaty (SALT) agreements signed in the 1970s by the United States and the Soviet Union were efforts to

(1) reduce Cold War tensions
(2) establish a worldwide human rights policy
(3) increase cooperation in the United Nations
(4) negotiate a lasting peace in the Middle East

48 **"Troops Break Up Bonus Army Protest"**
"FDR Proclaims Bank Holiday"
"Misery Created by Dust Bowl"

These headlines concern events that occurred during the

(1) Civil War
(2) Progressive Era
(3) Great Depression
(4) Cold War

Base your answers to questions 49 and 50 on the cartoon below and on your knowledge of social studies.

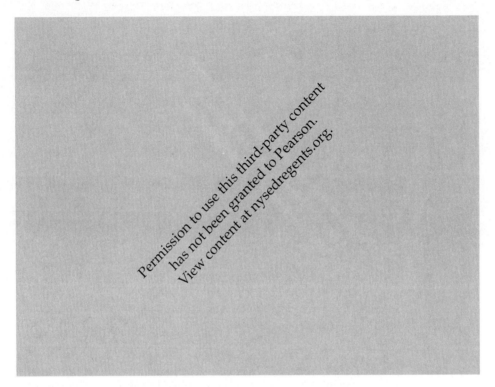

Permission to use this third-party content has not been granted to Pearson. View content at nysedregents.org.

49 The opinion expressed by the cartoonist is that the USA Patriot Act allows the federal government to

(1) set new term limits for federal judges

(2) restrict the investigative powers of the police

(3) violate freedoms guaranteed in the Bill of Rights

(4) eliminate States rights reserved in the 10th amendment

50 This cartoon was published in response to federal actions that followed which event?

(1) passage of the Espionage Act (1917) and the Sedition Act (1918)

(2) Supreme Court decision in *Korematsu* v. *United States* (1944)

(3) civil rights march on Washington, D.C. (1963)

(4) attacks on the World Trade Center and the Pentagon (2001)

Answers to the essay questions are to be written in the separate essay booklet.

In developing your answer to Part II, be sure to keep these general definitions in mind:
    (a) <u>describe</u> means "to illustrate something in words or tell about it"
    (b) <u>discuss</u> means "to make observations about something using facts, reasoning, and argument; to present in some detail"

Part II

THEMATIC ESSAY QUESTION

Directions: Write a well-organized essay that includes an introduction, several paragraphs addressing the task below, and a conclusion.

Theme: Organizations

> Throughout United States history, individuals and groups have formed organizations to achieve specific reforms. The reform efforts of these organizations have met with varying degrees of success.

Task:

> Identify *two* organizations that were formed to achieve a specific reform and for *each*
>
> • Describe the historical circumstances surrounding the formation of the organization
> • Discuss the degree to which the organization's reform efforts were successful

    You may use any organization from your study of United States history. Some suggestions you might wish to consider include the American Anti-Slavery Society (1833), the National Woman Suffrage Association (1869), the Woman's Christian Temperance Union (1874), the American Federation of Labor (1886), the Populist Party (1890), the Anti-Defamation League (1913), the United Farm Workers (1966), and the National Organization for Women (1966).

You are *not* limited to these suggestions.

Guidelines:

    In your essay, be sure to:
    • Develop all aspects of the task
    • Support the theme with relevant facts, examples, and details
    • Use a logical and clear plan of organization, including an introduction and a conclusion that are beyond a restatement of the theme

This page left blank intentionally.

GO ON TO THE NEXT PAGE ⇨

NAME _____ SCHOOL _____

Part III

DOCUMENT-BASED QUESTION

This question is based on the accompanying documents. The question is designed to test your ability to work with historical documents. Some of these documents have been edited for the purposes of this question. As you analyze the documents, take into account the source of each document and any point of view that may be presented in the document. Keep in mind that the language used in a document may reflect the historical context of the time in which it was written.

Historical Context:

> Throughout United States history, presidents have taken actions that have had a significant impact on the United States and American society. Three such presidential actions were **Andrew Jackson's Indian removal policy, Theodore Roosevelt's support for consumer protection,** and **Lyndon Johnson's support for civil rights.**

Task: Using the information from the documents and your knowledge of United States history, answer the questions that follow each document in Part A. Your answers to the questions will help you write the Part B essay in which you will be asked to

> Choose *two* presidential actions mentioned in the historical context and for *each*
> - Describe the historical circumstances surrounding the president's action
> - Discuss the impact of the president's action on the United States and/or on American society

In developing your answers to Part III, be sure to keep these general definitions in mind:
   (a) <u>describe</u> means "to illustrate something in words or tell about it"
   (b) <u>discuss</u> means "to make observations about something using facts, reasoning, and argument; to present in some detail"

Part A
Short-Answer Questions

Directions: Analyze the documents and answer the short-answer questions that follow each document in the space provided.

Document 1

> … The Southeastern Indians were particularly vulnerable. The traffic in deerskins, in which they had been intimately involved, had increasingly been replaced by a thriving cotton trade— spurred on by the invention of the cotton gin…[1793]—in which they were at best marginal producers and at worst obstacles to land-hungry whites. Much of their remaining territory was rich farmland, and the more they 'improved' it in the hope of turning themselves into acceptable neighbours, the more desirable they made it to would-be plantation-owners. A popular song at the time went:
>
> > All I ask in this creation
> >
> > Is a pretty little wife and a big plantation
> >
> > Way up yonder in the Cherokee Nation….

Source: James Wilson, *The Earth Shall Weep: A History of Native America,* Grove Press, 1998 (adapted)

1 According to James Wilson, what was **one** reason Native American Indians in the Southeast were removed from their native lands? [1]

_____

_____

Score ☐

Document 2

President Andrew Jackson had signed the Indian Removal Act on May 28, 1830.

… The consequences of a speedy removal will be important to the United States, to individual States, and to the [Native American] Indians themselves. The pecuniary [financial] advantages which it promises to the Government are the least of its recommendations. It puts an end to all possible danger of collision between the authorities of the General [Federal] and State Governments on account of the Indians. It will place a dense and civilized population in large tracts of country now occupied by a few savage hunters. By opening the whole territory between Tennessee on the north and Louisiana on the south to the settlement of the whites it will incalculably [greatly] strengthen the SW [southwestern] frontier and render the adjacent States strong enough to repel future invasions without remote aid. It will relieve the whole State of Mississippi and the western part of Alabama of Indian occupancy, and enable those States to advance rapidly in population, wealth, and power. It will separate the Indians from immediate contact with settlements of whites; free them from the power of the States; enable them to pursue happiness in their own way and under their own rude [primitive] institutions; will retard [slow] the progress of decay, which is lessening their numbers, and perhaps cause them gradually, under the protection of the Government and through the influence of good counsels, to cast off their savage habits and become an interesting, civilized, and Christian community. These consequences, some of them so certain and the rest so probable, make the complete execution of the plan sanctioned by Congress [Indian Removal Act] at their last session an object of much solicitude [concern]….

Source: President Andrew Jackson, Second Annual Message to Congress, December 6, 1830

2 According to President Andrew Jackson, what were **two** reasons for establishing an Indian removal policy? [2]

(1)_____

_____

Score ☐

(2)_____

_____

Score ☐

Document 3a

Indian Removal, 1830–1854

Source: Irving F. Ahlquist et al., *United States History,* Addison-Wesley, 1984 (adapted)

Document 3b

…It was natural, at a time when the national territory seemed almost illimitable [unlimited] and contained many millions of acres far outside the bounds of civilized settlements, that a policy should have been initiated which more than aught [anything] else has been the fruitful source of our [Native American] Indian complications.

I refer, of course, to the policy of dealing with the various Indian tribes as separate nationalities, of relegating them by treaty stipulations to the occupancy of immense reservations in the West, and of encouraging them to live a savage life, undisturbed by any earnest and well-directed efforts to bring them under the influences of civilization.

The unsatisfactory results which have sprung from this policy are becoming apparent to all.

As the white settlements have crowded the borders of the reservations, the Indians, sometimes contentedly and sometimes against their will, have been transferred to other hunting grounds, from which they have again been dislodged whenever their new-found homes have been desired by the adventurous settlers.

These removals and the frontier collisions by which they have often been preceded have led to frequent and disastrous conflicts between the races.…

Source: President Chester A. Arthur, Message to Congress, December 6, 1881

3 Based on these documents, what were *two* effects of federal removal policies on Native American Indians? [2]

(1)_____

_____

Score ☐

(2)_____

_____

Score ☐

Document 4a

In 1906 President Theodore Roosevelt appointed a commission to investigate practices in meatpacking plants. This is an excerpt from the commission's findings that were presented to Congress.

> ...The results of our observations have already been partly given. Other instances of how products may be made up, and still secure the stamp of government inspection, are here given. In one well-known establishment we came upon fresh meat being shoveled into barrels, and a regular proportion being added of stale scraps that had lain on a dirty floor in the corner of a room for some days previous. In another establishment equally well known, a long table was noted covered with several hundred pounds of cooked scraps of beef and other meats. Some of these meat scraps were dry, leathery and unfit to be eaten; and in the heap were found pieces of pigskin, and even some bits of rope strands and other rubbish. Inquiry evoked the frank admission from the man in charge that this was to be ground up and used in making "potted ham."...

Source: *Locomotive Firemen's Magazine*, July–December, 1906

Document 4b

A NAUSEATING JOB, BUT IT MUST BE DONE.

Source: *Utica Saturday Globe*, 1906 (adapted)

4 Based on these documents, what is **one** reason President Theodore Roosevelt supported consumer protection laws? [1]

_____

_____

Score ☐

Document 5

> # Postum Cereal Co., Ltd.
> ## Guarantee on Their Products.
>
> We warrant and guarantee that all packages of Postum Cereal, Grape-Nuts and Elijah's Manna hereafter sold by any jobber or retailer, comply with the provisions of the National Pure Food Law,* and are not and shall not be adulterated or mis-branded within the meaning of said Act of Congress approved June 30, 1906, and entitled, "An act for preventing the manufacture, sale and transportation of adulterated or mis-branded or poisonous or deleterious foods, drugs, medicines, liquors, and for regulating traffic therein for other purposes."
>
> POSTUM CEREAL CO., LTD.,
> C. W. Post, Chairman,
> Battle Creek, Mich.
>
> Dec. 12, 1906.
>
> Subscribed and sworn to before me this 15th day of December, 1906.
>
> BENJAMIN F. REID,
> Notary Public.
>
> My commision expires July 1, 1907.
>
> Our goods are pure, they always have been and always will be, they are not mis-branded. We have always since the beginning of our business, printed a truthful statement on the package of the ingredients contained therein and we stand back of every package.
>
> # Postum Cereal   Grape=Nuts
> ## Elijah's Manna.

Source: *New York Times,* December 30, 1906 (adapted)

*Pure Food and Drug Act

5 Based on this advertisement, state *one* way the Pure Food and Drug Act would protect consumers. [1]

_____

_____

Score ☐

Document 6

Eight months ago I signed into law the Wholesome Meat Act of 1967. That landmark bill capped a crusade that had begun 60 years ago—[in the presidency of Theodore Roosevelt] to assure American housewives that the meat they served their families was pure, not harmful or dirty or diseased.

Today I am proud to sign a bill that will extend the same coverage to all poultry products. It is the fulfillment of a promise I made to every housewife—in my first consumer message just after I became President.

In the early days of this century, Americans took for granted that there were risks in buying food. They even joked about it in print. One newspaper printed a little poem:

"Mary had a little lamb,

And when she saw it sicken,

She shipped it off to packing town,

And now it's labeled chicken."

In 1968, we cannot tolerate the image, or the fact, of unwholesome food:

—Not when Americans last year consumed more than 12 billion pounds of poultry.

—Not when a full 13 percent of that supply—or 1.6 billion pounds—was subject to little or no inspection because it didn't cross State lines….

The Wholesome Poultry Products Act of 1968 will insure that dirty plants will have to clean up or close down….

Source: President Lyndon B. Johnson, Statement Upon Signing the Wholesome Poultry Products Act, August 19, 1968

6 Based on this document, how did President Lyndon B. Johnson continue the consumer protection action begun by President Theodore Roosevelt? [1]

_____

_____

Score ☐

Document 7

...It ought to be possible, in short, for every American to enjoy the privileges of being American without regard to his race or his color. In short, every American ought to have the right to be treated as he would wish to be treated, as one would wish his children to be treated. But this is not the case....

The heart of the question is whether all Americans are to be afforded equal rights and equal opportunities, whether we are going to treat our fellow Americans as we want to be treated. If an American, because his skin is dark, cannot eat lunch in a restaurant open to the public, if he cannot send his children to the best public school available, if he cannot vote for the public officials who represent him, if, in short, he cannot enjoy the full and free life which all of us want, then who among us would be content to have the color of his skin changed and stand in his place? Who among us would then be content with the counsels of patience and delay?...

Now the time has come for this Nation to fulfill its promise. The events in Birmingham and elsewhere have so increased the cries for equality that no city or State or legislative body can prudently choose to ignore them....

We face, therefore, a moral crisis as a country and as a people. It cannot be met by repressive police action. It cannot be left to increase demonstrations in the streets. It cannot be quieted by token moves or talk. It is a time to act in the Congress, in your State and local legislative body and, above all, in all of our daily lives....

Source: President John F. Kennedy, Radio and Television Report to the American People on Civil Rights, June 11, 1963

7 According to President John F. Kennedy, what is **one** inequality African Americans continued to face in 1963? [1]

_____

_____

Score ☐

Document 8

President Lyndon B. Johnson addresses the nation as he prepares to sign the Civil Rights Act of 1964.

My fellow Americans:

I am about to sign into law the Civil Rights Act of 1964. I want to take this occasion to talk to you about what that law means to every American....

Americans of every race and color have died in battle to protect our freedom. Americans of every race and color have worked to build a nation of widening opportunities. Now our generation of Americans has been called on to continue the unending search for justice within our own borders.

We believe that all men are created equal. Yet many are denied equal treatment....

We believe that all men are entitled to the blessings of liberty. Yet millions are being deprived of those blessings—not because of their own failures, but because of the color of their skin.

The reasons are deeply imbedded in history and tradition and the nature of man. We can understand—without rancor or hatred—how this all happened.

But it cannot continue. Our Constitution, the foundation of our Republic, forbids it. The principles of our freedom forbid it. Morality forbids it. And the law I will sign tonight forbids it....

Source: President Lyndon B. Johnson, Radio and Television Remarks upon Signing the Civil Rights Bill, July 2, 1964, Lyndon B. Johnson Library & Museum (adapted)

8 Based on this document, what is **one** reason President Lyndon B. Johnson supported the Civil Rights Act of 1964? [1]

_____

_____

Score ___

Document 9a

...The Civil Rights Act of 1964 also revealed that Congress really can change conditions in the United States if it truly wishes to do so. The act ended virtually immediately and completely all forms of public segregation in the nation, both North and South. The threat of cutting off U.S. funds to government programs and business concerns that discriminate against minorities has made "equal employment opportunity" and "affirmative action in hiring" fixed institutions in American life. The act empowered the attorney general of the United States to sue for the desegregation of schools, a program that has resulted in the use of school busing to achieve racial balance in the nation's schools. The act was the first national law to guarantee significant equal rights for women, and it set the precedent for using cloture to stop a filibuster on a civil rights bill—a precedent that was used in...[1968] to pass a national law [the Fair Housing Act] guaranteeing equal housing opportunity....

Source: Robert D. Loevy, "A Brief History of the Civil Rights Act of 1964," in Kozak and Ciboski, eds., *The American Presidency*, Nelson Hall, 1985 (adapted)

9a According to Robert D. Loevy, what were **two** effects of the Civil Rights Act of 1964? [2]

(1)_____

_____

Score ☐

(2)_____

_____

Score ☐

Document 9b

The Voting Rights Act was signed by President Lyndon B. Johnson in 1965.

> ...The [social and economic] system was working hard, by the late sixties and early seventies, to contain the frightening explosiveness of the black [African American] upsurge. Blacks were voting in large numbers in the South, and in the 1968 Democratic Convention three blacks were admitted into the Mississippi delegation. By 1977, more than two thousand blacks held office in eleven southern states (in 1965 the number was seventy-two). There were two Congressmen, eleven state senators, ninety-five state representatives, 267 county commissioners, seventy-six mayors, 824 city council members, eighteen sheriffs or chiefs of police, 508 school board members. It was a dramatic advance. But blacks, with 20 percent of the South's population, still held less than 3 percent of the elective offices. A *New York Times* reporter, analyzing the new situation in 1977, pointed out that even where blacks held important city offices: "Whites almost always retain economic power." After Maynard Jackson, a black, became mayor of Atlanta, "the white business establishment continued to exert its influence."...

Source: Howard Zinn, *A People's History of the United States*, Harper Perennial, 2003

9b Based on this document, what was **one** effect of the Voting Rights Act of 1965? [1]

_____

_____

Score ☐

Part B
Essay

Directions: Write a well-organized essay that includes an introduction, several paragraphs, and a conclusion. Use evidence from *at least* ***four*** documents in your essay. Support your response with relevant facts, examples, and details. Include additional outside information.

Historical Context:

Throughout United States history, presidents have taken actions that have had a significant impact on the United States and American society. Three such presidential actions were **Andrew Jackson's Indian removal policy, Theodore Roosevelt's support for consumer protection,** and **Lyndon Johnson's support for civil rights.**

Task: Using the information from the documents and your knowledge of United States history, write an essay in which you

Choose ***two*** presidential actions mentioned in the historical context and for ***each***
- Describe the historical circumstances surrounding the president's action
- Discuss the impact of the president's action on the United States and/or on American society

Guidelines:

In your essay, be sure to
- Develop all aspects of the task
- Incorporate information from *at least* ***four*** documents
- Incorporate relevant outside information
- Support the theme with relevant facts, examples, and details
- Use a logical and clear plan of organization, including an introduction and a conclusion that are beyond a restatement of the theme